TOYOTA CAMRY
1983-96 REPAIR MANUAL

CHILTON'S

Covers all U.S. and Canadian models of Toyota Camry

by Dawn M. Hoch, S.A.E.

 *CHILTON* Automotive Books

PUBLISHED BY **HAYNES NORTH AMERICA, Inc.**

Manufactured in USA
© 1998 Haynes North America, Inc.
ISBN 0-8019-8955-8
Library of Congress Catalog Card No. 89-71352
6789012345 9876543210

Haynes Publishing Group
Sparkford Nr Yeovil
Somerset BA22 7JJ England

Haynes North America, Inc
861 Lawrence Drive
Newbury Park
California 91320 USA

ABCD

10F3

Contents

Contents

SAFETY NOTICE

Proper service and repair procedures are vital to the safe, reliable operation of all motor vehicles, as well as the personal safety of those performing repairs. This manual outlines procedures for servicing and repairing vehicles using safe, effective methods. The procedures contain many NOTES, CAUTIONS and WARNINGS which should be followed, along with standard procedures to eliminate the possibility of personal injury or improper service which could damage the vehicle or compromise its safety.

It is important to note that repair procedures and techniques, tools and parts for servicing motor vehicles, as well as the skill and experience of the individual performing the work vary widely. It is not possible to anticipate all of the conceivable ways or conditions under which vehicles may be serviced, or to provide cautions as to all possible hazards that may result. Standard and accepted safety precautions and equipment should be used when handling toxic or flammable fluids, and safety goggles or other protection should be used during cutting, grinding, chiseling, prying, or any other process that can cause material removal or projectiles.

Some procedures require the use of tools specially designed for a specific purpose. Before substituting another tool or procedure, you must be completely satisfied that neither your personal safety, nor the performance of the vehicle will be endangered.

Although information in this manual is based on industry sources and is complete as possible at the time of publication, the possibility exists that some car manufacturers made later changes which could not be included here. While striving for total accuracy, the authors or publishers cannot assume responsibility for any errors, changes or omissions that may occur in the compilation of this data.

PART NUMBERS

Part numbers listed in this reference are not recommendations by Haynes North America, Inc. for any product brand name. They are references that can be used with interchange manuals and aftermarket supplier catalogs to locate each brand supplier's discrete part number.

SPECIAL TOOLS

Special tools are recommended by the vehicle manufacturer to perform their specific job. Use has been kept to a minimum, but where absolutely necessary, they are referred to in the text by the part number of the tool manufacturer. These tools can be purchased, under the appropriate part number, from your local dealer or regional distributor, or an equivalent tool can be purchased locally from a tool supplier or parts outlet. Before substituting any tool for the one recommended, read the SAFETY NOTICE at the top of this page.

ACKNOWLEDGMENTS

The publisher expresses appreciation to Toyota Motor Corporation for their generous assistance.

1

GENERAL
INFORMATION
AND
MAINTENANCE

HOW TO USE THIS BOOK

This Chilton's Total Car Care manual is intended to help you learn more about the inner workings of your Toyota Camry while saving you money on its upkeep and operation.

The beginning of the book will likely be referred to the most, since that is where you will find information for maintenance and tune-up. The other sections deal with the more complex systems of your vehicle. Systems (from engine through brakes) are covered to the extent that the average do-it-yourselfer can attempt. This book will not explain such things as rebuilding a differential because the expertise required and the special tools necessary make this uneconomical. It will, however, give you detailed instructions to help you change your own brake pads and shoes, replace spark plugs, and perform many more jobs that can save you money and help avoid expensive problems.

A secondary purpose of this book is a reference for owners who want to understand their vehicle and/or their mechanics better.

Where to Begin

Before removing any bolts, read through the entire procedure. This will give you the overall view of what tools and supplies will be required. So read ahead and plan ahead. Each operation should be approached logically and all procedures thoroughly understood before attempting any work.

If repair of a component is not considered practical, we tell you how to remove the part and then how to install the new or rebuilt replacement. In this way, you at least save labor costs.

Avoiding Trouble

Many procedures in this book require you to "label and disconnect . . ." a group of lines, hoses or wires. Don't be think you can remember where everything goes—you won't. If you hook up vacuum or fuel lines incorrectly, the vehicle may run poorly, if at all. If you hook up electrical wiring incorrectly, you may instantly learn a very expensive lesson.

You don't need to know the proper name for each hose or line. A piece of masking tape on the hose and a piece on its fitting will allow you to assign your own label. As long as you remember your own code, the lines can be reconnected by matching your tags. Remember that tape will dissolve in gasoline or solvents; if a part is to be washed or cleaned, use another method of identification. A permanent felt-tipped marker or a metal scribe can be very handy for marking metal parts. Remove any tape or paper labels after assembly.

Maintenance or Repair?

Maintenance includes routine inspections, adjustments, and replacement of parts which show signs of normal wear. Maintenance compensates for wear or deterioration. Repair implies that something has broken or is not working. A need for a repair is often caused by lack of maintenance. for example: draining and refilling automatic transmission fluid is maintenance recommended at specific intervals. Failure to do this can shorten the life of the transmission/transaxle, requiring very expensive repairs. While no maintenance program can prevent items from eventually breaking or wearing out, a general rule is true: MAINTENANCE IS CHEAPER THAN REPAIR.

Two basic mechanic's rules should be mentioned here. First, whenever the left side of the vehicle or engine is referred to, it means the driver's side. Conversely, the right side of the vehicle means the passenger's side. Second, screws and bolts are removed by turning counterclockwise, and tightened by turning clockwise unless specifically noted.

Safety is always the most important rule. Constantly be aware of the dangers involved in working on an automobile and take the proper precautions. Please refer to the information in this section regarding SERVICING YOUR VEHICLE SAFELY and the SAFETY NOTICE on the acknowledgment page.

Avoiding the Most Common Mistakes

Pay attention to the instructions provided. There are 3 common mistakes in mechanical work:

1. Incorrect order of assembly, disassembly or adjustment. When taking something apart or putting it together, performing steps in the wrong order usually just costs you extra time; however, it CAN break something. Read the entire procedure before beginning. Perform everything in the order in which the instructions say you should, even if you can't see a reason for it. When you're taking apart something that is very intricate, you might want to draw a picture of how it looks when assembled in order to make sure you get everything back in its proper position. When making adjustments, perform them in the proper order. One adjustment possibly will affect another.

2. Overtorquing (or undertorquing). While it is more common for overtorquing to cause damage, undertorquing may allow a fastener to vibrate loose causing serious damage. Especially when dealing with aluminum parts, pay attention to torque specifications and utilize a torque wrench in assembly. If a torque figure is not available, remember that if you are using the right tool to perform the job, you will probably not have to strain yourself to get a fastener tight enough. The pitch of most threads is so slight that the tension you put on the wrench will be multiplied many times in actual force on what you are tightening.

There are many commercial products available for ensuring that fasteners won't come loose, even if they are not torqued just right (a very common brand is Loctite®). If you're worried about getting something together tight enough to hold, but loose enough to avoid mechanical damage during assembly, one of these products might offer substantial insurance. Before choosing a threadlocking compound, read the label on the package and make sure the product is compatible with the materials, fluids, etc. involved.

3. Crossthreading. This occurs when a part such as a bolt is screwed into a nut or casting at the wrong angle and forced. Crossthreading is more likely to occur if access is difficult. It helps to clean and lubricate fasteners, then to start threading the bolt, spark plug, etc. with your fingers. If you encounter resistance, unscrew the part and start over again at a different angle until it can be inserted and turned several times without much effort. Keep in mind that many parts have tapered threads, so that gentle turning will automatically bring the part you're threading to the proper angle. Don't put a wrench on the part until it's been tightened a couple of turns by hand. If you suddenly encounter resistance, and the part has not seated fully, don't force it. Pull it back out to make sure it's clean and threading properly.

Be sure to take your time and be patient, and always plan ahead. Allow yourself ample time to perform repairs and maintenance.

TOOLS AND EQUIPMENT

▶ **See Figures 1 thru 15**

Without the proper tools and equipment it is impossible to properly service your vehicle. It would be virtually impossible to catalog every tool that you would need to perform all of the operations in this book. It would be unwise for the amateur to rush out and buy an expensive set of tools on the theory that he/she may need one or more of them at some time.

The best approach is to proceed slowly, gathering a good quality set of those tools that are used most frequently. Don't be misled by the low cost of bargain tools. It is far better to spend a little more for better quality. Forged wrenches, 6 or 12-point sockets and fine tooth ratchets are by far preferable to their less expensive counterparts. As any good mechanic can tell you, there are few worse experiences than trying to work on a vehicle with bad tools. Your monetary savings will be far outweighed by frustration and mangled knuckles.

Begin accumulating those tools that are used most frequently: those associated with routine maintenance and tune-up. In addition to the normal assortment of screwdrivers and pliers, you should have the following tools:

• Wrenches/sockets and combination open end/box end wrenches in sizes ⅛–¾ in. and/or 3mm–19mm ¹³⁄₁₆ in. or ⅝ in. spark plug socket (depending on plug type).

➡**If possible, buy various length socket drive extensions. Universal-joint and wobble extensions can be extremely useful, but be careful when using them, as they can change the amount of torque applied to the socket.**

• Jackstands for support.
• Oil filter wrench.
• Spout or funnel for pouring fluids.

• Grease gun for chassis lubrication (unless your vehicle is not equipped with any grease fittings)

• Hydrometer for checking the battery (unless equipped with a sealed, maintenance-free battery).

• A container for draining oil and other fluids.

• Rags for wiping up the inevitable mess.

In addition to the above items there are several others that are not absolutely necessary, but handy to have around. These include an equivalent oil absorbent gravel, like cat litter, and the usual supply of lubricants, antifreeze and fluids. This is a basic list for routine maintenance, but only your personal needs and desire can accurately determine your list of tools.

After performing a few projects on the vehicle, you'll be amazed at the other tools and non-tools on your workbench. Some useful household items are: a large turkey baster or siphon, empty coffee cans and ice trays (to store parts), a ball of twine, electrical tape for wiring, small rolls of colored tape for tagging lines or hoses, markers and pens, a note pad, golf tees (for plugging vacuum lines), metal coat hangers or a roll of mechanic's wire (to hold things out of the way), dental pick or similar long, pointed probe, a strong magnet, and a small mirror (to see into recesses and under manifolds).

A more advanced set of tools, suitable for tune-up work, can be drawn up easily. While the tools are slightly more sophisticated, they need not be outrageously expensive. There are several inexpensive tach/dwell meters on the market that are every bit as good for the average mechanic as a professional model. Just be sure that it goes to a least 1200–1500 rpm on the tach scale and that it works on 4, 6 and 8-cylinder engines. The key to these purchases is to make them with an eye towards adaptability and wide range. A basic list of tune-up tools could include:

• Tach/dwell meter.

• Spark plug wrench and gapping tool.

• Feeler gauges for valve adjustment.

• Timing light.

The choice of a timing light should be made carefully. A light which works on the DC current supplied by the vehicle's battery is the best choice; it should have a xenon tube for brightness. On any vehicle with an electronic ignition sys-

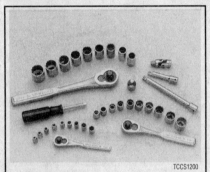

Fig. 1 All but the most basic procedures will require an assortment of ratchets and sockets

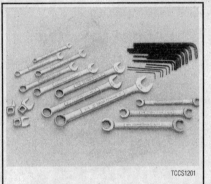

Fig. 2 In addition to ratchets, a good set of wrenches and hex keys will be necessary

Fig. 3 A hydraulic floor jack and a set of jackstands are essential for lifting and supporting the vehicle

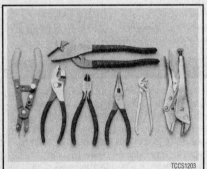

Fig. 4 An assortment of pliers, grippers and cutters will be handy for old rusted parts and stripped bolt heads

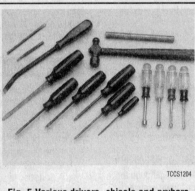

Fig. 5 Various drivers, chisels and prybars are great tools to have in your toolbox

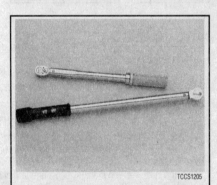

Fig. 6 Many repairs will require the use of a torque wrench to assure the components are properly fastened

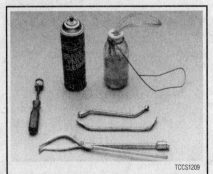

Fig. 7 Although not always necessary, using specialized brake tools will save time

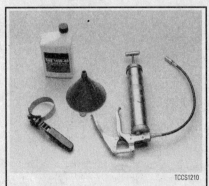

Fig. 8 A few inexpensive lubrication tools will make maintenance easier

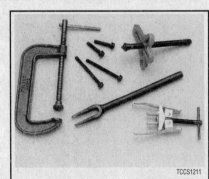

Fig. 9 Various pullers, clamps and separator tools are needed for many larger, more complicated repairs

Fig. 10 A variety of tools and gauges should be used for spark plug gapping and installation

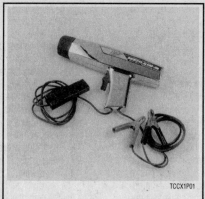

Fig. 11 Inductive type timing light

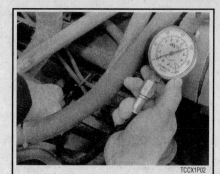

Fig. 12 A screw-in type compression gauge is recommended for compression testing

Fig. 13 A vacuum/pressure tester is necessary for many testing procedures

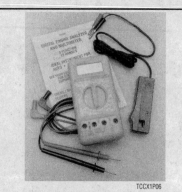

Fig. 14 Most modern automotive multimeters incorporate many helpful features

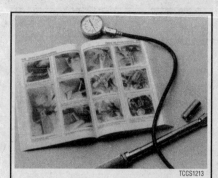

Fig. 15 Proper information is vital, so always have a Chilton Total Car Care manual handy

tem, a timing light with an inductive pickup that clamps around the No. 1 spark plug cable is preferred.

In addition to these basic tools, there are several other tools and gauges you may find useful. These include:

• Compression gauge. The screw-in type is slower to use, but eliminates the possibility of a faulty reading due to escaping pressure.
• Manifold vacuum gauge.
• 12V test light.
• A combination volt/ohmmeter
• Induction Ammeter. This is used for determining whether or not there is current in a wire. These are handy for use if a wire is broken somewhere in a wiring harness.

As a final note, you will probably find a torque wrench necessary for all but the most basic work. The beam type models are perfectly adequate, although the newer click types (breakaway) are easier to use. The click type torque wrenches tend to be more expensive. Also keep in mind that all types of torque wrenches should be periodically checked and/or recalibrated. You will have to decide for yourself which better fits your pocketbook, and purpose.

Special Tools

Normally, the use of special factory tools is avoided for repair procedures, since these are not readily available for the do-it-yourself mechanic. When it is possible to perform the job with more commonly available tools, it will be pointed out, but occasionally, a special tool was designed to perform a specific function and should be used. Before substituting another tool, you should be convinced that neither your safety nor the performance of the vehicle will be compromised.

Special tools can usually be purchased from an automotive parts store or from your dealer. In some cases special tools may be available directly from the tool manufacturer.

DIAGNOSTIC TEST EQUIPMENT

Modern vehicles equipped with computer-controlled fuel, emission and ignition systems require modern electronic tools to diagnose problems. Many of these tools are designed solely for the professional mechanic and are too costly and difficult to use for the average do-it-yourselfer. However, various automotive aftermarket companies have introduced products that address the needs of the average home mechanic, providing sophisticated information at affordable cost. Consult your local auto parts store to determine what is available for your vehicle.

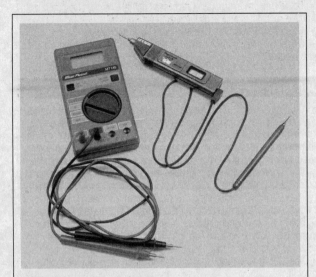

Digital multimeters come in a variety of styles and are a "must-have" for any serious home mechanic. Digital multimeters measure voltage (volts), resistance (ohms) and sometimes current (amperes). These versatile tools are used for checking all types of electrical or electronic components

Trouble code tools allow the home mechanic to extract the "fault code" number from an on-board computer that has sensed a problem (usually indicated by a Check Engine light). Armed with this code, the home mechanic can focus attention on a suspect system or component

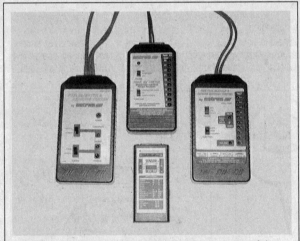

Sensor testers perform specific checks on many of the sensors and actuators used on today's computer-controlled vehicles. These testers can check sensors both on or off the vehicle, as well as test the accompanying electrical circuits

Hand-held scanners represent the most sophisticated of all do-it-yourself diagnostic tools. These tools do more than just access computer codes like the code readers above; they provide the user with an actual interface into the vehicle's computer. Comprehensive data on specific makes and models will come with the tool, either built-in or as a separate cartridge

SERVICING YOUR VEHICLE SAFELY

▶ **See Figures 16, 17 and 18**

It is virtually impossible to anticipate all of the hazards involved with automotive maintenance and service, but care and common sense will prevent most accidents.

The rules of safety for mechanics range from "don't smoke around gasoline," to "use the proper tool(s) for the job." The trick to avoiding injuries is to develop safe work habits and to take every possible precaution.

Do's

- Do keep a fire extinguisher and first aid kit handy.
- Do wear safety glasses or goggles when cutting, drilling, grinding or prying, even if you have 20–20 vision. If you wear glasses for the sake of vision, wear safety goggles over your regular glasses.
- Do shield your eyes whenever you work around the battery. Batteries contain sulfuric acid. In case of contact with, flush the area with water or a mixture of water and baking soda, then seek immediate medical attention.
- Do use safety stands (jackstands) for any undervehicle service. Jacks are for raising vehicles; jackstands are for making sure the vehicle stays raised until you want it to come down.
- Do use adequate ventilation when working with any chemicals or hazardous materials. Like carbon monoxide, the asbestos dust resulting from some brake lining wear can be hazardous in sufficient quantities.
- Do disconnect the negative battery cable when working on the electrical system. The secondary ignition system contains EXTREMELY HIGH VOLTAGE. In some cases it can even exceed 50,000 volts.
- Do follow manufacturer's directions whenever working with potentially hazardous materials. Most chemicals and fluids are poisonous.
- Do properly maintain your tools. Loose hammerheads, mushroomed punches and chisels, frayed or poorly grounded electrical cords, excessively worn screwdrivers, spread wrenches (open end), cracked sockets, slipping ratchets, or faulty droplight sockets can cause accidents.
- Likewise, keep your tools clean; a greasy wrench can slip off a bolt head, ruining the bolt and often harming your knuckles in the process.
- Do use the proper size and type of tool for the job at hand. Do select a wrench or socket that fits the nut or bolt. The wrench or socket should sit straight, not cocked.
- Do, when possible, pull on a wrench handle rather than push on it, and adjust your stance to prevent a fall.

- Do be sure that adjustable wrenches are tightly closed on the nut or bolt and pulled so that the force is on the side of the fixed jaw.
- Do strike squarely with a hammer; avoid glancing blows.
- Do set the parking brake and block the drive wheels if the work requires a running engine.

Don'ts

- Don't run the engine in a garage or anywhere else without proper ventilation—EVER! Carbon monoxide is poisonous; it takes a long time to leave the human body and you can build up a deadly supply of it in your system by simply breathing in a little at a time. You may not realize you are slowly poisoning yourself. Always use power vents, windows, fans and/or open the garage door.
- Don't work around moving parts while wearing loose clothing. Short sleeves are much safer than long, loose sleeves. Hard-toed shoes with neoprene soles protect your toes and give a better grip on slippery surfaces. Watches and jewelry is not safe working around a vehicle. Long hair should be tied back under a hat or cap.
- Don't use pockets for toolboxes. A fall or bump can drive a screwdriver deep into your body. Even a rag hanging from your back pocket can wrap around a spinning shaft or fan.
- Don't smoke when working around gasoline, cleaning solvent or other flammable material.
- Don't smoke when working around the battery. When the battery is being charged, it gives off explosive hydrogen gas.
- Don't use gasoline to wash your hands; there are excellent soaps available. Gasoline contains dangerous additives which can enter the body through a cut or through your pores. Gasoline also removes all the natural oils from the skin so that bone dry hands will suck up oil and grease.
- Don't service the air conditioning system unless you are equipped with the necessary tools and training. When liquid or compressed gas refrigerant is released to atmospheric pressure it will absorb heat from whatever it contacts. This will chill or freeze anything it touches.
- Don't use screwdrivers for anything other than driving screws! A screwdriver used as an prying tool can snap when you least expect it, causing injuries. At the very least, you'll ruin a good screwdriver.
- Don't use an emergency jack (that little ratchet, scissors, or pantograph jack supplied with the vehicle) for anything other than changing a flat! These jacks are only intended for emergency use out on the road; they are NOT designed as a maintenance tool. If you are serious about maintaining your vehicle yourself, invest in a hydraulic floor jack of at least a 1½ ton capacity, and at least two sturdy jackstands.

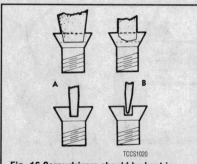

Fig. 16 Screwdrivers should be kept in good condition to prevent injury or damage which could result if the blade slips from the screw

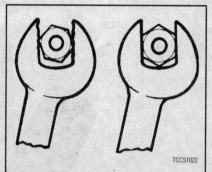

Fig. 17 Using the correct size wrench will help prevent the possibility of rounding off a nut

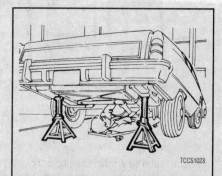

Fig. 18 NEVER work under a vehicle unless it is supported using safety stands (jackstands)

FASTENERS, MEASUREMENTS AND CONVERSIONS

Bolts, Nuts and Other Threaded Retainers

▶ **See Figures 19 and 20**

Although there are a great variety of fasteners found in the modern car or truck, the most commonly used retainer is the threaded fastener (nuts, bolts, screws, studs, etc.). Most threaded retainers may be reused, provided that they are not damaged in

use or during the repair. Some retainers (such as stretch bolts or torque prevailing nuts) are designed to deform when tightened or in use and should not be reinstalled.

Whenever possible, we will note any special retainers which should be replaced during a procedure. But you should always inspect the condition of a retainer when it is removed and replace any that show signs of damage. Check all threads for rust or corrosion which can increase the torque necessary to achieve the desired clamp load for which that fastener was originally selected.

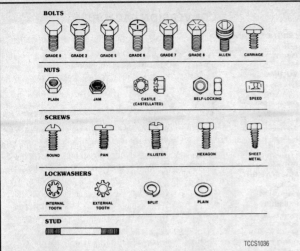

Fig. 19 There are many different types of threaded retainers found on vehicles

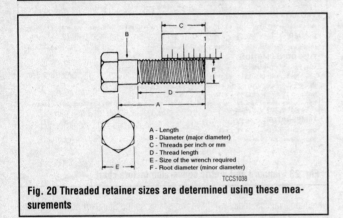

A - Length
B - Diameter (major diameter)
C - Threads per inch or mm
D - Thread length
E - Size of the wrench required
F - Root diameter (minor diameter)

Fig. 20 Threaded retainer sizes are determined using these measurements

Additionally, be sure that the driver surface of the fastener has not been compromised by rounding or other damage. In some cases a driver surface may become only partially rounded, allowing the driver to catch in only one direction. In many of these occurrences, a fastener may be installed and tightened, but the driver would not be able to grip and loosen the fastener again.

If you must replace a fastener, whether due to design or damage, you must ALWAYS be sure to use the proper replacement. In all cases, a retainer of the same design, material and strength should be used. Markings on the heads of most bolts will help determine the proper strength of the fastener. The same material, thread and pitch must be selected to assure proper installation and safe operation of the vehicle afterwards.

Thread gauges are available to help measure a bolt or stud's thread. Most automotive and hardware stores keep gauges available to help you select the proper size. In a pinch, you can use another nut or bolt for a thread gauge. If the bolt you are replacing is not too badly damaged, you can select a match by finding another bolt which will thread in its place. If you find a nut which threads properly onto the damaged bolt, then use that nut to help select the replacement bolt.

✳✳ WARNING

Be aware that when you find a bolt with damaged threads, you may also find the nut or drilled hole it was threaded into has also been damaged. If this is the case, you may have to drill and tap the hole, replace the nut or otherwise repair the threads. NEVER try to force a replacement bolt to fit into the damaged threads.

Torque

Torque is defined as the measurement of resistance to turning or rotating. It tends to twist a body about an axis of rotation. A common example of this would be tightening a threaded retainer such as a nut, bolt or screw. Measuring

torque is one of the most common ways to help assure that a threaded retainer has been properly fastened.

When tightening a threaded fastener, torque is applied in three distinct areas, the head, the bearing surface and the clamp load. About 50 percent of the measured torque is used in overcoming bearing friction. This is the friction between the bearing surface of the bolt head, screw head or nut face and the base material or washer (the surface on which the fastener is rotating). Approximately 40 percent of the applied torque is used in overcoming thread friction. This leaves only about 10 percent of the applied torque to develop a useful clamp load (the force which holds a joint together). This means that friction can account for as much as 90 percent of the applied torque on a fastener.

TORQUE WRENCHES

▶ See Figure 21

In most applications, a torque wrench can be used to assure proper installation of a fastener. Torque wrenches come in various designs and most automotive supply stores will carry a variety to suit your needs. A torque wrench should be used any time we supply a specific torque value for a fastener. Again, the general rule of "if you are using the right tool for the job, you should not have to strain to tighten a fastener" applies here.

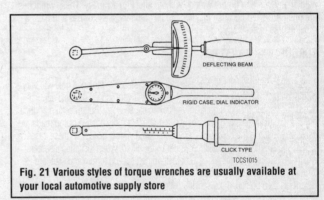

Fig. 21 Various styles of torque wrenches are usually available at your local automotive supply store

Beam Type

The beam type torque wrench is one of the most popular types. It consists of a pointer attached to the head that runs the length of the flexible beam (shaft) to a scale located near the handle. As the wrench is pulled, the beam bends and the pointer indicates the torque using the scale.

Click (Breakaway) Type

Another popular design of torque wrench is the click type. To use the click type wrench you pre-adjust it to a torque setting. Once the torque is reached, the wrench has a reflex signaling feature that causes a momentary breakaway of the torque wrench body, sending an impulse to the operator's hand.

Pivot Head Type

▶ See Figure 22

Some torque wrenches (usually of the click type) may be equipped with a pivot head which can allow it to be used in areas of limited access. BUT, it must be used properly. To hold a pivot head wrench, grasp the handle lightly, and as you pull on the handle, it should be floated on the pivot point. If the handle comes in contact with the yoke extension during the process of pulling, there is a very good chance the torque readings will be inaccurate because this could alter the wrench loading point. The design of the handle is usually such as to make it inconvenient to deliberately misuse the wrench.

➡ **It should be mentioned that the use of any U-joint, wobble or extension will have an effect on the torque readings, no matter what type of wrench you are using. For the most accurate readings, install the socket directly on the wrench driver. If necessary, straight extensions (which hold a socket directly under the wrench driver) will have the least effect on the torque reading. Avoid any extension that alters the length of the wrench from the handle to the head/driving point (such as a crow's foot). U-joint or wobble extensions can greatly affect the readings; avoid their use at all times.**

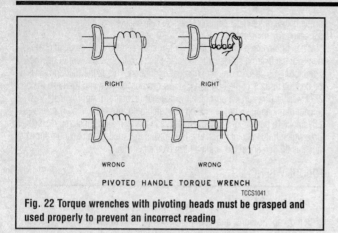

Fig. 22 Torque wrenches with pivoting heads must be grasped and used properly to prevent an incorrect reading

Rigid Case (Direct Reading)

A rigid case or direct reading torque wrench is equipped with a dial indicator to show torque values. One advantage of these wrenches is that they can be held at any position on the wrench without affecting accuracy. These wrenches are often preferred because they tend to be compact, easy to read and have a great degree of accuracy.

TORQUE ANGLE METERS

Because the frictional characteristics of each fastener or threaded hole will vary, clamp loads which are based strictly on torque will vary as well. In most applications, this variance is not significant enough to cause worry. But, in certain applications, a manufacturer's engineers may determine that more precise clamp loads are necessary (such is the case with many aluminum cylinder heads). In these cases, a torque angle method of installation would be specified. When installing fasteners which are torque angle tightened, a predetermined seating torque and standard torque wrench are usually used first to remove any compliance from the joint. The fastener is then tightened the specified additional portion of a turn measured in degrees. A torque angle gauge (mechanical protractor) is used for these applications.

Standard and Metric Measurements

▶ See Figure 23

Throughout this manual, specifications are given to help you determine the condition of various components on your vehicle, or to assist you in their installation. Some of the most common measurements include length (in. or cm/mm), torque (ft. lbs., inch lbs. or Nm) and pressure (psi, in. Hg, kPa or mm Hg). In most cases, we strive to provide the proper measurement as determined by the manufacturer's engineers.

Though, in some cases, that value may not be conveniently measured with what is available in your toolbox. Luckily, many of the measuring devices

CONVERSION FACTORS

LENGTH–DISTANCE

Inches (in.)	x 25.4	= Millimeters (mm)	x .0394	= Inches
Feet (ft.)	x .305	= Meters (m)	x 3.281	= Feet
Miles	x 1.609	= Kilometers (km)	x .0621	= Miles

VOLUME

Cubic Inches (in3)	x 16.387	= Cubic Centimeters	x .061	= in3
IMP Pints (IMP pt.)	x .568	= Liters (L)	x 1.76	= IMP pt.
IMP Quarts (IMP qt.)	x 1.137	= Liters (L)	x .88	= IMP qt.
IMP Gallons (IMP gal.)	x 4.546	= Liters (L)	x .22	= IMP gal.
IMP Quarts (IMP qt.)	x 1.201	= US Quarts (US qt.)	x .833	= IMP qt.
IMP Gallons (IMP gal.)	x 1.201	= US Gallons (US gal.)	x .833	= IMP gal.
Fl. Ounces	x 29.573	= Milliliters	x .034	= Ounces
US Pints (US pt.)	x .473	= Liters (L)	x 2.113	= Pints
US Quarts (US qt.)	x .946	= Liters (L)	x 1.057	= Quarts
US Gallons (US gal.)	x 3.785	= Liters (L)	x .264	= Gallons

MASS–WEIGHT

Ounces (oz.)	x 28.35	= Grams (g)	x .035	= Ounces
Pounds (lb.)	x .454	= Kilograms (kg)	x 2.205	= Pounds

PRESSURE

Pounds Per Sq. In. (psi)	x 6.895	= Kilopascals (kPa)	x .145	= psi
Inches of Mercury (Hg)	x .4912	= psi	x 2.036	= Hg
Inches of Mercury (Hg)	x 3.377	= Kilopascals (kPa)	x .2961	= Hg
Inches of Water (H_2O)	x .07355	= Inches of Mercury	x 13.783	= H_2O
Inches of Water (H_2O)	x .03613	= psi	x 27.684	= H_2O
Inches of Water (H_2O)	x .248	= Kilopascals (kPa)	x 4.026	= H_2O

TORQUE

Pounds–Force Inches (in-lb)	x .113	= Newton Meters (N·m)	x 8.85	= in-lb
Pounds–Force Feet (ft-lb)	x 1.356	= Newton Meters (N·m)	x .738	= ft-lb

VELOCITY

Miles Per Hour (MPH)	x 1.609	= Kilometers Per Hour (KPH)	x .621	= MPH

POWER

Horsepower (Hp)	x .745	= Kilowatts	x 1.34	= Horsepower

FUEL CONSUMPTION*

Miles Per Gallon IMP (MPG)	x .354	= Kilometers Per Liter (Km/L)	
Kilometers Per Liter (Km/L)	x 2.352	= IMP MPG	
Miles Per Gallon US (MPG)	x .425	= Kilometers Per Liter (Km/L)	
Kilometers Per Liter (Km/L)	x 2.352	= US MPG	

*It is common to covert from miles per gallon (mpg) to liters/100 kilometers (1/100 km), where mpg (IMP) x 1/100 km = 282 and mpg (US) x 1/100 km = 235.

TEMPERATURE

Degree Fahrenheit (°F)	= (°C x 1.8) + 32
Degree Celsius (°C)	= (°F – 32) x .56

Fig. 23 Standard and metric conversion factors chart

which are available today will have two scales so the Standard or Metric measurements may easily be taken. If any of the various measuring tools which are available to you do not contain the same scale as listed in the specifications, use the accompanying conversion factors to determine the proper value.

The conversion factor chart is used by taking the given specification and multiplying it by the necessary conversion factor. For instance, looking at the first line, if you have a measurement in inches such as "free-play should be 2 in." but your ruler reads only in millimeters, multiply 2 in. by the conversion factor of 25.4 to get the metric equivalent of 50.8mm. Likewise, if the specification was given only in a Metric measurement, for example in Newton Meters (Nm), then look at the center column first. If the measurement is 100 Nm, multiply it by the conversion factor of 0.738 to get 73.8 ft. lbs.

SERIAL NUMBER IDENTIFICATION

Vehicle

▶ See Figures 24, 25, 26 and 27

All models have the vehicle identification number (VIN) stamped on a plate which is attached to the left side of the instrument panel. This plate is visible through the windshield. The VIN is the legal identifier of your vehicle. The VIN consists of seventeen digits (letters and numbers). The first three digits "JT2" (for example) of the VIN is the World Manufacture Identification number. The next five digits are the Vehicle Description Section. The remaining nine digits are the production numbers including various codes on body style, trim level (base, luxury, ect.) and safety equipment or other information.

The VIN on most models is also stamped on the manufacturer's plate in the engine compartment which is usually located on the firewall cowl panel and on the certification regulation plate affixed to the driver's door post.

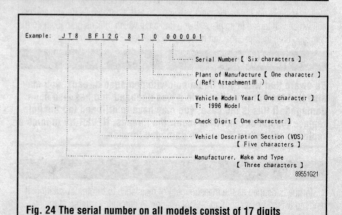

Fig. 24 The serial number on all models consist of 17 digits

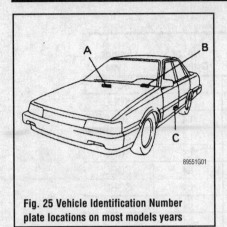

Fig. 25 Vehicle Identification Number plate locations on most models years

Fig. 26 The VIN plate is visible through the windshield of the vehicle

Fig. 27 Another label with the VIN can be found attached to the driver's door

VEHICLE IDENTIFICATION CHART

	Engine Code						Model Year	
Code	Liters	Cubic Centemeters	Cyl.	Fuel Sys.	Eng. Mfg.		Code	Year
1C-LTC	1.8	1839	4	Turbo DSL	Toyota		D	1983
2C-LTC	2.0	1974	4	Turbo DSL	Toyota		E	1984
2S-ELC	2.0	1995	4	MFI	Toyota		F	1985
2VZ-FE	2.5	2507	6	MFI	Toyota		G	1986
3S-FE	2.0	1998	4	MFI	Toyota		H	1987
3VZ-FE	3.0	2959	6	MFI	Toyota		J	1988
5S-FE	2.2	2164	4	MFI	Toyota		K	1989
1MZ-FE	3.0	2995	6	MFI	Toyota		L	1990
							M	1991
							N	1992
							P	1993
							R	1994
							S	1995
							T	1996

89551C05

Engine

Each engine is referred to by both its family designation, such as 3S-FE, and its production or serial number. The serial number can be important when ordering parts. Certain changes may have been made during production of the engine; different parts will be required if the engine was assembled before or after the change date. Generally, parts stores and dealers list this data in their catalogs, so have the engine number handy when you go.

It's a good idea to record the engine number while the vehicle is new. Jotting it inside the cover of the owner's manual or similar easy-to-find location will prevent having to scrape many years of grime off the engine when the number is finally needed.

The engine serial number consists of an engine series identification number, followed by a 6–digit production number.

On the 2S-ELC series engines, the serial numbers are stamped on the right side of the cylinder block, below the oil filter. On the 3S-FE and 5S-FE engine series, the engine serial number is stamped on the left rear side of the engine block. The 1MZ-FE engine stamping is located in the middle of the front of the engine. On the 2VZ-FE and 3VZ-FE series engines, the serial numbers are stamped on the front right side of the cylinder block, below the oil filter.

Transaxle

Transaxle identification codes are located on the vehicle identification number label under the hood and may also be stamped on the transaxle assembly housing.

Transfer Case

Transfer case identification codes are located on the vehicle identification number label under the hood and may also be stamped on the transfer case housing.

ENGINE IDENTIFICATION

Year	Model	Engine Displacement Liters (cc)	Engine Series (ID/VIN)	Fuel System	No. of Cylinders	Engine Type
1983	Camry	2.0 (1995)	2S-ELC	MFI	L4	SOHC
1984	Camry	2.0 (1995)	2S-ELC	MFI	L4	SOHC
	Camry	1.8 (1839)	1C-LTC	Turbo DSL	L4	SOHC
1985	Camry	2.0 (1995)	2S-ELC	MFI	L4	SOHC
	Camry	1.8 (1839)	1C-LTC	Turbo DSL	L4	SOHC
1986	Camry	2.0 (1995)	2S-ELC	MFI	L4	SOHC
	Camry	2.0 (1974)	2C-LTC	Turbo DSL	L4	SOHC
1987	Camry	2.0 (1998)	3S-FE	MFI	L4	DOHC
1988	Camry	2.0 (1998)	3S-FE	MFI	L4	DOHC
1989	Camry	2.0 (1998)	3S-FE	MFI	L4	DOHC
	Camry	2.5 (2507)	2VZ-FE	MFI	V6	DOHC
1990	Camry	2.0 (1998)	3S-FE	MFI	L4	DOHC
	Camry	2.5 (2507)	2VZ-FE	MFI	V6	DOHC
1991	Camry	2.0 (1998)	3S-FE	MFI	L4	DOHC
	Camry	2.5 (2507)	2VZ-FE	MFI	V6	DOHC
1992	Camry	2.2 (2164)	5S-FE	MFI	L4	DOHC
	Camry	3.0 (2959)	3VZ-FE	MFI	V6	DOHC
1993	Camry	2.2 (2164)	5S-FE	MFI	L4	DOHC
	Camry	3.0 (2959)	3VZ-FE	MFI	V6	DOHC
1994	Camry	2.2 (2164)	5S-FE	MFI	L4	DOHC
	Camry	3.0 (2995)	1MZ-FE	MFI	V6	DOHC
1995	Camry	2.2 (2164)	5S-FE	MFI	L4	DOHC
	Camry	3.0 (2995)	1MZ-FE	MFI	V6	DOHC
1996	Camry	2.2 (2164)	5S-FE	MFI	L4	DOHC
	Camry	3.0 (2995)	1MZ-FE	MFI	V6	DOHC

DSL: Diesel
MFI: Multiport Injection
DOHC: Dual Over head Cam
SOHC: Single Over head Cam

89551C04

ROUTINE MAINTENANCE AND TUNE-UP

▶ **See Figures 28, 29, 30, 31 and 32**

Proper maintenance and tune-up is the key to long and trouble-free vehicle life, and the work can yield its own rewards. Studies have shown that a properly tuned and maintained vehicle can achieve better gas mileage than an out-of-tune vehicle. As a conscientious owner and driver, set aside a Saturday morning, say once a month, to check or replace items which could cause major problems later. Keep your own personal log to jot down which services you performed, how much the parts cost you, the date, and the exact odometer reading at the time. Keep all receipts for such items as engine oil and filters, so that they may be referred to in case of related problems or to determine operating expenses. As a do-it-yourselfer, these receipts are the only proof you have that the required maintenance was performed. In the event of a warranty problem, these receipts will be invaluable.

The literature provided with your vehicle when it was originally delivered includes the factory recommended maintenance schedule. If you no longer have this literature, replacement copies are usually available from the dealer. A maintenance schedule is provided later in this section, in case you do not have the factory literature.

Air Cleaner (Element)

The element should be replaced at the recommended intervals shown in the Maintenance Intervals chart later in this section. If your car is operated under severely dusty conditions or severe operating conditions, more frequent changes will certainly be necessary. Inspect the element at least twice a year. Early spring and early fall are always good times for inspection. Remove the element and check for any perforations or tears in the filter. Check the cleaner housing for signs of dirt or dust that may have leaked through the filter element or in through the snorkel tube. Position a droplight on one side of the element and look through the filter at the light. If no glow of light can be seen through the element material, replace the filter. If holes in the filter element are apparent or signs of dirt seepage through the filter are evident, replace the filter.

MAINTENANCE COMPONENT LOCATIONS—V6 ENGINE

1. Engine oil filler cap
2. Coolant filler cap
3. Brake master cylinder
4. Coolant reservoir
5. Power steering reservoir
6. Windshield washer reservoir
7. Air cleaner
8. Battery
9. Radiator
10. Engine oil dipstick
11. Automatic transaxle dipstick
12. Fuse block
13. Ignition coils and spark plugs (under cover)
14. Radiator hose

8951P01

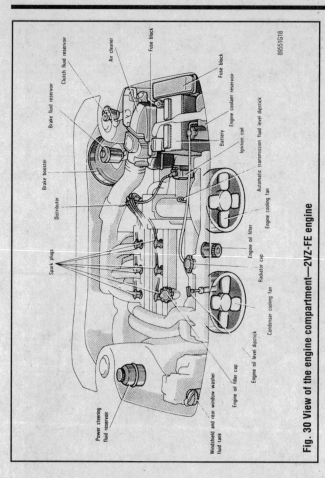

Fig. 30 View of the engine compartment—2VZ-FE engine

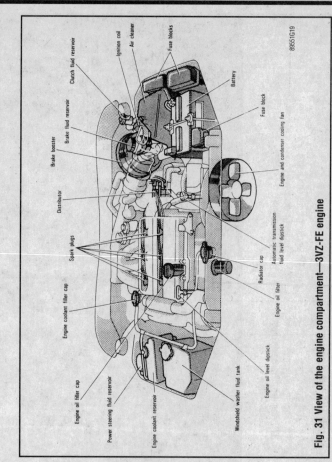

Fig. 31 View of the engine compartment—3VZ-FE engine

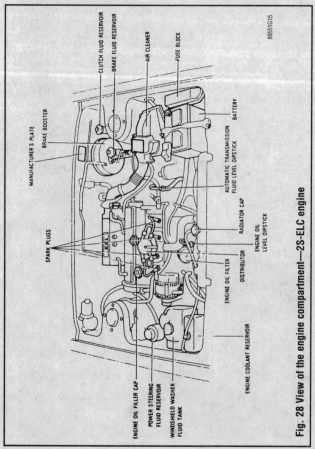

Fig. 28 View of the engine compartment—2S-ELC engine

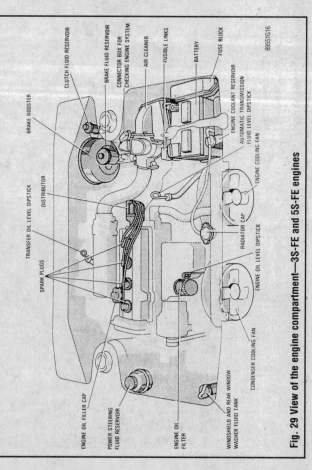

Fig. 29 View of the engine compartment—3S-FE and 5S-FE engines

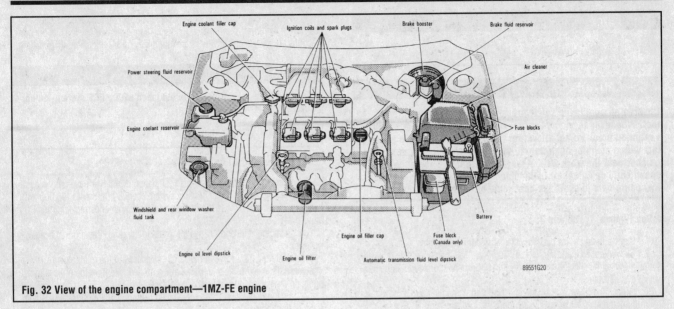

Fig. 32 View of the engine compartment—1MZ-FE engine

REMOVAL & INSTALLATION

▶ **See Figures 33, 34, 35 and 36**

1. On models equipped with cruise control, the cable may need to be released from the clamp attached to the side of the air cleaner.

2. Release the clips holding the top of the air box and lift the lid. Note that some of these clips may be in close quarters against bodywork or other components; don't pry or force the clips.

3. Separate any wiring that may be in the way of cover separation.

4. Position the cover with the air flow meter and the air cleaner flexible hose off to the side. If necessary, unplug the electrical connector.

5. Withdraw the element from the housing and discard it.

6. With a clean rag, remove any dirt or dust from the front cover and also from the element seating surface.

✳✳ CAUTION

Do not drive the vehicle with air cleaner removed. Doing so will allow dirt and a variety of other foreign particles to enter the engine and cause damage and wear. Also, backfiring could cause a fire in the engine compartment.

To install:

7. Position and install the new filter element so that it seats properly in the housing.

8. Position the cover with the attached air flow meter and hose over the element. Secure it with the retaining clips. Engage the electrical connector if applicable.

Fig. 33 The air cleaner cover is usually secured with clamps

Fig. 34 Release the clamps securing the cover

Fig. 35 If applicable, unplug the mass air flow sensor connector

Fig. 36 Lift the cover off and remove the filter element

Fuel Filter

REMOVAL & INSTALLATION

✳✳ CAUTION

Observe all applicable safety precautions when working around fuel. Whenever servicing the fuel system, always work in a well ventilated area. Do not allow fuel spray or vapors to come in contact with a spark or open flame. Keep a dry chemical fire extinguisher near the work area. Always keep fuel in a container specifically designed for fuel storage; also, always properly seal fuel containers to avoid the possibility of fire or explosion.

▶ See Figures 37, 38 and 39

1. Place a drain pan or plastic container under the fuel filter.
2. Slowly loosen the lower flare nut fitting until all the pressure is relieved and all the fuel is collected. Refer to Section 5 for more information on depressurizing the system.
3. Loosen the union bolt on the upper portion of the filter and remove the banjo fitting and two metal gaskets. Discard the gaskets.
4. Pull the filter from the mounting bracket.
To install:
5. Place a new filter into position.
6. Install the banjo fitting with a new metal gasket on each side and install the union bolt. Tighten the union bolt to 22 ft. lbs. (30 Nm).
7. Attach the flare nut to the lower connection and hand tighten. Tighten the flare nut to 22 ft. lbs. (30 Nm).
8. Remove the drain pan and/or rags and connect the negative battery cable.

9. Start the engine and visually inspect the upper and lower connections for leaks. Run the tip of your finger around both connections to ensure that the connections are leak-free. If any leaks are found they must be repaired immediately.

PCV Valve

➡ The 3S-FE engine series, while equipped with a PCV system, do not utilize a PCV valve.

REMOVAL & INSTALLATION

▶ See Figures 40, 41 and 42

The PCV valve regulates crankcase ventilation during various engine operating conditions. Inspect the PCV valve system every 60,000 miles (96,000 km) or every 36 months. Toyota Motor Corporation recommends replacing the PCV valve every 15,000 miles (24,000 km).

1. Check the ventilation hoses for leaks or clogging. Clean or replace as necessary.
2. Locate the PCV valve in the valve cover or from the manifold-to-crankcase hose and remove it. Clean any gum deposits from the orifices by spraying the valve with carburetor or contact cleaner.
3. Test the PCV valve, if the valve failed testing, it will require replacement. Refer to Section 4.
4. Visually inspect all hose connections and hoses for cracks, clogs or deterioration and replace as necessary.
5. Install the PCV valve. Make sure all hose connections are tight.

Evaporative Canister

To reduce hydrocarbon emissions, evaporated fuel is routed through the charcoal canister into the intake manifold where it is used for combustion in the cylinders.

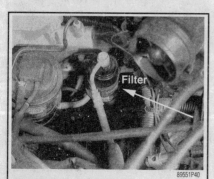

Fig. 37 The fuel filter can be found in the engine compartment (shown) or near the gas tank

Fig. 38 Once the filter is removed, discard the gaskets (1) and keep the union bolt (2)

Fig. 39 When installing the fuel filter, be sure to use new gaskets on both sides of the union

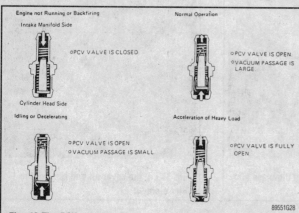

Fig. 40 The PCV valve regulates crankcase ventilation according to engine running conditions

SERVICING

▶ See Figures 43, 44, 45 and 46

1. Note which pipe connections on the canister the vacuum lines go to and disconnect them. This can be done easily with lettered or numbered strips of masking tape.
2. Remove the charcoal canister.
3. The canister should be checked for clogging and a stuck check valve. Using low pressure compressed air, blow into the tank pipe, and place your hand over the other pipes to ensure that the air flows freely. Blow compressed air into the purge pipe and make sure that air does not flow from the other pipes. If the air does not flow as outlined, replace the canister.
4. If the canister is clogged, it may be cleaned using low pressure compressed air. To clean the canister, blow low pressure compressed air into the tank pipe while holding the upper canister pipe closed. If any of the activated carbon comes out, replace the canister.

➡ Do not attempt to wash the canister to clean it.

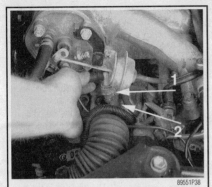

Fig. 41 Pull the PCV valve (1) from the grommet (2)

Fig. 42 Now pull the valve from the hose

Fig. 43 The canister can usually be found in the engine compartment

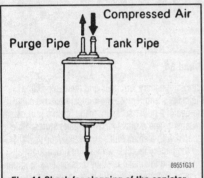

Fig. 44 Check for clogging of the canister on 2S-ELC, 3S-FE and 2VZ-FE engines as shown

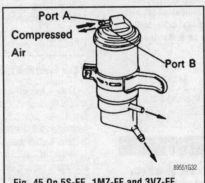

Fig. 45 On 5S-FE, 1MZ-FE and 3VZ-FE engines, check for a clogged canister as shown

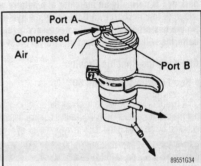

Fig. 46 Place a finger over the purge pipe and blow air into the tank pipe to clean the filter—5S-FE, 1MZ-FE and 3VZ-FE engines

5. The charcoal canister vacuum lines and pipe connections should be checked for clogging, pinching, looseness and cracks. Replace all damaged vacuum lines.

6. Install the charcoal canister and connect the canister hoses to their proper connections.

Battery

PRECAUTIONS

Always use caution when working on or near the battery. Never allow a tool to bridge the gap between the negative and positive battery terminals. Also, be careful not to allow a tool to provide a ground between the positive cable/terminal and any metal component on the vehicle. Either of these conditions will cause a short circuit, leading to sparks and possible personal injury.

Do not smoke or all open flames/sparks near a battery; the gases contained in the battery are very explosive and, if ignited, could cause severe injury or death.

All batteries, regardless of type, should be carefully secured by a battery hold-down device. If not, the terminals or casing may crack from stress during vehicle operation. A battery which is not secured may allow acid to leak, making it discharge faster. The acid can also eat away at components under the hood.

Always inspect the battery case for cracks, leakage and corrosion. A white corrosive substance on the battery case or on nearby components would indicate a leaking or cracked battery. If the battery is cracked, it should be replaced immediately.

GENERAL MAINTENANCE

Always keep the battery cables and terminals free of corrosion. Check and clean these components about once a year.

Keep the top of the battery clean, as a film of dirt can help discharge a battery that is not used for long periods. A solution of baking soda and water may be used for cleaning, but be careful to flush this off with clear water. DO NOT let any of the solution into the filler holes. Baking soda neutralizes battery acid and will de-activate a battery cell.

Batteries in vehicles which are not operated on a regular basis can fall victim to parasitic loads (small current drains which are constantly drawing current from the battery). Normal parasitic loads may drain a battery on a vehicle that is in storage and not used for 6–8 weeks. Vehicles that have additional accessories such as a phone or an alarm system may discharge a battery sooner. If the vehicle is to be stored for longer periods in a secure area and the alarm system is not necessary, the negative battery cable should be disconnected to protect the battery.

Remember that constantly deep cycling a battery (completely discharging and recharging it) will shorten battery life.

BATTERY FLUID

▶ See Figure 47

Check the battery electrolyte level at least once a month, or more often in hot weather or during periods of extended vehicle operation. On non-sealed batter-

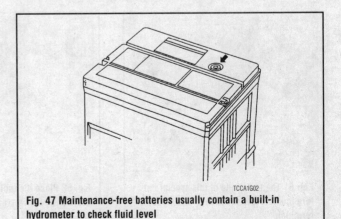

Fig. 47 Maintenance-free batteries usually contain a built-in hydrometer to check fluid level

ies, the level can be checked either through the case (if translucent) or by removing the cell caps. The electrolyte level in each cell should be kept filled to the split ring inside each cell, or the line marked on the outside of the case.

If the level is low, add only distilled water through the opening until the level is correct. Each cell must be checked and filled individually. Distilled water should be used, because the chemicals and minerals found in most drinking water are harmful to the battery and could significantly shorten its life.

If water is added in freezing weather, the vehicle should be driven several miles to allow the water to mix with the electrolyte. Otherwise, the battery could freeze.

Although some maintenance-free batteries have removable cell caps, the electrolyte condition and level on all sealed maintenance-free batteries must be checked using the built-in hydrometer "eye." The exact type of eye will vary. But, most battery manufacturers, apply a sticker to the battery itself explaining the readings.

➡**Although the readings from built-in hydrometers will vary, a green eye usually indicates a properly charged battery with sufficient fluid level. A dark eye is normally an indicator of a battery with sufficient fluid, but which is low in charge. A light or yellow eye usually indicates that electrolyte has dropped below the necessary level. In this last case, sealed batteries with an insufficient electrolyte must usually be discarded.**

Checking the Specific Gravity

▶ **See Figures 48, 49 and 50**

A hydrometer is required to check the specific gravity on all batteries that are not maintenance-free. On batteries that are maintenance-free, the specific gravity is checked by observing the built-in hydrometer "eye" on the top of the battery case.

✳✳ CAUTION

Battery electrolyte contains sulfuric acid. If you should splash any on your skin or in your eyes, flush the affected area with plenty of clear water. If it lands in your eyes, get medical help immediately.

The fluid (sulfuric acid solution) contained in the battery cells will tell you many things about the condition of the battery. Because the cell plates must be kept submerged below the fluid level in order to operate, the fluid level is extremely important. And, because the specific gravity of the acid is an indication of electrical charge, testing the fluid can be an aid in determining if the battery must be replaced. A battery in a vehicle with a properly operating charging system should require little maintenance, but careful, periodic inspection should reveal problems before they leave you stranded.

At least once a year, check the specific gravity of the battery. It should be between 1.20 and 1.26 on the gravity scale. Most auto stores carry a variety of inexpensive battery hydrometers. These can be used on any non-sealed battery to test the specific gravity in each cell.

The battery testing hydrometer has a squeeze bulb at one end and a nozzle at the other. Battery electrolyte is sucked into the hydrometer until the float is lifted from its seat. The specific gravity is then read by noting the position of the float. If gravity is low in one or more cells, the battery should be slowly charged and checked again to see if the gravity has come up. Generally, if after charging, the specific gravity between any two cells varies more than 50 points (0.50), the battery should be replaced, as it can no longer produce sufficient voltage to guarantee proper operation.

CABLES

▶ **See Figures 51, 52, 53 and 54**

Once a year (or as necessary), the battery terminals and the cable clamps should be cleaned. Loosen the clamps and remove the cables, negative cable first. On top post batteries, the use of a puller specially made for this purpose is recommended. These are inexpensive and available in most parts stores. Side terminal battery cables are secured with a small bolt.

Clean the cable clamps and the battery terminal with a wire brush, until all corrosion, grease, etc., is removed and the metal is shiny. It is especially important to clean the inside of the clamp thoroughly (an old knife is useful here), since a small deposit of oxidation there will prevent a sound connection and inhibit starting or charging. Special tools are available for cleaning these parts,

Fig. 48 On non-sealed batteries, the fluid level can be checked by removing the cell caps

Fig. 49 If the fluid level is low, add only distilled water until the level is correct

Fig. 50 Check the specific gravity of the battery's electrolyte with a hydrometer

Fig. 51 The underside of this special battery tool has a wire brush to clean post terminals

Fig. 52 Place the tool over the battery posts and twist to clean until the metal is shiny

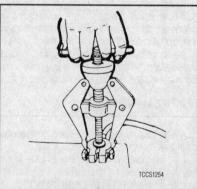

Fig. 53 A special tool is available to pull the clamp from the post

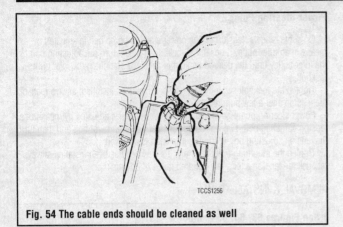

Fig. 54 The cable ends should be cleaned as well

one type for conventional top post batteries and another type for side terminal batteries. It is also a good idea to apply some dielectric grease to the terminal, as this will aid in the prevention of corrosion.

After the clamps and terminals are clean, reinstall the cables, negative cable last; DO NOT hammer the clamps onto battery posts. Tighten the clamps securely, but do not distort them. Give the clamps and terminals a thin external coating of grease after installation, to retard corrosion.

Check the cables at the same time that the terminals are cleaned. If the cable insulation is cracked or broken, or if the ends are frayed, the cable should be replaced with a new cable of the same length and gauge.

CHARGING

✳✳ CAUTION

The chemical reaction which takes place in all batteries generates explosive hydrogen gas. A spark can cause the battery to explode and splash acid. To avoid personal injury, be sure there is proper ventilation and take appropriate fire safety precautions when working with or near a battery.

A battery should be charged at a slow rate to keep the plates inside from getting too hot. However, if some maintenance-free batteries are allowed to discharge until they are almost "dead," they may have to be charged at a high rate to bring them back to "life." Always follow the charger manufacturer's instructions on charging the battery.

REPLACEMENT

When it becomes necessary to replace the battery, select one with an amperage rating equal to or greater than the battery originally installed. Deterioration and just plain aging of the battery cables, starter motor, and associated wires makes the battery's job harder in successive years. This makes it prudent to install a new battery with a greater capacity than the old.

Belts

INSPECTION

▶ **See Figures 55, 56, 57, 58 and 59**

Inspect the belts for signs of glazing or cracking. A glazed belt will be perfectly smooth from slippage, while a good belt will have a slight texture of fabric visible. Cracks will usually start at the inner edge of the belt and run outward. All worn or damaged drive belts should be replaced immediately. It is best to replace all drive belts at one time, as a preventive maintenance measure, during this service operation.

ADJUSTMENT

▶ **See Figures 60 and 61**

Belts are normally adjusted by loosening the bolts of the accessory being driven and moving that accessory on its pivot points until the proper tension is applied to the belt. The accessory is held in this position while the bolts are tightened. To determine proper belt tension, you can purchase a belt tension gauge or simply use the deflection method. To determine deflection, press inward on the belt at the mid-point of its longest straight run. The belt should deflect (move inward) ⅜–½ in. (10–13mm). Some long V-belts and

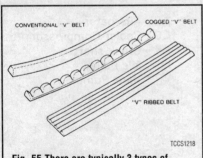

Fig. 55 There are typically 3 types of accessory drive belts found on vehicles today

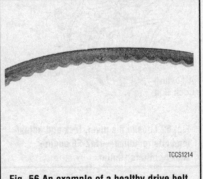

Fig. 56 An example of a healthy drive belt

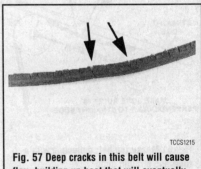

Fig. 57 Deep cracks in this belt will cause flex, building up heat that will eventually lead to belt failure

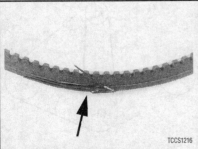

Fig. 58 The cover of this belt is worn, exposing the critical reinforcing cords to excessive wear

Fig. 59 Installing too wide a belt can result in serious belt wear and/or breakage

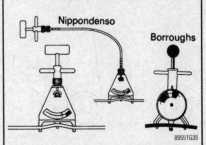

Fig. 60 The Nippondenso and Burroughs tension gauges may be found at retail auto parts stores

most serpentine belts have idler pulleys which are used for adjusting purposes. Just loosen the idler pulley and move it to take up or release tension on the belt.

➡️**Proper belt tension is important because it will allow the belt to run quietly and will maximize the belt's service life.**

Alternator

▶ See Figure 62

To adjust the tension of the alternator drive belt, loosen the pivot and mounting bolts on the alternator. Using a wooden hammer handle or a broomstick, or even your hand if you're strong enough, move the alternator one way or the other until the tension is within acceptable limits.

❊❊ CAUTION

Never use a screwdriver or any other metal device such as a prybar, as a lever when adjusting the alternator belt tension!

Tighten the mounting bolts securely. If a new belt has been installed, always recheck the tension after a few hundred miles of driving.

Alternator belt tension on all other engines is adjusted by means of a tension adjusting bolt. Loosen the alternator pivot bolt and the locking bolt, then turn the tension adjusting bolt until proper tension is achieved.

Tighten the mounting bolts securely. If a new belt has been installed, always recheck the tension after a few hundred miles of driving.

Air Conditioning Compressor

Tension on the air conditioning compressor belt is adjusted by means of an idler pulley. Loosen the lockbolt and then turn the adjusting bolt on the idler pulley until the desired tension is achieved. Retighten the idler pulley lockbolt.

Tighten the lockbolt securely. If a new belt has been installed, always recheck the tension after a few hundred miles of driving.

Power Steering Pump

On some models, tension on the power steering pump belt is adjusted by means of an idler pulley. Loosen the lockbolt and then turn the adjusting bolt on the idler pulley until the desired tension is achieved. Retighten the idler pulley lockbolt.

Tighten the lockbolt securely. If a new belt has been installed, always recheck the tension after a few hundred miles of driving.

Power steering pump belt tension on other models is adjusted by means of a tension adjusting bolt. Loosen the power steering pump pivot bolt and then turn the tension adjusting bolt until proper tension is achieved.

Tighten the mounting bolts securely. If a new belt has been installed, always recheck the tension after a few hundred miles of driving.

REMOVAL & INSTALLATION

▶ See Figures 63, 64, 65 and 66

If a belt must be replaced, the driven unit must be loosened and moved to its extreme loosest position, generally by moving it toward the center of the motor. After removing the old belt, check the pulleys for dirt or built-up material which could affect belt contact. Carefully install the new belt, remembering that it is new and unused — it may appear to be just a little too small to fit over the pulley flanges. Fit the belt over the largest pulley (usually the crankshaft pulley at the bottom center of the motor) first, then work on the smaller one(s). Gentle pressure in the direction of rotation is helpful. Some belts run around a third or idler pulley, which acts as an additional pivot in the belt's path. It may be possible to loosen the idler pulley as well as the main component, making your job much easier. Depending on which belt(s) you are changing, it may be necessary to loosen or remove other interfering belts to get at the one(s) you want.

When buying replacement belts, remember that the fit is critical according to the length of the belt, the width of the belt, the depth of the belt and the angle or profile of the V shape (always match up old belt with new belt if possible). The belt shape should exactly match the shape of the pulley; belts that are not an exact match can cause noise, slippage and premature failure.

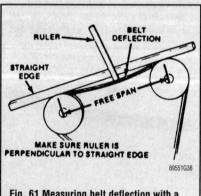

Fig. 61 Measuring belt deflection with a ruler and straight edge

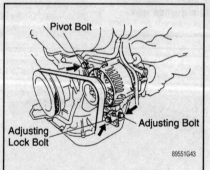

Fig. 62 Loosen the pivot, lock and adjusting bolts to adjust—1MZ-FE engine shown, others similar

AL : Alternator
CC : Cooler Compressor
CK : Crank shaft
IP : Idle Pulley
VP : Vane Pump

Fig. 63 Listing of pulley abbreviations

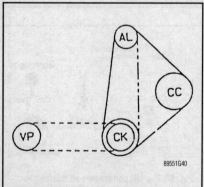

Fig. 64 Belt routings on the 5S-FE and 3S-FE engines

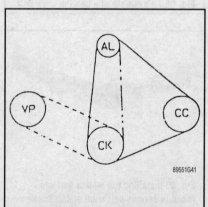

Fig. 65 Belt routings on the 3VZ-FE engine

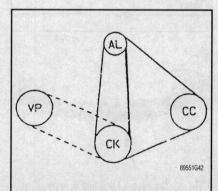

Fig. 66 Belt routings on the 1MZ-FE engine

After the new belt is installed, draw tension on it by moving the driven unit away from the motor and tighten its mounting bolts. This is sometimes a three- or four-handed job; you may find an assistant helpful. Make sure that all the bolts you loosened get retightened and that any other loosened belts also have the correct tension. A new belt can be expected to stretch a bit after installation so be prepared to re-adjust your new belt.

➡ **After installing a new belt, run the engine for about 5 minutes and then recheck the belt tension.**

Timing Belts

INSPECTION

▶ **See Figures 67 thru 72**

All 1983–96 Toyota Camry engines utilize a timing belt to drive the camshaft from the crankshaft's turning motion and to maintain proper valve timing. Some

but a damaged belt (which could give out suddenly) may not give as much warning. In general, any time the engine timing cover(s) is(are) removed you should inspect the belt for premature parting, severe cracks or missing teeth.

Hoses

INSPECTION

▶ **See Figures 73, 74, 75, 76 and 77**

Upper and lower radiator hoses along with the heater hoses should be checked for deterioration, leaks and loose hose clamps at least every 15,000 miles (24,000 km). It is also wise to check the hoses periodically in early spring and at the beginning of the fall or winter when you are performing other maintenance. A quick visual inspection could discover a weakened hose which might have left you stranded if it had remained unrepaired.

Whenever you are checking the hoses, make sure the engine and cooling system are cold. Visually inspect for cracking, rotting or collapsed hoses, and replace

Fig. 67 Do not bend, twist or turn the timing belt inside out. Never allow oil, water or steam to contact the belt

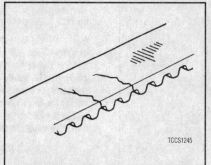

Fig. 68 Look for noticeable cracks or wear on the belt face

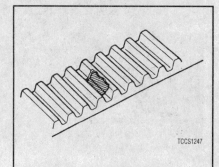

Fig. 69 Foreign materials can get in between the teeth and cause damage

Fig. 70 Inspect the timing belt for cracks, fraying, glazing or damage of any kind

Fig. 71 Damage on only one side of the timing belt may indicate a faulty guide

Fig. 72 ALWAYS replace the timing belt at the interval specified by the manufacturer

manufacturer's schedule periodic timing belt replacement to assure optimum engine performance, to make sure the motorist is never stranded should the belt break (as the engine will stop instantly) and for some (manufacturer's with interference motors) to prevent the possibility of severe internal engine damage should the belt break.

Although these engines are not listed as interference motors (it is not listed by the manufacturer as a motor whose valves might contact the pistons if the camshaft was rotated separately from the crankshaft) the first 2 reasons for periodic replacement still apply. Toyota does recommend replacement for these motors at 60,000 miles (96,000 km) if your vehicle is driven under conditions of extensive idling or low speed driving for a long distance such as a police car, taxi or door-to-door delivery usage. You will have to decide for yourself if the peace of mind offered by a new belt is worth it on higher mileage engines.

Whether or not you decide to replace it, you would be wise to check it periodically to make sure it has not become damaged or worn. Generally speaking, a severely damaged belt will show as engine performance would drop dramatically,

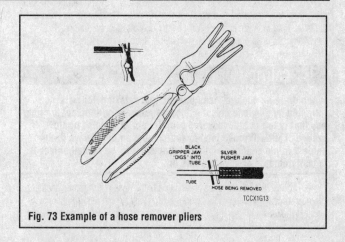

Fig. 73 Example of a hose remover pliers

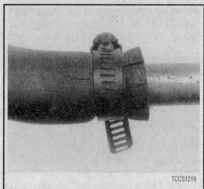

Fig. 74 The cracks developing along this hose are a result of age-related hardening

Fig. 75 A hose clamp that is too tight can cause older hoses to separate and tear on either side of the clamp

Fig. 76 A soft spongy hose (identifiable by the swollen section) will eventually burst and should be replaced

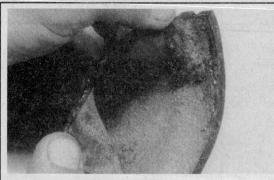

Fig. 77 Hoses are likely to deteriorate from the inside if the cooling system is not periodically flushed

as necessary. Run your hand along the length of the hose. If a weak or swollen spot is noted when squeezing the hose wall, the hose should be replaced.

REMOVAL & INSTALLATION

1. Remove the radiator pressure cap.

❊❊ CAUTION

Never remove the pressure cap while the engine is running, or personal injury from scalding hot coolant or steam may result. If possible, wait until the engine has cooled to remove the pressure cap. If this is not possible, wrap a thick cloth around the pressure cap and turn it slowly to the stop. Step back while the pressure is released from the cooling system. When you are sure all the pressure has been released, use the cloth to turn and remove the cap.

2. Position a clean container under the radiator and/or engine draincock or plug, then open the drain and allow the cooling system to drain to an appropriate level. For some upper hoses, only a little coolant must be drained. To remove hoses positioned lower on the engine, such as a lower radiator hose, the entire cooling system must be emptied.

❊❊ CAUTION

When draining coolant, keep in mind that cats and dogs are attracted by ethylene glycol antifreeze, and are quite likely to drink any that is left in an uncovered container or in puddles on the ground. This will prove fatal in sufficient quantity. Always drain coolant into a sealable container. Coolant may be reused unless it is contaminated or several years old.

3. Loosen the hose clamps at each end of the hose requiring replacement. Clamps are usually either of the spring tension type (which require pliers to squeeze the tabs and loosen) or of the screw tension type (which require screw

or hex drivers to loosen). Pull the clamps back on the hose away from the connection.

4. Twist, pull and slide the hose off the fitting, taking care not to damage the neck of the component from which the hose is being removed.

➡ **If the hose is stuck at the connection, do not try to insert a screwdriver or other sharp tool under the hose end in an effort to free it, as the connection and/or hose may become damaged. Heater connections especially may be easily damaged by such a procedure. If the hose is to be replaced, use a single-edged razor blade to make a slice along the portion of the hose which is stuck on the connection, perpendicular to the end of the hose. Do not cut deep so as to prevent damaging the connection. The hose can then be peeled from the connection and discarded.**

5. Clean both hose mounting connections. Inspect the condition of the hose clamps and replace them, if necessary.

To install:

6. Dip the ends of the new hose into clean engine coolant to ease installation.

7. Slide the clamps over the replacement hose, then slide the hose ends over the connections into position.

8. Position and secure the clamps at least ¼ in. (6.35mm) from the ends of the hose. Make sure they are located beyond the raised bead of the connector.

9. Close the radiator or engine drains and properly refill the cooling system with the clean drained engine coolant or a suitable mixture of ethylene glycol coolant and water.

10. If available, install a pressure tester and check for leaks. If a pressure tester is not available, run the engine until normal operating temperature is reached (allowing the system to naturally pressurize), then check for leaks.

❊❊ CAUTION

If you are checking for leaks with the system at normal operating temperature, BE EXTREMELY CAREFUL not to touch any moving or hot engine parts. Once temperature has been reached, shut the engine OFF, and check for leaks around the hose fittings and connections which were removed earlier.

CV-Boots

INSPECTION

▸ **See Figures 78 and 79**

Toyota recommends inspecting the CV boots every 7500 miles (12,000 km) or every 12 months whichever comes first. The CV (Constant Velocity) boots should be checked for damage each time the oil is changed and any other time the vehicle is raised for service. These boots keep water, grime, dirt and other damaging matter from entering the CV-joints. Any of these could cause early CV-joint failure which can be expensive to repair. Heavy grease thrown around the inside of the front wheel(s) and on the brake caliper/drum can be an indication of a torn boot. Thoroughly check the boots for missing clamps and tears. If the boot is damaged, it should be replaced immediately.

Fig. 78 CV-boots must be inspected periodically for damage

Fig. 79 A torn boot should be replaced immediately

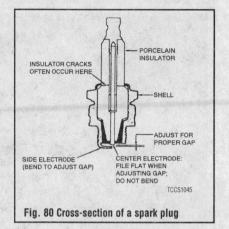

Fig. 80 Cross-section of a spark plug

Spark Plugs

▶ See Figures 80 and 81

➡Spark plugs are only used on vehicles with gasoline engines.

A typical spark plug consists of a metal shell surrounding a ceramic insulator. A metal electrode extends downward through the center of the insulator and protrudes a small distance. Located at the end of the plug and attached to the side of the outer metal shell is the side electrode. The side electrode bends in at a 90° angle so that its tip is just past and parallel to the tip of the center electrode. The distance between these two electrodes (measured in thousandths of an inch or hundredths of a millimeter) is called the spark plug gap.

The spark plug does not produce a spark but instead provides a gap across which the current can arc. The coil produces anywhere from 20,000 to 50,000 volts (depending on the type and application) which travels through the wires to the spark plugs. The current passes along the center electrode and jumps the gap to the side electrode, and in doing so, ignites the air/fuel mixture in the combustion chamber.

SPARK PLUG HEAT RANGE

▶ See Figures 81 and 82

Spark plug heat range is the ability of the plug to dissipate heat. The longer the insulator (or the farther it extends into the engine), the hotter the plug will operate; the shorter the insulator (the closer the electrode is to the block's cooling passages) the cooler it will operate. A plug that absorbs little heat and remains too cool will quickly accumulate deposits of oil and carbon since it is not hot enough to burn them off. This leads to plug fouling and consequently to misfiring. A plug that absorbs too much heat will have no deposits but, due to the excessive heat, the electrodes will burn away quickly and might possibly lead to preignition or other ignition problems. Preignition takes place when plug tips get so hot that they glow sufficiently to ignite the air/fuel mixture before the actual spark occurs. This early ignition will usually cause a pinging during low speeds and heavy loads.

The general rule of thumb for choosing the correct heat range when picking a spark plug is: if most of your driving is long distance, high speed travel, use a colder plug; if most of your driving is stop and go, use a hotter plug. Original equipment plugs are generally a good compromise between the 2 styles and most people never have the need to change their plugs from the factory-recommended heat range.

REMOVAL & INSTALLATION

▶ See Figures 83 thru 84

On the 2S-ELC, 3S-FE and 1992 5S-FE engines, the spark plugs require replacement at 30,000 miles (48,000 km). On all other engines the spark plugs are platinum and require replacement every 60,000 miles (96,000 km). In normal operation plug gap increases about 0.001 inch (0.025mm) for every 2500 miles (4000 km). As the gap increases, the plug's voltage requirement also increases. It requires a greater voltage to jump the wider gap and about two to three times as much voltage to fire the plug at high speeds than at idle. The improved air/fuel ratio control of modern fuel injection combined with the higher voltage output of modern ignition systems will often allow an engine to run significantly longer on a set of standard spark plugs, but keep in mind that efficiency will drop as the gap widens (along with fuel economy and power).

When you're removing spark plugs, work on one at a time. Don't start by removing the plug wires all at once, because, unless you number them, they may become mixed up. Take a minute before you begin and number the wires with tape.

1. Disconnect the negative battery cable. If the vehicle has been run recently, allow the engine to thoroughly cool.

2. If applicable, remove the cap nuts and valve bank cover(s).

3. On 1MZ-FE engines, disconnect the ignition coil wiring from the right and left cylinder heads. Remove the ignition coils from the cylinder heads. Arrange the coils in order on a table.

4. Carefully twist the spark plug wire boot to loosen it, then pull upward and remove the boot from the plug. Be sure to pull on the boot and not on the wire, otherwise the connector located inside the boot may become separated.

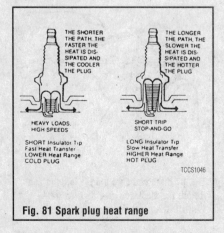

Fig. 81 Spark plug heat range

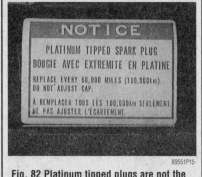

Fig. 82 Platinum tipped plugs are not the same as regular, check for a label specifying the type you have

Fig. 83 Use an extension to help reach the spark plug

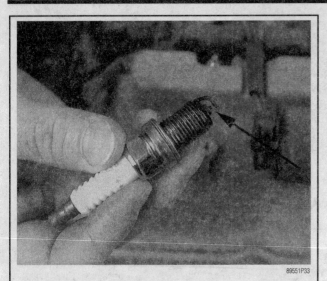

Fig. 84 Withdraw the spark plug and examine the tip

5. Using compressed air, blow any water or debris from the spark plug well to assure that no harmful contaminants are allowed to enter the combustion chamber when the spark plug is removed. If compressed air is not available, use a rag or a brush to clean the area.

➡ **Remove the spark plugs when the engine is cold, if possible, to prevent damage to the threads. If removal of the plugs is difficult, apply a few drops of penetrating oil or silicone spray to the area around the base of the plug, and allow it a few minutes to work.**

6. Using a spark plug socket that is equipped with a rubber insert to properly hold the plug, turn the spark plug counterclockwise to loosen and remove the spark plug from the bore.

❊❊ WARNING

Be sure not to use a flexible extension on the socket. Use of a flexible extension may allow a shear force to be applied to the plug. A shear force could break the plug off in the cylinder head, leading to costly and frustrating repairs.

To install:

7. Inspect the spark plug boot for tears or damage. If a damaged boot is found, the spark plug wire must be replaced.

8. Using a wire feeler gauge, check and adjust the spark plug gap. When using a gauge, the proper size should pass between the electrodes with a slight drag. The next larger size should not be able to pass while the next smaller size should pass freely.

9. Carefully thread the plug into the bore by hand. If resistance is felt before the plug is almost completely threaded, back the plug out and begin threading again. In small, hard to reach areas, an old spark plug wire and boot

could be used as a threading tool. The boot will hold the plug while you twist the end of the wire and the wire is supple enough to twist before it would allow the plug to crossthread.

❊❊ WARNING

Do not use the spark plug socket to thread the plugs. Always carefully thread the plug by hand or using an old plug wire to prevent the possibility of crossthreading and damaging the cylinder head bore.

10. Carefully tighten the spark plug. If the plug you are installing is equipped with a crush washer, seat the plug, then tighten about ¼ turn to crush the washer. If you are installing a tapered seat plug, tighten the plug to specifications provided by the vehicle or plug manufacturer.

11. Apply a small amount of silicone dielectric compound to the end of the spark plug lead or inside the spark plug boot to prevent sticking, then install the boot to the spark plug and push until it clicks into place. The click may be felt or heard, then gently pull back on the boot to assure proper contact.

12. On 1MZ-FE engines, install the ignition coils in their original locations. Tighten the bolts to 69 inch lbs. (8 Nm). Reattach the coil wiring.

13. If applicable, install the valve bank cover.

INSPECTION & GAPPING

▶ **See Figures 85, 86, 87 and 88**

Check the plugs for deposits and wear. If they are not going to be replaced, clean the plugs thoroughly. Remember that any kind of deposit will decrease the efficiency of the plug. Plugs can be cleaned on a spark plug cleaning machine, which can sometimes be found in service stations, or you can do an acceptable job of cleaning with a stiff brush. If the plugs are cleaned, the electrodes must be filed flat. Use an ignition points file, not an emery board or the like, which will leave deposits. The electrodes must be filed perfectly flat with sharp edges; rounded edges reduce the spark plug voltage by as much as 50%.

Check spark plug gap before installation. The ground electrode (the L-shaped one connected to the body of the plug) must be parallel to the center electrode and the specified size wire gauge (please refer to the Tune-Up Specifications chart for details) must pass between the electrodes with a slight drag.

➡ **NEVER adjust the gap on a used platinum type spark plug.**

Always check the gap on new plugs as they are not always set correctly at the factory. Do not use a flat feeler gauge when measuring the gap on a used plug, because the reading may be inaccurate. A round-wire type gapping tool is the best way to check the gap. The correct gauge should pass through the electrode gap with a slight drag. If you're in doubt, try one size smaller and one larger. The smaller gauge should go through easily, while the larger one shouldn't go through at all. Wire gapping tools usually have a bending tool attached. Use that to adjust the side electrode until the proper distance is obtained. Absolutely never attempt to bend the center electrode. Also, be careful not to bend the side electrode too far or too often as it may weaken and break off within the engine, requiring removal of the cylinder head to retrieve it.

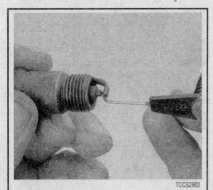

Fig. 85 Checking the spark plug gap with a feeler gauge

Fig. 86 Adjusting the spark plug gap

Fig. 87 If the standard plug is in good condition, the electrode may be filed flat—
WARNING: do not file platinum plugs

A **normally worn** spark plug should have light tan or gray deposits on the firing tip.

A **carbon fouled** plug, identified by soft, sooty, black deposits, may indicate an improperly tuned vehicle. Check the air cleaner, ignition components and engine control system.

This spark plug has been **left in the engine too long,** as evidenced by the extreme gap- Plugs with such an extreme gap can cause misfiring and stumbling accompanied by a noticeable lack of power.

An **oil fouled** spark plug indicates an engine with worn poston rings and/or bad valve seals allowing excessive oil to enter the chamber.

A **physically damaged** spark plug may be evidence of severe detonation in that cylinder. Watch that cylinder carefully between services, as a continued detonation will not only damage the plug, but could also damage the engine.

A **bridged or almost bridged** spark plug, identified by a build-up between the electrodes caused by excessive carbon or oil build-up on the plug.

TCCA1P40

Fig. 88 Inspect the spark plug to determine engine running conditions

Spark Plug Wires

TESTING

▶ **See Figure 89**

Spark plug wires are usually replaced in sets. If a wire is found faulty, it is recommended to replace all of them and not just the one or two that are bad.

At every tune-up/inspection, visually check the spark plug cables for burns cuts, or breaks in the insulation. Check the boots and the nipples on the distributor cap and/or coil. Replace any damaged wiring.

Every 50,000 miles (80,000 Km) or 60 months, the resistance of the wires should be checked with an ohmmeter. Wires with excessive resistance will cause misfiring, and may make the engine difficult to start in damp weather.

To check resistance, on the 4 cylinder engines, remove the distributor cap, leaving the wires attached. Connect one lead of an ohmmeter to an electrode within the

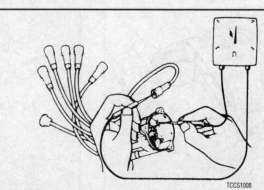
TCCS1008

Fig. 89 Checking plug wire resistance through the distributor cap with an ohmmeter

cap; connect the other lead to the corresponding spark plug terminal (remove it from the plug for this test). Replace any wire which shows a resistance of over 25,000 ohms. Test the high tension lead from the coil by connecting the ohmmeter between the center contact in the distributor cap and either of the primary terminals of the coil (remember, on the 3S-FE engine, the coil is in the cap). If resistance is more than 25,000 ohms, remove the cable from the coil and check the resistance of the cable alone. Anything over 15,000 ohms is cause for replacement.

To check the resistance on the V6 engines, remove the V-bank cover and then disconnect the wire at the plug. Trace the wire back to the distributor cap, pry up the lock claw and disconnect the holder from the cap and then disconnect the wire at the grommet. Connect one lead of an ohmmeter to each end of the spark plug wire. Replace any wire which shows resistance over 25,000 ohms. Test the high tension lead from the coil by connecting the ohmmeter between the center contact in the distributor cap and either of the primary terminals of the coil. If the resistance is more than 25,000 ohms, remove the cable from the coil and check the resistance of the able alone. Anything over 15,000 ohms is cause for replacement.

It should remembered that resistance is also a function of length; longer the cable, the greater the resistance. Thus, if the cause on your car are longer than the factory originally, resistance will be higher, quite possibly outside these limits.

REMOVAL & INSTALLATION

▶ **See Figures 90, 91, 92 and 93**

➡ **The 1987–91 3S-FE engine spark plug wires can not be removed from the distributor cap. They are replaced as one unit.**

1. Disconnect the negative battery cable.
2. Label and disconnect the wires from each spark plug one at a time.
3. Remove the spark plug wires from the distributor cap. On some models you may need to use a flat bladed tool to lift up the lock claw and disconnect the holder from the cap. Separate the wires at the grommet.

✳✳ WARNING

Do not pull on the plug wires to remove them, this may damage the conductor inside.

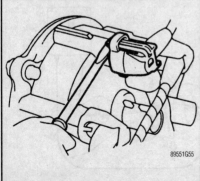

Fig. 90 Make sure to remove the spark plug wires from the boot end and not from the wire itself

4. Pull the plug wires from the retaining clamps.
To install:
5. Attach the holder and grommet portion to the distributor cap. Make sure that the holder is installed correctly to the grommet and cap.
6. Check that the lock claw of the holder is engaged by lightly pulling on the holder.
7. On the center cord, insert the grommet and holder together.
8. Secure the wires with the clamps.

Distributor Cap and Rotor

REMOVAL & INSTALLATION

➡ **The 1987–91 3S-FE engine spark plug wires can not be removed from the distributor cap. They are replaced as one unit.**

1. Disconnect the negative battery cable.
2. If equipped, remove the distributor cap rubber boot.
3. On some models the air cleaner tube may need to be removed to access the distributor cap.
4. Loosen the screws securing the cap on the distributor.
5. Tag the wires leading to the cap for easy identification upon installation.
6. Lift the cap off the distributor. Pulling from the wire boot, remove the plug wires from the cap.
7. If necessary to remove the rotor, some models you simply lift it straight off the shaft. On others, you may need to remove the rotor retaining screws, then lift up the unit.
To install:
8. Install the rotor onto the distributor shaft. The rotor only goes on one way so there should be no mix-up in replacement.
9. Apply a small amount of dielectric grease on the tip of the rotor and the inside of the cap carbon ends.
10. Attach the tagged wires to their proper locations on the cap.
11. Fit the cap onto the distributor, then tighten the bolts.
12. Make sure all the wires are secure on the cap and spark plugs. Connect the negative battery cable.
13. Start the vehicle and check for proper operation.

INSPECTION

When inspecting a cap and rotor, look for signs of cracks, carbon tracking, burns and wear. The inside of the cap may be burnt or have wear on the carbon ends. On the rotor, look at the tip for burning and excessive wear.

Ignition Timing

GENERAL INFORMATION

Ignition timing is the measurement (in degrees) of crankshaft position at the instant the spark plug fires. Ignition timing is adjusted by loosening the distributor locking device and turning the distributor in the engine.

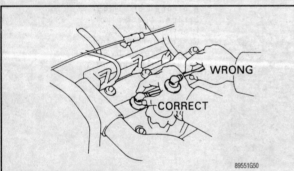

Fig. 91 Lift up the lock claw and disconnect the holder from the cap

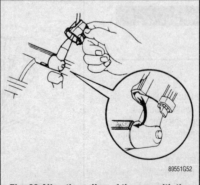

Fig. 92 Align the spline of the cap with the spline groove of the holder

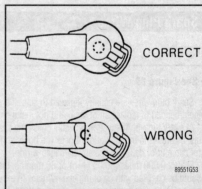

Fig. 93 Make sure the holder is correctly installed to the grommet

It takes a fraction of a second for the spark from the plug to completely ignite the mixture in the cylinder. Because of this, the spark plug must fire before the piston reaches TDC (top dead center, the highest point in its travel), if the mixture is to be completely ignited as the piston passes TDC. This measurement is given in degrees (of crankshaft rotation) before the piston reaches top dead center (BTDC). If the ignition timing setting for your engine is 10° BTDC, this means that the spark plug must fire at a time when the piston for that cylinder is 10° before top dead center of its compression stroke. However, this only holds true while your engine is at idle speed.

As you accelerate from idle, the speed of your engine (rpm) increases. The increase in rpm means that the pistons are now traveling up and down much faster. Because of this, the spark plugs will have to fire even sooner if the mixture is to be completely ignited as the piston passes TDC. To accomplish this, the distributor incorporates means to advance the timing of the spark as the engine speed increases.

The distributor in your Toyota has two means of advancing the ignition timing. One is called vacuum advance and is controlled by that large circular housing on the side of the distributor. This type of distributor is found on vehicles produced in the US from 1983–85 and also those produced in Canada in 1986. The other Electronic Spark Advance (ESA) and is controlled by a microcomputer in 1986–96.

In addition, some distributors have a vacuum retard mechanism which is contained in the same housing on the side of the distributor as the vacuum advance. The function of this mechanism is to retard the timing of the ignition spark under certain engine conditions. This causes more complete burning of the air/fuel mixture in the cylinder and consequently lowers exhaust emissions.

Because these mechanisms change ignition timing, it is necessary to disconnect and plug the one or two vacuum lines from the distributor when setting the basic ignition timing, if the distributor is equipped with a vacuum advancer.

If the ignition timing is set too far advanced (BTDC), the ignition and expansion of the air/fuel mixture in the cylinder will try to force the piston down while it is still traveling upward. This causes engine ping, a sound which resembles marbles being dropped into an empty tin can. If the ignition timing is too far retarded (after, or ATDC), the piston will have already started down on the power stroke when the air/fuel mixture ignites and expands. This will cause the piston to be forced down only a portion of its travel. This results in poor engine performance and lack of power.

Ignition timing adjustment is checked with a timing light. This instrument is connected to the number one (No. 1) spark plug of the engine. The timing light flashes every time an electrical current is sent from the distributor through the No. 1 spark plug wire to the spark plug. The crankshaft pulley and the front cover of the engine are marked with a timing pointer and a timing scale.

When the timing pointer is aligned with the 0 mark on the timing scale, the piston in the No. 1 cylinder is at TDC of it compression stroke. With the engine running, and the timing light aimed at the timing pointer and timing scale, the stroboscopic (periodic) flashes from the timing light will allow you to check the ignition timing setting of the engine. The timing light flashes every time the spark plug in the No. 1 cylinder of the engine fires. Since the flash from the timing light makes the crankshaft pulley seem to stand still for a moment, you will be able to read the exact position of the piston in the No. 1 cylinder on the timing scale on the front of the engine.

If you're buying a timing light, make sure the unit you select is rated for electronic or solid-state ignitions. Generally, these lights have two wires which connect to the battery with alligator clips and a third wire which connects to the No. 1 plug wire. The best lights have an inductive pick-up on the third wire; this allows you to simply clip the small box over the wire. Older lights may require the removal of the plug wire and the installation of an in-line adapter. Since the spark plugs in the twin-cam engines are in deep wells, rigging the adapter can be difficult. Buy quality the first time and the tool will give lasting results and ease of use.

INSPECTION & ADJUSTMENT

Canada and 1983–85 US Models

▶ See Figures 94, 97 and 101

1. Warm up the engine, apply the parking brake and block the wheels. Stop the engine when warm.
2. Locate the IIA service connector coming from the distributor and remove the rubber protective cap.
3. Attach the test probe of the tachometer to the service connector. Check the idle speed with the tachometer and make sure that it is correct. Adjust as necessary.
4. Attach the timing light to the engine according to the manufactures instructions. If the timing marks are not visible, use chalk or a dab of paint to mark them.
5. Disconnect the two vacuum lines from the vacuum advance and plug the lines.
6. Start the engine and run it at idle with the transaxle in Neutral on manual transaxles and Park on automatics. Make sure the parking rake is securely set and that the wheels are blocked.
7. Point the timing light at the timing marks. With the engine at idle, the timing mark on the crankshaft pulley should be aligned with the degree mark specified in the tune-up chart or according to the values listed on the emissions label.
8. If the timing is not specified, loosen the pinch bolt at the base of the distributor and move the unit to advance or retard the timing as required.
9. Stop the engine and tighten the pinch bolt. Start the engine and recheck the timing and the idle speed.
10. Stop the engine and disconnect the timing light and the tachometer. Install the rubber cap on the service connector.
11. Reconnect the vacuum lines to the advancer.

1986–95 Models

EXCEPT 1MZ-FE

▶ See Figures 94 thru 101

This service procedure is for setting base ignition timing. Refer to underhood emission sticker for any additional service procedure steps and/or specifications.

1. Warm the engine to normal operating temperature. Turn off all electrical accessories. Do not attempt to check timing specification or idle speed on a cold engine.
2. Connect a tachometer (as shown in the illustrations) and check the engine idle speed to be sure it is within the specification given in the Tune-Up Specifications chart or underhood emission sticker.

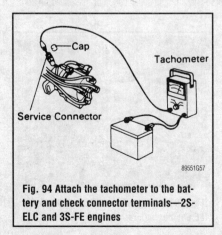

Fig. 94 Attach the tachometer to the battery and check connector terminals—2S-ELC and 3S-FE engines

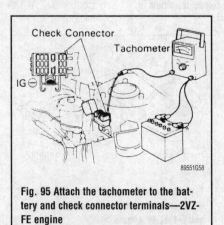

Fig. 95 Attach the tachometer to the battery and check connector terminals—2VZ-FE engine

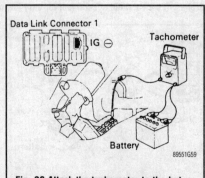

Fig. 96 Attach the tachometer to the battery and check connector terminals—3VZ-FE and 5S-FE engines

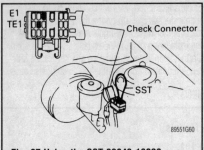

Fig. 97 Using the SST 09843-18020 or a jumper wire, connect terminals TE1 and E1 of the DLC1—2S-ELC and 3S-FE engines

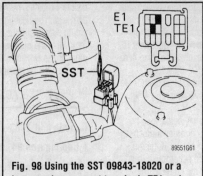

Fig. 98 Using the SST 09843-18020 or a jumper wire, connect terminals TE1 and E1 of the DLC1—2VZ-FE engine

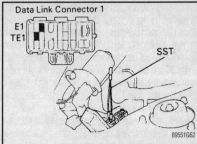

Fig. 99 Using the SST 09843-18020 or a jumper wire, connect terminals TE1 and E1 of the DLC1—3VZ-FE and 5S-FE engines

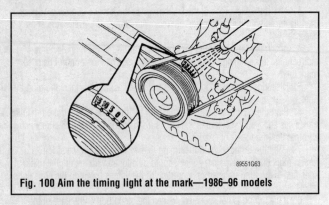

Fig. 100 Aim the timing light at the mark—1986–96 models

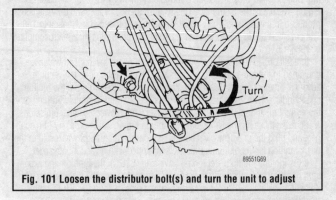

Fig. 101 Loosen the distributor bolt(s) and turn the unit to adjust

3. Remove the cap on the diagnostic check connector. Using a small jumper wire or Special Service Tool SST 09843-18020, short terminals at **T** and **E1** (1986–88) and TE1 and E1 together (1989–96).

4. If the timing marks are difficult to see, shut the engine **OFF** and use a dab of paint or chalk to make them more visible.

5. Connect a timing light according to the manufacturer's instructions.

6. Start the engine and use the timing light to observe the timing marks. With the jumper wire in the check connector the timing should be to specifications (refer to underhood emission sticker as necessary) with the engine fully warmed up (at correct idle speed) and the transmission in correct position. If the timing is not correct, loosen the bolts at the distributor just enough so that the distributor can be turned. Turn the distributor to advance or retard the timing as required. Once the proper marks are seen to align with the timing light, timing is correct.

7. Without changing the position of the distributor, tighten the distributor bolts and double check the timing with the light (check idle speed as necessary). Tighten the pinch bolt to 9 ft. lbs. (13 Nm) on 2S-ELC and 3S-FE engine, 14 ft. lbs. (19 Nm) on 5S-FE engines or 13 ft. lbs. (18 Nm) on the 2VZ-FE and 3VZ-FE engines.

8. Disconnect the jumper wire or Special Service Tool (SST) at the diagnostic check connector.

➥This jumper will be used repeatedly during diagnostics in later sections. Take the time to make a proper jumper with correct terminals or probes. It's a valuable special tool for very low cost.

9. Refer to the underhood emission sticker for timing specification and any additional service procedure steps. If necessary, repeat the timing adjustment procedure.

10. Shut the engine OFF and disconnect all test equipment. Roadtest the vehicle for proper operation.

1MZ-FE ENGINE

♦ See Figures 102, 103 and 104

➥This procedure only applies to the 1994 1MZ-FE engine. The timing on 1995 engines is not adjustable.

This service procedure is for setting base ignition timing. Refer to underhood emission sticker for any additional service procedure steps and/or specifications.

These engines require a tachometer hook-up to the check connector—see illustrations. NEVER allow the tachometer terminal to become grounded; severe and expensive damage can occur to the coil and/or igniter.

Some tachometers are not compatible with this ignition system, confirm the compatibility of your unit before using.

1. Warm the engine to normal operating temperature. Turn off all electrical accessories. Do not attempt to check timing specification or idle speed on a cold engine.

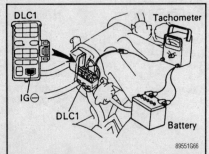

Fig. 102 Attach the tachometer to the battery and check connector terminals—1MZ-FE engine

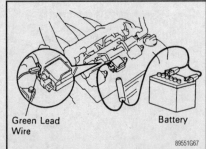

Fig. 103 Attach the timing light clip to the green wire of the lead wire on the No. 4 coil—1MZ-FE engine

Fig. 104 Timing mark at TDC—1994 1MZ-FE engine

2. Connect a tachometer (+) terminal to the terminal IG- of the data link connector.

3. Connect a timing light according to the manufacturer's instructions. On the 1MZ-FE engines, using a 5mm hexagon wrench, remove the two cap nuts and valve bank cover. Attach the timing light pick-up clip on the green lead wire for the No. 4 ignition coil. The timing light will detect the primary signal.

4. Race the engine speed at 2500 rpms for approximately 90 seconds. Check the idle speed.

5. Using SST 09843-18020 or its equivalent jumper wire, connect terminals TE1 and E1 of the DLC1 under the hood.

6. Check the ignition timing, the reading should be 8–12° BTDC at idle.

7. Remove the jumper wire from the DLC1.

8. Recheck the timing, the mark ranges from 7°–17° BTDC at idle. The timing mark will move in the range specified.

9. Disconnect the timing light. Install the valve bank cover and tighten the cap nuts.

10. Disconnect the tachometer from the engine.

11. Roadtest the vehicle for proper operation.

1995 1MZ-FE and 1996 Models

The ignition timing is not adjustable on these engines.

Valve Lash

GENERAL INFORMATION

➡ Check and adjust the valve clearance every 60,000 miles or 72 months.

Valve clearance is one factor which determines how far the intake and exhaust valves will open into the cylinder. If the valve clearance is too large, part of the lift of the camshaft will be used up in removing the excessive clearance, thus the valves will not be opened far enough. This condition has two effects, the valve train components will emit a tapping noise as they take up the excessive clearance, and the engine will perform poorly, since the less the intake valve opens,

the smaller the amount of air/fuel mixture that will be admitted to the cylinders. The less the exhaust valves open, the greater the back-pressure in the cylinder which prevents the proper air/fuel mixture from entering the cylinder.

If the valve clearance is too small, the intake and exhaust valves will not fully seat on the cylinder head when they close. When a valve seats on the cylinder head it does two things, it seals the combustion chamber so none of the gases in the cylinder can escape and it cools itself by transferring some of the heat it absorbed from the combustion process through the cylinder head and into the engine cooling system. Therefore, if the valve clearance is too small, the engine will run poorly due to gases escaping from the combustion chamber, and the valves will overheat and warp since they cannot transfer heat unless they are touching the seat in the cylinder head.

ADJUSTMENT

2S-ELC Engine

These engines are equipped with hydraulic valve adjusters in the valve train. The adjusters automatically maintain a zero valve clearance between the rocker arm and valve stem and no periodic adjustment is possible or necessary. The best way to maintain hydraulic lash adjusters is through regular and frequent oil filter changes.

3S-FE and 5S-FE Engines

▶ See Figures 105 thru 112

➡ **The use of the correct special tools or their equivalent is REQUIRED for this procedure. The valve adjustment requires removal of the adjusting shims (Tool kit J–37141 available from Kent-Moore Tool or a Toyota equivalent No. 09248–55010, 09248–55020 or 09248–55040) and accurate measurement of the shims with a micrometer. A selection of replacement shims (refer to parts department of your Toyota dealer) is also required. Do not attempt this procedure if you are not equipped with the proper tools. Valves on these engines are adjusted with the engine cold. Do not attempt adjustment if the engine has been run within the previous 4 hours. An overnight cooling period is recommended.**

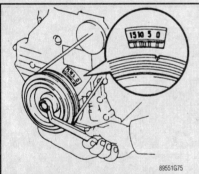

Fig. 105 Turn the crankshaft pulley and align its groove with the timing mark on 0 of the No. 1 timing cover

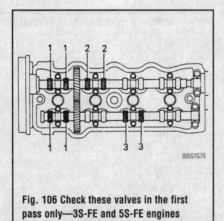

Fig. 106 Check these valves in the first pass only—3S-FE and 5S-FE engines

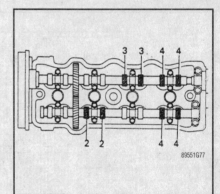

Fig. 107 Check these valves in the second pass only—3S-FE and 5S-FE engines

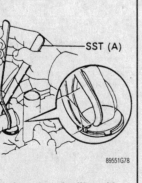

Fig. 108 Press down the valve lifter with SST-A and hold the lifter down with SST-B

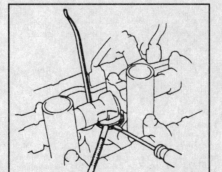

Fig. 109 Remove the adjusting shim with a flatbladded tool and a magnetic finger

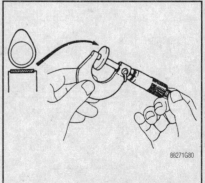

Fig. 110 Using a micrometer, measure the removed adjusting shim size

Adjusting Shim Selection Chart (Intake)

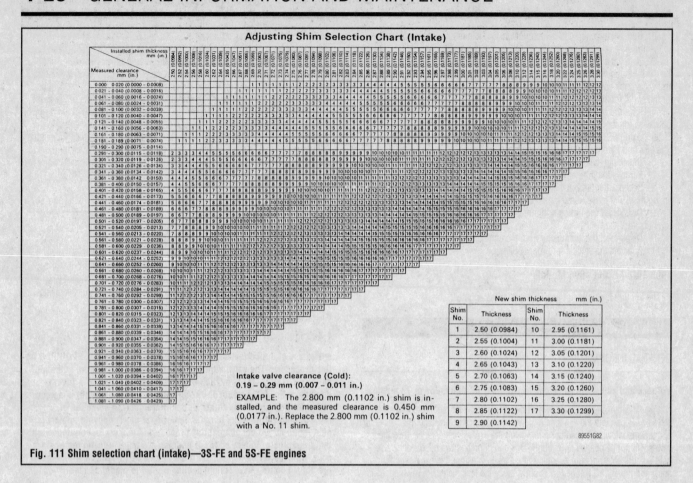

Intake valve clearance (Cold):
0.19 – 0.29 mm (0.007 – 0.011 in.)

EXAMPLE: The 2.800 mm (0.1102 in.) shim is installed, and the measured clearance is 0.450 mm (0.0177 in.). Replace the 2.800 mm (0.1102 in.) shim with a No. 11 shim.

Shim No.	Thickness	Shim No.	Thickness
1	2.50 (0.0984)	10	2.95 (0.1161)
2	2.55 (0.1004)	11	3.00 (0.1181)
3	2.60 (0.1024)	12	3.05 (0.1201)
4	2.65 (0.1043)	13	3.10 (0.1220)
5	2.70 (0.1063)	14	3.15 (0.1240)
6	2.75 (0.1083)	15	3.20 (0.1260)
7	2.80 (0.1102)	16	3.25 (0.1280)
8	2.85 (0.1122)	17	3.30 (0.1299)
9	2.90 (0.1142)		

New shim thickness   mm (in.)

89551G82

Fig. 111 Shim selection chart (intake)—3S-FE and 5S-FE engines

Adjusting Shim Selection Chart (Exhaust)

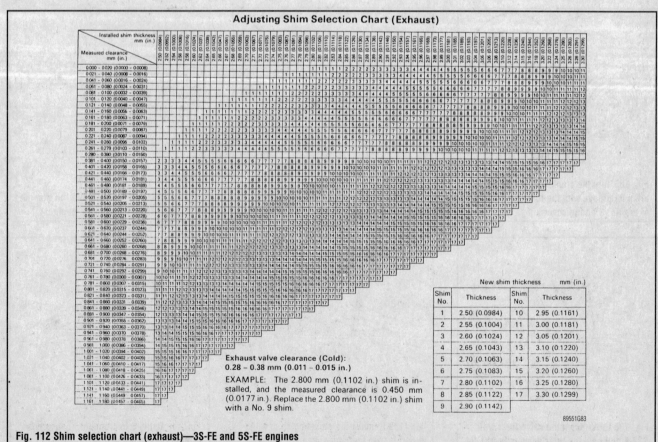

Exhaust valve clearance (Cold):
0.28 – 0.38 mm (0.011 – 0.015 in.)

EXAMPLE: The 2.800 mm (0.1102 in.) shim is installed, and the measured clearance is 0.450 mm (0.0177 in.). Replace the 2.800 mm (0.1102 in.) shim with a No. 9 shim.

Shim No.	Thickness	Shim No.	Thickness
1	2.50 (0.0984)	10	2.95 (0.1161)
2	2.55 (0.1004)	11	3.00 (0.1181)
3	2.60 (0.1024)	12	3.05 (0.1201)
4	2.65 (0.1043)	13	3.10 (0.1220)
5	2.70 (0.1063)	14	3.15 (0.1240)
6	2.75 (0.1083)	15	3.20 (0.1260)
7	2.80 (0.1102)	16	3.25 (0.1280)
8	2.85 (0.1122)	17	3.30 (0.1299)
9	2.90 (0.1142)		

New shim thickness   mm (in.)

89551G83

Fig. 112 Shim selection chart (exhaust)—3S-FE and 5S-FE engines

1. Remove the spark plug wires from the valve cover.

2. Remove the valve cover following procedures discussed in Section 3.

3. Turn the crankshaft to align the groove in the crankshaft pulley with the **0** mark on the timing belt cover. Removing the spark plugs makes this easier, but is not required.

4. Check that the lifters on No.1 cylinder are loose and those on No.4 are tight. If not, turn the crankshaft pulley one full revolution (360°).

5. Using the feeler gauge, measure the clearance on the valves in the positions shown in the diagram labeled First Pass. Make a written record of any measurements which are not within specification.

6. Rotate the crankshaft pulley one full turn (360°) and check the clearance on the other valves. The positions are shown on the diagram labeled Second Pass. Any measurements not within specification should be added to your written record.

- Intake clearance COLD: 0.007–0.011 inch (0.19–0.29mm)
- Exhaust clearance COLD: 0.011–0.015 inch (0.28–0.38mm)

7. For ANY given valve needing adjustment:

a. Turn the crankshaft pulley until the camshaft lobe points upward over the valve. This takes the tension off the valve and spring.

b. Using the forked tool (SST-A), press the valve lifter downward and hold it there. Some tool kits require a second tool for holding the lifter in place (SST-B), allowing the first to be removed.

c. Using small magnetic tools, remove the adjusting shim from the top of the lifter.

d. Use the micrometer and measure the thickness of the shim removed. Determine the thickness of the new shim using the formula below or the selection charts. For the purposes of the following formula, T = Thickness of the old shim; A = Valve clearance measured; N = Thickness of the new shim

- Intake side (camshaft nearest intake manifold): N = T + (A—0.009 inch (0.24mm))
- Exhaust side (camshaft nearest exhaust manifold): N = T + (A—0.013 inch (0.33mm))

8. Select a shim closest to the calculated thickness. Use the lifter depressor tool to press down the lifter and install the shim. Shims are available in 17 sizes from 0.0984–0.1299 inch (2.50mm–3.30mm). The standard increment is 0.0020 inch (0.05mm).

9. Repeat steps a through e for each valve needing adjustment.

10. Reinstall the valve cover, following the procedures outlined in Section 3.

11. Install the spark plug wires.

12. Check and adjust the timing and idle speed, following the procedures outlined in this section. Road test the vehicle for proper operation.

2VZ-FE and 3VZ-FE Engines

▶ See Figures 108, 110, 113 thru 118

➥Adjust the valve clearance when the engine is cold.

1. Disconnect the negative battery cable.

2. Remove the air intake chamber.

3. Remove the cylinder head cover as described in Section 3.

4. Turn the crankshaft to align the groove in the crankshaft pulley with the **0** mark on the timing belt cover. Removing the spark plugs makes this easier, but is not required.

5. Check that the lifters on No.1 intake are loose and those on No. 1 exhaust are tight. If not, turn the crankshaft pulley one full revolution (360°).

6. Using the feeler gauge, measure the clearance on the valves in the positions shown in the diagram labeled First Pass. Make a written record of any measurements which are not within specification.

7. Rotate the crankshaft pulley ⅔ turn (240°) and check the clearance on the other valves. The positions are shown on the diagram labeled Second Pass. Any measurements not within specification should be added to your written record.

8. Turn the crankshaft a further ⅔ turn (240°), and check only the valves indicated in the Third pass. Measure the valve clearance.

9. Turn the crankshaft to position the cam lobe of the camshaft on the adjusting valve upward. press down the valve lifter with SST 09248–55011 (A), then place SST 09248–55021 (B) between the camshaft and the valve lifter. Remove SST tool (A). Before pressing down on the valve lifter, position the notch toward the spark plug. Remove the adjusting shim with a small screwdriver and magnetic finger.

10. Determine the replacement adjusting shim size by following the formulas or charts. For the purposes of the following formula, T = Thickness of the old shim; A = Valve clearance measured; N = Thickness of the new shim

- Intake side (camshaft nearest intake manifold): N = T + (A - 0.007 inch [0.19mm])
- Exhaust side (camshaft nearest exhaust manifold): N = T + (A - 0.013 inch [0.32mm])

11. Select a shim closest to the calculated thickness. Use the lifter depressor tool to press down the lifter and install the shim. Shims are available in 17 sizes from 0.0984–0.1299 inch (2.50mm–3.30mm). The standard increment is 0.0020 in. (0.05mm).

12. Repeat the previous steps for each valve needing adjustment.

13. Reinstall the valve cover, using all new gaskets following the procedures outlined in Section 3.

14. Install the air intake chamber as outlined in Section 3.

15. Connect the negative battery cable.

16. Check and adjust the timing and idle speed, following the procedures outlined in this section. Road test the vehicle for proper operation.

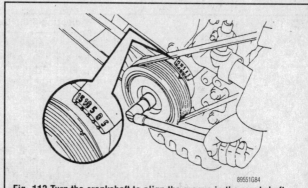

Fig. 113 Turn the crankshaft to align the groove in the crankshaft pulley with the 0 mark

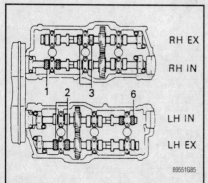

Fig. 114 Check these valves in the first pass only—2VZ-FE and 3VZ-FE engines

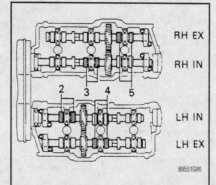

Fig. 115 Check these valves in the second pass only—2VZ-FE and 3VZ-FE engines

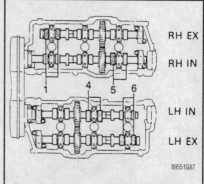

Fig. 116 Check these valves in the third pass only—2VZ-FE and 3VZ-FE engines

Adjusting Shim Selection Chart (Intake)

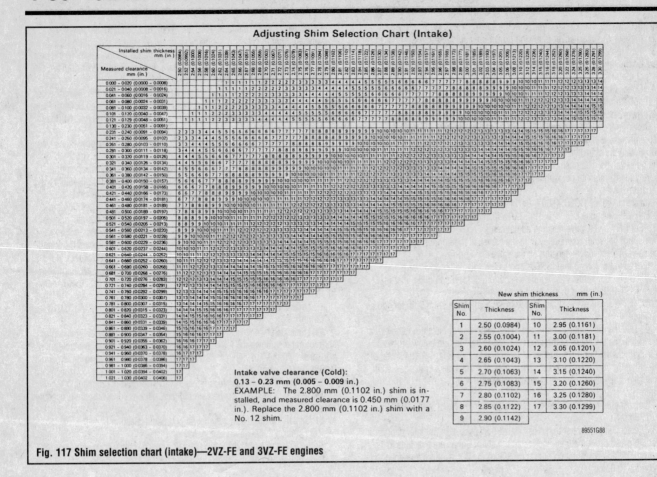

Intake valve clearance (Cold):
0.13 – 0.23 mm (0.005 – 0.009 in.)
EXAMPLE: The 2.800 mm (0.1102 in.) shim is installed, and measured clearance is 0.450 mm (0.0177 in.). Replace the 2.800 mm (0.1102 in.) shim with a No. 12 shim.

Shim No.	Thickness	Shim No.	Thickness
1	2.50 (0.0984)	10	2.95 (0.1161)
2	2.55 (0.1004)	11	3.00 (0.1181)
3	2.60 (0.1024)	12	3.05 (0.1201)
4	2.65 (0.1043)	13	3.10 (0.1220)
5	2.70 (0.1063)	14	3.15 (0.1240)
6	2.75 (0.1083)	15	3.20 (0.1260)
7	2.80 (0.1102)	16	3.25 (0.1280)
8	2.85 (0.1122)	17	3.30 (0.1299)
9	2.90 (0.1142)		

89551G88

Fig. 117 Shim selection chart (intake)—2VZ-FE and 3VZ-FE engines

Adjusting Shim Selection Chart (Exhaust)

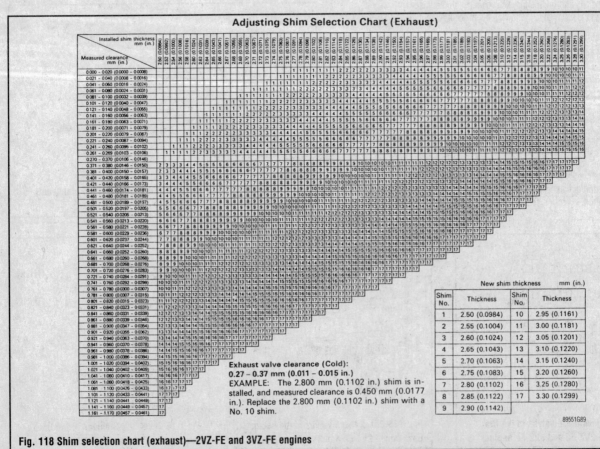

Exhaust valve clearance (Cold):
0.27 – 0.37 mm (0.011 – 0.015 in.)
EXAMPLE: The 2.800 mm (0.1102 in.) shim is installed, and measured clearance is 0.450 mm (0.0177 in.). Replace the 2.800 mm (0.1102 in.) shim with a No. 10 shim.

Shim No.	Thickness	Shim No.	Thickness
1	2.50 (0.0984)	10	2.95 (0.1161)
2	2.55 (0.1004)	11	3.00 (0.1181)
3	2.60 (0.1024)	12	3.05 (0.1201)
4	2.65 (0.1043)	13	3.10 (0.1220)
5	2.70 (0.1063)	14	3.15 (0.1240)
6	2.75 (0.1083)	15	3.20 (0.1260)
7	2.80 (0.1102)	16	3.25 (0.1280)
8	2.85 (0.1122)	17	3.30 (0.1299)
9	2.90 (0.1142)		

89551G89

Fig. 118 Shim selection chart (exhaust)—2VZ-FE and 3VZ-FE engines

1MZ-FE Engine

▶ See Figures 110, 119 thru 125

➡Inspect and adjust the valve clearance while the engine is cold.

1. Disconnect the negative battery cable.
2. Remove the right side fender apron seal.
3. Drain the engine coolant.
4. Remove the valve bank cover using a 5mm wrench.
5. Remove the spark plug wires from the valve cover.
6. Remove the air intake chamber assembly, refer to Section 3.
7. Remove the ignition coils. Make sure to arrange them in the order of removal.
8. Disconnect the radiator hose from the water outlet.
9. Remove the valve cover and gasket as described in Section 3.
10. Set the No. 1 cylinder to TDC by turning the crankshaft pulley and align its groove with the timing mark "0" of the No. 1 timing cover. Check that the valve lifters on the No. 1 intake and exhaust are loose. If not, turn the crankshaft one revolution (360°) and align the mark.
11. Using the feeler gauge, measure the clearance on the valves in the positions shown in the diagram labeled first pass. Make a written record of any measurements which are not within specification.
   - Intake COLD: 0.006–0.010 in. (0.15–0.25mm)
   - Exhaust COLD: 0.010–0.014 in. 90.25–0.35mm)
12. Rotate the crankshaft pulley ⅔ turn (240°) and check the clearance on the other valves. The positions are shown on the diagram labeled second pass. Any measurements not within specification should be added to your written record.
13. Turn the crankshaft a further ⅔ turn (240°), and check only the valves indicated in the third pass. Measure the valve clearance.
14. To remove the adjusting shim, turn the camshaft so that the cam lobe for the valve to be adjusted faces up. Turn the valve lifter with a screwdriver so that the notches are perpendicular to the camshaft. Using SST (A) 09278–05410 or

equivalent, press down the valve lifter and place the SST (B) 09248–05420 between the camshaft and valve lifter. Remove SST (A).
15. Apply SST (B) 09248–05420 or equivalent at a slight angle on the side marked with **9 or 7 at the position shown in the illustration. When the SST (B) is inserted too deeply, it will get pinched by the shim. To prevent it from being stuck, insert it gently from the intake side, at a slight angle.**
16. Remove the adjusting shim with a small flat bladed tool and magnetic finger.
17. Determine the replacement adjusting shim size according to the formula or charts. For the purposes of the following formula, T = Thickness of the old shim; A = Valve clearance measured; N = Thickness of the new shim
   - Intake side (camshaft nearest intake manifold): N = T + (A –; 0.007 inch (0.19mm))
   - Exhaust side (camshaft nearest exhaust manifold): N = T + (A –; 0.013 inch (0.32mm))
18. Select a shim closest to the calculated thickness. Use the lifter depressor tool to press down the lifter and install the shim. Shims are available in 17 sizes from 0.0984–0.1299 inch (2.50mm–3.30mm). The standard increment is 0.0020 in. (0.05mm).
19. Install the new adjusting shim on the valve lifter. Place a new shim on the valve lifter with the numbers facing down. Using the SST-A or equivalent, press down the valve lifter and remove SST-B.
20. Recheck the valve clearance.
21. Install the valve cover. Attach the radiator hose to the water outlet.
22. Install the ignition coils. Make sure they are in the exact places where they were removed from.
23. Install the air intake chamber assembly, refer to Section 3.
24. Attach the valve bank cover. Fill the engine coolant system.
25. Connect the negative battery cable.
26. Start the engine and top off the coolant level. install the right hand fender apron seal.

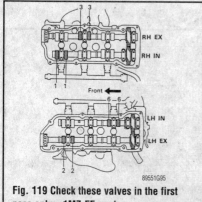

Fig. 119 Check these valves in the first pass only—1MZ-FE engine

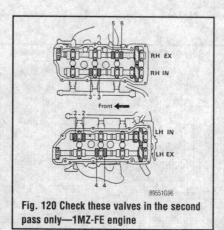

Fig. 120 Check these valves in the second pass only—1MZ-FE engine

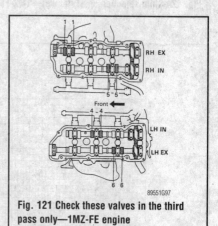

Fig. 121 Check these valves in the third pass only—1MZ-FE engine

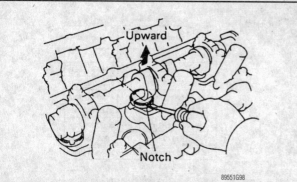

Fig. 122 Turn the camshaft so that the cam lobe for the valve to be adjusted faces upward—1MZ-FE engine

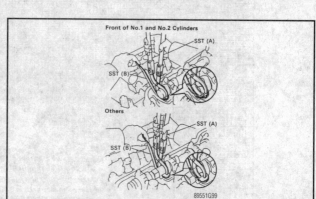

Fig. 123 When installing the new shim, apply SST (B) at a slight angle on the side that is marked at the position shown—1MZ-FE engine

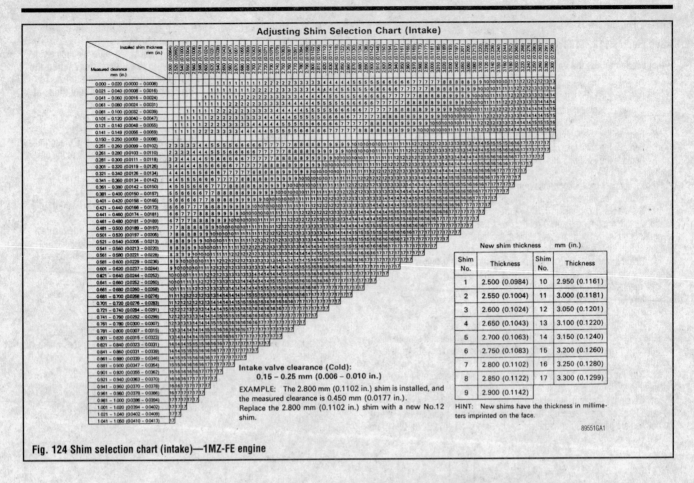

Intake valve clearance (Cold):
0.15 – 0.25 mm (0.006 – 0.010 in.)

EXAMPLE: The 2.800 mm (0.1102 in.) shim is installed, and the measured clearance is 0.450 mm (0.0177 in.).
Replace the 2.800 mm (0.1102 in.) shim with a new No.12 shim.

New shim thickness   mm (in.)

Shim No.	Thickness	Shim No.	Thickness
1	2.500 (0.0984)	10	2.950 (0.1161)
2	2.550 (0.1004)	11	3.000 (0.1181)
3	2.600 (0.1024)	12	3.050 (0.1201)
4	2.650 (0.1043)	13	3.100 (0.1220)
5	2.700 (0.1063)	14	3.150 (0.1240)
6	2.750 (0.1083)	15	3.200 (0.1260)
7	2.800 (0.1102)	16	3.250 (0.1280)
8	2.850 (0.1122)	17	3.300 (0.1299)
9	2.900 (0.1142)		

HINT: New shims have the thickness in millimeters imprinted on the face.

89551GA1

Fig. 124 Shim selection chart (intake)—1MZ-FE engine

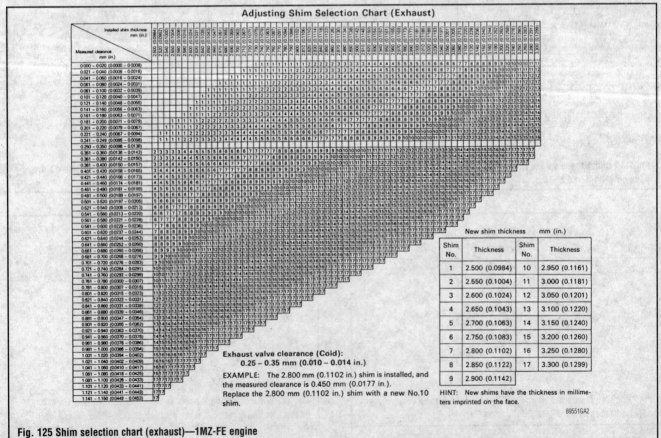

Exhaust valve clearance (Cold):
0.25 – 0.35 mm (0.010 – 0.014 in.)

EXAMPLE: The 2.800 mm (0.1102 in.) shim is installed, and the measured clearance is 0.450 mm (0.0177 in.).
Replace the 2.800 mm (0.1102 in.) shim with a new No.10 shim.

New shim thickness   mm (in.)

Shim No.	Thickness	Shim No.	Thickness
1	2.500 (0.0984)	10	2.950 (0.1161)
2	2.550 (0.1004)	11	3.000 (0.1181)
3	2.600 (0.1024)	12	3.050 (0.1201)
4	2.650 (0.1043)	13	3.100 (0.1220)
5	2.700 (0.1063)	14	3.150 (0.1240)
6	2.750 (0.1083)	15	3.200 (0.1260)
7	2.800 (0.1102)	16	3.250 (0.1280)
8	2.850 (0.1122)	17	3.300 (0.1299)
9	2.900 (0.1142)		

HINT: New shims have the thickness in millimeters imprinted on the face.

89551GA2

Fig. 125 Shim selection chart (exhaust)—1MZ-FE engine

Idle Speed and Mixture Adjustment

IDLE SPEED ADJUSTMENT

Follow the correct service adjustment procedure for your engine. Review the complete procedure before starting.

One of the merits of electronic fuel injection is that it requires so little adjustment. The computer (ECM) does most of the work in compensating for changes in climate, engine temperature, electrical load and driving conditions. The idle on the fuel injected engines should be checked periodically (15,000 miles or 24 months) but not adjusted unless out of specifications by more than 50 rpm.

The idle speed adjusting screw is located on the side of the throttle body. You can find the throttle body by following the accelerator cable to its end. The adjusting screw may have a cap over it. If so, pop the cap off with a small screwdriver.

If for any reason the idle cannot be brought into specification by this adjustment procedure, return the screw to its original setting and follow other diagnostic procedures to find the real cause of the problem. Do not try to cure other problems with this adjustment.

2S-ELC Engine

▶ See Figures 126 and 127

1. Leave the air cleaner installed and all the air pipes and hoses of the air intake system connected. Leave all vacuum lines connected to the ESA and EGR systems, etc.
2. Make sure that the electronic fuel injection system wiring connectors are fully plugged in. Apply the emergency brake and block the wheels. Start the engine and allow it to warm up.
3. Turn all the accessories off and place the transaxle in the Neutral range.
4. Remove the rubber cap from the IIA service connector coming from the distributor. Remove the plug covering the idle speed adjusting screw. Place a cap and the plug in your pocket. Do not loose them.
5. Attach the test probe of the tachometer to the service connector. Please refer to the illustrations in the Ignition Timing.

❈❈ WARNING

Never allow the tachometer terminal to touch the ground as it could result in damage to the Igniter and/or the ignition coil.

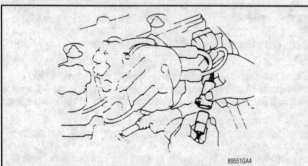

Fig. 126 Disconnect the Idle Speed Control (ISC) valve—2S-ELC engine

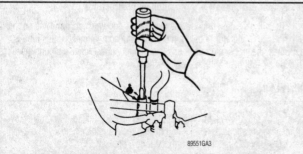

Fig. 127 The idle speed screw is located on the throttle body

6. Race the engine at 2500 rpms for approximately two minutes. Return the engine to idle and disconnect the Vacuum Switching Valve (VSV) for the Idle Speed Control (ISC).
7. Set the idle speed by turning the adjusting screw. Check the Tune-up chart or label under the hood for the correct speed.
8. After setting the idles speed, shut the engine off. Connect the VSV connector and remove the tachometer. Install the plug and the rubber cap.

3S-FE Engine

▶ See Figure 127

1. Leave the air cleaner installed and all the air pipes and hoses of the air intake system connected. Leave all vacuum lines connected to the ESA and EGR systems, ect.
2. Make sure that the electronic fuel injection system wiring connectors are fully plugged in. Apply the emergency brake and block the wheels. Start the engine and allow it to warm up.
3. Turn all the accessories off and place the transaxle in the Neutral range.
4. Remove the rubber cap from the IIA service connector coming from the distributor. Remove the plug covering the idle speed adjusting screw. Place a cap and the plug in your pocket. Do not loose them.

➡**These engines require the use of a special tachometer that can be attached to this service connector. Many tachometers are not compatible with this hook-up, so it is recommended that you consult your manufacture before purchasing a certain type.**

5. Connect the test probe of the tachometer to the service connector. Please refer to the illustrations in the Ignition Timing.

❈❈ WARNING

Never allow the tachometer terminal to touch the ground as it could result in damage to the Igniter and/or the ignition coil.

6. Open the lid of the check connector. Using a suitable jumper wire, short the E1 and T terminals on 1987–88 models and **E1** and **TE1** terminals on the 1988–91 models.
7. Check the idle speed by turning the idle adjusting screw. The idle speed should be as specified in the Tune-up chart or on your label under the hood.
8. Remove the jumper wire and close the lid of the service connector. Disconnect the tachometer and install the plug and rubber boot.

1994 1MZ-FE And 1992–95 5S-FE Engines

1. Idle speed adjustment is performed under the following conditions:
• Engine at normal operating temperature
• Air cleaner installed
• Air pipes and hoses of the air induction and EGR systems properly connected
• All vacuum lines and electrical wires connected and plugged in properly
• All electrical accessories in the **OFF** position
• Transaxle in the **N** position
2. Connect a tachometer to the engine. Connect the probe of the tachometer to terminal IG- of the check connector.
3. Run the engine at 2500 rpm for 90 seconds.
4. Short the check connector at terminals **TE1** and **E1** using a suitable jumper wire or special service tool 09843–18020.
5. Adjust the idle speed by turning the idle speed adjusting screw to specification.

➡**Refer to underhood emission sticker to confirm idle speed specification. Always follow the emission sticker specification.**

6. Remove the jumper wire or special service tool from the connector terminals.
7. Disconnect the tachometer. Road test the vehicle for proper operation.

1995–96 1MZ-FE, 1996 5S-FE Engines, 2VZ-FE And 3VZ-FE Engines

Idle speed on these engines is controlled completely by the Electronic Control Module (ECM). The idle speed is not adjustable on these engines.

GASOLINE ENGINE TUNE-UP SPECIFICATIONS

Year	Engine ID/VIN	Engine Displacement Liters (cc)	Spark Plugs Gap (in.)	Ignition Timing (deg.) MT	Ignition Timing (deg.) AT	Fuel Pump (psi)	Idle Speed (rpm) MT	Idle Speed (rpm) AT	Valve Clearance In.	Valve Clearance Ex.
1983	2S-ELC	2.0 (1995)	0.43	5B	5B	28-36	700	700	Hyd.	Hyd.
1984	2S-ELC	2.0 (1995)	0.43	5B	5B	28-36	700	700	Hyd.	Hyd.
1985	2S-ELC	2.0 (1995)	0.43	5B	5B	33-38	700	750	Hyd.	Hyd.
1986	2S-ELC	2.0 (1995)	0.43	10B ①	10B ①	33-38	700	750	Hyd.	Hyd.
1987	3S-FE	2.0 (1998)	0.43	10B ①	10B ①	38-44	650	650	0.007-0.011	0.011-0.015
1988	3S-FE	2.0 (1998)	0.43	10B ①	10B ①	38-44	650	650	0.007-0.011	0.011-0.015
1989	3S-FE	2.0 (1998)	0.43	10B ①	10B ①	38-44	700	700	0.007-0.011	0.011-0.015
	2VZ-FE	2.5 (2507)	0.43	10B ①	10B ①	38-44	700	700	0.005-0.009	0.011-0.015
1990	3S-FE	2.0 (1998)	0.43	10B ①	10B ①	38-44	700	700	0.007-0.011	0.011-0.015
	2VZ-FE	2.5 (2507)	0.43	10B ①	10B ①	38-44	700	700	0.005-0.009	0.011-0.015
1991	3S-FE	2.0 (1998)	0.43	10B ①	10B ①	38-44	650	650	0.007-0.011	0.011-0.015
	3VZ-FE	3.0 (2959)	0.43	10B ①	10B ①	38-44	700	700	0.005-0.009	0.011-0.015
1992	5S-FE	2.2 (2164)	0.43	10B ①	10B ①	38-44	750	750	0.007-0.011	0.011-0.015
	3VZ-FE	3.0 (2959)	0.43	10B ①	10B ①	38-44	700	700	0.005-0.009	0.011-0.015
1993	5S-FE	2.2 (2164)	0.43	10B ①	10B ①	38-44	750	750	0.007-0.011	0.011-0.015
	3VZ-FE	3.0 (2959)	0.43	10B ①	10B ①	38-44	700	700	0.005-0.009	0.011-0.015
1994	5S-FE	2.2 (2164)	0.43	10B ①	10B ①	38-44	750	750	0.007-0.011	0.011-0.015
	1MZ-FE	3.0 (2995)	0.43	10B ①	10B ①	38-44	700	700	0.006-0.010	0.010-0.014
1995	5S-FE	2.2 (2164)	0.43	10B ①	10B ②	38-44	750	750	0.007-0.011	0.011-0.015
	1MZ-FE	3.0 (2995)	0.43	10B ①	10B ②	38-44	700	700	0.006-0.010	0.010-0.014
1996	5S-FE	2.2 (2164)	0.43	10B ①	10B ①	38-44	750	750	0.007-0.011	0.011-0.015
	1MZ-FE	3.0 (2995)	0.43	10B ②	10B ②	38-44	700	700	0.006-0.010	0.010-0.014

① Use the TE1 and E1 of the DLC1
② Use the OBD II scan tester on the DLC3

89551C01

Air Conditioning System

SYSTEM SERVICE & REPAIR

➡**It is recommended that the A/C system be serviced by an EPA Section 609 certified automotive technician utilizing a refrigerant recovery/recycling machine.**

The do-it-yourselfer should not service his/her own vehicle's A/C system for many reasons, including legal concerns, personal injury, environmental damage and cost.

According to the U.S. Clean Air Act, it is a federal crime to service or repair (involving the refrigerant) a Motor Vehicle Air Conditioning (MVAC) system for money without being EPA certified. It is also illegal to vent R-12 and R-134a refrigerants into the atmosphere. State and/or local laws may be more strict than the federal regulations, so be sure to check with your state and/or local authorities for further information.

➡**Federal law dictates that a fine of up to $25,000 may be levied on people convicted of venting refrigerant into the atmosphere.**

When servicing an A/C system you run the risk of handling or coming in contact with refrigerant, which may result in skin or eye irritation or frostbite. Although low in toxicity (due to chemical stability), inhalation of concentrated refrigerant fumes is dangerous and can result in death; cases of fatal cardiac arrhythmia have been reported in people accidentally subjected to high levels of refrigerant. Some early symptoms include loss of concentration and drowsiness.

➡**Generally, the limit for exposure is lower for R-134a than it is for R-12. Exceptional care must be practiced when handling R-134a.**

Also, some refrigerants can decompose at high temperatures (near gas heaters or open flame), which may result in hydrofluoric acid, hydrochloric acid and phosgene (a fatal nerve gas).

It is usually more economically feasible to have a certified MVAC automotive technician perform A/C system service on your vehicle.

R-12 Refrigerant Conversion

If your vehicle still uses R-12 refrigerant, one way to save A/C system costs down the road is to investigate the possibility of having your system converted to R-134a. The older R-12 systems can be easily converted to R-134a refrigerant by a certified automotive technician by installing a few new components and changing the system oil.

The cost of R-12 is steadily rising and will continue to increase, because it is no longer imported or manufactured in the United States. Therefore, it is often possible to have an R-12 system converted to R-134a and recharged for less than it would cost to just charge the system with R-12.

If you are interested in having your system converted, contact local automotive service stations for more details and information.

PREVENTIVE MAINTENANCE

Although the A/C system should not be serviced by the do-it-yourselfer, preventive maintenance should be practiced to help maintain the efficiency of the vehicle's A/C system. Be sure to perform the following:

• The easiest and most important preventive maintenance for your A/C system is to be sure that it is used on a regular basis. Running the system for five minutes each month (no matter what the season) will help ensure that the seals and all internal components remain lubricated.

➡**Some vehicles automatically operate the A/C system compressor whenever the windshield defroster is activated. Therefore, the A/C system would not need to be operated each month if the defroster was used.**

• In order to prevent heater core freeze-up during A/C operation, it is necessary to maintain proper antifreeze protection. Be sure to properly maintain the engine cooling system.

• Any obstruction of or damage to the condenser configuration will restrict air flow which is essential to its efficient operation. Keep this unit clean and in proper physical shape.

➡**Bug screens which are mounted in front of the condenser (unless they are original equipment) are regarded as obstructions.**

• The condensation drain tube expels any water which accumulates on the bottom of the evaporator housing into the engine compartment. If this tube is obstructed, the air conditioning performance can be restricted and condensation buildup can spill over onto the vehicle's floor.

SYSTEM INSPECTION

Although the A/C system should not be serviced by the do-it-yourselfer, system inspections should be performed to help maintain the efficiency of the vehicle's A/C system. Be sure to perform the following:

The easiest and often most important check for the air conditioning system consists of a visual inspection of the system components. Visually inspect the system for refrigerant leaks, damaged compressor clutch, abnormal compressor drive belt tension and/or condition, plugged evaporator drain tube, blocked condenser fins, disconnected or broken wires, blown fuses, corroded connections and poor insulation.

A refrigerant leak will usually appear as an oily residue at the leakage point in the system. The oily residue soon picks up dust or dirt particles from the surrounding air and appears greasy. Through time, this will build up and appear to be a heavy dirt impregnated grease.

For a thorough visual and operational inspection, check the following:

• Check the surface of the radiator and condenser for dirt, leaves or other material which might block air flow.

• Check for kinks in hoses and lines. Check the system for leaks.

• Make sure the drive belt is properly tensioned. During operation, make sure the belt is free of noise or slippage.

• Make sure the blower motor operates at all appropriate positions, then check for distribution of the air from all outlets.

➡**Remember that in high humidity, air discharged from the vents may not feel as cold as expected, even if the system is working properly. This is because moisture in humid air retains heat more effectively than dry air, thereby making humid air more difficult to cool.**

Windshield Wipers

ELEMENT (REFILL) CARE & REPLACEMENT

▶ **See Figures 128, 129 and 130**

For maximum effectiveness and longest element life, the windshield and wiper blades should be kept clean. Dirt, tree sap, road tar and so on will cause streaking, smearing and blade deterioration if left on the glass. It is advisable to wash the windshield carefully with a commercial glass cleaner at least once a month. Wipe off the rubber blades with the wet rag afterwards. Do not attempt to move wipers across the windshield by hand; damage to the motor and drive mechanism will result.

Tires and Wheels

Common sense and good driving habits will afford maximum tire life. Make sure that you don't overload the vehicle or run with incorrect pressure in the tires. Either of these will increase tread wear. Fast starts, sudden stops and sharp cornering are hard on tires and will shorten their useful life span.

➡**For optimum tire life, keep the tires properly inflated, rotate them often and have the wheel alignment checked periodically.**

Inspect your tires frequently. Be especially careful to watch for bubbles in the tread or sidewall, deep cuts or underinflation. Replace any tires with bubbles in the sidewall. If cuts are so deep that they penetrate to the cords, discard the tire. Any cut in the sidewall of a radial tire renders it unsafe. Also look for uneven tread wear patterns that may indicate the front end is out of alignment or that the tires are out of balance.

TIRE ROTATION

▶ **See Figure 131**

Tires must be rotated periodically to equalize wear patterns that vary with a tire's position on the vehicle. Tires will also wear in an uneven way as the front steering/suspension system wears to the point where the alignment should be reset.

Rotating the tires will ensure maximum life for the tires as a set, so you will not have to discard a tire early due to wear on only part of the tread. Regular rotation is required to equalize wear.

When rotating "unidirectional tires," make sure that they always roll in the same direction. This means that a tire used on the left side of the vehicle must not be switched to the right side and vice-versa. Such tires should only be rotated front-to-rear or rear-to-front, while always remaining on the same side of the vehicle. These tires are marked on the sidewall as to the direction of rotation; observe the marks when reinstalling the tire(s).

Some styled or "mag" wheels may have different offsets front to rear. In these cases, the rear wheels must not be used up front and vice-versa. Furthermore, if these wheels are equipped with unidirectional tires, they cannot be rotated unless the tire is remounted for the proper direction of rotation.

Fig. 128 Most aftermarket blades are available with multiple adapters to fit different vehicles

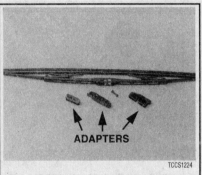

Fig. 129 Choose a blade which will fit your vehicle, and that will be readily available next time you need blades

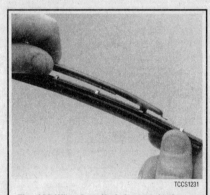

Fig. 130 When installed, be certain the blade is fully inserted into the backing

To inspect and/or replace the wiper blade elements, place the wiper switch in the **LOW** speed position and the ignition switch in the **ACC** position. When the wiper blades are approximately vertical on the windshield, turn the ignition switch to **OFF**.

Examine the wiper blade elements. If they are found to be cracked, broken or torn, they should be replaced immediately. Replacement intervals will vary with usage, although ozone deterioration usually limits element life to about one year. If the wiper pattern is smeared or streaked, or if the blade chatters across the glass, the elements should be replaced. It is easiest and most sensible to replace the elements in pairs.

If your vehicle is equipped with aftermarket blades, there are several different types of refills and your vehicle might have any kind. Aftermarket blades and arms rarely use the exact same type blade or refill as the original equipment.

Regardless of the type of refill used, be sure to follow the part manufacturer's instructions closely. Make sure that all of the frame jaws are engaged as the refill is pushed into place and locked. If the metal blade holder and frame are allowed to touch the glass during wiper operation, the glass will be scratched.

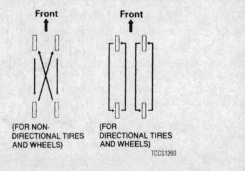

Fig. 131 Compact spare tires must **NEVER** be used in the rotation pattern

➡The compact or space-saver spare is strictly for emergency use. It must never be included in the tire rotation or placed on the vehicle for everyday use.

TIRE DESIGN

▶ **See Figure 132**

For maximum satisfaction, tires should be used in sets of four. Mixing of different brands or types (radial, bias-belted, fiberglass belted) should be avoided. In most cases, the vehicle manufacturer has designated a type of tire on which the vehicle will perform best. Your first choice when replacing tires should be to use the same type of tire that the manufacturer recommends.

When radial tires are used, tire sizes and wheel diameters should be selected to maintain ground clearance and tire load capacity equivalent to the original specified tire. Radial tires should always be used in sets of four.

✳✳ CAUTION

Radial tires should never be used on only the front axle.

When selecting tires, pay attention to the original size as marked on the tire. Most tires are described using an industry size code sometimes referred to as P-Metric. This allows the exact identification of the tire specifications, regardless of the manufacturer. If selecting a different tire size or brand, remember to check the installed tire for any sign of interference with the body or suspension while the vehicle is stopping, turning sharply or heavily loaded.

Snow Tires

Good radial tires can produce a big advantage in slippery weather, but in snow, a street radial tire does not have sufficient tread to provide traction and control. The small grooves of a street tire quickly pack with snow and the tire behaves like a billiard ball on a marble floor. The more open, chunky tread of a snow tire will self-clean as the tire turns, providing much better grip on snowy surfaces.

To satisfy municipalities requiring snow tires during weather emergencies, most snow tires carry either an M + S designation after the tire size stamped on the sidewall, or the designation "all-season." In general, no change in tire size is necessary when buying snow tires.

Most manufacturers strongly recommend the use of 4 snow tires on their vehicles for reasons of stability. If snow tires are fitted only to the drive wheels, the opposite end of the vehicle may become very unstable when braking or turning on slippery surfaces. This instability can lead to unpleasant endings if the driver can't counteract the slide in time.

Note that snow tires, whether 2 or 4, will affect vehicle handling in all non-snow situations. The stiffer, heavier snow tires will noticeably change the turning and braking characteristics of the vehicle. Once the snow tires are installed, you must re-learn the behavior of the vehicle and drive accordingly.

➡**Consider buying extra wheels on which to mount the snow tires. Once done, the "snow wheels" can be installed and removed as needed. This eliminates the potential damage to tires or wheels from seasonal removal and installation. Even if your vehicle has styled wheels, see if inexpensive steel wheels are available. Although the look of the vehicle will change, the expensive wheels will be protected from salt, curb hits and pothole damage.**

TIRE STORAGE

If they are mounted on wheels, store the tires at proper inflation pressure. All tires should be kept in a cool, dry place. If they are stored in the garage or basement, do not let them stand on a concrete floor; set them on strips of wood, a mat or a large stack of newspaper. Keeping them away from direct moisture is of paramount importance. Tires should not be stored upright, but in a flat position.

INFLATION & INSPECTION

▶ **See Figures 133 thru 138**

The importance of proper tire inflation cannot be overemphasized. A tire employs air as part of its structure. It is designed around the supporting

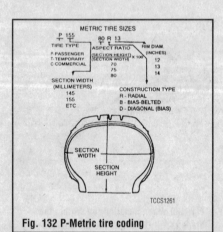

Fig. 132 P-Metric tire coding

Fig. 133 Tires with deep cuts, or cuts which bulge, should be replaced immediately

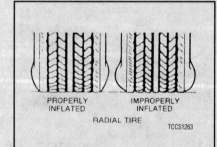

Fig. 134 Radial tires have a characteristic sidewall bulge; don't try to measure pressure by looking at the tire. Use a quality air pressure gauge

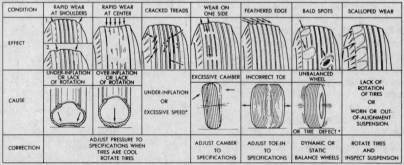

Fig. 135 Common tire wear patterns and causes

Fig. 136 Tread wear indicators will appear when the tire is worn

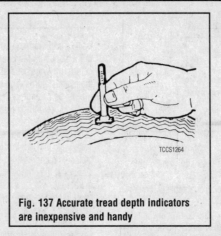

Fig. 137 Accurate tread depth indicators are inexpensive and handy

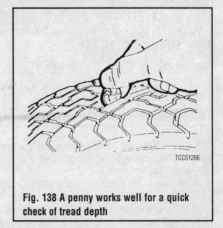

Fig. 138 A penny works well for a quick check of tread depth

strength of the air at a specified pressure. For this reason, improper inflation drastically reduces the tire's ability to perform as intended. A tire will lose some air in day-to-day use; having to add a few pounds of air periodically is not necessarily a sign of a leaking tire.

Two items should be a permanent fixture in every glove compartment: an accurate tire pressure gauge and a tread depth gauge. Check the tire pressure (including the spare) regularly with a pocket type gauge. Too often, the gauge on the end of the air hose at your corner garage is not accurate because it suffers too much abuse. Always check tire pressure when the tires are cold, as pressure increases with temperature. If you must move the vehicle to check the tire inflation, do not drive more than a mile before checking. A cold tire is generally one that has not been driven for more than three hours.

A plate or sticker is normally provided somewhere in the vehicle (door post, hood, tailgate or trunk lid) which shows the proper pressure for the tires. Never counteract excessive pressure build-up by bleeding off air pressure (letting some air out). This will cause the tire to run hotter and wear quicker.

✳✳ CAUTION

Never exceed the maximum tire pressure embossed on the tire! This is the pressure to be used when the tire is at maximum loading, but it is rarely the correct pressure for everyday driving. Consult the owner's manual or the tire pressure sticker for the correct tire pressure.

Once you've maintained the correct tire pressures for several weeks, you'll be familiar with the vehicle's braking and handling personality. Slight adjustments in tire pressures can fine-tune these characteristics, but never change the cold pressure specification by more than 2 psi. A slightly softer tire pressure will give a softer ride but also yield lower fuel mileage. A slightly harder tire will give crisper dry road handling but can cause skidding on wet surfaces. Unless you're fully attuned to the vehicle, stick to the recommended inflation pressures.

All automotive tires have built-in tread wear indicator bars that show up as ½ in. (13mm) wide smooth bands across the tire when ¹⁄₁₆ in. (1.5mm) of tread remains. The appearance of tread wear indicators means that the tires should be replaced. In fact, many states have laws prohibiting the use of tires with less than this amount of tread.

You can check your own tread depth with an inexpensive gauge or by using a Lincoln head penny. Slip the Lincoln penny (with Lincoln's head upside-down) into several tread grooves. If you can see the top of Lincoln's head in 2 adjacent grooves, the tire has less than ¹⁄₁₆ in. (1.5mm) tread left and should be replaced. You can measure snow tires in the same manner by using the "tails" side of the Lincoln penny. If you can see the top of the Lincoln memorial, it's time to replace the snow tire(s).

FLUIDS AND LUBRICANTS

Fluid Disposal

Used fluids such as engine oil, transmission fluid, antifreeze and brake fluid are hazardous wastes and must be disposed of properly. Before draining any fluids, consult with your local authorities; in many areas waste oil, etc. is being accepted as a part of recycling programs. A number of service stations and auto parts stores are also accepting waste fluids for recycling.

Be sure of the recycling center's policies before draining any fluids, as many will not accept different fluids that have been mixed together.

Fuel and Engine Oil Recommendations

OIL

▶ **See Figures 139, 140, 141 and 142**

The SAE (Society of Automotive Engineers) grade number indicates the viscosity of the engine oil; its resistance to flow at a given temperature. The lower the SAE grade number, the lighter the oil. For example, the mono-grade oils begin with SAE 5 weight, which is a thin light oil, and continue in viscosity up

Fig. 139 Look for the API oil identification label when choosing your engine oil

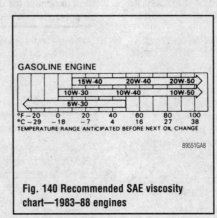

Fig. 140 Recommended SAE viscosity chart—1983–88 engines

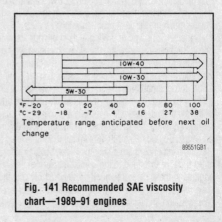

Fig. 141 Recommended SAE viscosity chart—1989–91 engines

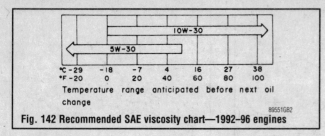

Fig. 142 Recommended SAE viscosity chart—1992–96 engines

to SAE 80 or 90 weight, which are heavy gear lubricants. These oils are also known as "straight weight", meaning they are of a single viscosity, and do not vary with engine temperature.

Multi-viscosity oils offer the important advantage of being adaptable to temperature extremes. These oils have designations such as 10W-40, 20W-50, etc. The "10W-40" means that in winter (the "W" in the designation) the oil acts like a thin 10 weight oil, allowing the engine to spin easily when cold and offering rapid lubrication. Once the engine has warmed up, however, the oil acts like a straight 40 weight, maintaining good lubrication and protection for the engine's internal components. A 20W-50 oil would therefore be slightly heavier than and not as ideal in cold weather as the 10W-40, but would offer better protection at higher rpm and temperatures because when warm it acts like a 50 weight oil. Whichever oil viscosity you choose when changing the oil, make sure you are anticipating the temperatures your engine will be operating in until the oil is changed again. Refer to the oil viscosity chart for oil recommendations according to temperature.

The API (American Petroleum Institute) designation indicates the classification of engine oil used under certain given operating conditions. Only oils designated for use "Service SH" (or its superceding type) should be used. Oils of the SH type perform a variety of functions inside the engine in addition to the basic function as a lubricant. Through a balanced system of metallic detergents and polymeric dispersants, the oil prevents the formation of high and low temperature deposits and also keeps sludge and particles of dirt in suspension. Acids, particularly sulfuric acid, as well as other by-products of combustion, are neutralized. Both the SAE grade number and the APE designation can be found on top of the oil can.

For recommended oil viscosity's, refer to the chart. Note that 10W-30 and 10W-40 grade oils are not recommended for sustained high speed driving when the temperature rises above the indicated limit.

Synthetic Oil

There are many excellent synthetic and fuel-efficient oils currently available that can provide better gas mileage, longer service life, and in some cases better engine protection. These benefits do not come without a few hitches, however, the main one being the price of synthetic oils, which is three or four times the price per quart of conventional oil.

Synthetic oil is not for every car and every type of driving, so you should consider your engine's condition and your type of driving. Also, check your car's warranty conditions regarding the use of synthetic oils.

Both brand new engines and older, high mileage engines are the wrong candidates for synthetic oil. The synthetic oils are so slippery that they can prevent the proper break-in of new engines; most manufacturer's recommend that you wait until the engine is properly broken in 5,000 miles (8,046km) before using synthetic oil. Older engines with wear have a different problem with synthetics: they use (consume during operation) more oil as they age. Slippery synthetic oils get past these worn parts easily. If your engine is using conventional oil, it will use synthetics much faster. If your car is leaking oil past old seals you'll have a much greater leak problem with synthetics.

Consider your type of driving. If most of your accumulated mileage is high speed, highway type driving, the more expensive synthetic oils may be of benefit. Extended highway driving gives the engine a chance to warm up, accumulating less acids in the oil and putting less stress on the engine over the long run. Under these conditions, the oil change interval can be extended (as long as your oil filter can last the extended life of the oil) up to the advertised mileage claims of the synthetics. Cars with synthetic oils may show increased fuel economy in highway driving, due to less internal friction. However, many automotive experts agree that 50,000 miles (80,465km) is too long to keep any oil in your engine.

Cars used under harder circumstances, such as stop-and-go, city type driving, short trips, or extended idling, should be serviced more frequently. For the engines in these cars, the much greater cost of synthetic or fuel-efficient oils may not be worth the investment. Internal wear increases much quicker on these cars, causing greater oil consumption and leakage.

FUEL

It is important to use fuel of the proper octane rating in your car. Octane rating is based on the quantity of anti-knock compounds added to the fuel and it determines the speed at which the gas will burn. The lower the octane rating, the faster it burns. The higher the octane, the slower the fuel will burn and a greater percentage of compounds in the fuel prevent spark ping (knock), detonation and preignition (dieseling).

As the temperature of the engine increases, the air/fuel mixture exhibits a tendency to ignite before the spark plug is fired. If fuel of an octane rating too low for the engine is used, this will allow combustion to occur before the piston has completed its compression stroke, thereby creating a very high pressure very rapidly.

Fuel of the proper octane rating, for the compression ratio and ignition timing of your car, will slow the combustion process sufficiently to allow the spark plug enough time to ignite the mixture completely and smoothly. Many non-catalyst models are designed to run on regular fuel. The use of some super-premium fuel is no substitution for a properly tuned and maintained engine. Chances are that if your engine exhibits any signs of spark ping, detonation or pre-ignition when using regular fuel, the ignition timing should be checked against specifications or the cylinder head should be removed for decarbonizing.

Vehicles equipped with catalytic converters must use UNLEADED GASOLINE ONLY. Use of unleaded fuel shortened the life of spark plugs, exhaust systems and EGR valves and can damage the catalytic converter. Most converter equipped models are designed to operate using unleaded gasoline with a minimum rating of 87 octane. Use of unleaded gas with octane ratings lower than 87 can cause persistent spark knock which could lead to engine damage.

Light spark knock may be noticed when accelerating or driving up hills. The slight knocking may be considered normal (with 87 octane) because the maximum fuel economy is obtained under condition of occasional light spark knock. Gasoline with an octane rating higher than 87 may be used, but it is not necessary (in most cases) for proper operation.

If spark knock is constant, when using 87 octane, at cruising speeds on level ground, ignition timing adjustment may be required.

➡**Your engine's fuel requirement can change with time, mainly due to carbon buildup, which changes the compression ratio. If your engine pings, knocks or runs on, switch to a higher grade of fuel. Sometimes just changing brands will cure the problem. If it becomes necessary to retard the timing from specifications, don't change it more than a few degrees. Retarded timing will reduce power output and fuel mileage and will increase the engine temperature.**

OPERATION IN FOREIGN COUNTRIES

If you plan to drive your car outside the United States or Canada, there is a possibility that fuels will be too low in anti-knock quality and could produce engine damage. It is wise to consult with local authories upon arrival in a foreign county to determine the best fuels available.

Engine

✳✳ CAUTION

Prolonged and repeated skin contact with used engine oil, with no effort to remove the oil, may be harmful. Always follow these simple precautions when handling used motor oil:

- Avoid prolonged skin contact with used motor oil.
- Remove oil from skin by washing thoroughly with soap and water or waterless hand cleaner. Do not use gasoline, thinners or other solvents.
- Avoid prolonged skin contact with oil-soaked clothing.

OIL LEVEL CHECK

◗ **See Figures 143 and 144**

Every time you stop for fuel, check the engine oil as follows:
1. Park the car on level ground.
2. When checking the oil level it is best for the engine to be at operating temperature, although checking the oil immediately after a stopping will lead to a false reading. Wait a few minutes after turning off the engine to allow the oil to drain back into the crankcase.

3. Open the hood and locate the dipstick which is on the left side of the engine. Pull the dipstick from its tube, wipe it clean and reinsert it.

4. Pull the dipstick out again and, holding it horizontally, read the oil level. The oil should be between the **F** and **L** marks on the dipstick. If the oil is below the **L** mark, add oil of the proper viscosity through the capped opening on the top of the cylinder head cover.

5. Replace the dipstick and check the oil level again after adding any oil. Be careful not to overfill the crankcase. Approximately one quart of oil will raise the level from the **L** to the **F**. Excess oil will generally be consumed at an accelerated rate.

OIL & FILTER CHANGE

▶ **See Figures 145 thru 152**

The oil should be changed every 7500 miles (12,000 km). Toyota recommends changing the oil filter with every other oil change; we suggest that the filter be changed with every oil change. There is approximately 1 quart of dirty oil left remaining in the old oil filter if it is not changed! A few dollars more every year seems a small price to pay for extended engine life so change the filter every time you change the oil!

✳✳ CAUTION

Prolonged and repeated skin contact with used engine oil, with no effort to remove the oil, may be harmful. Always follow these simple precautions when handling used motor oil.

- Avoid prolonged skin contract with used motor oil.
- Remove oil from skin by washing thoroughly with soap and water or waterless hand cleaner. Do not use gasoline, thinners or other solvents.
- Avoid prolonged skin contact with oil-soaked clothing.

1. Warm the oil by running the engine for a short period of time or at least until the needle on the temperature gauge rises above the **C** mark. This will make the oil flow more freely from the oil pan.

2. Park on a level surface, apply the parking brake and block the wheels. Stop the engine. Raise the hood and remove the oil filler cap from the top of the valve cover. This allows the air to enter the engine as the oil drains. Remove the dipstick, wipe it off and set it aside.

3. Position a suitable oil drain pan under the drain plug.

4. With the proper size metric socket or closed end wrench (DO NOT use pliers or vise grips), loosen the drain plug. Back out the drain plug while maintaining a slight upward force on it to keep the oil from running out around it (and your hand). Allow the oil to drain into the drain pan. It is recommended to discard the old gasket and replace with a new one each oil change.

✳✳ CAUTION

The engine oil will be hot. Keep your arms, face and hands away from the oil as it is draining

5. Remove the drain pan and wipe any excess oil from the area around the hole using a clean rag. Clean the threads of the drain plug and the drain plug gasket to remove any sludge deposits that may have accumulated.

6. With a filter wrench, loosen the oil filter counterclockwise and back the filter off the filter post the rest of the way by hand. Keep the filter end up so that the oil does not spill out. Tilt the filter into the drain pan to drain the oil.

7. Remove the drain pan from under the vehicle and position it off to the side.

8. With a clean rag, wipe off the filter seating surface to ensure a proper seal. Make sure that the old gasket is not stuck to the seating surface. If it is, remove it and thoroughly clean the seating surface of the old gasket material.

9. Open a container of new oil and smear some of this oil onto the rubber gasket of the new oil filter. Get a feel for where the filter post is and start the filter by hand until the gasket contacts the seat. Using the filter wrench, turn the filter an additional ¾ turn.

10. Install the drain plug and metal gasket. Be sure that the plug is tight enough that the oil does not leak out, but not tight enough to strip the threads. Over time you will develop a sense of what the proper tightness of the drain plug is. If a torque wrench is available, tighten the plug to the following specifications:

Fig. 143 The engine oil dipstick is usually marked and in clear view

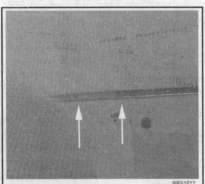

Fig. 144 The engine oil dipstick is marked with a full and low level on the indicator

Fig. 145 Remove the engine oil pan drain plug . . .

Fig. 146 . . . this allows the old engine oil to flow out of the crankcase

Fig. 147 Inspect the threads of the drain plug and discard the old gasket

Fig. 148 On the 1MZ-FE engine, the oil filter is located under the front exhaust manifold

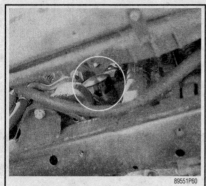

Fig. 149 Some oil filters are accessed from the bottom of the vehicle

89551P60

Fig. 150 Make sure the oil filter mounting boss is clean

89551P62

TCCS1901

Fig. 151 Before installing a new oil filter, lightly coat the rubber gasket with clean oil

89551P23

Fig. 152 Fill the oil crankcase system through the valve cover opening

- 2S-ELC engine—18 ft. lbs. (25 Nm)
- 3S-FE, 5S-FE engines—29 ft. lbs. (39 Nm)
- 2VZ-FE engines—18 ft. lbs. (25 Nm)
- 3VZ-FE engines—27 ft. lbs. (37 Nm)
- 1MZ-FE engines—33 ft. lbs. (45 Nm)

➥Replace the drain plug gasket at every time you change the oil to be sure of no leakage.

11. Through a suitable plastic or metal funnel, add clean new oil of the proper grade and viscosity through the oil filler on the top of the valve cover. Be sure that the oil level registers near the **F** (full) mark on the dipstick.

12. Install and tighten the oil filler cap.

13. Start the engine and allow it to run for several minutes. Check for leaks at the filter and drain plug. Sometimes leaks will not be revealed until the engine reaches normal operating temperature.

14. Stop the engine and recheck the oil level. Add oil as necessary.

Manual Transaxle

FLUID RECOMMENDATIONS

- 1983–90 2WD 4 cyl. models: DEXRON® II ATF
- 1991–96 2WD 4 cyl. models: multipurpose gear oil API GL-4 or GL-5; SAE 80W–90
- All 2WD 6 cyl. models: multipurpose gear oil API GL-4 or GL-5; SAE 80W–90
- All 4WD models: multipurpose gear oil API GL-4; SAE 75W–90 or 80W–90

LEVEL CHECK

▶ See Figure 153

The oil in the manual transaxle should be checked at least every 15,000 miles (24,000 km) and replaced every 25,000–30,000 miles (40,000–48,000 km), even more frequently if driven in deep water.

1. With the car parked on a level surface, remove the filler plug (24mm hex head) from the front side of the transaxle housing.

2. If the lubricant begins to trickle out of the hole, there is enough. Otherwise, carefully insert your finger (watch out for sharp threads!) and check to see if the oil is up to the edge of the hole.

3. If not, add oil through the hole until the level is at the edge of the hole. Most gear lubricants come in a plastic squeeze bottle with a nozzle; making additions simple. You can also use a common everyday kitchen baster.

4. Replace the filler plug and tighten it to 36 ft. lbs. (49 Nm). Run the engine and check for leaks.

DRAIN & REFILL

▶ See Figures 153, 154 and 155

Once every 30,000 miles (48,000 km), the oil in the manual transaxle should be changed.

1. The transaxle oil should be hot before it is drained. If the engine is at normal operating temperature, the transaxle oil should be hot enough.

2. Raise the car and support it properly on jackstands so that you can safely work underneath. You will probably not have enough room to work if the car is not raised.

3. Remove the filler plug from the side of the transaxle case. It is on the front side. There is usually a gasket underneath this plug. Replace it if damaged.

4. The drain plug is located on the bottom of the transaxle, it should be a 24mm hex head. Place a pan under the drain plug and remove it. Keep a slight upward pressure on the plug while unscrewing it, this will keep the oil from pouring out until the plug is removed.

❊❊ CAUTION

The oil will be HOT! Be careful when you remove the plug so that you don't take a bath in hot gear oil.

5. Allow the oil to drain completely. Clean off the plug and replace it, tightening it until it is just snug 36 ft. lbs. (49 Nm).

6. Fill the transaxle, with the proper lubricant, through the filler plug hole as detailed previously. Refer to the Capacities Chart for the amount of oil needed to refill your transaxle.

7. The oil level should come right up to the edge of the hole. You can stick your finger in to verify this. Watch out for sharp threads!

8. Replace the filler plug and gasket, lower the car, and check for leaks. Dispose of the old oil in the proper manner.

Automatic Transaxle

FLUID RECOMMENDATIONS

All 2WD models use DEXRON® II (or its superceding type) ATF fluid whereas all 4WD models use type T ATF.

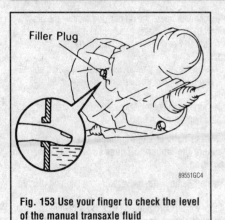

Fig. 153 Use your finger to check the level of the manual transaxle fluid

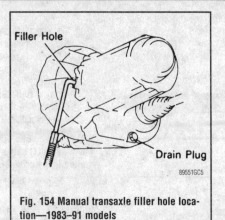

Fig. 154 Manual transaxle filler hole location—1983-91 models

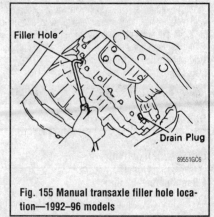

Fig. 155 Manual transaxle filler hole location—1992-96 models

LEVEL CHECK

▶ **See Figures 156, 157 and 158**

Check the automatic transmission fluid level at least every 15,000 miles (24,000 km). The dipstick is located in the engine compartment. The fluid level should be checked only when the transmission is hot (normal operating temperature). The transmission is considered hot after about 20 miles of highway driving.

1. Park the car on a level surface with the engine idling. Shift the transmission into **P** and set the parking brake.

2. Remove the dipstick, wipe it clean and reinsert if firmly. Be sure that it has been pushed all the way in. Remove the dipstick and check the fluid level while holding it horizontally. All models have a HOT and a COLD side to the dipstick.

- **COLD**—The fluid level should fall in this range when the engine has been running for only a short time.
- **HOT**—The fluid level should fall in this range when the engine has reached normal running temperatures.

3. If the fluid level is not within the proper area on either side of the dipstick, pour ATF into the dipstick tube. This is easily done with the aid of a funnel. Check the level often as you are filling the transaxle. Be extremely careful not to overfill it. Overfilling will cause slippage, seal damage and overheating. Approximately one pint of ATF will raise the level from one notch to the other.

➡ **The fluid on the dipstick should always be a bright red color. It if is discolored (brown or black), or smells burnt, serious transmission troubles, probably due to overheating, should be suspected. The transmission should be inspected by a qualified service technician to locate the cause of the burnt fluid.**

DRAIN & REFILL

▶ **See Figures 159, 160 and 161**

The automatic transaxle fluid should be changed at least every 25,000-30,000 miles (40,000-48,000 km). If the car is normally used in severe service, such as stop-and-go driving, trailer towing or the like, the interval should be halved. The fluid should be hot before it is drained; a 20 minute drive will accomplish this.

1. Remove the dipstick from the filler tube and install a funnel in the opening.

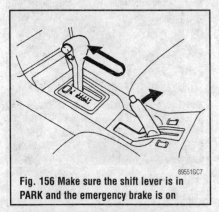

Fig. 156 Make sure the shift lever is in PARK and the emergency brake is on

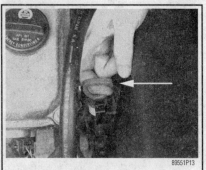

Fig. 157 The automatic transaxle dipstick is marked on the head of the indicator

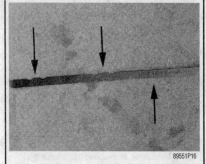

Fig. 158 The automatic transaxle dipstick shows the fluid type and level indicators

Fig. 159 Remove the transaxle drain plug

Fig. 160 Allow the fluid to drain form the transaxle pan into a container

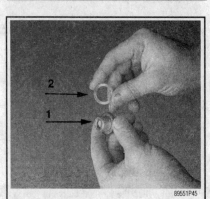

Fig. 161 Inspect the plug threads (1) and gasket (2) prior to installation

2. Position a suitable drain pan under the drain plug. Loosen the drain plug with a 10mm hex head wrench and allow the fluid to drain.

3. Install and tighten the drain plug to 36 ft. lbs. (49 Nm).

4. Through the filler tube opening, add the proper amount of transmission fluid as specified in the Capacities Chart.

5. Check the fluid level and add as required.

✹✹ WARNING

Do not overfill the transaxle.

PAN & FILTER SERVICE

◆ **See Figures 162 thru 171**

1. To avoid contamination of the transaxle, thoroughly clean the exterior of the oil pan and surrounding area to remove any deposits of dirt and grease.

2. Position a suitable drain pan under the oil pan and remove the drain plug. Allow the oil to drain from the pan. Set the drain plug aside.

3. Loosen and remove all but two of the oil pan retaining bolts. Try to remove them in a crisscross pattern.

4. Support the pan by hand and slowly remove the remaining two bolts.

5. Carefully lower the pan to the ground. There will be some fluid still inside the pan, so be careful.

6. Remove the three oil strainer attaching bolts and carefully remove the strainer. The strainer will also contain some fluid.

➡ **One of the three oil strainer bolts is slightly longer than the other two. Make a mental note of where the longer bolt goes so that it may be reinstalled in the original position.**

7. Remove the oil strainer. Remove the gasket from the pan and discard it.

8. Drain the remainder of the fluid from the oil pan and wipe the pan clean with a rag. With a gasket scraper, remove any old gasket material from the

Fig. 162 Transaxle pan retaining bolt locations

Fig. 163 Loosen and remove all of the bolts in a crisscross fashion

Fig. 164 Be careful when lowering the pan. There is still some fluid left in it

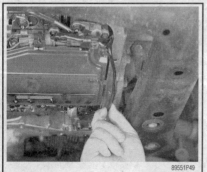

Fig. 165 Some transaxles may have wires attached on the side of the valve body; detach them

Fig. 166 There are usually three bolts retaining the strainer to the valve body—A541E transaxle shown

Fig. 167 Unbolt and remove the oil strainer

Fig. 168 When the strainer bolts are loosened, some fluid may still come from the valve body; be prepared

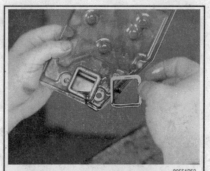

Fig. 169 Check for a gasket once the strainer is removed. It may need to be scraped from the valve body

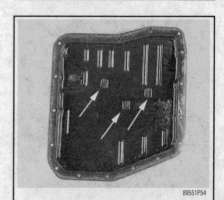

Fig. 170 Remove and clean the magnets on the bottom of the pan

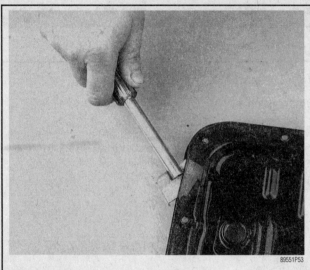

Fig. 171 Scrape all old gasket material off the pan

flanges of the pan and the transaxle. Remove the gasket from the drain plug and replace it with a new one.

➡️**Depending on the year and maintenance schedule of the vehicle, there may be from one to three small magnets on the bottom of the pan. These magnets were installed by the manufacturer at the time the transaxle was assembled. The magnets function to collect metal chips and filings from clutch plates, bushings and bearings that accumulate during the normal break-in process that a new transaxle experiences. So, don't be alarmed if such accumulations are present. Clean the magnets and reinstall them. They are useful tools for determining transaxle component wear.**

To install:

9. Install the new oil strainer. Tighten the retaining bolts in their proper locations.

10. Install the new gasket onto the oil pan making sure that the holes in the gasket are aligned evenly with those of the pan. Position the magnets so that they will not interfere with the oil tubes.

11. Raise the pan and gasket into position on the transaxle and install the retaining bolts. Tighten the retaining bolts in a crisscross pattern to 43 inch lbs. (5 Nm).

12. Install and tighten the drain plug to 36 ft. lbs. (49 Nm).

13. Fluid is added only through the dipstick tube. Use only the proper automatic transmission fluid; do not overfill.

14. Replace the dipstick after filling. Start the engine and allow it to idle. DO NOT race the engine!

15. After the engine has idled for a few minutes, shift the transmission slowly through the gears and then return it to **P**. With the engine still idling,

check the fluid level on the dipstick. If necessary, add more fluid to raise the level to where it is supposed to be.

> ❊ **CAUTION**
>
> **Check the fluid in the drain pan, it should always be a bright red color. It if is discolored (brown or black), or smells burnt, serious transmission troubles, probably due to overheating, should be suspected. The transmission should be inspected by a qualified service technician to locate the cause of the burnt fluid.**

Transfer Case

FLUID RECOMMENDATIONS

All models use multipurpose gear oil API GL-5; SAE 75W–90 or 80W–90.

LEVEL CHECK

The oil in the transfer case should be checked at least every 15,000 miles (24,000 km) and replaced every 25,000–30,000 miles (40,000–48,000 km), even more frequently if driven in deep water or mud.

Manual Transaxle

▶ **See Figures 172 and 173**

1. With the car parked on a level surface, remove the filler plug from the front of the transaxle housing. The plug should use a 24mm hex head wrench.

2. If the lubricant begins to trickle out of the hole, there is enough. Otherwise, carefully insert your finger (watch out for sharp threads!) and check to see if the oil is up to the edge of the hole.

3. If not, add oil through the hole until the level is at the edge of the hole. Most gear lubricants come in a plastic squeeze bottle with a nozzle; making additions simple. You can also use a common everyday kitchen baster.

4. Replace the filler plug and tighten it to 36 ft. lbs. (49 Nm). Run the engine and check for leaks.

Automatic Transaxle

▶ **See Figure 174**

1. Park the car on a level surface with the engine idling. Shift the transmission into **P** and set the parking brake.

2. Remove the dipstick, wipe it clean and reinsert if firmly. Be sure that it has been pushed all the way in. Remove the dipstick and check the fluid level while holding it horizontally. All models have a LOW and a HIGH notch on the dipstick.

3. If the fluid level is not within the proper area on either side of the dipstick, pour the proper lubricant into the dipstick tube. This is easily done with the aid of a funnel. Check the level often as you are filling the transfer case. Be extremely careful not to overfill it.

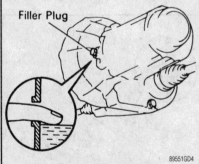

Fig. 172 Place your finger inside the fill hole to inspect the level of the fluid in the transfer case

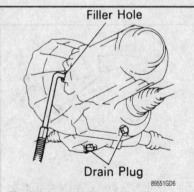

Fig. 173 Add fluid through the filler hole of the manual transaxle transfer case

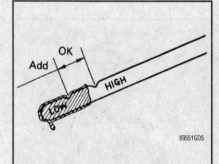

Fig. 174 On automatic transfer cases, inspect the level of the fluid on the dipstick

DRAIN & REFILL

▶ **See Figures 175 and 176**

Once every 30,000 miles (48,000 km), the oil in the transfer case should be changed.

1. The transfer case oil should be hot before it is drained. If the engine is at normal operating temperature, the oil should be hot enough.

2. Raise the car and support it properly on jackstands so that you can safely work underneath. You will probably not have enough room to work if the car is not raised.

3. The drain plug is located on the bottom of the transfer case. It should require a hex head wrench (24mm on models with MT and 10mm on those with AT). Place a pan under the drain plug and remove it. Keep a slight inward pressure on the plug while unscrewing it, this will keep the oil from pouring out until the plug is removed.

✳✳ CAUTION

The oil will be HOT. Be careful when you remove the plug so that you don't take a bath in hot gear oil.

4. Allow the oil to drain completely. Clean off the plug and replace it, tightening it until it is just snug 36 ft. lbs. (49 Nm).

5. Remove the filler plug from the side of the case on models with MT. There will be a gasket underneath this plug. Replace it if damaged.

6. Fill the transfer case with gear oil through the filler plug hole as detailed previously (remember, on models with AT, simply use the dipstick tube!). Refer to the Capacities Chart for the amount of oil needed to refill your transfer case.

7. The oil level should come right up to the edge of the hole. You can stick your finger in to verify this. Watch out for sharp threads. On models with AT, use the dipstick as detailed previously.

8. Replace the filler plug and gasket, lower the car, and check for leaks. Dispose of the old oil in the proper manner.

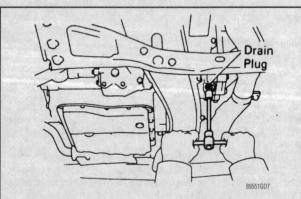

Fig. 175 Automatic transaxle transfer case drain plug location

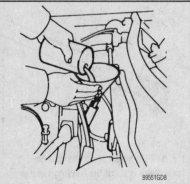

Fig. 176 Fill the transfer case through the dipstick tube on automatic models

Drive Axles

FLUID RECOMMENDATIONS

Front

1983–89 MODELS

- All AT models—DEXRON® II ATF
- All 2WD models (4 cyl., MT)—DEXRON® II ATF
- All 2WD models (6 cyl., MT)—Hypoid gear oil API GL-4, SAE 75W-90
- All 4WD models—Hypoid gear oil API GL-5, SAE 80W-90

1990–96 MODELS

All models use DEXRON® II ATF.

Rear

All 4WD models use Hypoid gear oil API GL-5, SAE 80W-90.

LEVEL CHECK

▶ **See Figures 177 and 178**

The oil in the front and/or rear differential should be checked at least every 15,000 miles (24,000 km) and replaced every 25,000–30,000 miles (40,000–48,000 km). If driven in deep water it should be replaced immediately.

1. With the car parked on a level surface, remove the filler plug (usually a 10mm hex head) from the back of the differential.

➡**The plug on the bottom is the drain plug on rear differentials and most front. The lower of the two plugs on the back of the housing is the drain plug on the front differential of models with V6 engines.**

2. If the oil begins to trickle out of the hole, there is enough. Otherwise, carefully insert your finger (watch out for sharp threads!) into the hole and check to see if the oil is up to the bottom edge of the filler hole.

3. If not, add oil through the hole until the level is at the edge of the hole. Most gear oils come in a plastic squeeze bottle with a nozzle, making additions simple. You can also use a common kitchen baster.

4. Replace the filler plug and drive the car for a while. Stop and check for leaks. Tighten the plug to 36 ft. lbs. (49 Nm).

DRAIN & REFILL

▶ **See Figures 179, 180 and 181**

The gear oil in the front or rear differential should be changed at least every 25,000–30,000 miles (40,000–48,000 km); immediately if driven in deep water.

To drain and fill the differential, proceed as follows:

1. Park the vehicle on a level surface. Set the parking brake.

2. Remove the filler (upper) plug. Place a container which is large enough to catch all of the differential oil, under the drain plug.

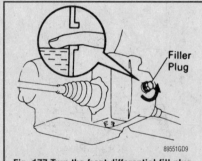

Fig. 177 Turn the front differential fill plug counterclockwise on most models to remove, then check the level of the fluid with your finger

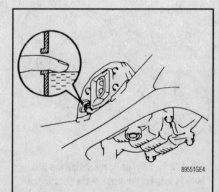

Fig. 178 Location of the rear differential fill plug on 4WD models

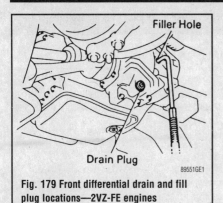

Fig. 179 Front differential drain and fill plug locations—2VZ-FE engines

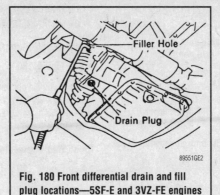

Fig. 180 Front differential drain and fill plug locations—5SF-E and 3VZ-FE engines

Fig. 181 Front differential drain and fill plug locations—2S-ELC and 3S-FE engines

3. Remove the drain (lower) plug (usually a 10mm hex head) and gasket, if so equipped. Allow all of the oil to drain into the container.

4. Install the drain plug. Tighten it so that it will not leak, but do not over-tighten. Tighten to 36 ft. lbs. (49 Nm).

➥**Its usually a good idea to replace the drain plug gasket at this time.**

5. Refill with the proper grade and viscosity of axle lubricant. Be sure that the level reaches the bottom of the filler plug. DO NOT overfill!

6. Install the filler plug and check for leakage.

Cooling System

FLUID RECOMMENDATIONS

The correct coolant is any permanent, high quality ethylene glycol antifreeze mixed in a 50/50 concentration with water. This mixture gives the best combination of antifreeze and anti-boil characteristics within the engine.

LEVEL CHECK

▶ **See Figures 182, 183, 184 and 185**

✳✳ CAUTION

Always allow the car to sit and cool for an hour or so (longer is better) before removing the radiator cap. To avoid injury when working on a warm engine, cover the radiator cap with a thick cloth and turn it slowly counterclockwise until the pressure begins to escape. After the pressure is completely removed, remove the cap. Never remove the cap until the pressure is gone. There should be no excessive rust deposits around the radiator cap or filler tube. The coolant should be free from any oil. On a COLD engine, place your finger in the coolant and check for oil or rust deposits.

It's best to check the coolant level when the engine is COLD. The radiator coolant level should be between the LOW and the FULL lines on the expansion tank when the engine is cold. If low, check for leakage and add coolant up to the FULL line but do not overfill.

➥**Check the freeze protection rating of the antifreeze at least once a year or as necessary with a suitable antifreeze tester.**

DRAIN & REFILL

▶ **See Figures 186 and 187**

✳✳ CAUTION

When draining the coolant, keep in mind that cats and dogs are attracted by ethylene glycol antifreeze, and are quite likely to drink any that is left in an uncovered container or in puddles on the ground. This will prove fatal in sufficient quantity. Always drain the coolant into a sealable container. Coolant should be reused unless it is contaminated or several years old.

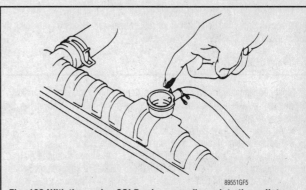

Fig. 182 With the engine COLD, place your finger into the radiator opening and check for oil or excessive dirt

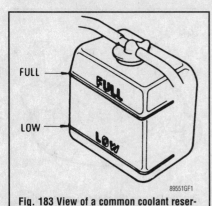

Fig. 183 View of a common coolant reservoir tank with markings

Fig. 184 The cap lifts off the reservoir to allow addition of fluid if necessary

Fig. 185 Using the appropriate amount of coolant and water mixture, top off the coolant system

Completely draining and refilling the cooling system every two years at least will remove accumulated rust, scale and other deposits.

➡ **Use a good quality antifreeze with water pump lubricants, rust inhibitors and other corrosion inhibitors along with acid neutralizers.**

1. Drain the existing antifreeze and coolant. Open the radiator and engine drain petcocks. Some engines have two petcocks, but most are equipped with one. The easiest way to drain the system is to disconnect the bottom radiator hose, at the radiator outlet. Set the heater temperature controls to the full HOT position.

➡ **Before opening the radiator petcock, spray it with some penetrating lubricant.**

2. Close the petcock and tighten the drain plug(s) to 9 ft. lbs. (13 Nm) on 4 cyl. engines or 22 ft. lbs. (29 Nm) on 6 cyl. engines or reconnect the lower hose. Open the air relief plug (2VZ-FE) until you can see the hole.

3. Determine the capacity of your cooling system (see Capacities specifications). Add a 50/50 mix of quality antifreeze (ethylene glycol) and water to provide the desired protection. Add through the radiator filler neck until full and then fill the expansion tank to the **FULL** line. It is recommended that you fill the system with the engine off, then start the engine and top off the levels once the engine is warmed up.

FLUSHING & CLEANING THE SYSTEM

Proceed with draining the system as outlined above. When the system has drained, reconnect any hoses close to the radiator draincock. Move the temperature control for the heater to its hottest position; this allows the heater core to be flushed as well. Using a garden hose or bucket, fill the radiator and allow the water to run out the engine drain cock. Continue until the water runs clear. Be sure to clean the expansion tank as well.

If the system is badly contaminated with rust or scale, you can use a commercial flushing solution to clean it out. Follow the manufacturer's instructions. Some causes of rust are air in the system, failure to change the coolant regularly, use of excessively hard or soft water, and/or failure to use the correct mix of antifreeze and water.

After the system has been flushed, continue with the refill procedures outlined above. Check the condition of the radiator cap and its gasket, replacing the radiator cap as necessary.

SYSTEM INSPECTION

Most permanent antifreeze/coolant have a colored dye added which makes the solution an excellent leak detector. When servicing the cooling system, check for leakage at:

- All hoses and hose connections.
- Radiator seams, radiator core, and radiator draincock.
- All engine block and cylinder head freeze (core) plugs, and drain plugs.
- Edges of all cooling system gaskets (head gaskets, thermostat gasket).
- Transmission fluid cooler.
- Heating system components, water pump.
- Check the engine oil dipstick for signs of coolant in the engine oil.

- Check the coolant in the radiator for signs of oil in the coolant. Investigate and correct any indication of coolant leakage.

Check the Radiator Cap

▶ **See Figure 188**

While you are checking the coolant level, check the radiator cap for a worn or cracked gasket. If the cap doesn't seal properly, fluid will be lost and the engine will overheat.

A worn cap should be replaced with a new one.

Clean Radiator of Debris

▶ **See Figure 189**

Periodically clean any debris such as leaves, paper, insects, etc., from the radiator fins. Pick the large pieces off by hand. The smaller pieces can be washed away with water pressure from a hose.

Carefully straighten any bent radiator fins with a pair of needle nose pliers. Be careful, the fins are very soft. Don't wiggle the fins back and forth too much. Straighten them once and try not to move them again.

CHECKING SYSTEM PROTECTION

A 50/50 mix of coolant concentrate and water will usually provide protection to 35°F (37°C). Freeze protection may be checked by using a cooling system hydrometer. Inexpensive hydrometers (floating ball types) may be obtained from a local department store (automotive section) or an auto supply store. Follow the directions packaged with the coolant hydrometer when checking protection.

Brake Master Cylinder

FLUID RECOMMENDATIONS

All vehicles use DOT 3 or SAE J1703 brake fluid.

LEVEL CHECK

▶ **See Figures 190 and 191**

The brake master cylinder is located under the hood, in the left rear section of the engine compartment. It is made of translucent plastic so that the levels may be checked without removing the top. The fluid level in the reservoir should be checked at least every 15,000 miles (24,000km) or 1 year. The fluid level should be maintained at the uppermost mark on the side of the reservoir. Any sudden decrease in the level indicates a possible leak in the system and should be checked out immediately.

When adding fluid, use only fresh, uncontaminated brake fluid meeting or exceeding DOT 3 standards. Be careful not to spill any brake fluid on painted surfaces, as it eats the paint. Do not allow the brake fluid container or the master cylinder reservoir to remain open any longer than necessary; brake fluid absorbs moisture from the air, reducing its effectiveness and causing corrosion in the lines.

Fig. 186 Loosen the radiator drain plug . . .

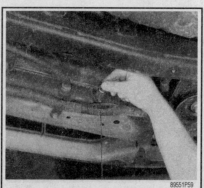

Fig. 187 . . . to allow the coolant to flow out

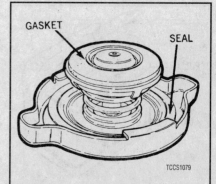

Fig. 188 Be sure the rubber gasket on the radiator cap has a tight seal

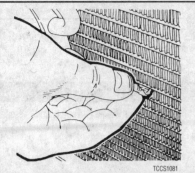

Fig. 189 Periodically remove all debris from the radiator fins

Fig. 190 The reservoir is translucent enabling easy level checks

Fig. 191 Always clean the area around the lid prior to removal

Clutch Master Cylinder

FLUID RECOMMENDATIONS

All vehicles use DOT 3 or SAE J1703 brake fluid.

LEVEL CHECK

The clutch master cylinder is located under the hood, in the left rear section of the engine compartment near the brake master. The clutch master is made of a translucent plastic so that the levels may be checked without removing the top. The fluid level in the reservoir should be checked at least every 15,000 miles (24,000 km) or 1 year. The fluid level should be maintained at the uppermost mark on the side of the reservoir. Any sudden decrease in the level indicates a possible leak in the system and should be checked out immediately.

When adding fluid, use only fresh, uncontaminated brake fluid meeting or exceeding DOT 3 standards. Be careful not to spill any brake fluid on painted surfaces, as it eats the paint. Do not allow the brake fluid container or the master cylinder reservoir to remain open any longer than necessary; brake fluid absorbs moisture from the air, reducing its effectiveness and causing corrosion in the lines.

Power Steering Pump

FLUID RECOMMENDATIONS

All vehicles use DEXRON®II (or its superceding fluid type) automatic transmission fluid in the power steering system.

FLUID LEVEL CHECK

▶ **See Figures 192, 193 and 194**

Check the power steering fluid level every 6 months or 6000 miles (9600 km).
1. Make sure that the vehicle is level. If the reservoir is dirty, wipe it off.
2. Start the engine and allow it to idle.

3. With the engine at idle, move the steering wheel from LOCK to LOCK several times to raise the temperature of the fluid.
4. The power steering pump reservoir is translucent, so the fluid level may be checked without removing the cap. Look through the reservoir and check for foaming or emulsification.

➡**Foaming or emulsification indicates the either there is air in the system or the fluid level is low.**

5. Check the fluid level in the reservoir. The fluid should be within the **HOT LEVEL** of the reservoir. If the fluid is checked when cold, the level should be within the **COLD LEVEL** of the reservoir.
6. Add fluid as required until the proper level is reached. To add fluid, remove the filler cap by turning it counterclockwise and lifting up. After the proper amount of fluid is added, replace the cap making sure that the arrows on the cap are properly aligned with the arrows on the tank.
7. While your in the neighborhood, check the steering box case, vane pump and hose connections for leaks and damage. Simple preventative maintenance checks like these can identify minor problems before turn into major problems and also increase your familiarity with the locations of steering system components.

Chassis Greasing

The Toyota Camry does not require any chassis greasing, all components are sealed.

Body Lubrication And Maintenance

There is no set period recommended by Toyota for body lubrication. However, it is a good idea to lubricate the following body points at least once a year, especially in the fall before cold weather.

LOCK CYLINDERS

Apply graphite lubricant sparingly thought the key slot. Insert the key and operate the lock several times to be sure that the lubricant is worked into the lock cylinder.

Fig. 192 The power steering reservoir is clearly marked for identification

Fig. 193 The levels are clearly marked on the outside of the power steering reservoir

Fig. 194 Carefully add fluid using a funnel to top off the power steering system

DOOR HINGES & HINGE CHECKS

Spray a silicone lubricant or apply white lithium grease on the hinge pivot points to eliminate any binding conditions. Open and close the door several times to be sure that the lubricant is evenly and thoroughly distributed. When applying grease, the use of a small acid brush is very helpful in getting the grease to those hard to reach areas.

TAILGATE

Spray a silicone lubricant on all of the pivot and friction surfaces to eliminate any squeaks or binds. Work the tailgate to distribute the lubricant

JUMP STARTING A DEAD BATTERY

♦ See Figure 195

Whenever a vehicle is jump started, precautions must be followed in order to prevent the possibility of personal injury. Remember that batteries contain a small amount of explosive hydrogen gas which is a by-product of battery charging. Sparks should always be avoided when working around batteries, especially when attaching jumper cables. To minimize the possibility of accidental sparks, follow the procedure carefully.

☀☀ CAUTION

NEVER hook the batteries up in a series circuit or the entire electrical system will go up in smoke, including the starter!

Vehicles equipped with a diesel engine may utilize two 12 volt batteries. If so, the batteries are connected in a parallel circuit (positive terminal to positive terminal, negative terminal to negative terminal). Hooking the batteries up in parallel circuit increases battery cranking power without increasing total battery voltage output. Output remains at 12 volts. On the other hand, hooking two 12 volt batteries up in a series circuit (positive terminal to negative terminal, positive terminal to negative terminal) increases total battery output to 24 volts (12 volts plus 12 volts).

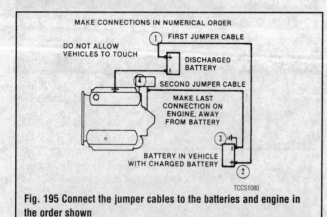

Fig. 195 Connect the jumper cables to the batteries and engine in the order shown

Jump Starting Precautions

- Be sure that both batteries are of the same voltage. Vehicles covered by this manual and most vehicles on the road today utilize a 12 volt charging system.
- Be sure that both batteries are of the same polarity (have the same terminal, in most cases NEGATIVE grounded).
- Be sure that the vehicles are not touching or a short could occur.
- On serviceable batteries, be sure the vent cap holes are not obstructed.
- Do not smoke or allow sparks anywhere near the batteries.
- In cold weather, make sure the battery electrolyte is not frozen. This can occur more readily in a battery that has been in a state of discharge.
- Do not allow electrolyte to contact your skin or clothing.

BODY DRAIN HOLES

Be sure that the drain holes in the doors and rocker panels are cleared of obstruction. A small screwdriver can be used to clear them of any debris.

Wheel Bearings

The Toyota Camry models are equipped with sealed hub and bearing assemblies. The hub and bearing assemblies are nonserviceable. If the assembly is damaged, the complete unit must be replaced.

Jump Starting Procedure

1. Make sure that the voltages of the 2 batteries are the same. Most batteries and charging systems are of the 12 volt variety.
2. Pull the jumping vehicle (with the good battery) into a position so the jumper cables can reach the dead battery and that vehicle's engine. Make sure that the vehicles do NOT touch.
3. Place the transmissions/transaxles of both vehicles in **Neutral** (MT) or **P** (AT), as applicable, then firmly set their parking brakes.

➡ **If necessary for safety reasons, the hazard lights on both vehicles may be operated throughout the entire procedure without significantly increasing the difficulty of jumping the dead battery.**

4. Turn all lights and accessories OFF on both vehicles. Make sure the ignition switches on both vehicles are turned to the **OFF** position.
5. Cover the battery cell caps with a rag, but do not cover the terminals.
6. Make sure the terminals on both batteries are clean and free of corrosion or proper electrical connection will be impeded. If necessary, clean the battery terminals before proceeding.
7. Identify the positive (+) and negative (-;) terminals on both batteries.
8. Connect the first jumper cable to the positive (+) terminal of the dead battery, then connect the other end of that cable to the positive (+) terminal of the booster (good) battery.
9. Connect one end of the other jumper cable to the negative (-;) terminal on the booster battery and the final cable clamp to an engine bolt head, alternator bracket or other solid, metallic point on the engine with the dead battery. Try to pick a ground on the engine that is positioned away from the battery in order to minimize the possibility of the 2 clamps touching should one loosen during the procedure. DO NOT connect this clamp to the negative (−) terminal of the bad battery.

☀☀ CAUTION

Be very careful to keep the jumper cables away from moving parts (cooling fan, belts, etc.) on both engines.

10. Check to make sure that the cables are routed away from any moving parts, then start the donor vehicle's engine. Run the engine at moderate speed for several minutes to allow the dead battery a chance to receive some initial charge.
11. With the donor vehicle's engine still running slightly above idle, try to start the vehicle with the dead battery. Crank the engine for no more than 10 seconds at a time and let the starter cool for at least 20 seconds between tries. If the vehicle does not start in 3 tries, it is likely that something else is also wrong or that the battery needs additional time to charge.
12. Once the vehicle is started, allow it to run at idle for a few seconds to make sure that it is operating properly.
13. Turn ON the headlights, heater blower and, if equipped, the rear defroster of both vehicles in order to reduce the severity of voltage spikes and subsequent risk of damage to the vehicles' electrical systems when the cables are disconnected. This step is especially important to any vehicle equipped with computer control modules.
14. Carefully disconnect the cables in the reverse order of connection. Start with the negative cable that is attached to the engine ground, then the negative cable on the donor battery. Disconnect the positive cable from the donor battery and finally, disconnect the positive cable from the formerly dead battery. Be careful when disconnecting the cables from the positive terminals not to allow the alligator clips to touch any metal on either vehicle or a short and sparks will occur.

JACKING

▶ **See Figures 196 thru 200**

Your vehicle was supplied with a jack for emergency road repairs. This jack is fine for changing a flat tire or other short term procedures not requiring you to go beneath the vehicle. If it is used in an emergency situation, carefully follow the instructions provided either with the jack or in your owner's manual. Do not attempt to use the jack on any portions of the vehicle other than specified by the vehicle manufacturer. Always block the diagonally opposite wheel when using a jack.

A more convenient way of jacking is the use of a garage or floor jack. You may use the floor jack raise the vehicle and place stands on the jacking points under the vehicle.

Never place the jack under the radiator, engine or transmission components. Severe and expensive damage will result when the jack is raised. Additionally, never jack under the floorpan or bodywork; the metal will deform.

Whenever you plan to work under the vehicle, you must support it on jackstands or ramps. Never use cinder blocks or stacks of wood to support the vehicle, even 'f you're only going to be under it for a few minutes. Never crawl under the vehicle when it is supported only by the tire-changing jack or other floor jack.

➡ **Always position a block of wood or small rubber pad on top of the jack or jackstand to protect the lifting point's finish when lifting or supporting the vehicle.**

Small hydraulic, screw, or scissors jacks are satisfactory for raising the vehicle. Drive-on trestles or ramps are also a handy and safe way to both raise and support the vehicle. Be careful though, some ramps may be too steep to drive your vehicle onto without scraping the front bottom panels. Never support the vehicle on any suspension member (unless specifically instructed to do so by a repair manual) or by an underbody panel.

Jacking Precautions

The following safety points cannot be overemphasized:
• Always block the opposite wheel or wheels to keep the vehicle from rolling off the jack.
• When raising the front of the vehicle, firmly apply the parking brake.
• When the drive wheels are to remain on the ground, leave the vehicle in gear to help prevent it from rolling.
• Always use jackstands to support the vehicle when you are working underneath. Place the stands beneath the vehicle's jacking brackets. Before climbing underneath, rock the vehicle a bit to make sure it is firmly supported.

Fig. 196 When raising the front of the vehicle, place the jack under the front crossmember

Fig. 197 Place the jack under the rear crossmember to support the rear of the vehicle

Fig. 198 Be careful not to place the jackstand on the seam, damage will occur

Fig. 199 Jackstand placement for the rear of the vehicle

Fig. 200 Jackstand placement for the front of the vehicle

MAINTENANCE SCHEDULE—1983-84

Maintenance operations: A = Check and/or adjust if necessary; R = Replace, change or lubricate; I = Inspect and correct or replace if necessary

System	Maintenance items		Miles x 1,000 / 15	30	45	60	SV series	CV series
			Kilometers x 1,000 / 24	48	72	96		
			Months / 12	24	36	48		
ENGINE	Valve clearance [2] (Diesel)		A	A	A	A	●	—
	Timing belt (Diesel)					R	—	●
	Drive belts [4] (including PS and A/C drive belt)	Gasoline		A		A	●	●
		Diesel		I		R	●	—
	Engine oil and oil filter [1]	Gasoline	Change every 10,000 miles (16,000 km) or 8 months				●	●
		Diesel	Change every 5,000 miles (8,000 km) or 4 months				●	—
	Engine coolant [5]					R	●	●
	Vacuum pump oil hoses (Diesel)			I		R	●	—
	Exhaust pipes and mountings [1]			I		R	●	●
FUEL	Idle speed [2]	Gasoline	A*	A*	A*	A*	●	●
		Diesel	A	A	A	A	●	—
	Fuel filter (Diesel)			R		R	●	—
	Air filter [1]			R		R	●	●
	Fuel lines and connections			I		I	●	●
	Fuel filler cap gasket			R		R	—	●
IGNITION	Spark plugs (Gasoline)			R		R	●	●
	Ignition wiring and distributor cap [1] (Gasoline)				(3)		●	●
EMISSION CONTROL	Charcoal canister (Gasoline)					I	—	●
	Fuel evaporative emission control system, hoses and connections (Gasoline)					I	●	●
TRANSAXLE	Transmission and differential oil [1]			I		I	●	●
BRAKES	Brake lining and drums [1]			I		I	●	●
	Brake pads and discs [6]			I		I	—	●
	Brake line pipes and hoses [6]			I		I	●	●
CHASSIS	Steering linkage [1],[6]			I		I	●	●
	Drive shaft boots [1],[6]			I		I	●	●
	Ball joints and dust covers [1],[6]			I		I	—	●
	Bolts and nuts on chassis and body [1]			I		I	●	●

Service interval: Odometer reading or months, whichever comes first

* The items marked with an asterisk are recommended maintenance items for California vehicles only, but are required for Federal and Canada.

89551C20

MAINTENANCE SCHEDULE—1983-84

NOTE:

(1) For vehicles normally used under any of the following severe conditions, the applicable items of maintenance should be performed as indicated in the table below.

Maintenance items			Service interval	Severe condition
Engine oil and oil filter	Gasoline	R	Every 3,750 miles (6,000 km) or 3 months	A . . . . F
	Diesel	R	Every 1,875 miles (3,000 km) or 1.5 months	A . . D . F
Exhaust pipes and mountings		I	Every 7,500 miles (12,000 km) or 6 months	A B C . E .
Air filter	Gasoline	I	Every 3,750 miles (6,000 km) or 3 months	. . . . . E
	Diesel	R	Every 30,000 miles (48,000 km) or 24 months	. . . D . .
Ignition wiring [3] (Gasoline)		I	Every 12 months	. . . . . E
Distributor cap [3] (Gasoline)		I	Every 12 months	. . . . . E
Brake linings and drums		I	Every 7,500 miles (12,000 km) or 6 months	A B C D
Brake pads and discs		I	Every 7,500 miles (12,000 km) or 6 months	A B C D
Steering linkage, gear housing and steering wheel freeplay		I	Every 7,500 miles (12,000 km) or 6 months	. . C
Ball joints and dust covers		I	Every 7,500 miles (12,000 km) or 6 months	. . C D E
Drive shaft boots		I	Every 7,500 miles (12,000 km) or 6 months	. . C . E
Transmission and differential oil		R	Every 15,000 miles (24,000 km) or 12 months	A . C
Automatic transmission fluid		R	Every 15,000 miles (24,000 km) or 12 months	A . C
Bolts and nuts on chassis and body		I	Every 7,500 miles (12,000 km) or 6 months	. . C

"Severe conditions"

A – Pulling trailers
B – Repeated short trips
C – Driving on rough and/or muddy roads
D – Driving on dusty roads
E – Operating in extremely cold weather and/or driving in areas using road salt
F – Repeated short trips in extremely cold weather

(2) Specifications appear on the information label.

(3) In areas where road salt is used, inspection and cleaning of the distributor cap and ignition wiring should be performed each year just after the snow season.

(4) Inspect every 15,000 miles (24,000 km) or 12 months after 60,000 miles (96,000 km) or 48 months.

(5) Replace every 30,000 miles (48,000 km) or 24 months after 60,000 miles (96,000 km) or 48 months, due to possible use of poor quality coolant locally available.

(6) First inspection at 30,000 miles (48,000 km) or 24 months and every 15,000 miles (24,000 km) or 12 months thereafter.

89551C21

NORMAL MAINTENANCE SCHEDULE—1985-86 (GASOLINE ENGINE)

Maintenance operations: A = Check and/or adjust if necessary; R = Replace, change or lubricate; I = Inspect and correct or replace if necessary

Service interval (Odometer reading or months, whichever comes first)

Maintenance services beyond 60,000 miles (96,000 km) should be performed at the same intervals shown in each maintenance schedule.

System	Maintenance items	Miles x 1,000: 10 / Km 16 / Mo 12	20 / 32 / 24	30 / 48 / 36	40 / 64 / 48	50 / 80 / 60	60 / 96 / 72
ENGINE	Drive belts (V-ribbed belt)(1)						I
	Engine oil and oil filter ★★	R	R	R	R	R	R
	Engine coolant(2)						R
	Exhaust pipes and mountings			I			I
FUEL	Idle speed ★(3)			A			A
	Air filter ★★			R			R
	Fuel line and connections						I
	Fuel filler cap gasket						R
IGNITION	Spark plugs ★★			R			R
EVAP	Charcoal canister						
BRAKES	Brake lining and drums	I	I	I	I	I	I
	Brake pads and discs	I	I	I	I	I	I
	Brake line pipes and hoses	I	I	I	I	I	I
CHASSIS	Steering linkage	I	I	I	I	I	I
	Drive shaft boots	I	I	I	I	I	I
	Ball joints and dust covers	I	I	I	I	I	I
	Automatic transaxle, manual transaxle, differential and steering gear housing oil						
	Bolts and nuts on chassis and body						

Maintenance services indicated by a star (★) or asterisk (*) are required under the terms of the Emission Control Systems Warranty (ECSW). See Owner's Guide for complete warranty information.
★ For vehicles sold in California
* For vehicles sold outside California

NOTE:
(1) After 60,000 miles (96,000 km) or 72 months, inspect every 10,000 miles (16,000 km) or 12 months.
(2) After 60,000 miles (96,000 km) or 72 months, replace every 30,000 miles (48,000 km) or 36 months.
(3) After 30,000 miles (48,000 km) or 36 months, adjust every 30,000 miles (48,000 km) or 36 months.
Maintenance services performed only at 30,000 miles (48,000 km) or 36 months under the terms of the ECSW.

88551C22

SEVERE MAINTENANCE SCHEDULE—1985-86

Follow the severe condition schedule if vehicle is operated mainly under one or more of the following severe conditions:
● Pulling a trailer
● Repeated short trips
● Driving on rough and/or muddy roads
● Driving on dusty roads
● Driving in extremely cold weather and/or on salted roads

Service interval (Odometer reading or months, whichever comes first)

Maintenance services beyond 60,000 miles (96,000 km) should be performed at the same intervals shown in each maintenance schedule.

System	Maintenance items	5/8/6	10/16/12	15/24/18	20/32/24	25/40/30	30/48/36	35/56/42	40/64/48	45/72/54	50/80/60	55/88/66	60/96/72
ENGINE	Drive belts (V-ribbed belt)(1)												R
	Engine oil and oil filter ★	R	R	R	R	R	R	R	R	R	R	R	R
	Engine coolant(2)												R
	Exhaust pipes and mountings				I				I				I
FUEL	Idle speed ★(3)						A						A
	Air filter ★★(5)						R						R
	Fuel line and connections												I
	Fuel filler cap gasket												R
IGNITION	Spark plugs ★★						R						R
	Ignition wiring and distributor cap ★★						(4)						
EVAP	Charcoal canister												
BRAKES	Brake lining and drums		I		I		I		I		I		I
	Brake pads and discs		I		I		I		I		I		I
	Brake line pipes and hoses		I		I		I		I		I		I
CHASSIS	Steering linkage(6)						R						R
	Drive shaft boots						I						I
	Ball joints and dust covers						R						R
	Automatic transaxle, manual transaxle, differential and steering gear housing(7) oil						R						R
	Bolts and nuts on chassis and body(6)												R

Maintenance servies indicated by a star (★) or asterisk (*) are required under the terms of the Emission Control Systems Warranty (ECSW).
See Owner's Guide for complete warranty information.
★ For vehicles sold in California
* For vehicles sold outside California

NOTE:
(1) After 60,000 miles (96,000 km) or 72 months, inspect every 10,000 miles (16,000 km) or 12 months.
(2) After 60,000 miles (96,000 km) or 72 months, replace every 30,000 miles (48,000 km) or 36 months.
(3) After 30,000 miles (48,000 km) or 36 months, adjust every 30,000 miles (48,000 km) or 36 months.
Maintenance services performed only at 30,000 miles (48,000 km) or 36 months under the terms of the ECSW.
(4) In areas where road salt is used, inspect and clean each year just after the snow season.
(5) Applicable when operating mainly on dusty roads. If not, follow the normal condition schedule.
(6) Applicable when operating mainly on rough and/or muddy roads. If not, follow the normal condition schedule.
(7) Inspect the steering gear housing for oil leakage only.

88551C23

NORMAL MAINTENANCE SCHEDULE—1987-88

Maintenance operations: A = Check and adjust if necessary; R = Replace, change or lubricate; I = Inspect and correct or replace if necessary

Maintenance services beyond 60,000 miles (96,000 km) should be performed at the same intervals shown in each maintenance schedule.

System	Maintenance items	Miles × 1,000	10	20	30	40	50	60
		Km × 1,000	16	32	48	64	80	96
		Months	12	24	36	48	60	72
ENGINE	Valve clearance							A
	Drive belts(1)							I
	Engine oil and oil filter★		R	R	R	R	R	R
	Engine coolant(2)				I			R
	Exhaust pipes and mountings							
FUEL	Air filter★				R			R
	Fuel lines and connections				I			I
	Fuel tank cap gasket							R
IGNITION	Spark plugs★★			R		R		R
EVAP	Charcoal canister							I
BRAKES	Brake linings and drums			I		I		I
	Brake pads and discs			I		I		I
	Brake line pipes and hoses				I			I
CHASSIS	Steering linkage				I			I
	Drive shaft boots			I		I		I
	Ball joints and dust covers				I			I
	Automatic transaxle, manual transaxle, differential and steering gear housing oil(3)				R			R
	Bolts and nuts on chassis and body			I		I		I

Maintenance services indicated by a star (★) or asterisk (*) are required under the terms of the Emission Control Systems Warranty (ECSW). See Owner's Guide or Warranty Booklet for complete warranty information.
★ For vehicles sold in California
* For vehicles sold outside California

NOTE:
(1) After 60,000 miles (96,000 km), inspect every 10,000 miles (16,000 km) or 12 months.
(2) After 60,000 miles (96,000 km), replace every 30,000 miles (48,000 km) or 36 months.
(3) Inspect the steering gear housing oil for leakage only.

8955IC26

SEVERE MAINTENANCE SCHEDULE—1987-88

Follow the severe condition schedule if vehicle is operated mainly under one or more of the following severe conditions:
• Towing a trailer, using a camper or car top carrier.
• Repeat short trips less than 5 miles (8 km) and outside temperatures remain below freezing.
• Extensive idling and/or low speed driving for a long distance such as police, taxi or door-to-door delivery use.
• Operating on dusty, rough, muddy or salt spread roads.

Maintenance services beyond 60,000 miles (96,000 km) should be performed at the same intervals shown in each maintenance schedule.

System	Maintenance items	Miles × 1,000	5	10	15	20	25	30	35	40	45	50	55	60
		Km × 1,000	8	16	24	32	40	48	56	64	72	80	88	96
		Months	6	12	18	24	30	36	42	48	54	60	66	72
ENGINE	Timing belt							R(1)						A
	Valve clearance													A
	Drive belts(2)													I
	Engine oil and oil filter★		R	R	R	R	R	R	R	R	R	R	R	R
	Engine coolant(3)													R
	Exhaust pipes and mountings													I
FUEL	Air filter★ (4)				R			R			R			R
	Fuel line and connections							I						I
	Fuel tank cap gasket													R
IGNITION	Spark plugs★★							R						R
EVAP	Charcoal canister													I
BRAKES	Brake linings and drums			I		I		I		I		I		I
	Brake pads and discs			I		I		I		I		I		I
	Brake line pipes and hoses							I						I
CHASSIS	Steering linkage(5)							I						I
	Drive shaft boots							I						I
	Ball joints and dust covers							I						I
	Transaxle, rear differential, and steering gear housing(6) oil							R						R
	Bolts and nuts on chassis and body(5)							I						I

Maintenance services indicated by a star (★) or asterisk (*) are required under the terms of the Emission Control Systems Warranty (ECSW). See Owner's Guide for complete warranty information.
★ For vehicles sold in California
* For vehicles sold outside California

NOTE:
(1) For the vehicles frequently idled for extensive periods and/or driven for long distance at low speeds such as taxi, police and door-to-door delivery, it is recommended to change at 60,000 miles (96,000 km).
(2) After 60,000 miles (96,000 km), inspect every 10,000 miles (16,000 km) or 12 months.
(3) After 60,000 miles (96,000 km), replace every 30,000 miles (48,000 km) or 36 months.
(4) Applicable when operating mainly on dusty roads. If not, follow the normal condition schedule.
(5) Applicable when operating mainly on rough and/or muddy roads. If not, follow the normal condition schedule.
(6) Inspect the steering gear housing for oil leakage only.

8955IC27

NORMAL MAINTENANCE SCHEDULE—1989

Maintenance operations:
A = Check and adjust if necessary;
R = Replace, change or lubricate;
I = Inspect and correct or replace if necessary

CONDITIONS:
- Towing a trailer, using a camper or car top carrier.
- Repeated short trips less than 5 miles (8 km) and outside temperatures remain below freezing.
- Extensive idling and/or low speed driving for a long distance such as police, taxi or door-to-door delivery use.
- Operating on dusty, rough, muddy or salt spread roads.

Maintenance services beyond 60,000 miles (96,000 km) should be performed at the same intervals shown in each maintenance schedule.

System	Maintenance items		Miles × 1,000	5	10	15	20	25	30	35	40	45	50	55	60
			Km × 1,000	8	16	24	32	40	48	56	64	72	80	88	96
			Months	6	12	18	24	30	36	42	48	54	60	66	72
ENGINE	Timing belt														R(1)
	Valve clearance														A
	Drive belts(2)														I
	Engine oil and oil filter*			R	R	R	R	R	R	R	R	R	R	R	R
	Engine coolant(3)								R						R
	Exhaust pipes and mountings								I						I
FUEL	Air filter*(4)								R						R
	Fuel lines and connections														I
	Fuel tank cap gasket														R
IGNITION	Spark plugs	3S-FE**							R						R
		2VZ-FE													R
EVAP	Charcoal canister														I
BRAKES	Brake linings and drums				I		I		I		I		I		I
	Brake pads and discs				I		I		I		I		I		I
	Brake line pipes and hoses														I
CHASSIS	Steering linkage(5)														I
	Drive shaft boots														I
	Ball joints and dust covers														I
	Automatic transaxle, manual transaxle, transfer differential and steering gear housing(6) oil								R						R
	Bolts and nuts on chassis and body(5)														I

Maintenance services indicated by a star (★) or asterisk (*) are required under the terms of the Emission Control Systems Warranty (ECSW). See Owner's Guide or Warranty Booklet for complete warranty information.
 ★ For vehicles sold in California
 * For vehicles sold outside California

NOTE:
(1) For vehicles frequently idled for extensive periods and/or driven for long distance at low speeds such as taxi, police and door-to-door delivery, it is recommended to change at 60,000 miles (96,000 km).
(2) After 60,000 miles (96,000 km) or 72 months, inspect every 10,000 miles (16,000 km) or 12 months
(3) After 60,000 miles (96,000 km) or 72 months, replace every 30,000 miles (48,000 km) or 36 months
(4) Applicable when operating mainly on dusty roads. If not, follow the schedule B
(5) Applicable when operating mainly on rough and/or muddy roads. If not, follow the schedule B
(6) Inspect the steering gear housing for oil leakage only

SEVERE MAINTENANCE SCHEDULE—1989

CONDITIONS: Conditions other than those listed for SCHEDULE A.

Maintenance services beyond 60,000 miles (96,000 km) should be performed at the same intervals shown in each maintenance schedule.

System	Maintenance items		Miles × 1,000	10	20	30	40	50	60
			Km × 1,000	16	32	48	64	80	96
			Months	12	24	36	48	60	72
ENGINE	Valve clearance								A
	Drive belts(1)								I
	Engine oil and filter*			R	R	R	R	R	R
	Engine coolant(2)								R
	Exhaust pipes and mountings								
FUEL	Air filter*					R			R
	Fuel lines and connections								I
	Fuel tank cap gasket								R
IGNITION	Spark plugs	3S-FE engine**				R			R
		2VZ-FE engine							R
EVAP	Charcoal canister								
BRAKES	Brake linings and drums				I		I		I
	Brake pads and discs				I		I		I
	Brake line pipes and hoses								I
CHASSIS	Steering linkage								
	Drive shaft boots								
	Ball joints and dust covers								R
	Automatic transaxle, manual transaxle, transfer differential and steering gear housing oil								R
	Bolts and nuts on chassis and body								

Maintenance services indicated by a star (★) or asterisk (*) are required under the terms of the Emission Control Systems Warranty (ECSW). See Owner's Guide or Warranty Booklet for complete warranty information.
 ★ For vehicles sold in California
 * For vehicles sold outside California

NOTE:
(1) After 60,000 miles (96,000 km) or 72 months, inspect every 10,000 miles (16,000 km) or 12 months.
(2) After 60,000 miles (96,000 km) or 72 months, replace every 30,000 miles (48,000 km) or 36 months.

NORMAL RECOMMENDED MAINTENANCE INTERVALS (1990-95)

VEHICLE MAINTENANCE INTERVAL

Component	6 / 3.75	12 / 7.5	18 / 11.25	24 / 15	30 / 18.75	36 / 22.5	42 / 26.25	48 / 30	54 / 33.75	60 / 37.5	66 / 41.25	72 / 45	78 / 48.75	84 / 52.5	90 / 56.25	96 / 60	Months
Engine oil and filter	R	R	R	R	R	R	R	R	R	R	R	R	R	R	R	R	I: Every 6
Timing Belt																R	R: Every 72
Valve clearance										A						A	
Drive belts										A						I	
Engine coolant								R								R	R: Every 24
Exhaust pipes					−							−					I: Every 24
Air cleaner filter								R								R	I: Every 6
Fuel lines and connections							−										I: Every 36
Fuel tank cap gasket																R	R: Every 72
Spark plugs-non platinum								R								R	R: Every 36
Spark plugs-platinum																R	R: Every 72
Charcoal canister																−	I: Every 72
Brake linings and drums		−		−		−		−		−		−		−		−	I: Every 12
Brake pads and discs		−		−		−		−		−		−		−		−	I: Every 12
Brake line hose and connections				−				−				−				−	I: Every 24
Steering linkage				−				−				−				−	I: Every 12
SRS air bags																−	I: Every 12
Ball joints and dust covers				−				−				−				−	I: Every 12
Drive shaft boots				−				−				−				−	I: Every 12
Transaxles				R				R				R				R	R: Every 24
Steering gear box				−				−				−				−	I: Every 24
Bolts and nuts on chassis and body				−				−				−				−	I: Every 24

I: Inspect
R: Replace
A: Adjust

89551CM1

SEVERE RECOMMENDED MAINTENANCE INTERVALS (1990-95)

VEHICLE MAINTENANCE INTERVAL

Component	6 / 3.75	12 / 7.5	18 / 11.25	24 / 15	30 / 18.75	36 / 22.5	42 / 26.25	48 / 30	54 / 33.75	60 / 37.5	66 / 41.25	72 / 45	78 / 48.75	84 / 52.5	90 / 56.25	96 / 60	Months
Engine oil and filter	R	R	R	R	R	R	R	R	R	R	R	R	R	R	R	R	I: Every 6
Timing Belt																R	R: Every 72
Valve clearance										A	A					A	R: Every 72
Drive belts										A	A					I	I: Every 72
Engine coolant								R				−				R	R: Every 24
Exhaust pipes					−			−				−				−	I: Every 24
Air cleaner filter								R								R	I: Every 6
Fuel lines and connections								−				−				−	I: Every 36
Fuel tank cap gasket																R	R: Every 72
Spark plugs-non platinum								R								R	R: Every 36
Spark plugs-platinum																R	R: Every 72
Charcoal canister																−	I: Every 72
Brake linings and drums		−		−		−		−		−		−		−		−	I: Every 12
Brake pads and discs		−		−		−		−		−		−		−		−	I: Every 12
Brake line hose and connections				−				−				−				−	I: Every 24
Steering linkage				−				−				−				−	I: Every 12
SRS air bags																−	I: Every 12
Ball joints and dust covers				−				−				−				−	I: Every 12
Drive shaft boots				−				−				−				−	I: Every 12
Transaxles				R				R				R				R	R: Every 24
Steering gear box				−				−				−				−	I: Every 24
Bolts and nuts on chassis and body				−				−				−				−	I: Every 24

I: Inspect
R: Replace
A: Adjust

89551CM2

SEVERE RECOMMENDED MAINTENANCE INTERVALS (1996)

Component	\[km (x1000)\] 6	12	18	24	30	36	42	48	54	60	66	72	78	84	90	96	Months
Miles (x1000)	3.75	7.5	11.25	15	18.75	22.5	26.25	30	33.75	37.5	41.25	45	48.75	52.5	56.25	60	
Engine oil and filter	R	R	R	R	R	R	R	R	R	R	R	R	R	R	R	R	I: Every 4
Timing Belt																R	R
Valve clearance										A						A	R: Every 48
Drive belts										A							
Engine coolant								R								R	R
Exhaust pipes				I				I				I				I	I: Every 24
Air cleaner filter				I				R				I				R	I: Every 6
Fuel lines and connections				I				I				I				I	I: Every 24
Fuel tank cap																	
Fuel tank cap gasket												R					R: Every 72
Spark plugs–non platinum				R				R				R				R	R: Every 24
Spark plugs–platinum												R					R: Every 72
Charcoal canister								I								I	I: Every 48
Brake linings and drums		I		I		I		I		I		I		I		I	I: Every 12
Brake pads and discs		I		I		I		I		I		I		I		I	I: Every 12
Brake line hose and connections				I				I				I				I	I: Every 24
Steering linkage		I		I		I		I		I		I		I		I	I: Every 12
SRS air bags		I		I		I		I		I		I		I		I	I: Every 12
Ball joints and dust covers		I		I		I		I		I		I		I		I	I: Every 12
Drive shaft boots		I		I		I		I		I		I		I		I	I: Every 12
Transaxles				R				R				R				R	R: Every 24
Steering gear box				I				I				I				I	I: Every 24
Bolts and nuts on chassis and body				I				I				I				I	I: Every 24

I: Inspect R: Replace A: Adjust

89551CM4

NORMAL RECOMMENDED MAINTENANCE INTERVALS (1996)

Component	\[km (x1000)\] 6	12	18	24	30	36	42	48	54	60	66	72	78	84	90	96	Months
Miles (x1000)	3.75	7.5	11.25	15	18.75	22.5	26.25	30	33.75	37.5	41.25	45	48.75	52.5	56.25	60	
Engine oil and filter	R	R	R	R	R	R	R	R	R	R	R	R	R	R	R	R	I: Every 4
Timing Belt																R	R
Valve clearance										A						A	R: Every 48
Drive belts										A							
Engine coolant								R								R	R
Exhaust pipes				I				I				I				I	I: Every 24
Air cleaner filter				I				R				I				R	I: Every 6
Fuel lines and connections				I				I				I				I	I: Every 24
Fuel tank cap																	
Fuel tank cap gasket												R					R: Every 72
Spark plugs–non platinum				R				R				R				R	R: Every 24
Spark plugs–platinum												R					R: Every 72
Charcoal canister								I								I	I: Every 48
Brake linings and drums		I		I		I		I		I		I		I		I	I: Every 12
Brake pads and discs		I		I		I		I		I		I		I		I	I: Every 12
Brake line hose and connections				I				I				I				I	I: Every 24
Steering linkage		I		I		I		I		I		I		I		I	I: Every 12
SRS air bags		I		I		I		I		I		I		I		I	I: Every 12
Ball joints and dust covers		I		I		I		I		I		I		I		I	I: Every 12
Drive shaft boots		I		I		I		I		I		I		I		I	I: Every 12
Transaxles				R				R				R				R	R: Every 24
Steering gear box				I				I				I				I	I: Every 24
Bolts and nuts on chassis and body				I				I				I				I	I: Every 24

I: Inspect R: Replace A: Adjust

89551CM3

CAPACITIES

Year	Model	Engine ID/VIN	Engine Displacement Liters (cc)	Engine Oil with Filter	Transaxle (pts.) 5-Spd	Transaxle (pts.) Auto.	Transfer Case (pts.)	Drive Axle Front (pts.)	Drive Axle Rear (pts.)	Fuel Tank (gal.)	Cooling System (qts.)
1983	Camry	2S-ELC	2.0 (1995)	4.2	5.4	5.0	-	4.4 ②	-	14.5	7.4
1984	Camry	2S-ELC	2.0 (1995)	4.2	5.4	5.0	-	4.4 ②	-	14.5	7.4
	Camry	1C-TLC	1.8 (1839)	4.5	5.4	-	-	4.4 ②	-	14.5	7.9
1985	Camry	2S-ELC	2.0 (1995)	4.2	5.4	①	-	4.4 ②	-	14.5	7.4
	Camry	1C-TLC	1.8 (1839)	4.5	5.4	-	-	4.4 ②	-	14.5	8.9
1986	Camry	2S-ELC	2.0 (1995)	4.2	5.4	①	-	3.4 ②	-	14.5	7.4
	Camry	2C-TLC	2.0 (1974)	4.5	5.4	-	-	3.4 ②	-	14.5	8.9
1987	Camry	3S-FE	2.0 (1998)	4.3	5.4	5.2	-	3.4 ②	-	15.9	6.8
1988	Camry (2wd)	3S-FE	2.0 (1998)	4.1	5.4	5.2	-	3.4 ②	-	15.9	6.8
	Camry (4wd)	3S-FE	2.0 (1998)	4.1	11 ③	-	④	④	2.4	15.9	6.8
1989	Camry (2wd)	3S-FE	2.0 (1998)	4.1	5.4	5.2	-	3.4 ②	-	15.9	6.8
	Camry (2wd)	2VZ-FE	2.5 (2507)	4.1	8.8	5.2	-	2.2 ②	-	15.9	9.0
	Camry (4wd)	3S-FE	2.0 (1998)	4.1	11	5.2	④	2.2 ②	2.4	15.9	6.8
1990	Camry (2wd)	3S-FE	2.0 (1998)	4.1	5.4	5.2	-	3.4 ②	-	15.9	6.8
	Camry (2wd)	2VZ-FE	2.5 (2507)	4.1	8.8	5.2	-	2.2 ②	-	15.9	9.9
	Camry (4wd)	3S-FE	2.0 (1998)	4.1	10.6	5.2	④	3.4	2.4	15.9	6.8
1991	Camry (2wd)	3S-FE	2.0 (1998)	4.3	5.4	5.2	-	3.4 ②	-	15.9	6.8
	Camry (2wd)	2VZ-FE	2.5 (2507)	4.1	8.8	5.2	-	2.2 ②	-	15.9	9.9
	Camry (4wd)	3VZ-FE	3.0 (2959)	4.3	-	7.0	1.5	3.4	2.4	15.9	6.8
1992	Camry	5S-FE	2.2 (2164)	3.8	5.4	5.2	-	3.4	-	18.5	6.7
	Camry	3VZ-FE	3.0 (2959)	4.5	8.8	5.2	-	1.6	-	18.5	9.0
1993	Camry	5S-FE	2.2 (2164)	3.8	8.8	8.8	-	3.4	-	18.5	6.7
	Camry	3VZ-FE	3.0 (2959)	4.5	-	6.6	-	1.6	-	18.5	9.0
1994	Camry	5S-FE	2.2 (2164)	3.8	5.4	9.4	-	3.4	-	18.5	6.7
	Camry	1MZ-FE	3.0 (2995)	5.0	-	6.6	-	1.6	-	18.5	9.2
1995	Camry	5S-FE	2.2 (2164)	3.8	5.4	9.4	-	3.4	-	18.5	6.7
	Camry	1MZ-FE	3.0 (2995)	5.0	-	6.6	-	1.8	-	18.5	9.2
1996	Camry	5S-FE	2.2 (2164)	3.8	5.4	9.4	-	3.4	-	18.5	6.7
	Camry	1MZ-FE	3.0 (2995)	5.0	-	6.6	-	1.8	-	18.5	9.2

Note: All capacities are approximate. Add fluid gradually and check to be sure a proper fluid level is obtained.

① A140E: 5.0
   A140L: 4.2

② AT only, MT included w/transaxle capacity

③ Includes differential and transfer case

④ Included w/transaxle capacity

89551C03

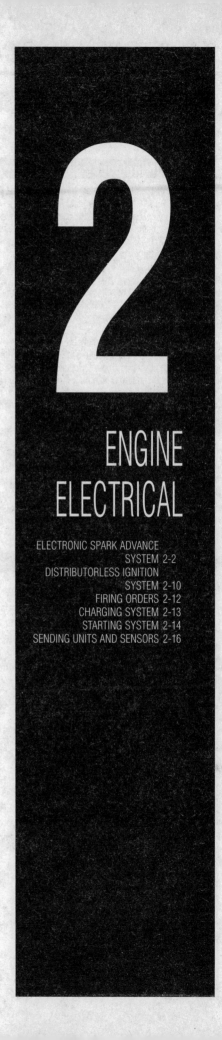

2

ENGINE
ELECTRICAL

ELECTRONIC SPARK ADVANCE SYSTEM

→For information on understanding electricity and troubleshooting electrical circuits, please refer to Section 6 of this manual.

General Information

The Integrated Ignition Assembly (IIA) system or the Electronic Spark Advance (ESA) system is used on most Toyota Camrys with gasoline engines. The diesel engines do not require the use of ignition systems. The electronic ignition system offers many advantages over the conventional breaker points ignition system. By eliminating the points, maintenance requirements are greatly reduced. An electronic ignition system is capable of producing a much higher voltage which in turn aide in starting, reduces spark fouling and provides emission control.

The distributor used on vehicles sold in the United States from 1983–85 was discontinued in 1986 and appeared in Canadian vehicles sold in that year. That distributor used a vacuum advancer to control spark advance electronically thought a micro-computer.

The Integrated Ignition Assembly (IIA) ignition system consists of a distributor with a signal generator, ignition coil (s), electronic igniter and a micro-computer called an Electronic Control Module (ECM). The ECM is programmed with data for optimum ignition timing for a wide range of driving and operating conditions. Using data provided by the various engine mounting sensors (intake air volume, engine temperature, rpm, etc.), the ECM converts the data into a reference voltage signal and sends this signal to the igniter mounted inside the distributor. The signal generator receives a reference voltage from the ECM and activates the components of the igniter. The signal generator consists of three main components: the signal rotor, pick-up coil and the permanent magnet. The signal rotor revolves with the distributor shaft, while the pick-up coil and permanent magnet are stationary. as the signal; rotor spins the teeth on it pass a projection leading from the pick-up coil. When this occurs, voltage is allowed to flow through the system and fire the spark plugs. This process happens without physical contact or electrical arching; therefore, there is no need to replace burnt or worn parts.

Diagnosis and Testing

ON VEHICLE INSPECTION SPARK TEST

2S-ELC, 3S-FE and 5S-FE Engines

▶ See Figures 1, 2, 3 and 4

→DO NOT use this test for the 1994–95 5S-FE California or any 1996 models.

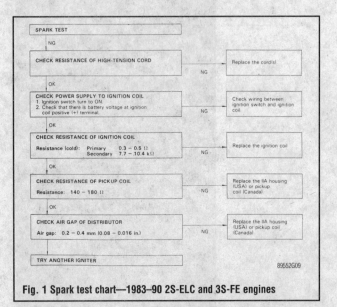

Fig. 1 Spark test chart—1983–90 2S-ELC and 3S-FE engines

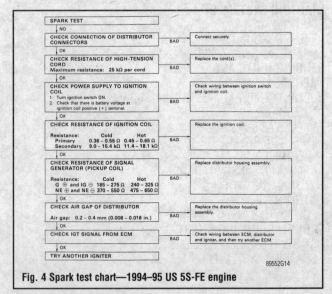

Fig. 2 Spark test chart—1991 3S-FE engine

Fig. 3 Spark test chart—1992–93 5S-FE engine

Fig. 4 Spark test chart—1994–95 US 5S-FE engine

1. Tag and disconnect the spark plug wires from the spark plugs.
2. Remove the spark plugs and install the spark plug wires to each spark plug.
3. Ground (do not hold spark plug) the spark plug; check if spark occurs while engine is being cranked.

➡**Crank the engine for no more than 2 seconds at a time to prevent flooding the engine with gasoline.**

4. If good spark does not occur, follow the correct diagnostic flow chart (engine and year) and necessary service procedures.

2VZ-FE, 3VZ-FE and 5S-FE Engines

◆ **See Figures 5, 6, 7 and 8**

➡**Use this test for the 1994–95 5S-FE California and 1996 5S-FE models.**

1. Disconnect the coil wire from distributor. Hold the coil wire end about ½ inch (12.5mm) from a good body ground; check if spark occurs while engine is being cranked.

➡**Crank the engine for no more than 2 seconds at a time to prevent flooding the engine with gasoline.**

2. If good spark does not occur, follow the correct diagnostic flow chart (engine and year) and necessary service procedures.

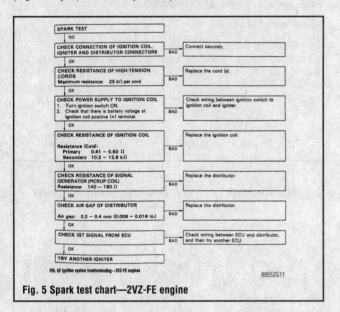

Fig. 5 Spark test chart—2VZ-FE engine

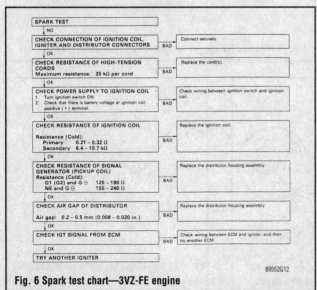

Fig. 6 Spark test chart—3VZ-FE engine

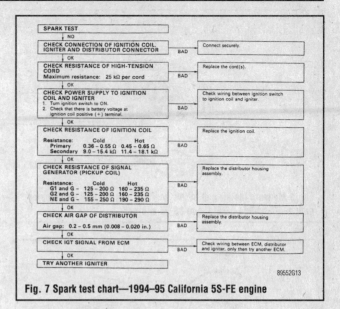

Fig. 7 Spark test chart—1994–95 California 5S-FE engine

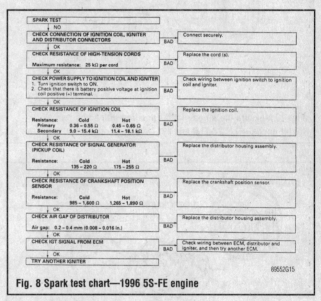

Fig. 8 Spark test chart—1996 5S-FE engine

SIGNAL GENERATOR AIR-GAP INSPECTION

2S-ELC and 3S-FE Engines

◆ **See Figures 9, 10 and 11**

➡**The air gap in the distributor should be check periodically. Distributor air gap may only be checked and can only be adjusted by component replacement.**

Remove the hold-down bolts from the top of the distributor gap.
1. Remove the distributor cap from the housing without disconnecting the ignition wires.
2. Pull the ignition rotor (not the signal rotor) straight up and remove it. If the contacts are worn, pitted or burnt, replace it. Do not file the contacts.
3. Remove the dust shield.
4. Turn the crankshaft (a socket wrench on the front pulley bolt may be used to do this) until a tooth on the signal rotor aligns with the projection of the pickup coil.
5. Using a non-ferrous feeler gauge (brass, copper or plastic) measure the gap between the signal rotor and the pick-up coil projection. DO NOT USE AND ORDINARY METAL FEELER GAUGE! The gauge should just touch either side of the gap (snug fit). The acceptable range for the air gap is 0.008–0.016 inch (0.20–0.40mm).

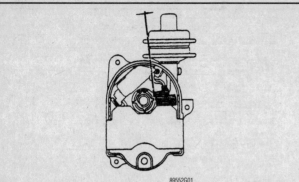

Fig. 9 Measure the air gap in this position with a non-ferrous feeler gauge—Canadian 2S-ELC and 3S-FE engines

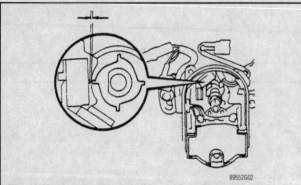

Fig. 10 Measure the air gap in this position with a non-ferrous feeler gauge—U.S.2S-ELC and 1987–89 3S-FE engines

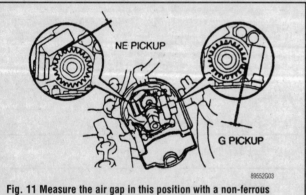

Fig. 11 Measure the air gap in this position with a non-ferrous feeler gauge—1990-91 3S-FE engine

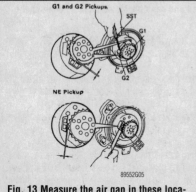

Fig. 13 Measure the air gap in these locations—3VZ-FE engine

Fig. 14 Measuring the air gap—1992-96 except 1994-95 California 5S-FE engine

6. On all US models, if the air gap is not within specifications, replace the IIA distributor housing. On Canadian models, replace the breaker plate and pick-up coil assembly.

7. Check to make sure the housing gasket is in position on the housing.

8. Install the rotor and dust shield.

9. Install the distributor cap with attached wiring. Attach the cap to the housing and tighten the hold-down bolts.

2VZ-FE and 3VZ-FE Engines

♦ See Figures 12 and 13

1. Remove the distributor cap.

2. Use SST 09240–00020 or equivalent wire gauge set on G1 and G2 and a non-ferrous feeler gauge (use paper, brass or plastic gauge) on NE pick-up. Measure the air gap between the signal rotor and pick-up coil projection. Measure the gap between the signal rotor and the pick-up coil projection, by using). The acceptable range for the air gap is:
   - 2VZ-FE engines—0.008–0.016 inch (0.20–0.40mm)
   - 3VZ-FE engines—0.008–0.020 inch (0.20–0.50mm)

3. If the air gap is not within specifications, replace the IIA distributor housing.

5S-FE Engine

1992–96 EXCEPT 1994–95 CALIFORNIA

♦ See Figures 14 and 15

1. Remove the distributor cap.

2. Measure the gap between the signal rotor and the pick-up coil projection, by using a non-ferrous feeler gauge (use paper, brass or plastic gauge). Or use SST 09240–00020 wire gauge set.

3. The air gap should be 0.008–0.0016 inch (0.2–0.4mm).

4. If the air gap is not correct, replace the distributor housing.

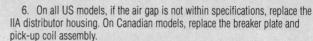

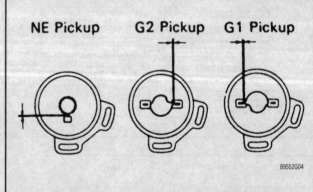

Fig. 12 Measure the air gap in these locations—2VZ-FE engine

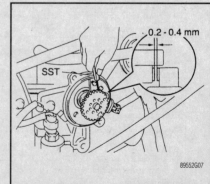

Fig. 15 Measuring the air gap—1996 5S-FE engine

1994–95 CALIFORNIA

▶ **See Figure 16**

1. Remove the distributor cap.
2. Use SST 09240–00020 or equivalent wire gauge set on G1 and G2 and a feeler gauge on NE pick-up. Measure the air gap between the signal rotor and pick-up coil projection.
3. The air gap should read 0.008–0.020 inch (0.20–0.50mm).
4. If the air gap is not within specifications, replace the distributor housing assembly.

SIGNAL GENERATOR (PICK-UP) RESISTANCE TEST

3S-FE Engine

▶ **See Figure 17**

1. Using a suitable ohmmeter, check the resistance cold between terminals G1 and G- and NE and G- of the signal generator.
2. The signal generator (pick-up coil) resistance cold should be 140–180 ohms (1987–90 and 205–255 ohms (1991)
3. If the resistance is not correct, replace the distributor housing assembly.

5S-FE Engine

1992–93 MODELS

▶ **See Figure 18**

1. Using a suitable ohmmeter, check the resistance cold between terminals G and G- and NE and NE- of the signal generator.
2. The signal generator (pick-up coil) resistance cold should be 185–265 ohms at G and G-, and 370–530 ohms at NE and NE-.
3. If the resistance is not correct, replace the distributor housing.

1994–95 MODELS EXCEPT CALIFORNIA

▶ **See Figure 19**

1. Using a suitable ohmmeter, check the resistance cold between terminals G and G- and NE and NE- of the signal generator.
2. The signal generator (pick-up coil) resistance cold should be 185–275 ohms at G and G-, and 370–550 ohms at NE and NE-.
3. If the resistance is not correct, replace the distributor housing.

1994–95 CALIFORNIA MODELS

▶ **See Figure 20**

1. Using a suitable ohmmeter, check the resistance cold between terminals G1 and G-, G2 and G- then NE and G- of the signal generator.
2. The signal generator (pick-up coil) resistance cold should be:
- G1 and G——125–200 ohms
- G2 and G——125–200 ohms
- NE and G——155–250 ohms
3. If the resistance is not correct, replace the distributor housing.

1996 MODELS

▶ **See Figure 21**

1. Using a suitable ohmmeter, check the resistance of the signal generator.
2. Pick up coil resistance should be 135–220 ohms.
3. If the resistance is not correct, replace the distributor housing assembly.

2VZ-FE Engine

▶ **See Figure 22**

1. Using a suitable ohmmeter, check the resistance cold between terminals G1 and G-, G2 and G- then NE and G- of the signal generator.
2. The signal generator (pick-up coil) resistance cold should be:

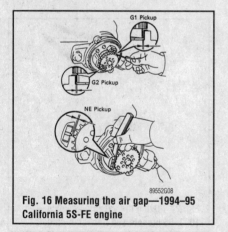

Fig. 16 Measuring the air gap—1994–95 California 5S-FE engine

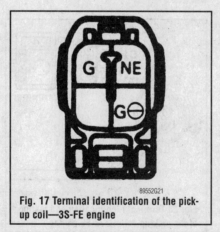

Fig. 17 Terminal identification of the pick-up coil—3S-FE engine

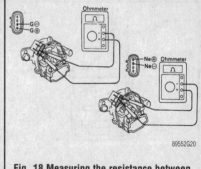

Fig. 18 Measuring the resistance between terminals of the pick-up coil—1992–93 5S-FE engine

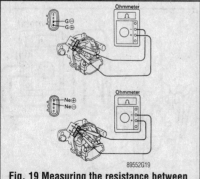

Fig. 19 Measuring the resistance between terminals of the pick-up coil—1994–95 5S-FE engine except California

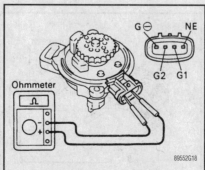

Fig. 20 Measuring the resistance between terminals of the pick-up coil—1994–95 5S-FE engine California models

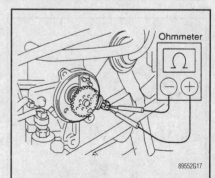

Fig. 21 Measuring the resistance between terminals of the pick-up coil—1996 5S-FE engine

- G1 and G——140–180 ohms
- G2 and G——140–180 ohms
- NE and G——140–180 ohms

3. If the resistance is not correct, replace the distributor housing.

3VZ-FE Engine

♦ **See Figure 23**

1. Using a suitable ohmmeter, check the resistance cold between terminals G1 and G-, G2 and G- then NE and G- of the signal generator.
2. The signal generator (pick-up coil) resistance cold should be:
- G1 and G——125–190 ohms
- G2 and G——125–190 ohms
- NE and G——155–240 ohms

3. If the resistance is not correct, replace the distributor housing.

VACUUM ADVANCE

1983–85 and Canadian Models

♦ **See Figure 24**

Inspect the vacuum advance by disconnecting the vacuum hose and attaching a vacuum pump to the diaphragms. Apply vacuum and check that the advancer moves freely. It does not respond to the test, replace the advancer.

GOVENER ADVANCE

1983–85 and Canadian Models

♦ **See Figure 25**

Inspect the governor advance by turning the rotor shaft counterclockwise, then release it and check that the rotor turns slightly clockwise. Check that the rotor shaft is not excessively loose.

All adjustments in the ignition system are controlled by the ECM for optimum performance. No adjustments are possible.

Ignition Coil

TESTING

♦ **See Figures 26, 27, 28 and 29**

➡**Prior to testing the coil, perform a secondary spark test. If spark occurs at the spark plug, the coil is functioning properly.**

The ignition coil is found in the distributor on all models except the 2VZ-FE, 3VZ-FE and 1994–95 California 5S-FE and 1996 5S-FE engines. On most of these engines the coil is located on the left fender well, near the fuse block.

1. Turn the ignition key to the OFF position.
2. Perform a visual inspection of the coil. If the coil is cracked, damaged or oil is leaking from the coil, the coil is faulty.
3. Label and disconnect the electrical harness from the ignition coil.
4. Inspect the harness connector and ignition coil terminals for dirt, corrosion or damage. Repair as necessary.
5. Using an ohmmeter, measure coil primary resistance between the ignition coil terminals. Resistance cold should be approximately:
- 2S-ELC engine; 1983–86 US—0.3–0.5 ohms
- 2S-ELC engine; 1983–86 Canada—1.2–1.5 ohms
- 3S-FE engine—0.38–0.46 ohms
- 5S-FE engine; 1992–93 All—0.4–0.5 ohms
- 5S-FE engine; 1994–96 All—0.36–0.55 ohms
- 2VZ-FE engine—0.41–0.50 ohms
- 3VZ-FE engine—0.21–0.32 ohms

6. Measure coil secondary resistance between the ignition coil terminals and the distributor cap high tension lead terminals. resistance cold should be approximately:

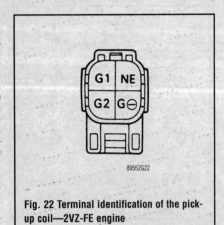

Fig. 22 Terminal identification of the pick-up coil—2VZ-FE engine

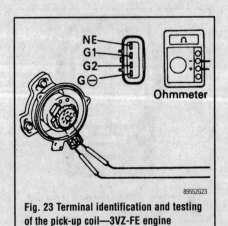

Fig. 23 Terminal identification and testing of the pick-up coil—3VZ-FE engine

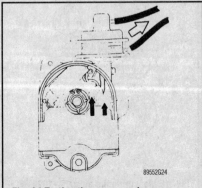

Fig. 24 Testing the vacuum advance—1983–85 models and Canadian models

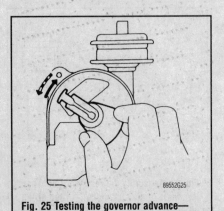

Fig. 25 Testing the governor advance—1983–85 models and Canadian models

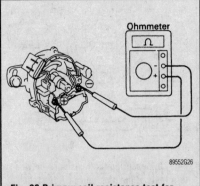

Fig. 26 Primary coil resistance test for coils located inside the distributor

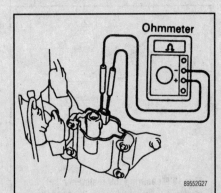

Fig. 27 Primary coil resistance testing for external coils

- 2S-ELC and 3S-FE engines; 1983–88—7.5–10.5 kilohms
- 3S-FE engine; 1989–91—7.7–10.4 kilohms
- 5S-FE engine; 1992–93 All—10.2–14.3 kilohms
- 5S-FE engine; 1994–96 All—9.0–15.4 kilohms
- 2VZ-FE engine—10.2–13.8 kilohms
- 3VZ-FE engine—6.4–10.7 kilohms
7. If resistance is not within specification, the coil may be faulty.

REMOVAL & INSTALLATION

External Coils

1. Turn the ignition key to the OFF position. Disconnect the negative battery cable. Wait at least 90 seconds from the time the negative battery was disconnected to start work.
2. Disconnect the high tension wire or coil wire (running between the coil and the distributor) from the coil.
3. Disconnect the low tension wires from the coil.
4. Loosen the coil bracket and remove the coil.
5. Installation is the reverse of removal.

Internal Coils

▶ See Figures 30, 31, 32, 33 and 34

The internal coil found within the distributor and can be changed without removing the distributor (a selection of various short screwdrivers may be required for access to the screws) but it is recommended to remove the distributor and then replace the coil assembly.

1. Disconnect the negative battery cable.

☀ CAUTION

On models with an airbag, wait at least 90 seconds from the time that the ignition switch is turned to the LOCK position and the bat-

tery is disconnected before performing any further work. Refer to Section 7 for all air bag warnings.

2. Lable and disconnect the distributor wiring.
3. Lable and disconnect the vacuum advance hoses (if equipped).
4. Lable and disconnect the plug wires from the distributor.
5. Mark the location of the distributor. Remove the hold-down bolts and pull out the distributor.
6. Mark the location and remove the distributor rotor with O-ring (if equipped). Discard the O-ring.
7. Remove the dust cover(s) over the ignition coil.

➡Note position and routing of all internal distributor assembly wiring.

8. Remove the nuts and disconnect the wiring from the ignition coil.
9. Remove the screws and the ignition coil and gasket from the distributor.

To install:

10. Install the ignition coil, gasket, screws and secure its wiring. Again, watch the wiring positions.
11. Install a new gasket to the housing when attaching the dust cover.
12. Install the distributor rotor.
13. Set the No. 1 cylinder to TDC of the compression stroke. Turn the crankshaft clockwise, and position the slit of the intake camshaft as shown in distributor Removal and Installation.
14. Apply a light coat of engine oil to the new O-ring and install it to the distributor housing. align the cutout portion of the coupling with the protrusion of the housing. Insert the distributor, aligning the center of the flange with that of the bolt hole on the cylinder head. Lightly tighten the 2 mounting bolts. Install all remaining components in the reverse order of removal.
15. Reset any digital equipment such as radio memory and the clock if necessary.

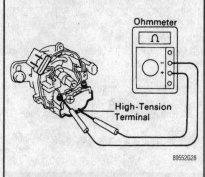

Fig. 28 Secondary coil resistance test for coils located inside the distributor

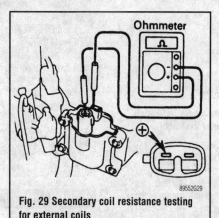

Fig. 29 Secondary coil resistance testing for external coils

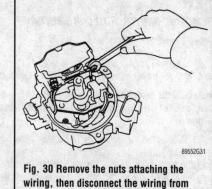

Fig. 30 Remove the nuts attaching the wiring, then disconnect the wiring from the coil

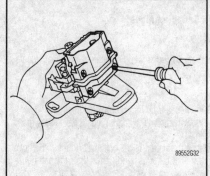

Fig. 31 Remove the screws attaching the coil to the distributor

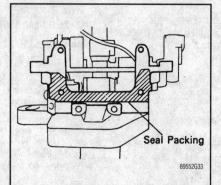

Fig. 32 Replace the seal packing prior to coil installation

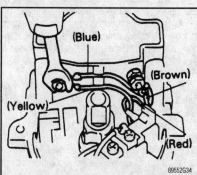

Fig. 33 Attach the wiring in the correct places—1983–85 US and 1983–86 Canadian models

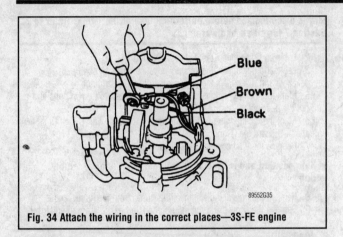

Fig. 34 Attach the wiring in the correct places—3S-FE engine

Blue
Brown
Black

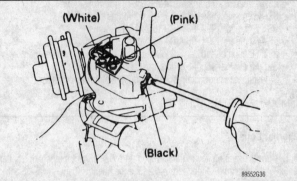

Fig. 35 Make sure you remember where the colored wires attach for installation—2S-ELC engine

(White) (Pink)

(Black)

Ignition Module

REMOVAL & INSTALLATION

External

All engines, except the 2S-ELC, have an external igniter.
1. Turn the ignition key to the **OFF** position. Disconnect the negative battery cable.
2. Separate the wiring harness connections.
3. Unbolt the igniter.
4. Loosen the nut holding the wire lead onto the coil.
5. Tag and disconnect the wire lead.
6. Lift the igniter off its mount.
7. Installation is the reverse of removal.

Internal

REMOVING IGNITER WITH DISTRIBUTOR

▶ See Figure 35

The internal igniter is only applicable to 2S-ELC engine Camry models. All other engines are equipped with an external igniter assembly.

➡Review the complete service procedure before this repair. Note position, color of wire and routing of all internal distributor assembly wiring.

1. Disconnect the cable from the negative battery terminal.
2. Remove the number one spark plug. Place a finger over the spark plug hole and rotate the crankshaft clockwise to top dead center. When there is pressure felt on the finger at the spark plug hole, this will be top dead center of the compression stroke on number one cylinder. If not, repeat the procedure. Install the number one spark plug.
3. Mark the position of the distributor flange in relation to the camshaft housing. Remove the IIA distributor assembly.
4. Remove the distributor cap with the wires attached, and remove the packing. Mark the position of the rotor relative to the housing and pull the rotor straight up and off the shaft. The distributor cap is held to the housing with three retaining screws.
5. Remove the ignition coil dust cover.
6. Remove the two nuts and spring washers and disconnect the four wires from the terminals on the side of the ignition coil. The wires are color coded yellow, blue, brown and red.
7. Remove the four retaining screws and remove the ignition coil and packing.
8. Remove the nuts and disconnect the pink, white and black wires from the igniter terminals. Remove the two igniter retaining screws and remove the igniter.
To install:
9. Attach the new igniter with the two retaining screws. Connect the pink, black and white wires to their respective terminals and install the nuts. Make

sure that the pick-up coil wires are secured in their clips and that there is slack in the wires.
10. Install the ignition coil and attach it with the four retaining screws.
11. Connect the four ignition coil wires to their respective terminals and install the two nuts and springs washers.
12. The remainder of installation is the reverse of removal. Tighten each component to specifications.
13. Connect a tachometer and timing light to the engine and adjust the ignition timing.
14. Reset any digital equipment such as radio memory and the clock if necessary.

REMOVING IGNITER WITHOUT REMOVING DISTRIBUTOR

1. Remove the distributor cap, rotor and di-electric insulator covers. Disconnect the red and yellow wires from the coil and the pink, white and black wires from the igniter.
2. Remove the igniter. It may be necessary to mark and rotate the distributor to gain access to the igniter retaining screws. The timing should be checked after the distributor is returned to the mark.
To install:
3. Install the new igniter using the two new retaining screws.
4. Twist the pick-up coil wires together, install the white wire first then pink and black wires to their original locations. Make sure the wires do not touch the housing generator or advance plate.
5. Route the red and yellow wires from the igniter so they do not contact moving parts. Connect the red wire to the right coil terminal (with the brown wire) and the yellow wire to the left terminal (with the blue wire). Replace the covers, rotor and cap.
6. Connect a tachometer and timing light to the engine and adjust the ignition timing.

Distributor

REMOVAL & INSTALLATION

1983–85 US and 1983–86 Canadian Models

▶ See Figures 36, 37 and 38

1. Turn the ignition key to the **OFF** position. Disconnect the negative battery cable. Wait at least 90 seconds from the time the negative battery was disconnected to start work.
2. Disconnect the IIA wiring.
3. Label and disconnect the hoses from he vacuum advancer.
4. Label and disconnect the wires from the spark plugs. Leave the wires connected to the distributor cap.
5. Mark the distributor flange in relation to the camshaft housing. Remove the hold-down bolts and pull the distributor assembly from the camshaft housing.
6. Before the distributor can be installed (especially in cases where the engine has been disturbed, cranked or dismantled) set the No. 1 piston at TDC by performing the following:

a. Remove the right front wheel and fender apron seal.

b. Remove the inspection plug from the hole of the No. 2 timing belt cover.

c. With the use of a mirror, align the oil seal retainer mark with the center of the small hole on the camshaft timing pulley. Perform the alignment by turning the crankshaft pulley clockwise using a socket wrench.

d. Install the inspection plug and the right fender seal.

e. Also the timing mark on the crankshaft pulley should be aligned with the **0** mark on the timing indicator.

7. Installation is the reverse of removal. Coat the spiral gear and governor shaft tip with clean engine oil.

8. Align the protrusions on the housing with the spiral gear.

9. Insert the distributor by aligning the center of the flange with the hole in the camshaft housing. Lightly tighten the hold-down bolts.

10. Connect a tachometer and timing light to the engine and adjust the ignition timing.

1986–96 Models

▶ See Figures 39 thru 46

1. Disconnect the cable from the negative battery terminal.

2. Remove the air cleaner hose. On the 5S-FE, disconnect the accelerator cable from the throttle linkage and the remove the air cleaner cap, resonator and the air cleaner hose.

3. Disconnect the wiring from the distributor.

4. Label and disconnect the spark plug wires from the spark plugs. Leave the wires connected to the distributor cap.

5. Mark the distributor flange in relation to the cylinder head. Loosen and remove the distributor hold-down bolt(s) and pull out the distributor assembly.

6. Remove the O-ring from the distributor housing and discard.

7. Before the distributor can be installed (especially in cases where the engine has been disturbed, cranked or dismantled), set the No. 1 piston at TDC by performing the following: with a socket wrench or equivalent, turn the crank-

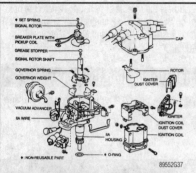

Fig. 36 Exploded view of the distributor assembly—1983–85 US and 1983–86 Canadian Models

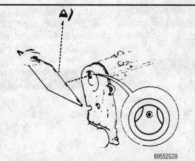

Fig. 37 To set the No. 1 cylinder at TDC, align the oil seal retainer mark with the small hole on the crankshaft—2S-ELC engines

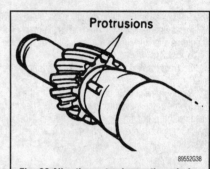

Fig. 38 Align the protrusion on the spiral gear with the protrusions on the housing—1983–85 US and 1983–86 Canadian Models

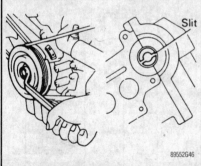

Fig. 39 Setting the No. 1 cylinder to TDC by positioning the intake camshaft slit—2VZ-FE and 3VZ-FE engines

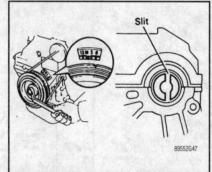

Fig. 40 Setting the No. 1 cylinder to TDC by positioning the intake camshaft slit—5S-FE engine

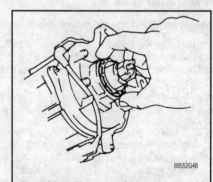

Fig. 41 Installing a new O-ring with clean engine oil on the end of the distributor shaft—2VZ-FE and 3VZ-FE engines

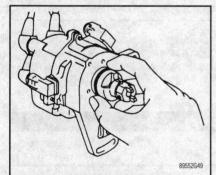

Fig. 42 Installing a new O-ring with clean engine oil on the end of the distributor shaft—2VZ-FE and 3VZ-FE engines

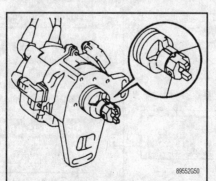

Fig. 43 Align the cutout of the coupling with the line on the housing—5S-FE engine

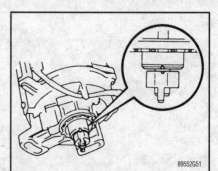

Fig. 44 Align the cutout of the coupling with the line on the housing—2VZ-FE and 3VZ-FE engine

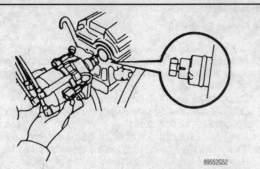

Fig. 45 Insert the distributor while aligning the line on the housings with that of the cutout on the bearing cap—1986 2S-ELC and all 3S-FE engines

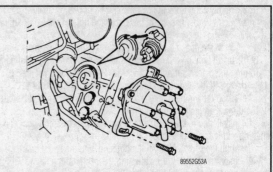

Fig. 46 Insert the distributor while aligning the line on the housings with that of the cutout on the bearing cap—1986 2S-ELC and all 3S-FE engines

shaft clockwise and position the slit in the intake camshaft as shown in the accompanying illustrations. Also the timing mark on the crankshaft pulley should be aligned with the **0** mark on the No. 1 timing belt cover indicator.

To install:

8. Coat the new distributor housing O-ring with clean engine oil and install the O-ring.

9. Align the cut-out of the coupling with the line of the housing.

10. Insert the distributor into the cylinder head by aligning the center of the flange with the bolt hole in the cylinder head. Now align the flange with the match mark made previously on the cylinder head. Lightly tighten the hold-down bolts.

11. The remainder of installation is the reverse of removal. Tighten the hold-down bolts to 9 ft. lbs. (13 Nm) on 2S-E and 3S-FE engines; 14 ft. lbs. (19 Nm) on 5S-FE engines; or, 13 ft. lbs. (18 Nm) on 2VZ-FE and 3VZ-FE engines.

12. Recheck the ignition timing.

Crankshaft and Camshaft Position Sensors

Refer to Electronic Engine Controls in Section 4 for information on servicing the position sensors.

DISTRIBUTORLESS IGNITION SYSTEM

General Information

▶ **See Figures 47 and 48**

➡ **Only the 1MZ-FE engine uses a distributorless ignition.**

The Engine Control Module (ECM) is programmed with data for optimum ignition timing under all operating conditions. Using data provided by sensors which monitor various engine functions (RPM, intake air volume, engine temperature, etc.) the ECM triggers the spark at precisely the right instant.

The ECM monitors the engine condition signals from each sensor, calculates the ignition timing and sends an ignition signal to the igniter. High voltage from the ignition is distributed to each spark plug in the appropriate order to generate a spark between the electrodes, which ignites the air fuel mixture.

The igniter interrupts the primary current with the ignition signal (IGT signal) from the ECM and generates sparks at the spark plug. Also, as a fail-safe measure, when ignition occurs an ignition confirms signal (IGF signal) is sent to the ECM.

The ignition coil uses a closed core coil with the primary coil wrapped around the core and the secondary coil wrapped around the primary coil. This allows the generation of a high voltage sufficient to cause a spark to jump

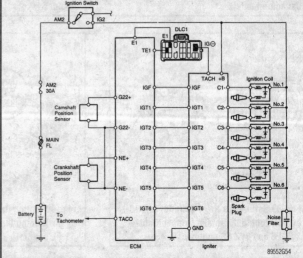

Fig. 48 Distributorless ignition system circuit—1MZ-FE engines

across the spark plug gap. The camshaft position sensor detects the camshaft position and the crankshaft position sensor detects the crankshaft position.

To maintain the most appropriate ignition timing, the ECM sends a control signal so that the igniter will pass the current to the ignition coils and spark plugs to produce a spark.

Diagnosis and Testing

ON VEHICLE SPARK TEST

▶ **See Figure 49**

1. Remove an ignition coil as described in this section.
2. Remove the spark plug.

Fig. 47 Exploded view of the distributorless ignition system—1MZ-FE engine

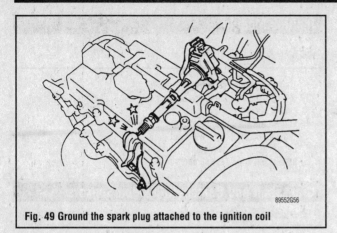

Fig. 49 Ground the spark plug attached to the ignition coil

3. Install the spark plug to the ignition coil, than attach the ignition coil wiring.

4. Ground the spark plug.

5. Check to see if spark occurs while the engine is being cranked. To prevent gasoline from being injected out during this test, crank the engine for no more than 2 seconds at a time.

6. If spark does not occur, perform the complete spark test as detailed in the chart.

Adjustments

All adjustments in the ignition system are controlled by the ECM for optimum performance. No adjustments are possible.

Ignition Coil

TESTING

1994–95 Models

▶ See Figures 50, 51 and 52

1. Turn the ignition key to the OFF position. Disconnect the negative battery cable. Wait at least 90 seconds from the time the negative battery was disconnected to start work.

✳✳ CAUTION

Work must be started after 90 seconds from the time that the ignition switch is turned to the LOCK position and the negative battery cable is disconnected from the battery.

2. Using a 5mm hexagon wrench, remove the 2 cap nuts and the V-bank cover.

3. Disconnect the ignition coil wiring from the coil being tested.

4. Inspect the primary coil resistance using an ohmmeter. Measure the resistance (cold) between the positive and negative terminals. Resistance should be between 0.54–0.84 ohms.

5. If the resistance is not within specifications, replace the ignition coil.

6. Reattach the ignition coil wiring.

7. Reinstall the V-bank cover. Push on the cover until a click is felt, then tighten the cap nuts.

8. Connect the negative battery cable. Reset any digital equipment such as radio memory and the clock if necessary.

1996 Models

▶ See Figures 52 and 53

➡ **The ignition coils should be removed and tested one at a time so not to mix them up.**

1. Disconnect and label the wires from the coils.

2. Disconnect the ignition coil harness.

3. Using an ohmmeter, measure the resistance between the positive and negative terminals of the coil. Primary coil, resistance (cold) should be between 0.70–0.94 ohms.

4. Remove the ignition coil.

5. Using an ohmmeter, measure the resistance between the positive and negative terminals of the coil. Secondary coil, resistance (cold) should be between 10.8–14.9 ohms.

6. If the resistance is not within specifications, replace the ignition coil that is faulty.

7. Reinstall the coil.

8. Reattach the coil harness.

9. Attach the coil wires to the appropriate coil.

10. Start the engine and check for proper operation.

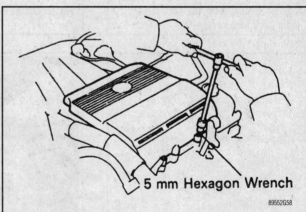

Fig. 50 Remove the V-bank cover, a 5mm hexagon wrench will be needed—1MZ-FE engine

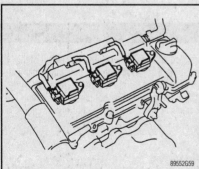

Fig. 51 Disconnect the ignition coil wiring from the component being tested—1MZ-FE engine

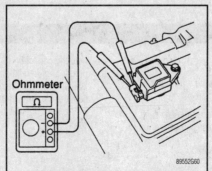

Fig. 52 Attach an ohmmeter to the positive and negative terminals of the coil—1MZ-FE engine

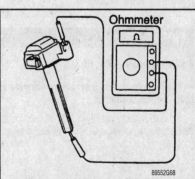

Fig. 53 With the coil removed measure the secondary resistance—1996 1MZ-FE engine

REMOVAL & INSTALLATION

▶ **See Figures 54 thru 59**

1. Turn the ignition key to the **OFF** position.
2. Using a 5mm hexagon wrench, remove the 2 cap nuts and the V-bank cover.

➡**The rear coils may be hard to access, a little bit of maneuvering may be necessary.**

3. Lable and disconnect the ignition coil wiring from the coils.
4. Remove the bolts retaining the right side coils from the cylinder head. Place each coil into position where it was taken from on a table. Do the same for the left side.
5. Installation is the reverse of removal. Secure all components accordingly.

Ignition Module

REMOVAL & INSTALLATION

1. Turn the ignition key to the OFF position.
2. Separate the wiring harness connections.
3. Unbolt the igniter.
4. Loosen the nut holding the wire lead onto the coil.
5. Tag and disconnect the wire lead.
6. Lift the igniter off its mount.
7. Installation is the reverse of removal.

Crankshaft and Camshaft Position Sensors

Refer to Electronic Engine Controls in Section 4 for information on servicing the position sensors.

Fig. 54 Remove these two 5mm screws from the V-bank cover—1MZ-FE engine

Fig. 55 Lift the V-bank cover off to access the coils

Fig. 56 The ignition coils are located on the top of the cylinder heads

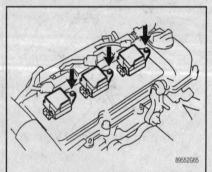

Fig. 57 Remove the bolts retaining the coils to the cylinder heads, one side at a time—1MZ-FE engine

Fig. 58 Pull the coil out of the spark plug hole

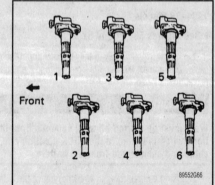

Fig. 59 Arrange the coils on a table in order—1MZ-FE engine

FIRING ORDERS

▶ **See Figures 60, 61, 62 and 63**

➡**To avoid confusion, label and remove the spark plug wires one at a time, for replacement.**

If a distributor is not keyed for installation with only one orientation, it could have been removed previously and rewired. The resultant wiring would hold the correct firing order, but could change the relative placement of the plug towers in relation to the engine. For this reason it is imperative that you label all wires before disconnecting any of them. Also, before removal, compare the current wiring with the accompanying illustrations. If the current wiring does not match, make notes in your book to reflect how your engine is wired.

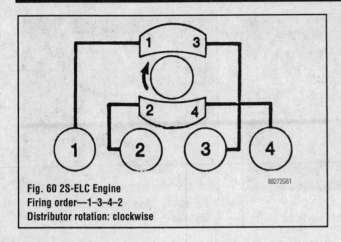

Fig. 60 2S-ELC Engine
Firing order—1–3–4–2
Distributor rotation: clockwise

88272G61

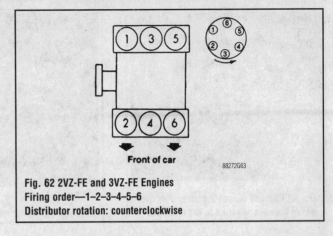

Front of car

Fig. 62 2VZ-FE and 3VZ-FE Engines
Firing order—1–2–3–4–5–6
Distributor rotation: counterclockwise

88272G63

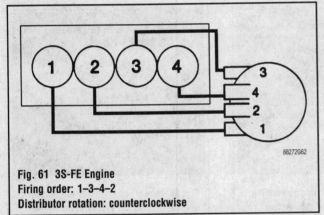

88272G62

Fig. 61 3S-FE Engine
Firing order: 1–3–4–2
Distributor rotation: counterclockwise

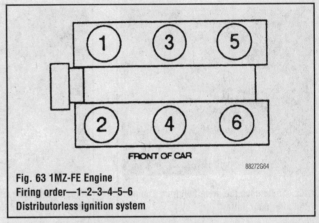

FRONT OF CAR

88272G64

Fig. 63 1MZ-FE Engine
Firing order—1–2–3–4–5–6
Distributorless ignition system

CHARGING SYSTEM

Alternator Precautions

To prevent damage to the alternator and regulator, the following precautionary measures must be taken when working with the electrical system.

1. Never reverse the battery connections. Always check the battery polarity visually. This is to be done before any connections are made to ensure that all of the connections correspond to the battery ground polarity of the car.

2. Booster batteries must be connected properly. Make sure the positive cable of the booster battery is connected to the positive terminal of the battery which is getting the boost.

3. Disconnect the battery cables before using a fast charger; the charger has a tendency to force current through the diodes in the opposite direction for which they were designed.

4. Never use a fast charger as a booster for starting the car.

5. Never disconnect the voltage regulator while the engine is running, unless as noted for testing purposes.

6. Do not ground the alternator output terminal.

7. Do not operate the alternator on an open circuit with the field energized.

8. Do not attempt to polarize the alternator.

9. Disconnect the battery cables and remove the alternator before using an electric arc welder on the car.

10. Protect the alternator from excessive moisture. If the engine is to be steam cleaned, cover or remove the alternator.

Alternator

TESTING

The easiest way to test the performance of the alternator is to perform a regulated voltage test.

1. Start the engine and allow it to reach operating temperature.

2. Connect a voltmeter between the positive and negative terminals of the battery.

3. Voltage should be 14.1–14.7 volts.

4. If voltage is higher or lower than specification, connect a voltmeter between the battery positive (B+) voltage output terminal of the alternator and a good engine ground.

5. Voltage should be 14.1–14.7 volts.

6. If voltage is still out of specification, a problem exists in the alternator or voltage regulator.

7. If voltage is now within specification, a problem exists in the wiring to the battery or in the battery itself.

➡**Many automotive parts stores have alternator bench testers available for use by customers. An alternator bench test is the most definitive way to determine the condition of your alternator.**

REMOVAL & INSTALLATION

▶ **See Figures 64 thru 69**

1. Turn the ignition key to the OFF position. Disconnect the negative battery cable. Wait at least 90 seconds from the time the negative battery was disconnected to start work.

✳✳ CAUTION

On models with an airbag, wait at least 90 seconds from the time that the ignition switch is turned to the LOCK position and the battery is disconnected before performing any further work.

2. Remove the two bolts and the No. 3 right hand engine mounting stay on the 3VZ-FE. Remove the bolt and nut and then remove the No. 2 right hand engine mounting stay on 2VZ-FE and 3VZ-FE engines.

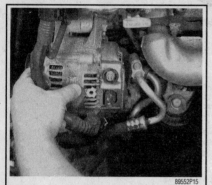

Fig. 64 Remove the rubber cover over the wiring harness attached to the alternator

Fig. 65 Remove the pivot bolt first . . .

Fig. 66 . . . then remove the two adjusting bolts

Fig. 67 Remove the drive belt from around the alternator pulley

Fig. 68 Disconnect the wiring by pushing the clip in and pulling out the harness

Fig. 69 Once all components are disconnected, remove the unit form the engine

3. Disconnect the electrical harness and wire (and nut) from the alternator.

4. Remove the air cleaner (2S-E), if necessary, to gain access to the alternator.

5. Unfasten the bolts which attach the adjusting link to the alternator.

6. Remove the alternator drive belt from the pulley.

7. Unfasten the alternator attaching bolt and then withdraw the alternator from its bracket.

8. Installation is the reverse of removal. Install the drive belt onto the pulley making sure that the grooves on the belt and the grooves on the pulley are properly aligned.

9. Adjust the drive belt tension and properly tighten the pivot and adjusting bolts.

10. Start the engine and allow it warm to warm up. Visually inspect the drive belt and listen for any abnormal vibration. Stop the engine and recheck the belt tension.

STARTING SYSTEM

Starter

TESTING

❄❄ WARNING

This test must be performed within 3 to 5 seconds to avoid burning out the coil.

Pull-in

▶ See Figure 70

Disconnect the field coil lead from the terminal C. Connect the battery to the solenoid switch as shown. See if the clutch pinion gear movement is outward. If the gear does not move perform the hold-in test.

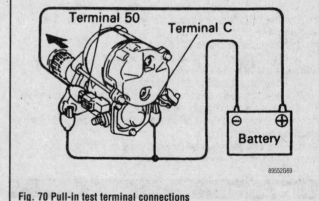

Fig. 70 Pull-in test terminal connections

Hold-in

▶ **See Figure 71**

Attach the battery to the starter as shown and with the clutch pinion gear out, disconnect the negative lead from terminal C. Check to make sure the pinion gear stays in the outward position. If the clutch gear returns inwards, perform the clutch pinion gear return test.

Clutch Pinion Gear Return

▶ **See Figure 72**

Disconnect the negative lead from the solenoid body. Check the clutch pinion gear returns inward. If not perform the no-load test.

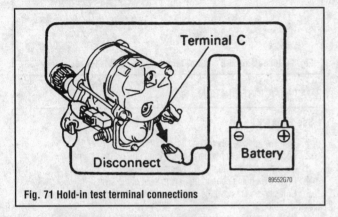

Fig. 71 Hold-in test terminal connections

No-load

▶ **See Figure 73**

Attach a battery and ammeter to the starter. Check that the starter rotates smoothly and steadily with the pinion gear moving out. Check the ammeter shows the correct current. 90 amps or less at 11.5 volts on gasoline engines and 180 amps or less at 11.0 volts on diesel engines. If not replace the starter.

REMOVAL & INSTALLATION

▶ **See Figures 74, 75, 76 and 77**

1. Disconnect the cable from the negative terminal of the battery.
2. On 1992–96 models with cruise control, remove the battery.
3. Also on 1992–96 models with cruise control, remove the actuator cover and disconnect the wiring harness. Remove the three bolts and then lift out the cruise control actuator. Remove the bracket from beneath the actuator and put aside.
4. Peel the rubber boot away and remove the nut and disconnect the negative battery cable from the magnetic switch terminal on the starter. Disconnect the electrical connector also located on the magnetic switch.
5. Support the starter by hand and remove the two mounting bolts.
6. Remove the starter from the transaxle.
7. Installation is the reverse of removal. Secure the two mounting bolts and tighten them to 29–31 ft. lbs. (39–42 Nm).
8. The remainder of installation is the reverse of removal. Tighten each component to specifications. Using the ignition switch, "bump" the starter over a few times and check for proper operation.

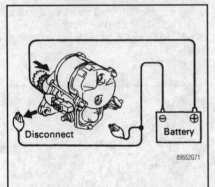

Fig. 72 Clutch pinion gear return terminal connections

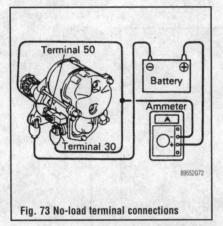

Fig. 73 No-load terminal connections

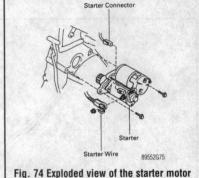

Fig. 74 Exploded view of the starter motor mounting—5S-FE engine shown, others similar

Fig. 75 Lift the cruise control, actuator cover off

Fig. 76 Remove the rubber boot and the nut retaining the starter wiring

Fig. 77 Remove the these two starter mounting bolts . . .

SENDING UNITS AND SENSORS

→This section describes the operating principles of sending units, warning lights and gauges. Sensors which provide information to the Electronic Control Module (ECM) are covered in Section 4 of this manual.

Instrument panels contain a number of indicating devices (gauges and warning lights). These devices are composed of two separate components. One is the sending unit, mounted on the engine or other remote part of the vehicle, and the other is the actual gauge or light in the instrument panel.

Several types of sending units exist, however most can be characterized as being either a pressure type or a resistance type. Pressure type sending units convert liquid pressure into an electrical signal which is sent to the gauge or warning light. Resistance type sending units are most often used to measure temperature and use variable resistance to control the current flow back to the indicating device. Both types of sending units are connected in series by a wire to the battery (through the ignition switch). When the ignition is turned **ON**, current flows from the battery through the indicating device and on to the sending unit.

Coolant Temperature Sender

TESTING

♦ See Figures 78, 79 and 80

Using an ohmmeter, measure the resistance between the terminals. Refer to the appropriate chart for your engine. If the resistance is not as specified, replace the sender.

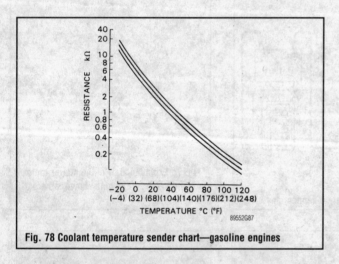

Fig. 78 Coolant temperature sender chart—gasoline engines

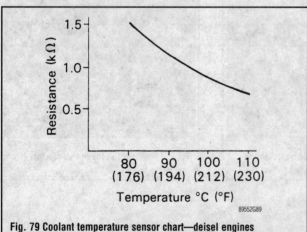

Fig. 79 Coolant temperature sensor chart—deisel engines

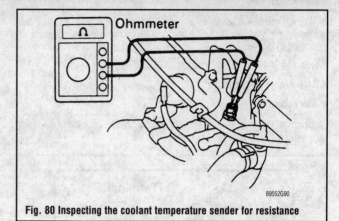

Fig. 80 Inspecting the coolant temperature sender for resistance

REMOVAL & INSTALLATION

♦ See Figure 81

1. Turn the ignition key to the OFF position.
2. Locate the coolant temperature sending unit on the engine.
3. Disconnect the sending unit electrical harness.
4. Drain the engine coolant below the level of the switch.
5. Unfasten and remove the sending unit from the engine. Discard the old gasket if equipped.
6. Installation is the reverse of removal. Coat the new sending unit with Teflon® tape or electrically conductive sealer. Place a new gasket on the sender. Install the sending unit and tighten to 12–18 ft. lbs. (16–24 Nm).
7. Fill the engine with coolant. Start the engine, allow it to reach operating temperature and check for leaks.
8. Check for proper sending unit operation.

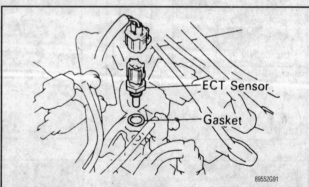

Fig. 81 All ECT sensors have an electrical harness attached to it and a gasket on the bottom

Oil Pressure Sender

TESTING

A quick way to determine if the gauge (idiot light) or sending unit is faulty is to disconnect the sending unit electrical harness and ground it (if two terminal, jumper between the terminals). If the gauge responds, the sending unit may be faulty. Proceed with the sending unit test.

1. Disconnect the sending unit electrical harness.
2. Using an ohmmeter, check continuity between the sending unit terminals (sending unit terminal and ground).
3. With the engine stopped, continuity should exist.
4. With the engine running, continuity should not exist.
5. If continuity does not exist as stated, the sending unit is faulty.

REMOVAL & INSTALLATION

1. Turn the ignition key to the OFF position.
2. Locate the oil pressure sending unit on the engine.
3. Disconnect the sending unit electrical harness.
4. Unfasten and remove the sending unit from the engine.
5. Installation is the reverse of removal. Coat the new sending unit with Teflon® tape or electrically conductive sealer.
6. Start the engine, allow it to reach operating temperature and check for leaks.

Electric Fan Switch

TESTING

▶ **See Figure 82**

3S-FE and 5S-FE Engines

1. Disconnect the sending unit electrical harness.
2. Using an ohmmeter, check that there is no continuity between the terminals when the coolant temperature is above 199° F (93°) C.
3. Using an ohmmeter, check that there is continuity between the terminals when the coolant temperature is below 181° F (83°) C.
4. If resistance does not respond as specified, the sending unit is faulty.

1MZ-FE Engine

▶ **See Figure 83**

NO. 1 SWITCH

▶ **See Figure 84**

1. Disconnect the sending unit electrical harness.
2. Using an ohmmeter, check that there is no continuity between the terminals when the coolant temperature is above 208° F (98°) C.

3. Using an ohmmeter, check that there is continuity between the terminals when the coolant temperature is below 190° F (88°) C.
4. If resistance does not respond as specified, the sending unit is faulty.

NO. 2 SWITCH

▶ **See Figure 85**

1. Disconnect the sending unit electrical harness.
2. Using an ohmmeter, check that there is no continuity between the terminals when the coolant temperature is above 199° F (93° C.
3. Using an ohmmeter, check that there is continuity between the terminals when the coolant temperature is below 181° F (83° C.
4. If resistance does not respond as specified, the sending unit is faulty.

2VZ-FE Engine

▶ **See Figure 86**

1. Remove the switch from the engine.
2. Using an ohmmeter, measure the resistance between terminals.
- Approximately 1.53 kilo ohms at 176°F (80°) C
- Approximately 1.18 kilo ohms at 194°F (90°) C
- Approximately 1.03 kilo ohms at 203°F (95°) C
3. If the continuity is not as specified, replace the switch.

REMOVAL & INSTALLATION

1. Turn the ignition key to the OFF position.
2. Drain the cooling system.
3. Disconnect the switch electrical wiring.
4. Remove the switch from the thermostat housing.
5. Installation is the reverse of removal. Coat the new sending unit with Teflon® tape or electrically conductive sealer.
6. Start the engine, allow it to reach operating temperature and check for leaks.

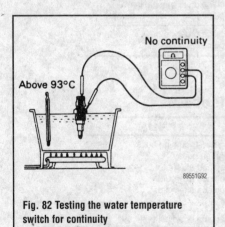

Fig. 82 Testing the water temperature switch for continuity

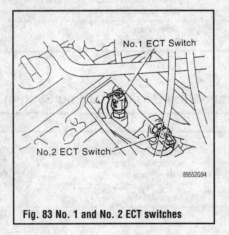

Fig. 83 No. 1 and No. 2 ECT switches

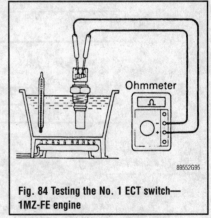

Fig. 84 Testing the No. 1 ECT switch— 1MZ-FE engine

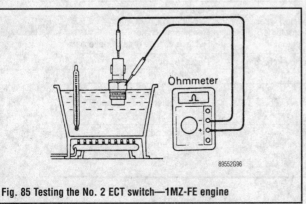

Fig. 85 Testing the No. 2 ECT switch—1MZ-FE engine

Check for	Tester connection	Condition		Specified valve
Continuity	2 – Ground	–		Continuity
Voltage	3 – Ground	Ignition switch ON		Battery voltage
Voltage	4 – Ground	Ignition switch ON		Battery voltage
Resistance	5 – 7	Coolant temp.	80°C (176°F)	Approx. 1.53 kΩ
			90°C (194°F)	Approx. 1.18 kΩ
			95°C (203°F)	Approx. 1.03 kΩ
Continuity	6 – Ground	–		Continuity

Fig. 86 Water temperature sensor chart—2VZ-FE engine

Troubleshooting Basic Starting System Problems

Problem	Cause	Solution
Starter motor rotates engine slowly	• Battery charge low or battery defective	• Charge or replace battery
	• Defective circuit between battery and starter motor	• Clean and tighten, or replace cables
	• Low load current	• Bench-test starter motor. Inspect for worn brushes and weak brush springs.
	• High load current	• Bench-test starter motor. Check engine for friction, drag or coolant in cylinders. Check ring gear-to-pinion gear clearance.
Starter motor will not rotate engine	• Battery charge low or battery defective	• Charge or replace battery
	• Faulty solenoid	• Check solenoid ground. Repair or replace as necessary.
	• Damaged drive pinion gear or ring gear	• Replace damaged gear(s)
	• Starter motor engagement weak	• Bench-test starter motor
	• Starter motor rotates slowly with high load current	• Inspect drive yoke pull-down and point gap, check for worn end bushings, check ring gear clearance
	• Engine seized	• Repair engine
Starter motor drive will not engage (solenoid known to be good)	• Defective contact point assembly	• Repair or replace contact point assembly
	• Inadequate contact point assembly ground	• Repair connection at ground screw
	• Defective hold-in coil	• Replace field winding assembly
Starter motor drive will not disengage	• Starter motor loose on flywheel housing	• Tighten mounting bolts
	• Worn drive end busing	• Replace bushing
	• Damaged ring gear teeth	• Replace ring gear or driveplate
	• Drive yoke return spring broken or missing	• Replace spring
Starter motor drive disengages prematurely	• Weak drive assembly thrust spring	• Replace drive mechanism
	• Hold-in coil defective	• Replace field winding assembly
Low load current	• Worn brushes	• Replace brushes
	• Weak brush springs	• Replace springs

TCCS2C01

Troubleshooting Basic Charging System Problems

Problem	Cause	Solution
Noisy alternator	• Loose mountings	• Tighten mounting bolts
	• Loose drive pulley	• Tighten pulley
	• Worn bearings	• Replace alternator
	• Brush noise	• Replace alternator
	• Internal circuits shorted (High pitched whine)	• Replace alternator
Squeal when starting engine or accelerating	• Glazed or loose belt	• Replace or adjust belt
Indicator light remains on or ammeter indicates discharge (engine running)	• Broken belt	• Install belt
	• Broken or disconnected wires	• Repair or connect wiring
	• Internal alternator problems	• Replace alternator
	• Defective voltage regulator	• Replace voltage regulator/alternator
Car light bulbs continually burn out—battery needs water continually	• Alternator/regulator overcharging	• Replace voltage regulator/alternator
Car lights flare on acceleration	• Battery low	• Charge or replace battery
	• Internal alternator/regulator problems	• Replace alternator/regulator
Low voltage output (alternator light flickers continually or ammeter needle wanders)	• Loose or worn belt	• Replace or adjust belt
	• Dirty or corroded connections	• Clean or replace connections
	• Internal alternator/regulator problems	• Replace alternator/regulator

TCCS2C02

3

ENGINE AND
ENGINE
OVERHAUL

ENGINE MECHANICAL

2S-ELC ENGINE SPECIFICATIONS

	English	Metric
Camshaft lobe height	1.5325-1.5365 inch	38.926-39.026mm
Journal diameter		
No. 1	1.8291-1.8297 inch	46.459-46.475mm
No. 2	1.892-1.8199 inch	46.209-46.225mm
No. 3	1.8094-1.100 inch	45.959-45.975mm
No. 4	1.7995-1.8002 inch	45.709-45.725mm
No. 5	1.9897-1.7904 inch	45.459-45.475mm
No. 6	1.7799-1.7805 inch	45.209-45.225mm
Journal oil clearance	0.0010-0.0026 inch	0.025-0.067mm
Thrust clearance	0.0031-0.0091 inch	0.08-0.23mm
Camshaft runout	0.0016 inch	0.04mm
Cylinder block		
Cylinder bore diameter	3.3071-3.3083 inch	84.0-84.03mm
Wear	3.3181 inch	84.28mm
Warpage	0.0020 inch	0.05mm
Cylinder head		
Valve stem diameter intake	0.3138-0.3134 inch	7.970-7.985mm
exhaust	0.3136-0.3142 inch	7.965-7.980mm
Valve stem-to-guide clearance intake	0.0010-0.0024 inch	0.025-0.060mm
exhaust	0.0012-0.0026 inch	0.030-0.065mm
Valve face angle	45.5 deg	45.5 deg
Valve seat angle	45 deg	45 deg
Valve spring pressure	68 lbs. @ 1.555 inch	302N @ 39.5mm
Valve spring free length	1.839 inch	46.7mm
Valve overall length intake	4.319 inch	109.7mm
exhaust	4.303 inch	109.3mm
Piston and connecting rod piston diameter	3.3061-3.3073 inch	83.975-84.005mm
Piston bore clearance	0.0006-0.0014 inch	0.015-0.035mm
Pin diameter	1.8892-1.8898 inch	47.985-48.000mm
Pin-to-bushing clearance	0.0009-0.0022 inch	0.024-0.055mm
Ring groove clearance	0.0012-0.0028 inch	0.03-0.07mm
Ring end gap		
No. 1	0.0110-0.0197 inch	0.28-0.50mm
No. 2	0.0079-0.0177 inch	0.20-0.45mm
oil	0.0079-0.0311 inch	0.20-0.79mm
Connecting rod alignment		
twist	0.0059 inch per 3.94 inch	0.015mm per 100mm
bend	0.0020 inch per 3.94 inch	0.05mm per 100mm
Connecting rod thrust clearance	0.0063-0.0083 inch	0.16-0.21mm
Connecting rod oil clearance	0.0009-0.0022 inch	0.024-0.055mm
Crankshaft		
Main journal diameter	2.1648-2.1654 inch	54.985-55.000mm
Journal out-of-round limit	0.0008 inch	0.02mm
Journal oil clearance		
No. 3	0.0012-0.0022 inch	0.030-0.057mm
all others	0.0008-0.0019 inch	0.020-0.047mm

89553C14

2S-ELC ENGINE SPECIFICATIONS

	English	Metric
Connecting rod journal diameter	1.8892-1.8898 inch	47.985-48.000mm
Connecting rod out-of-round	0.0008 inch	0.02mm
Rod bearing-to-crankshaft oil clearance	0.0009-0.0022 inch	0.024-0.055mm
Crankshaft runout	0.0024 inch	0.06mm
Crankshaft thrust clearance	0.0008-0.0087 inch	0.02-0.22mm
Oil pump		
body clearance	0.0039-0.0067 inch	0.10-0.17mm
tip clearance	0.0016-0.0063 inch	0.04-0.016mm

89553C15

3S-FE ENGINE SPECIFICATIONS

	English	Metric
Compression pressure		
STD	178 psi	1226 kPa
Limit	142 psi	981 kPa
Difference of pressure between cylinders	14 psi or less	98 kPa or less
Cylinder head		
Block side warpage	0.0020 inch	0.05mm
Manifold side warpage	0.0031 inch	0.08mm
Valve		
refacing angle	30, 45, 75 deg	30, 45, 75 deg
contacting angle	45 deg	45 deg
contacting width	0.039-0.055 inch	1.0-1.4mm
Valve guide bushing		
Inside diameter	0.2366-0.2374 inch	6.010-6.030mm
Outside diameter STD	0.4350-0.4354 inch	11.048-11.059mm
O/S 0.05	0.4369-0.4374 inch	11.098-11.109mm
Valve		
Overall length STD intake	3.9606 inch	100.60mm
exhaust	3.9547 inch	100.45mm
limit intake	3.941 inch	100.1mm
exhaust	3.937 inch	100.0mm
Face angle	44.5 deg	44.5 deg
Stem diameter intake	0.2350-0.2356 inch	5.970-5.985mm
exhaust	0.2348-0.2354 inch	5.965-5.980mm
Stem oil clearance STD intake	0.0010-0.0024 inch	0.025-0.060mm
exhaust	0.0012-0.0024 inch	0.030-0.065mm
limit intake	0.0031 inch	0.08mm
exhaust	00039 inch	0.10mm
Margin thickness STD	0.031-0.047 inch	0.8-1.2mm
limit	0.020 inch	0.5mm
Valve spring		
Free length	1.772 inch	45.0mm
Installed load	36.8-42.5 lb	164-189 N
Squareness	0.075 inch	2.0mm
Valve lifter		
Lifter diameter	1.1014-1.1018 inch	27.975-27.985mm
Head lifter bore diameter	1.1024-1.1032 inch	28.000-28.021mm
Oil clearance STD	0.0005-0.0018 inch	0.015-0.046mm
limit	0.0028 inch	0.07mm
Camshaft and gear		
Thrust clearance STD intake	0.0018-0.0039 inch	0.045-0.100mm
exhaust	0.0012-0.0033 inch	0.030-0.085mm

89553C16

3S-FE ENGINE SPECIFICATIONS

		English	Metric
Thrust clearance			
limit	intake	0.0047 inch	0.12mm
	exhaust	0.0039 inch	0.10mm
Journal oil clearance			
STD		0.0010-0.0024 inch	0.025-0.062mm
limit		0.0039 inch	0.10mm
Journal diameter		1.0614-1.0620 inch	26.959-26.975mm
Circle runout		0.0016 inch	0.04mm
Cam lobe height			
STD	intake	1.3744-1.3787 inch	34.910-35.101mm
	exhaust	1.4000-1.4039 inch	35.560-35.660mm
limit	intake	1.3701 inch	34.80mm
	exhaust	1.3957 inch	35.45mm
Camshaft gear backlash			
STD		0.0008-0.0078 inch	0.020-0.200mm
limit		0.0188 inch	0.30mm
Gear spring and free distance		0.886-0.902 inch	22.5-22.9mm
Idler pulley tension spring			
Free length		1.815 inch	46.1mm
Installed load		59-69 N	6.0-7.0kg
Piston and ring			
Piston diameter			
mark 1		3.3836-3.3840 inch	85.945-85.955mm
mark 2		3.3840-3.3844 inch	85.955-85.965mm
mark 3		3.3844-3.3848 inch	85.965-89.975mm
Piston oil clearance			
STD		0.0018-0.0024 inch	0.045-0.065mm
limit		0.0033 inch	0.085mm
Ring-to-ring groove clearance		0.0012-0.0028 inch	0.030-0.070mm
Piston ring end gap			
STD	No. 1	0.0106-0.0197 inch	0.270-0.500mm
	No. 2	0.0106-0.0201 inch	0.270-0.510mm
	oil	0.0079-0.0217 inch	0.200-0.550mm
limit	No. 1	0.0433 inch	1.10mm
	No. 2	0.0437 inch	1.11mm
	oil	0.0453 inch	1.15mm
Connecting rod			
Thrust clearance			
STD		0.0063-0.0123 inch	0.160-0.312mm
limit		0.0138 inch	0.35mm
Connecting rod bearing center thickness			
mark 1		0.0584-0.0586 inch	1.484-1.488mm
mark 2		0.0586-0.0587 inch	1.488-1.492mm
mark 3		0.0587-0.0589 inch	1.492-1.496mm
Connecting rod oil clearance			
STD		0.0009-0.0022 inch	0.024-0.055mm
U/S 0.25		0.0009-0.0027 inch	0.023-0.069mm
limit		0.0031 inch	0.08mm
Rod bending per 3.94 inch (100mm)		0.0020 inch	0.05mm

89553C17

3S-FE ENGINE SPECIFICATIONS

		English	Metric
Rod twist per 3.94 inch (100mm)		0.0059 inch	0.15mm
Crankshaft			
Thrust clearance			
STD		0.0008-0.0087 inch	0.020-0.220mm
limit		0.0118 inch	0.30mm
Thrust washer thickness		0.0961-0.0980 inch	2.440-2.490mm
Main journal oil clearance			
STD	No. 3	0.0010-0.0017 inch	0.025-0.044mm
	others	0.0006-0.0013 inch	0.015-0.034mm
limit		0.0031 inch	0.08mm
Main bearing center wall thickness			
No. 3	mark 1	0.0784-0.0785 inch	1.992-1.995mm
	mark 2	0.0785-0.0787 inch	1.995-1.998mm
	mark 3	0.0787-0.0788 inch	1.998-2.001mm
	mark 4	0.0788-0.0789 inch	2.001-2.004mm
	mark 5	0.0789-0.0790 inch	2.004-2.007mm
others	mark 1	0.0786-0.0787 inch	1.997-2.000mm
	mark 2	0.0787-0.0789 inch	2.000-2.0003mm
	mark 3	0.0789-0.0790 inch	2.003-2.006mm
	mark 4	0.0790-0.0791 inch	2.006-2.009mm
	mark 5	0.0791-0.0792 inch	2.009-2.012mm
Crank pin diameter			
STD		1.8892-1.8898 inch	47.985-48.00mm
U/S 0.25		1.8797-1.8801 inch	47.745-47.755mm
Circle runout		0.0024 inch	0.06mm
Main journal taper out-of-round		0.0008 inch	0.02mm
Crank pin journal taper and out-of-round		0.0008 inch	0.02mm

89553C18

5S-FE ENGINE SPECIFICATIONS

		English	Metric
Compression pressure		178 psi	1226 kPa
		142 psi	981 kPa
Differential of pressure between each cylinder		14 psi or less	98 kPa or less
Valve clearance			
Cold	intake	0.007-0.011 inch	0.19-0.29mm
	exhaust	0.011-0.015 inch	0.28-0.38mm
Adjusting shims	mark 2.500	0.0984 inch	2.500mm
	mark 2.550	0.1004 inch	2.550mm
	mark 2.600	0.1024 inch	2.600mm
	mark 2.650	0.1043 inch	2.650mm
	mark 2.700	0.1063 inch	2.700mm
	mark 2.750	0.1083 inch	2.750mm
	mark 2.800	0.1102 inch	2.800mm
	mark 2.850	0.1122 inch	2.850mm
	mark 2.900	0.1142 inch	2.900mm
	mark 2.950	0.1161 inch	2.950mm
	mark 3.000	0.1181 inch	3.000mm
	mark 3.050	0.1201 inch	3.050mm
	mark 3.100	0.1220 inch	3.100mm
	mark 3.150	0.1240 inch	3.150mm
	mark 3.200	0.1260 inch	3.200mm
	mark 3.250	0.1280 inch	3.250mm
	mark 3.300	0.1299 inch	3.300mm
Balance shaft			
Thrust clearance	STD	0.0026-0.0043 inch	0.065-0.110mm
	maximum	0.0043 inch	0.110mm
Backlash			
crankshaft-to-No. 1 balance shaft	off-vehicle	0-0.0024 inch	0-0.06mm
	on-vehicle	0.0010-0.0035	0.025-0.090mm
No. 1 balance shaft-to-No. 2 shaft	D mark	0.0008-0.0030 inch	0.020-0.075mm
	E mark	0.0002-0.0030 inch	0.005-0.075mm
	F mark	0.0002-0.0022 inch	0.005-0.055mm
Spacer thickness	No. 01	0.0685 inch	1.74mm
	No. 03	0.0693 inch	1.76mm
	No. 05	0.0701 inch	1.78mm
	No. 07	0.0709 inch	1.80mm
	No. 09	0.0717 inch	1.82mm
	No. 11	0.0724 inch	1.84mm
	No. 13	0.0732 inch	1.86mm
	No. 15	0.0740 inch	1.88mm
	No. 17	0.0748 inch	1.90mm
	No. 19	0.0756 inch	1.92mm
	No. 21	0.0764 inch	1.94mm

89553C19

5S-FE ENGINE SPECIFICATIONS

			English	Metric
Spacer thickness	No. 23		0.0772 inch	1.96mm
	No. 25		0.0780 inch	1.98mm
	No. 27		0.0787 inch	2.00mm
	No. 29		0.0795 inch	2.02mm
	No. 31		0.0803 inch	2.04mm
	No. 33		0.0811 inch	2.06mm
	No. 35		0.0819 inch	2.08mm
	No. 37		0.0827 inch	2.10mm
	No. 39		0.0835 inch	2.12mm
Balance shaft housing bolt diameter	STD		0.2559-0.2638 inch	6.5-6.7mm
	minimum		0.2480 inch	6.3mm
Idler pulley tension spring	Free length		1.811 inch	48.0mm
	loaded @ 1.988 inch (50.5mm)		7.2-8.3 lbf	32-37 N
Cylinder head				
Warpage	block side	maximum	0.0020 inch	0.05mm
	manifold side	maximum	0.0031 inch	0.08mm
Valve seat	refacing angle		30, 45, 75 deg	30, 45, 75 deg
	contacting angle		45 deg	45 deg
	contacting width		0.039-0.055 inch	1.0-1.4mm
Valve guide bushing				
Inside diameter			0.2366-0.2374 inch	6.0410-6.030mm
Outside diameter	STD		0.4331-0.4342 inch	11.000-11.027mm
	O/S 0.05		0.4350-0.4361 inch	11.050-11.077mm
Valve				
Overall length	STD	intake	3.8425 inch	97.60mm
		exhaust	3.8760 inch	98.45mm
	minimum	intake	3.823 inch	97.1mm
		exhaust	3.858 inch	98.0mm
Valve face angle			44.5 deg	44.5 deg
Stem diameter	intake		0.2350-0.2356 inch	5.970-5.995mm
	exhaust		0.2348-0.2354 inch	5.965-5.980mm
Stem oil clearance	STD	intake	0.0010-0.0024 inch	0.025-0.060mm
		exhaust	0.0012-0.0026 inch	0.030-0.065mm
	maximum	intake	0.0031 inch	0.08mm
		exhaust	0.0039 inch	0.010mm
Margin thickness	STD		0.031-0.047 inch	0.8-1.2mm
	minimum		0.020 inch	0.5mm
Valve spring	Deviation		0.079 inch	2.0mm

89553C20

5S-FE ENGINE SPECIFICATIONS

			English	Metric
Valve spring				
Free length			1.6520-1.6531 inch	41.96-41.99mm
Installed tension @ 1.366 inch (34.7mm)			36.8-42.5 lbf	164-189 N
Valve lifter				
Lifter diameter			1.2191-1.2195 inch	30.966-30.976mm
Bore diameter			1.2205-1.2212 inch	31.000-31.018mm
Oil clearance	STD		0.0009-0.0020 inch	0.024-0.052mm
	maximum		0.0028 inch	0.07mm
Camshaft				
Thrust clearance	STD	intake	0.0018-0.0039 inch	0.045-0.100mm
		exhaust	0.0012-0.0033 inch	0.030-0.085mm
	maximum	intake	0.0047 inch	0.12mm
		exhaust	0.0039 inch	0.10mm
Journal clearance	STD		0.0010-0.0024 inch	0.025-0.062mm
	maximum		0.0039 inch	0.10mm
Journal diameter			1.0614-1.0620 inch	26.959-26.975mm
Circle runout			0.0016 inch	0.04mm
Cam lobe height	STD	intake	1.6539-1.6579 inch	42.01-42.11mm
		exhaust	1.5772-1.5811 inch	40.06-40.16mm
	minimum	intake	1.6496 inch	41.90mm
		exhaust	1.5728 inch	39.95mm
Camshaft gear backlash	STD		0.0008-0.0079 inch	0.020-0.200mm
	maximum		0.0188 inch	0.30mm
Camshaft gear spring and free distance			0.886-0.902 inch	22.5-22.9mm
Piston and ring				
Piston diameter	STD	mark 1	3.4193-3.4197 inch	86.850-86.860mm
		mark 2	3.4197-3.4201 inch	86.860-86.870mm
		mark 3	3.4201-3.4205 inch	86.870-86.880mm
		O/S 0.50	3.4390-3.4402 inch	87.350-87.380mm
Piston oil clearance	STD		0.0055-0.0063 inch	0.14-0.016mm
	maximum		0.0071 inch	0.18mm
Piston ring groove clearance	No. 1		0.0016-0.0031 inch	0.040-0.080mm
	No. 2		0.0012-0.0028 inch	0.030-0.070mm
Piston ring end gap	STD	No. 1	0.0106-0.0197 inch	0.270-0.500mm
		No. 2	0.0138-0.0236 inch	0.350-0.600mm
		oil	0.0079-0.0217 inch	0.200-0.550mm
	maximum	No. 1	0.0433 inch	1.10mm
		No. 2	0.0472 inch	1.20mm
		oil	0.0453 inch	1.15mm

5S-FE ENGINE SPECIFICATIONS

			English	Metric
Connecting rod				
Thrust clearance	STD		0.0063-0.0123 inch	0.160-0.312mm
	maximum		0.0138 inch	0.35mm
Bearing center wall thickness	STD	mark 1	0.0584-0.0586 inch	1.484-1.488mm
Bearing center wall thickness (continued)		mark 2	0.0586-0.0587 inch	1.488-1.492mm
		mark 3	0.0587-0.0589 inch	1.492-1.496mm
Rod oil clearance	STD		0.0009-0.0022 inch	0.024-0.055mm
	U/S 0.25		0.0009-0.0027 inch	0.023-0.069mm
	maximum		0.0031 inch	0.08mm
Rod-out-of-alignment	maximum per 3.94 inch (100mm)		0.0020 inch	0.05mm
Rod twist	maximum per 3.94 inch (100mm)		0.0059 inch	0.15mm
Busing inside diameter			0.8663-0.8668 inch	22.005-22.017mm
Piston pin diameter			0.8660-0.8665 inch	21.997-22.009mm
Crankshaft				
Thrust clearance	STD		0.0008-0.0087 inch	0.020-0.220mm
	maximum		0.0118 inch	0.30mm
Thrust washer thickness			0.961-0.980 inch	2.440-2.490mm
Main journal oil clearance	STD	No. 3 STD	0.0010-0.0017 inch	0.025-0.044mm
		others	0.0011-0.0026 inch	0.024-0.067mm
	U/S 0.25	STD	0.0006-0.0013 inch	0.015-0.034mm
		U/S 0.25	0.0007-0.0023 inch	0.019-0.059mm
	maximum		0.0031 inch	0.08mm
Main journal diameter	STD		2.1653-2.655 inch	54.988-55.003mm
	U/S 0.25		2.1553-2.1557 inch	54.745-54.755mm
Main bearing center wall thickness	STD- No. 3	mark 1	0.0784-0.0785 inch	1.992-1.995mm
		mark 2	0.0785-0.0787 inch	1.995-1.998mm
		mark 3	0.00787-0.0788 inch	1.998-2.001mm
		mark 4	0.0788-0.0789 inch	2.001-2.004mm
		mark 5	0.0789-0.0790 inch	2.004-2.007mm
	others	mark 1	0.0786-0.0787 inch	1.997-2.000mm
		mark 2	0.0787-0.0789 inch	2.000-2.003mm
		mark 3	0.0789-0.0790 inch	2.003-2.006mm
		mark 4	0.0790-0.0791 inch	2.006-2.009mm
		mark 5	0.0791-0.0792 inch	2.009-2.012mm
Crank pin diameter	STD		2.0466-2.0472 inch	51.985-52.000mm
	U/S 0.25		2.0372-2.0376 inch	51.745-51.755mm
Circle runout	maximum		0.0024 inch	0.06mm

89553C21

89553C22

5S-FE ENGINE SPECIFICATIONS

		English	Metric
Main journal taper out-of-round		0.0008 inch	0.02mm
Pin taper and out-of-round	maximum	0.0008 inch	0.02mm

89553C23

2VZ-FE AND 3VZ-FE ENGINE SPECIFICATIONS

			English	Metric
Compression pressure	STD		178 psi	1226 kPa
	Limit		142 psi	981 kPa
	Difference of pressure between cylinders		14 psi or less	98 kPa or less
Cylinder head	Block surface warpage		0.0039 inch	0.10mm
	Valve seat-refacing angle		30, 45, 60 deg	30, 45, 60 deg
	Valve seat-contacting angle		45 deg	45 deg
	Valve-contacting width		0.039-0.055 inch	1.0-1.4mm
Valve guide bushing	Inside diameter		0.2366-0.2374 inch	6.010-6.030mm
	Outside diameter	STD	0.4350-0.4354 inch	11.048-11.059mm
		O/S 0.05	0.4369-0.4374 inch	11.098-11.109mm
Valve	Overall length STD 2VZ-FE	intake	3.783 inch	96.1mm
		exhaust	3.787 inch	96.2mm
	3VZ-FE	intake	3.7461 inch	95.15mm
		exhaust	3.7362 inch	94.90mm
	Limit 2VZ-FE	intake	3.764 inch	95.6mm
		exhaust	3.768 inch	95.7mm
	3VZ-FE	intake	3.724 inch	94.6mm
		exhaust	3.717 inch	94.4mm
	Face angle		44.5 deg	44.5 deg
	Stem diameter	intake	0.2350-0.2356 inch	5.970-5.985mm
		exhaust	0.2348-0.2354 inch	5.965-5.980mm
	Oil clearance STD	intake	0.0010-0.0024 inch	0.025-0.060mm
		exhaust	0.0012-0.0026 inch	0.030-0.065mm
	limit	intake	0.0031 inch	0.08mm
		exhaust	0.0039 inch	0.10mm
	Margin thickness 2VZ-FE	STD	0.039 inch	1.0mm
		limit	0.020 inch	0.5mm
	3VZ-FE	STD	0.0394 inch	1.0mm
		limit	0.0197 inch	0.5mm
Valve spring	Free length	2VZ-FE	1.677 inch	42.6mm
		3VZ-FE	1.630 inch	41.4mm
	Installed tension @ 1.311 inch (33.3mm)	2VZ-FE	41.0-47.2 lb	182-210 N
		3VZ-FE	38.4-42.4 lbf	186-206 N
	Squareness		0.075 inch	2.0mm
Valve lifter	Lifter diameter		1.2191-1.2195 inch	30.966-30.976mm
	Lifter bore diameter		1.2201-1.2212 inch	31.000-31.018mm

89553C24

2VZ-FE AND 3VZ-FE ENGINE SPECIFICATIONS

			English	Metric
Valve lifter (continued)	Oil clearance	STD	0.0009-0.0020 inch	0.024-0.052mm
		limit	0.0031 inch	0.08mm
Camshaft	Thrust clearance 2VZ-FE	STD	0.0012-0.0031 inch	0.030-0.080mm
		limit	0.0047 inch	0.12mm
	3VZ-FE	STD	0.0013-0.0031 inch	0.033-0.080mm
		limit	0.0047 inch	0.12mm
	Journal oil clearance 2VZ-FE	STD	0.0014-0.0028 inch	0.035-0.072mm
		limit	0.0039 inch	0.10mm
	3VZ-FE	STD	0.0014-0.0028 inch	0.035-0.072mm
		limit	0.0039 inch	0.10mm
	Journal diameter		1.0610-1.616 inch	26.949-26.965mm
	Circle runout		0.0024 inch	0.06mm
	Cam lobe height 2VZ-FE STD	intake	1.5555-1.5594 inch	39.510-39.610mm
		exhaust	1.5339-1.5378 inch	38.860-39.060
	limit	intake	1.5496 inch	39.36mm
		exhaust	1.5279 inch	38.81mm
	3VZ-FE STD	intake	1.6598-1.6636 inch	42.160-42.260mm
		exhaust	1.6520-1.6559 inch	41.96-42.06mm
	limit	intake	16.539 inch	42.01mm
		exhaust	16.461 inch	41.81mm
	Camshaft gear spring end free distance		0.712-0.740 inch	18.2-18.8mm
	Camshaft gear backlash	STD	0.0008-0.0079 inch	0.020-0.200mm
		limit	0.0188 inch	0.30mm
Timing belt tensioner	Protrusion	2VZ-FE	0.413-0.453 inch	10.5-11.5mm
		3VZ-FE	0.394-0.425 inch	10.0-10.8mm
Block	Head warpage surface		0.0020 inch	0.05mm
	Bore diameter STD	mark 1	3.4449-3.4453 inch	87.500-87.510mm
		mark 2	3.4453-3.4457 inch	87.510-87.520mm
		mark 3	3.4457-3.4461 inch	87.520-87.530mm
	limit	STD	2.439 inch	87.73mm
		O/S 0.50	3.4736 inch	88.23mm

89553C25

2VZ-FE AND 3VZ-FE ENGINE SPECIFICATIONS

				English	Metric
Piston and ring					
Piston diameter					
2VZ-FE	STD	mark 1		3.4427-3.4431 inch	87.445-87.455mm
		mark 2		3.4431-3.4435 inch	87.455-87.465mm
		mark 3		3.4435-3.4439 inch	87.465-87.475mm
	O/S 0.50			3.4624-3.4636 inch	87.945-87.975mm
3VZ-FE	STD	mark 1		3.4394-3.4398 inch	87.360-87.370mm
		mark 2		3.4398-3.4402 inch	87.370-87.380mm
		mark 3		3.4402-3.4405 inch	87.380-87.390mm
	O/S 0.50			3.4413-3.4425 inch	87.410-87.440mm
Oil clearance					
2VZ-FE	STD			0.0018-0.0026 inch	0.045-0.065mm
	limit			0.0033 inch	0.085mm
3VZ-FE	STD			0.0051-0.0059 inch	0.13-0.15mm
	limit			0.0067 inch	0.17mm
Ring groove clearance					
		No. 1		0.0004-0.0031 inch	0.010-0.080mm
		No. 2		0.0012-0.0028 inch	0.010-0.080mm
Ring end gap					
2VZ-FE	STD	No. 1		0.0118-0.0205 inch	0.300-0.520mm
		No. 2		0.0138-0.0236 inch	0.350-0.600mm
		oil		0.0079-0.0217 inch	0.200-0.550mm
	limit	No. 1		0.0441 inch	1.12mm
		No. 2		0.0472 inch	1.20mm
		oil		0.0453 inch	1.15mm
3VZ-FE	STD	No. 1		0.00110-0.0197 inch	0.280-0.500mm
		No. 2		0.0150-0.0236 inch	0.380-0.600mm
		oil		0.0059-0.0224 inch	0.150-0.570mm
	limit	No. 1		0.0433 inch	1.10mm
		No. 2		0.0472 inch	1.20mm
		oil		0.0431 inch	1.17mm
Connecting rod and bearing					
Thrust clearance					
2VZ-FE	STD			0.0059-0.0130 inch	0.150-0.330mm
	limit			0.0150 inch	0.38mm
3VZ-FE	STD			0.0059-0.0118 inch	0.15-0.30mm
	limit			0.0150 inch	0.38mm
Connecting rod bearing center wall thickness					
		mark 1		0.0584-0.0586 inch	1.484-1.488mm
		mark 2		0.0586-0.0587 inch	1.488-1.492mm
		mark 3		0.0587-0.0589 inch	1.492-1.496mm

89553C26

2VZ-FE AND 3VZ-FE ENGINE SPECIFICATIONS

			English	Metric
Connecting rod oil clearance				
	STD		0.0011-0.0026 inch	0.028-0.065mm
	limit		0.0031 inch	0.08mm
Rod out of alignment			0.0020 inch	0.05mm
Rod twist			0.0059 inch	0.15mm
Piston pin diameter	3VZ-FE		0.8660-0.8664 inch	21.997-22.006mm
Crankshaft				
Thrust clearance	STD		0.0008-0.0087 inch	0.020-0.220m
	limit		0.0118 inch	0.30mm
Thrust washer thickness			0.0961-0.0980 inch	2.440-2.490mm
Main journal oil clearance	STD		0.0011-0.0022 inch	0.029-0.056mm
	limit		0.0031 inch	0.08mm
Main journal diameter	STD		2.5191-2.5197 inch	63.985-64.000mm
	U/S 0.25		2.5096-2.5100 inch	63.745-63.755mm
Main bearing wall thickness				
	mark 1		0.0783-0.0784 inch	1.989-1.992mm
	mark 2		0.0784-0.0785 inch	1.992-1.995mm
	mark 3		0.0785-0.0787 inch	1.995-1.998mm
	mark 4		0.0787-0.0788 inch	1.998-2.001mm
	mark 5		0.0788-0.0789 inch	2.001-2.004mm
Crank pin diameter				
	2VZ-FE		1.8892-1.8898 inch	47.987-48.000mm
	3VZ-FE		2.0863-2.0866 inch	52.992-53.000mm
Circle runout limit			0.0024 inch	0.06mm
Main journal taper and out-of-round limit			0.0008 inch	0.02mm
Crank pin journal taper and out-of-round limit			0.0008 inch	0.02mm

89553C27

1MZ-FE ENGINE SPECIFICATIONS

Description		English	Metric
Compression pressure		218 psi	1500 kPa
		145 psi	1000 kPa
Differential of pressure between each cylinder		15 psi or less	100 kPa or less
Valve clearance			
Cold	intake	0.006-0.010 inch	0.15-0.25mm
	exhaust	0.010-0.014 inch	0.25-0.35mm
Adjusting shims	mark 2.500	0.0984 inch	2.500mm
	mark 2.550	0.1004 inch	2.550mm
	mark 2.600	0.1024 inch	2.600mm
	mark 2.650	0.1043 inch	2.650mm
	mark 2.700	0.1063 inch	2.700mm
	mark 2.750	0.1083 inch	2.750mm
	mark 2.800	0.1102 inch	2.800mm
	mark 2.850	0.1122 inch	2.850mm
	mark 2.900	0.1142 inch	2.900mm
	mark 2.950	0.1161 inch	2.950mm
	mark 3.000	0.1181 inch	3.000mm
	mark 3.050	0.1201 inch	3.050mm
	mark 3.100	0.1220 inch	3.100mm
	mark 3.150	0.1240 inch	3.150mm
	mark 3.200	0.1260 inch	3.200mm
	mark 3.250	0.1280 inch	3.250mm
	mark 3.300	0.1299 inch	3.300mm
Intake manifold vacuum		17.7 in. Hg or more	60 kPa
Timing belt tensioner			
Protrusion from housing side		0.394-0.425 inch	10.0-10.8mm
Cylinder head			
Warpage		0.039 inch	0.10mm
Valve seat			
refacing angle		30, 45, 75 degrees	30, 45, 75 degrees
contacting angle		45 degrees	45 degrees
contacting width		0.039-0.055 inch	1.0-1.4mm
Valve guide bushing bore diameter			
STD		0.4053-0.4060 inch	10.295-10.313mm
O/S 0.05		0.4073-0.4080 inch	10.345-10.363mm
12 pointed head bolt diameter			
STD		0.3524-0.3563 inch	8.95-9.05mm
minimum		0.3445 inch	8.75mm
Valve guide busing			
Inside diameter		0.2169-0.2177 inch	5.510-5.530mm
STD		0.4068-0.4072 inch	10.333-10.344mm
O/S 0.50		0.4088-0.4092 inch	10.383-10.394mm
Valve			
Overall length			
STD	intake	3.5779 inch	95.45mm
	exhaust	3.7559 inch	95.40mm
minimum	intake	3.3782 inch	94.95mm
	exhaust	3.37362 inch	94.90mm

1MZ-FE ENGINE SPECIFICATIONS

Description			English	Metric
Valve (continued)				
Valve face angle			44.5 degrees	44.5 degrees
Stem oil clearance	intake		0.0010-0.0024 inch	0.025-0.060mm
	exhaust		0.0012-0.0026 inch	0.030-0.065mm
Margin thickness		STD	0.0039 inch	1.0mm
		Limit	0.020 inch	0.5mm
Valve spring				
Deviation	maximum		0.079 inch	2.0mm
Free length			1.7913 inch	45.50mm
Installed load @ 1.331 inch (33.8mm)			41.9-46.3lbf	186-206 N
Valve lifter				
Outer diameter			1.2191-2.2195 inch	30.966-30.976mm
Inner diameter			1.2205-1.2211 inch	31.000-31.016mm
Lifter-to-head oil clearance		STD	0.0009-0.0020 inch	0.024-0.050mm
		limit	0.0028 inch	0.07mm
Camshaft				
Thrust clearance		STD	0.0016-0.0035 inch	0.040-0.090mm
		maximum	0.0047 inch	0.12mm
Journal oil clearance		STD	0.0014-0.0028 inch	0.035-0.072mm
		maximum	0.0039 inch	0.10mm
Journal diameter	intake		1.0610-1.616 inch	26.949-26.965mm
	exhaust		1.0614-1.0620 inch	26.959-26.975mm
Circle runout			0.0024 inch	0.06mm
Cam lobe height				
STD	intake		1.6579-1.6618 inch	42.11-42.21mm
	exhaust		1.6520-1.6559 inch	41.96-42.06mm
minimum	intake		16.520 inch	41.96mm
	exhaust		16.461 inch	41.81mm
Camshaft gear spring end free distance			0.712-0.740 inch	18.2-18.8mm
Camshaft gear backlash		STD	0.0008-0.0079 inch	0.020-0.200mm
		maximum	0.0188 inch	0.30mm
Cylinder block				
Cylinder head surface warpage limit			0.0028 inch	0.07mm
Cylinder bore diameter		STD	3.4449-3.4453 inch	87.500-87.512mm
		maximum	3.4457 inch	87.52mm
Piston and Ring				
Piston diameter			3.4412-3.4416 inch	87.408-87.416mm
Piston to cylinder clearance		STD	0.0033-0.0042 inch	0.084-0.106mm
		maximum	0.00051 inch	0.13mm

1MZ-FE ENGINE SPECIFICATIONS

Description			English	Metric
Piston ring end gap				
	STD	No. 1	0.0098-0.0138 inch	0.25-0.35mm
		No.2	0.0138-0.0177 inch	0.35-0.45mm
Piston ring end gap (continued)				
		oil	0.0059-0.0157 inch	0.15-0.40mm
	maximum	No. 1	0.0374 inch	0.95mm
		No. 2	0.0413 inch	1.05mm
		oil	0.0394 inch	1.00mm
Connecting rod and bearing				
Thrust clearance				
	STD		0.0059-0.0118 inch	0.15-0.30mm
	maximum		0.0138 inch	0.35mm
Connecting rod bearing center wall thickness				
	mark 1		0.0584-0.0585 inch	1.484-1.487mm
	mark 2		0.0585-0.0587 inch	1.487-1.490mm
	mark 3		0.0587-0.0588 inch	1.490-1.493mm
	mark 4		0.0588-0.0589 inch	1.493-1.496mm
Connecting rod oil clearance				
	STD		0.0015-0.0025 inch	0.038-0.064mm
	maximum		0.0031 inch	0.08mm
Rod out of alignment			0.0020 inch	0.05mm
Rod twist			0.0059 inch	0.15mm
Piston pin diameter			0.8660-0.8664 inch	21.997-22.006mm
Connecting rod bolt diameter				
	STD		0.284-0.287 inch	7.2-7.3mm
	minimum		0.276 inch	7.0mm
Crankshaft				
Thrust clearance				
	STD		0.0016-0.0095 inch	0.04-0.24m
	maximum		0.0118 inch	0.30mm
Thrust washer thickness			0.0760-0.0780 inch	1.930-1.980mm
Main journal oil clearance				
	STD		0.0010-0.0018 inch	0.026-0.046mm
	maximum		0.0024 inch	0.06mm
Main journal diameter			2.4011-2.4016 inch	60.988-61.000mm
Main bearing wall thickness				
	mark 1		0.0979-0.0980 inch	2.486-2.489mm
	mark 2		0.0980-0.0981 inch	2.489-2.492mm
	mark 3		0.0981-0.0982 inch	2.492-2.495mm
	mark 4		0.0982-0.0983 inch	2.495-2.498mm
	mark 5		0.0983-0.0985 inch	2.498-2.501mm
Crank pin diameter			2.0863-2.866 inch	52.992-53.000mm
Circle runout limit			0.0024 inch	0.06mm
Main journal taper and out-of-round limit			0.0008 inch	0.02mm
Crank pin journal taper and out-of-round limit			0.0008 inch	0.02mm

89553C30

Engine

REMOVAL & INSTALLATION

In the process of removing the engine, you will come across a number of steps which call for the removal of a separate component or system, such as "disconnect the exhaust system" or "remove the radiator." In most instances, a detailed removal procedure can be found elsewhere in this manual.

It is virtually impossible to list each individual wire and hose which must be disconnected, simply because so many different model and engine combinations have been manufactured. Careful observation and common sense are the best possible approaches to any repair procedure.

Removal and installation of the engine can be made easier if you follow these basic points:

- If you have to drain any of the fluids, use a suitable container.
- Always tag any wires or hoses and, if possible, the components they came from before disconnecting them.
- Because there are so many bolts and fasteners involved, store and label the retainers from components separately in muffin pans, jars or coffee cans. This will prevent confusion during installation.
- After unbolting the transmission or transaxle, always make sure it is properly supported.
- If it is necessary to disconnect the air conditioning system, have this service performed by a qualified technician using a recovery/recycling station. If the system does not have to be disconnected, unbolt the compressor and set it aside.
- When unbolting the engine mounts, always make sure the engine is properly supported. When removing the engine, make sure that any lifting devices are properly attached to the engine. It is recommended that if your engine is supplied with lifting hooks, your lifting apparatus be attached to them.
- Lift the engine from its compartment slowly, checking that no hoses, wires or other components are still connected.
- After the engine is clear of the compartment, place it on an engine stand or workbench.
- After the engine has been removed, you can perform a partial or full teardown of the engine using the procedures outlined in this manual.

2-Wheel Drive

1. Drain the engine coolant from the radiator and engine drain cocks.

✳✳ CAUTION

Never open, service or drain the radiator or cooling system when hot; serious burns can occur from the steam and hot coolant. Also, when draining engine coolant, keep in mind that cats and dogs are attracted to ethylene glycol antifreeze and could drink any that is left in an uncovered container or in puddles on the ground. This will prove fatal in sufficient quantities. Always drain coolant into a sealable container. Coolant should be reused unless it is contaminated or is several years old.

2. Remove the hood. Disconnect and remove the battery, on some models it may be necessary to remove the battery tray also. On vehicles equipped with an automatic transaxle, disconnect the throttle cable and bracket from the throttle body.

✳✳ CAUTION

Some models covered by this manual may be equipped with a Supplemental Restraint System (SRS), which uses an air bag. Whenever working near any of the SRS components, such as the impact sensors, the air bag module, steering column and instrument panel, disable the SRS, as described in Section 6.

3. Disconnect and label all cables, electrical wires and vacuum lines attached to various engine parts.
4. Remove the cruise control actuator and bracket. Disconnect the radiator and heater hoses. Disconnect the automatic transaxle cooler lines. Remove the radiator. On some models it may be necessary to remove the washer fluid reservoir.
5. Remove the air cleaner assembly and air flow meter. Disconnect all wiring and linkage at the transaxle.
6. Pull out the fuel injection system wiring harness. Secure the assembly to the right side of fender apron.
7. Disconnect and plug the fuel lines at the fuel filter and return pipes. Unbolt the air conditioning compressor and position it out of the way. DO NOT disconnect any refrigerant lines.
8. Disconnect the speedometer cable at the transaxle. Remove the clutch release cylinder without disconnecting the fluid line.
9. Disconnect any engine wiring attached to the cabin of the vehicle.
10. Raise and support the vehicle safely. Drain the engine oil. Remove the engine under covers.
11. Remove the suspension lower crossmember. Drain the transaxle fluid. Wrap both driveshaft boots with shop towels an unbolt both halfshafts.
12. Unbolt the power steering pump (leaving the hoses connected) and position it out of the way. Disconnect the exhaust pipe from the manifold. Disconnect the front, rear and center engine mounts at the frame member. On some models a center crossmember may need to be removed also.
13. Attach an engine hoist chain to the lifting eyes and connect a suitable engine lifting device to the hoist. Take up the engine weight with the crane and remove the right and left side engine mounts.
14. Carefully, raise and remove the engine and transaxle assembly from the vehicle. Clear the right side of the mounting while lowering the transaxle and clear the power steering gear while lowering the neutral start switch. Make sure that the engine clears all wiring hoses and cables.
15. Position the engine in a suitable engine holding stand and disconnect the lifting device and the chains.

To install:

16. Connect the engine hoist chains to the lifting eyes and connect the lifting device to the hoist. Remove the engine from the holding stand.
17. Carefully lower the engine and transaxle assembly into the engine compartment. Keep the engine level and align each mounting with its bracket. Temporarily install engine mounting through their nuts and bolts. Remove the lifting device and chain hoist from the engine.
18. Raise the vehicle and support safely. Install the front and rear mounting insulators onto the frame member. Tighten the bolts to specifications. Refer to the Torque Specification chart in this section.
19. Install all other components previously removed. Route, connect and clamp all the electrical wires to their various engine parts. Connect all the vacuum hoses. adjust the tension of all drive belts.
20. Fill the radiator with coolant to the proper level. Fill the transaxle with ATF. Install a new oil filter and replace the engine oil.
21. Start the engine and check for leaks of any kind. Correct all leaks as necessary.
22. Adjust the engine idle and maximum idle speeds.
23. Install and adjust the hood.
24. Perform a road test. Recheck the coolant and engine oil levels.

All-Trac 4-Wheel Drive

1. Disconnect the negative battery cable and drain the engine coolant. Remove the hood.
2. Disconnect the accelerator cable from the throttle body. Remove the radiator.
3. Disconnect the heater hoses.
4. Disconnect the inlet hose at the fuel filter. Disconnect the return hose at the fuel return pipe.

✳✳ CAUTION

Observe all applicable safety precautions when working around fuel. Whenever servicing the fuel system, always work in a well ventilated area. Do not allow fuel spray or vapors to come in contact with a spark or open flame. Keep a dry chemical fire extinguisher near the work area. Always keep fuel in a container specifically designed for fuel storage; also, always properly seal fuel containers to avoid the possibility of fire or explosion.

5. Disconnect and remove the cruise control actuator.

6. Remove the air cleaner assembly.

7. Remove the clutch slave cylinder and hose bracket without disconnecting the hose. Position the assembly out of the way. Disconnect the speedometer cable and the transaxle control cables.

8. Disconnect and remove the air conditioning compressor with the refrigerant lines still attached; position it out of the way. DO NOT disconnect the refrigerant lines.

9. Disconnect and label all wires, connectors and vacuum lines from their various engine parts.

10. Raise the front of the vehicle so that there is sufficient clearance to lower the engine. Drain the engine oil and remove the engine undercovers.

11. Remove the lower suspension crossmember and the halfshafts. Disconnect and remove the propeller shaft. Cover the drive boots with shop towels.

12. Remove the power steering pump with the hydraulic lines still attached and place it against the cowl. Secure the pump with a piece of string or wire. Remove the front exhaust pipe.

13. Remove the engine mounting center member and the stabilizer bar. Lower the vehicle.

14. Unplug the TCCS (Toyota Computer Control System) and ECU (Electronic Control Unit) connectors and pull them out through the firewall. Remove the power steering pump reservoir tank mounting bolts.

15. Attach an engine lifting device to the engine lift brackets. Remove the right side engine mount stay and then remove the insulator and bracket. Remove the left side engine mount insulator and bracket.

16. Lower the engine and transaxle as an assembly from the engine compartment. Be careful not to hit the power steering gear housing or the neutral safety switch.

17. Place the engine in a suitable engine holding stand.

To install:

18. Remove the engine from the holding stand. Carefully raise the engine into the engine compartment being careful not to strike the power steering gear housing or the neutral start switch.

19. Keep the engine level and align each mounting with the bracket. Install the left and right mounting insulators and temporarily install the through bolts. Tighten the left mount bolts to 38 ft. lbs. (52 Nm), the thru-bolt to 64 ft. lbs. (87 Nm) and right mounting bracket bolts to 64 ft. lbs. (87 Nm), the nuts to 38 ft. lbs. (52 Nm) and the right mounting stay bolt and nut to 54 ft. lbs. (73 Nm). Remove the lifting device from the engine.

20. Install the power steering pump reservoir mounting bolts. Engage the TCCS and ECU connectors. Raise the vehicle and support safely.

21. Install the stabilizer bar. Install the engine mounting center member and tighten the member body bolts to 29 ft. lbs. (39 Nm) and all other member bolts to 38 ft. lbs. (52 Nm).

22. Install the front exhaust pipe and tighten the bolts to 46 ft. lbs. (62 Nm). Attach the power steering pump to the bracket. Install the propeller shaft and connect the front driveshafts. Install the suspension lower crossmember. Tighten the member body bolts to 153 ft. lbs. (207 Nm) and all other member bolts to 29 ft. lbs. (39 Nm).

23. Install the engine covers and lower the vehicle. Connect all electrical wires, connectors and vacuum hoses. Install the air conditioning compressor and the drive belt.

24. Connect the transaxle control and speedometer cables. Install the clutch release cylinder and release bracket.

25. Install the air cleaner, air cleaner hose and flow meter assembly. Install the cruise control actuator.

26. Unplug and connect the fuel hoses. Connect the heater water hoses.

27. Install the radiator. Install the accelerator cable and adjust it. Install the battery.

28. Fill the engine with coolant to the proper level. Install a new oil filter and replace the engine oil. Start the engine and check for leaks of any kind. Correct all leaks as necessary.

29. Adjust the power steering pump and the alternator drive belt tension. Adjust the ignition timing and the valve clearance.

30. Install the hood and check the toe-in.

31. Perform a road test. Recheck the coolant and engine oil levels.

Rocker Arm (Valve) Cover

REMOVAL & INSTALLATION

2S-ELC, 3S-FE and 5S-FE Engines

▶ See Figures 1, 2 and 3

➡It is recommended when replacing the valve cover gasket you replace the seal nuts also. They may be reused only if they do not seem to be damaged.

1. Remove and label all electrical wiring, connectors and vacuum hoses necessary to gain removal clearance.

2. Remove the spark plug wires. Disconnect the PCV hose.

3. Remove the four nuts and grommets located on top of the cylinder head cover.

➡On 3S-FE engines, label or arrange the grommets so that they may be reinstalled in the same order. This will minimize the possibility of oil leakage when the cylinder head cover is reinstalled.

4. Remove the cylinder head cover and the cover gasket from the cylinder head. Discard the gasket and replace with a new one.

To install:

5. With a wire brush or gasket scraper, remove all the old gasket material from the cylinder head and the cylinder head cover gasket surfaces.

6. When the cylinder head surfaces are free and clean, apply beads of sealant to the cylinder head in the locations shown in the accompanying illustrations.

7. Install the new cylinder head gasket in the cover. Make sure that the gasket seats evenly. Place the cylinder head cover with the gasket onto the cylinder head.

8. Install the four grommets and nuts. Uniformly tighten the nuts in several passes to 13 ft. lbs. (18 Nm) on the 2S-ELC; 17 ft. lbs. (23 Nm) on the 3S-FE and 5S-FE.

➡On 3S-FE engines, align the grommets as shown in the accompanying illustration to ensure proper sealing of the cylinder head cover.

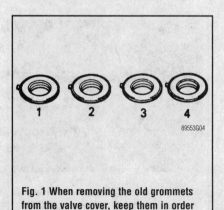

Fig. 1 When removing the old grommets from the valve cover, keep them in order of removal—3S-FE and 5S-FE engines

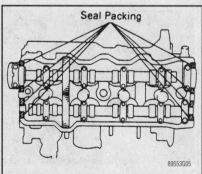

Fig. 2 Before installing the valve cover, apply sealant to the head in these locations—3S-FE engine

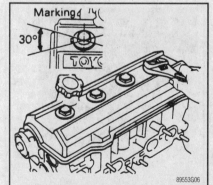

Fig. 3 Align the grommets on the cover as shown—3S-FE engine shown

9. Connect the PCV hose. Connect all removed vacuum hoses, connectors and electrical wiring. Connect the negative battery cable. Start the engine and inspect for oil leaks. Repair any leaks as necessary.

2VZ-FE and 3VZ-FE Engines

♦ See Figure 4

➥It is recommended when replacing the valve cover gasket you replace the seal nuts also. They may be reused only if they do not seem to be damaged.

1. Turn the ignition key to the OFF position. Disconnect the negative battery cable. Wait at least 90 seconds from the time the negative battery was disconnected to start work.
2. Remove and label all electrical wiring, connectors and vacuum hoses necessary to gain removal clearance.
3. On the 3VZ-FE, remove the V-bank cover.
4. Remove the spark plug wires. Disconnect the PCV hose.
5. Remove the six (2VZ-FE) or eight (3VZ-FE) nuts and seal washers located on top of the cylinder head cover.
6. Remove the cylinder head cover and the cover gasket from the cylinder head. Discard the gasket and replace with a new one.
7. Installation is the reverse of removal. When the cylinder head surfaces are free and clean, apply beads of sealant to the cylinder head in the locations shown in the accompanying illustrations.
8. Install the six/eight nuts and seal washers. Uniformly tighten the nuts in several passes to 52 inch lbs. (6 Nm). Start the engine and inspect for oil leaks. Repair any leaks as necessary.

1MZ-FE Engine

♦ See Figures 5 thru 9

1. Drain and recycle the engine coolant.
2. Disconnect the radiator inlet hose.
3. Disconnect the throttle and accelerator cables.

4. Remove the air cleaner cap assembly.
5. Remove the V-bank cover. Use a 5mm hexagon wrench to loosen the nuts.
6. Label and remove all emission control valve hoses. Disconnect any wiring interfering with the valve cover removal.
7. Remove the air intake chamber. This will gain you access to the back valve cover.
8. Disconnect the engine wire from the left hand side, No. 3 timing belt cover, rear side and right hand side. Most of the wiring is secured by nuts and or bolts to the body of the vehicle.
9. Remove the ignition coils, make sure the place them in order on a table so not to mix them up.
10. Remove the 8 bolts retaining the valve covers and gasket.
   To install:
11. Clean the mating area of the valve cover and cylinder heads well. If necessary, scrape any left gasket from either surface.
12. Apply seal packing to the cylinder heads and place new gaskets into position.
13. Attach the valve covers. Uniformly tighten the bolts in several passes to 69 inch lbs. (8 Nm).
14. The remainder of installation is the reverse of removal. Tighten each component to specifications.

Rocker Arms

REMOVAL & INSTALLATION

♦ See Figure 10

The 2S-ELC engine is the only engine in the Camry family that uses rocker arms to activate the valves. Valve operation in on all other engines is accomplished directly by the camshaft and accessory valve components.
1. Disconnect the negative battery cable.
2. Remove the cylinder head cover and gasket.
3. Remove the rocker arms and lash adjusters retainers. Label each rocker

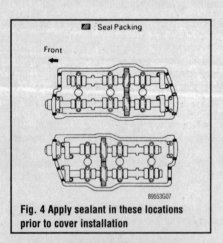

Fig. 4 Apply sealant in these locations prior to cover installation

Fig. 5 To remove the valve cover, remove the bolts and set them aside . . .

Fig. 6 . . . then remove the cover from the cylinder head

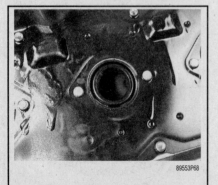

Fig. 7 Inspect the seals in the top of the valve cover and replace if necessary

Fig. 8 Remove the gasket from the edge of the cover and discard

Fig. 9 Inspect the cylinder head end seals. Replace with new packing material if necessary

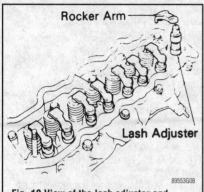

Fig. 10 View of the lash adjuster and rocker arm assembly locations

Fig. 11 Remove the thermostat housing from the engine with the coolant temperature sensor—1MZ-FE engine

Fig. 12 Removing the thermostat from the engine—1MZ-FE engine

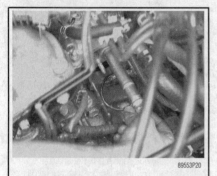

Fig. 13 Always discard the old O-ring from the thermostat, if reusing the old component

Fig. 14 Always replace the thermostat with the correct temperature specification

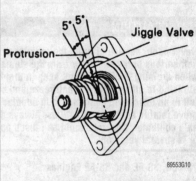

Fig. 15 Line-up the jiggle valve with the protrusion on the housing—5S-FE engine

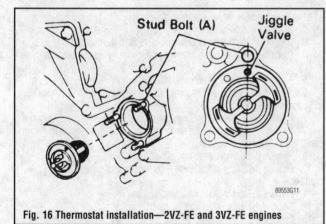

Fig. 16 Thermostat installation—2VZ-FE and 3VZ-FE engines

arm/lash adjuster pair as it is removed so that they are installed in their original positions.

4. Installation is the reverse of removal. Install the rocker arms and lash adjuster in the same order as they were removed.

Thermostat

On both diesel and gasoline engines, the thermostat is located in the water inlet housing connected to the lower radiator hose.

REMOVAL & INSTALLATION

✳✳ CAUTION

Never open, service or drain the radiator or cooling system when hot; serious burns can occur from the steam and hot coolant. Also, when draining engine coolant, keep in mind that cats and dogs are attracted to ethylene glycol antifreeze and could drink any that is left in an uncovered container or in puddles on the ground. This will prove fatal in sufficient quantities. Always drain coolant into a sealable container. Coolant should be reused unless it is contaminated or is several years old.

▶ See Figures 11 thru 16

1. Position a suitable drain pan under the radiator drain cock and drain the cooling system.
2. On the 1MZ-FE engine, remove the air cleaner cap assembly. Be sure to label all wiring disconnected.
3. Disconnect the water temperature switch harness from the water inlet housing (except 5S-FE engines).
4. Remove the oil filter on 5S-FE engines. On the 1MZ-FE engines, remove the heater hose covering the housing.
5. Loosen the hose clamp and disconnect the lower radiator hose from the water inlet housing.
6. Remove the two nuts from the water inlet housing and remove the housing from the water pump studs.
7. Remove the thermostat and rubber O-ring gasket from the water inlet housing.
   To install:
8. Make sure all the gasket surfaces are clean. Clean the inside of the inlet housing and the radiator hose connection with a rag.
9. Install the new rubber O-ring gasket onto the thermostat. On 2SE and 3S-FE engines, align the jiggle valve of the thermostat with the protrusion on the water inlet housing. On 5S-FE engines, align the jiggle valve with the upper side of the stud bolt. On 2VZ-FE and 3VZ-FE engines, align the jiggle valve with the stud bolt. Insert the thermostat into the housing.
10. Position the water inlet housing with the thermostat over the studs on the water pump and install the two nuts. Tighten the two nuts to 78 inch lbs. (9 Nm) on 4 cyl. engines, 2VZ-FE and 3VZ-FE; 14 ft. lbs. (20 Nm) and 69 inch lbs. (8 Nm) on 1MZ-FE engines.

➡**Don't forget to install a new O-ring onto the water inlet pipe. Apply soapy water to the O-ring prior to installation.**

11. Connect the lower radiator hose to the inlet housing and install the hose clamp. On the 3VZ-FE, tighten the bolt holding the water inlet hose to the alternator belt adjusting bar to 14 ft. lbs. (20 Nm). On the 1MZ-FE engine, tighten the bolt retaining the water inlet pipe to the cylinder head to 14 ft. lbs. (20 Nm).

12. Attach the water temperature switch connector.

13. On the 1MZ-FE engines, install the heater hose removed.

14. Install the oil filter and check the oil level if removed. Install the air cleaner cap assembly on the 1MZ-FE engines.

15. Fill the cooling system with a good brand of ethylene glycol based coolant.

16. Start the engine and inspect for leaks.

Intake Manifold

REMOVAL & INSTALLATION

✳ CAUTION

Never open, service or drain the radiator or cooling system when hot; serious burns can occur from the steam and hot coolant. Also, when draining engine coolant, keep in mind that cats and dogs are attracted to ethylene glycol antifreeze and could drink any that is left in an uncovered container or in puddles on the ground. This will prove fatal in sufficient quantities. Always drain coolant into a sealable container. Coolant should be reused unless it is contaminated or is several years old.

2S-ELC, 3S-FE and 5S-FE Engines

▶ **See Figure 17**

1. Disconnect the negative battery cable.

2. Position a suitable drain pan under the radiator drain cock and drain the cooling system.

3. Remove the accelerator cable return spring along with the cable and bracket from the throttle body.

4. Loosen the clamp and disconnect the air cleaner hose.

5. Disconnect the throttle position sensor harness. On 3S-FE engines, disconnect the Idle Speed Control (ISC) valve wiring also.

6. Disconnect, label and plug the following hoses:
- Two water by-pass hoses.
- PCV hoses from the throttle body.

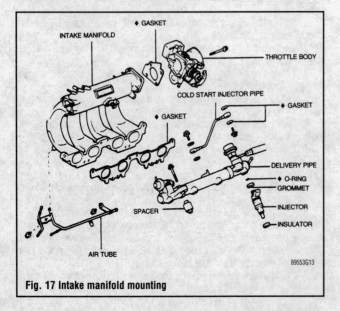

Fig. 17 Intake manifold mounting

- Inlet hose to the air valve.
- All emission vacuum hoses attached to the throttle body.
- Vacuum hose between the EGR valve and modulator.
- Power steering pump air hose (if equipped).

7. Loosen the union nut of the EGR pipe. Remove the two bolts, EGR valve modulator and gasket. Remove the bolt and the EGR valve.

8. Remove the bolts attaching the throttle body to the intake manifold. Remove the throttle body and gasket.

9. Remove the intake manifold stays and on the 5S-FE engine, the No. 1 air intake chamber.

10. Disconnect the vacuum sensing hose.

11. Remove the two nuts and seven bolts (1983–85 2S-ELC engines) or two nuts and six bolts (1986 2S-ELC and all 3S-FE and 5S-FE engines) that attach the intake manifold to the cylinder head.

12. On 5S-FE engines, remove the bolt, vacuum hose bracket and the main engine wire harness. On Calif. 5S-FE, remove the wire bracket.

13. Remove the intake manifold and gasket from the cylinder head.

To install:

14. Thoroughly clean the intake manifold and cylinder head surfaces. Using a machinist's straight edge and a feeler gauge, check the surface of the intake manifold for warpage. If the warpage is greater than 0.0118 inch (0.300mm), replace the intake manifold.

15. Place a new gasket onto the intake manifold and position the intake manifold onto the cylinder head with the proper amount of nuts and bolts. On 1983–85 2S-ELC engines tighten the nuts and bolts to 31 ft. lbs. (42 Nm). On all other engines, tighten the nuts and bolts to 14 ft. lbs. (19 Nm).

16. Install the intake manifold stays. Tighten the 12mm bolts to 14 ft. lbs. (19 Nm) and the 14mm bolts to 31 ft. lbs. (42 Nm).

17. The remainder of installation is the reverse of removal. Tighten each component to specifications.

18. Place a new gasket onto the throttle body and attach the unit to the intake manifold with the four bolts. Uniformly tighten the bolts in several passes to 14 ft. lbs. (19 Nm).

19. Start the engine and inspect for leaks.

2VZ-FE and 3VZ-FE Engines

1. Disconnect the negative battery cable.

2. Drain the engine coolant.

3. Disconnect the throttle/accelerator cable from the throttle body.

4. Disconnect the air cleaner hose at the air intake chamber and remove it.

5. Remove the V-bank cover on the 3VZ-FE engine.

6. Tag and disconnect all lines and hoses and then remove both the ISC valve and the throttle body.

7. Remove the EGR valve and vacuum modulator. Remove the distributor.

8. On the 3VZ-FE, remove the emission control valve set and then disconnect the left side engine harness.

9. Remove the cylinder head rear plate.

10. Remove the intake chamber stays, any wires and remove the air intake chamber.

11. Remove the fuel injection delivery pipe and the injectors.

12. Remove the water outlet and the by-pass outlet.

13. Remove the two bolts and the No. 2 idler pulley bracket stay. Remove the eight bolts and four nuts and then lift out the intake manifold.

To install:

14. Thoroughly clean the intake manifold and cylinder head surfaces. Using a machinist's straight edge and a feeler gauge, check the surface of the intake manifold for warpage. If the warpage is greater than 0.0039 inch (0.10mm), replace the intake manifold.

15. Place new gaskets onto the intake manifold and position the intake manifold between the cylinder heads. Tighten the nuts and bolts to 13 ft. lbs. (18 Nm). Tighten the No. 2 pulley bracket bolts to 13 ft. lbs. (18 Nm).

16. Install the water by-pass outlet and tighten the bolts to 14 ft. lbs. (20 Nm) on the 2VZ-FE, or 74 inch lbs. (8 Nm) on the 3VZ-FE. Tighten the water outlet to 74 inch lbs. (8 Nm).

17. Install the injectors and delivery pipe.

18. Install the air intake chamber and tighten the two bolts and two nuts to 32 ft. lbs. (43 Nm). Install the chamber stays and tighten the mounting bolts to 27 ft. lbs. (37 Nm) on the 2VZ-FE, or 29 ft. lbs. (39 Nm) on the 3VZ-FE.

19. Install the distributor. Install the emission control valve set on the 3VZ-FE and tighten the two bolts to 73 inch lbs. (8 Nm).

20. The remainder of installation is the reverse of removal. Tighten each component to specifications.

- EGR valve and modulator—13 ft. lbs. (18 Nm)
- Throttle body—14 ft. lbs. (19 Nm)
- ISC valve—9 ft. lbs. (13 Nm).

21. Fill the cooling system to the proper level and connect the negative battery cable. Start the engine and inspect for leaks.

1MZ-FE Engine

▶ See Figures 18 thru 24

1. Remove the battery and battery tray.
2. Drain and recycle the engine coolant.

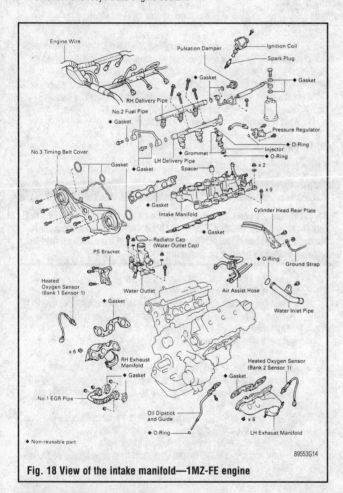

Fig. 18 View of the intake manifold—1MZ-FE engine

3. Disconnect the accelerator cable on automatic transaxles. Disconnect the throttle cable.

4. Remove the air cleaner cap assembly. Disconnect and label any wiring or hoses interfering with removal.

5. Remove the right side engine mounting stay.

6. Disonnect the radiator and heater hoses in the way of the intake manifold removal.

7. Remove the V-bank cover.

8. Disconnect all the vacuum hose and wiring for the emission control valve set and remove.

9. Unbolt and remove the air intake chamber. Label all wiring and hoses. Discard the old gasket.

10. Remove the EGR pipe discard the old gaskets.

11. Unbolt and remove the hydraulic motor pressure hose from the air intake chamber.

12. Disconnect, unbolt and label the engine wiring harnesses from the left side, right side, rear and No. 3 timing belt cover.

13. Disconnect the front exhaust pipe and remove if necessary.

14. Remove the timing belt, camshaft timing pulleys, No. 2 idler pulley and No. 3 timing belt cover.

Unbolt and remove the cylinder head rear plate.

15. Remove the two bolts, nuts and plate washers with the intake manifold. The delivery pipes with injectors will be attached to the manifold. Remove any other fuel related components such as the No. 2 fuel pipe and pulsation damper if needed.

16. Separate the delivery pipes from the intake manifold. Refer to Section 5.

17. Clean and inspect the intake manifold mating surfaces. Scrape all old gasket martial off.

To install:

18. Install the delivery pipes with injectors to the intake manifold. Make sure to place 4 spacers in position on the manifold. Temporarily install 4 bolts to retain the delivery pipes to the manifold. Inspect the injectors for smooth rotation. Refer to Section 5. Once the injectors are seated properly, tighten the delivery pipes retaining bolts to 7 ft. lbs. (10 Nm).

19. Install the No. 2 fuel pipe with union bolts and gaskets. Tighten the bolts to 24 ft. lbs. (32 Nm).

20. Install the No. 1 fuel pipe with pulsation damper, 4 new gaskets and the bolt, tighten the damper to 35 ft. lbs. (32 Nm) and the bolt to 11 ft. lbs. (15 Nm).

21. Install the fuel pressure regulator if removed, refer to Section 5.

22. Attach the intake manifold and tighten the nine retaining bolts and two nuts in a crisscross pattern to 11 ft. lbs. (15 Nm). Make sure the gasket is in place properly prior to tightening.

23. The remainder of installation is the reverse of removal. Tighten each component to specifications.

24. Tighten the air intake chamber bolts and nuts to 32 ft. lbs. (43 Nm), the EGR pipe nuts to 9 ft. lbs. (12 Nm), the emission control valve set to 69 inch lbs. (8 Nm).

25. Fill the cooling system to the proper level and connect the negative battery cable.

26. Start the engine and inspect for leaks.

Fig. 19 View of the intake manifold prior to component removal

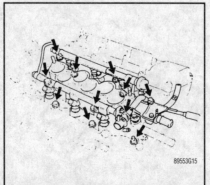

Fig. 20 Remove these bolts retaining the intake manifold—1MZ-FE engine

Fig. 21 Remove the manifold gasket . . .

Fig. 22 . . . then scrape all remaining materials from the mating surfaces

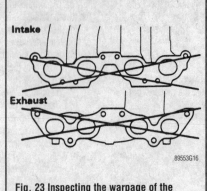

Fig. 23 Inspecting the warpage of the intake and exhaust manifolds

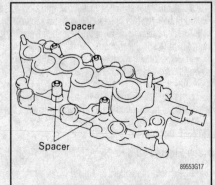

Fig. 24 Place the 4 spacers correctly into position on the intake manifold

Exhaust Manifold

REMOVAL & INSTALLATION

2S-ELC Engines

❄❄ CAUTION

Be careful when working on or near the catalytic converter. External temperatures can reach 1,500°F (816°C) and more causing severe burns. Removal and installation of the exhaust manifold should be accomplished only on a cold engine.

1. Disconnect the negative battery cable.
2. Raise the front of the vehicle and support safely.
3. Disconnect the oxygen sensor wiring (USA only). The oxygen sensor is located in the exhaust manifold.
4. Loosen the front and rear flange bolts of the catalytic converter so that they can be turned by hand (there are two nuts and bolts per flange).
5. Support the catalytic converter and disconnect the exhaust pipe by removing the loosened flange bolts and nuts. Remove the flange gaskets and set them aside.
6. Remove the exhaust pipe stay bolts from the cylinder block.
7. Remove the three nuts from the exhaust manifold flange.
8. Disconnect the exhaust pipe from the manifold and remove the two exhaust manifold gaskets. You may have to "coax" the manifold from the block with a few sharp blows from a heavy rubber mallet. Remove the two exhaust manifold gaskets.

❄❄ WARNING

When removing the exhaust manifold, be careful not to damage the oxygen sensor.

9. With a brush and solvent, thoroughly clean the surfaces of the exhaust manifold and cylinder block to remove any carbon or gasket material residue. While you are in the area, run a wire brush across the converter flange also. If the converter flange gaskets are damaged, replace them with new ones.
10. Installation is the reverse of removal. Tighten the manifold nuts to 31 ft. lbs. (42 Nm).
11. Start the engine and inspect for exhaust leaks.

3S-FE Engines

▶ See Figures 25, 26 and 27

❄❄ CAUTION

Be careful when working on or near the catalytic converter. External temperatures can reach 1,500°F (816°C) and more causing severe burns. Removal and installation of the exhaust manifold should be accomplished only on a cold engine.

1. Raise the front of the vehicle and support safely.
2. Disconnect the oxygen sensor wiring.
3. Loosen the bolt and disconnect the clamp from the catalytic converter bracket. Remove the nuts and disconnect the exhaust pipe from the catalytic converter. Remove the gasket and discard it.
4. Remove the upper manifold heat insulator by removing the six retaining bolts.
5. Remove the six nuts and lower the exhaust manifold and catalytic converter assembly. Discard the nuts and replace with new.
6. Disconnect the catalytic converter stay by removing the two bolts and two nuts.
7. To separate the exhaust manifold from the converter, proceed as follows:
   a. Unbolt the five lower manifold heat insulator bolts.
   b. Remove the catalytic converter heat insulator bolts.
   c. Unbolt and separate the exhaust manifold from the catalytic converter.
   d. Remove the gasket, retainer and cushion.

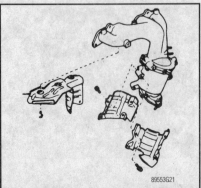

Fig. 25 Exploded view of the converter heat insulators from the exhaust manifold

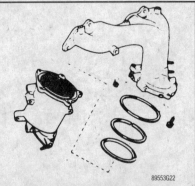

Fig. 26 Exploded view of the catalytic converter from the exhaust manifold

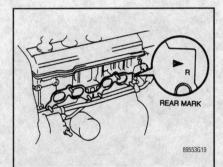

Fig. 27 Place the new gasket onto the engine with the letter R facing towards the back as shown for the intake manifold

8. Thoroughly clean the exhaust manifold and cylinder block to remove any carbon or gasket material deposits. Replace the two exhaust manifold gaskets, catalytic converter gasket, retainer and cushion.

To install:

9. Attach the two converter heat insulators with the eight bolts. Place the new cushion, retainer and gasket on the converter. Position the converter onto the exhaust manifold and install the three bolts and two nuts. Tighten the nuts and bolts to 22 ft. lbs. (29 Nm).

10. Place a new gasket on the engine so that the **R** mark is facing the back (not all models will have this mark). If the gasket is not installed properly, it will not seal.

11. Support the exhaust manifold and catalytic converter assembly by hand and guide the assembly over the mounting studs. Install the six new nuts and tighten them to 31 ft. lbs. (41 Nm) on 1987–88 models , or 37 ft. lbs. (48 Nm) on 1989–91 models.

12. Install the converter stay with the two bolts and two nuts and tighten to 31 ft. lbs. (41 Nm).

13. Install the manifold upper heat insulator with the six bolts. Install and secure all remaining components.

14. Start the engine and inspect for leaks.

5S-FE Engines

▶ **See Figures 28 and 29**

1. Raise the front of the vehicle and support safely.
2. Disconnect the oxygen sensor wiring.
3. Loosen the two bolts and disconnect the front exhaust pipe bracket. Disconnect the exhaust pipe from the catalytic converter. Remove the gasket and discard it.
4. On models except California perform the following:
   a. Remove the upper manifold heat insulator by removing the six retaining bolts.
   b. Remove the two manifold stays.
   c. Remove the six nuts and lower the exhaust manifold. Discard the nuts and replace with new ones.
   d. Remove the four bolts and lift off the lower heat insulator.
5. On California models perform the following:
   a. Remove the upper manifold heat insulator by removing the four retaining bolts.
   b. Remove the two manifold stays.
   c. Remove the six nuts and lower the exhaust manifold and catalytic converter assembly. Discard the nuts and replace with new ones.
6. To separate the exhaust manifold from the converter, proceed as follows:
   a. Unbolt the lower manifold heat insulator (three bolts).
   b. Unbolt the two catalytic converter heat insulators (eight bolts).
   c. Unbolt and separate the exhaust manifold from the catalytic converter (three bolts and two nuts).
   d. Remove the gasket, retainer and cushion.
7. Thoroughly clean the exhaust manifold and cylinder block to remove

any carbon or gasket material deposits. Replace the exhaust manifold gaskets, catalytic converter gasket, retainer and cushion.

To install:

8. To assemble the exhaust manifold to the converter on California models, attach these components in this order:
   a. Three-way catalytic converter
   b. Cushion
   c. Retainier
   d. Gasket
   e. Exhaust manifold
   f. Bolts and nuts; tighten the nuts to 22 ft. lbs. (29 Nm).
   g. Heat insulators
   h. Eight bolts
   i. Manifold lower heat insulator
   j. Three bolts
9. For California models, install a new gasket, the exhaust manifold and catalytic converter assembly with the six nuts. Uniformly tighten the nuts in several passes to 36 ft. lbs. (49 Nm).
   a. Install the manifold stay with the bolt and nut and tighten to 31 ft. lbs. (42 Nm). Install the No. 1 manifold stay and tighten to 31 ft. lbs. (42 Nm).
   b. Install the manifold upper heat insulator with the four bolts and attach the two oxygen sensor wiring harnesses.
10. On non-California models perform the following:
    a. Install the lower heat insulator with the four bolts securely.
    b. Install a new gasket and attach the exhaust manifold with six new nuts; uniformly tighten them to 36 ft. lbs. (49 Nm).
    c. Attach the manifold stay with the bolt and nut and tighten to 31 ft. lbs. (42 Nm).
    d. Attach the No. 1 manifold stay and tighten that to 31 ft. lbs. (42 Nm).
    e. Attach the manifold upper heat insulator with six new bolts and tighten them securely. Connect the oxygen sensor wiring.
11. The remainder of installation is the reverse of removal. Tighten each component to specifications.

2VZ-FE Engines

1. Raise the car, support it on safety stands and then remove the engine under covers.
2. Remove the lower suspension crossmember. Remove the two front exhaust pipe stay bolts. Disconnect the front pipe from the center pipe and remove the gasket. Loosen the three nuts and then remove the front pipe.
3. Remove the six nuts and two bolts and lift out the upper crossover pipe and its gaskets.
4. Disconnect the O_2 sensor at the right side manifold. Remove the three mounting nuts and lift off the outside heat insulator.
5. Remove the six nuts and lift off the right side manifold and gasket. Remove the bolt and pull off the inner insulator.
6. Loosen the two nuts and lift off the left side heat insulator. Remove the six nuts and lift off the left side manifold and gaskets.

To install:

7. Scrape the mating surfaces of all old gasket material.
8. Install the right inner heat insulator and then position the manifold with a new gasket. Tighten the nuts to 29 ft. lbs. (39 Nm). Install the outer insulator.

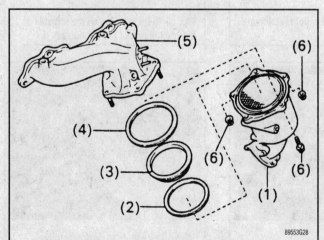

89553G28

Fig. 28 Assemble the exhaust manifold components in this order— 5S-FE California engines

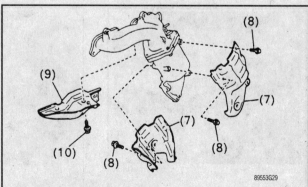

89553G29

Fig. 29 Assemble the exhaust manifold components in this order— 5S-FE California engines continued

9. Use a new gasket and install the left manifold. Tighten the nuts to 29 ft. lbs. (39 Nm). Install the outer insulator.

10. The remainder of installation is the reverse of removal. Tighten each component to specifications.

3VZ-FE Engines

1. Raise the car, support it on safety stands and then remove the engine under covers.

2. Remove the two front exhaust pipe stay bolts. Disconnect the front pipe from the center pipe and remove the gasket. Loosen the three nuts and then remove the front pipe.

3. Disconnect the O$_2$sensor at the right side manifold. Remove the three mounting nuts and lift off the outside heat insulator.

4. Remove the six nuts and lift off the right side manifold and gasket.

5. Loosen the two nuts and bolt and lift off the left side heat insulator. Remove the six nuts and lift off the left side manifold and gaskets.

To install:

6. Scrape the mating surfaces of all old gasket material.

7. Install the right manifold with a new gasket. Tighten the nuts to 29 ft. lbs. (39 Nm). Install the outer insulator.

8. Use a new gasket and install the left manifold. Tighten the nuts to 29 ft. lbs. (39 Nm). Install the outer insulator.

9. The remainder of installation is the reverse of removal. Tighten each component to specifications.

1MZ-FE Engines

FRONT MANIFOLD

▶ See Figures 30 thru 38

➡ Removing the oil filter helps gain access to a lower bolt in the front exhaust manifold.

Fig. 30 Front exhaust manifold-to-front pipe mounting nut locations

Fig. 31 Rear exhaust manifold-to-front pipe mounting

Fig. 32 Lowering the exhaust pipe from the front and rear exhaust manifolds

Fig. 33 Always discard old exhaust gaskets

Fig. 34 Front exhaust manifold retaining nut locations

Fig. 35 There is a stay on the left side of the front manifold to be removed

Fig. 36 Remove the exhaust manifold and discard the old gasket

Fig. 37 Always scrape old materials from the cylinder head

Fig. 38 . . . and manifold prior to installation

1. Disconnect the negative battery cable from the battery.
2. Raise and safely support the vehicle.
3. Remove the engine undercovers from the vehicle.
4. From below the engine, disconnect the front exhaust pipe from the exhaust manifolds by removing the nuts.

➡**Check for access to some of the manifold lower bolts, if so remove any possible.**

5. Lower the vehicle to access the upper manifold bolts.
6. Disconnect and remove the heated oxygen sensor.
7. Remove the exhaust manifold stay by removing the bolt and nut.
8. Remove the remaining nuts to the exhaust manifold and separate the exhaust manifold from the engine.
9. Installation is the reverse of removal. Using a new gasket, install the exhaust manifold to the engine and install the six nuts. Uniformly tighten the bolts to 36 ft. lbs. (49 Nm).
10. Install exhaust manifold stay and install the bolt and nut. Tighten the bolt and nut to 15 ft. lbs. (20 Nm).

REAR MANIFOLD

1. Disconnect the negative battery cable from the battery.
2. Raise and safely support the vehicle.
3. Remove the engine undercovers from the vehicle.
4. From below the engine, disconnect the front exhaust pipe from both exhaust manifolds.
5. Remove the EGR pipe from the rear exhaust manifold by removing four nuts.
6. Disconnect the heated oxygen sensor wiring to the right exhaust manifold.
7. Remove the exhaust manifold stay by removing the bolt and nut.
8. Remove the six nuts to the exhaust manifold and separate the exhaust manifold from the engine.
9. Installation is the reverse of removal. Using a new gasket, install the exhaust manifold to the engine and install the six nuts. Uniformly tighten and then tighten the bolts to 36 ft. lbs. (49 Nm).

10. Install the exhaust manifold stay and install the bolt and nut. Tighten the bolt and nut to 15 ft. lbs. (20 Nm).

Air Intake Chamber

REMOVAL & INSTALLATION

▶ **See Figures 39 thru 46**

This procedure applies to 1MZ-FE engines only.
1. Remove the battery and battery tray.
2. Drain and recycle the engine coolant.
3. Disconnect the accelerator cable on automatic transaxles. Disconnect the throttle cable.
4. Remove the air cleaner cap assembly. Disconnect and label any wiring or hoses interfering with removal.
5. Remove the V-bank cover.
6. Disconnect the heater hoses in the way of the intake manifold removal.
7. Disconnect all the vacuum hose and wiring for the emission control valve set and remove.
8. Disconnect the following hoses for the air intake chamber:
    a. Brake booster vacuum hose
    b. PCV hose
    c. Air control valve vacuum hose
9. Unplug the DLC1 connector. Remove the nut and disconnect the 2 ground straps.
10. Unbolt and remove the hydraulic motor pressure hose from the air intake chamber.
11. Remove the bolt and disconnect the ground strap.
12. Disconnect the right side oxygen sensor wiring clamp from the power steering tube. Remove the two nuts and disconnect the tube.
13. Remove the 2 bolts and the No. 1 engine hanger. Remove the air intake chamber stay.
14. Remove the EGR pipe discard the old gaskets.

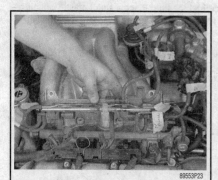

Fig. 39 Label and remove the emission control valve set

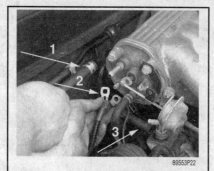

Fig. 40 Brake booster vacuum line, (1), ground straps (2) and PCV valve hose (3) removal component locations

Fig. 41 Remove the rear engine stay mounted behind the throttle body

Fig. 42 The hydraulic fan pressure hose (2) must be removed to separate the ground strap (1) in the rear of the air intake chamber

Fig. 43 Remove the two hex head bolts and the two regular nuts from the air intake chamber

Fig. 44 Lift the air intake chamber off the intake manifold

Fig. 45 Never reuse old gaskets

Fig. 46 Once the air intake chamber is removed, other components may be extracted

15. Disconnect the throttle position sensor wiring, IAC valve connector, EGR temperature sensor and A/C idle-up connector. Disconnect the 2 vacuum hoses from the throttle vacuum valve and the vacuum hose form the cylinder head rear plate. Disconnect the vacuum hose form the charcoal canister.

16. Dsiconnect the 2 water bypass hoses and the air assist hose.

17. Using an 8mm hexagon wrench, remove the 2 bolts, 2 nuts and the air intake chamber and gasket.

18. Clean and inspect the air intake chamber mating surfaces. Scrape all old gasket material off.

To install:

19. Install a new gasket and the air intake chamber with the 2 bolts and nuts. Tighten them to 32 ft. lbs. (43 Nm). Connect the water and vacuum hoses along with wiring for the air intake chamber.

20. Install any remaining components, remember to use all new gaskets.

21. Tighten the following components:
- Air intake chamber bolts and nuts to 32 ft. lbs. (43 Nm)
- EGR pipe nuts to 9 ft. lbs. (12 Nm)
- Emission control valve set to 69 inch lbs. (8 Nm)
- No. 1 engine hanger to 19 ft. lbs. (39 Nm)
- Air intake chamber stay to 14 ft. lbs. (20 Nm)

22. The remainder of installation is the reverse of removal. Tighten each component to specifications.

Radiator

REMOVAL & INSTALLATION

✲✲ CAUTION

Never open, service or drain the radiator or cooling system when hot; serious burns can occur from the steam and hot coolant. Also, when draining engine coolant, keep in mind that cats and dogs are attracted to ethylene glycol antifreeze and could drink any that is left in an uncovered container or in puddles on the ground. This will prove fatal in sufficient quantities. Always drain coolant into a sealable container. Coolant should be reused unless it is contaminated or is several years old.

2S-ELC, 3S-FE, 5S-FE and 2VZ-FE Engines

♦ See Figure 47

1. Position a suitable drain pan under the radiator and drain the cooling system by opening the radiator draincock.

2. Disconnect the coolant reservoir hose.

3. Remove the battery. On 2VZ-FE models, remove the ignition coil/ignition assembly. On 5S-FE models, remove the cruise control actuator cover.

4. Unfasten the engine and air conditioning cooling fan motor connectors. On the 5S-FE, disconnect the water temperature switch at the fan shroud.

5. Disconnect the upper and lower hoses from the radiator.

6. Unbolt and remove the engine electric cooling fan assembly (shroud and motor).

7. On vehicles equipped with air conditioning, remove the air conditioning electric cooling fan assembly (shroud and motor).

8. On vehicles equipped with automatic transaxle, disconnect the two cooler hoses from the cooler pipes at the bottom of the radiator.

➡ **Take care when disconnecting the cooler lines because some of the transmission oil will leak from the line. Place a small plastic container under the lines to collect the oil and plug each connection to prevent further leakage.**

9. Support the radiator by hand and remove the two bolts and radiator supports.

10. Remove the radiator from the vehicle.

11. Installation is the reverse of removal. Secure the radiator in position and support it by hand. Install the two radiator supports with bolts. Tighten the bolts to 9 ft. lbs. (13 Nm). Make sure that the rubber cushion of each support is not depressed or crimped.

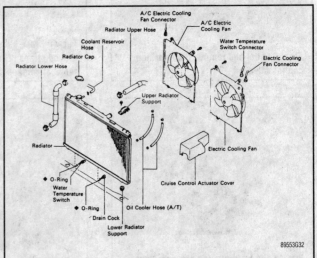

Fig. 47 Exploded view of the radiator and cooling fans—5S-FE engine

12. Start the engine and inspect for leaks. Remember to check the transmission fluid level on cars with automatic transaxles. Add fluid as required.

1MZ-FE and 3VZ-FE Engines

▶ **See Figures 48, 49, 50, 51 and 52**

1. Disconnect the cable at the negative battery terminal.

✳✳ CAUTION

On models with an air bag, wait at least 90 seconds from the time that the ignition switch is turned to the LOCK position and the battery is disconnected before performing any further work.

2. Drain the engine coolant into a suitable container.
3. Remove the cruise control actuator cover on the 3VZ-FE and wire clamp on the 1MZ-FE engine.
4. Remove the union bolt and gasket and then disconnect the pressure line from the hydraulic fan motor. You may lose some hydraulic fluid here, so have a container ready.
5. Disconnect the upper radiator hose and the coolant reservoir hose. Disconnect the hydraulic return hose.
6. Remove the engine under cover.
7. Disconnect the lower radiator hose and the oil cooler lines.
8. On the Canadian 1MZ-FE engines, remove the No. 7 relay block.
9. Remove the two bolts and the upper supports and lift out the radiator/fan assembly. Remove the bolts and separate the fan from the radiator.
10. Installation is the reverse of removal. Secure the fan assembly to the radiator and then install the radiator. Tighten the support bolts to 9 ft. lbs. (13 Nm). Be sure that the rubber support cushions are not pinched.
11. Fill the engine with coolant, connect the battery, start the car and check for leaks.

BLEEDING

▶ **See Figures 53, 54 and 55**

This procedure applies to 1MZ-FE and 3VZ-FE engines only.
1. Check the level in the reservoir tank. If low add ATF DEXRON II.

➡**Check that the level is within the HOT level on the reservoir tank. If the fluid is cold, check that the level is in the COLD level on the tank.**

2. Using a jumper wire connect terminals OP1 and E1 of the DLC1.

➡**When the terminals OP1 and E1 are connected, the circuit of the ECT sensor is grounded, fixing the coolant fan speed at approximately 1100 rpm.**

3. Start the engine without depressing the accelerator pedal.
4. Leave the engine running for several seconds.
5. Check that there is no foaming and emulsification of the fluid in the reservoir tank.
6. Remove the jumper wire from the DLC1.

89553P07

Fig. 48 Remove the cruise control wire clamp

89553P08

Fig. 49 Remove the union bolt and gasket from the pressure line for the hydraulic fan motor

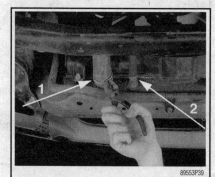

89553P39

Fig. 50 Disconnect the lower radiator hose (1) and the oil cooler lines (2)

89553P10

Fig. 51 Remove the two upper supports retaining the radiator

89553P11

Fig. 52 Extract the radiator from the engine compartment

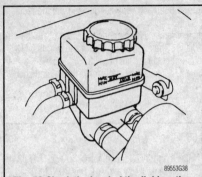

Fig. 53 Check the level of the fluid on the side of the reservoir—1MZ-FE and 3VZ-FE engines

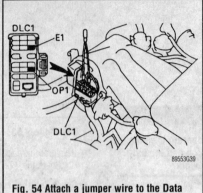

Fig. 54 Attach a jumper wire to the Data Link Connector 1 (DLC1)

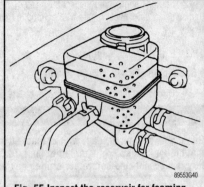

Fig. 55 Inspect the reservoir for foaming, there should be NONE

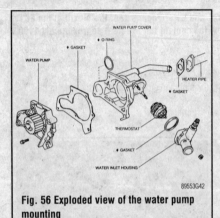

Fig. 56 Exploded view of the water pump mounting

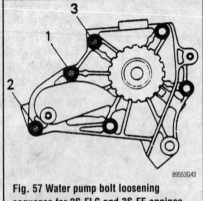

Fig. 57 Water pump bolt loosening sequence for 2S-ELC and 3S-FE engines

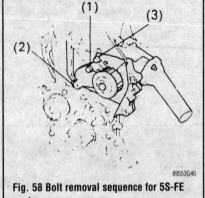

Fig. 58 Bolt removal sequence for 5S-FE engines

Water Pump

REMOVAL & INSTALLATION

❊❊ CAUTION

Never open, service or drain the radiator or cooling system when hot; serious burns can occur from the steam and hot coolant. Also, when draining engine coolant, keep in mind that cats and dogs are attracted to ethylene glycol antifreeze and could drink any that is left in an uncovered container or in puddles on the ground. This will prove fatal in sufficient quantities. Always drain coolant into a sealable container. Coolant should be reused unless it is contaminated or is several years old.

2S-ELC Engines

♦ **See Figures 56 and 57**

1. Drain the cooling system.
2. Remove the timing belt as described in this section.
3. Remove the alternator adjusting bar.
4. Disconnect the lower radiator hose from the water inlet housing.
5. Disconnect the water temperature switch from the water inlet housing.
6. Disconnect the water by-pass hose from the water pump.
7. Remove the two heater pipe clamp bolt. Remove the two nuts and heater pipe with gasket. Replace the gasket.
8. Loosen the three water pump mounting bolts in the indicated sequence.
9. Remove the water pump and O-ring. If the water pump is stubborn, tap it a few times with a rubber mallet.
10. Installation is the reverse of removal. Make sure all the water pump and engine contact surfaces are clean and install the new O-ring into the pump cover groove.

11. Install the water pump with the three bolts. Tighten the bolts in sequence to 82 inch lbs. (9 Nm).
12. Fill the cooling system to the proper level with a good brand of ethylene glycol based coolant. Start the engine and inspect for leaks.

3S-FE Engines

♦ **See Figure 57**

1. Drain the cooling system.
2. Disconnect the water temperature switch connector from the water inlet housing.
3. Disconnect the lower radiator hose from the water inlet housing.
4. Remove the timing belt and timing belt pulleys as described in this section.
5. Remove the two nuts attaching the water by-pass pipe to the water pump cover.
6. Remove the three water pump-to-engine attaching bolts.
7. Pull the water pump and the water pump cover out from the engine.
8. Remove the two O-rings and gasket. Discard them and replace with new.
9. Installation is the reverse of removal. Secure the water pump onto the engine and install the three bolts. Tighten the bolts in an alternate pattern to 82 inch lbs. (9 Nm). Install the by-pass pipe attaching nuts and tighten them to 82 inch lbs. (9 Nm) also.
10. Fill the cooling system to the proper level with coolant.
11. Start the engine and check for leaks.

5S-FE Engine

♦ **See Figure 58**

1. Drain the engine coolant.
2. Remove the timing belt.
3. Remove the No. 1 idler pulley and tension spring. Remove the No. 2 idler pulley.
4. Disconnect the lower radiator hose at the water inlet.
5. Remove the alternator belt adjusting bar.

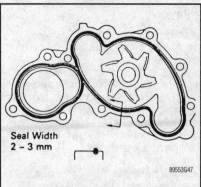

Fig. 59 Apply sealant on the surface of the water pump as shown

Fig. 60 Unbolt the No. 3 timing belt cover from the engine

Fig. 61 Water pump mounting bolt and nut locations

Fig. 62 Pull the water pump from the engine and remove it from the vehicle

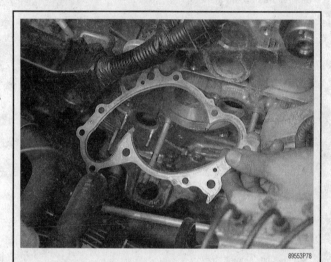

Fig. 63 Always discard the old gasket

6. Loosen the two nuts and disconnect the water by-pass pipe.

7. Remove the three pump mounting bolts in sequence (middle, top, bottom) and then pull out the water pump and cover. Remove the gasket and two O-rings.

To install:

8. Replace the two O-rings and gasket with new ones, coat the by-pass O-ring with soapy water and then connect the pump cover to the by-pass pipe. Do not install the nuts yet!

9. With the pump loosely connected to the pipe, install the pump and tighten the three bolts to 82 inch lbs. (9 Nm), in sequence (top, bottom, middle). Install the two by-pass pipe nuts and tighten them to 78 inch lbs. (9 Nm).

10. The remainder of installation is the reverse of removal. Tighten each component to specifications.

2VZ-FE and 3VZ-FE Engines

▶ See Figure 59

1. Drain the engine coolant.
2. Disconnect the lower radiator hose at the water inlet.
3. Disconnect the timing belt from the water pump pulley.
4. Remove the bolt holding the inlet pipe to the alternator belt adjusting bar and then remove the inlet pipe and O-ring.
5. Remove the water inlet and thermostat.
6. Remove the seven bolts and then pry off the water pump.

To install:

7. Scrape any remaining gasket material off the pump mating surface. Apply a 0.08–0.12 inch (2–3mm) bead of sealant to the groove in the pump and then install the pump. Tighten the bolts to 14 ft. lbs. (20 Nm).

8. The remainder of installation is the reverse of removal. Tighten each component to specifications. Connect the radiator hose and fill the engine with coolant.

1MZ-FE Engine

▶ See Figures 60, 61, 62 and 63

1. Drain the engine coolant.
2. Remove the timing belt.
3. Mark the left and right camshaft pulleys with a touch of paint. Using a spanner wrench, remove the bolts to the right and left camshaft pulleys. Separate the pulleys from the engine. Be sure not to mix up the pulleys.
4. Remove the No. 2 idler pulley by removing the bolt.
5. Disconnect the three clamps and engine wire from the rear timing belt cover.
6. Remove the six bolts holding the No. 3 timing belt cover to the engine block.
7. Remove the bolts and nuts to the extract the water pump.
8. Raise the engine slightly and remove the water pump and the gasket from the engine.

To install:

9. Check that the water pump turns smoothly. Also check the air hole for coolant leakage.

10. Using a new gasket, apply liquid sealer to the gasket, water pump and engine block.

11. Install the gasket and pump to the engine and install the four bolts and two nuts. Tighten the nuts and bolts to 53 inch lbs. (6 Nm).

12. The remainder of installation is the reverse of removal. Tighten each component to specifications.
   • Rear timing belt cover—74 inch lbs. (9 Nm).
   • No. 2 idler pulley—32 ft. lbs. (43 Nm)

13. Fill the engine coolant. Connect the negative battery cable to the battery and start the engine.

14. Top off the engine coolant and check for leaks.

Cylinder Head

REMOVAL & INSTALLATION

❋❋ CAUTION

When draining the coolant, keep in mind that cats and dogs are attracted by ethylene glycol antifreeze, and are quite likely to drink any that is left in an uncovered container or in puddles on the ground. This will prove fatal in sufficient quantity. Always drain the coolant into a sealable container. Coolant should be reused unless it is contaminated or several years old.

2S-ELC Engine

▶ See Figures 64, 65 and 66

1. Disconnect the negative battery cable.
2. Drain the cooling system.
3. On vehicles equipped with AT, disconnect the cable and bracket from the throttle body.
4. Disconnect the accelerator cable from the throttle body.
5. Remove the air pipe and hoses.
6. Disconnect and label the following wires and electrical wiring.
- Ground strap connector
- IIA connector
- Igniter connector (USA only)
- Water temperature sensor gauge connector
- Idle-up VSV connector (USA) only
- Water temperature switch connector (automatic transmission only)
- Alternator terminal wiring and connector
7. Disconnect and label the following vacuum hoses:
- Air conditioning idle-up vacuum hoses
- Cruise control actuator vacuum hose
- Brake booster vacuum hose from the air intake manifold
- Vacuum hose to the charcoal canister
- Emission control hoses
8. Remove the vacuum pipe from the head cover.
9. Disconnect and label the following wires
- Oxygen sensor connector (USA only)
- Cold start injector time switch connector
- Injector connectors
- Throttle position sensor connector
- Air flow meter connector
- Check connector
- Solenoid resistor connector
- LH fender apron connectors
- Air valve connector
- Water temperature sensor connector
- Start injector time switch connector (normal)
- Engine ground strap

10. Pull the EFI harness to the right fender apron side.
11. Remove the alternator.
12. Remove the distributor assembly.
13. Remove the upper radiator hose and bypass hose, water outlet housing and the heater water outlet hose.
14. Disconnect the two air hoses from the fuel injection air valve.
15. Unbolt and remove the rear end housing with the air valve attached.
16. Remove the heater pipe by disconnecting the water by-pass and heater water inlet hoses and removing the two nuts with the gasket.
17. Disconnect the fuel line at the filter and the fuel return line at the return pipe. Collect all the excess fuel in a small plastic container.
18. Raise and support the vehicle on jackstands.
19. Drain the oil.
20. Disconnect the exhaust pipe at the manifold.
21. Disconnect the two power steering pump vacuum hoses.
22. Remove the intake manifold stay.
23. Lower the vehicle.
24. Remove the timing belt from the camshaft pulley.
25. Remove the No. 1 idler pulley and tension spring.
26. Remove the throttle body.
27. Disconnect the PCV hoses and remove the valve cover.
28. Unbolt and remove the camshaft housing using a small prybar positioned between the cylinder head and camshaft housing projections. Loosen the bolts gradually in the sequence shown.

❋❋ WARNING

If the bolts are loosened out of sequence, warpage could occur.

29. Remove the rocker arms and lash adjusters. Label each assembly as it is removed and keep all the assemblies together.
30. Loosen and remove the head bolts evenly, in three passes, in the order shown. Carefully lift the head from the engine and place it on wood blocks in a clean work area.
31. Remove the cylinder head gasket and purchase a new one (cylinder head gaskets must never be re-used). With a gasket scraper, remove all the old gasket material from the cylinder head and engine block surfaces.
To install:
32. Place the new cylinder head gasket onto the cylinder block. Place the cylinder head onto the gasket.
33. Coat the threads of the eighteen cylinder head bolts with clean engine oil and install the bolts into the cylinder head. Uniformly tighten the bolts in three passes to 15 ft. lbs. (20 Nm), 30 ft. lbs. (47 Nm), 47 ft. lbs. (64 Nm) using the sequence shown.
34. Install the rocker arms and lash adjusters in their original locations.
35. Install the camshaft housing by performing the following:
   a. Using a gasket scraper, thoroughly clean all the old packing material from the gasket surfaces and sealing grooves. Clean the surfaces again with a suitable cleaning solvent.
   b. Apply a bead of seal packing (No. 08826-00080 or equivalent) to the camshaft housing contact surface. Do not use to much sealant. The sealant hardens within 3 minutes after application. If the sealant hardens, it must be removed and reapplied.

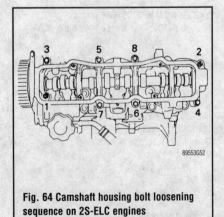

Fig. 64 Camshaft housing bolt loosening sequence on 2S-ELC engines

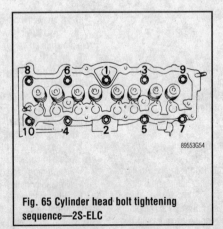

Fig. 65 Cylinder head bolt tightening sequence—2S-ELC

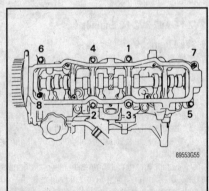

Fig. 66 Camshaft housing tightening sequence

c. Place the camshaft housing onto the cylinder head.

d. Install the camshaft housing bolts. Tighten the bolts in three passes to 11 ft. lbs. (16 Nm).

e. Install the vacuum idle-up pipe.

36. Install the valve cover with a new gasket. Connect the PCV hoses to the cover.

37. The remainder of installation is the reverse of removal. Tighten each component to specifications.

38. Fill the cooling system to the proper level. Connect the negative battery cable.

39. Start and warm up the engine. Inspect for leaks. Adjust the ignition timing and the idle speed.

40. Road test the vehicle and check for unusual noise, shock, slippage, correct shift points and smooth operation. Recheck the coolant and engine oil levels.

3S-FE and 5S-FE Engines

▶ See Figures 67, 68 and 69

1. Drain the cooling system.

2. On vehicles equipped with automatic transmission, disconnect the throttle cable and bracket from the throttle body.

3. Disconnect the accelerator cable and bracket from the throttle body and intake chamber.

4. On vehicles equipped with cruise control, remove the actuator and bracket (3S-FE).

5. Remove the air cleaner hose.

6. Remove the alternator.

7. Remove the oil pressure gauge, engine hangers and alternator upper bracket.

8. Loosen the lug nuts on the right wheel and raise and support the vehicle safely.

9. Remove the right tire and wheel assembly.

10. Remove the right under cover.

11. Remove the suspension lower crossmember (3S-FE).

12. Disconnect the exhaust pipe from the catalytic converter.

13. Separate the exhaust pipe from the catalytic converter.

14. Remove the distributor.

15. Disconnect the water temperature sender gauge connector, water temperature sensor connector, cold start injector time switch connector, upper radiator hose, water hoses, and the emission control vacuum hoses. Unbolt and remove the water outlet and gaskets.

16. Remove the water bypass pipe with O-rings and gasket.

17. Remove the EGR valve and vacuum modulator.

18. Remove the throttle body.

19. Remove the cold start injector pipe (3S-FE).

20. Disconnect the air chamber hose, throttle body air hose and power steering hoses (if equipped). Remove the air tube.

21. Remove the intake manifold stay and disconnect the vacuum sensing hose. Remove the intake manifold and gasket. Purchase a new gasket.

22. Remove the fuel delivery pipe and the injectors.

23. Remove the spark plugs.

24. Remove the camshaft timing pulley. Remove the No. 1 idler pulley and

tension spring. Remove the No. 3 timing belt cover. Properly support the timing belt so that meshing of the crankshaft timing pulley does not occur and the timing belt does not shift.

25. Remove the cylinder head cover. Label and arrange the grommets in order so that they can be reinstalled in the correct order. Remove the engine hangers, and the alternator bracket on the 5S-FE.

26. Remove the intake and exhaust camshafts as described in this section.

27. Loosen and remove the ten head bolts evenly, in three passes, in the order shown. Carefully lift the head from the engine and place it on wood blocks in a clean work area.

✳✳ WARNING

If the cylinder head bolts are loosened out of sequence, warpage or cracking could result.

28. Remove the cylinder head gasket and purchase a new one (cylinder head gaskets must never be re-used). With a gasket scraper, remove all the old gasket material from the cylinder head and engine block surfaces.

To install:

29. Place the new cylinder head gasket onto the cylinder block. Place the cylinder head onto the gasket.

30. Coat the threads of the ten cylinder head bolts with clean engine oil and install the bolts into the cylinder head. Uniformly tighten the bolts in three passes to 47 ft. lbs. (64 Nm) on 1986–88 models, or 36 ft. lbs. (49 Nm) on 1989–96 models, using the sequence shown. If any of the bolts does not meet the torque, replace it. On 1989–96 models, mark the forward edge of each bolt with paint and then retighten each bolt an additional 90°. Check that each painted mark is now at a 90° angle to the front.

31. The remainder of installation is the reverse of removal. Tighten each component to specifications.

32. Fill the cooling system to the proper level with a good brand of ethylene glycol coolant.

33. Start the engine and check for leaks. Adjust the valves and the ignition timing.

34. Road test the vehicle and check for unusual noise, shock, slippage, correct shift points and smooth operation. Recheck the coolant and engine oil levels.

2VZ-FE and 3VZ-FE Engines

▶ See Figures 70, 71 and 72

1. Drain the cooling system.

2. On vehicles equipped with automatic transmission, disconnect the throttle cable and bracket from the throttle body.

3. Disconnect the accelerator cable and bracket from the throttle body and intake chamber.

4. On vehicles equipped with cruise control, remove the actuator, vacuum pump and bracket (2VZ-FE).

5. Remove the air cleaner hose.

6. Remove the alternator.

7. Remove the oil pressure gauge, engine hangers and alternator upper bracket.

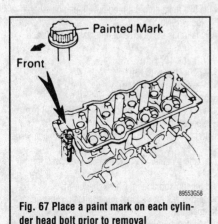

Fig. 67 Place a paint mark on each cylinder head bolt prior to removal

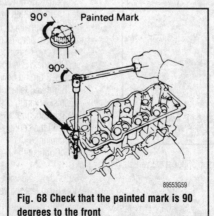

Fig. 68 Check that the painted mark is 90 degrees to the front

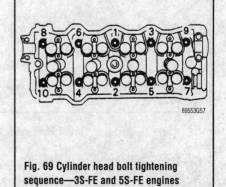

Fig. 69 Cylinder head bolt tightening sequence—3S-FE and 5S-FE engines

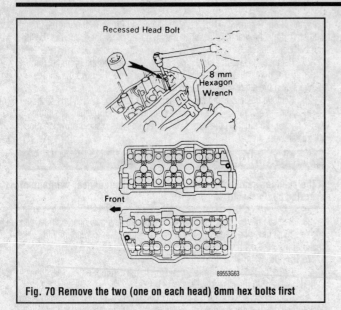

Fig. 70 Remove the two (one on each head) 8mm hex bolts first

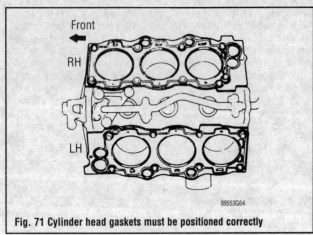

Fig. 71 Cylinder head gaskets must be positioned correctly

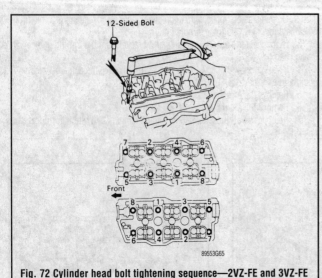

Fig. 72 Cylinder head bolt tightening sequence—2VZ-FE and 3VZ-FE engines

8. Loosen the lug nuts on the right wheel and raise and support the vehicle safely.

9. Remove the right tire and wheel assembly.

10. Remove the right under cover.

11. Remove the suspension lower crossmember (2VZ-FE).

12. Disconnect the exhaust pipe from the catalytic converter.

13. Separate the exhaust pipe from the catalytic converter.

14. Remove the distributor. Remove the V-bank cover on the 3VZ-FE.

15. Disconnect the water temperature sender gauge connector, water temperature sensor connector, cold start injector time switch connector, upper radiator hose, water hoses, and the emission control vacuum hoses. Unbolt and remove the water outlet and gaskets.

16. Remove the water bypass pipe with O-rings and gasket.

17. Remove the EGR valve and vacuum modulator. Remove the exhaust crossover pipe.

18. Remove the throttle body.

19. Remove the cold start injector pipe (2VZ-FE).

20. Disconnect the air chamber hose, throttle body air hose and power steering hoses (if equipped). Remove the air tube.

21. Remove the intake manifold stay and disconnect the vacuum sensing hose. Remove the intake manifold and gasket. Purchase a new gasket.

22. Remove the fuel delivery pipe and the injectors.

23. Remove the rear cylinder head plate. On the 3VZ-FE, remove the emission control valve set and the left side engine harness.

24. Remove the exhaust manifolds. Remove the spark plugs. On the 3VZ-FE, remove the oil dipstick.

25. Remove the timing belt, all camshaft timing pulleys and the No. 2 idler pulley.

26. Remove the No. 3 timing belt cover. Support the belt carefully so that the belt and pulley mesh does not shift.

27. Remove the cylinder head covers. Remove the spark plug tube gaskets on the 2VZ-FE.

28. Remove the intake and exhaust camshafts from each head as described in this section.

29. On the 3VZ-FE, remove the power steering pump bracket and the left side engine hanger.

30. Remove the two (one on each head) 8mm hex bolts. Loosen and remove the eight head bolts evenly, in three passes, in the order shown. Carefully lift the head from the engine and place it on wood blocks in a clean work area.

✳✳ WARNING

If the cylinder head bolts are loosened out of sequence, warpage or cracking could result.

31. Remove the cylinder head gasket and purchase a new one (cylinder head gaskets must never be re-used). With a gasket scraper, remove all the old gasket material from the cylinder head and engine block surfaces.

To install:

32. Place the new cylinder head gasket onto the cylinder block. Place the cylinder head onto the gasket.

33. Coat the threads of the eight cylinder head bolts (12-sided) with clean engine oil and install the bolts into the cylinder head. Uniformly tighten the bolts in three passes to 25 ft. lbs. (34 Nm), using the sequence shown. If any of the bolts does not meet the torque, replace it.

34. Mark the forward edge of each bolt with paint and then retighten each bolt an additional 90°, in the order shown. Now repeat the process once more, for an additional 90°. Check that each painted mark is now at a 180° angle to the front, facing the rear.

35. Coat the threads of the two remaining 8mm bolts with engine oil and install them. Tighten to 13 ft. lbs. (18 Nm).

36. The remainder of installation is the reverse of removal. Tighten each component to specifications.

- Left engine hanger—27 ft. lbs. (37 Nm)
- Cylinder head covers—52 inch lbs. (6 Nm)
- No. 3 timing belt cover—65 inch lbs. (7 Nm)
- Right and left side exhaust manifolds—29 ft. lbs. (39 Nm)
- Intake manifold and the No. 2 idler pulley bracket—13 ft. lbs. (18 Nm)
- Injectors and delivery pipe—9 ft. lbs. (13 Nm)

37. Fill the cooling system to the proper level with a good brand of ethylene glycol coolant.

38. Connect the negative battery cable. Start the engine and check for leaks.

39. Adjust the valves and the ignition timing. Check the toe-in.

40. Road test the vehicle and check for unusual noise, shock, slippage, correct shift points and smooth operation.

41. Recheck the coolant and engine oil levels.

1MZ-FE Engine

♦ **See Figures 73 thru 84**

1. Relieve the fuel pressure.
2. Drain the cooling system.
3. Disconnect the accelerator cable and the throttle cable on vehicles equipped with an automatic transaxle.
4. Remove the air cleaner cover, air flow meter, and the air duct.
5. Remove the cruise control actuator and bracket, if equipped.
6. Disconnect the two engine ground straps.
7. Remove the right engine mounting support.
8. Disconnect the radiator hoses.
9. Disconnect the two heater hoses.
10. Disconnect and plug the fuel feed and return lines from the fuel rail assembly.
11. Disconnect and plug the pressure hose from the hydraulic motor.
12. Remove the V-bank cover.
13. Disconnect the following vacuum hoses:
• Fuel pressure control VSV
• Fuel pressure regulator
• Cylinder head rear plate
• Intake air control valve VSV
• EGR vacuum modulator
• EGR valve
14. Disconnect the following wiring and hoses:
• Intake air control valve

Fig. 73 Remove the emission control valve set. Make sure to label each connection

Fig. 74 Disconnect the vacuum hoses and remove the cylinder head rear plate

Fig. 75 Unbolt and remove the oil dipstick from the front of the engine

Fig. 76 There are bolts recessed in the cylinder heads, remove these first

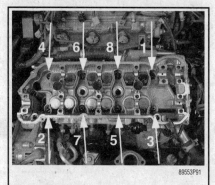

Fig. 77 Left side cylinder head bolt loosening sequence

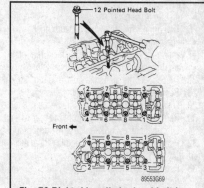

Fig. 78 Right side cylinder head bolt loosening sequence

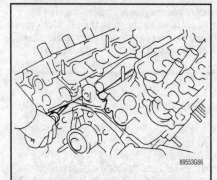

Fig. 79 Use a prybar to help separate the head from the block

Fig. 80 Lift the cylinder head off the block

Fig. 81 Remove the old head gasket and discard

Fig. 82 Scrape the old gasket material off the mating surfaces

Fig. 83 Only use a torque wrench to tighten the cylinder head bolts

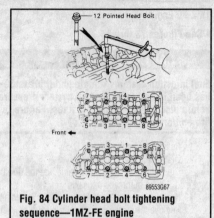

Fig. 84 Cylinder head bolt tightening sequence—1MZ-FE engine

- Fuel pressure regulator
- EGR VSV
15. Remove the two nuts and the emission control valve set.
16. Disconnect the following hoses;
- Brake booster vacuum hose
- PCV hose
- Intake air control valve vacuum hose
17. Remove the data link connector from the mounting bracket.
18. Remove the two ground straps from the intake chamber.
19. Remove the hydraulic motor pressure hose from the intake chamber.
20. Remove the right oxygen sensor connector from the pressure tube.
21. Remove the two nuts and the pressure tube from the intake chamber.
22. Disconnect the two air hoses.
23. Remove the engine hanger and the intake chamber support.
24. Remove the EGR pipe and gaskets.
25. Disconnect the following wiring;
- Throttle position sensor connector
- IAC valve connector
- EGR gas temperature connector
- A/C idle up connector
26. Disconnect the following vacuum hoses:
- Two vacuum hoses from the TVV
- Vacuum hose from the cylinder head rear plate
- Vacuum hose from the charcoal canister
27. Disconnect the air assist hose and the two water bypass hoses.
28. Remove the air intake chamber.
29. Disconnect the left engine wire harness and position it out of the way.
30. Remove the wire harness from the rear of the engine.
31. Disconnect the right engine wire harness and position it out of the way.
32. Remove the ignition coils and lay them aside in the exact positions where they are placed in the heads.
33. Remove the timing belt.
34. Remove the camshaft pulleys and the timing belt rear cover.
35. Remove the cylinder head rear plate.
36. Remove the water inlet pipe.
37. Remove the air assist hose and vacuum hose.
38. Remove the intake manifold and fuel rail assembly.
39. Remove the water outlet.
40. Remove the EGR pipe from the right exhaust manifold.
41. Remove the front exhaust pipe and exhaust manifolds.
42. Remove the dipstick assembly and the pump bracket.
43. Remove the valve covers and the camshaft position sensor.
44. Remove the camshafts following the proper sequences and procedures.
45. Make sure the engine is at or near ambient temperature and remove the two (one on each head) 8mm recessed hex bolts. Loosen and remove the 8 head bolts evenly, in 3 passes, in the reverse order of the installation sequence. Carefully lift the head from the engine; if it is necessary to pry the head loose, take great care not to damage the mating surfaces. Place the head on wood blocks in a clean work area.

✱✱ WARNING

If the cylinder head bolts are loosened out of sequence, warpage or cracking could result.

46. Remove the cylinder head gasket. With a gasket scraper, carefully remove all the old gasket material from the cylinder head and engine block surfaces.
To install:
47. Place the new cylinder head gasket onto the cylinder block. Place the cylinder head onto the gasket.
48. Coat the threads of the 8 cylinder head bolts (12-sided) with clean engine oil and install the bolts into the cylinder head. Uniformly tighten the bolts in sequence in three steps to 40 ft. lbs. (54 Nm), using the proper sequence. If any bolt does not meet the torque, replace it.
49. Mark the forward edge of each bolt with paint and then tighten each bolt, in proper sequence, an additional 90 °. Check that each painted mark is now at a 90 ° angle to the front. The paint mark should have been applied to the bolt in the 9 o'clock position and should now be in the 12 o'clock position.
50. Coat the threads of the two remaining 8mm bolts with engine oil and install them. Tighten to 13 ft. lbs. (18 Nm).
51. Install the camshafts following the proper sequences and procedures. Apply sealant to the cylinder heads where the camshaft supports meet the cylinder heads.
52. The remainder of installation is the reverse of removal. Tighten each component to specifications.
53. Fill the cooling system to the proper level with coolant. Connect the negative battery cable.
54. Start the engine and check for leaks. Bleed the air from the cooling system.
55. Adjust the ignition timing. Road test the vehicle and check for unusual noise, shock, slippage, correct shift points and smooth operation. Recheck the coolant and engine oil levels.

Oil Pan

REMOVAL & INSTALLATION

✱✱ CAUTION

The EPA warns that prolonged contact with used engine oil may cause a number of skin disorders, including cancer! You should make every effort to minimize your exposure to used engine oil. Protective gloves should be worn when changing the oil. Wash your hands and any other exposed skin areas as soon as possible after exposure to used engine oil. Soap and water, or waterless hand cleaner should be used.

Except 1MZ-FE

▶ See Figures 85, 86 and 87

1. Raise the support the front end on jackstands.
2. Drain the oil and remove the dipstick.
3. Remove the right engine undercover or covers (exc. 2S-ELC).
4. On all engines except the 2S-ELC, disconnect the exhaust pipe, remove the lower suspension crossmember, engine mounting center member and the stiffener plate.
5. Remove the nuts and bolts from the oil pan flange.

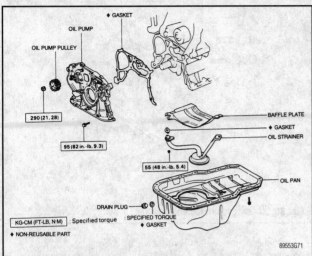

Fig. 85 Exploded view of the oil pan assembly found on 2S-ELC, 3S-FE and 5S-FE engines

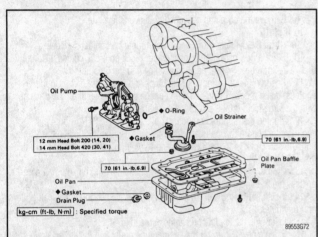

Fig. 86 Exploded view of the oil pump and pan used on 23VZ-FE and 3VZ-FE engines

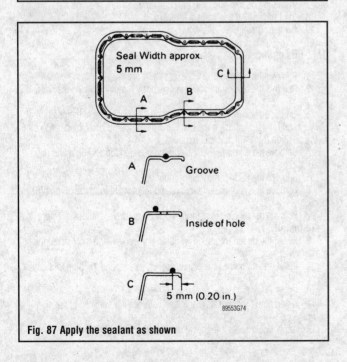

Fig. 87 Apply the sealant as shown

6. Separate the oil pan from the cylinder block.

7. Lower the oil pan to the ground being careful not to damage the oil pan flange.

To install:

8. Using a gasket scraper and a wire brush, remove all the old packing material from the oil pan and cylinder block gasket surfaces. Wipe the oil pan interior with a rag. Clean the contact surfaces with a non-residue type solvent.

9. Apply a thin ⅛ inch bead of No. 102 seal packing or equivalent to the oil pan as shown in the illustration. To ensure the proper size bead, cut the nozzle on the tube.

➥**Avoid applying too much sealant to the oil pan.**

10. Place the oil pan against the block and install the bolts and nuts. Tighten the nuts and bolts to 4 ft. lbs. (5 Nm)

11. Install the stiffener plate and tighten the mounting bolts to 27 ft. lbs. (37 Nm). Install the engine mounting center member. Connect the exhaust pipe.

12. Install the right engine cover or covers. Fill the engine with oil to the proper level.

13. Start the engine and check for leaks. Recheck the engine oil level.

1MZ-FE Engine

▶ **See Figure 88**

1. Raise and safely support the front of the vehicle.

2. Remove the right front wheel.

3. Remove the fender apron seal.

4. Remove the engine undercover.

5. Drain the engine oil from the engine.

6. Remove the front exhaust pipe.

7. Remove the front exhaust pipe bracket from the No. 1 oil pan.

8. Remove the flywheel housing undercover.

9. Remove the ten bolts and two nuts to the No. 2 oil pan.

10. Insert the blade of SST tool 09032–00100 or equivalent between the No. 1 and No. 2 oil pans. Clean the surfaces of the oil pans.

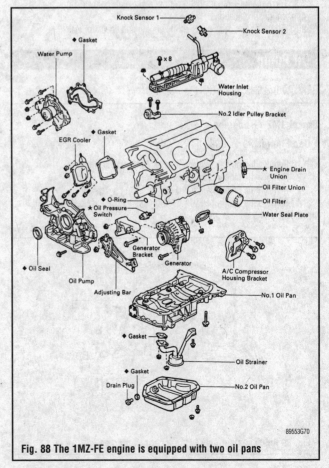

Fig. 88 The 1MZ-FE engine is equipped with two oil pans

11. Remove the oil strainer and gasket from the engine by removing the three nuts.

12. Remove the No.1 oil pan as follows:

a. Remove the two bolts to the flywheel housing undercover. Remove the flywheel undercover.

b. Remove the 17 bolts and 2 nuts to the No. 1 oil pan. Make a note of the position of the each bolt. When replacing the bolts into the oil pan, place each bolt in the position from which it was removed.

c. Remove the oil pan by prying portions between the cylinder block and the oil pan. Be careful not to damage the contact surfaces.

13. Remove the baffle plate from the No. 1 oil pan.

To install:

14. Clean all mating surfaces of the oil pans.

15. Install the baffle plate to the No. 1 oil pan and tighten to 69 inch lbs. (8 Nm).

16. Install the No. 1 oil pan as follows:

a. Using a non residue solvent, clean both sealing surfaces to the oil pan.

b. Apply liquid sealant to the oil pan and engine block.

c. Install the oil pan with the 17 bolts and 2 nuts. Uniformly tighten the bolts and nuts in several passes.

d. Tighten the bolts as follows:

- 10mm head bolt–69 inch lbs. (8 Nm)
- 12mm head bolt–14 ft. lbs. (20 Nm)
- 14mm head bolt–27 ft. lbs. (37 Nm)

e. Install the flywheel housing undercover with the two bolts. Tighten the bolts to 69 inch lbs. (8 Nm).

17. Install the oil strainer with the three nuts. Tighten the nuts to 69 inch lbs. (8 Nm).

18. Install the No. 2 oil pan as follows:

a. Using a non residue solvent, clean both sealing surfaces to the oil pan.

b. Apply liquid sealant to the oil pan and engine block.

c. Install the No. 2 oil pan with the ten bolts and two nuts. Uniformly tighten the bolts and nuts in several passes. Tighten the bolts to 69 inch lbs. (8 Nm).

19. The remainder of installation is the reverse of removal. Tighten each component to specifications.

20. Fill the engine with oil. Start the engine and check for leaks.

Oil Pump

REMOVAL & INSTALLATION

Except 1MZ-FE Engines

▶ See Figures 89 and 90

1. Remove the oil pan as described earlier in this section.
2. Remove the oil pan baffle plate.
3. Remove the oil strainer and O-ring.
4. Remove the timing belt. On V6 engines, remove the No. 1 idler and the crankshaft timing pulleys.

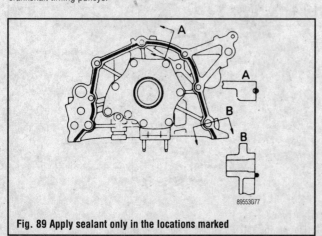

Fig. 89 Apply sealant only in the locations marked

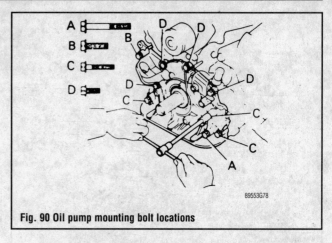

Fig. 90 Oil pump mounting bolt locations

5. On the V6, remove the alternator and the A/C compressor. Also, remove the compressor bracket and the power steering pump adjusting bar.

6. Remove the twelve (nine on V6) oil pump retaining bolts.

7. With a soft-faced hammer or rubber mallet, tap the oil pump loose from the block.

8. Remove the oil pump gasket and replace a new one.

To install:

9. Clean the cylinder block and oil pump gasket contact surfaces.

10. Place a new gasket onto the cylinder block on 4 cyl. engines. On the V6, draw a 2–3mm bead of seal packing as shown in the illustration.

11. Position the oil pump onto the block and install the bolts. On the V6 engines, insert a new O-ring and then engage the spline teeth on the drive gear with the large teeth on the end of the crankshaft.

12. Tighten the oil pump mounting bolts to 7 ft. lbs. (9 Nm) on 4 cyl. engines; the bottom two bolts are the long ones. On the V6, tighten the 12mm bolts (C and D) to 14 ft. lbs. (20 Nm) and the 14mm bolts (A and B) to 30 ft. lbs. (41 Nm).

13. On the V6, install the power steering belt adjusting bar, the A/C compressor bracket and the alternator.

14. Install the timing belt. Don't forget the No. 1 idler and crankshaft pulleys on V6 engines.

15. Install the baffle plate on engines so equipped.

16. Place a new O-ring on the strainer pipe outlet and install the strainer. Tighten the four bolts on 4 cyl. engines to 4 ft. lbs. (6 Nm). On V6 engines, tighten the bolt and two nuts to 61 inch lbs. (7 Nm).

17. Install the oil pan and refill the engine oil.

18. Start the engine and inspect for leaks.

19. Recheck the engine oil level.

1MZ-FE Engines

1. Remove the oil pan.

2. Remove the crankshaft position sensor by removing the connector and bolt.

3. On the oil pump, remove the nine bolts. Make a note of the position of the each bolt. When replacing the bolts into the oil pump body, place each bolt in the position from which it was removed.

4. Remove the oil pump body by prying between the oil pump and main bearing cap.

5. Remove the O-ring from the cylinder block.

6. Remove the plug, gasket, spring, and relief valve from the oil pump body.

7. Remove the nine screws, pump body cover, drive, and driven rotors.

To install:

8. Install the driven rotors, drive, pump body cover, and then install the nine screws.

9. Install the oil pump relief valve, spring, gasket, and the plug to the oil pump body.

10. Place a new O-ring on the cylinder block.

11. Using a non residue solvent, clean both sealing surfaces to the oil pump.

12. Apply liquid sealant to the oil pump and engine block.

13. Install the oil pump to the engine block. Make sure to engage the spline teeth of the oil pump drive gear with the large teeth of the crankshaft.

14. Install the nine bolts to the oil pump and uniformly tighten the bolts in several passes. Tighten the bolts as follows:
- 10mm head–69 inch lbs. (8 Nm)
- 12mm head–14 ft. lbs. (20 Nm)

15. Install the crankshaft position sensor and install the bolt. Tighten the bolt to 69 inch lbs. (8 Nm).

16. Install the baffle plate to the oil pan and tighten to 69 inch lbs. (8 Nm).

17. Install the No. 1 oil pan, oil strainer and No. 2 oil pan.

18. Refill the engine with oil.

19. Start the engine and inspect for leaks.

20. Recheck the engine oil level.

Timing Belt Cover and Seal

REMOVAL & INSTALLATION

2S-ELC, 3S-FE and 5S-FE Engines

▶ See Figures 91 thru 99

1. On some models the engine coolant reservoir must be removed.
2. Remove the right front wheel.
3. Remove the fender apron liner and right engine under cover.
4. Remove the drive belts.
5. Remove the cruise control actuator and bracket.

6. On 2S-ELC engines, remove the power steering reservoir and belt. On 3S-FE and 5S-FE engines, remove the alternator and alternator bracket.

7. Using a wood block on the jack, raise the engine enough to relieve the weight from the engine on the right mounting side.

8. Remove the right engine mounting insulator and bracket. On the 5S-FE, remove the engine moving control rod.

9. Remove the spark plugs.

10. Remove the five bolts and remove the upper (No. 2) timing belt cover with gasket.

11. Set the No. 1 cylinder to TDC of the compression stroke as follows:

   a. **2S-ELC/USA**: Align the oil seal retainer mark with the center of the small hole **E** mark on the camshaft timing pulley by turning the crankshaft pulley clockwise.

   b. **2S-ELC/Canada**: Align the oil seal retainer with the center of the small hole on the camshaft timing pulley by turning the pulley clockwise.

   c. **3S-FE and 5S-FE**: Check that the hole in the camshaft timing pulley is aligned with the bearing cap alignment mark. If hole and timing mark are not in alignment, turn the crankshaft one complete revolution (360°) and align them.

12. Matchmark the timing belt with the camshaft timing pulley. Also, mark the belt where it meets the edge of the lower timing belt cover. Loosen the No. 1 idler pulley set bolt and shift the pulley toward the left as far as it will go, and temporarily tighten the bolt. Remove the timing belt from the camshaft timing pulley.

13. Using spanner wrench to hold the camshaft timing pulley, remove the pulley setbolt. Remove the pulley and bolt. On 3S-FE and 5S-FE engines, remove the plate washer also.

14. Using a spanner wrench to hold the crankshaft pulley, remove the pulley setbolt. Remove the pulley using a puller.

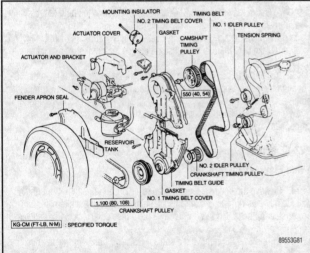

Fig. 91 Exploded view of the timing belt and front cover—2S-ELC engines

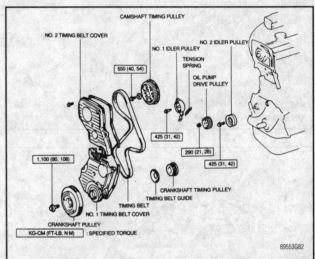

Fig. 92 Exploded view of the timing belt and front cover—3S-FE and 5S-FE engines

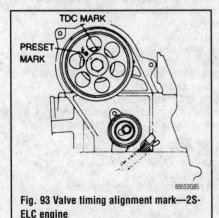

Fig. 93 Valve timing alignment mark—2S-ELC engine

Fig. 94 Valve timing alignment mark—3S-FE and 5S-FE engines

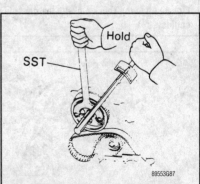

Fig. 95 Using a spanner wrench to retain the camshaft pulley while removing the setbolt

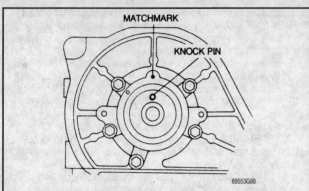

Fig. 96 Align the camshaft knock pin with the matchmarks on the oil seal retainer

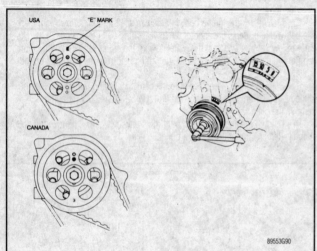

Fig. 97 Align the knock pin with this marking—2S-ELC Canadian and US engines

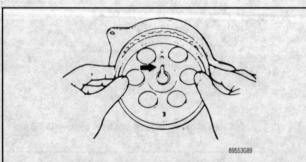

Fig. 98 Align the knock pin with the pin hole on the pulley—2S-ELC engine

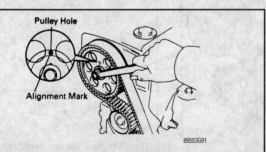

Fig. 99 Align the hole in the camshaft pulley with the mark on the camshaft bearing—3S-FE and 5S-FE engines

15. Remove the four bolts and remove the lower (No. 1) timing belt cover with gaskets.

16. Discard the upper and lower timing belt gaskets and purchase new ones. Make sure the gasket surfaces are clean.

To install:

17. Install the lower (No.1) timing belt cover and new gasket with the four bolts.

18. Align the crankshaft pulley key with the pulley key groove. Install the pulley. Tighten the pulley bolt to 80 ft. lbs. (108 Nm).

19. On **2S-ELC** engines, turn the crankshaft pulley and align the **0** mark on the lower (No. 1) timing belt cover.

20. Align the camshaft knock pin with the matchmarks on the oil seal retainer.

21. On **2S-ELC/USA** engines, align the knock pin with the pin hole on the timing pulley **E** mark side. On **2S-ELC/Canadian** engines, align the knock pin with the pin hole on the timing pulley. On **3S-FE** and **5S-FE** engines, align the knock pin with the groove of the pulley, and slide the pulley onto the camshaft with the plate washer and set bolt.

➡**On 2S-ELC engines, make sure that the matchmark on the oil seal retainer and center hole of the small hole on the camshaft timing pulley are aligned.**

22. Using the removal tool to hold the pulley stationary, install and tighten the pulley set bolt to 40 ft. lbs. (54 Nm) on the 2S-ELC and the 3S-FE. On the 5S-FE, tighten the set bolt to 27 ft. lbs. (37 Nm).

23. On 3S-FE and 5S-FE engines, turn the crankshaft pulley and align the **0** mark on the lower (No. 1) timing belt cover.

24. Install the timing belt and check the valve timing as follows:

    a. Align the matchmarks that you made previously, and install the timing belt onto the camshaft pulley.

    b. Loosen the No. 1 idler pulley set bolt ½ turn.

    c. Turn the crankshaft pulley two complete revolutions TDC to TDC. ALWAYS turn the crankshaft CLOCKWISE. Check that the pulleys are still in alignment with the timing marks.

    d. Tighten the No. 1 idler pulley set bolt to 31 ft. lbs. (42 Nm).

    e. Make sure there is belt tension between the crankshaft and camshaft timing pulleys.

25. Install the upper (No. 2) timing cover with a new gasket(s). On the 5S-FE, align the two clamps for the engine wiring harness with the cover mounting bolts.

26. The remainder of installation is the reverse of removal. Tighten each component to specifications.

2VZ-FE and 3VZ-FE Engines

▶ **See Figures 100 thru 110**

1. Remove the power steering pump reservoir and position it out of the way. Remove the right fender apron seal and then remove the alternator and power steering belts. On 2VZ-FE, remove the cruise control actuator and vacuum pump.

2. On the 3VZ-FE, remove the coolant reservoir hose, the washer tank and then the coolant overflow tank.

3. Remove the right side engine mount stays.

4. Position a piece of wood on a floor jack and then slide the jack under the oil pan. Raise the jack slightly until the pressure is off the engine mounts.

5. On the 2VZ-FE, remove the right side engine mount insulator. On 3VZ-FE, remove the engine control rod.

6. Remove the spark plugs.

7. Remove the right side engine mounting bracket.

8. Remove the eight bolts and lift off the upper (No. 2) cover.

9. Paint matchmarks on the timing belt at all points where it meshes with the pulleys and the lower timing cover.

10. Set the No. 1 cylinder to TDC of the compression stroke and check that the timing marks on the camshaft timing pulleys are aligned with those on the No. 3 timing cover. If not, turn the engine one complete revolution (360°) and check again.

11. Remove the timing belt tensioner and the dust boot.

12. Turn the right camshaft pulley clockwise slightly to release tension and then remove the timing belt from the pulleys.

13. Use a spanner wrench to hold the pulley, loosen the set bolt and then remove the camshaft timing pulleys along with the knock pin. Be sure to keep track of which is which.

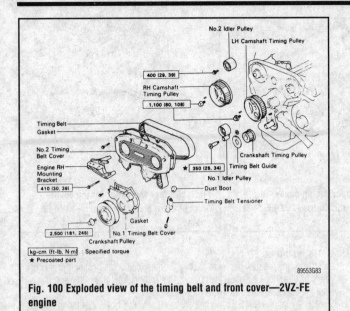

Fig. 100 Exploded view of the timing belt and front cover—2VZ-FE engine

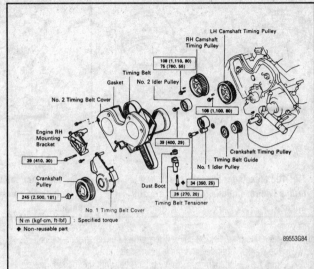

Fig. 101 Exploded view of the timing belt and front cover—3VZ-FE engine

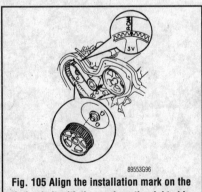

Fig. 102 Mark the belt where it passes the lower timing cover

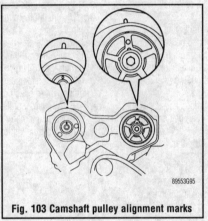

Fig. 103 Camshaft pulley alignment marks

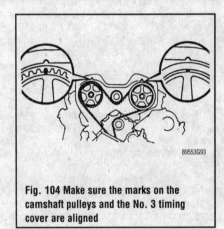

Fig. 104 Make sure the marks on the camshaft pulleys and the No. 3 timing cover are aligned

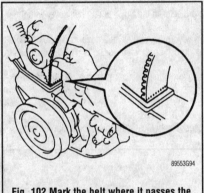

Fig. 105 Align the installation mark on the timing belt with the mark on the right side camshaft pulley

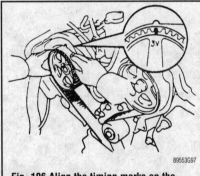

Fig. 106 Align the timing marks on the right pulley with the one on the No. 3 cover, then slide the pulley on

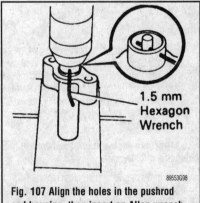

Fig. 107 Align the holes in the pushrod and housing, then insert an Allen wrench

14. Remove the No. 2 idler pulley.
15. Remove the crankshaft pulley and then pull off the lower (No. 1) timing belt cover.

To install:
16. Install the lower (No. 1) timing cover and tighten the bolts.
17. Align the crankshaft pulley set key with the key groove on the pulley and slide the pulley on. Tighten the bolt to 181 ft. lbs. (245 Nm).
18. Install the No. 2 idler pulley and tighten the bolt to 29 ft. lbs. (39 Nm). Check that the pulley moves smoothly.
19. Install the left camshaft pulley with the flange side outward. Align the

knock pin hole in the camshaft with the knock pin groove on the pulley and then install the pin. Tighten the bolt to 80 ft. lbs. (108 Nm).
20. Set the No. 1 cylinder to TDC again. Turn the right camshaft until the knock pin hole is aligned with the timing mark on the No. 3 belt cover. Turn the left pulley until the marks on the pulley are aligned with the mark on the No. 3 timing cover.
21. Check that the mark on the belt matches with the edge of the lower cover. If not, shift it on the crank pulley until it does. Turn the left pulley clockwise a bit and align the mark on the timing belt with the timing mark on the pulley. Slide the belt over the left pulley. Now move the pulley until the marks on it

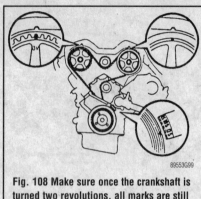

Fig. 108 Make sure once the crankshaft is turned two revolutions, all marks are still aligned

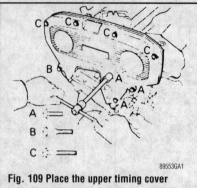

Fig. 109 Place the upper timing cover bolts in there correct locations—2VZ-FE engine

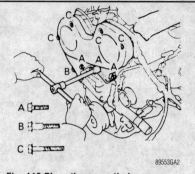

Fig. 110 Place the upper timing cover bolts in there correct locations—3VZ-FE engine

align with the one on the No. 3 cover. There should be tension on the belt between the crankshaft pulley and the left camshaft pulley.

22. Align the installation mark on the timing belt with the mark on the right side camshaft pulley. Hang the belt over the pulley with the flange facing inward. Align the timing marks on the right pulley with the one on the No. 3 cover and slide the pulley onto the end of the camshaft. Move the pulley until the camshaft knock pin hole is aligned with the groove in the pulley and then install the knock pin. Tighten the bolt to 55 ft. lbs. (75 Nm).

23. Position a plate washer between the timing belt tensioner and the a block and then press in the pushrod until the holes are aligned between it and the housing. Slide a 1.27mm (3VZ-FE 1.5mm) Allen wrench through the hole to keep the push rod set. Install the dust boot and then install the tensioner. Tighten the bolts to 20 ft. lbs. (26 Nm). Don't forget to pull out the Allen wrench!

24. Turn the crankshaft **clockwise** two complete revolutions and check that all marks are still in alignment. If they aren't, remove the timing belt and start over again.

25. Install the right engine mount bracket and tighten it to 30 ft. lbs. (39 Nm).

26. Position a new gasket and then install the upper (No. 2) timing cover. Refer to the illustration for bolt positioning.

27. The remainder of installation is the reverse of removal. Tighten each component to specifications. Connect the battery cable, start the car and check for any leaks.

1MZ-FE Engine

▶ See Figures 111 thru 128

1. Remove the engine coolant reservoir tank and the alternator belt.
2. Remove the right front wheel and the splash shield.
3. Remove the power steering pump drive belt by loosening the two bolts.
4. Disconnect the two ground wire connectors.
5. Remove the right engine mounting stay.
6. Remove the engine moving control rod and the No. 2 right engine mounting bracket.

➡To extract the engine bracket and control rod, you will need to raise the engine slightly.

7. Remove the No. 2 alternator bracket.
8. Using a prybar and wrench or SST tool 09213–54015 and 09330–00021, remove the crankshaft pulley bolt.
9. Using a puller, remove the crankshaft pulley.
10. Remove the No. 1 timing belt cover by removing four bolts.
11. Remove the No. 2 timing belt cover as follows:
   a. Remove the bolt and disconnect the engine wire protector from the No. 3 (rear) timing belt cover.
   b. Disconnect the engine wire protector clamp from the No. 3 timing belt cover.
   c. Remove the five bolts from the No. 2 timing belt cover.
   d. Remove the No. 2 cover from the engine.

To install:

12. Apply the new gasket to the No. 2 timing belt cover. Install it evenly to the part of the belt cover shaded black. After installation, press down on it so that the adhesive sticks to the belt cover firmly.

13. Install the No. 2 timing belt cover with the five bolts. Tighten the bolts to 74 inch lbs. (8 Nm).

14. Install the engine wire protector clamp to the No. 3 timing belt cover.

15. Install the engine wire protector to the No. 3 timing belt cover with the bolt.

16. Apply new gasket the way you did on the No. 2 cover on the No. 1 timing cover. Secure the No. 1 timing belt cover with four bolts. Tighten the bolts to 74 inch lbs. (8 Nm).

17. The remainder of installation is the reverse of removal. Tighten each component to specifications.
   • Crankshaft pulley—159 ft. lbs. (215 Nm)
   • No. 2 alternator bracket—21 ft. lbs. (28 Nm)

18. Start the vehicle and check for any leaks. Recheck the ignition timing.

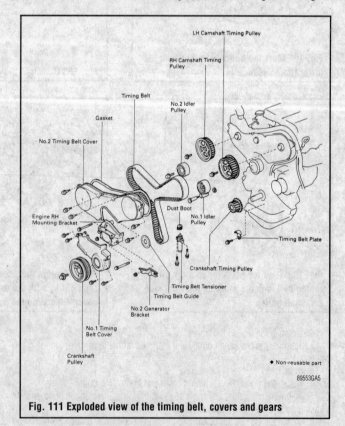

Fig. 111 Exploded view of the timing belt, covers and gears

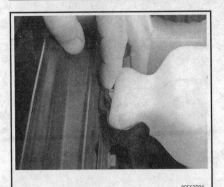

Fig. 112 Remove the engine coolant reservoir by pushing the retaining clip

Fig. 113 Loosen the bolts to loosen the power steering drive belt

Fig. 114 Slip the power steering drive belt off

Fig. 115 Remove the bolts retaining the engine control rod

Fig. 116 Remove the engine control rod (1) and No. 2 right engine bracket (2)

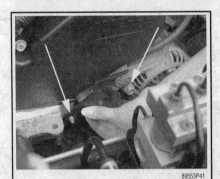

Fig. 117 The No. 2 alternator bracket is held in by a bolt and stud

Fig. 118 Using a prybar to retain the pulley, remove the bolt

Fig. 119 If necessary, use a puller to remove the crankshaft pulley

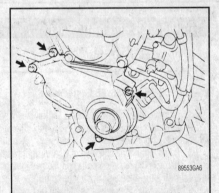

Fig. 120 Remove the four bolts retaining the timing belt cover

Fig. 121 Note the timing marks are on the lower cover

Fig. 122 On the passengers side near the firewall is a bolt retaining the engine wiring. Remove this . . .

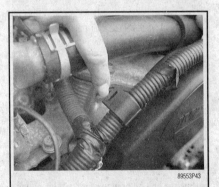

Fig. 123 . . . then push the retaining clip to release the harness

Fig. 124 Now simply lift the harness up and tie it up it out of the way

Fig. 125 The No. 2 timing belt cover is secured by 5 bolts

Fig. 126 Lift and remove the No. 2 timing belt cover from the engine

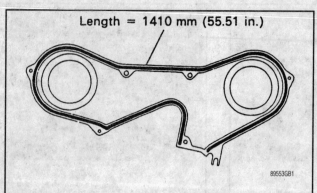

Fig. 127 Place the new gasket on the No. 2 timing cover till it sticks firmly

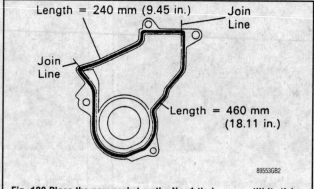

Fig. 128 Place the new gasket on the No. 1 timing cover till it sticks firmly

Timing Belt and Sprockets

REMOVAL & INSTALLATION

2S-ELC, 3S-FE and 5S-FE Engines

1. Remove the timing belt covers as previously detailed.
2. Raise the engine just enough to remove the weight from the engine mount on the right side.
3. Remove the thru-bolt, two nuts, and right hand mounting insulator.
4. Remove the retaining bolts and remove the right hand mounting bracket (from the side the alternator was removed from).
5. Remove the timing belt and timing belt guide. If the timing belt is to be reused, draw a directional arrow on the timing belt in the direction of engine rotation (clockwise) and place matchmarks on the timing belt and crankshaft gear.
6. Remove the bolt retaining the No. 1 idler pulley and tension spring.
7. Remove the No. 2 idler pulley.
8. Remove the crankshaft timing gear , if it can not be removed by hand, use two flat bladed tools to pry it off. Make sure to position shop rags to prevent damages to the components.
9. Remove the nut retaining the oil pump pulley.

To install:

10. Align the cutouts of the oil pump pulley and shaft, and slide the pulley on. Retain the pulley while tightening the nut to 21 ft. lbs. (28 Nm).
11. Align the crankshaft timing pulley set key with the key groove of the crankshaft pulley, then slide the pulley on.
12. Install the No. 2 idler pulley with the bolt and tighten to 31 ft. lbs. (42 Nm). Be sure the pulley moves smoothly.

➡Remove any oil or water on the idler pulley and keep it clean.

13. Temporarily install the No. 1 idler pulley with the retaining bolt. Hint: use a 1.65 inch (42mm) bolt in length. Do not tighten the bolt yet. Install the

tension spring. Pry the pulley toward the left as far as it will go, then tighten the bolt.
14. Turn the crankshaft until the key groove in the crankshaft timing pulley is facing upward. Install the timing belt on the crankshaft timing, oil pump, No. 2 idler and water pump pulleys.

➡If the old timing belt is being reinstalled, make sure the directional arrow is facing in the original direction and that the belt and crankshaft gear matchmarks are properly aligned.

15. Install the lower (No. 1) timing belt cover and new gasket with the four bolts.
16. Align the crankshaft pulley set key with the pulley key groove. Install the pulley. Tighten the pulley bolt to 80 ft. lbs. (108 Nm).
17. On 2S-ELC engines, turn the crankshaft pulley and align the **0** mark on the lower (No. 1) timing belt cover.
18. Align the camshaft knock pin with the matchmarks on the oil seal retainer.
19. On 2S-ELC/USA engines, align the knock pin with the pin hole on the timing pulley **E** mark side. On 2S-ELC/Canadian engines, align the knock pin with the pin hole on the timing pulley. On 3S-FE and 5S-FE engines, align the knock pin with the groove of the pulley, and slide the pulley onto the camshaft with the plate washer and set bolt.

➡On 2S-ELC engines, make sure that the Matchmark on the oil seal retainer and center hole of the small hole on the camshaft timing pulley are aligned.

20. Using the removal tool to hold the pulley stationary, install and tighten the pulley set bolt to 40 ft. lbs. (54 Nm) on the 2S-ELC and the 3S-FE. On the 5S-FE, tighten the set bolt to 27 ft. lbs. (37 Nm).
21. On 3S-FE and 5S-FE engines, turn the crankshaft pulley and align the **0** mark on the lower (No. 1) timing belt cover.
22. Install the timing belt and check the valve timing as follows:
    a. Align the matchmarks that you made previously, and install the timing belt onto the camshaft pulley.

b. Loosen the No. 1 idler pulley set bolt ½ turn.

c. Turn the crankshaft pulley two complete revolutions TDC to TDC. ALWAYS turn the crankshaft CLOCKWISE. Check that the pulleys are still in alignment with the timing marks.

d. Tighten the No. 1 idler pulley set bolt to 31 ft. lbs. (42 Nm).

e. Make sure there is belt tension between the crankshaft and camshaft timing pulleys.

23. Install the upper (No. 2) timing cover with a new gasket(s). On the 5S-FE, align the two clamps for the engine wiring harness with the cover mounting bolts.

24. Install the spark plugs.

25. The remainder of installation is the reverse of removal. Tighten each component to specifications.

2VZ-FE and 3VZ-FE Engines

▶ See Figure 129

1. Remove the upper and lower timing belt covers as previously detailed.
2. Remove the timing belt guide.
3. Remove the timing belt.

➡**If the timing belt is to be reused, draw a directional arrow on the timing belt in the direction of engine rotation (clockwise) and place matchmarks on the timing belt and crankshaft gear to match the drilled mark on the pulley.**

4. With a 10mm hex wrench, remove the setbolt, plate washer and the No. 1 idler pulley.

5. Remove the crankshaft timing pulley, if it can not be removed by hand, use two flat bladed tools. Position shop rags on the components to prevent damage.

To install:

6. Turn the crankshaft until the key groove in the crankshaft timing pulley is facing upward. Slide the timing pulley on so that the flange side faces inward.

7. Apply bolt adhesive to the first few threads of the No. 1 idler pulley setbolt, install the plate washer and pulley and then tighten the bolt to 25 ft. lbs. (34 Nm).

8. Install the timing belt on the crankshaft timing, No. 1 idler and water pump pulleys.

➡**If the old timing belt is being reinstalled, make sure the directional arrow is facing in the original direction and that the belt and crankshaft gear matchmarks are properly aligned.**

9. Install the lower (No. 1) timing cover and tighten the bolts.

10. Align the crankshaft pulley set key with the key groove on the pulley and slide the pulley on. Tighten the bolt to 181 ft. lbs. (245 Nm).

11. Install the No. 2 idler pulley and tighten the bolt to 29 ft. lbs. (39 Nm). Check that the pulley moves smoothly.

12. Slide the left pulley, facing the flange side outward. Align the knock pin hole of the camshaft with the knockpin of the timing pulley, then install the knock pin. Tighten the left camshaft timing pulley bolt to 80 ft. lbs. (108 Nm).

13. Set the No. 1 cylinder to TDC again. Turn the right camshaft until the

knock pin hole is aligned with the timing mark on the No. 3 belt cover. Turn the left pulley until the marks on the pulley are aligned with the mark on the No. 3 timing cover.

14. Check that the mark on the belt matches with the edge of the lower cover. If not, shift it on the crank pulley until it does. Turn the left pulley clockwise a bit and align the mark on the timing belt with the timing mark on the pulley. Slide the belt over the left pulley. Now move the pulley until the marks on it align with the one on the No. 3 cover. There should be tension on the belt between the crankshaft pulley and the left camshaft pulley.

15. Align the installation mark on the timing belt with the mark on the right side camshaft pulley. Hang the belt over the pulley with the flange facing inward. Align the timing marks on the right pulley with the one on the No. 3 cover and slide the pulley onto the end of the camshaft. Move the pulley until the camshaft knock pin hole is aligned with the groove in the pulley and then install the knock pin. Tighten the bolt to 55 ft. lbs. (75 Nm).

16. Position a plate washer between the timing belt tensioner and the a block and then press in the pushrod until the holes are aligned between it and the housing. Slide a 1.27mm (3VZ-FE 1.5mm) Allen wrench through the hole to keep the push rod set. Install the dust boot and then install the tensioner. Tighten the bolts to 20 ft. lbs. (26 Nm). Don't forget to pull out the Allen wrench!

17. Turn the crankshaft **clockwise** two complete revolutions and check that all marks are still in alignment. If they aren't, remove the timing belt and start over again.

18. Install the right engine mount bracket and tighten it to 30 ft. lbs. (39 Nm).

19. Position a new gasket and then install the upper (No. 2) timing cover. refer to the illustration for bolt positioning.

20. The remainder of installation is the reverse of removal. Tighten each component to specifications.

21. Connect the battery cable, start the car and check for any leaks.

1MZ-FE Engine

▶ See Figures 130 thru 155

1. Remove the timing belt covers as described earlier in this section.

2. Remove the right engine mounting bracket by removing the nut and two bolts.

3. Remove the crankshaft timing belt guide.

4. Temporarily install the crankshaft pulley bolt.

5. Turn the crankshaft and align the crankshaft timing pulley groove with the oil pump alignment mark. Always turn the engine clockwise.

6. Ensure the timing mark of the camshaft timing pulleys and rear timing belt cover are aligned. If not, turn the engine over an additional 360 °.

7. Remove the crankshaft pulley bolt.

➡**If the belt is to be reused, align the installation marks on the belt to the marks on the pulleys. If the marks have worn off, make new ones.**

8. Alternately loosen the two timing belt tensioner bolts. Remove the tensioner and dust boot.

9. Remove the timing belt.

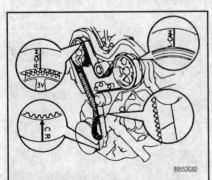

Fig. 129 Prior to timing belt removal, make sure all the matchmarks are there—2VZ-FE and 3VZ-FE engines

Fig. 130 Remove the right engine mounting bracket bolts and nut . . .

Fig. 131 . . . then lift the right engine bracket from the engine

Fig. 132 Slide the timing belt guide off the crankshaft pulley

Fig. 133 Place matchmarks on the pulley and cover

Fig. 134 Turn the crankshaft clockwise to align the crankshaft timing pulley grove with the oil pump mark

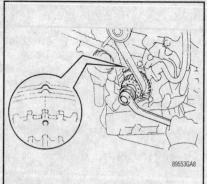

Fig. 135 Align the timing marks to set No. 1 cylinder to TDC

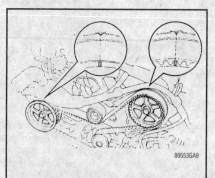

Fig. 136 If the timing marks are not aligned, turn the crankshaft one full revolution (360 degrees)

Fig. 137 Make sure the timing belt marks are aligned with the camshaft pulley and No. 3 timing belt cover

Fig. 138 Unbolt the timing belt tensioner . . .

Fig. 139 . . . and only carry it in the upright position

Fig. 140 Place a directional arrow on the belt if reusing it

Fig. 141 Slip the belt off the lower and upper pulleys and extract it from the engine

Fig. 142 Remove the camshaft pulley bolt and pulleys

Fig. 143 Label the camshaft pulleys with an L and R to identify them

Fig. 144 Remove the No. 1 idler pulley and bolt

Fig. 145 Remove the bolt retaining the No. 1 idler pulley, then slide the pulley off

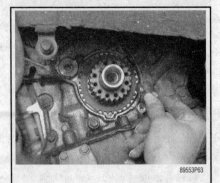

Fig. 146 Remove the crankshaft timing belt plate . . .

Fig. 147 . . . then remove the crankshaft pulley gear

Fig. 148 Look for seal leakage and replace if noticeable

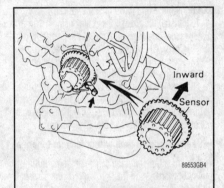

Fig. 149 Install the crankshaft timing pulley with the sensor facing inward

Fig. 150 Install the No. 2 idler pulley with the bolt and washer in these locations

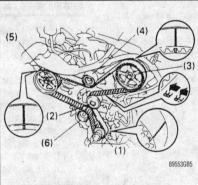

Fig. 151 Install the timing belt components in this order

Fig. 152 Remove the boot from the tensioner

Fig. 153 Measure the protrusion of the rod from the housing end

Fig. 154 Press the rod facing upwards only to see if it moves

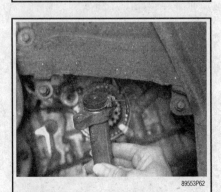

Fig. 155 Insert an Allen head wrench through the hole of the tensioner

10. Using a spanner wrench, remove the right side camshaft timing pulley. Do the same for the left side.

➡**Make sure the left and right side camshaft pulleys are arranged on the table correctly. Do not mix them up! It is recommended to mark them with an L and R.**

11. Remove the bolt retaining the No. 2 idler pulley, the slide the pulley off.

12. Using a 10mm hexagon wrench, remove the bolt and No. 1 idler pulley with plate washer.

13. Remove the crankshaft bolt and timing belt plate. Using a gear puller, separate the crankshaft pulley from the engine.

➡**Do not scratch the sensor portion of the crankshaft timing pulley.**

14. Inspect the seal for leakage and replace if necessary.

To install:

15. When installing the crankshaft timing pulley, along the pulley set key with the key groove of the pulley, then slide the pulley on. Install the crankshaft timing pulley, with the sensor side facing inward. Install the timing belt plate and tighten the bolt to 69 inch lbs. (8 Nm).

16. Install the No. 1 idler pulley using a 10mm hexagon wrench, install the plate washer and idler pulley with the pivot bolt. tighten the pivot bolt to 25 ft. lbs. (34 Nm). Check that the pulley moves freely.

17. Install the No. 2 idler pulley and tighten to 32 ft. lbs. (43 Nm). Check that the pulley moves smoothly.

18. Install the right side camshaft timing pulley, face the flange side of the pulley outward. Align the knock pin on the camshaft with the knock pin groove of the timing pulley, then slide the right hand camshaft pulley on. Install the pulley bolt and tighten to 65 ft. lbs. (88 Nm).

➡**Use a torque wrench with a fulcrum length of 13.39 inch (340mm).**

19. Install the left side camshaft timing pulley, face the flange side of the pulley outward. Align the knock pin on the camshaft with the knock pin groove of the timing pulley, then slide the left side camshaft pulley on. Install the pulley bolt and tighten to 94 ft. lbs. (125 Nm).

20. Temporarily install the crankshaft pulley bolt of the crankshaft. Turn the crankshaft, and align the timing marks of the crankshaft timing pulley and oil pump body.

21. Using a spanner wrench, turn the camshaft pulley, align the timing marks of the timing pulley and the No. 3 timing belt cover.

22. Remove any dirt or oil from the pulleys and keep them clean. Only wipe the pulleys. Face the front mark of the timing belt forward. align the installation mark on the belt with the timing mark of the crankshaft timing pulley. Align the installation marks on the timing belt with the timing marks on the camshaft timing pulleys.

23. Install the timing belt in the following order:
   a. Crankshaft pulley
   b. Water pump pulley
   c. Left camshaft pulley
   d. No. 2 idler pulley
   e. Right camshaft pulley
   f. No. 1 idler pulley

24. Inspect the tensioner prior to installation of the old one as follows:
   a. Visually check for any oil leakage. If there is only the faintest trace of oil on the seal on the push rod side, the tensioner is still useable.

   b. Using force against an sturdy object facing upwards only, press the rod to see if there is no movement. If the rod moves, replace the tensioner.
   c. Measure the protrusion. It should be 0.394–0.425 in, (10.0–10.8mm)
   d. Using a press, slowly press the timing belt tensioner until the holes of the pushrod and housing align. Insert a 1.27mm hexagon Allen wrench through the holes to preserve the setting position.

25. Install the dust boot to the tensioner.

26. Install the tensioner with the two bolts. Alternately tighten and then tighten the bolts to 20 ft. lbs. (27 Nm). Remove the Allen wrench.

27. Turn the crankshaft clockwise and align the crankshaft timing pulley groove with the oil pump alignment mark.

28. Ensure the camshaft timing marks align with the timing marks on the rear timing belt cover.

29. Install the timing belt guide.

30. The remainder of installation is the reverse of removal. Tighten the crankshaft pulley bolt to 159 ft. lbs. (215 Nm).

31. Start the vehicle and check for any leaks.

32. Recheck the ignition timing.

Camshaft and Bearings

REMOVAL & INSTALLATION

2S-ELC Engines

▶ **See Figures 156, 157 and 158**

The camshaft is located in the camshaft housing.

1. Disconnect the negative battery cable.
2. Remove the valve cover.
3. Loosen the camshaft housing bolts gradually in the sequence shown in Cylinder Head Removal and Installation procedure.

☀ CAUTION

If the bolts are loosened out of sequence, warpage of the camshaft housing could occur.

4. Position a small prybar between the cylinder head and camshaft housing projections, separate the camshaft housing from the cylinder head.

5. Once separated, lift the housing from the engine and place it on a clean work bench.

6. Using a spanner wrench, hold the camshaft pulley stationary and remove the pulley set bolt. Remove the pulley.

7. Inspect the camshaft thrust clearance as follows:
   a. Mount a dial indicator (of recent calibration) to the pulley end of the camshaft.
   b. Preload the dial indicator and zero it.
   c. Move the camshaft back and forth by hand and record the thrust clearance. The standard thrust clearance is 0.0031–0.0090 inch (0.0787–0.228mm). Maximum thrust clearance is 0.0138 inch (0.35mm).
   d. If the thrust is greater than the maximum limit, replace the camshaft and/or the camshaft housing.

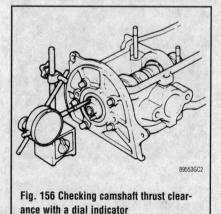

Fig. 156 Checking camshaft thrust clearance with a dial indicator

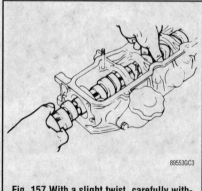

Fig. 157 With a slight twist, carefully withdraw the camshaft from the housing

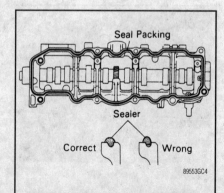

Fig. 158 It is very important to apply the sealant to the camshaft housing correctly

8. Remove the five bolts that attach the oil seal retainer to the housing. Remove the oil seal retainer and O-ring. Discard the O-ring.

9. With a slight twisting motion, slowly withdraw the camshaft from the camshaft housing. This must be done slowly to avoid damaging the housing.

10. With a gasket scraper and cleaning solvent, remove the old sealing material from the housing and head contact surfaces.

11. Inspect the camshaft and camshaft housing.

To install:

12. Good maintenance practice suggests that whenever a seal is removed or disturbed, it should be replaced. Replace the camshaft oil seal as follows:

    a. Tap the old seal from the retainer with a screwdriver and hammer.

    b. Install the new seal by pressing it in with the proper size deep well socket.

    c. Lubricate the new seal with multi-purpose grease.

13. Slowly insert the camshaft into the housing.

14. Clean the retainer bolts thoroughly with a wire brush to remove all the old sealant, grease or dirt.

15. Apply sealant to the last two or three threads of the bolt end.

16. Place the new O-ring into the retainer and attach the retainer with the five bolts. Tighten the bolts to 82 inch lbs. (9 Nm).

17. Remove any oil or grease from the camshaft pulley and then install it as previously detailed.

18. Apply a bead of sealant to the camshaft housing contact surface. Do not use too much sealant. The sealant hardens within 3 minutes after application. If the sealant hardens, it must be removed and re-applied.

19. Place the camshaft housing onto the cylinder head. Install the camshaft housing bolts. Tighten the bolts in three passes to 11 ft. lbs. (15 Nm) in the sequence shown in the Cylinder Head Removal and Installation section.

20. Install the head cover. Connect the negative battery cable. Start and warm up the engine. Inspect for leaks. Adjust the ignition timing and the idle speed.

3S-FE and 5S-FE Engines

▶ **See Figures 159 thru 167**

1. Remove the cylinder head cover.

➡ **Being that the thrust clearance on both the intake and exhaust camshafts is small, the camshafts must be kept level during removal. If the camshafts are removed without being kept level, the camshaft may be caught in the cylinder head causing the head to break or the camshaft to seize.**

2. To remove the exhaust camshaft proceed as follows:

    a. Set the knock pin of the intake camshaft at 10–45° BTDC of camshaft angle. This angle will help to lift the exhaust camshaft level and evenly by pushing No. 2 and No. 4 cylinder camshaft lobes of the exhaust camshaft toward their valve lifters.

    b. Secure the exhaust camshaft sub-gear to the main gear using a service bolt. The manufacturer recommends a bolt 0.63–0.79 inch (16–20mm) long with a thread diameter of 6mm and a 1mm thread pitch. When removing the exhaust camshaft be sure that the torsional spring force of the sub-gear has been eliminated.

    c. Remove the No. 1 and No. 2 rear bearing cap bolts and remove the cap. Uniformly loosen and remove bearing cap bolts No. 3 to No. 8 in several passes and in the proper sequence. Do not remove bearing cap bolts No. 9 and 10 at this time. Remove the No. 1, 2, and 4 bearing caps.

    d. Alternately loosen and remove bearing cap bolts No. 9 and 10. As these bolts are loosened, check to see that the camshaft is being lifted out straight and level.

➡ **If the camshaft is not lifting out straight and level, retighten No. 9 and 10 bearing cap bolts. Reverse the order of Steps c through a and reset the intake camshaft knock pin to 10-45 ° BTDC and repeat Steps a through c again. Do not attempt to pry the camshaft from its mounting.**

    e. Remove the No. 3 bearing cap and exhaust camshaft from the engine.

3. To remove the intake camshaft, proceed as follows:

    a. Set the knock pin of the intake camshaft at 80–115° BTDC of camshaft angle. This angle will help to lift the intake camshaft level and evenly by pushing No. 1 and No. 3 cylinder camshaft lobes of the intake camshaft toward their valve lifters.

    b. Remove the No. 1 and No. 2 front bearing cap bolts and remove the

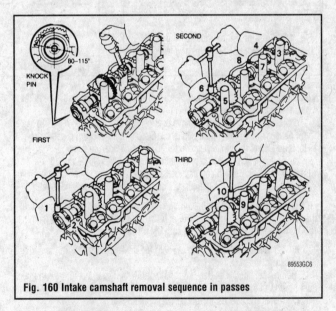

Fig. 160 Intake camshaft removal sequence in passes

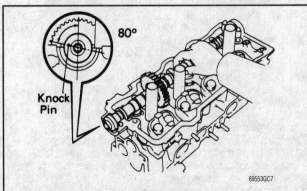

Fig. 161 Place the intake camshaft at 80–115° BTDC of the camshaft angle on the cylinder head

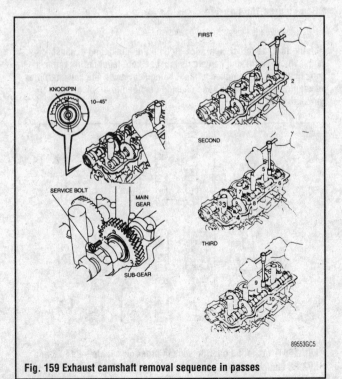

Fig. 159 Exhaust camshaft removal sequence in passes

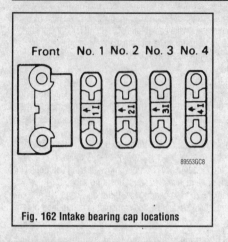

Fig. 162 Intake bearing cap locations

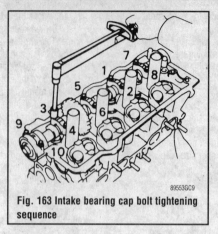

Fig. 163 Intake bearing cap bolt tightening sequence

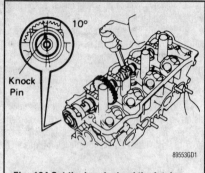

Fig. 164 Set the knock pin of the intake camshaft at 10° BTDC of the camshaft angle

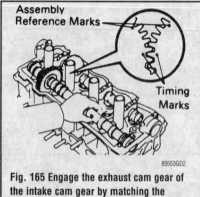

Fig. 165 Engage the exhaust cam gear of the intake cam gear by matching the marks

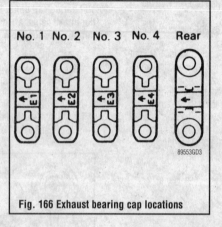

Fig. 166 Exhaust bearing cap locations

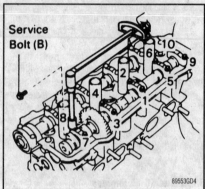

Fig. 167 Exhaust camshaft bearing cap tightening sequence

front bearing cap and oil seal. If the cap will not come apart easily, leave it in place without the bolts.

c. Uniformly loosen and remove bearing cap bolts No. 3 to No. 8 in several phases and in the proper sequence. Do not remove bearing cap bolts No. 9 and 10 at this time. Remove No. 1, 3, and 4 bearing caps.

d. Alternately loosen and remove bearing cap bolts No. 9 and 10. As these bolts are loosened and after breaking the adhesion on the front bearing cap, check to see that the camshaft is being lifted out straight and level.

➡️If the camshaft is not lifting out straight and level retighten No. 9 and 10 bearing cap bolts. Reverse Steps b through d, than start over from Step b. Do not attempt to pry the camshaft from its mounting.

e. Remove the No. 2 bearing cap with the intake camshaft from the engine.

To install:

4. Before installing the intake camshaft, apply multi-purpose grease to the thrust portion of the camshaft.

5. To install the intake camshaft, proceed as follows:
a. Position the camshaft at 80–115° BTDC of camshaft angle on the cylinder head.
b. Apply sealant to the front bearing cap.
c. Coat the bearing cap bolts with clean engine oil.
d. Tighten the camshaft bearing caps evenly and in several passes to 14 ft. lbs. (19 Nm) in the proper sequence.

6. To install the exhaust camshaft, proceed as follows:
a. Set the knock pin of the camshaft at 10–45° BTDC of camshaft angle.
b. Apply multipurpose grease to the thrust portion of the camshaft.
c. Position the exhaust camshaft gear with the intake camshaft gear so that the timing marks are in alignment with one another. Be sure to use the proper alignment marks on the gears. Do not use the assembly reference marks.
d. Turn the intake camshaft clockwise or counterclockwise little by little until the exhaust camshaft sits in the bearing journals evenly without rocking the camshaft on the bearing journals.
e. Coat the bearing cap bolts with clean engine oil.
f. Tighten the camshaft bearing caps evenly and in several passes to 14 ft. lbs. (19 Nm). Remove the service bolt from the assembly.

7. Install the head cover.
8. Start the engine and check for leaks.
9. Adjust the valves and the ignition timing.

2VZ-FE and 3VZ-FE Engines

▶ See Figures 168 thru 174

1. Remove the cylinder head covers.

➡️Being that the thrust clearance on both the intake and exhaust camshafts is small, the camshafts must be kept level during removal. If the camshafts are removed without being kept level, the camshaft may be caught in the cylinder head causing the head to break or the camshaft to seize.

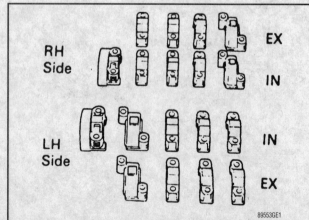

Fig. 168 Arrange the bearing caps in order on a table—2VZ-FE and 3VZ-FE engines

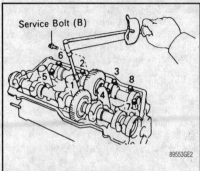

Fig. 169 Right exhaust camshaft bearing cap bolt tightening sequence—2VZ-FE and 3VZ-FE engines

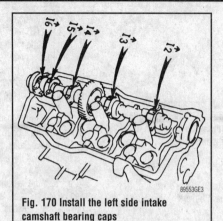

Fig. 170 Install the left side intake camshaft bearing caps

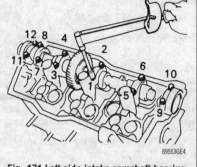

Fig. 171 Left side intake camshaft bearing cap bolt tightening sequence—2VZ-FE and 3VZ-FE engines

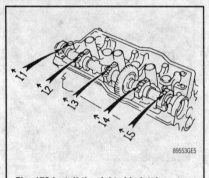

Fig. 172 Install the right side intake camshaft bearing caps—2VZ-FE and 3VZ-FE engines

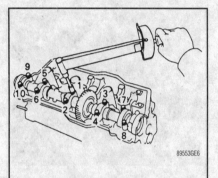

Fig. 173 Right side intake camshaft bearing cap bolt tightening sequence—2VZ-FE and 3VZ-FE engines

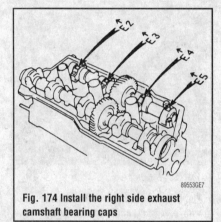

Fig. 174 Install the right side exhaust camshaft bearing caps

2. To remove the exhaust camshaft from the right side cylinder head, proceed as follows:

   a. Turn the camshaft with a wrench until the two pointed marks on the drive and driven gears are aligned.

   b. Secure the exhaust camshaft sub-gear to the main gear using a service bolt. The manufacturer recommends a bolt 0.63–0.79 inch (16–20mm) long with a thread diameter of 6mm and a 1mm thread pitch. When removing the exhaust camshaft be sure that the torsional spring force of the sub-gear has been eliminated (you guessed it; that's what the bolt is for!).

   c. Remove eight bearing cap bolts and remove the caps. Uniformly loosen and remove bearing cap bolts in several passes and in the proper sequence.

   d. Remove the exhaust camshaft from the engine.

3. Uniformly loosen and remove the ten bearing cap bolts in several passes, in the sequence shown. Remove the bearing caps and oil seal and then lift out the intake camshaft.

4. To remove the exhaust camshaft from the left side cylinder head, proceed as follows:

   a. Turn the camshaft with a wrench until the pointed marks on the drive and driven gears are aligned.

   b. Secure the exhaust camshaft sub-gear to the main gear using a service bolt. The manufacturer recommends a bolt 0.63–0.79 inch (16–20mm) long with a thread diameter of 6mm and a 1mm thread pitch. When removing the exhaust camshaft be sure that the torsional spring force of the sub-gear has been eliminated.

   c. Remove eight bearing cap bolts and remove the caps. Uniformly loosen and remove bearing cap bolts in several passes and in the proper sequence.

   d. Remove the exhaust camshaft from the engine.

5. Uniformly loosen and remove the ten bearing cap bolts in several passes, in the sequence shown. Remove the bearing caps and oil seal and then lift out the intake camshaft.

To install:

6. Before installing the intake camshaft in the right side cylinder head, apply multi-purpose grease to the thrust portion of the camshaft.

7. To install the intake camshaft, proceed as follows:

   a. Position the camshaft at a 90° angle to the two pointed marks on the cylinder head.

   b. Apply sealant to the No. 1 bearing cap.

   c. Coat the bearing cap bolts with clean engine oil.

   d. Tighten the camshaft bearing caps evenly and in several passes to 12 ft. lbs. (16 Nm) in the proper sequence.

8. Apply multi-purpose grease to the thrust portion of the exhaust camshaft (right side head).

9. Position the camshaft into the head so that the two pointed marks are aligned on the drive and driven gears. Install the bearing caps and tighten the bolts to 12 ft. lbs. (16 Nm), in several passes, in the sequence shown.

10. Remove the service bolt.

11. Before installing the intake camshaft in the left side cylinder head, apply multi-purpose grease to the thrust portion of the camshaft.

12. To install the intake camshaft, proceed as follows:

   a. Position the camshaft at a 90° angle to the pointed mark on the cylinder head.

   b. Apply sealant to the No. 1 bearing cap.

   c. Coat the bearing cap bolts with clean engine oil.

   d. Tighten the camshaft bearing caps evenly and in several passes to 12 ft. lbs. (16 Nm) in the proper sequence.

13. Apply multi-purpose grease to the thrust portion of the exhaust camshaft (left side head).

14. Position the camshaft into the head so that the pointed marks are aligned on the drive and driven gears. Install the bearing caps and tighten the bolts to 12 ft. lbs. (16 Nm), in several passes, in the sequence shown.

15. Remove the service bolt. Install the head cover, start the engine and check for leaks.

16. Adjust the valves and the ignition timing.

1MZ-FE Engine

▶ **See Figures 175 thru 189**

1. Remove the timing belt and idler pulley.
2. Remove the camshaft timing pulleys.
3. Remove the cylinder head covers.

➡**The thrust clearance on both the intake and exhaust camshafts is very small; the camshafts must be kept level during removal. If the camshafts are removed without being kept level, the camshaft may be caught in the cylinder head, causing the head to break or the camshaft to seize.**

4. To remove the exhaust and intake camshafts from the right side cylinder head:

   a. Turn the camshaft with a wrench until the 2 pointed marks drive and driven gears are aligned. (The right camshaft gears have 2 marks apiece; the left side camshaft gears have one mark each.)

b. Secure the exhaust camshaft sub-gear to the main gear using a service bolt. A bolt 0.63–0.79 in. (16–20mm) long with a 6mm thread diameter and a 1mm pitch is recommended. When removing the exhaust camshaft be sure the sub-gear is not loaded; all the force must be eliminated.

c. Uniformly loosen and remove the exhaust camshaft bearing cap bolts in several passes and in the proper sequence. Remove the eight bearing cap bolts and remove the caps, keeping them in the correct order.

d. Remove the exhaust camshaft from the engine.

e. Uniformly loosen and remove the 10 bearing cap bolts in several passes, in the proper sequence. Remove the bearing caps, keeping them in order, remove the oil seal and then lift out the intake camshaft.

5. To remove the exhaust and intake camshafts from the left side cylinder head:

   a. Turn the camshaft with a wrench until the pointed marks on the drive and driven gears are aligned. (The right camshaft gears have 2 marks apiece; the left side camshaft gears have one mark each.)

   b. Secure the exhaust camshaft sub-gear to the main gear using a service

Fig. 175 View of the left cylinder head with exhaust (1) and intake (2) camshafts

Fig. 176 Place a service bolt in the camshaft sub-gear to secure it

Fig. 177 Lift the caps and bolts up and place in order of removal—intake camshaft shown

Fig. 178 All bearing caps are marked with an E or I

Fig. 179 Carefully lift the camshaft out and carry in the vertical position shown—intake camshaft shown

Fig. 180 Removing the left side exhaust camshaft

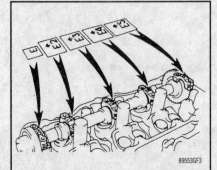

Fig. 181 Right exhaust bearing caps must be placed in their proper locations

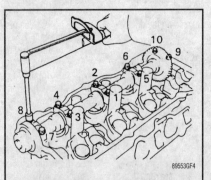

Fig. 182 Right exhaust camshaft bearing cap bolt tightening sequence—1MZ-FE engine

Fig. 183 Use a torque wrench to tighten the cap bolts

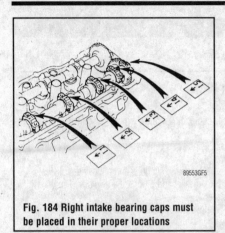

Fig. 184 Right intake bearing caps must be placed in their proper locations

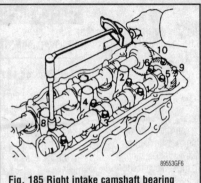

Fig. 185 Right intake camshaft bearing cap bolt tightening sequence—1MZ-FE engine

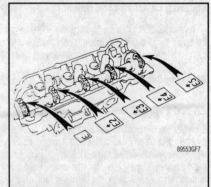

Fig. 186 Left exhaust bearing caps must be placed in their proper locations

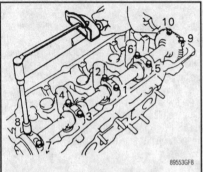

Fig. 187 Left exhaust camshaft bearing cap bolt tightening sequence—1MZ-FE engine

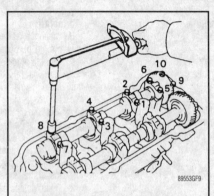

Fig. 188 Left intake camshaft bearing cap bolt tightening sequence—1MZ-FE engine

Fig. 189 The camshaft seals are on the end of the component

bolt. A bolt 0.63–0.79 inch (16–20mm) long with a 6mm thread diameter and a 1mm pitch is recommended. When removing the exhaust camshaft be sure the sub-gear is not loaded; all the force must be eliminated.

c. Uniformly loosen and remove the exhaust camshaft bearing cap bolts in several passes and in the proper sequence. Remove the eight bearing cap bolts and remove the caps. Keep the caps in the correct order.

d. Remove the exhaust camshaft from the engine.

e. Uniformly loosen and remove the 10 bearing cap bolts in several passes, in the reverse order of the installation sequence. Remove the bearing caps, keeping them in order, remove the oil seal and then lift out the intake camshaft.

6. Remove the valve lifter shims and hydraulic lifters. Identify each lifter and shim as it is removed so it can be reinstalled in the same position. If the lifters are to be reused, store them upside down in a sealed container.

To install:

7. Install the valve lifters into their original positions and install the shims. Check valve clearance and replace the shims as necessary.

8. When reinstalling, remember that the camshafts must be handled carefully and kept straight and level to avoid damage.

9. Before installing the camshafts in either cylinder head, apply multi-purpose grease to each camshaft.

10. To install the right camshafts:

a. Position the intake camshaft on the head so that the alignment marks are at a 90 degree angle from vertical. The mark should be at the "3 o'clock" position.

b. Apply sealant to the No. 1 bearing cap.

c. Apply a light coat of clean engine oil to the bolt threads and under the bolt head. Install the bearing caps to their proper position. Tighten the bolts evenly and in several passes to 12 ft. lbs. (16 Nm) in the proper sequence.

d. Position the exhaust camshaft on the head so that the alignment marks are at a 90 degree angle from vertical. The mark should be at the " o'clock" position and must align with the marks on the other gear.

e. Apply a light coat of clean engine oil to the bolt threads and under the

bolt head. Install the bearing caps to their proper position. Tighten the bolts evenly and in several passes to 12 ft. lbs. (16 Nm) in the proper sequence.

f. Remove the service bolt.

11. To install the left camshafts:

a. Position the intake camshaft on the head so that the alignment mark is at a 90 degree angle from vertical. The mark should be at the "9 o'clock" position.

b. Apply sealant to the No. 1 bearing cap.

c. Apply a light coat of clean engine oil to the bolt threads and under the bolt head. Install the bearing caps to their proper position. Tighten the bolts evenly and in several passes to 12 ft. lbs. (16 Nm) in the proper sequence.

d. Position the exhaust camshaft on the head so that the alignment marks are at a 90 degree angle from vertical. The mark should be at the "3 o'clock" position and must align with the marks on the other gear.

e. Apply a light coat of clean engine oil to the bolt threads and under the bolt head. Install the bearing caps to their proper position. Tighten the bolts evenly and in several passes to 12 ft. lbs. (16 Nm) in the proper sequence.

f. Remove the service bolt.

12. Apply multi-purpose grease to new camshaft oil seals. Install the seals.

13. Install the No. 3 (rear) timing belt cover. The remainder installation is the reverse of removal. Tighten each component to specifications.

14. Start the engine. Check the ignition timing. Test drive the vehicle and check all fluid levels.

INSPECTION

Checking Camshaft Runout

Camshaft runout should be checked when the camshaft has been removed from the engine. An accurate dial indicator is needed for this procedure; engine specialists and most machine shops have this equipment. If you have access to a dial indicator, or can take your camshaft to someone who does, measure the camshaft bearing journal runout. If the runout exceeds the limit replace the camshaft.

Checking Camshaft Lobe Height

Use a micrometer to check camshaft (lobe) height, making sure the anvil and the spindle of the micrometer are positioned directly on the heel and tip of the camshaft lobe as shown in the accompanying illustration.

Checking Bearing Oil Clearance

2S-ELC ENGINES ONLY

While the camshaft is still removed from the housing, the camshaft bearing journals should be measured with a micrometer. Compare the measurements with those listed in the Engine Mechanical Specifications chart in this section. If the measurements are less than the limits listed in the chart, the camshaft will require replacement, since the camshaft runs directly on the housing surface; no actual bearings or bushings are used, so no oversize bearings or bushings are available.

Using an inside dial gauge or inside micrometer, measure the inside diameter of the camshaft saddles (the camshaft mounts that are integrally cast as part of the housing. The inside diameter of the saddles is as follows:

- No. 1—1.8307–1.8317 inch (46.500–46.525mm)
- No. 2—1.8209–1.8218 inch (46.250–46.275mm)
- No. 3—1.8110–1.8120 inch (46.000–46.025mm)
- No. 4—1.8012–1.8022 inch (45.750–45.775mm)
- No. 5—1.7913–1.7923 inch (45.500–45.525mm)
- No. 6—1.7815–1.7825 inch (45.250–45.275mm)

The camshaft journal oil clearances are listed in the Engine Mechanical Specifications chart in this section. Simply subtract the journal diameter from the inside diameter. If clearances are off, the housing must be replaced (again, because oversize bearings or bushings are not available).

EXCEPT 2S-ELC

▶ **See Figure 190**

Measure the bearing oil clearance by placing a piece of Plastigage® on each bearing journal. Replace the bearing caps and tighten the bolts to the proper torque.

➡**Do not turn the camshaft.**

Remove the caps and measure each piece of Plastigage®. If the clearance is greater than the values on the Engine Mechanical Specifications chart, replace the camshaft. If necessary, replace the bearing caps and cylinder head as a set.

Check the camshaft bearings for flaking and scoring. If the bearings show any signs of damage, replace the bearing caps and the cylinder head as a set.

Checking Camshaft End-Play

After the camshaft has been installed, end-play should be checked. The camshaft sprocket should not be installed on the cam. Use a dial gauge to check the end-play, by moving the camshaft forward and backward in the cylinder head. End-play specifications should be as noted in the Engine Mechanical Specifications chart.

Rear Main Seal

REMOVAL & INSTALLATION

▶ **See Figures 191 and 192**

1. Remove the transaxle.
2. On manual transaxle equipped vehicles, remove the clutch cover assembly and flywheel.
3. On automatic transaxle equipped vehicles, remove the drive plate.
4. Remove the rear end plate.
5. On gasoline engines, remove the six bolts and remove the oil seal retainer and gasket. Discard the gasket and purchase a new one. The V6 engines use sealant instead of a gasket.
6. On diesel engines, remove the dust seal. Remove the five bolts and remove the oil seal retainer.
7. Use a small prybar to pry the oil seal from the retaining plate. Be careful not to damage the plate.

   To install:
8. Clean the retainer contact surfaces thoroughly and lubricate the new oil seal with multi-purpose grease.
9. Using a block of wood, drive the oil seal into the retainer until its surface is flush with the edge of the retainer. Make sure that the seal is installed evenly in the retainer to ensure proper sealing.
10. On V6 gasoline engines, apply a ⅛ inch bead of sealant to the oil seal retainer. Bolt the retainer with the five bolts (V6) and install the dust seal. Tighten the bolts on the V6 to 69 inch lbs. (8 Nm).
11. On 2S-ELC, 3S-FE and 5S-FE engines, install the oil seal retainer with the new gasket and attach with the six bolts. Tighten the bolts to 7 ft. lbs. (9 Nm) in a crisscross pattern.
12. Install the rear end plate.
13. On automatic transaxle equipped vehicles, install the drive plate.
14. On manual transaxle equipped vehicles, install the clutch disc and clutch cover.
15. Install the transaxle.

Flywheel/Flexplate

REMOVAL & INSTALLATION

▶ **See Figures 193 and 194**

➡**Vehicles equipped with manual transaxles are equipped with flywheels and automatic transaxles use drive plates (also known as flexplates). Drive plates and flywheels are removed and installed in the same manner.**

1. Remove the engine from the vehicle and disconnect the transaxle from the engine.
2. Loosen the eight bolts (six bolts on the 2S-ELC) that attach the flywheel/drive plate to the crankshaft.

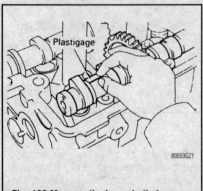

Fig. 190 Measure the journal oil clearance with Plastigage®

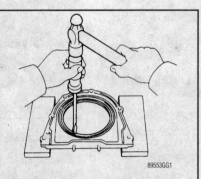

Fig. 191 Always place the seal on blocks of wood, then tap the seal from the retainer

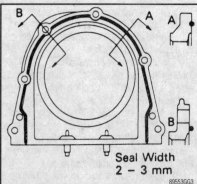

Seal Width
2 – 3 mm

Fig. 192 Apply sealant to the rear oil seal retainer

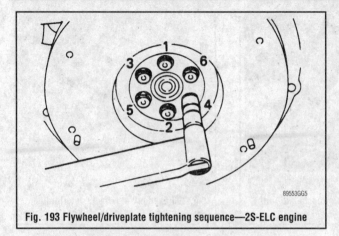

Fig. 193 Flywheel/driveplate tightening sequence—2S-ELC engine

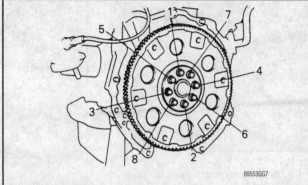

Fig. 194 Flywheel/driveplate tightening sequence—Except 2S-ELC engine

3. Pull the flywheel/drive plate from the crankshaft.

4. Wire brush the retaining bolts thoroughly to remove all the old sealant from the threads.

5. Remove any sealant or debris from the crankshaft and flywheel/drive plate bolt holes. If the holes are filled with oil and grease, clean them with a small wire brush and penetrating oil. You may have to run the proper size metric tap down each bolt hole several times to clear the hole.

6. Apply No. 08833-00070, THREE BOND®1324 or equivalent adhesive to the last two or three threads of each bolt.

7. Support and position the flywheel/drive plate onto the crankshaft.

8. On flywheel equipped engines, tighten the bolts in sequence to:
- 2S-ELC—72 ft. lbs. (98 Nm)
- 3S-FE, 5S-FE—65 ft. lbs. (88 Nm)
- 2VZ-FE, 3VZ-FE—61 ft. lbs. (83 Nm)

9. On drive plate equipped engines, tighten the bolts in sequence to:
- 2S-ELC—61 ft. lbs. (83 Nm)
- 3S-FE, 5S-FE—61 ft. lbs. (83 Nm)
- 1MZ-FE, 2VZ-FE, 3VZ-FE—61 ft. lbs. (83 Nm)

10. Attach the transaxle to the engine and install the engine into the vehicle.

EXHAUST SYSTEM

Inspection

♦ See Figures 195 thru 201

➡Safety glasses should be worn at all times when working on or near the exhaust system. Older exhaust systems will almost always be covered with loose rust particles which will shower you when disturbed. These particles are more than a nuisance and could injure your eye.

✳✳ CAUTION

Do NOT perform exhaust repairs or inspection with the engine or exhaust hot. Allow the system to cool completely before attempting any work. Exhaust systems are noted for sharp edges, flaking metal and rusted bolts. Gloves and eye protection are required. A healthy supply of penetrating oil and rags is highly recommended.

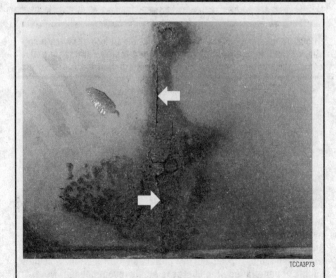

Fig. 195 Cracks in the muffler are a guaranteed leak

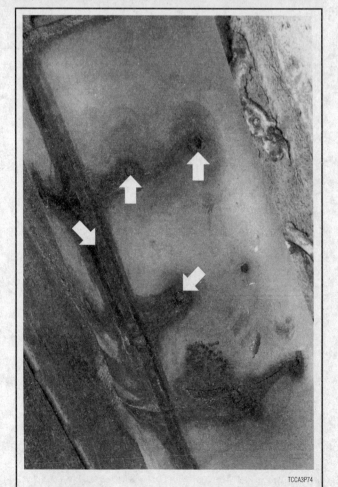

Fig. 196 Check the muffler for rotted spot welds and seams

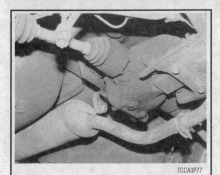

Fig. 197 Make sure the exhaust components are not contacting the body or suspension

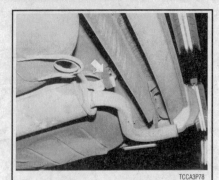

Fig. 198 Check for overstreached or torn exhaust hangers

Fig. 199 Example of a badly deteriorated exhaust pipe

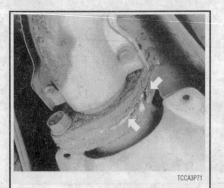

Fig. 200 Inspect flanges for gaskets that have deteriorated and need replacement

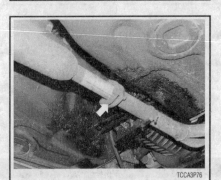

Fig. 201 Some systems, like this one, use large O-rings (donuts) in between the flanges

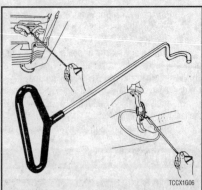

Fig. 202 Example of an exhaust doughnut expander

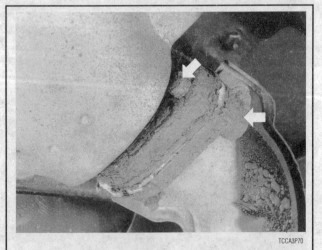

Fig. 203 Nuts and bolts will be extremely difficult to remove when deteriorated with rust

Your vehicle must be raised and supported safely to inspect the exhaust system properly. By placing 4 safety stands under the vehicle for support should provide enough room for you to slide under the vehicle and inspect the system completely. Start the inspection at the exhaust manifold or turbocharger pipe where the header pipe is attached and work your way to the back of the vehicle. On dual exhaust systems, remember to inspect both sides of the vehicle. Check the complete exhaust system for open seams, holes loose connections, or other deterioration which could permit exhaust fumes to seep into the passenger compartment. Inspect all mounting brackets and hangers for deterioration, some models may have rubber O-rings that can be overstretched and non-supportive. These components will need to be replaced if found. It has always been a practice to use a pointed tool to poke up into the exhaust system where the deterio-

ration spots are to see whether or not they crumble. Some models may have heat shield covering certain parts of the exhaust system , it will be necessary to remove these shields to have the exhaust visible for inspection also.

REPLACEMENT

▶ **See Figures 202 thru 207**

There are basically two types of exhaust systems. One is the flange type where the component ends are attached with bolts and a gasket in-between. The other exhaust system is the slip joint type. These components slip into one another using clamps to retain them together.

✳✳ CAUTION

Allow the exhaust system to cool sufficiently before spraying a solvent exhaust fasteners. Some solvents are highly flammable and could ignite when sprayed on hot exhaust components.

Before removing any component of the exhaust system, ALWAYS squirt a liquid rust dissolving agent onto the fasteners for ease of removal. A lot of knuckle skin will be saved by following this rule. It may even be wise to spray the fasteners and allow them to sit overnight.

Flange Type

▶ **See Figure 208**

✳✳ CAUTION

Do NOT perform exhaust repairs or inspection with the engine or exhaust hot. Allow the system to cool completely before attempting any work. Exhaust systems are noted for sharp edges, flaking metal and rusted bolts. Gloves and eye protection are required. A healthy supply of penetrating oil and rags is highly recommended. Never spray liquid rust dissolving agent onto a hot exhaust component.

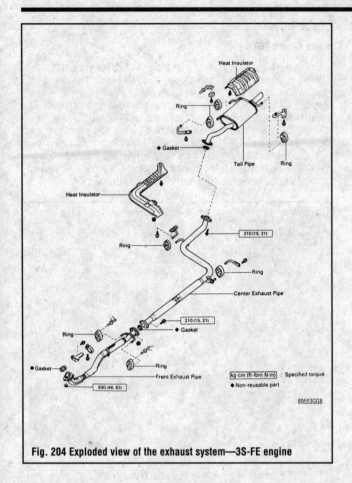

Fig. 204 Exploded view of the exhaust system—3S-FE engine

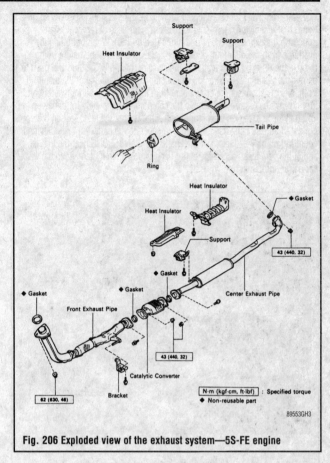

Fig. 206 Exploded view of the exhaust system—5S-FE engine

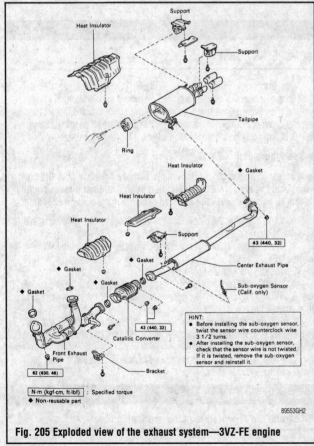

Fig. 205 Exploded view of the exhaust system—3VZ-FE engine

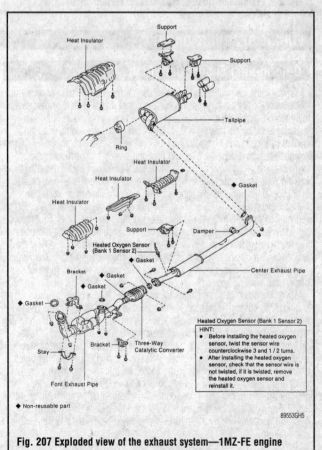

Fig. 207 Exploded view of the exhaust system—1MZ-FE engine

Before removing any component on a flange type system, ALWAYS squirt a liquid rust dissolving agent onto the fasteners for ease of removal. Start by unbolting the exhaust piece at both ends (if required). When unbolting the headpipe from the manifold, make sure that the bolts are free before trying to remove them. if you snap a stud in the exhaust manifold, the stud will have to be removed with a bolt extractor, which often means removal of the manifold itself. Next, disconnect the component from the mounting; slight twisting and turning may be required to remove the component completely from the vehicle. You may need to tap on the component with a rubber mallet to loosen the component. If all else fails, use a hacksaw to separate the parts. An oxy-acetylene cutting torch may be faster but the sparks are DANGEROUS near the fuel tank, and at the very least, accidents could happen, resulting in damage to the under-car parts, not to mention yourself.

Fig. 208 Example of a flange type exhaust system joint

Slip Joint Type

♦ **See Figure 209**

Before removing any component on the slip joint type exhaust system, ALWAYS squirt a liquid rust dissolving agent onto the fasteners for ease of removal. Start by unbolting the exhaust piece at both ends (if required). When unbolting the headpipe from the manifold, make sure that the bolts are free before trying to remove them. if you snap a stud in the exhaust manifold, the stud will have to be removed with a bolt extractor, which often means removal of the manifold itself. Next, remove the mounting U-bolts from around the exhaust pipe you are extracting from the vehicle. Don't be surprised if the U-bolts break while removing the nuts. Loosen the exhaust pipe from any mounting brackets retaining it to the floor pan and separate the components.

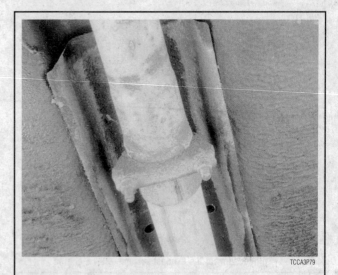

Fig. 209 Example of a common slip joint type system

ENGINE RECONDITIONING

Determining Engine Condition

Anything that generates heat and/or friction will eventually burn or wear out (for example, a light bulb generates heat, therefore its life span is limited). With this in mind, a running engine generates tremendous amounts of both; friction is encountered by the moving and rotating parts inside the engine and heat is created by friction and combustion of the fuel. However, the engine has systems designed to help reduce the effects of heat and friction and provide added longevity. The oiling system reduces the amount of friction encountered by the moving parts inside the engine, while the cooling system reduces heat created by friction and combustion. If either system is not maintained, a break-down will be inevitable. Therefore, you can see how regular maintenance can affect the service life of your vehicle. If you do not drain, flush and refill your cooling system at the proper intervals, deposits will begin to accumulate in the radiator, thereby reducing the amount of heat it can extract from the coolant. The same applies to your oil and filter; if it is not changed often enough it becomes laden with contaminates and is unable to properly lubricate the engine. This increases friction and wear.

There are a number of methods for evaluating the condition of your engine. A compression test can reveal the condition of your pistons, piston rings, cylinder bores, head gasket(s), valves and valve seats. An oil pressure test can warn you of possible engine bearing, or oil pump failures. Excessive oil consumption, evidence of oil in the engine air intake area and/or bluish smoke from the tailpipe may indicate worn piston rings, worn valve guides and/or valve seals. As a general rule, an engine that uses no more than one quart of oil every 1000 miles is in good condition. Engines that use one quart of oil or more in less than 1000 miles should first be checked for oil leaks. If any oil leaks are present, have them fixed before determining how much oil is consumed by the engine, especially if blue smoke is not visible at the tailpipe.

COMPRESSION TEST

A noticeable lack of engine power, excessive oil consumption and/or poor fuel mileage measured over an extended period are all indicators of internal engine wear. Worn piston rings, scored or worn cylinder bores, blown head gaskets, sticking or burnt valves, and worn valve seats are all possible culprits. A check of each cylinder's compression will help locate the problem.

♦ **See Figure 210**

➡**A screw-in type compression gauge is more accurate than the type you simply hold against the spark plug hole. Although it takes slightly longer to use, it's worth the effort to obtain a more accurate reading.**

1. Make sure that the proper amount and viscosity of engine oil is in the crankcase, then ensure the battery is fully charged.
2. Warm-up the engine to normal operating temperature, then shut the engine **OFF**.
3. Disable the ignition system.
4. Label and disconnect all of the spark plug wires from the plugs.
5. Thoroughly clean the cylinder head area around the spark plug ports, then remove the spark plugs.
6. Set the throttle plate to the fully open (wide-open throttle) position. You can block the accelerator linkage open for this, or you can have an assistant fully depress the accelerator pedal.
7. Install a screw-in type compression gauge into the No. 1 spark plug hole until the fitting is snug.

✳✳ WARNING

Be careful not to crossthread the spark plug hole.

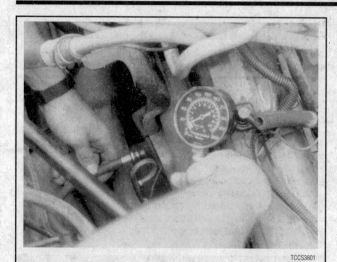

Fig. 210 A screw-in type compression gauge is more accurate and easier to use without an assistant

8. According to the tool manufacturer's instructions, connect a remote starting switch to the starting circuit.

9. With the ignition switch in the **OFF** position, use the remote starting switch to crank the engine through at least five compression strokes (approximately 5 seconds of cranking) and record the highest reading on the gauge.

10. Repeat the test on each cylinder, cranking the engine approximately the same number of compression strokes and/or time as the first.

11. Compare the highest readings from each cylinder to that of the others. The indicated compression pressures are considered within specifications if the lowest reading cylinder is within 75 percent of the pressure recorded for the highest reading cylinder. For example, if your highest reading cylinder pressure was 150 psi (1034 kPa), then 75 percent of that would be 113 psi (779 kPa). So the lowest reading cylinder should be no less than 113 psi (779 kPa).

12. If a cylinder exhibits an unusually low compression reading, pour a tablespoon of clean engine oil into the cylinder through the spark plug hole and repeat the compression test. If the compression rises after adding oil, it means that the cylinder's piston rings and/or cylinder bore are damaged or worn. If the pressure remains low, the valves may not be seating properly (a valve job is needed), or the head gasket may be blown near that cylinder. If compression in any two adjacent cylinders is low, and if the addition of oil doesn't help raise compression, there is leakage past the head gasket. Oil and coolant in the combustion chamber, combined with blue or constant white smoke from the tailpipe, are symptoms of this problem. However, don't be alarmed by the normal white smoke emitted from the tailpipe during engine warm-up or from cold weather driving. There may be evidence of water droplets on the engine dipstick and/or oil droplets in the cooling system if a head gasket is blown.

OIL PRESSURE TEST

Check for proper oil pressure at the sending unit passage with an externally mounted mechanical oil pressure gauge (as opposed to relying on a factory installed dash-mounted gauge). A tachometer may also be needed, as some specifications may require running the engine at a specific rpm.

1. With the engine cold, locate and remove the oil pressure sending unit.

2. Following the manufacturer's instructions, connect a mechanical oil pressure gauge and, if necessary, a tachometer to the engine.

3. Start the engine and allow it to idle.

4. Check the oil pressure reading when cold and record the number. You may need to run the engine at a specified rpm, so check the specifications.

5. Run the engine until normal operating temperature is reached (upper radiator hose will feel warm).

6. Check the oil pressure reading again with the engine hot and record the number. Turn the engine **OFF**.

7. Compare your hot oil pressure reading to specification. If the reading is low, check the cold pressure reading against the chart. If the cold pressure is well above the specification, and the hot reading was lower than the specifica-

tion, you may have the wrong viscosity oil in the engine. Change the oil, making sure to use the proper grade and quantity, then repeat the test.

Low oil pressure readings could be attributed to internal component wear, pump related problems, a low oil level, or oil viscosity that is too low. High oil pressure readings could be caused by an overfilled crankcase, too high of an oil viscosity or a faulty pressure relief valve.

Buy or Rebuild?

Now if you have determined that your engine is worn out, you must make some decisions. The question of whether or not an engine is worth rebuilding is largely a subjective matter and one of personal worth. Is the engine a popular one, or is it an obsolete model? Are parts available? Will it get acceptable gas mileage once it is rebuilt? Is the car it's being put into worth keeping? Would it be less expensive to buy a new engine, have your engine rebuilt by a pro, rebuild it yourself or buy a used engine from a salvage yard? Or would it be simpler and less expensive to buy another car? If you have considered all these matters, and have still decided to rebuild the engine, then it is time to decide how you will rebuild it.

➡ **The editors at Chilton feel that most engine machining should be performed by a professional machine shop. Think of it as an assurance that the job has been done right the first time. There are many expensive and specialized tools required to perform such tasks as boring and honing an engine block or having a valve job done on a cylinder head. Even inspecting the parts requires expensive micrometers and gauges to properly measure wear and clearances. A machine shop can deliver to you clean, and ready to assemble parts, saving you time and aggravation. Your maximum savings will come from performing the removal, disassembly, assembly and installation of the engine and purchasing or renting only the tools required to perform these tasks.**

A complete rebuild or overhaul of an engine involves replacing all of the moving parts (pistons, rods, crankshaft, camshaft, etc.) with new ones and machining the non-moving wearing surfaces of the block and heads. Unfortunately, this may not be cost effective. For instance, your crankshaft may have been damaged or worn, but it can be machined undersize for a minimal fee.

So although you can replace everything inside the engine, it is usually wiser to replace only those parts which are really needed, and, if possible, repair the more expensive ones. Later in this section, we will break the engine down into its two main components: the cylinder head and the engine block. We will discuss each component, and the recommended parts to replace during a rebuild on each.

Engine Overhaul Tips

Most engine overhaul procedures are fairly standard. In addition to specific parts replacement procedures and specifications for your individual engine, this section is also a guide to acceptable rebuilding procedures. Examples of standard rebuilding practice are given and should be used along with specific details concerning your particular engine.

Competent and accurate machine shop services will ensure maximum performance, reliability and engine life. In most instances it is more profitable for the do-it-yourself mechanic to remove, clean and inspect the component, buy the necessary parts and deliver these to a shop for actual machine work.

Much of the assembly work (crankshaft, bearings, piston rods, and other components) is well within the scope of the do-it-yourself mechanic's tools and abilities. You will have to decide for yourself the depth of involvement you desire in an engine repair or rebuild.

TOOLS

The tools required for an engine overhaul or parts replacement will depend on the depth of your involvement. With a few exceptions, they will be the tools found in a mechanic's tool kit·(see Section 1 of this manual). More in-depth work will require some or all of the following:

- A dial indicator (reading in thousandths) mounted on a universal base
- Micrometers and telescope gauges
- Jaw and screw-type pullers
- Scraper
- Valve spring compressor

- Ring groove cleaner
- Piston ring expander and compressor
- Ridge reamer
- Cylinder hone or glaze breaker
- Plastigage®
- Engine stand

The use of most of these tools is illustrated in this section. Many can be rented for a one-time use from a local parts jobber or tool supply house specializing in automotive work.

Occasionally, the use of special tools is called for. See the information on Special Tools and the Safety Notice in the front of this book before substituting another tool.

OVERHAUL TIPS

Aluminum has become extremely popular for use in engines, due to its low weight. Observe the following precautions when handling aluminum parts:
- Never hot tank aluminum parts (the caustic hot tank solution will eat the aluminum.)
- Remove all aluminum parts (identification tag, etc.) from engine parts prior to the tanking.
- Always coat threads lightly with engine oil or anti-seize compounds before installation, to prevent seizure.
- Never overtighten bolts or spark plugs especially in aluminum threads.

When assembling the engine, any parts that will be exposed to frictional contact must be prelubed to provide lubrication at initial start-up. Any product specifically formulated for this purpose can be used, but engine oil is not recommended as a prelube in most cases.

When semi-permanent (locked, but removable) installation of bolts or nuts is desired, threads should be cleaned and coated with Loctite, or another similar, commercial non-hardening sealant.

CLEANING

▶ **See Figures 211, 212, 213 and 214**

Before the engine and its components are inspected, they must be thoroughly cleaned. You will need to remove any engine varnish, oil sludge and/or carbon deposits from all of the components to insure an accurate inspection. A crack in the engine block or cylinder head can easily become overlooked if hidden by a layer of sludge or carbon.

Most of the cleaning process can be carried out with common hand tools and readily available solvents or solutions. Carbon deposits can be chipped away using a hammer and a hard wooden chisel. Old gasket material and varnish or sludge can usually be removed using a scraper and/or cleaning solvent. Extremely stubborn deposits may require the use of a power drill with a wire brush. If using a wire brush, use extreme care around any critical machined surfaces (such as the gasket surfaces, bearing saddles, cylinder bores, etc.). USE OF A WIRE BRUSH IS NOT RECOMMENDED ON ANY ALUMINUM COMPONENTS. Always follow any safety recommendations given by the manufacturer of the tool and/or solvent.

■✳■ **CAUTION**

Always wear eye protection during any cleaning process involving scraping, chipping or spraying of solvents.

An alternative to the mess and hassle of cleaning the parts yourself is to drop them off at a local garage or machine shop. They should have the necessary equipment to properly clean all of the parts for a nominal fee.

Remove any oil galley plugs, freeze plugs and/or pressed-in bearings and carefully wash and degrease all of the engine components including the fasteners and bolts. Small parts such as the valves, springs, etc., should be placed in a metal basket and allowed to soak. Use pipe cleaner type brushes, and clean all passageways in the components.

Use a ring expander and remove the rings from the pistons. Clean the piston ring grooves with a special tool or a piece of broken ring. Scrape the carbon off of the top of the piston. You should never use a wire brush on the pistons. After preparing all of the piston assemblies in this manner, wash and degrease them again.

■✳■ **WARNING**

Use extreme care when cleaning around the cylinder head valve seats. A mistake or slip may cost you a new seat.

When cleaning the cylinder head, remove carbon from the combustion chamber with the valves installed. This will avoid damaging the valve seats.

REPAIRING DAMAGED THREADS

▶ **See Figures 215, 216, 217, 218 and 219**

Several methods of repairing damaged threads are available. Heli-Coil, (shown here), Keenserts, and Microdot, are among the most widely used. All involve basically the same principle—drilling out stripped threads, tapping the hole and installing a prewound insert—making welding, plugging and oversize fasteners unnecessary.

Two types of thread repair inserts are usually supplied: a standard type for most inch coarse, inch fine, metric course and metric fine thread sizes and a spark lug type to fit most spark plug port sizes. Consult the individual tool manufacturer's catalog to determine exact applications. Typical thread repair kits will contain a selection of prewound threaded inserts, a tap (corresponding to the outside diameter threads of the insert) and an installation tool. Spark plug inserts usually differ because they require a tap equipped with pilot threads and a combined reamer/tap section. Most manufacturers also supply blister-packed thread repair inserts separately in addition to a master kit containing a variety of taps and inserts plus installation tools.

Before attempting to repair a threaded hole, remove any snapped, broken or damaged bolts or studs. Penetrating oil can be used to free frozen threads. The offending item can usually be removed with locking pliers or using a screw/stud extractor. After the hole is clear, the thread can be repaired as shown in the kit manufacturer's instructions.

TCCS3132

Fig. 211 Use a gasket scraper to remove the old gasket material from the mating surfaces

TCCS3211

Fig. 212 Before cleaning and inspection, use a ring expander tool to remove the piston rings

TCCS3208

Fig. 213 Clean the piston ring grooves using a ring groove cleaner tool, or . . .

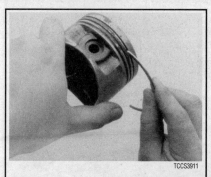

Fig. 214 . . . use a piece of an old ring to clean the grooves. Be careful, the ring can be quite sharp

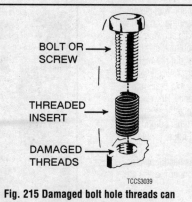

Fig. 215 Damaged bolt hole threads can be replaced with thread repair inserts

Fig. 216 Standard thread repair insert (left), and spark plug thread insert

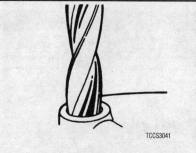

Fig. 217 Drill out the damaged threads with the specified size bit. Be sure to drill completely through the hole or to the bottom of a blind hole

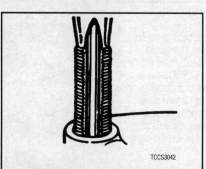

Fig. 218 Using the kit, tap the hole in order to receive the thread insert. Keep the tap well oiled and back it out frequently to avoid clogging the threads

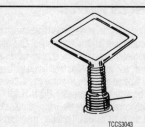

Fig. 219 Screw the insert onto the installer tool until the tang engages the slot. Thread the insert into the hole until it is ¼–½ turn below the top surface, then remove the tool and break off the tang using a punch

Engine Preparation

To properly rebuild an engine, you must first remove it from the vehicle, then disassemble and diagnose it. Ideally you should place your engine on an engine stand. This affords you the best access to the engine components. Remove the flywheel or flexplate before installing the engine to the stand.

Now that you have the engine on a stand, and assuming that you have drained the oil and coolant from the engine, it's time to strip it of all but the necessary components. Before you start disassembling the engine, you may want to take a moment to draw some pictures, or fabricate some labels or containers to mark the locations of various components and the bolts and/or studs which fasten them. Modern day engines use a lot of little brackets and clips which hold wiring harnesses and such, and these holders are often mounted on studs and/or bolts that can be easily mixed up. The manufacturer spent a lot of time and money designing your vehicle, and they wouldn't have wasted any of it by haphazardly placing brackets, clips or fasteners on the vehicle. If it's present when you disassemble it, put it back when you assemble, you will regret not remembering that little bracket which holds a wire harness out of the path of a rotating part.

You should begin by unbolting any accessories still attached to the engine, such as the water pump, power steering pump, alternator, etc. Then, unfasten any manifolds (intake or exhaust) which were not removed during the engine removal procedure. Finally, remove any covers remaining on the engine such as the rocker arm, front or timing cover and oil pan. Some front covers may require the vibration damper and/or crank pulley to be removed beforehand. The idea is to reduce the engine to the bare necessities of cylinder head(s), valve train, engine block, crankshaft, pistons and connecting rods, plus any other `in block' components such as oil pumps, balance shafts and auxiliary shafts.

Finally, remove the cylinder head(s) from the engine block and carefully place on a bench. Disassembly instructions for each component follow later in this section.

Cylinder Head

There are two basic types of cylinder heads used on today's automobiles: the Overhead Valve (OHV) and the Overhead Camshaft (OHC). The latter can also be broken down into two subgroups: the Single Overhead Camshaft (SOHC) and the Dual Overhead Camshaft (DOHC). Generally, if there is only a single camshaft on a head, it is just referred to as an OHC head. Also, an engine with an OHV cylinder head is also known as a pushrod engine.

Most cylinder heads these days are made of an aluminum alloy due to its light weight, durability and heat transfer qualities. However, cast iron was the material of choice in the past, and is still used on many vehicles. Whether made from aluminum or iron, all cylinder heads have valves and seats. Some use two valves per cylinder, while the more hi-tech engines will utilize a multi-valve configuration using 3, 4 and even 5 valves per cylinder. When the valve contacts the seat, it does so on precision machined surfaces, which seals the combustion chamber. All cylinder heads have a valve guide for each valve. The guide centers the valve to the seat and allows it to move up and down within it. The clearance between the valve and guide can be critical. Too much clearance and the engine may consume oil, lose vacuum and/or damage the seat. Too little, and the valve can stick in the guide causing the engine to run poorly if at all, and possibly causing severe damage. The last component all automotive cylinder heads have are valve springs. The spring holds the valve against its seat. It also returns the valve to this position when the valve has been opened by the valve train or camshaft. The spring is fastened to the valve by a retainer and valve locks (sometimes called keepers). Aluminum heads will also have a valve spring shim to keep the spring from wearing away the aluminum.

An ideal method of rebuilding the cylinder head would involve replacing all of the valves, guides, seats, springs, etc. with new ones. However, depending on how the engine was maintained, often this is not necessary. A major cause of valve, guide and seat wear is an improperly tuned engine. An engine that is running too rich, will often wash the lubricating oil out of the guide with gasoline, causing it to wear rapidly. Conversely, an engine which is running too lean will place higher combustion temperatures on the valves and seats allowing them to wear or even burn. Springs fall victim to the driving habits of the individual. A driver who often runs the engine rpm to the redline will wear out or break the springs faster then one that stays well below it. Unfortunately, mileage takes it toll on all of the parts. Generally, the valves, guides, springs and seats in a cylinder head can be machined and re-used, saving you money. However, if a valve is burnt, it may be wise to replace all of the valves, since they were all operating in the same environment. The same goes for any other component on the cylinder head. Think of it as an insurance policy against future problems related to that component.

Unfortunately, the only way to find out which components need replacing, is to disassemble and carefully check each piece. After the cylinder head(s) are disassembled, thoroughly clean all of the components.

DISASSEMBLY

▶ **See Figures 220 and 221**

Whether it is a single or dual overhead camshaft cylinder head, the disassembly procedure is relatively unchanged. One aspect to pay attention to is careful labeling of the parts on the dual camshaft cylinder head. There will be an intake camshaft and followers as well as an exhaust camshaft and followers and they must be labeled as such. In some cases, the components are identical and could easily be installed incorrectly. DO NOT MIX THEM UP! Determining which is which is very simple; the intake camshaft and components are on the same side of the head as was the intake manifold. Conversely, the exhaust camshaft and components are on the same side of the head as was the exhaust manifold.

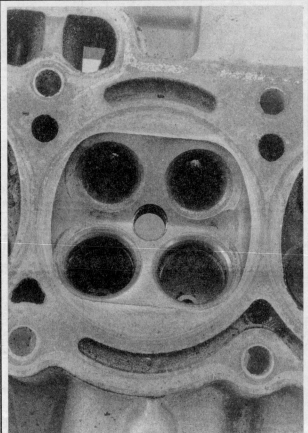

TCCA3P62

Fig. 221 Example of a multi-valve cylinder head. Note how it has 2 intake and 2 exhaust valve ports

Cup Type Camshaft Followers

▶ **See Figures 222, 223 and 224**

Most cylinder heads with cup type camshaft followers will have the valve spring, retainer and locks recessed within the follower's bore. You will need a

TCCA3P54

Fig. 220 Exploded view of a valve, seal, spring, retainer and locks from an OHC cylinder head

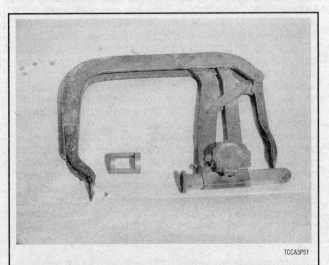

TCCA3P51

Fig. 222 C-clamp type spring compressor and an OHC spring removal tool (center) for cup type followers

Fig. 223 Most cup type follower cylinder heads retain the camshaft using bolt-on bearing caps

Fig. 224 Position the OHC spring tool in the follower bore, then compress the spring with a C-clamp type tool

C-clamp style valve spring compressor tool, an OHC spring removal tool (or equivalent) and a small magnet to disassemble the head.

   1. If not already removed, remove the camshaft(s) and/or followers. Mark their positions for assembly.

   2. Position the cylinder head to allow use of a C-clamp style valve spring compressor tool.

➡It is preferred to position the cylinder head gasket surface facing you with the valve springs facing the opposite direction and the head laying horizontal.

   3. With the OHC spring removal adapter tool positioned inside of the follower bore, compress the valve spring using the C-clamp style valve spring compressor.

   4. Remove the valve locks. A small magnetic tool or screwdriver will aid in removal.

   5. Release the compressor tool and remove the spring assembly.

   6. Withdraw the valve from the cylinder head.

   7. If equipped, remove the valve seal.

➡Special valve seal removal tools are available. Regular or needlenose type pliers, if used with care, will work just as well. If using ordinary pliers, be sure not to damage the follower bore. The follower and its bore are machined to close tolerances and any damage to the bore will effect this relationship.

   8. If equipped, remove the valve spring shim. A small magnetic tool or screwdriver will aid in removal.

   9. Repeat Steps 3 through 8 until all of the valves have been removed.

Rocker Arm Type Camshaft Followers

◆ See Figures 225 thru 233

Most cylinder heads with rocker arm-type camshaft followers are easily disassembled using a standard valve spring compressor. However, certain models may not have enough open space around the spring for the standard tool and may require you to use a C-clamp style compressor tool instead.

   1. If not already removed, remove the rocker arms and/or shafts and the camshaft. If applicable, also remove the hydraulic lash adjusters. Mark their positions for assembly.

   2. Position the cylinder head to allow access to the valve spring.

   3. Use a valve spring compressor tool to relieve the spring tension from the retainer.

➡Due to engine varnish, the retainer may stick to the valve locks. A gentle tap with a hammer may help to break it loose.

   4. Remove the valve locks from the valve tip and/or retainer. A small magnet may help in removing the small locks.

   5. Lift the valve spring, tool and all, off of the valve stem.

   6. If equipped, remove the valve seal. If the seal is difficult to remove with the valve in place, try removing the valve first, then the seal. Follow the steps below for valve removal.

   7. Position the head to allow access for withdrawing the valve.

Fig. 225 Example of the shaft mounted rocker arms on some OHC heads

Fig. 226 Another example of the rocker arm type OHC head. This model uses a follower under the camshaft

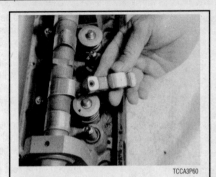

Fig. 227 Before the camshaft can be removed, all of the followers must first be removed . . .

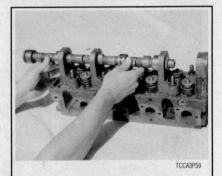

Fig. 228 . . . then the camshaft can be removed by sliding it out (shown), or unbolting a bearing cap (not shown)

Fig. 229 Compress the valve spring . . .

Fig. 230 . . . then remove the valve locks from the valve stem and spring retainer

Fig. 231 Remove the valve spring and retainer from the cylinder head

Fig. 232 Remove the valve seal from the guide. Some gentle prying or pliers may help to remove stubborn ones

Fig. 233 All aluminum and some cast iron heads will have these valve spring shims. Remove all of them as well

Fig. 234 Valve stems may be rolled on a flat surface to check for bends

➡Cylinder heads that have seen a lot of miles and/or abuse may have mushroomed the valve lock grove and/or tip, causing difficulty in removal of the valve. If this has happened, use a metal file to carefully remove the high spots around the lock grooves and/or tip. Only file it enough to allow removal.

   8. Remove the valve from the cylinder head.

   9. If equipped, remove the valve spring shim. A small magnetic tool or screwdriver will aid in removal.

   10. Repeat Steps 3 though 9 until all of the valves have been removed.

INSPECTION

   Now that all of the cylinder head components are clean, it's time to inspect them for wear and/or damage. To accurately inspect them, you will need some specialized tools:

  • A 0–1 in. micrometer for the valves

  • A dial indicator or inside diameter gauge for the valve guides

  • A spring pressure test gauge

   If you do not have access to the proper tools, you may want to bring the components to a shop that does.

Valves

▸ **See Figures 234 and 235**

   The first thing to inspect are the valve heads. Look closely at the head, margin and face for any cracks, excessive wear or burning. The margin is the best place to look for burning. It should have a squared edge with an even width all around the diameter. When a valve burns, the margin will look melted and the edges rounded. Also inspect the valve head for any signs of tulipping. This will show as a lifting of the edges or dishing in the center of the head and will usually not occur to all of the valves. All of the heads should look the same, any that seem dished more than others are probably bad. Next, inspect the valve lock grooves and valve tips. Check for any burrs around the lock grooves, espe-

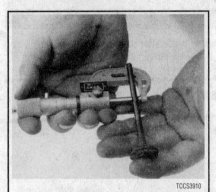

Fig. 235 Use a micrometer to check the valve stem diameter

Fig. 236 Use a caliper to check the valve spring free-length

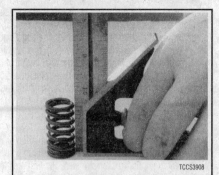

Fig. 237 Check the valve spring for squareness on a flat surface; a carpenter's square can be used

Fig. 238 A dial gauge may be used to check valve stem-to-guide clearance; read the gauge while moving the valve stem

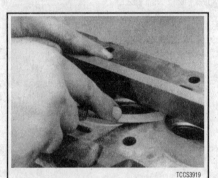

Fig. 239 Check the head for flatness across the center of the head surface using a straightedge and feeler gauge

Fig. 240 Checks should also be made along both diagonals of the head surface

cially if you had to file them to remove the valve. Valve tips should appear flat, although slight rounding with high mileage engines is normal. Slightly worn valve tips will need to be machined flat. Last, measure the valve stem diameter with the micrometer. Measure the area that rides within the guide, especially towards the tip where most of the wear occurs. Take several measurements along its length and compare them to each other. Wear should be even along the length with little to no taper. If no minimum diameter is given in the specifications, then the stem should not read more than 0.001 in. (0.025mm) below the unworn portion of the stem. Any valves that fail these inspections should be replaced.

Springs, Retainers and Valve Locks

▶ See Figures 236 and 237

The first thing to check is the most obvious, broken springs. Next check the free length and squareness of each spring. If applicable, insure to distinguish between intake and exhaust springs. Use a ruler and/or carpenter's square to measure the length. A carpenter's square should be used to check the springs for squareness. If a spring pressure test gauge is available, check each springs rating and compare to the specifications chart. Check the readings against the specifications given. Any springs that fail these inspections should be replaced.

The spring retainers rarely need replacing, however they should still be checked as a precaution. Inspect the spring mating surface and the valve lock retention area for any signs of excessive wear. Also check for any signs of cracking. Replace any retainers that are questionable.

Valve locks should be inspected for excessive wear on the outside contact area as well as on the inner notched surface. Any locks which appear worn or broken and its respective valve should be replaced.

Cylinder Head

There are several things to check on the cylinder head: valve guides, seats, cylinder head surface flatness, cracks and physical damage.

VALVE GUIDES

▶ See Figure 238

Now that you know the valves are good, you can use them to check the guides, although a new valve, if available, is preferred. Before you measure anything, look at the guides carefully and inspect them for any cracks, chips or breakage. Also if the guide is a removable style (as in most aluminum heads), check them for any looseness or evidence of movement. All of the guides should appear to be at the same height from the spring seat. If any seem lower (or higher) from another, the guide has moved. Mount a dial indicator onto the spring side of the cylinder head. Lightly oil the valve stem and insert it into the cylinder head. Position the dial indicator against the valve stem near the tip and zero the gauge. Grasp the valve stem and wiggle towards and away from the dial indicator and observe the readings. Mount the dial indicator 90 degrees from the initial point and zero the gauge and again take a reading. Compare the two readings for an out of round condition. Check the readings against the specifications given. An Inside Diameter (I.D.) gauge designed for valve guides will give you an accurate valve guide bore measurement. If the I.D. gauge is used, compare the readings with the specifications given. Any guides that fail these inspections should be replaced or machined.

VALVE SEATS

A visual inspection of the valve seats should show a slightly worn and pitted surface where the valve face contacts the seat. Inspect the seat carefully for severe pitting or cracks. Also, a seat that is badly worn will be recessed into the cylinder head. A severely worn or recessed seat may need to be replaced. All cracked seats must be replaced. A seat concentricity gauge, if available, should be used to check the seat run-out. If run-out exceeds specifications the seat must be machined (if no specification is available given use 0.002 in. or 0.051mm).

CYLINDER HEAD SURFACE FLATNESS

▶ See Figures 239 and 240

After you have cleaned the gasket surface of the cylinder head of any old gasket material, check the head for flatness.

Place a straightedge across the gasket surface. Using feeler gauges, determine the clearance at the center of the straightedge and across the cylinder head at several points. Check along the centerline and diagonally on the head surface. If the warpage exceeds 0.003 in. (0.076mm) within a 6.0 in. (15.2cm) span, or 0.006 in. (0.152mm) over the total length of the head, the cylinder head must be resurfaced. After resurfacing the heads of a V-type engine, the intake manifold flange surface should be checked, and if necessary, milled proportionally to allow for the change in its mounting position.

CRACKS AND PHYSICAL DAMAGE

Generally, cracks are limited to the combustion chamber, however, it is not uncommon for the head to crack in a spark plug hole, port, outside of the head or in the valve spring/rocker arm area. The first area to inspect is always the hottest: the exhaust seat/port area.

A visual inspection should be performed, but just because you don't see a crack does not mean it is not there. Some more reliable methods for inspecting for cracks include Magnaflux®, a magnetic process or Zyglo®, a dye penetrant. Magnaflux® is used only on ferrous metal (cast iron) heads. Zyglo® uses a spray on fluorescent mixture along with a black light to reveal the cracks. It is strongly recommended to have your cylinder head checked professionally for cracks, especially if the engine was known to have overheated and/or leaked or consumed coolant. Contact a local shop for availability and pricing of these services.

Physical damage is usually very evident. For example, a broken mounting ear from dropping the head or a bent or broken stud and/or bolt. All of these defects should be fixed or, if unrepairable, the head should be replaced.

Camshaft and Followers

Inspect the camshaft(s) and followers as described earlier in this section.

REFINISHING & REPAIRING

Many of the procedures given for refinishing and repairing the cylinder head components must be performed by a machine shop. Certain steps, if the inspected part is not worn, can be performed yourself inexpensively. However, you spent a lot of time and effort so far, why risk trying to save a couple bucks if you might have to do it all over again?

Valves

Any valves that were not replaced should be refaced and the tips ground flat. Unless you have access to a valve grinding machine, this should be done by a machine shop. If the valves are in extremely good condition, as well as the valve seats and guides, they may be lapped in without performing machine work.

It is a recommended practice to lap the valves even after machine work has been performed and/or new valves have been purchased. This insures a positive seal between the valve and seat.

LAPPING THE VALVES

➡Before lapping the valves to the seats, read the rest of the cylinder head section to insure that any related parts are in acceptable enough condition to continue. Also, remember that before any valve seat machining and/or lapping can be performed, the guides must be within factory recommended specifications.

1. Invert the cylinder head.
2. Lightly lubricate the valve stems and insert them into the cylinder head in their numbered order.
3. Raise the valve from the seat and apply a small amount of fine lapping compound to the seat.
4. Moisten the suction head of a hand-lapping tool and attach it to the head of the valve.
5. Rotate the tool between the palms of both hands, changing the position of the valve on the valve seat and lifting the tool often to prevent grooving.
6. Lap the valve until a smooth, polished circle is evident on the valve and seat.
7. Remove the tool and the valve. Wipe away all traces of the grinding compound and store the valve to maintain its lapped location.

✳✳ WARNING

Do not get the valves out of order after they have been lapped. They must be put back with the same valve seat with which they were lapped.

Springs, Retainers and Valve Locks

There is no repair or refinishing possible with the springs, retainers and valve locks. If they are found to be worn or defective, they must be replaced with new (or known good) parts.

Cylinder Head

Most refinishing procedures dealing with the cylinder head must be performed by a machine shop. Read the sections below and review your inspection data to determine whether or not machining is necessary.

VALVE GUIDE

➡If any machining or replacements are made to the valve guides, the seats must be machined.

Unless the valve guides need machining or replacing, the only service to perform is to thoroughly clean them of any dirt or oil residue.

There are only two types of valve guides used on automobile engines: the replaceable-type (all aluminum heads) and the cast-in integral-type (most cast iron heads). There are four recommended methods for repairing worn guides.
- Knurling
- Inserts
- Reaming oversize
- Replacing

Knurling is a process in which metal is displaced and raised, thereby reducing clearance, giving a true center, and providing oil control. It is the least expensive way of repairing the valve guides. However, it is not necessarily the best, and in some cases, a knurled valve guide will not stand up for more than a short time. It requires a special knurlizer and precision reaming tools to obtain proper clearances. It would not be cost effective to purchase these tools, unless you plan on rebuilding several of the same cylinder head.

Installing a guide insert involves machining the guide to accept a bronze insert. One style is the coil-type which is installed into a threaded guide. Another is the thin-walled insert where the guide is reamed oversize to accept a split-sleeve insert. After the insert is installed, a special tool is then run through the guide to expand the insert, locking it to the guide. The insert is then reamed to the standard size for proper valve clearance.

Reaming for oversize valves restores normal clearances and provides a true valve seat. Most cast-in type guides can be reamed to accept an valve with an oversize stem. The cost factor for this can become quite high as you will need to purchase the reamer and new, oversize stem valves for all guides which were reamed. Oversizes are generally 0.003–0.030 in. (0.076–0.762mm), with 0.015 in. (0.381mm) being the most common.

To replace cast-in type valve guides, they must be drilled out, then reamed to accept replacement guides. This must be done on a fixture which will allow centering and leveling off of the original valve seat or guide, otherwise a serious guide-to-seat misalignment may occur making it impossible to properly machine the seat.

Replaceable-type guides are pressed into the cylinder head. A hammer and a stepped drift or punch may be used to install and remove the guides. Before removing the guides, measure the protrusion on the spring side of the head and record it for installation. Use the stepped drift to hammer out the old guide from the combustion chamber side of the head. When installing, determine whether or not the guide also seals a water jacket in the head, and if it does, use the recommended sealing agent. If there is no water jacket, grease the valve guide and its bore. Use the stepped drift, and hammer the new guide into the cylinder head from the spring side of the cylinder head. A stack of washers the same thickness as the measured protrusion may help the installation process.

VALVE SEATS

➡Before any valve seat machining can be performed, the guides must be within factory recommended specifications. If any machining occurred or if replacements were made to the valve guides, the seats must be machined.

If the seats are in good condition, the valves can be lapped to the seats, and the cylinder head assembled. See the valves section for instructions on lapping.

If the valve seats are worn, cracked or damaged, they must be serviced by a machine shop. The valve seat must be perfectly centered to the valve guide, which requires very accurate machining.

CYLINDER HEAD SURFACE

If the cylinder head is warped, it must be machined flat. If the warpage is extremely severe, the head may need to be replaced. In some instances, it may be possible to straighten a warped head enough to allow machining. In either case, contact a professional machine shop for service.

➡Any OHC cylinder head that shows excessive warpage should have the camshaft bearing journals align bored after the cylinder head has been resurfaced.

❋❋ WARNING

Failure to align bore the camshaft bearing journals could result in severe engine damage including but not limited to: valve and piston damage, connecting rod damage, camshaft and/or crankshaft breakage.

CRACKS AND PHYSICAL DAMAGE

Certain cracks can be repaired in both cast iron and aluminum heads. For cast iron, a tapered threaded insert is installed along the length of the crack. Aluminum can also use the tapered inserts, however welding is the preferred method. Some physical damage can be repaired through brazing or welding. Contact a machine shop to get expert advice for your particular dilemma.

ASSEMBLY

The first step for any assembly job is to have a clean area in which to work. Next, thoroughly clean all of the parts and components that are to be assembled. Finally, place all of the components onto a suitable work space and, if necessary, arrange the parts to their respective positions.

Cup Type Camshaft Followers

▸ See Figure 241

To install the springs, retainers and valve locks on heads which have these components recessed into the camshaft follower's bore, you will need a small screwdriver-type tool, some clean white grease and a lot of patience. You will also need the C-clamp style spring compressor and the OHC tool used to disassemble the head.

1. Lightly lubricate the valve stems and insert all of the valves into the cylinder head. If possible, maintain their original locations.

TCCA3P64

Fig. 241 Once assembled, check the valve clearance and correct as needed

2. If equipped, install any valve spring shims which were removed.
3. If equipped, install the new valve seals, keeping the following in mind:
   • If the valve seal presses over the guide, lightly lubricate the outer guide surfaces.
   • If the seal is an O-ring type, it is installed just after compressing the spring but before the valve locks.
4. Place the valve spring and retainer over the stem.
5. Position the spring compressor and the OHC tool, then compress the spring.
6. Using a small screwdriver as a spatula, fill the valve stem side of the lock with white grease. Use the excess grease on the screwdriver to fasten the lock to the driver.
7. Carefully install the valve lock, which is stuck to the end of the screwdriver, to the valve stem then press on it with the screwdriver until the grease squeezes out. The valve lock should now be stuck to the stem.
8. Repeat Steps 6 and 7 for the remaining valve lock.
9. Relieve the spring pressure slowly and insure that neither valve lock becomes dislodged by the retainer.
10. Remove the spring compressor tool.
11. Repeat Steps 2 through 10 until all of the springs have been installed.
12. Install the followers, camshaft(s) and any other components that were removed for disassembly.

Rocker Arm Type Camshaft Followers

1. Lightly lubricate the valve stems and insert all of the valves into the cylinder head. If possible, maintain their original locations.
2. If equipped, install any valve spring shims which were removed.
3. If equipped, install the new valve seals, keeping the following in mind:
   • If the valve seal presses over the guide, lightly lubricate the outer guide surfaces.
   • If the seal is an O-ring type, it is installed just after compressing the spring but before the valve locks.
4. Place the valve spring and retainer over the stem.
5. Position the spring compressor tool and compress the spring.
6. Assemble the valve locks to the stem.
7. Relieve the spring pressure slowly and insure that neither valve lock becomes dislodged by the retainer.
8. Remove the spring compressor tool.
9. Repeat Steps 2 through 8 until all of the springs have been installed.
10. Install the camshaft(s), rockers, shafts and any other components that were removed for disassembly.

Engine Block

GENERAL INFORMATION

A thorough overhaul or rebuild of an engine block would include replacing the pistons, rings, bearings, timing belt/chain assembly and oil pump. For OHV engines also include a new camshaft and lifters. The block would then have the cylinders bored and honed oversize (or if using removable cylinder sleeves, new sleeves installed) and the crankshaft would be cut undersize to provide new wearing surfaces and perfect clearances. However, your particular engine may not have everything worn out. What if only the piston rings have worn out and the clearances on everything else are still within factory specifications? Well, you could just replace the rings and put it back together, but this would be a very rare example. Chances are, if one component in your engine is worn, other components are sure to follow, and soon. At the very least, you should always replace the rings, bearings and oil pump. This is what is commonly called a "freshen up".

Cylinder Ridge Removal

Because the top piston ring does not travel to the very top of the cylinder, a ridge is built up between the end of the travel and the top of the cylinder bore.

Pushing the piston and connecting rod assembly past the ridge can be difficult, and damage to the piston ring lands could occur. If the ridge is not removed before installing a new piston or not removed at all, piston ring breakage and piston damage may occur.

➡It is always recommended that you remove any cylinder ridges before removing the piston and connecting rod assemblies. If you know that new pistons are going to be installed and the engine block will be bored oversize, you may be able to forego this step. However, some ridges may actually prevent the assemblies from being removed, necessitating its removal.

There are several different types of ridge reamers on the market, none of which are inexpensive. Unless a great deal of engine rebuilding is anticipated, borrow or rent a reamer.

1. Turn the crankshaft until the piston is at the bottom of its travel.
2. Cover the head of the piston with a rag.
3. Follow the tool manufacturers instructions and cut away the ridge, exercising extreme care to avoid cutting too deeply.
4. Remove the ridge reamer, the rag and as many of the cuttings as possible. Continue until all of the cylinder ridges have been removed.

DISASSEMBLY

▶ See Figures 242 and 243

The engine disassembly instructions following assume that you have the engine mounted on an engine stand. If not, it is easiest to disassemble the engine on a bench or the floor with it resting on the bell housing or transmission mounting surface. You must be able to access the connecting rod fasteners and turn the crankshaft during disassembly. Also, all engine covers (timing, front, side, oil pan, whatever) should have already been removed. Engines which are seized or locked up may not be able to be completely disassembled, and a core (salvage yard) engine should be purchased.

If not done during the cylinder head removal, remove the timing chain/belt and/or gear/sprocket assembly. Remove the oil pick-up and pump assembly and, if necessary, the pump drive. If equipped, remove any balance or auxiliary shafts. If necessary, remove the cylinder ridge from the top of the bore. See the cylinder ridge removal procedure earlier in this section.

Rotate the engine over so that the crankshaft is exposed. Use a number punch or scribe and mark each connecting rod with its respective cylinder number. The cylinder closest to the front of the engine is always number 1. However, depending on the engine placement, the front of the engine could either be the flywheel or damper/pulley end. Generally the front of the engine faces the front of the vehicle. Use a number punch or scribe and also mark the main bearing caps from front to rear with the front most cap being number 1 (if there are five caps, mark them 1 through 5, front to rear).

❊❊ WARNING

Take special care when pushing the connecting rod up from the crankshaft because the sharp threads of the rod bolts/studs will score the crankshaft journal. Insure that special plastic caps are installed over them, or cut two pieces of rubber hose to do the same.

Fig. 242 Place rubber hose over the connecting rod studs to protect the crankshaft and cylinder bores from damage

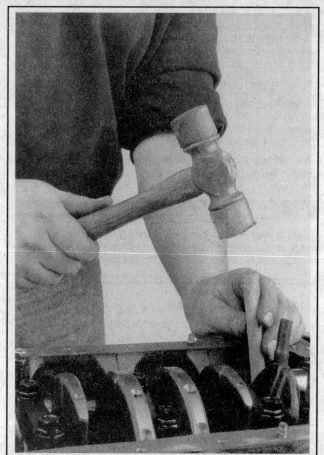

Fig. 243 Carefully tap the piston out of the bore using a wooden dowel

Again, rotate the engine, this time to position the number one cylinder bore (head surface) up. Turn the crankshaft until the number one piston is at the bottom of its travel, this should allow the maximum access to its connecting rod. Remove the number one connecting rods fasteners and cap and place two lengths of rubber hose over the rod bolts/studs to protect the crankshaft from damage. Using a sturdy wooden dowel and a hammer, push the connecting rod up about 1 in. (25mm) from the crankshaft and remove the upper bearing insert. Continue pushing or tapping the connecting rod up until the piston rings are out of the cylinder bore. Remove the piston and rod by hand, put the upper half of the bearing insert back into the rod, install the cap with its bearing insert installed, and hand-tighten the cap fasteners. If the parts are kept in order in this manner, they will not get lost and you will be able to tell which bearings came form what cylinder if any problems are discovered and diagnosis is necessary. Remove all the other piston assemblies in the same manner. On V-style engines, remove all of the pistons from one bank, then reposition the engine with the other cylinder bank head surface up, and remove that banks piston assemblies.

The only remaining component in the engine block should now be the crankshaft. Loosen the main bearing caps evenly until the fasteners can be turned by hand, then remove them and the caps. Remove the crankshaft from the engine block. Thoroughly clean all of the components.

INSPECTION

Now that the engine block and all of its components are clean, it's time to inspect them for wear and/or damage. To accurately inspect them, you will need some specialized tools:

• Two or three separate micrometers to measure the pistons and crankshaft journals
• A dial indicator

- Telescoping gauges for the cylinder bores
- A rod alignment fixture to check for bent connecting rods

If you do not have access to the proper tools, you may want to bring the components to a shop that does.

Generally, you shouldn't expect cracks in the engine block or its components unless it was known to leak, consume or mix engine fluids, it was severely overheated, or there was evidence of bad bearings and/or crankshaft damage. A visual inspection should be performed on all of the components, but just because you don't see a crack does not mean it is not there. Some more reliable methods for inspecting for cracks include Magnaflux®, a magnetic process or Zyglo®, a dye penetrant. Magnaflux® is used only on ferrous metal (cast iron). Zyglo® uses a spray on fluorescent mixture along with a black light to reveal the cracks. It is strongly recommended to have your engine block checked professionally for cracks, especially if the engine was known to have overheated and/or leaked or consumed coolant. Contact a local shop for availability and pricing of these services.

Engine Block

ENGINE BLOCK BEARING ALIGNMENT

Remove the main bearing caps and, if still installed, the main bearing inserts. Inspect all of the main bearing saddles and caps for damage, burrs or high spots. If damage is found, and it is caused from a spun main bearing, the block will need to be align-bored or, if severe enough, replacement. Any burrs or high spots should be carefully removed with a metal file.

Place a straightedge on the bearing saddles, in the engine block, along the centerline of the crankshaft. If any clearance exists between the straightedge and the saddles, the block must be align-bored.

Align-boring consists of machining the main bearing saddles and caps by means of a flycutter that runs through the bearing saddles.

DECK FLATNESS

The top of the engine block where the cylinder head mounts is called the deck. Insure that the deck surface is clean of dirt, carbon deposits and old gasket material. Place a straightedge across the surface of the deck along its centerline and, using feeler gauges, check the clearance along several points. Repeat the checking procedure with the straightedge placed along both diagonals of the deck surface. If the reading exceeds 0.003 in. (0.076mm) within a 6.0 in. (15.2cm) span, or 0.006 in. (0.152mm) over the total length of the deck, it must be machined.

CYLINDER BORES

▶ See Figure 244

The cylinder bores house the pistons and are slightly larger than the pistons themselves. A common piston-to-bore clearance is 0.0015–0.0025 in. (0.0381mm–0.0635mm). Inspect and measure the cylinder bores. The bore

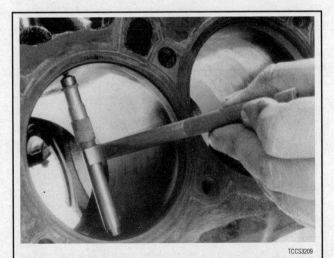

TCCS3209

Fig. 244 Use a telescoping gauge to measure the cylinder bore diameter—take several readings within the same bore

should be checked for out-of-roundness, taper and size. The results of this inspection will determine whether the cylinder can be used in its existing size and condition, or a rebore to the next oversize is required (or in the case of removable sleeves, have replacements installed).

The amount of cylinder wall wear is always greater at the top of the cylinder than at the bottom. This wear is known as taper. Any cylinder that has a taper of 0.0012 in. (0.305mm) or more, must be rebored. Measurements are taken at a number of positions in each cylinder: at the top, middle and bottom and at two points at each position; that is, at a point 90 degrees from the crankshaft centerline, as well as a point parallel to the crankshaft centerline. The measurements are made with either a special dial indicator or a telescopic gauge and micrometer. If the necessary precision tools to check the bore are not available, take the block to a machine shop and have them mike it. Also if you don't have the tools to check the cylinder bores, chances are you will not have the necessary devices to check the pistons, connecting rods and crankshaft. Take these components with you and save yourself an extra trip.

For our procedures, we will use a telescopic gauge and a micrometer. You will need one of each, with a measuring range which covers your cylinder bore size.

1. Position the telescopic gauge in the cylinder bore, loosen the gauges lock and allow it to expand.

➡**Your first two readings will be at the top of the cylinder bore, then proceed to the middle and finally the bottom, making a total of six measurements.**

2. Hold the gauge square in the bore, 90 degrees from the crankshaft centerline, and gently tighten the lock. Tilt the gauge back to remove it from the bore.
3. Measure the gauge with the micrometer and record the reading.
4. Again, hold the gauge square in the bore, this time parallel to the crankshaft centerline, and gently tighten the lock. Again, you will tilt the gauge back to remove it from the bore.
5. Measure the gauge with the micrometer and record this reading. The difference between these two readings is the out-of-round measurement of the cylinder.
6. Repeat steps 1 through 5, each time going to the next lower position, until you reach the bottom of the cylinder. Then go to the next cylinder, and continue until all of the cylinders have been measured.

The difference between these measurements will tell you all about the wear in your cylinders. The measurements which were taken 90 degrees from the crankshaft centerline will always reflect the most wear. That is because at this position is where the engine power presses the piston against the cylinder bore the hardest. This is known as thrust wear. Take your top, 90 degree measurement and compare it to your bottom, 90 degree measurement. The difference between them is the taper. When you measure your pistons, you will compare these readings to your piston sizes and determine piston-to-wall clearance.

Crankshaft

Inspect the crankshaft for visible signs of wear or damage. All of the journals should be perfectly round and smooth. Slight scores are normal for a used crankshaft, but you should hardly feel them with your fingernail. When measuring the crankshaft with a micrometer, you will take readings at the front and rear of each journal, then turn the micrometer 90 degrees and take two more readings, front and rear. The difference between the front-to-rear readings is the journal taper and the first-to-90 degree reading is the out-of-round measurement. Generally, there should be no taper or out-of-roundness found, however, up to 0.0005 in. (0.0127mm) for either can be overlooked. Also, the readings should fall within the factory specifications for journal diameters.

If the crankshaft journals fall within specifications, it is recommended that it be polished before being returned to service. Polishing the crankshaft insures that any minor burrs or high spots are smoothed, thereby reducing the chance of scoring the new bearings.

Pistons and Connecting Rods

PISTONS

▶ See Figure 245

The piston should be visually inspected for any signs of cracking or burning (caused by hot spots or detonation), and scuffing or excessive wear on the skirts. The wrist pin attaches the piston to the connecting rod. The piston

Fig. 245 Measure the piston's outer diameter, perpendicular to the wrist pin, with a micrometer

Fig. 246 Use a ball type cylinder hone to remove any glaze and provide a new surface for seating the piston rings

Fig. 247 Most pistons are marked to indicate positioning in the engine (usually a mark means the side facing the front)

should move freely on the wrist pin, both sliding and pivoting. Grasp the connecting rod securely, or mount it in a vise, and try to rock the piston back and forth along the centerline of the wrist pin. There should not be any excessive play evident between the piston and the pin. If there are C-clips retaining the pin in the piston then you have wrist pin bushings in the rods. There should not be any excessive play between the wrist pin and the rod bushing. Normal clearance for the wrist pin is approx. 0.001–0.002 in. (0.025mm–0.051mm).

Use a micrometer and measure the diameter of the piston, perpendicular to the wrist pin, on the skirt. Compare the reading to its original cylinder measurement obtained earlier. The difference between the two readings is the piston-to-wall clearance. If the clearance is within specifications, the piston may be used as is. If the piston is out of specification, but the bore is not, you will need a new piston. If both are out of specification, you will need the cylinder rebored and oversize pistons installed. Generally if two or more pistons/bores are out of specification, it is best to rebore the entire block and purchase a complete set of oversize pistons.

CONNECTING ROD

You should have the connecting rod checked for straightness at a machine shop. If the connecting rod is bent, it will unevenly wear the bearing and piston, as well as place greater stress on these components. Any bent or twisted connecting rods must be replaced. If the rods are straight and the wrist pin clearance is within specifications, then only the bearing end of the rod need be checked. Place the connecting rod into a vice, with the bearing inserts in place, install the cap to the rod and torque the fasteners to specifications. Use a telescoping gauge and carefully measure the inside diameter of the bearings. Compare this reading to the rods original crankshaft journal diameter measurement. The difference is the oil clearance. If the oil clearance is not within specifications, install new bearings in the rod and take another measurement. If the clearance is still out of specifications, and the crankshaft is not, the rod will need to be reconditioned by a machine shop.

➡You can also use Plastigage® to check the bearing clearances. The assembling section has complete instructions on its use.

Camshaft

Inspect the camshaft and lifters/followers as described earlier in this section.

Bearings

All of the engine bearings should be visually inspected for wear and/or damage. The bearing should look evenly worn all around with no deep scores or pits. If the bearing is severely worn, scored, pitted or heat blued, then the bearing, and the components that use it, should be brought to a machine shop for inspection. Full-circle bearings (used on most camshafts, auxiliary shafts, balance shafts, etc.) require specialized tools for removal and installation, and should be brought to a machine shop for service.

Oil Pump

➡The oil pump is responsible for providing constant lubrication to the whole engine and so it is recommended that a new oil pump be installed when rebuilding the engine.

Completely disassemble the oil pump and thoroughly clean all of the components. Inspect the oil pump gears and housing for wear and/or damage. Insure that the pressure relief valve operates properly and there is no binding or sticking due to varnish or debris. If all of the parts are in proper working condition, lubricate the gears and relief valve, and assemble the pump.

REFINISHING

▶ See Figure 246

Almost all engine block refinishing must be performed by a machine shop. If the cylinders are not to be rebored, then the cylinder glaze can be removed with a ball hone. When removing cylinder glaze with a ball hone, use a light or penetrating type oil to lubricate the hone. Do not allow the hone to run dry as this may cause excessive scoring of the cylinder bores and wear on the hone. If new pistons are required, they will need to be installed to the connecting rods. This should be performed by a machine shop as the pistons must be installed in the correct relationship to the rod or engine damage can occur.

Pistons and Connecting Rods

▶ See Figure 247

Only pistons with the wrist pin retained by C-clips are serviceable by the home-mechanic. Press fit pistons require special presses and/or heaters to remove/install the connecting rod and should only be performed by a machine shop.

All pistons will have a mark indicating the direction to the front of the engine and the must be installed into the engine in that manner. Usually it is a notch or arrow on the top of the piston, or it may be the letter F cast or stamped into the piston.

C-CLIP TYPE PISTONS

1. Note the location of the forward mark on the piston and mark the connecting rod in relation.
2. Remove the C-clips from the piston and withdraw the wrist pin.

➡Varnish build-up or C-clip groove burrs may increase the difficulty of removing the wrist pin. If necessary, use a punch or drift to carefully tap the wrist pin out.

3. Insure that the wrist pin bushing in the connecting rod is usable, and lubricate it with assembly lube.
4. Remove the wrist pin from the new piston and lubricate the pin bores on the piston.
5. Align the forward marks on the piston and the connecting rod and install the wrist pin.
6. The new C-clips will have a flat and a rounded side to them. Install both C-clips with the flat side facing out.
7. Repeat all of the steps for each piston being replaced.

ASSEMBLY

Before you begin assembling the engine, first give yourself a clean, dirt free work area. Next, clean every engine component again. The key to a good assembly is cleanliness.

Mount the engine block into the engine stand and wash it one last time using water and detergent (dishwashing detergent works well). While washing it, scrub the cylinder bores with a soft bristle brush and thoroughly clean all of the oil passages. Completely dry the engine and spray the entire assembly down with an anti-rust solution such as WD-40® or similar product. Take a clean lint-free rag and wipe up any excess anti-rust solution from the bores, bearing saddles, etc. Repeat the final cleaning process on the crankshaft. Replace any freeze or oil galley plugs which were removed during disassembly.

Crankshaft

▶ See Figures 248, 249, 250 and 251

1. Remove the main bearing inserts from the block and bearing caps.
2. If the crankshaft main bearing journals have been refinished to a definite

Fig. 248 Apply a strip of gauging material to the bearing journal, then install and torque the cap

undersize, install the correct undersize bearing. Be sure that the bearing inserts and bearing bores are clean. Foreign material under inserts will distort bearing and cause failure.

3. Place the upper main bearing inserts in bores with tang in slot.

➡The oil holes in the bearing inserts must be aligned with the oil holes in the cylinder block.

4. Install the lower main bearing inserts in bearing caps.
5. Clean the mating surfaces of block and rear main bearing cap.
6. Carefully lower the crankshaft into place. Be careful not to damage bearing surfaces.
7. Check the clearance of each main bearing by using the following procedure:

   a. Place a piece of Plastigage® or its equivalent, on bearing surface across full width of bearing cap and about ¼ in. off center.

   b. Install cap and tighten bolts to specifications. Do not turn crankshaft while Plastigage® is in place.

   c. Remove the cap. Using the supplied Plastigage® scale, check width of Plastigage® at widest point to get maximum clearance. Difference between readings is taper of journal.

   d. If clearance exceeds specified limits, try a 0.001 in. or 0.002 in. undersize bearing in combination with the standard bearing. Bearing clearance must be within specified limits. If standard and 0.002 in. undersize bearing does not bring clearance within desired limits, refinish crankshaft journal, then install undersize bearings.

8. Install the rear main seal.
9. After the bearings have been fitted, apply a light coat of engine oil to the journals and bearings. Install the rear main bearing cap. Install all bearing caps except the thrust bearing cap. Be sure that main bearing caps are installed in original locations. Tighten the bearing cap bolts to specifications.
10. Install the thrust bearing cap with bolts finger-tight.
11. Pry the crankshaft forward against the thrust surface of upper half of bearing.
12. Hold the crankshaft forward and pry the thrust bearing cap to the rear. This aligns the thrust surfaces of both halves of the bearing.
13. Retain the forward pressure on the crankshaft. Tighten the cap bolts to specifications.
14. Measure the crankshaft end-play as follows:

    a. Mount a dial gauge to the engine block and position the tip of the gauge to read from the crankshaft end.

    b. Carefully pry the crankshaft toward the rear of the engine and hold it there while you zero the gauge.

    c. Carefully pry the crankshaft toward the front of the engine and read the gauge.

    d. Confirm that the reading is within specifications. If not, install a new thrust bearing and repeat the procedure. If the reading is still out of specifications with a new bearing, have a machine shop inspect the thrust surfaces of the crankshaft, and if possible, repair it.

15. Rotate the crankshaft so as to position the first rod journal to the bottom of its stroke.

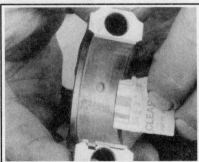

Fig. 249 After the cap is removed again, use the scale supplied with the gauging material to check the clearance

Fig. 250 A dial gauge may be used to check crankshaft end-play

Fig. 251 Carefully pry the crankshaft back and forth while reading the dial gauge for end-play

Pistons and Connecting Rods

▶ See Figures 252, 253, 254 and 255

1. Before installing the piston/connecting rod assembly, oil the pistons, piston rings and the cylinder walls with light engine oil. Install connecting rod bolt protectors or rubber hose onto the connecting rod bolts/studs. Also perform the following:

   a. Select the proper ring set for the size cylinder bore.

   b. Position the ring in the bore in which it is going to be used.

   c. Push the ring down into the bore area where normal ring wear is not encountered.

   d. Use the head of the piston to position the ring in the bore so that the ring is square with the cylinder wall. Use caution to avoid damage to the ring or cylinder bore.

   e. Measure the gap between the ends of the ring with a feeler gauge. Ring gap in a worn cylinder is normally greater than specification. If the ring gap is greater than the specified limits, try an oversize ring set.

   f. Check the ring side clearance of the compression rings with a feeler gauge inserted between the ring and its lower land according to specification. The gauge should slide freely around the entire ring circumference without binding. Any wear that occurs will form a step at the inner portion of the lower land. If the lower lands have high steps, the piston should be replaced.

2. Unless new pistons are installed, be sure to install the pistons in the cylinders from which they were removed. The numbers on the connecting rod and bearing cap must be on the same side when installed in the cylinder bore. If a connecting rod is ever transposed from one engine or cylinder to another, new bearings should be fitted and the connecting rod should be numbered to correspond with the new cylinder number. The notch on the piston head goes toward the front of the engine.

3. Install all of the rod bearing inserts into the rods and caps.

4. Install the rings to the pistons. Install the oil control ring first, then the second compression ring and finally the top compression ring. Use a piston ring expander tool to aid in installation and to help reduce the chance of breakage.

5. Make sure the ring gaps are properly spaced around the circumference of the piston. Fit a piston ring compressor around the piston and slide the piston and connecting rod assembly down into the cylinder bore, pushing it in with the wooden hammer handle. Push the piston down until it is only slightly below the top of the cylinder bore. Guide the connecting rod onto the crankshaft bearing journal carefully, to avoid damaging the crankshaft.

6. Check the bearing clearance of all the rod bearings, fitting them to the crankshaft bearing journals. Follow the procedure in the crankshaft installation above.

7. After the bearings have been fitted, apply a light coating of assembly oil to the journals and bearings.

8. Turn the crankshaft until the appropriate bearing journal is at the bottom of its stroke, then push the piston assembly all the way down until the connecting rod bearing seats on the crankshaft journal. Be careful not to allow the bearing cap screws to strike the crankshaft bearing journals and damage them.

9. After the piston and connecting rod assemblies have been installed, check the connecting rod side clearance on each crankshaft journal.

10. Prime and install the oil pump and the oil pump intake tube.

11. Install the auxiliary/balance shaft(s)/assembly(ies).

Cylinder Head(S)

1. Install the cylinder head(s) using new gaskets.
2. Install the timing sprockets/gears and the belt/chain assemblies.

Engine Covers and Components

Install the timing cover(s) and oil pan. Refer to your notes and drawings made prior to disassembly and install all of the components that were removed. Install the engine into the vehicle.

TCCS3923

Fig. 252 Checking the piston ring-to-ring groove side clearance using the ring and a feeler gauge

TCCS3917

Fig. 253 The notch on the side of the bearing cap matches the tang on the bearing insert

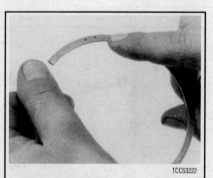

TCCS3222

Fig. 254 Most rings are marked to show which side of the ring should face up when installed to the piston

TCCS3914

Fig. 255 Install the piston and rod assembly into the block using a ring compressor and the handle of a hammer

Engine Start-up and Break-in

STARTING THE ENGINE

Now that the engine is installed and every wire and hose is properly connected, go back and double check that all coolant and vacuum hoses are connected. Check that your oil drain plug is installed and properly tightened. If not already done, install a new oil filter onto the engine. Fill the crankcase with the proper amount and grade of engine oil. Fill the cooling system with a 50/50 mixture of coolant/water.

1. Connect the vehicle battery.
2. Start the engine. Keep your eye on your oil pressure indicator; if it does not indicate oil pressure within 10 seconds of starting, turn the vehicle **OFF**.

✳✳ WARNING

Damage to the engine can result if it is allowed to run with no oil pressure. Check the engine oil level to make sure that it is full. Check for any leaks and if found, repair the leaks before continuing. If there is still no indication of oil pressure, you may need to prime the system.

3. Confirm that there are no fluid leaks (oil or other).
4. Allow the engine to reach normal operating temperature (the upper radiator hose will be hot to the touch).
5. At this point any necessary checks or adjustments can be performed, such as ignition timing.
6. Install any remaining components or body panels which were removed.

BREAKING IT IN

Make the first miles on the new engine, easy ones. Vary the speed but do not accelerate hard. Most importantly, do not lug the engine, and avoid sustained high speeds until at least 100 miles. Check the engine oil and coolant levels frequently. Expect the engine to use a little oil until the rings seat. Change the oil and filter at 500 miles, 1500 miles, then every 3000 miles past that.

KEEP IT MAINTAINED

Now that you have just gone through all of that hard work, keep yourself from doing it all over again by thoroughly maintaining it. Not that you may not have maintained it before, heck you could have had one to two hundred thousand miles on it before doing this. However, you may have bought the vehicle used, and the previous owner did not keep up on maintenance. Which is why you just went through all of that hard work. See?

TORQUE SPECIFICATIONS

1C-TLC and 2C-TLC Engines:

		US	METRIC
A/C Compressor		20 ft. lbs.	27 Nm
Camshaft bearing cap		13 ft. lbs.	18 Nm
Camshaft timing pulley		65 ft. lbs.	88 Nm
Coolant temperature sensor		15 ft. lbs.	20 Nm
Crankshaft pulley		72 ft. lbs.	98 Nm
Cylinder head	1C-TLC	62 ft. lbs.	84 Nm
	2C-TLC 1st	33 ft. lbs.	44 Nm
	2nd	90 deg.	90 deg.
	3rd	90 deg.	90 deg.
Cylinder head cover		65 inch lbs.	8 Nm
Drive plate		65 ft. lbs.	88 Nm
Injection pump drive pulley		47 ft. lbs.	64 Nm
No. 1 idler pulley		65 inch lbs.	7 Nm
No. 2 idler pulley		27 ft. lbs.	37 Nm
Right side engine mounting bracket	10mm	27 ft. lbs.	37 Nm
	12mm	47 ft. lbs.	64 Nm
Exhaust manifold		34 ft. lbs.	47 Nm
Exhaust pipe-to-turbine elbow		9 ft. lbs.	13 Nm
Intake manifold		13 ft. lbs.	18 Nm
Turbocharger		38 ft. lbs.	52 Nm
Turbocharger oil pipe flange nuts		13 ft. lbs.	18 Nm
Turbocharger oil pipe	inlet	18 ft. lbs.	25 Nm
	outlet	34 ft. lbs.	47 Nm
Oil cooler pipe	cooler	42 ft. lbs.	56 Nm
	pipe	38 ft. lbs.	51 Nm
Flywheel		65 ft. lbs.	88 Nm
Fuel filter inlet nut		22 ft. lbs.	29 Nm
Oil pan		5 ft. lbs.	7 Nm
Oil pump		13 ft. lbs.	18 Nm
Power steering pump		31 ft. lbs.	43 Nm
Radiator		9 ft. lbs.	13 Nm
Starter		29 ft. lbs.	39 Nm
Thermostat housing		65 inch lbs.	7 Nm
Water pump		13 ft. lbs.	18 Nm

2S-ELC Engine:

		US	METRIC
A/C Compressor		20 ft. lbs.	27 Nm
Camshaft timing pulley		40 ft. lbs.	54 Nm
Coolant temperature sensor		15 ft. lbs.	20 Nm
Crankshaft pulley		80 ft. lbs.	108 Nm
Cylinder head bolts	1st	15 ft. lbs.	20 Nm
	2nd	30 ft. lbs.	47 Nm
	3rd	47 ft. lbs.	64 Nm
Cylinder head cover		13 ft. lbs.	18 Nm

TORQUE SPECIFICATIONS

2S-ELC Engine: (continued)

		US	METRIC
Distributor pinch bolt		9 ft. lbs.	13 Nm
Drive plate		61 ft. lbs.	83 Nm
EGR valve	pipe	43 ft. lbs.	59 Nm
	bolt	9 ft. lbs.	13 Nm
Engine mounts		29 ft. lbs.	39 Nm
Exhaust manifold		31 ft. lbs.	42 Nm
Exhaust pipe		46 ft. lbs.	62 Nm
Flywheel		31 ft. lbs.	42 Nm
Fuel filter inlet nut		22 ft. lbs.	29 Nm
Fuel sender		17 inch lbs.	2 Nm
Idler pulley		31 ft. lbs.	42 Nm
Intake manifold	1983-85	31 ft. lbs.	42 Nm
	1986	14 ft. lbs.	19 Nm
Oil pan		4 ft. lbs.	5 Nm
Oil pan stiffener plate		27 ft. lbs.	37 Nm
Oil pump		7 ft. lbs.	9 Nm
Oil pump relief valve plug		27 ft. lbs.	37 Nm
Power steering pump		31 ft. lbs.	43 Nm
Rear main seal retainer		7 ft. lbs.	9 Nm
Radiator		9 ft. lbs.	13 Nm
Starter		29 ft. lbs.	39 Nm
Thermostat housing		78 inch lbs.	9 Nm
Throttle body		14 ft. lbs.	20 Nm
Water pump		82 inch lbs.	9 Nm

3S-FE Engine:

		US	METRIC
Oil pump pulley-to-pump drive shat		21 ft. lbs.	28 Nm
No. 1 idler pulley-to-cylinder head		31 ft. lbs.	42 Nm
No. 2 idler pulley-to-cylinder block		31 ft. lbs.	42 Nm
Camshaft timing pulley		40 ft. lbs.	54 Nm
Crankshaft pulley		80 ft. lbs.	108 Nm
Spark plug tube		29 ft. lbs.	39 Nm
Cylinder head bolts	1st	36 ft. lbs.	49 Nm
	2nd	90 deg.	90 deg.
Camshaft bearing cap		14 ft. lbs.	19 Nm
Cylinder head cover		17 ft. lbs.	23 Nm
Intake manifold		14 ft. lbs.	19 Nm
Intake manifold stay-to-head		14 ft. lbs.	19 Nm
Intake manifold stay-to-block		31 Nm	42 Nm
EGR valve-to-intake manifold		9 ft. lbs.	13 Nm
EGR pipe		43 ft. lbs.	59 Nm
Water outlet-to-head		11 ft. lbs.	15 Nm
Exhaust manifold-to-catalyst		21 ft. lbs.	29 Nm
Exhaust manifold-to-head		36 ft. lbs.	49 Nm

89553C02

89553C03

TORQUE SPECIFICATIONS

3S-FE Engine: (continued)

	US	METRIC
Engine hanger-to-head	31 ft. lbs.	42 Nm
Alternator bracket	31 ft. lbs.	42 Nm
Rear oil seal retainer	82 inch lbs.	9 Nm
Rear end plate	82 inch lbs.	9 Nm
Flywheel	65 ft. lbs.	88 Nm
Drive plate	61 ft. lbs.	83 Nm
Suspension lower crossmember-to-body	154 ft. lbs.	208 Nm
Suspension crossmember-to-center member	29 ft. lbs.	39 Nm
Engine mounting center-to-body	29 ft. lbs.	39 Nm
Engine mounting center member-to-insulator		
nuts	35 ft. lbs.	48 Nm
bolts	54 ft. lbs.	73 Nm
RH engine mounting bracket-to-block	38 ft. lbs.	52 Nm
RH engine insulator-to-engine bracket	38 ft. lbs.	52 Nm
RH engine insulator-to-body (2WD)	47 ft. lbs.	64 Nm
RH engine insulator-to-body (4WD) bolt	65 ft. lbs.	88 Nm
nut	64 ft. lbs.	87 Nm
RH engine stay-to-insulator	54 ft. lbs.	73 Nm
RH engine stay-to-alternator bracket	54 ft. lbs.	73 Nm
LH engine bracket-to-transaxle	38 ft. lbs.	52 Nm
LH engine insulator-to-engine mounting insulator	38 ft. lbs.	52 Nm
LH engine insulator-to-engine insulator (AT)	15 ft. lbs.	21 Nm
LH engine stay-to-transaxle (AT)	15 ft. lbs.	21 Nm
Engine front mounting bracket-to-transaxle	57 ft. lbs.	77 Nm
Engine front insulator-to-bracket	64 ft. lbs.	87 Nm
Engine center bracket-to-block (2WD)	35 ft. lbs.	48 Nm
Engine rear mounting-to-transaxle	57 ft. lbs.	77 Nm
Engine rear insulator-to-bracket	64 ft. lbs.	87 Nm
Front pipe-to-catalyst	46 ft. lbs.	62 Nm
Front pipe-to-center pipe	32 ft. lbs.	43 Nm

2VZ-FE Engine:

	US	METRIC
Camshaft timing pulley	80 ft. lbs.	108 Nm
Crankshaft pulley	181 ft. lbs.	245 Nm
No. 1 idler pulley-to-block	25 ft. lbs.	34 Nm
No. 2 idler pulley-to-bracket	29 ft. lbs.	39 Nm
RH engine mounting bracket-to-block	30 ft. lbs.	39 Nm
Timing belt tensioner-to-oil pump	20 ft. lbs.	26 Nm
Cylinder head bolts 1st	25 ft. lbs.	34 Nm
2nd	90 deg.	90 deg.
3rd	90 deg.	90 deg.
recessed bolt	13 ft. lbs.	18 Nm
LH engine hanger-to-LH head	27 ft. lbs.	37 Nm
Camshaft bearing cap	12 ft. lbs.	16 Nm
Cylinder head cover	52 inch lbs.	6 Nm

89563C04

TORQUE SPECIFICATIONS

2VZ-FE Engine: (continued)

		US	METRIC
No. 3 timing belt cover-to-head		65 inch lbs.	7 Nm
No. 3 timing belt cover-to-block		65 inch lbs.	7 Nm
Exhaust manifold		29 ft. lbs.	39 Nm
Intake manifold		13 ft. lbs.	18 Nm
No. 2 idler pulley bracket stay-to-head		13 ft. lbs.	18 Nm
No. 2 idler pulley bracket stay-to-No. 2 pulley bracket		13 ft. lbs.	18 Nm
Water by-pass outlet-to-head		14 ft. lbs.	20 Nm
Water outlet-to-head		73 inch lbs.	8 Nm
Air intake chamber-to-intake manifold		32 ft. lbs.	43 Nm
Air intake chamber stay-to-air intake chamber		27 ft. lbs.	37 Nm
Air intake chamber stay-to-head		27 ft. lbs.	37 Nm
Crossover pipe-to-manifold		29 ft. lbs.	39 Nm
Crossover pipe-to-head		25 ft. lbs.	34 Nm
Crossover pipe-to-block		25 ft. lbs.	34 Nm
EGR valve-to-air intake chamber		13 ft. lbs.	18 Nm
EGR pipe-to-EGR valve		58 ft. lbs.	78 Nm
EGR pipe-to-RH exhaust manifold		69 inch lbs.	8 Nm
Rear oil seal retainer		27 ft. lbs.	37 Nm
No. 2 idler pulley bracket-to-block		74 inch lbs.	8 Nm
Water by-pass pipe-to-block		65 inch lbs.	7 Nm
Rear end plate-to-block		61 ft. lbs.	83 Nm
Flywheel		61 ft. lbs.	83 Nm
Drive plate		38 ft. lbs.	52 Nm
RH engine insulator-to-bracket		47 ft. lbs.	64 Nm
RH engine insulator-to-body	bolt	65 ft. lbs.	88 Nm
	nut	38 ft. lbs.	52 Nm
LH engine insulator-to-bracket		64 ft. lbs.	87 Nm
LH engine insulator-to-body		38 ft. lbs.	52 Nm
No. 1 engine RH stay-to-air intake chamber		38 ft. lbs.	52 Nm
No. 1 engine RH stay-to-RH insulator		38 ft. lbs.	52 Nm
No. 2 engine RH stay-to-alternator		38 ft. lbs.	52 Nm
No. 2 engine RH stay-to-RH insulator		48 ft. lbs.	66 Nm
LH engine stay-to-transaxle MT bolt		14 ft. lbs.	19 Nm
nut		38 ft. lbs.	52 Nm
AT 12mm nut		15 ft. lbs.	21 Nm
14mm nut		38 ft. lbs.	52 Nm
LH engine stay-to-insulator		38 ft. lbs.	52 Nm
Engine front insulator-to-block		38 ft. lbs.	52 Nm
Engine front insulator-to-transaxle		57 ft. lbs.	77 Nm
Engine front insulator-to-mounting bracket		64 ft. lbs.	87 Nm
Engine center mounting bracket-to-block		38 ft. lbs.	52 Nm
Engine rear insulator-to-transaxle		57 ft. lbs.	77 Nm
Engine rear insulator-to-bracket		64 ft. lbs.	87 Nm
Engine center member-to-body		29 ft. lbs.	39 Nm
Engine center member-to-front insulator		54 ft. lbs.	73 Nm
Engine center member-to-center insulator		54 ft. lbs.	73 Nm

89563C05

TORQUE SPECIFICATIONS

	US		METRIC
2VZ-FE Engine: (continued)			
Engine center member-to-rear insulator	54 ft. lbs.		73 Nm
Front pipe-to-manifold	46 ft. lbs.		62 Nm
Front pipe-to-catalyst	32 ft. lbs.		43 Nm
Suspension lower member-to-body	153 ft. lbs.		207 Nm
Suspension lower member-to-engine center member	29 ft. lbs.		39 Nm
3S-FE Engine:			
Oil pump pulley	21 ft. lbs.		28 Nm
No. 1 idler pulley-to-cylinder head	31 ft. lbs.		42 Nm
No. 2 idler pulley-to-cylinder head	31 ft. lbs.		42 Nm
Camshaft timing pulley-to-camshaft	40 ft. lbs.		54 Nm
Crankshaft pulley-to-crankshaft	80 ft. lbs.		108 Nm
Cylinder head-to-block	36 ft. lbs.	1st	49 Nm
	90 deg. turn	2nd	90 deg. turn
Spark plug tube-to-head	29 ft. lbs.		39 Nm
Camshaft bearing cap-to-head	14 ft. lbs.		19 Nm
Cylinder head cover-to-head	17 ft. lbs.		23 Nm
Intake manifold-to-head	14 ft. lbs.		19 Nm
Intake manifold stay-to-head	14 ft. lbs.		19 Nm
Intake manifold stay-to-block	31 ft. lbs.		42 Nm
EGR valve-to-intake manifold	9 ft. lbs.		13 Nm
EGR pipe-to-head	43 ft. lbs.		59 Nm
Water outlet-to-head	11 ft. lbs.		15 Nm
Exhaust manifold-to-catalytic converter	21 ft. lbs.		29 Nm
Exhaust manifold-to-head	36 ft. lbs.		49 Nm
Engine hanger-to-head	31 ft. lbs.		42 Nm
Alternator bracket-to-head	31 ft. lbs.		42 Nm
Main bearing cap-to-block	43 ft. lbs.		59 Nm
Connecting rod cap-to-rod	36 ft. lbs.		49 Nm
Rear oil seal retainer-to-block	82 inch lbs.		9 Nm
Rear end plate-to-block	82 inch lbs.		9 Nm
Flywheel-to-crankshaft	65 ft. lbs.		88 Nm
Driveplate-to-crankshaft	61 ft. lbs.		83 Nm
Suspension lower member-to-body	154 ft. lbs.		208 Nm
Suspension lower member-to-engine center mounting	29 ft. lbs.		39 Nm
Engine center member-to-body	29 ft. lbs.		39 Nm
Engine center member-to-insulator	35 ft. lbs.	nuts	48 Nm
	54 ft. lbs.	bolts	73 Nm
Engine RH bracket-to-block	38 ft. lbs.		52 Nm
Engine RH insulator-to-engine mounting bracket	38 ft. lbs.		52 Nm
Engine RH insulator-to-body (2WD)	47 ft. lbs.	bolt	64 Nm
	65 ft. lbs.	nuts	88 Nm
Engine RH insulator-to-body (4WD)	64 ft. lbs.		87 Nm
Engine RH stay-to-engine mounting insulator	54 ft. lbs.		73 Nm
Engine RH stay-to-alternator bracket	54 ft. lbs.		73 Nm
Engine LH mounting bracket-to-transaxle	38 ft. lbs.		52 Nm
Engine LH insulator-to-insulator	38 ft. lbs.		52 Nm

TORQUE SPECIFICATIONS

	US		METRIC
3S-FE Engine: (continued)			
Engine LH stay-to-insulator	15 ft. lbs.	AT	21 Nm
Engine LH stay-to-transaxle	15 ft. lbs.	AT	21 Nm
Engine front mounting bracket-to-transaxle	57 ft. lbs.		77 Nm
Engine front insulator-to-mounting bracket	64 ft. lbs.		87 Nm
Engine center bracket-to-block (2WD)	35 ft. lbs.		48 Nm
Engine rear mounting-to-transaxle	57 ft. lbs.		77 Nm
Engine rear insulator-to-engine mounting bracket	64 ft. lbs.		87 Nm
3VZ-FE Engine:			
Cylinder head cover-to-head	52 inch lbs.		6 Nm
Air intake chamber-to-intake manifold	32 ft. lbs.		43 Nm
EGR pipe-to-exhaust manifold	58 ft. lbs.		78 Nm
EGR pipe-to-air intake chamber	13 ft. lbs.		18 Nm
Hydraulic pressure pipe-to-air intake chamber	14 ft. lbs.		20 Nm
Air intake stay-to-air intake chamber	29 ft. lbs.		39 Nm
Air intake stay-to-head	29 ft. lbs.		39 Nm
No. 1 engine hanger-to-air intake chamber	29 ft. lbs.		39 Nm
No. 1 engine hanger-to-head	29 ft. lbs.		39 Nm
Cold start injector pipe (No. 2)-to-cold start injector	11 ft. lbs.		15 Nm
Spark plug-to-head	13 ft. lbs.		18 Nm
No. 1 idler pulley-to-oil pump	25 ft. lbs.		34 Nm
Crankshaft pulley-to-crankshaft	181 ft. lbs.		245 Nm
No. 2 idler pulley-to-pulley bracket	29 ft. lbs.		39 Nm
Camshaft timing pulley-to-camshaft	80 ft. lbs.		108 Nm
Timing belt tensioner-to-oil pump	20 ft. lbs.		26 Nm
Engine RH bracket-to-block	30 ft. lbs.		39 Nm
Engine moving control rod-to-NO. 2 RH engine bracket	47 ft. lbs.		64 Nm
RH engine stay-to-intake manifold	23 ft. lbs.		31 Nm
RH engine stay-to-No. 2 RH engine bracket	23 ft. lbs.		31 Nm
No. 2 RH engine stay bolt	55 ft. lbs.		75 Nm
No. 2 RH engine stay nut	48 ft. lbs.		62 Nm
No. 3 RH engine stay bolt	54 ft. lbs.		73 Nm
Head-to-block 1st pass	25 ft. lbs.		34 Nm
Head-to-block 2nd pass	turn 90 deg.		turn 90 deg.
Head-to-block 3rd pass	turn 90 deg.		turn 90 deg.
Head-to-block recessed head bolt	13 ft. lbs.		18 Nm
LH engine hanger-to-LH head	29 ft. lbs.		39 Nm
PS pump bracket-to-RH head	32 ft. lbs.		43 Nm
Camshaft bearing cap-to-head	12 ft. lbs.		16 Nm
No. 3 timing belt cover-to-head	65 inch lbs.		7 Nm
No. 3 timing belt cover-to-block	65 inch lbs.		7 Nm
Exhaust manifold-to-head	29 ft. lbs.		39 Nm
Intake manifold-to-head	13 ft. lbs.		18 Nm
Air pipe-to-intake manifold	74 inch lbs.		8 Nm
No. 2 idler pulley bracket stay-to-intake manifold	13 ft. lbs.		18 Nm
No. 2 idler pulley bracket stay-to-No. 2 pulley bracket	13 ft. lbs.		18 Nm
Water by-pass outlet-to-intake manifold	74 inch lbs.		8 Nm

TORQUE SPECIFICATIONS

3VZ-FE Engine: (continued)

Fastener	US	METRIC
Delivery pipe-to-intake manifold	9 ft. lbs.	13 Nm
No. 1 EGR cooler-to-air intake chamber	13 ft. lbs.	18 Nm
Water outlet-to-intake manifold	74 inch lbs.	8 Nm
Emission control valve set-to-intake chamber	74 inch lbs.	8 Nm
EGR valve-to-air intake chamber	13 ft. lbs.	18 Nm
Throttle body-to-intake chamber	9 ft. lbs.	13 Nm
Front pipe-to-exhaust manifold	46 ft. lbs.	62 Nm
Front exhaust manifold-to-catalytic converter	32 ft. lbs.	43 Nm
Main bearing cap-to-block — 1st	45 ft. lbs.	61 Nm
Main bearing cap-to-block — 2nd	turn 90 deg.	turn 90 deg.
Connecting rod cap-to-rod — 1st	18 ft. lbs.	25 Nm
Connecting rod cap-to-rod — 2nd	turn 90 deg.	turn 90 deg.
Rear oil seal retainer-to-block	69 inch lbs.	8 Nm
No. 2 idler pulley bracket-to-block	27 ft. lbs.	37 Nm
Knock sensor-to-block	33 ft. lbs.	44 Nm
Water by-pass pipe-to-block	74 inch lbs.	9 Nm
Coolant petcock-to-block	29 ft. lbs.	39 Nm
Drain hose clamp-to-block	14 ft. lbs.	20 Nm
Rear end plate-to-block	74 inch lbs.	9 Nm
Flywheel-to-crankshaft	61 ft. lbs.	83 Nm
Driveplate-to-crankshaft	61 ft. lbs.	83 Nm
RR engine insulator-to-block	57 ft. lbs.	77 Nm
FR engine insulator-to-block	57 ft. lbs.	77 Nm
FR engine insulator-to-front suspension member	59 ft. lbs.	80 Nm
Engine mounting absorber-to-front suspension member	35 ft. lbs.	48 Nm
Engine mounting absorber-to-transaxle	35 ft. lbs.	48 Nm
RR engine insulator-to-front suspension member	59 ft. lbs.	80 Nm
LH engine insulator-to-transaxle	47 ft. lbs.	64 Nm
PS pump-to-pump bracket	31 ft. lbs.	43 Nm
Fuel inlet hose-to-fuel filter	20 ft. lbs.	27 Nm
Center exhaust pipe-to-tail pipe	32 ft. lbs.	43 Nm

5S-FE Engine:

Fastener	US	METRIC
Cylinder head cover-to-head	17 ft. lbs.	23 Nm
Spark plug-to-head	13 ft. lbs.	18 Nm
Oil pump pulley-to-oil pump drive shaft	21 ft. lbs.	28 Nm
No. 2 idler pulley-to-block	31 ft. lbs.	42 Nm
Crankshaft pulley-to-crankshaft	80 ft. lbs.	108 Nm
Camshaft timing pulley-to-camshaft	40 ft. lbs.	54 Nm
No. 1 idler pulley-to-head	31 ft. lbs.	42 Nm
No. 2 engine mounting bracket-to-block	38 ft. lbs.	52 Nm
Engine control rod-to-fender apron	47 ft. lbs.	64 Nm
Engine control rod-to-No. 2 engine mounting bracket	47 ft. lbs.	64 Nm
Cylinder head-to-block — 1st	36 ft. lbs.	49 Nm
Cylinder head-to-block — 2nd	turn 90 deg.	turn 90 deg.
Spark plug tube-to-head	29 ft. lbs.	39 Nm
Camshaft bearing cap-to-head	14 ft. lbs.	19 Nm

TORQUE SPECIFICATIONS

5S-FE Engine: (continued)

Fastener	US	METRIC
Alternator bracket-to-head	31 ft. lbs.	42 Nm
Engine hanger-to-head	18 ft. lbs.	25 Nm
No. 3 timing belt cover-to-head	69 inch lbs.	8 Nm
Delivery pipe-to-head	9 ft. lbs.	13 Nm
Pulsation damper-to-head	25 ft. lbs.	34 Nm
Intake manifold-to-head	14 ft. lbs.	19 Nm
Intake manifold stay-to-intake manifold	16 ft. lbs.	22 Nm
Intake manifold stay-to-block	31 ft. lbs.	42 Nm
No. 1 air intake chamber stay-to-intake manifold	31 ft. lbs.	42 Nm
No. 1 air intake chamber stay-to-head	31 ft. lbs.	42 Nm
EGR valve-to-intake manifold	9 ft. lbs.	13 Nm
EGR pipe-to-head	43 ft. lbs.	59 Nm
Throttle body-to-intake manifold	11 ft. lbs.	15 Nm
Water by-pass pipe-to-water pump cover	78 inch lbs.	9 Nm
Water outlet-to-head	36 ft. lbs.	49 Nm
Exhaust manifold-to-head	31 ft. lbs.	42 Nm
Exhaust manifold stay-to-block	31 ft. lbs.	42 Nm
No. 1 exhaust manifold stay-to-exhaust manifold	31 ft. lbs.	42 Nm
No. 1 exhaust manifold stay-to-FR engine insulator	31 ft. lbs.	42 Nm
Catalytic converter-to-exhaust manifold (Calif.)	22 ft. lbs.	29 Nm
Exhaust manifold stay-to-converter (Calif.)	31 ft. lbs.	42 Nm
No. 1 exhaust manifold stay-to-converter (Calif.)	31 ft. lbs.	42 Nm
Main bearing cap-to-block	43 ft. lbs.	59 Nm
Connecting rod cap-to-rod — 1st	18 ft. lbs.	25 Nm
Connecting rod cap-to-rod — 2nd	turn 90 deg.	turn 90 deg.
No. 1 balance shaft housing-to-No. 2 — 1st	16 ft. lbs.	22 Nm
balance shaft housing — 2nd	turn 90 deg.	turn 90 deg.
Engine balancer-to-block	36 ft. lbs.	49 Nm
Rear oil seal retainer-to-block	82 inch lbs.	9 Nm
Knock sensor-to-block	27 ft. lbs.	37 Nm
PS pump bracket-to-block	32 ft. lbs.	43 Nm
Rear end plate-to-block	82 inch lbs.	9 Nm
Flywheel-to-crankshaft	65 ft. lbs.	88 Nm
Driveplate-to-crankshaft	61 ft. lbs.	83 Nm
RR engine insulator-to-block	57 ft. lbs.	77 Nm
FR engine insulator-to-block	57 ft. lbs.	77 Nm
FR engine insulator-to-front suspension crossmember	59 ft. lbs.	80 Nm
RR engine insulator-to-front suspension crossmemeber	48 ft. lbs.	66 Nm
LH engine insulator-to-transaxle	47 ft. lbs.	64 Nm
PS pump-to-PS bracket	31 ft. lbs.	43 Nm

1MZ-FE Engine:

Fastener	US	METRIC
Timing belt plate	69 inch lbs.	8 Nm
No. 1 idler pulley-to-oil pump	25 ft. lbs.	34 Nm
No. 2 idler pulley-to-No. 2 pulley bracket	32 ft. lbs.	43 Nm
Camshaft timing pulley-to-camshaft	94 ft. lbs.	125 Nm

89553C08

89553C09

TORQUE SPECIFICATIONS

1MZ-FE Engine: (continued)

	US	METRIC
Knock sensor-to-block	29 ft. lbs.	39 Nm
No. 2 idler pulley bracket-to-block	21 ft. lbs.	28 Nm
Water seal plate-to-block	13 ft. lbs.	18 Nm
Alternator bracket-to-block	32 ft. lbs.	43 Nm
Driveplate-to-crankshaft	61 ft. lbs.	83 Nm
Transaxle-to-engine	47 ft. lbs.	64 Nm
No. 1 oil pan-to-transaxle	27 ft. lbs.	37 Nm
Drive plate-to-torque converter clutch	30 ft. lbs.	41 Nm
Flywheel housing under cover-to-transaxle	69 inch lbs.	8 Nm
RR engine insulator-to-block	47 ft. lbs.	64 Nm
FR engine insulator-to-block	47 ft. lbs.	64 Nm
Engine control rod-to-engine RH bracket	47 ft. lbs.	64 Nm
Engine control rod-to-RH fender apron	47 ft. lbs.	64 Nm
RH engine stay-to-water outlet	23 ft. lbs.	31 Nm
RH engine stay-to-engine control rod	23 ft. lbs.	31 Nm
RH engine stay-to-No. 2 RH engine bracket	23 ft. lbs.	31 Nm
FR engine insulator-to-front frame TMC	59 ft. lbs.	81 Nm
TMM	48 ft. lbs.	66 Nm
Engine absorber-to-front frame	35 ft. lbs.	48 Nm
Engine absorber-to-transaxle	35 ft. lbs.	48 Nm
RR engine insulator-to-front frame	48 ft. lbs.	66 Nm
LH engine insulator-to-transaxle	47 ft. lbs.	64 Nm
PS pump-to-PS bracket	31 ft. lbs.	43 Nm
Alternator adjusting bar-to-belt bracket	13 ft. lbs.	18 Nm
Fuel inlet hose-to-fuel filter	21 ft. lbs.	29 Nm
Front exhaust pipe bracket-to-No. 1 oil pan	15 ft. lbs.	21 Nm
Front pipe-to-manifold	46 ft. lbs.	62 NM
Front pipe-to-center pipe	41 ft. lbs.	56 Nm
Front pipe stay-to-front support bracket	22 ft. lbs.	30 Nm
Front pipe support bracket-to-front frame	14 ft. lbs.	19 Nm
Center pipe-to-tailpipe	32 ft. lbs.	43 Nm
Oil pump-to-block 10mm	69 inch lbs.	8 Nm
12mm	14 ft. lbs.	20 Nm
No. 1 oil pan-to-oil pump	69 inch lbs.	8 Nm
No. 1 oil pan-to-real oil seal retainer	69 inch lbs.	8 Nm
No. 1 oil pan-to-cylinder block	14 ft. lbs.	20 Nm
Oil strainer-to-main bearing cap	69 inch lbs.	8 Nm
Oil strainer-to-oil pump	69 inch lbs.	8 Nm
No. 2 oil pan-to-No. 1 oil pan	69 inch lbs.	8 Nm

89553C11

TORQUE SPECIFICATIONS

1MZ-FE Engine: (continued)

	US	METRIC
Timing belt tensioner-to- oil pump	20 ft. lbs.	27 Nm
RH engine bracket-to-block	21 ft. lbs.	28 Nm
No. 2 timing belt cover-to-No. 3 belt cover	74 inch lbs.	9 Nm
No. 1 timing belt cover-to-oil pump	74 inch lbs.	9 Nm
Crankshaft pulley-to-crankshaft	159 ft. lbs.	215 Nm
No. 2 alternator bracket-to-RH engine bracket	21 ft. lbs.	28 Nm
Cylinder head-to-block 1st	40 ft. lbs.	54 Nm
2nd	turn 90 deg.	turn 90 deg.
recessed	13 ft. lbs.	19 Nm
Camshaft bearing cap-to-head	12 ft. lbs.	16 Nm
Cylinder head cover-to-head	69 inch lbs.	8 Nm
Exhaust manifold-to-head	36 ft. lbs.	49 NM
Exhaust manifold stay-to-exhaust manifold	15 ft. lbs.	20 Nm
Exhaust manifold stay-to-transaxle housing	15 ft. lbs.	20 Nm
No. 1 EGR pipe-to-RH exhaust manifold	9 ft. lbs.	12 Nm
No. 1 EGR pipe-to-EGR cooler	9 ft. lbs.	12 Nm
PS pump bracket-to-RH head	32 ft. lbs.	43 Nm
Oil dipstick guide-to-LH head	69 inch lbs.	8 Nm
Heated oxygen sensor-to-exhaust manifold	33 ft. lbs.	44 Nm
Water outlet-to-intake manifold	11 ft. lbs.	15 Nm
Delivery pipe-to-intake manifold	7 ft. lbs.	10 Nm
No. 2 fuel pipe-to-delivery pipe	24 ft. lbs.	33 Nm
Pulsation damper-to-delivery pipe	24 ft. lbs.	33 Nm
No. 1 fuel pipe-to-intake manifold	11 ft. lbs.	15 Nm
TVV-to-intake manifold	22 ft. lbs.	30 Nm
Intake manifold-to-head	11 ft. lbs.	15 Nm
Water inlet pipe-to-LH cylinder head	14 ft. lbs.	20 Nm
Cylinder head rear plate-to-LH head	69 inch lbs.	8 Nm
No. 3 timing belt cover-to-head	74 inch lbs.	9 Nm
Air intake chamber-to-intake manifold	32 ft. lbs.	43 Nm
EGR valve-to-air intake chamber	9 ft. lbs.	12 Nm
Throttle body-to-intake chamber	14 ft. lbs.	20 Nm
Intake air control-to-air intake chamber	10 ft. lbs.	15 Nm
No. 2 EGR pipe-to-air intake chamber	9 ft. lbs.	12 Nm
No. 2 EGR pipe-to-EGR cooler	9 ft. lbs.	12 Nm
No. 1 engine hanger-to-air intake chamber	29 ft. lbs.	39 Nm
No. 1 engine hanger-to-RH head	29 ft. lbs.	39 Nm
Air intake stay-to-air intake chamber	14 ft. lbs.	20 Nm
Air intake stay-to-RH head	14 ft. lbs.	20 Nm
Emission control valve set-to-air intake chamber	69 inch lbs.	8 Nm
Main bearing cap-to-block 1st	16 ft. lbs.	22 Nm
2nd	turn 90 deg.	turn 90 deg.
6 pointed	20 ft. lbs.	27 Nm
Connecting rod cap-to-rod 1st	18 ft. lbs.	25 Nm
2nd	turn 90 deg.	turn 90 deg.
Rear oil seal retainer-to-block	69 inch lbs.	8 Nm
EGR cooler-to-block	78 inch lbs.	9 Nm
Engine coolant drain cock-to-block	29 ft. lbs.	39 Nm

89553C10

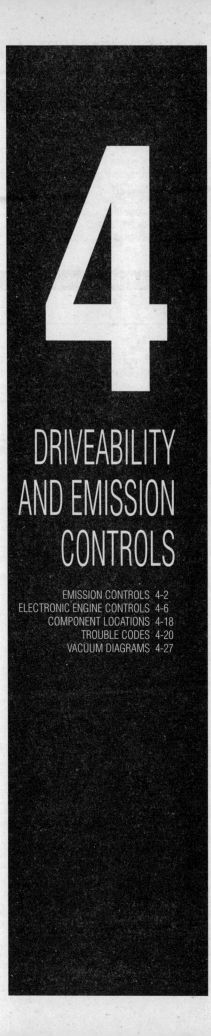

4

DRIVEABILITY AND EMISSION CONTROLS

EMISSION CONTROLS

▶ **See Figure 1**

Due to varying state, federal, and provincial regulations, specific emission control equipment may vary by area of sale. The US emission equipment is divided into two categories: California and 49 State (or Federal). In this section, the term "California" applies only to cars originally built to be sold in California. Some California emissions equipment is not shared with equipment installed on cars built to be sold in the other 49 states. Models built to be sold in Canada also have specific emissions equipment, although in many cases the 49 State and Canadian equipment is the same.

Crankcase Ventilation System

OPERATION

▶ **See Figure 2**

A Positive Crankcase Ventilation (PCV) system is used on all Toyota gasoline engines. Exhaust blow-by gasses are routed from the crankcase to the intake manifold, where they are combined with the fuel/air mixture and burned during combustion. This reduces the amount of hydrocarbons emitted by the exhaust.

A valve is used in the line to prevent the gases in the crankcase from being ignited in case of a backfire. The amount of blow-by gasses entering the mixture is also regulated by the PCV valve, which is spring loaded and has a variable orifice.

The components of the PCV system consist of the following:
- PCV valve
- Valve cover
- Air intake chamber
- Ventilation case
- Hoses, connections and gaskets

COMPONENT TESTING

▶ **See Figures 3, 4 and 5**

Inspect the PCV system hoses and connections at each tune-up and replace any deteriorated hoses. Check the PCV valve at every tune-up and replace it at 30,000 mile (48,000 km) intervals. The PCV system is easily checked with the engine running at normal idle speed (warmed up).

1. Remove the PCV valve from the valve cover or intake manifold, but leave it connected to its hose.
2. Start the engine.
3. Place your thumb over the end of the valve to check for vacuum. If there is no vacuum, check for plugged hoses or ports. If these are open, the valve is faulty.
4. With the engine **OFF**, remove the valve completely. Shake it end-to-end, listening for the rattle of the needle inside the valve. If no rattle is heard, the needle is jammed (probably due to oil sludge) and the valve should be replaced.

✴✴ CAUTION

Don't blow directly into the valve; petroleum deposits within the valve can be harmful. Use a separate air source or attach a length of clean hose to the valve.

5. Blow air from the cylinder head side of the PCV valve. It should flow easily. Air should pass with difficulty from the manifold side.

Evaporative Emission Controls

OPERATION

▶ **See Figure 6**

The Evaporative Emission Control (EVAP) system is designed to prevent fuel tank vapors from being emitted into the atmosphere. When the engine is not

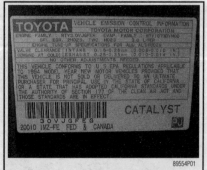

Fig. 1 The vehicle emission control label can be found under the hood—1994 1MZ-FE engine shown

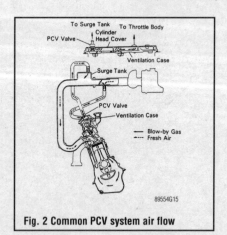

Fig. 2 Common PCV system air flow

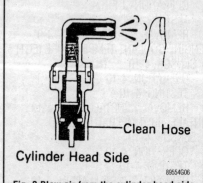

Fig. 3 Blow air from the cylinder head side of the PCV valve, it should flow easily

Fig. 4 Blow air from the air manifold side, check that the air passes with difficulty

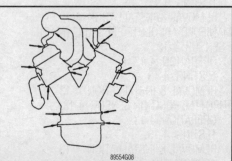

Fig. 5 Leaks at gaskets or hose connections can cause the PCV system to malfunction

running, fuel vapors from the tank are stored in a charcoal canister. The charcoal canister absorbs the vapors and stores them until certain engine conditions are met and the vapors can be purged and burned by the engine. In some vehicles, any liquid fuel entering the canister goes into a reservoir in the bottom of the canister to protect the integrity of the carbon element in the canister above. These systems employ the following components:

2S-ELC, 3VZ-FE and 3S-FE engines:
- Fuel tank cap
- Charcoal canister
- Bi-metal Vacuum Switching Valve (BVSV)
- Check valve
- Jet (Canada)

2VZ-FE engine:
- Bimetal Vacuum Switching Valve (BVSV)
- Check valve
- Charcoal canister
- Fuel tank cap

5S-FE and 1MZ-FE engines:
- Charcoal canister
- Fuel tank cap
- Thermal Vacuum Valve (TVV)
- Check valve
- Heated Oxygen sensors

REMOVAL & INSTALLATION

➡ **When replacing any EVAP system hoses, always use hoses that are fuel-resistant or are marked EVAP. Use of hose which is not fuel-resistant will lead to premature hose failure.**

Charcoal Canister

Label and disconnect the lines running to the canister. Remove the fasteners, then remove the charcoal canister from the vehicle. Do not attempt to wash the charcoal canister. Installation is the reverse of removal.

To install:
4. Apply adhesive to 2 or 3 of the threads of the TVV, then tighten the valve to 22 ft. lbs. (29 Nm).
5. Reattach the vacuum hoses.
6. Refill the engine with coolant. Start the engine, check and top off the fluid level.

Dash Pot (DP) System

SYSTEM OPERATION

▶ **See Figure 9**

The operation of this system reduces the HC and CO emissions. When decelerating, the dash pot opens the throttle valve slightly more than at idle. This causes the air-fuel mixture to burn completely. This system is only applicable to the 1989–91 2VZ-FE engines.

ADJUSTMENT

1. Warm up and stop engine.
2. Check idle speed.
3. Disconnect the throttle cables from the throttle cam.
4. Remove the VTV cap, filter and separator from the dash pot.
5. Adjust DP setting speed as follows:
   a. Race the engine at 2500 rpm for a few seconds. Plug the VTV hole with your finger in the dash pot assembly.
   b. Release the throttle valve.
   c. Check the DP setting speed. The DP setting speed is 2000 rpm with cooling fan OFF.
   d. Adjust the DP setting speed by turning the DP adjusting screw.
6. Reinstall the DP separator, filter and VTV cap.
7. Connect the throttle cables to the throttle cam.

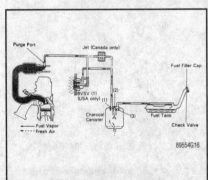

Fig. 6 Evaporative Emission Control (EVAP) system components—2S-ELC engine shown, others similar

Fig. 7 Tag and disconnect the lines leading to the Thermal Vacuum Valve (TVV)

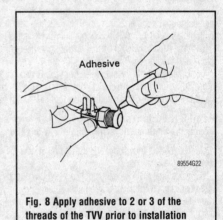

Fig. 8 Apply adhesive to 2 or 3 of the threads of the TVV prior to installation

Bimetal Vacuum Switching Valve (BVSV)

1. Drain the engine coolant from the radiator into a suitable container.
2. Unscrew the BVSV from the engine.

To install:
3. Apply liquid sealer to the threads of the BVSV. Carefully thread the valve into the engine.
4. Fill the radiator with coolant. Start the engine, check and top off the fluid level.

Thermal Vacuum Valve (TVV)

▶ **See Figures 7 and 8**

1. Drain the coolant the from the radiator.
2. Disconnect the vacuum hoses from the charcoal canister (lower-2) and throttle body (upper-1).
3. Remove the TVV valve from the engine.

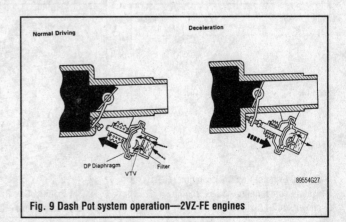

Fig. 9 Dash Pot system operation—2VZ-FE engines

8. Check system operation by racing the engine at 2500 rpm for a few seconds, release the throttle valve and check that the engine returns to idle speed in a few seconds.

REMOVAL & INSTALLATION

1. To remove the dash pot assembly, unplug the vacuum hose then remove the dash pot mounting screws.
2. Remove the assembly from the throttle body.
3. Installation is the reverse of removal. Replace the dash pot assembly and adjust if necessary.

Exhaust Gas Recirculation System

OPERATION

The EGR system reduces oxides of nitrogen. This is accomplished by recirculating some of the exhaust gases through the EGR valve to the intake manifold, lowering peak combustion temperatures.

TESTING

2SE-LC and 3S-FE Engines

SYSTEM CHECK

▶ See Figure 10

1. Check and clean the filter in the EGR vacuum modulator. Use compressed air (if possible) to blow the dirt out of the filters and check the filters for contamination or damage.
2. Using a tee (3-way connector), connect a vacuum gauge to the hose between the EGR valve and the vacuum modulator.
3. Check the seating of the EGR valve by starting the engine and seeing that it runs at a smooth idle. If the valve is not completely closed, the idle will be rough.
4. With the engine coolant temperature below 113°F (45°C), the vacuum gauge should read 0 at 2500 rpm. This indicates that the Bimetal Vacuum Switching Valve (BVSV) is functioning correctly at this temperature range.
5. Warm the engine to normal operating temperature. Check the vacuum gauge and confirm low vacuum at 2500 rpm.
6. Disconnect the vacuum hose from the **R** port on the EGR vacuum modulator and, using another piece of hose, connect the **R** port directly to the intake manifold. Check that the vacuum gauge indicates high vacuum at 2500 rpm.

➡**Port R is the lower of the two ports. As a large amount of exhaust gas enters, the engine will misfire slightly at this time.**

7. Disconnect the vacuum gauge and reconnect the vacuum hoses to their proper locations.
8. Check the EGR valve by applying vacuum directly to the valve with the engine at idle. (This may be accomplished either by bridging vacuum directly from the intake manifold or by using a hand-held vacuum pump.) The engine should falter and die as the full load of recalculated gasses enters the engine.

9. If no problem is found with this inspection, the system is OK; otherwise inspect each part.

2VZ-FE Engine

SYSTEM CHECK

▶ See Figure 11

1. Check and clean the filter in the EGR vacuum modulator. Use compressed air (if possible) to blow the dirt out of the filters and check the filters for contamination or damage.
2. Using a tee (3-way connector), connect a vacuum gauge to the hose between the EGR valve and the vacuum modulator.
3. Check the seating of the EGR valve by starting the engine and seeing that it runs at a smooth idle. If the valve is not completely closed, the idle will be rough.
4. With the engine coolant temperature below 104°F (40°C), the vacuum gauge should read 0 at 2500 rpm. This indicates that the Bimetal Vacuum Switching Valve (BVSV) is functioning correctly at this temperature range.
5. Warm the engine to normal operating temperature. Check the vacuum gauge and confirm low vacuum at 2500 rpm.
6. Disconnect the vacuum hose from the **R** port on the EGR vacuum modulator and, using another piece of hose, connect the **R** port directly to the intake manifold. Check that the vacuum gauge indicates high vacuum at 3500 rpm.

➡**Port R is the lower of the two ports. As a large amount of exhaust gas enters, the engine will misfire slightly at this time.**

7. Disconnect the vacuum gauge and reconnect the vacuum hoses to their proper locations.
8. Check the EGR valve by applying vacuum directly to the valve with the engine at idle. (This may be accomplished either by bridging vacuum directly from the intake manifold or by using a hand-held vacuum pump.) The engine should falter and die as the full load of recalculated gasses enters the engine.
9. If no problem is found with this inspection, the system is OK; otherwise inspect each part.

3VZ-FE Engine

SYSTEM CHECK

▶ See Figure 12

1. Check and clean the filter in the EGR vacuum modulator. Use compressed air (if possible) to blow the dirt out of the filters and check the filters for contamination or damage.
2. Using a tee (3-way connector), connect a vacuum gauge to the hose between the EGR valve and the vacuum modulator.
3. Check the seating of the EGR valve by starting the engine and seeing that it runs at a smooth idle. If the valve is not completely closed, the idle will be rough.
4. Inspect the Thermal Vacuum Valve (TVV) with the engine coolant temperature below 95°F (35°C), the vacuum gauge should read 0 at 2500 rpm.
5. Warm the engine to normal operating temperature. Check the vacuum gauge and confirm low vacuum at 2500 rpm.

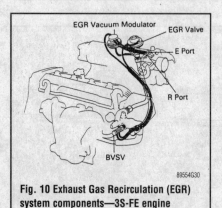

Fig. 10 Exhaust Gas Recirculation (EGR) system components—3S-FE engine shown, 2SE-LC similar

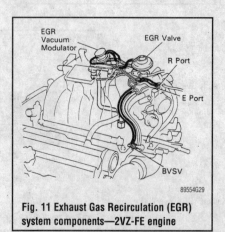

Fig. 11 Exhaust Gas Recirculation (EGR) system components—2VZ-FE engine

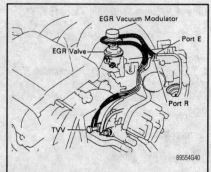

Fig. 12 Exhaust Gas Recirculation (EGR) system components found on 3VZ-FE engines

6. Disconnect the vacuum hose from the **R** port on the EGR vacuum modulator and, using another piece of hose, connect the **R** port directly to the intake manifold. Check that the vacuum gauge indicates high vacuum at 3500 rpm.

➡**Port R is the lower of the two ports. As a large amount of exhaust gas enters, the engine will misfire slightly at this time.**

7. Disconnect the vacuum gauge and reconnect the vacuum hoses to their proper locations.

8. Check the EGR valve by applying vacuum directly to the valve with the engine at idle. (This may be accomplished either by bridging vacuum directly from the intake manifold or by using a hand-held vacuum pump.) The engine should falter and die as the full load of recalculated gasses enters the engine.

9. If no problem is found with this inspection, the system is OK; otherwise inspect each part.

5S-FE Engine

SYSTEM CHECK

▶ **See Figures 13 and 14**

1. Check and clean the filter in the EGR vacuum modulator. Use compressed air (if possible) to blow the dirt out of the filters and check the filters for contamination or damage.

2. Using a tee (3-way connector), connect a vacuum gauge to the hose between the EGR valve and the vacuum modulator.

3. Check the seating of the EGR valve by starting the engine and seeing that it runs at a smooth idle. If the valve is not completely closed, the idle will be rough.

➡**The check connector is located near the air cleaner.**

4. Connect terminals TE$_1$ and E$_1$ in the check connector.

5. Inspect VSV and EGR vacuum modulator operation with hot engine. With the engine coolant temperature above 140°F (60°C) on AT and 131°F (55°C) on MT, check the vacuum gauge and confirm 0 vacuum at 2500 rpm.

6. Warm the engine up and check that the vacuum gauge indicates low vacuum at 2500 rpm.

7. Disconnect the hose from port R of the EGR vacuum modulator and connect port R directly to the intake manifold with another hose. Check the vacuum and make sure the reading is high at 2500 rpm.

➡**Port R is the lower of the two ports. As a large amount of exhaust gas enters, the engine will misfire slightly at this time.**

8. Disconnect the vacuum gauge, SST or jumper wire and reconnect the vacuum hoses to their proper locations.

9. Check the EGR valve by applying vacuum directly to the valve with the engine at idle. (This may be accomplished either by bridging vacuum directly from the intake manifold or by using a hand-held vacuum pump.) The engine should falter and die as the full load of recalculated gasses enters the engine.

10. Remove the jumper from the check connector.

11. If no problem is found with this inspection, the system is OK; otherwise inspect each part.

1MZ-FE Engine

SYSTEM CHECK

1. Check and clean the filter in the EGR vacuum modulator. Use compressed air (if possible) to blow the dirt out of the filters and check the filters for contamination or damage.

2. Using a tee (3-way connector), connect a vacuum gauge to the hose between the EGR valve and the vacuum modulator.

3. Check the seating of the EGR valve by starting the engine and seeing that it runs at a smooth idle. If the valve is not completely closed, the idle will be rough.

➡**The check connector is located near the air cleaner.**

4. Connect terminals TE$_1$ and E$_1$ in the check connector.

5. Inspect VSV and EGR vacuum modulator operation with hot engine. With the engine coolant temperature above 131°F (55°C), check the vacuum gauge and confirm 0 vacuum at 2800 rpm. Check that the EGR pipe is hot.

6. Warm the engine up and check that the vacuum gauge indicates low vacuum at 2800 rpm.

7. Disconnect the hose from port R of the EGR vacuum modulator and connect port R directly to the intake manifold with another hose. Check the vacuum and make sure the reading is high at 3500 rpm.

➡**Port R is the lower of the two ports. As a large amount of exhaust gas enters, the engine will misfire slightly at this time.**

8. Disconnect the vacuum gauge, SST or jumper wire and reconnect the vacuum hoses to their proper locations.

9. Check the EGR valve by applying vacuum directly to the valve with the engine at idle. (This may be accomplished either by bridging vacuum directly from the intake manifold or by using a hand-held vacuum pump.) The engine should falter and die as the full load of recalculated gasses enters the engine.

10. Remove the jumper from the check connector.

11. If no problem is found with this inspection, the system is OK; otherwise inspect each part.

REMOVAL & INSTALLATION

EGR Valve

▶ **See Figures 15, 16, 17 and 18**

1. Disconnect the negative battery cable.

2. Remove the air cleaner hose and lid. Disconnect the IAT sensor wiring.

3. Disconnect the accelerator cable bracket from the throttle body.

4. Remove the throttle body from the air intake chamber.

5. Unbolt and remove the engine hanger, air intake chamber stay and EGR vacuum modulator. Discard the vacuum modulator gasket.

6. Loosen the union nut of the EGR valve. Disconnect and label the hoses attached to the valve.

7. Disconnect the EGR gas temperature sensor wiring.

8. Remove the nuts, EGR valve and pipe. Discard the gaskets.

9. Installation is the reverse of removal. Place a new gasket on the cylinder head facing the protrusion downward. Install another gasket on the EGR valve and pipe and secure with the mounting nuts. Tighten them to 9 ft. lbs. (13 Nm).

10. Tighten the union nut on the EGR valve to 43 ft. lbs. (59 Nm).

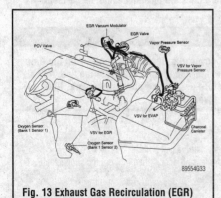

Fig. 13 Exhaust Gas Recirculation (EGR) system components—5S-FE engine

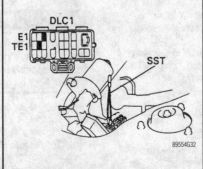

Fig. 14 Connect terminals TE$_1$ and E$_1$ in the data link connector

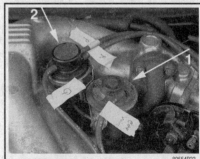

Fig. 15 Prior to EGR valve removal, label all hoses for the EGR valve (1) and vacuum modulator (2)

Fig. 16 Remove these three nuts to separate the EGR and modulator from the intake manifold

Fig. 17 Pull the unit from the engine . . .

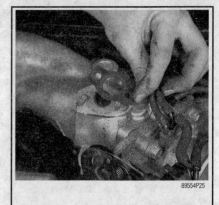

Fig. 18 . . . and discard the old gasket

ELECTRONIC ENGINE CONTROLS

General Information

The Electronic Fuel Injection (EFI) system precisely controls fuel injection to match engine requirements. This in turn reduces emissions and increases driveability. The ECM receives input from various sensors to determine engine operating conditions. These sensors provide the input to the control unit which determines the amount of fuel to be injected as well as other variables such as idle speed. These inputs and their corresponding sensors include:

- Intake manifold absolute pressure—MAP or Vacuum Sensor
- Intake air temperature—Intake Air Temperature Sensor
- Coolant temperature—Water Temperature Sensor
- Engine speed—Pulse signal from the distributor
- Throttle valve opening—Throttle Position Sensor
- Exhaust oxygen content—Oxygen Sensor

Engine Control Module (ECM)

OPERATION

The ECM receives signals from various sensors on the engine. It will then process this information and calculate the correct air/fuel mixture under all operating conditions. The ECM is a very fragile and expensive component. Always follow the precautions when servicing the electronic control system.

PRECAUTIONS

- Do not permit parts to receive a severe impact during removal or installation. Always handle all fuel injection parts with care, especially the ECM. DO NOT open the ECM cover!
- Before removing the fuel injected wiring connectors, terminals, etc., first disconnect the power by either disconnecting the negative battery cable or turning the ignition switch **OFF**.
- Do not be careless during troubleshooting as there are numerous amounts of transistor circuits; even a slight terminal contact can induce troubles.
- When inspecting during rainy days, take extra caution not to allow entry of water in or on the unit. When washing the engine compartment, prevent water from getting on the fuel injection parts and wiring connectors.

REMOVAL & INSTALLATION

▶ See Figures 19 and 20

Most ECM's are located in the passengers compartment under the dash behind the glovebox. Other models may have the unit on the drivers side near the center console.

1. Disconnect the negative battery cable.

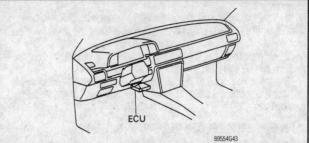

Fig. 19 Some ECM's are located under the dash on the drivers side of the vehicle . . .

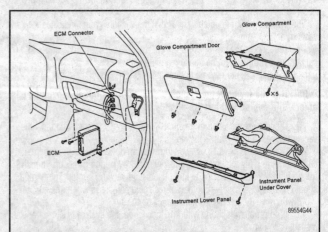

Fig. 20 . . . while other ECM's are located behind the glovebox

❊❊ CAUTION

On models with an airbag, wait at least 90 seconds from the time that the ignition switch is turned to the LOCK position and the battery is disconnected before performing any further work. Refer to Section 6 for all air bag warnings.

2. Remove any necessary trim panel to gain access to the ECM floor mat bracket bolts.
3. Remove the ECM floor mat bracket bolts.
4. Locate the ECM and release the lock, then pull out the connector. Pull on the connectors only!
5. Unbolt the ECM from its mounting area.
6. Installation is the reverse of removal. Start engine and check for proper operation.

Oxygen Sensor

OPERATION

The exhaust oxygen sensor or O2S, is mounted in the exhaust stream where it monitors oxygen content in the exhaust gas. The oxygen content in the exhaust is a measure of the air/fuel mixture going into the engine. The oxygen in the exhaust reacts with the oxygen sensor to produce a voltage which is read by the ECM.

There are two types of oxygen sensors used in these vehicles. They are the single wire oxygen sensor (O2S) and the heated oxygen sensor (HO2S). The oxygen sensor is a spark plug shaped device that is screwed into the exhaust manifold. It monitors the oxygen content of the exhaust gases and sends a voltage signal to the Electronic Control Module (ECM). The ECM monitors this voltage and, depending on the value of the received signal, issues a command to the mixture control solenoid on the carburetor to adjust for rich or lean conditions.

The heated oxygen sensor has a heating element incorporated into the sensor to aid in the warm up to the proper operating temperature and to maintain that temperature.

The proper operation of the oxygen sensor depends upon four basic conditions:
• Good electrical connections. Since the sensor generates low currents, good clean electrical connections at the sensor are a must.
• Outside air supply. Air must circulate to the internal portion of the sensor. When servicing the sensor, do not restrict the air passages.
• Proper operating temperatures. The ECM will not recognize the sensor's signals until the sensor reaches approximately 600°F (316°C).
• Non-leaded fuel. The use of leaded gasoline will damage the sensor very quickly.

TESTING

✳✳ WARNING

Do not pierce the wires when testing this sensor; this can lead to wiring harness damage. Backprobe the connector to properly read the voltage of the HO2S.

Single Wire Sensor

1. Start the engine and bring it to normal operating temperature, then run the engine above 1200 rpm for two minutes.
2. Backprobe with a high impedance averaging voltmeter (set to the DC voltage scale) between the oxygen sensor (O2S) and battery ground.
3. Verify that the O2S voltage fluctuates rapidly between 0.40–0.60 volts.
4. If the O2S voltage is stabilized at the middle of the specified range (approximately 0.45–0.55 volts) or if the O2S voltage fluctuates very slowly between the specified range (O2S signal crosses 0.5 volts less than 5 times in ten seconds), the O2S may be faulty.
5. If the O2S voltage stabilizes at either end of the specified range, the ECM is probably not able to compensate for a mechanical problem such as a vacuum leak or a faulty pressure regulator. These types of mechanical problems will cause the O2S to sense a constant lean or constant rich mixture. The mechanical problem will first have to be repaired and then the O2S test repeated.

6. Pull a vacuum hose located after the throttle plate. Voltage should drop to approximately 0.12 volts (while still fluctuating rapidly). This tests the ability of the O2S to detect a lean mixture condition. Reattach the vacuum hose.
7. Richen the mixture using a propane enrichment tool. Voltage should rise to approximately 0.90 volts (while still fluctuating rapidly). This tests the ability of the O2S to detect a rich mixture condition.
8. If the O2S voltage is above or below the specified range, the O2S and/or the O2S wiring may be faulty. Check the wiring for any breaks, repair as necessary and repeat the test.

Heated Oxygen Sensor

◆ See Figure 21

1. Start the engine and bring it to normal operating temperature, then run the engine above 1200 rpm for two minutes.
2. Turn the ignition **OFF** disengage the HO2S harness connector.
3. Connect an ohmmeter between terminals +B and HT of the sensor. Resistance should be 11–16 ohms at 68° F (20° C). If not, replace the sensor.
4. Start the engine and bring it to normal operating temperature, then run the engine above 1200 rpm for two minutes.
5. Backprobe with a high impedance averaging voltmeter (set to the DC voltage scale) between the oxygen sensor (O2S) signal wire and battery ground.
6. Verify that the O2S voltage fluctuates rapidly between 0.40–0.60 volts.
7. If the O2S voltage is stabilized at the middle of the specified range (approximately 0.45–0.55 volts) or if the O2S voltage fluctuates very slowly between the specified range (O2S signal crosses 0.5 volts less than 5 times in ten seconds), the O2S may be faulty.
8. If the O2S voltage stabilizes at either end of the specified range, the ECM is probably not able to compensate for a mechanical problem such as a vacuum leak or a faulty fuel pressure regulator. These types of mechanical problems will cause the O2S to sense a constant lean or constant rich mixture. The mechanical problem will first have to be repaired and then the O2S test repeated.
9. Pull a vacuum hose located after the throttle plate. Voltage should drop to approximately 0.12 volts (while still fluctuating rapidly). This tests the ability of the O2S to detect a lean mixture condition. Reattach the vacuum hose.
10. Richen the mixture using a propane enrichment tool. Voltage should rise to approximately 0.90 volts (while still fluctuating rapidly). This tests the ability of the O2S to detect a rich mixture condition.
11. If the O2S voltage is above or below the specified range, the O2S and/or the O2S wiring may be faulty. Check the wiring for any breaks, repair as necessary and repeat the test.

REMOVAL & INSTALLATION

◆ See Figures 22 and 23

The oxygen sensor can be located in several places. Either in the exhaust manifold, front pipe or catalytic converter.

✳✳ WARNING

Care should be used during the removal of the oxygen sensor. Both the sensor and its wire can be easily damaged.

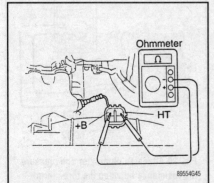

Fig. 21 Check the resistance of the heater portion of the sensor

Fig. 22 The heated oxygen sensor can be found mounted in the exhaust manifold on many models

Fig. 23 A special socket is available to remove the threaded type sensor

1. The best condition in which to remove the sensor is when the engine is moderately warm. This is generally achieved after two to five minutes (depending on outside temperature) of running after a cold start. The exhaust manifold has developed enough heat to expand and make the removal easier but is not so hot that it has become untouchable. Wearing heat resistant gloves is highly recommended during this repair.

2. With the ignition **OFF**, unplug the connector for the sensor.

3. Remove the two sensor attaching bolts. Some sensors do not use the two bolts and are threaded instead (looks similar to a spark plug). If this is the case, use a wrench to unscrew the sensor. A special socket with one side cut out (to allow the wire to hang out) is also available.

4. Remove the oxygen sensor from its mounting place and discard the gasket.

5. Installation is the reverse of removal.

➡**During and after the removal, use great care to protect the tip of the sensor if it is to be reused. Do not allow it to come in contact with fluids or dirt. Do not attempt to clean it or wash it.**

Knock Sensor

TESTING

1. Disconnect the wiring from the knock sensor.
2. Remove the knock sensor from the vehicle.
3. Using an ohmmeter, check that there is no continuity between the terminal and the sensor body.
4. If there is continuity, replace the sensor.
5. Install the knock sensor.
6. Connect the sensor wiring.

REMOVAL & INSTALLATION

▶ **See Figure 24**

1. Disconnect the wiring from the knock sensor.
2. Unscrew the knock sensor from the vehicle.
3. Installation is the reverse of removal. Secure the knock sensor to 33 ft. lbs. (44 Nm).

Idle Air Control (IAC) Valve

OPERATION

The ECM is programmed with specific engine speed values to respond to different engine conditions (coolant temperature, air conditioner on/off, etc.). Sensors transmit signals to the ECM which controls the flow of air through the bypass of the throttle valve and adjusts the idle speed to the specified value. Some vehicles use an Idle Speed Control (ISC) valve while others use an Air Valve (AV) or Idle Air Control (IAC) valve to control throttle body by-pass air flow.

TESTING

2S-ELC Engine

1. With the engine running and the coolant temperature below 140°F (60°C), pinch off the Air Valve hose and verify that the idle is reduced by no more than a 100 rpm.

2. Unplug the valve wire connector and measure the coil resistance with an ohmmeter. It should be 40–60 ohms with the coolant temperature at 176°F (80°C) and the air valve closed.

3. If not as specified, replace the valve.

3S-FE and 5S-FE Engines

▶ **See Figures 25, 26 and 27**

➡**The idle speed must be set correctly before testing the ISC valve.**

4. Bring the engine to normal operating temperature with transmission in N.

5. Using a jumper wire, connect the terminals TE1 and EI of the check connector (DLC 1).

6. The engine rpm should rise to 900–1300 rpms for 5 seconds. Check that it returns to idle speed. If rpm is as specified, the valve is functioning properly.

7. If rpm did not function as specified, stop the engine and disconnect the jumper wire.

8. Disengauge the ISC valve connector.

9. Using an ohmmeter, measure the resistance between the +B terminal (middle terminal) and the ISC1—ISC2 (3S-FE) and the ISCC—ISCO (5S-FE) outer terminals.

10. The resistance should be 16–17 ohms on the 3S-FE engine and 19.3–22.3 ohms on the 5S-FE engine.

11. If not as specified, replace the ISC valve.

1MZ-FE Engine

▶ **See Figures 28 and 29**

➡**The idle speed must be set correctly before testing the valve. Make sure the A/C is off during testing.**

1. Bring the engine to normal operating temperature with transmission in N.

2. Using a jumper wire, connect the terminals TE1 and EI of the check connector (DLC 1).

3. The engine rpm should rise to 1000 rpms for 5 seconds. Check that it returns to idle speed. If rpm is as specified, the valve is functioning properly.

4. If rpm did not function as specified, stop the engine and disconnect the jumper wire.

5. Disengage the ISC valve connector.

6. Using an ohmmeter, measure the resistance between the +B terminal (middle terminal) and the RSC and RSO outer terminals.

7. The resistance should be 21–28.5 ohms on a hot engine.

8. If not as specified, replace the ISC valve.

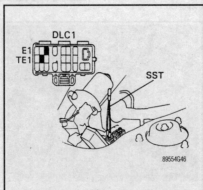

Fig. 24 Some 6-cylinder engines are equipped with two knock sensors. One for each cylinder bank

Fig. 25 Attach a jumper wire to the terminals TE1 and E1 in the DLC 1

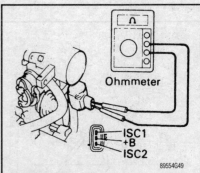

Fig. 26 Attach an ohmmeter and measure the resistance between the three terminals—3S-FE engine

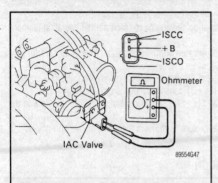

Fig. 27 Attach an ohmmeter and measure the resistance between the three terminals—5S-FE engine

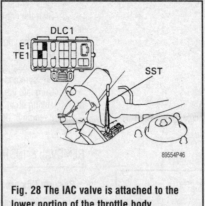

Fig. 28 The IAC valve is attached to the lower portion of the throttle body

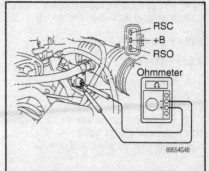

Fig. 29 Attach an ohmmeter and measure the resistance between the three terminals—1MZ-FE engine

2VZ-FE and 3VZ-FE Engines

▶ **See Figures 30, 31 and 32**

1. Disengage the ISC valve connector.
2. Using an ohmmeter, measure the resistance between the B1 terminal (lower middle terminal) and the S1 or S3 (lower outer terminals), and between B2 terminal (upper middle terminal) and the S2 or S4 (upper outer terminals).
3. If the resistance is not 10–30 ohms, replace the ISC valve.
4. Apply battery voltage to terminals B1 and B2 while repeatedly grounding S1, S2, S3, S4, S1 in sequence. Check that valve moves toward the closed position.
5. Apply battery voltage to terminals B1 and B2 while repeatedly Grounding S4, S3, S2, S1, S4 in sequence. Check that valve moves toward the opened position.
6. If valve does not function as specified, replace the ISC valve.

REMOVAL & INSTALLATION

2S-ELC Engine

1. Disconnect the air valve wiring.
2. Disconnect the air hoses attached to the valve.
3. Remove the two bolts and extract the valve from the cylinder head rear cover.
4. Installation is the reverse of removal.

1MZ-FE, 3S-FE and 5S-FE Engines

▶ **See Figures 33, 34 and 35**

1. Remove the throttle body from the vehicle.
2. Remove the four screws that attach the idle speed control (ISC) valve to the throttle body.
3. Lift the ISC valve from the throttle body and remove the gasket.

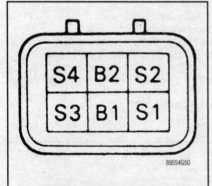

Fig. 30 ISC terminal identification—2VZ-FE and 3VZ-FE engines

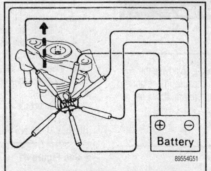

Fig. 31 Testing the IAC using battery voltage to see if the valve will close—2VZ-FE and 3VZ-FE engines

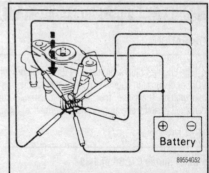

Fig. 32 Testing the IAC using battery voltage to open the valve—2VZ-FE and 3VZ-FE engines

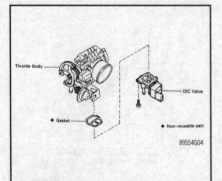

Fig. 33 Exploded view of the Idle Speed Control (ISC) valve

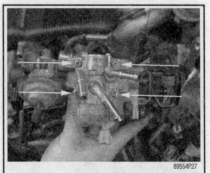

Fig. 34 The idle air control valve secured to the bottom of the throttle body with four screws—1MZ-FE engine shown

Fig. 35 Be sure to discard the old IAC gasket once the throttle body and valve are separated

4. Discard the gasket and purchase a new one.
5. Installation is the reverse of removal.

2VZ-FE and 3VZ-FE Engines

▶ **See Figure 36**

1. Drain the engine coolant.
2. Disengage the ISC connector.
3. Disconnect the air, vacuum and coolant by-pass hoses.
4. Free the wire harness from the clamp; remove the retaining bolts and remove the valve with the gasket.
5. Installation is the reverse of removal.

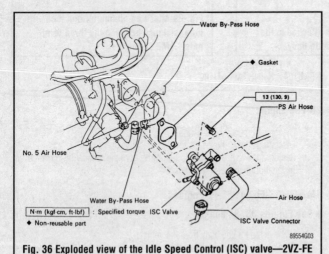

Fig. 36 Exploded view of the Idle Speed Control (ISC) valve—2VZ-FE and 3VZ-FE engines

Engine Coolant Temperature (ECT) Sensor

OPERATION

The Engine Coolant Temperature (ECT) sensor's function is to advise the ECM of changes in engine temperature by monitoring the changes in coolant temperature. The sensor must be handled carefully during removal. It can be damaged (thereby affecting engine performance) by impact.

TESTING

▶ **See Figures 37, 38 and 39**

1. Disconnect the engine wiring harness from the ECT sensor.
2. Connect an ohmmeter between the ECT sensor terminals.
3. With the engine cold and the ignition switch in the **OFF** position, measure and note the ECT sensor resistance.

4. Connect the engine wiring harness to the sensor.
5. Start the engine and allow the engine to reach normal operating temperature.
6. Once the engine has reached normal operating temperature, turn the engine **OFF**.
7. Once again, disconnect the engine wiring harness from the ECT sensor.
8. Measure and note the ECT sensor resistance with the engine hot.
9. Compare the cold and hot ECT sensor resistance measurements with the accompanying chart.
10. If readings do not approximate those in the chart, the sensor may be faulty.

REMOVAL & INSTALLATION

➡ **Perform this procedure only on a cold engine.**

1. Drain the coolant from the system low enough to remove the sensor.
2. Disconnect the sensor wiring.
3. Using a deep socket, remove the ECT sensor and gasket.
4. Installation is the reverse of removal. Secure to 9–14 ft. lbs. (12–20 Nm).
5. Refill the cooling system.

Intake Air Temperature (IAT) Sensor

OPERATION

The IAT sensor advises the ECM of changes in intake air temperature (and therefore air density). As air temperature of the intake varies, the ECM, by monitoring the voltage change, adjusts the amount of fuel injection according to the air temperature.

TESTING

▶ **See Figure 40**

1. Turn the ignition switch **OFF**.
2. Disconnect the wiring harness from the IAT sensor.
3. Measure the resistance between the sensor terminals.
4. Compare the resistance reading with the accompanying chart.
5. If the resistance is not within specification, the IAT may be faulty.
6. Heat the IAT sensor with a blow dryer while checking the resistance. Resistance should drop steadily. Any sudden changes in resistance can indicate a faulty sensor.
7. Connect the wiring harness to the sensor.

REMOVAL & INSTALLATION

▶ **See Figure 41**

1. Remove the air cleaner cover.
2. With the ignition **OFF**, unplug the electrical connector.
3. Push the IAT sensor out from inside the air cleaner housing.
4. Installation is the reverse of removal.

Fig. 37 Separate the harness connection (2) from the ECT sensor (1)

Fig. 38 Attach an ohmmeter to the sensor terminals and measure the resistance

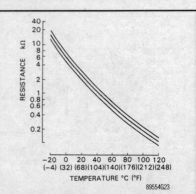

Fig. 39 Compare the resistance reading to this chart

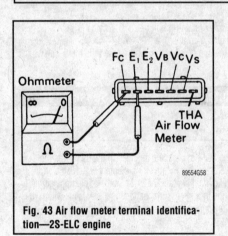

Fig. 40 Measure the resistance between the IAT sensor terminals with an ohmmeter, then compare the reading with this chart

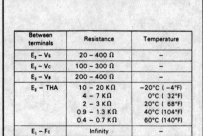

Fig. 41 The Intake Air Temperature (IAT) sensor is located in the side of the air cleaner housing—5S-FE engine shown, others similar

Mass Airflow Meter/Sensor

OPERATION

♦ See Figure 42

The Mass Air Flow Meter (MAF) contains a spring-loaded measuring plate or cone. The plate/cone is connected to a pointemeter which controls the signal to the ECM. In this way, the control unit is advised of intake air volume and can control injector duration and ignition advance accordingly. All engines except the 5S-FE engine uses an air flow meter. The 5S-FE engines uses a Manifold Air Pressure (MAP) sensor.

TESTING

♦ See Figures 43 thru 52

1. Disconnect the wiring from the air flow meter.
2. Using an ohmmeter, measure the resistance between each terminal as shown in the charts.
3. If the resistance is not as specified, replace the air flow meter.

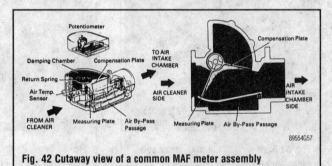

Fig. 42 Cutaway view of a common MAF meter assembly

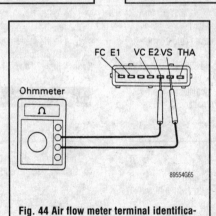

Fig. 43 Air flow meter terminal identification—2S-ELC engine

Fig. 44 Air flow meter terminal identification—3S-FE and 2VZ-FE engines

Fig. 45 Test the resistance of terminals E2 (1) and THA (2) of the MAF sensor—1MZ-FE engine

Between terminals	Resistance	Temperature
E₂ – Vs	20 – 400 Ω	–
E₂ – Vc	100 – 300 Ω	–
E₂ – Vs	200 – 400 Ω	–
E₂ – THA	10 – 20 KΩ	–20°C (–4°F)
	4 – 7 KΩ	0°C (32°F)
	2 – 3 KΩ	20°C (68°F)
	0.9 – 1.3 KΩ	40°C (104°F)
	0.4 – 0.7 KΩ	60°C (140°F)
E₁ – Fc	Infinity	–

Fig. 46 Air flow meter test values—2S-ELC engine

Between terminals	Resistance	Temperature
THA – E2	10 – 20 kΩ	–20°C (–4°F)
THA – E2	4 – 7 kΩ	0°C (32°F)
THA – E2	2 – 3 kΩ	20°C (68°F)
THA – E2	0.9 – 1.3 kΩ	40°C (104°F)
THA – E2	0.4 – 0.7 kΩ	60°C (140°F)

Fig. 47 Air flow meter test values—1MZ-FE engine

Between terminals		Resistance (Ω)	Temp. °C (°F)
VS — E2		200 — 600	—
VC — E2	3S-FE	3,000 — 7,000	—
	2VZ-FE	200 — 400	
THA — E2		10,000 — 20,000	–20 (–4)
		4,000 — 7,000	0 (32)
		2,000 — 3,000	20 (68)
		900 — 1,300	40 (104)
		400 — 700	60 (140)
FC — E1		Infinity	—

Fig. 48 Air flow meter test values—3S-FE and 2VZ-FE engines

Between terminals	Resistance (Ω)	Temp. °C (°F)
VS – E2	200 – 600	–
VC – E2	200 – 400	–
THA – E2	10,000 – 20,000	–20 (–4)
	4,000 – 7,000	0 (32)
FC – E1	Infinity	–

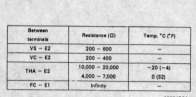

89554G64

Fig. 49 Air flow meter test values—3VZ-FE engine

89554P10

Fig. 50 Attach the test probe terminals to the E21 (first pin) and VG (fourth pin) from the left of the MAF meter—1994 1MZ-FE

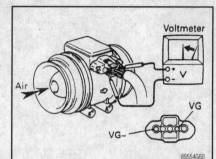

89554G60

Fig. 51 Attach the test probe terminals to the VG- (first pin) and VG (fourth pin) from the left of the MAF meter—1995–96 1MZ-FE

89554P12

Fig. 52 Blow air into the MAF meter and make sure the voltage fluctuates

89554P03

Fig. 53 Separate the harness connector from the Mass Air Flow (MAF) sensor

89554P04

Fig. 54 Disconnect the PCV hose before removing the MAF sensor

4. Inspect the meter operation. Connect the MAF meter wiring.

a. On 1994 models, connect a voltmeter to the positive (+) test probe to the VG and the negative (-) test probe to terminal E21.

b. On 1995–96 models, connect a voltmeter to the positive (+) test probe to the VG and the negative (-) test probe to terminal VG-.

5. Blow air into the meter and check that the voltage fluctuates.

6. If the operation is not as specified, replace the MAF meter.

REMOVAL & INSTALLATION

▶ **See Figures 53, 54, 55, 56 and 57**

1. Disconnect the air flow meter wiring harness from the unit.

2. Remove the air cleaner hose on the engine. First the PCV valve hose may need to be disconnected.

3. Loosen the air cleaner hose clamps and pull the unit off the engine.

4. Remove the MAF meter retaining bolts.

5. Lift the meter unit off the engine.

6. Installation is the reverse order of removal. Tighten the meter screws to 61 inch lbs. (7 Nm).

Manifold Absolute Pressure (MAP) Sensor

OPERATION

This sensor advises the ECM of pressure changes in the intake manifold. It consists of a semi-conductor pressure converting element which converts a pressure change into an electrical signal. The ECM sends a reference signal to the MAP sensor; the change in air pressure changes the resistance within the sensor. The ECM reads the change from its reference voltage and signals its systems to react accordingly.

89554P05

Fig. 55 Loosen the air cleaner hose clamps

89554P06

Fig. 56 Now the air hose can be pulled off the MAF and throttle body

89554P07

Fig. 57 Unbolt the MAF from the engine

TESTING

▶ See Figures 58, 59 and 60

➡Use only a 10 megaohm digital multi-meter when testing. The use of any other type of equipment may damage the ECM and other components.

1. Unplug the vacuum sensor connector.
2. Turn the ignition switch ON.
3. Using a voltmeter, measure the voltage between terminals **VC** and **E2** of the vacuum sensor connector. It should be between 4.75–5.25 volts.
4. Turn the ignition switch OFF.
5. Push the electrical connector back into place.
6. Disconnect the vacuum hose from the sensor.
7. Connect the voltmeter to terminals PIM and E2 of the ECM. Measure and record the output voltage under ambient atmospheric pressure.
8. Apply vacuum to the sensor according to the segments show on the chart. Measure each voltage drop and compare to the chart.
9. Reconnect the vacuum hose to the MAP sensor.

REMOVAL & INSTALLATION

Replacing the MAP sensor simply requires unplugging the vacuum and electrical connections, then unbolting the sensor. Inspect the vacuum hose over its entire length for any signs of cracking or splitting. The slightest leak can cause false messages to be send to the ECM.

Throttle Position Sensor

OPERATION

The Throttle Position (TP) sensor measures how far the throttle valve is open. Used in conjunction with the MAP or MAF sensors, it helps determine engine load.

TESTING

▶ See Figures 61 thru 81

1. Unplug the TP sensor connector.
2. For the 2S-ELC engine, make an angle gauge as shown in the illustration.
3. Except for the 2S-ELC engine, apply vacuum to the throttle opener.
4. Insert a thickness gauge between the throttle stop screw and the stop lever.
5. Using an ohmmeter, measure the applicable value between each terminal. Compare the readings to the appropriate chart.
6. Reconnect the sensor wiring.

REMOVAL & INSTALLATION

1. Remove the mounting screws and extract the sensor.
2. Make certain the throttle plate is fully closed. With the throttle body held in its normal orientation, place the sensor onto the throttle body so that the electrical connector is in the correct position.
3. Temporarily install the retaining screws for the sensor. Adjust the throttle position sensor.

ADJUSTMENT

2S-FE and 3S-FE Without ECT

▶ See Figures 82, 83 and 84

1. Loosen the sensor screw.
2. Insert a 0.028 inch (0.070mm) feeler gauge between the throttle stop screw and lever.
3. Connect an ohmmeter to terminals IDL and E1.
4. Gradually turn the sensor counterclockwise until the ohmmeter deflects and then tighten the screws.

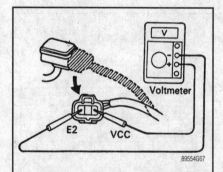

Fig. 58 Using a voltmeter, measure the voltage between the MAP connector terminals

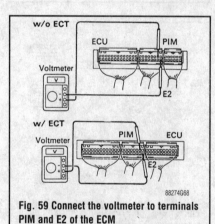

Fig. 59 Connect the voltmeter to terminals PIM and E2 of the ECM

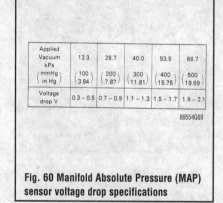

Applied Vacuum kPa (mmHg) (in.Hg)	13.3 (100) (3.94)	26.7 (200) (7.87)	40.0 (300) (11.81)	53.5 (400) (15.75)	66.7 (500) (19.69)
Voltage drop V	0.3 – 0.5	0.7 – 0.9	1.1 – 1.3	1.5 – 1.7	1.9 – 2.1

Fig. 60 Manifold Absolute Pressure (MAP) sensor voltage drop specifications

Fig. 61 Disconnect the TPS sensor wiring

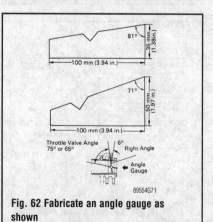

Fig. 62 Fabricate an angle gauge as shown

Fig. 63 Disconnect the hose form the throttle opener . . . .

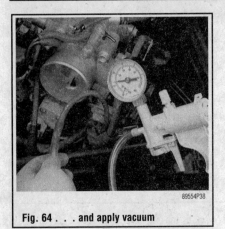

Fig. 64 . . . and apply vacuum

Fig. 65 Check the TPS for resistance without a gauge first—1MZ-FE engine

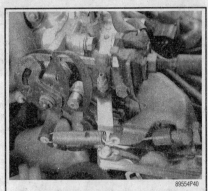

Fig. 66 Insert a thickness gauge between the throttle stop screw and lever

Fig. 67 Insert a 0.14 inch (0.35mm) gauge and check the reading—1MZ-FE engine

Fig. 68 Next insert a 0.28 inch (0.70mm) gauge and check for an infinite reading—1MZ-FE engine

Fig. 69 Holding the throttle fully open test the VTA and E2 terminals for resistance—1MZ-FE engine

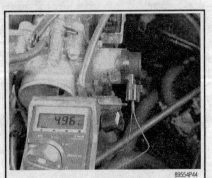

Fig. 70 Next test the TPS terminals VC and E2 and check for resistance between 2.7–7.7 kilo ohms

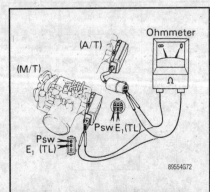

Fig. 71 Check for resistance between the terminals indicated—2S-ELC engine

Fig. 72 Throttle position sensor resistance chart—2S-ELC engine

Throttle valve opening angle	Continuity		
	IDL − E₁ (TL)	Psw − E₁ (TL)	IDL − Psw
71° from vertical	No continuity	No continuity	No continuity
81° from vertical	No continuity	Continuity	No continuity
Less than 7.5° from vertical	Continuity	No continuity	No continuity

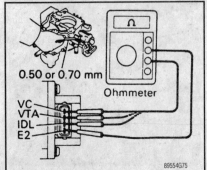

Fig. 73 Check for resistance between the terminals indicated—3S-FE engine with ECT

Fig. 74 Throttle position sensor resistance chart—3S-FE engine with ECT

Clearance between lever and stop screw	Between terminals	Resistance
0 mm (0 in.)	VTA — E2	0.2 − 0.8 kΩ
0.50 mm (0.020 in.)	IDL — E2	2.3 kΩ or less
0.70 mm (0.028 in.)	IDL — E2	Infinity
Throttle valve fully open	VTA — E2	3.3 − 10 kΩ
—	VC — E2	3 − 7 kΩ

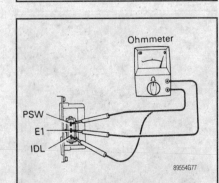

Fig. 75 Check for continuity between the terminals indicated—3S-FE engine without ECT

Throttle valve opening angle	Continuity	
	IDL — E1	PSW — E1
71° from vertical	No continuity	No continuity
81° from vertical	No continuity	Continuity
Less than 7.5° from vertical	Continuity	No continuity

89554G78

Fig. 76 Throttle position sensor continuity chart—3S-FE engine without ECT

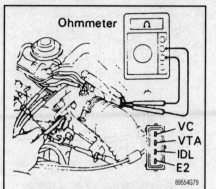

89554G79

Fig. 77 Check for resistance between the terminals indicated—2VZ-FE engine

Clearance between lever and stop screw	Between terminals	Resistance
0 mm (0 in.)	VTA — E2	0.3 — 6.3 kΩ
0.30 mm (0.012 in.)	IDL — E2	2.3 kΩ or less
0.70 mm (0.028 in.)	IDL — E2	Infinity
Throttle valve fully open	VTA — E2	3.5 — 10.3 kΩ
—	VC — E2	4.25 — 8.25 kΩ

89554G80

Fig. 78 Throttle position sensor resistance chart—2VZ-FE engine

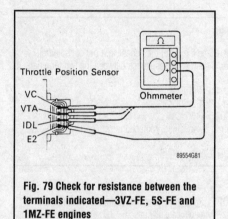

89554G81

Fig. 79 Check for resistance between the terminals indicated—3VZ-FE, 5S-FE and 1MZ-FE engines

Clearance between lever and stop screw	Between terminals	Resistance
0 mm (0 in.)	VTA — E2	0.28 — 6.4 kΩ
0.35 mm (0.014 in.)	IDL — E2	0.5 kΩ or less
0.70 mm (0.028 in.)	IDL — E2	Infinity
Throttle valve fully open	VTA — E2	2.0 — 11.6 kΩ
—	VC — E2	2.7 — 7.7 kΩ

89554G82

Fig. 80 Throttle position sensor resistance chart—3VZ-FE and 1MZ-FE engines

Clearance between lever and stop screw	Between terminals	Resistance
0 mm (0 in.)	VTA — E2	0.2 — 5.7 kΩ
0.50 mm (0.020 in.)	IDL — E2	2.3 kΩ or less
0.70 mm (0.028 in.)	IDL — E2	Infinity
Throttle valve fully open	VTA — E2	2.0 — 10.2 kΩ
—	VC — E2	2.5 — 5.9 kΩ

89554G89

Fig. 81 Throttle position sensor resistance chart—5S-FE engine

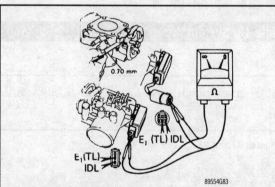

89554G83

Fig. 82 Adjusting the TPS using an ohmmeter and feeler gauge (first pass)—2S-FE and 3S-FE without ECT

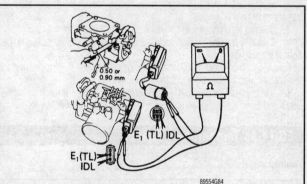

89554G84

Fig. 83 Adjusting the TPS using an ohmmeter and feeler gauge (second pass)—2S-FE and 3S-FE without ECT

Clearance between lever and stop screw	Continuity between terminals	
	IDL — E1	PSW — E1
0.50 mm (0.020 in.)	Continuity	No continuity
0.90 mm (0.035 in.)	No continuity	No continuity
Throttle valve fully open	No continuity	Continuity

89554G85

Fig. 84 Continuity chart for adjusting the TPS—2S-ELC and 3S-FE without ECT

5. Using a 0.020 inch (0.050mm) feeler gauge between the throttle stop and lever, verify with an ohmmeter that there is continuity.

6. Using a 0.0354 inch (0.090mm) feeler gage between the throttle stop screw and lever, verify with an ohmmeter that there is not continuity.

7. If non of the test is as specified, replace the sensor.

3S-FE With ECT

▶ See Figures 85, 86 and 87

➡This procedure is for vehicles with 3S-FE and Electronic Controlled Transmission.

1. Loosen the sensor screws. Apply vacuum to the throttle opener, if equipped.

2. Insert a 0.024 inch (0.060mm) feeler gauge between the throttle stop screw and lever.

3. Connect an ohmmeter to terminals IDL and E2 of the sensor.

4. Gradually turn the sensor clockwise until the ohmmeter deflects and then tighten the screws.

5. Using a 0.020 inch (0.050mm) feeler gauge between the throttle stop and lever, verify with an ohmmeter that there is continuity.

6. Using a 0.028 inch (0.070mm) feeler gage between the throttle stop screw and lever, verify with an ohmmeter that there is not continuity.

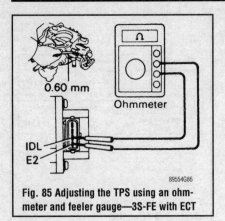

Fig. 85 Adjusting the TPS using an ohm-meter and feeler gauge—3S-FE with ECT

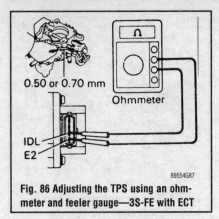

Fig. 86 Adjusting the TPS using an ohm-meter and feeler gauge—3S-FE with ECT

Clearance between lever and stop screw	Between terminals	Resistance
0 mm (0 in.)	VTA — E2	0.2 — 0.8 kΩ
0.50 mm (0.020 in.)	IDL — E2	2.3 kΩ or less
0.70 mm (0.028 in.)	IDL — E2	Infinity
Throttle valve fully opened	VTA — E2	3.3 — 10 kΩ
—	VC — E2	3 — 7 kΩ

Fig. 87 Continuity chart for adjusting the TPS—3S-FE with ECT

5S-FE Engine

1. Loosen the sensor screws. Apply vacuum to the throttle opener, if equipped.
2. Insert a 0.024 inch (0.060mm) feeler gauge between the throttle stop screw and lever.
3. Connect an ohmmeter to terminals IDL and E2 of the sensor.
4. Gradually turn the sensor clockwise until the ohmmeter deflects and then tighten the screws.
5. Using a 0.020 inch (0.050mm) feeler gauge between the throttle stop and lever, verify with an ohmmeter that there is continuity.
6. Using a 0.030 inch (0.070mm) feeler gage between the throttle stop screw and lever, verify with an ohmmeter that there is not continuity.
7. If non of the test is as specified, replace the sensor.

1MZ-FE Engine

▶ See Figure 88

1. Loosen the sensor screws. Apply vacuum to the throttle opener, if equipped.
2. Insert a 0.021 inch (0.054mm) feeler gauge between the throttle stop screw and lever.
3. Connect an ohmmeter to terminals IDL and E2 of the sensor.
4. Gradually turn the sensor clockwise until the ohmmeter deflects and then tighten the screws.
5. Using a 0.014 inch (0.035mm) feeler gauge between the throttle stop and lever, verify with an ohmmeter that there is continuity.
6. Using a 0.030 inch (0.070mm) feeler gauge between the throttle stop screw and lever, verify with an ohmmeter that there is not continuity.

EGR Gas Temperature Sensor

OPERATION

The EGR gas temperature sensor is used mostly on California models. It simply indicates the temperature of the EGR exhaust gas to the EGR system.

TESTING

▶ See Figures 89 and 90

1. Remove the sensor. Place the tip of the sensor in a pot of heated oil.
2. Using an ohmmeter, measure the resistance between the two terminals. It should be as follows:
   a. 64–97k ohms at 112°F(50°C)
   b. 11–16k ohms at 212°F(100°C)
   c. 2–4k ohms at 302°F (150°C)
3. If the resistance is not as specified, replace the sensor.

REMOVAL & INSTALLATION

▶ See Figure 91

1. With the ignition **OFF**, unplug the electrical connector to the sensor.
2. Using the proper sized wrench, carefully unscrew the sensor from the engine.
3. Installation is the reverse of removal. Refill the coolant to the proper level. Road test the vehicle for proper operation.

A/C Idle-Up System

OPERATION

The A/C idle-up valve is used to raise the engine idle when the A/C is turned on.

TESTING

▶ See Figures 92 and 93

1. Make sure all accessories are off.
2. Disconnect the idle-up valve wiring.
3. Label and remove the two hoses attached to the valve.
4. Remove the 2 bolts and the valve.

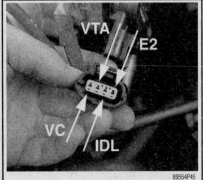

Fig. 88 TPS terminal harness identification—1MZ-FE engine

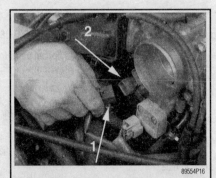

Fig. 89 The Exhaust Gas Temperature sensor wiring (1) and harness connector (2)—1MZ-FE engine shown

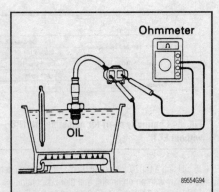

Fig. 90 Submerge the sensor tip in oil and measure the resistance of the sensor

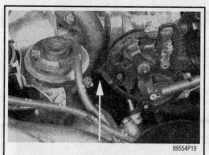

Fig. 91 The EGR temperature sensor located up underneath the throttle body

Fig. 92 Testing for continuity on the A/C idle-up valve

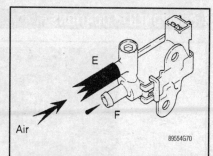

Fig. 93 Blow air into pipe E and check that it flows into pipe F of the VSV

5. Check the valve for and open circuit. Test the A/C idle-up valve using an ohmmeter, check that there is continuity between terminals. Resistance should be around 30–33 ohms at 68°F (20°C).

6. If it is not as specified, replace the VSV.

7. Check the valve for ground, with an ohmmeter, make sure there is not continuity between each terminal and the body.

8. If there is, replace the VSV.

9. Check the valve operation.

10. Check that air does not blow from pipe E to F.

11. Apply positive battery voltage across the terminals. Check that air flows from pipe E to F.

12. If operation is not as specified, replace the VSV.

REMOVAL & INSTALLATION

▶ **See Figure 94**

Replacing the various vacuum switches simply requires unplugging the vacuum and/or electrical connections, then unbolting the switch. Inspect the vacuum hose over its entire length for any signs of cracking or splitting. The slightest leak can cause improper operation.

Camshaft Position Sensor

OPERATION

The ECM uses the camshaft signal to determine the position of the No. 1 cylinder piston during its power stroke. The signal is used by the ECM to calculate fuel injection mode of operation.

If the cam signal is lost while the engine is running, the fuel injection system will shift to a calculated fuel injected mode based on the last fuel injection pulse, and the engine will continue to run.

TESTING

1. Check voltage between the camshaft position sensor terminals.

2. With engine running, voltage should be greater than 0.1 volt AC and vary with engine speed.

3. If voltage is not within specification, the sensor may be faulty.

REMOVAL & INSTALLATION

▶ **See Figure 95**

1. Disconnect the negative battery cable. Disconnect the camshaft position sensor wiring.

2. Remove the 2 bolts and the sensor from the vehicle.

3. Installation is the reverse of removal. Secure the sensor to the engine and tighten the retaining bolts to 69 inch lbs. (8 Nm).

Crankshaft Position Sensor

OPERATION

The Crankshaft Position (CKP) sensor provides a signal through the ignition module which the ECM uses as a reference to calculate rpm and crankshaft position.

TESTING

➡ **The crankshaft sensor should be tested either cold 14–122°F (-10–50°C) or hot at 122–212°F (50–100°C).**

1. Using an ohmmeter, measure the resistance between terminals. Resistance cold should read 1630–2740 ohms and hot; 2060–3225 ohms.

2. If resistance is not within specification, the sensor may be faulty.

REMOVAL & INSTALLATION

▶ **See Figure 96**

1. Disconnect the negative battery cable.

2. Remove the right hand engine under cover and the right side fender apron seal.

3. Remove the sensor wiring retaining nuts. Unbolt and disconnect the crankshaft position sensor wiring, then withdraw the sensor.

4. Installation is the reverse of removal. Secure the sensor and tighten to 69 inch lbs. (8 Nm).

Fig. 94 The A/C Idle-up valve is attached to the left side of the intake manifold

Fig. 95 Camshaft position sensor is located on the side of the cylinder head

Fig. 96 The crankshaft position sensor is located to the right of the water pump—1MZ-FE engine

COMPONENT LOCATIONS

EMISSION COMPONENT LOCATIONS—V6 ENGINE

1. Data Link Connector (DLC)
2. Heated oxygen sensor
3. Emission VSV set (under V-bank cover)
4. Throttle body (TPS and IAC attached)
5. Engine coolant sensor (next to inlet)
6. Intake air control valve
7. Mass Air Flow (MAF) meter
8. Camshaft position sensor

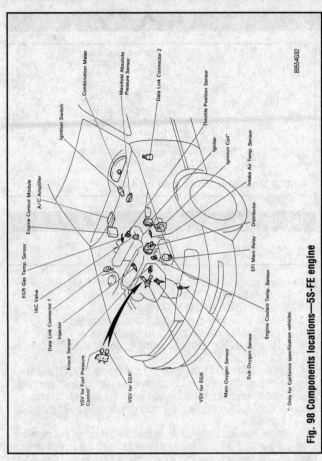

Fig. 98 Components locations—5S-FE engine

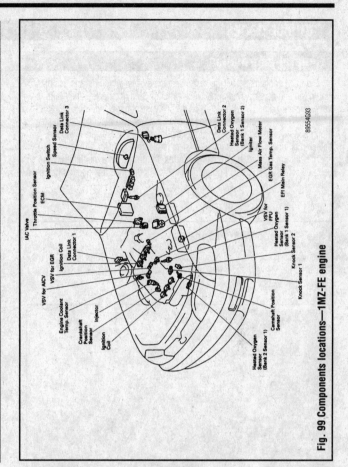

Fig. 99 Components locations—1MZ-FE engine

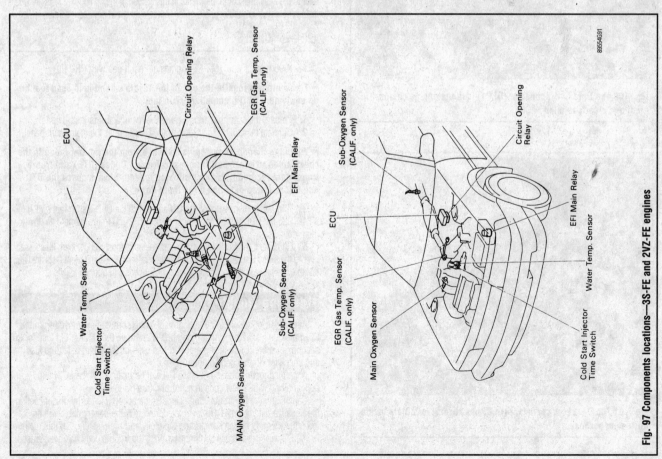

Fig. 97 Components locations—3S-FE and 2VZ-FE engines

TROUBLE CODES

General Information

The ECM contains a built-in, self-diagnosis system which detects troubles within the engine signal network. Once a malfunction is detected, the Malfunction Indicator Lamp (MIL), located on the instrument panel, will light.

By analyzing various signals, the ECM detects system malfunctions related to the operating sensors. The ECM stores the failure code associated with the detected failure until the diagnosis system is cleared.

The MIL on the instrument panel informs the driver that a malfunction has been detected. The light will go out automatically once the malfunction has been cleared.

DATA LINK CONNECTOR (DLC)

▶ See Figures 100, 101 and 102

The DLC1 is located in the engine compartment. The DLC3 is located in the interior of the vehicle, under the driver's side dash.

Fig. 100 The Data Link connector (DLC1) is in the engine compartment and clearly labeled

Fig. 101 The Data Link connector (DLC) has several terminals inside for testing purposes

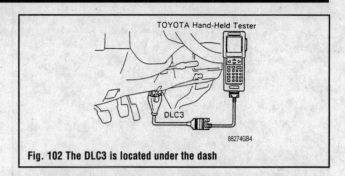

Fig. 102 The DLC3 is located under the dash

Reading Codes

1982–95 MODELS

All models except the 1MZ-FE engine is equipped with OBD I till 1995.
1. Make sure the battery voltage is at least 11 volts.
2. Make sure the throttle valve is fully closed.
3. Place the gear shift lever in Neutral. Turn all accessories off.
4. The engine should be at normal operating temperature.
5. Using a jumper wire, connect terminals TE1 and E1 of the Data Link Connector 1 (DLC1).
6. Turn the ignition switch **ON**, but do not start the engine. Read the diagnostic code by the counting the number of flashes of the malfunction indicator lamp.
7. Codes will flash in numerical order. If no faults are stored, the lamp flashes continuously every ½ second. This is sometimes called the Normal or System Clear signal.
8. After the diagnosis check, turn the ignition OFF and remove the jumper wire.
9. Compare the codes found to the applicable diagnostic code chart. If necessary, refer to the individual component tests in this section. If the component tests are OK, test the wire harness and connectors for shorts, opens and poor connections.

1994–96 MODELS

All 1996 models and 1MZ-FE engines are equipped with OBD II.

➡These models require the use of the Toyota's hand held scan tool or an equivalent OBD II compliant scan tool.

1. Prepare the scan tool according to the manufacturers instructions.
2. Connect the OBD II scan tool, to the DLC3 under the instrument panel.

➡When the diagnosis system is switched from the normal mode to the check mode, it erases all Diagnostic Trouble Codes (DTC) and freeze frame data recorded. Before switching modes, always check the DTC and freeze frame data and write them down.

3. Turn the ignition switch to the **ON** and switch the OBD II scan tool switch on.
4. Use the OBD II scan tool to check the DTC and freeze frame data. Write them down.
5. Compare the codes found to the applicable diagnostic code chart. If necessary, refer to the individual component tests in this section. If the component tests are OK, test the wire harness and connectors for shorts, opens and poor connections.

Clearing Trouble Codes

After repair of the circuit, the diagnostic code(s) must be removed from the ECM memory. With the ignition turned **OFF**, remove the 15 amp EFI fuse for 30 seconds or more. Once the time period has been observed, reinstall the fuse and check for normal code output.

If the diagnostic code is not erased, it will be retained by the ECM and appear along with a new code in event of future trouble.

Cancellation of the trouble code can also be accomplished by disconnecting the negative battery cable. However, disconnecting the battery cable will erase the other memory systems including the clock and radio settings. If this method is used, always reset these components once the trouble code has been erased.

DIAGNOSTIC CODES (3S-FE) (Cont'd)

Code No.	Number of blinks "CHECK" Engine Warning Light	System	"CHECK" Engine Warning Light	Diagnosis	Trouble Area	*2 Memory
*6 27		Sub-Oxygen Sensor Signal	ON	When sub-oxygen sensor is warmed up and full acceleration continued for 2 seconds, output of main oxygen sensor is 0.45 V or more (rich) and output of sub-oxygen sensor is 0.45 V or less (lean). (OX2) *6 (2 trip detection logic)	• Short or open in sub-oxygen sensor circuit • Sub-oxygen sensor • ECU	○
31		Air Flow Meter Signal	ON	At idling, open or short detected continuously for 500 msec. or more in air flow meter circuit. • Open – VC • Short – VC-E2	• Open or short in air flow meter circuit • Air flow meter • ECU	○
32		Air Flow Meter Signal	ON	Open or short detected continuously for 500 msec. or more in air flow meter circuit. • Open – E2 • Short – VS-VC		○
41		Throttle Position Sensor Signal	*3 ON	Open or short detected in throttle position sensor signal (VTA) for 500 msec. or more. (Vehicle w/ECT)	• Open or short in throttle position sensor circuit • Throttle position sensor • ECU	○
42		Vehicle Speed Sensor Signal	OFF	Low PSW signal is input continuously to the ECU for 500 msec. or more at idling (IDL contact is ON). (w/o ECT) SPD signal is not input to the ECU for at least 8 seconds during high load driving with engine speed between 2,500 rpm and 5,500 rpm.	• Open or short in vehicle speed sensor circuit • Vehicle speed sensor • ECU	○
43		Starter Signal	OFF	Starter signal (STA) is not input to ECU even once until engine reaches 800 rpm or more when cranking.	• Open or short in starter signal circuit • Open or short in IG SW circuit • ECU	○
*5 71		EGR System Malfunction	ON	EGR gas temp. sensor signal (THG) is below 70°C (158°F) after driving for 50 seconds in EGR operation range. *6 (2 trip detection logic)	• Open in EGR gas temp. sensor circuit • EGR vacuum hose disconnected, valve stuck • Clogged in EGR gas passage • ECU	○
51		Switch Condition Signal	OFF	Displayed when A/C is ON, IDL contact OFF or shift position in "R", "D", "2", or "1" ranges with the check terminals E1 and TE1 connected.	• A/C switch circuit • Throttle position sensor • IDL circuit • Neutral start switch circuit • Accelerator pedal, cable • ECU	×

REMARKS:

*1: "ON" displayed in the diagnosis mode column indicates that the "CHECK" Engine Warning Light is lighted up when a malfunction is detected.
"OFF" indicates that the "CHECK" does not light up during malfunction diagnosis, even if a malfunction is detected.

*2: "○" in the memory column indicates that a diagnostic code is recorded in the ECU memory when a malfunction occurs. "X" indicates that a diagnostic code is not recorded in the ECU memory even if a malfunction occurs. Accordingly, output of diagnostic results is performed with the IG SW ON.

*3: The "CHECK" Engine Warning Light comes on if malfunction occurs only for California specifications.

*4: No. (2) and (3) in the diagnostic contents of codes No. 25 and 26 apply to California specification vehicles only, while (1) applies to all models.

*5: Codes 27 and 71 are used only for California specifications.

*6: "2 trip detection logic"

Fig. 104 Diagnostic codes—3S-FE engine (continued)

DIAGNOSTIC CODES (3S-FE)

Code No.	Number of blinks "CHECK" Engine Warning Light	System	"CHECK" Engine Warning Light	Diagnosis	Trouble Area	*2 Memory
–		Normal	–	Output when no other code is recorded.	–	–
12		RPM Signal	ON	No G or NE signal is input to the ECU for 2 secs. or more after STA turns ON.	• Open or short in NE, G circuit • Distributor • Open or short in STA circuit • ECU	○
13		RPM Signal	ON	NE signal is not input to ECU for 50 msec. or more when engine speed is 1,000 rpm or more.	• Open or short in NE circuit • Distributor • ECU	○
14		Ignition Signal	ON	IGF signal from igniter is not input to ECU for 4 – 5 consecutive ignition.	• Open or short in IGF or IGT circuit from igniter to ECU • Igniter • ECU	○
16		ECT Control Signal	ON	Normal signal is not output from ECU of ECT.	• ECU	×
21		Main Oxygen Sensor Signal	ON	At normal driving speed (below 60 mph and engine speed is above 1,800 rpm), amplitude of main oxygen sensor signal OX1 is reduced to between 0.35 – 0.70 V continuously for 60 secs. or more	• Open or short in main oxygen sensor circuit • Main oxygen sensor • ECU	○
22		Water Temp. Sensor Signal	ON	Open or short in water temp. sensor circuit for 500 msec. or more. (THW)	• Open or short in water temp. sensor circuit. • Water temp. sensor • ECU	○
24		Intake Air Temp. Sensor Signal	*3 ON	Open or short in intake air temp. sensor circuit for 500 msec. or more. (THA)	• Open or short in intake air temp. circuit • Intake air temp. sensor • ECU	○
25		Air-Fuel Ratio Lean Malfunction	ON	(1) Oxygen sensor output is less than 0.45 V for at least 120 secs. when oxygen sensor is warmed up (racing at 2,000 rpm). – only for code 25 *4 (2) When air-fuel ratio feedback correction value or adaptive control value continues at the upper (lean) or lower (rich) limit for a certain period of time or adaptive control value is not renewed for a certain period of time.	• Engine ground bolt loose • Open in E1 circuit • Open in injector circuit (Injector blockage, etc.) • Fuel line pressure (Injector leakage, etc.) • Open or short in oxygen sensor circuit • Oxygen sensor • Water temp. sensor • Ignition system • Air flow meter (air intake) • ECU	○
26		Air-Fuel Ratio Rich Malfunction	ON	*4 (3) When the oxygen sensor feedback frequency is abnormally high during feedback condition. *6 (2 trip detection logic) (1) – (3)	• Engine ground bolt loose • Open in E1 circuit • Short in injector circuit • Fuel line pressure (Injector leakage, etc.) • Open or short in cold start injector circuit • Cold start injector • Open or short in oxygen sensor circuit • Oxygen sensor • Water temp. sensor • Air flow meter • Compression pressure • ECU	○

Fig. 103 Diagnostic codes—3S-FE engines

DIAGNOSTIC CODES (2VZ-FE) (Cont'd)

8954GA4

Code No.	Number of blinks "CHECK" Engine Warning Light	System	"CHECK" Engine Warning Light	Diagnosis	Trouble Area	Memory
27		Sub-Oxygen Sensor Signal	ON	When sub-oxygen sensor is warmed up and full acceleration continued for 2 seconds, output of main oxygen sensor is 0.45 V or more (rich) and output of sub-oxygen sensor is 0.45 V or less (lean). (OX2) *4 (2 trip detection logic)	• Short or open in sub-oxygen sensor circuit • Sub-oxygen sensor • ECU	O
31		Air Flow Meter Signal	ON	At idling, open or short detected continuously for 500 msec. or more in air flow meter circuit. • Open — VC • Short — VC-E2	• Open or short in air flow meter circuit • Air flow meter • ECU	O
32		Air Flow Meter Signal	ON	Open or short detected continuously for 500 msec. or more in air flow meter circuit. • Open — E2 • Short — VS-VC		O
41		Throttle Position Sensor Signal	ON	Open or short detected in throttle position sensor signal (VTA) for 500 msec. or more. IDL contact is ON and VTA output exceeds 1.45 V.	• Open or short in throttle position sensor circuit • Throttle position sensor • ECU	O
42		Vehicle Speed Sensor Signal	OFF	SPD signal is not input to the ECU for at least 8 seconds during high load driving with engine speed between 2,500 rpm and 4,500 rpm.	• Open or short in vehicle speed sensor circuit • Vehicle speed sensor • ECU	O
43		Starter Signal	OFF	Starter signal (STA) is not input to ECU even once until engine reaches 800 rpm or more when cranking.	• Open or short in starter signal circuit • Open or short in IG SW circuit • ECU	O
52		Knock Sensor Signal	ON	With engine speed between 1800 rpm – 5,200 rpm, signal from knock sensor is not input to ECU for 6 revolution. (KNK)	• Open or short in knock sensor circuit • Knock sensor (looseness etc.) • ECU	O
53		Knock Control Signal	ON	Engine speed is between 650 rpm and 5,200 rpm and engine control computer (for knock control) malfunction is detected.	• ECU	X
71		EGR System Malfunction	ON	EGR gas temp. sensor signal (THG) is below 55°C (131°F) for M/T, 60°C (140°F) for A/T after driving for 60 seconds in EGR operation range. *6 (2 trip detection logic)	• Open in EGR gas temp. sensor circuit • BVSV circuit for EGR • EGR vacuum hose disconnected, valve stuck • Clogged in EGR gas passage • ECU	O
51		Switch Condition Signal	OFF	Displayed when A/C is ON, IDL contact OFF or shift position in "R", "D", "2", or "1" ranges with the check terminals E1 and TE1 connected.	• A/C switch circuit • Throttle position sensor • IDL circuit • Neutral start switch circuit • Accelerator pedal, cable • ECU	X

REMARKS:
*1: "ON" displayed in the diagnosis mode column indicates that the ""CHECK"" Engine Warning Light is lighted up when a malfunction is detected. "OFF" indicates that the ""CHECK"" does not light up during malfunction diagnosis, even if a malfunction is detected.
*2: "O" in the memory column indicates that a diagnostic code is recorded in the ECU memory when a malfunction occurs. "X" indicates that a diagnostic code is not recorded in the ECU memory even if a malfunction occurs. Accordingly, output of diagnostic results is performed with the IG SW ON.
*3: The ""CHECK"" Engine Warning Light comes on if malfunction occurs only for California specifications.
*4: No. (2) and (3) in the diagnostic contents of codes No. 25 and 26 apply to California specification vehicles only, while (1) applies to all models.
*5: Codes 27 and 71 are used only for California specifications.
*6: "2 trip detection logic"

Fig. 106 Diagnostic codes—2VZ-FE engine (continued)

DIAGNOSTIC CODES (2VZ-FE)

8954GA3

Code No.	Number of blinks "CHECK" Engine Warning Light	System	"CHECK" Engine Warning Light	Diagnosis	Trouble Area	Memory
–		Normal	–	Output when no other code is recorded.	–	–
12		RPM Signal	ON	No G or NE signal is input to the ECU for 2 secs. or more after STA turns ON.	• Open or short in NE, G circuit • Distributor • Open or short in STA circuit • ECU	O
13		RPM Signal	ON	NE signal is not input to ECU for 50 msec. or more when engine speed is 1,000 rpm or more.	• Open or short in NE circuit • Distributor • ECU	O
14		Ignition Signal	ON	IGF signal from igniter is not input to ECU for 6 consecutive ignition.	• Open or short in IGF or IGT circuit from igniter to ECU • Igniter • ECU	O
16		ECT Control Signal	ON	Normal signal is not output from ECU of ECT.	• ECU	X
21		Main Oxygen Sensor Signal	ON	(1) Open or short in heater circuit of main oxygen sensor for 500 msec. or more. (HT) (2) At normal driving speed (below 60 mph and engine speed is above 1,500 rpm), amplitude of main oxygen sensor signal (OX1) is reduced to between 0.35 – 0.70 V continuously for 60 secs. or more. *4 (2 trip detection logic) (2)	• Open or short in heater circuit of main oxygen sensor • Main oxygen sensor heater • ECU • Open or short in main oxygen sensor circuit • Main oxygen sensor • ECU	O
22		Water Temp. Sensor Signal	ON	Open or short in water temp. sensor circuit for 500 msec. or more. (THW)	• Open or short in water temp. sensor circuit • Water temp. sensor • ECU	O
24		Intake Air Temp. Sensor Signal	*3 ON	Open or short in intake air temp. sensor circuit for 500 msec. or more. (THA)	• Open or short in intake air temp. circuit • Intake air temp. sensor • ECU	O
25		Air-Fuel Ratio Lean Malfunction	ON	(1) Oxygen sensor output is less than 0.45 V for at least 90 secs. when oxygen sensor is warmed up (racing at 2,000 rpm). – only for code 25 *4 (2) When air-fuel ratio feedback correction value or adaptive control value continues at the upper (lean) or lower (rich) limit for a certain period of time or adaptive control value is not renewed for a certain period of time.	• Engine ground bolt loose • Open in E1 circuit • Open in injector circuit • Fuel line pressure (injector blockage, etc.) • Open or short in oxygen sensor circuit • Oxygen sensor • Water temp. sensor • Ignition system • Air flow meter (air intake) • ECU	O
26		Air-Fuel Ratio Rich Malfunction	ON	*4 (3) When the oxygen sensor feedback frequency is abnormally high during feedback condition. *4 (2 trip detection logic) (1) ~ (3)	• Engine ground bolt loose • Open in E1 circuit • Short in injector circuit • Fuel line pressure (injector leakage, etc.) • Open or short in cold start injector circuit • Cold start injector • Open or short in oxygen sensor circuit • Oxygen sensor • Water temp. sensor • Air flow meter • Compression pressure • ECU	O

Fig. 105 Diagnostic codes—2VZ-FE engines

DIAGNOSTIC TROUBLE CODES (Cont'd)

Code No.	Number of blinks Malfunction Indicator Lamp	System	Malfunction Indicator Lamp Normal Mode	Malfunction Indicator Lamp Test Mode	Diagnosis	Trouble Area	Memory *2
27**		Sub-Oxygen Sensor Signal	ON	ON	When sub-oxygen sensor is warmed up and full acceleration continued for 2 seconds, output of main oxygen sensor is 0.45 V or more (rich) and output of sub-oxygen sensor is 0.45 V less (lean). (OX2) ** (2 trip detection logic)	• Short or open in sub-oxygen sensor signal circuit • Sub-oxygen sensor • ECM	○
31		Vacuum Sensor Signal	ON	ON	Open or short detected continuously for 500 msec. or more in vacuum sensor circuit (PIM)	• Open or short in vacuum sensor circuit • Vacuum sensor • ECM	○
41		Throttle Position Sensor Signal	ON*3	ON	Open or short detected continuously for 500 msec. or more when engine speed or more in throttle sensor (VTA) circuit.	• Open or short in throttle position sensor circuit • Throttle position sensor • ECM	○
42		Vehicle Speed Sensor Signal	OFF	OFF	(M/T) SPD signal is not input to ECM for at least 8 seconds during high load driving with engine speed between 3,100 rpm and 5,000 rpm. (A/T) PNP OFF and engine speed 3,100 rpm or more	• Open or short in vehicle speed sensor circuit • Vehicle speed sensor • ECM	○
43		Starter Signal	N.A.	OFF	No starter signal is not input to ECM even once after ignition.	• Open or short in starter signal circuit • Open or short in IG SW or main relay circuit • ECM	×
52		Knock Sensor Signal	N.A.	N.A.	In area of knock control signal from knock sensor is not input to ECM for 6 revolutions. (KNK)	• Open or short in knock sensor circuit • Knock sensor (looseness, etc.) • ECM	○
71**		EGR System Malfunction	ON	ON	50 seconds from start of EGR operation, EGR gas temp. is less than 70 °C with engine coolant temp. 80°C (176°F) or more.	• Open in EGR gas temp. sensor circuit • Open in VSV circuit for EGR • EGR vacuum hose disconnected, valve stuck • Clogged in EGR gas passage • ECM	○
51		Switch Condition Signal	N.A.	OFF	Displayed when A/C is ON IDL contact OFF or shift position in "R", "D", "2", or "L" positions with the check terminals E1 and TE1 connected.	• A/C switch system • Throttle position sensor • IDL circuit • Park/neutral position switch circuit • Accelerator pedal, cable • ECM	×

REMARKS:
*1: "ON" displayed in the diagnosis mode column indicates that the Malfunction Indicator Lamp is lighted up when a malfunction is detected. "OFF" indicates that the Malfunction Indicator Lamp does not light up during malfunction diagnosis, even if a malfunction is detected. "N.A." indicates that the item is not included in malfunction diagnosis.
*2: "○" in the memory column indicates that a diagnostic trouble code is recorded in the ECM memory when a malfunction occurs. "×" indicates that a diagnostic trouble code is not recorded in the ECM memory even if a malfunction occurs. Accordingly, output of diagnostic results in normal or test mode is performed with the IG SW ON.
*3: The Malfunction Indicator Lamp comes on if malfunction occurs only for California specification vehicles.
*4: Codes 26, 27 and 71 are used only for California specification vehicles.
*5: "2 trip detection logic"

Fig. 108 Diagnostic codes—25-ELC, 1992–95 3VZ-FE and 5S-FE engines (continued)

89554GA6

DIAGNOSTIC TROUBLE CODES

Code No.	Number of blinks Malfunction Indicator Lamp	System	Malfunction Indicator Lamp Normal Mode	Malfunction Indicator Lamp Test Mode	Diagnosis	Trouble Area	Memory *2
—		Normal	—	—	Output when no other code is recorded.	—	—
12		RPM Signal	ON	N.A.	(1) No NE signal is input to ECM for 2 secs. or more after STA turns ON. (2) No G Signal is input to ECM for 3 secs. or more between 600 – 4000 rpm.	• Open or short in NE, G circuit • Distributor • Open or short in STA circuit • ECM	○
13		RPM Signal	ON	ON	(1) NE signal is not input to ECM for 300 msec. or more when engine speed is 1,500 rpm or more. (2) No G signal is input to ECM for 4 NE signal. (Test mode only)	• Open or short in NE circuit • Distributor • ECM	○
14		Ignition Signal	ON	N.A.	IGF signal from igniter is not input to ECM for 4 – 5 consecutive ignition.	• Open on short in IGF or IGT circuit from igniter to ECM • Igniter • ECM	○
16		Electronic Controlled Transmission Control Signal	ON	N.A.	Normal signal is not output from ECM CPU.	• ECM	×
21		Main Oxygen Sensor Signal	ON	N.A.	At normal driving speed (below 60 mph and engine speed is above 1,500 rpm), amplitude of oxygen sensor signal (OX) is reduced to between 0.35 – 0.70 V continuously for 60 secs. or more.	• Open or short in oxygen sensor circuit • Oxygen sensor • ECM	○
22		Engine Coolant Temp. Sensor	ON	ON	Open or short in engine coolant temp. sensor circuit for 500 msec. or more. (THW)	• Open or short in engine coolant temp. sensor circuit • Engine coolant temp. sensor • ECM	○
24		Intake Air Temp. Sensor Signal	ON*3	ON	Open or short in intake air temp. sensor circuit for 500 msec. or more. (THA)	• Open or short in intake air temp. sensor circuit • Intake air temp. sensor • ECM	○
25		Air-Fuel Ratio Lean Malfunction	ON		(1) Oxygen sensor output is less than 0.45 V for at least 90 secs. when oxygen sensor is warmed up (racing at 2000 rpm) - only for code 25	• Engine ground bolt loose • Open in E1 circuit • Open in injector circuit • Fuel line pressure (Injector blockage, etc.) • Open or short in oxygen sensor circuit • Oxygen sensor • Ignition system • Engine coolant temp. sensor • Vacuum Sensor • ECM	○
26**		Air-Fuel Ratio Rich Malfunction	ON	ON	(2) When the engine speed varies by more than 20 rpm over the preceding crankshaft position period during a period of 20 seconds during idling with the engine coolant temp. 60°C (140°F) or more. *5 (2 trip detection logic) (1) and (2)	• Engine ground bolt loose • Open in E1 circuit • Short in injector circuit • Fuel line pressure (injector leakage, etc.) • Open or short in cold start injector circuit • Cold start injector • Open or short in oxygen sensor circuit • Oxygen sensor • Engine coolant temp. sensor • Vacuum sensor • Compression pressure • ECM	○

Fig. 107 Diagnostic codes—25-ELC, 1992–95 3VZ-FE and 5S-FE engines

89554GA5

DTC CHART (SAE Controlled)

HINT: Parameters listed in the chart may not be exactly the same as your reading due to the type of instrument or other factors.

If a malfunction code is displayed during the DTC check in check mode, check the circuit for that code listed in the table below.

DTC No.	Detection Item	Trouble Area	MIL*	Memory
P0105	Manifold Absolute Pressure/Barometric Pressure Circuit Malfunction	• Open or short in Manifold absolute pressure sensor circuit • Manifold absolute pressure sensor • ECM	○	○
P0106	Manifold Absolute Pressure/Barometric Pressure Circuit Range/Performance Problem	• Manifold absolute pressure sensor	○	○
P0110	Intake Air Temp. Circuit Malfunction	• Open or short in intake air temp. sensor circuit • Intake air temp. sensor • ECM	○	○
P0115	Engine Coolant Temp. Circuit Malfunction	• Open or short in engine coolant temp. sensor circuit • Engine coolant temp. sensor • ECM	○	○
P0116	Engine Coolant Temp. Circuit Range/Performance Problem	• Engine coolant temp. sensor • Cooling system	○	○
P0120	Throttle/Pedal Position Sensor/Switch "A" Circuit Malfunction	• Open or short in throttle position sensor circuit • Throttle position sensor • ECM	○	○
P0121	Throttle/Pedal Position Sensor/Switch "A" Circuit Range/Performance Problem	• Throttle position sensor	○	○
P0125	Insufficient Coolant Temp. for Closed Loop Fuel Control	• Open or short in oxygen sensor circuit • Oxygen sensor	○	○
P0130	Oxygen Sensor Circuit Malfunction (Bank 1 Sensor 1)	• Oxygen sensor • Fuel trim malfunction	○	○
P0133	Oxygen Sensor Circuit Slow Response (Bank 1 Sensor 1)	• Oxygen sensor	○	○

*: ○ ..... MIL lights up

Fig. 109 Diagnostic codes—1996 5S-FE engine

EG-194   5S-FE ENGINE TROUBLESHOOTING – DTC CHART

DTC CHART (Cont'd)

DTC No.	Detection Item	Trouble Area	MIL	Memory
P0136 (EG-226)	Oxygen Sensor Circuit Malfunction (Bank 1 Sensor 2)	• Oxygen sensor	○*1	○
P0171	System too Lean (Fuel Trim)	• Air intake (hose loose) • Fuel line pressure • Injector blockage • Oxygen sensor malfunction • Manifold absolute pressure sensor • Engine coolant temp. sensor	○*1	○
P0172	System too Rich (Fuel Trim)	• Fuel line pressure • Injector blockage, leak • Oxygen sensor malfunction • Manifold absolute pressure sensor • Engine coolant temp. sensor	○*1	○
P0300	Random/Multiple Cylinder Misfire Detected	• Ignition system • Injector • Fuel line pressure • EGR • Compression pressure • Valve clearance not to specification • Valve timing • Manifold absolute pressure sensor • Engine coolant temp. sensor	○*2	
P0301 P0302 P0303 P0304	Misfire Detected – Cylinder 1 – Cylinder 2 – Cylinder 3 – Cylinder 4			○
P0325	Knock Sensor 1 Circuit Malfunction	• Open or short in knock sensor 1 circuit • Knock sensor 1 (looseness) • ECM	○*1	○
P0335	Crankshaft Position Sensor Circuit "A" Malfunction	• Open or short in crankshaft position sensor circuit • Crankshaft position sensor • Starter • ECM	○*1	○
P0340	Camshaft Position Sensor Circuit Malfunction	• Open or short in camshaft position sensor circuit • Camshaft position sensor • Starter • ECM	○*1	○

*1: MIL lights up
*2: MIL lights up or blinking

Fig. 110 Diagnostic codes—1996 5S-FE engine (continued)

DTC CHART (Cont'd)

DTC No.	Detection Item	Trouble Area	MIL*	Memory
P0500	Vehicle Speed Sensor Malfunction	• Open or short in vehicle speed sensor circuit • Vehicle speed sensor • Combination meter • ECM	O	O
P0505	Idle Control System Malfunction	• IAC valve is stuck or closed • Open or short in IAC valve circuit • Open or short AC1 signal circuit • Air intake (hose loose)	O	O

DTC CHART (Manufacturer Controlled)

DTC No.	Detection Item	Trouble Area	MIL*	Memory
P1300	Igniter Circuit Malfunction	• Open or short in IGF or IGT circuit from igniter to ECM • Igniter • ECM	O	O
P1335	Crankshaft Position Sensor Circuit Malfunction (during engine running)	• Open or short in crankshaft position sensor circuit • Crankshaft position sensor • ECM	-	O
P1500	Starter Signal Circuit Malfunction	• Open or short in starter signal circuit • Open or short in ignition switch or starter relay circuit • ECM	-	O
P1600	ECM BATT Malfunction	• Open in back up power source circuit • ECM	O	O
P1780	Park/Neutral Position Switch Malfunction	• Short in park/neutral position switch circuit • Park/neutral position switch • ECM	O	O

*: - .... MIL does not light up
   O .... MIL lights up

Fig. 112 Diagnostic codes—1996 5S-FE engine (continued)

DTC CHART (Cont'd)

DTC No.	Detection Item	Trouble Area	MIL*1	Memory
P0401 (EG-238)	Exhaust Gas Recirculation Flow Insufficient Detected	• EGR valve stuck closed • Open or short in VSV circuit for EGR • Vacuum or EGR hose disconnected • Manifold absolute pressure sensor • EGR VSV open or close malfunction • ECM	O	O
P0402 (EG-242)	Exhaust Gas Recirculation Flow Excessive Detected	• EGR valve stuck open • Vacuum or EGR hose is connected to wrong post • Manifold absolute pressure sensor • ECM	O	O
P0420	Catalyst System Efficiency Below Threshold	• Three-way catalytic converter • Open or short in oxygen sensor circuit • Oxygen sensor	O	O
P0440 *2	Evaporative Emission Control System Malfunction	• Vapor pressure sensor • Fuel tank cap incorrectly installed • Fuel tank cap cracked or damaged • Vacuum hose cracked, holed, blocked, damaged or disconnected • Hose or tube cracked, holed, damaged or loose • Fuel tank cracked, holed or damaged • Charcoal canister cracked, holed or damaged	O	O
P0441 (EG-252) *2	Evaporative Emission Control System Incorrect Purge Flow	• Open or short in VSV circuit for vapor pressure sensor • VSV for vapor pressure sensor • Open or short in vapor pressure sensor circuit • Vapor pressure sensor	O	O
P0446 *2	Evaporative Emission Control System Vent Control Malfunction	• Open or short in VSV circuit for EVAP • VSV for EVAP • Vacuum hose cracks, hole, blocked, damaged or disconnected • Charcoal canister cracks, hole or damaged	O	O
P0450 *2	Evaporative Emission Control System Pressure Sensor Malfunction	• Open or short in vapor pressure sensor circuit • Vapor pressure sensor • ECM	O	O

*1: O .... MIL light up
*2: Only for A/T

Fig. 111 Diagnostic codes—1996 5S-FE engine (continued)

DIAGNOSTIC TROUBLE CODE CHART (SAE Controlled)

HINT: Parameters listed in the chart may not be exactly the same as your reading due to the type of instrument or other factors.

DTC No.	Detection Item	Diagnostic Trouble Code Detecting Condition
P0100	Mass Air Flow Circuit Malfunction	Open or short in mass air flow meter circuit with engine speed 4,000 rpm or less
P0101	Mass Air Flow Circuit Range/Performance Problem	Conditions a) and b) continue with engine speed 900 rpm or less: (2 trip detection logic) a) Closed throttle position switch: ON b) Mass air flow meter output > 2.2 V
P0110	Intake Air Temp. Circuit Malfunction	Open or short in intake air temp. sensor circuit
P0115	Engine Coolant Temp. Circuit Malfunction	Open or short in engine coolant temp. sensor circuit
P0116	Engine Coolant Temp. Circuit Range/Performance Problem	20 min. or more after starting engine, engine coolant temp. sensor value is 30°C (86°F) or less (2 trip detection logic)
P0120	Throttle Position Circuit Malfunction	Condition a) or b) continues: a) VTA < 0.1 V, and closed throttle position switch is OFF. b) VTA > 4.9 V
P0121	Throttle Position Circuit Range/Performance Problem	When closed throttle position switch is ON, condition a) continues: (2 trip detection logic) a) VTA > 2.0 V
P0125	Insufficient Coolant Temp. for Closed Loop Fuel Control	After the engine is warmed up, heated oxygen sensor output does not indicate RICH even once when conditions a) and b) continue for at least 2 minutes: a) Engine speed: 1,500 rpm or more b) Vehicle speed: 40 km/h (25 mph) or more
P0130	Heated Oxygen Sensor Circuit Malfunction (Bank 1 Sensor 1)	Voltage output of heated oxygen sensor remains at 0.4 V or more, or 0.55 V or less, during idling after the engine is warmed up (2 trip detection logic)
P0133	Heated Oxygen Sensor Circuit Slow Response (Bank 1 Sensor 1)	Response time for the heated oxygen sensor's voltage output to change from rich to lean, or from lean to rich, is 1 sec. or more during idling after the engine is warmed up (2 trip detection logic)

89654GB4

Fig. 113 Diagnostic codes—1MZ-FE engine

DIAGNOSTIC TROUBLE CODE CHART (Cont'd)

DTC No.	Detection Item	Diagnostic Trouble Code Detecting Condition
P0135	Heated Oxygen Sensor Heater Circuit Malfunction (Bank 1 Sensor 1)	When the heater operates, heater current exceeds 2 A or voltage drop for the heater circuit exceeds 5 V (2 trip detection logic) / Heater current of 0.25 A or less when the heater operates (2 trip detection logic)
P0136	Heated Oxygen Sensor Circuit Malfunction (Bank 1 Sensor 2)	Voltage output of the heated oxygen sensor (bank 1 sensor 2) remains at 0.4 V or more or 0.5 V or less when the vehicle is driven at 50 km/h (31 mph) or more after the engine is warmed up (2 trip detection logic)
P0141	Heated Oxygen Sensor Heater Circuit Malfunction (Bank 1 Sensor 2)	Same as DTC No. P0135
P0150	Heated Oxygen Sensor Circuit Malfunction (Bank 2 Sensor 1)	Same as DTC No. P0130
P0153	Heated Oxygen Sensor Circuit Slow Response (Bank 2 Sensor 1)	Same as DTC No. P0133
P0155	Heated Oxygen Sensor Heater Circuit Malfunction (Bank 2 Sensor 1)	Same as DTC No. P0135
P0170	Fuel Trim Malfunction	When the air fuel ratio feedback is stable after engine warming up, the fuel trim is considerably in error on the RICH side or the LEAN side (2 trip detection logic)
P0300	Random Misfire Detected	Misfiring of random cylinders is detected during any particular 200 or 1,000 revolutions
P0301 P0302 P0303 P0304 P0305 P0306	Misfire Detected - Cylinder 1 - Cylinder 2 - Cylinder 3 - Cylinder 4 - Cylinder 5 - Cylinder 6	For any particular 200 revolutions of the engine, misfiring is detected which can cause catalyst overheating (This causes MIL to blink) / For any particular 1,000 revolutions of the engine, misfiring is detected which causes a deterioration in emissions (2 trip detection logic)
P0325	Knock Sensor 1 Circuit Malfunction	No knock sensor 1 signal to ECM with engine speed 2,000 rpm or more
P0330	Knock Sensor 2 Circuit Malfunction	No knock sensor 2 signal to ECM with engine speed 2,000 rpm or more

89654GB5

Fig. 114 Diagnostic codes—1MZ-FE engine (continued)

DIAGNOSTIC TROUBLE CODE CHART
(Manufacturer Controlled)

DTC No.	Detection Item	Diagnostic Trouble Code Detecting Condition
P1300	Ignitier Circuit Malfunction	No IGF signal to ECM for 6 consecutive IGT signals during engine running
P1335	Crankshaft position Sensor Circuit Malfunction (during engine running)	No crankshaft position sensor signal to ECM with engine speed 1,000 rpm or more
P1500	Starter Signal Circuit Malfunction	No starter signal to ECM
P1600	ECM BATT Malfunction	Open in back up power source circuit
P1605	Knock Control CPU Malfunction	Engine control computer malfunction (for knock control)
P1780	Park/Neutral Position Switch Malfunction	Two or more switches are ON simultaneously for "N", "2" and "L" position (2 trip detection logic)
		When driving under conditions a) and b) for 30 sec. or more, the park/neutral position switch is ON (N position) (2 trip detection logic) a) Vehicle speed: 70 km/h (44 mph) or more b) Engine speed: 1,500 ~ 2,500 rpm

89554GB6

Fig. 115 Diagnostic codes continued—1MZ-FE engine (continued)

VACUUM DIAGRAMS

Following are vacuum diagrams for most of the engine and emissions package combinations covered by this manual. Because vacuum circuits will vary based on various engine and vehicle options, always refer first to the vehicle emission control information label, if present. Should the label be missing, or should vehicle be equipped with a different engine from the vehicle's original equipment, refer to the diagrams below for the same or similar configuration. If you wish to obtain a replacement emissions label, most manufacturers make the labels available for purchase. The labels can usually be ordered from a local dealer.

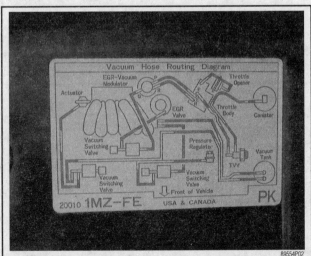

Fig. 116 A vacuum diagram label is located under the hood—1MZ-FE engine shown

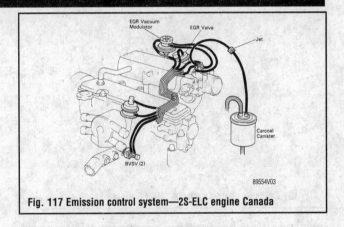

Fig. 117 Emission control system—2S-ELC engine Canada

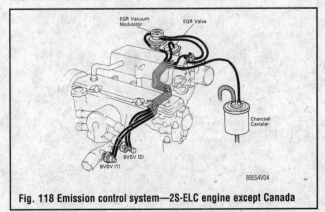

Fig. 118 Emission control system—2S-ELC engine except Canada

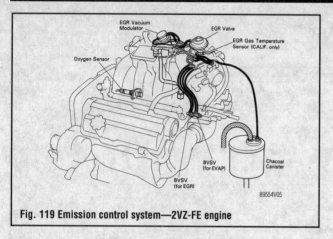

Fig. 119 Emission control system—2VZ-FE engine

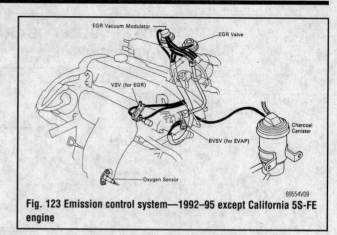

Fig. 123 Emission control system—1992–95 except California 5S-FE engine

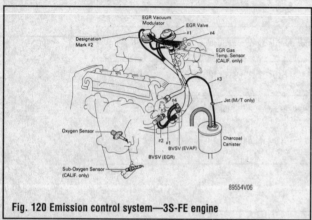

Fig. 120 Emission control system—3S-FE engine

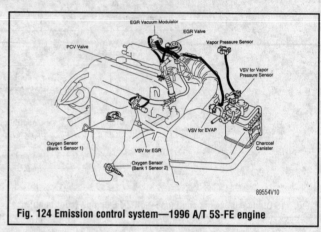

Fig. 124 Emission control system—1996 A/T 5S-FE engine

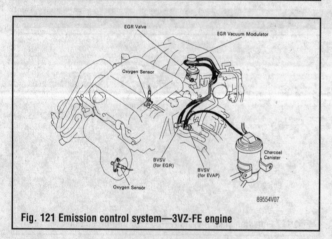

Fig. 121 Emission control system—3VZ-FE engine

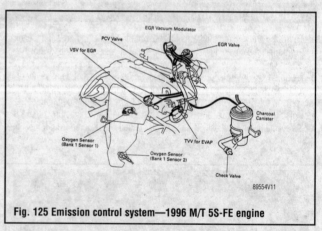

Fig. 125 Emission control system—1996 M/T 5S-FE engine

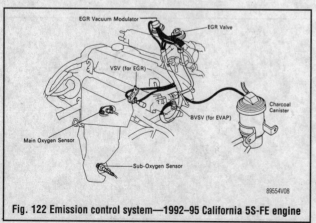

Fig. 122 Emission control system—1992–95 California 5S-FE engine

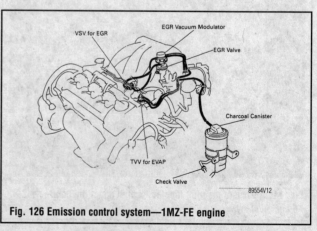

Fig. 126 Emission control system—1MZ-FE engine

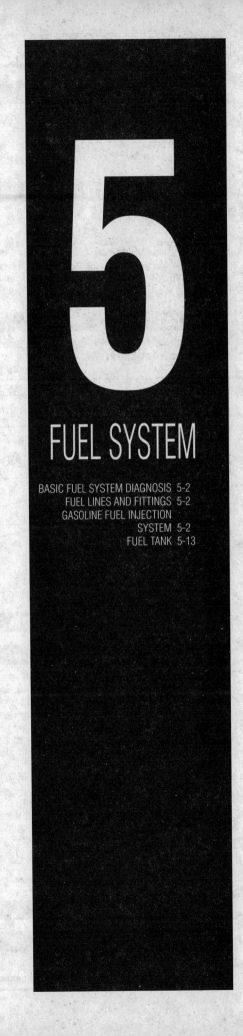

5

FUEL SYSTEM

BASIC FUEL SYSTEM DIAGNOSIS

When there is a problem starting or driving a vehicle, two of the most important checks involve the ignition and the fuel systems. The questions most mechanics attempt to answer first, "is there spark?" and "is there fuel?" will often lead to solving most basic problems. For ignition system diagnosis and testing, please refer to the information on engine electrical components and ignition systems found earlier in this manual. If the ignition system checks out (there is spark), then you must determine if the fuel system is operating properly (is there fuel?).

FUEL LINES AND FITTINGS

▶ **See Figures 1 and 2**

When working on the fuel system, insect the lines and connections for cracks, leakage and deformation. Inspect the fuel tank vapor vent system hose and connections for looseness, sharp bends or damage. Check the fuel tank for any deformation due to bad driving conditions. Inspect the bands for rust or cracks. The tank bands should be secure and not loose. Check the filler neck for damage or leakage.

- Place a container under the connection.
- Slowly loosen the connection. Have a rag handy to clean up any split fuel.
- Separate the connection.
- Plug the connection with a rubber plug.
- When connecting the union bolt on the high pressure line, always use a new gasket.
- Always tighten the union bolt by hand. Tighten the bolt to 22 ft. lbs. (29 Nm).

Union Bolt Type

When disconnecting the high pressure fuel line, a large amount of gasoline will spill out, so observe the following.

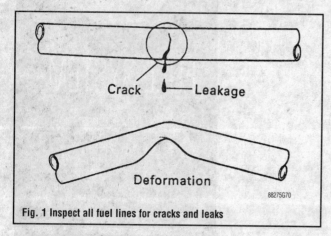

Fig. 1 Inspect all fuel lines for cracks and leaks

Flare Nut Type

Apply a light coat of engine oil to the flare and tighten the flare nut by hand. Using a torque wrench, tighten the flare nut to 22 ft. lbs. (30 Nm).

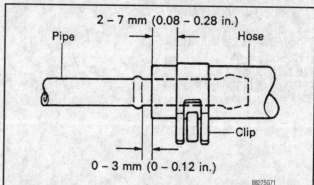

Fig. 2 When placing a hose clamp, install in the position illustrated for a secure hold

GASOLINE FUEL INJECTION SYSTEM

General Information

Fuel injected engines are equipped with the Toyota Computer Control System (TCCS). This integrated control system allows the Engine Control Module (ECM) to control other systems as well as the fuel injection. On earlier systems, the fuel management was performed by the EFI computer; in the current system, the control unit also oversees ignition timing and advance, EGR function, idle speed control (ISC system), Electronically Controlled Transmission (ECT) function as well as on-board diagnostics and back-up or fail-safe functions. The control unit is a sophisticated micro-computer, receiving input signals from many sources and locations on the vehicle. It is capable of rapid calculation of many variables and controls several output circuits simultaneously. This system is broken down into 3 major sub-systems: the Fuel System, Air Induction System and the Electronic Control System. Keeping these divisions in mind will shorten troubleshooting and diagnostic time. An electric fuel pump supplies sufficient fuel, under a constant pressure, to the injectors. These injectors allow a metered quantity of fuel into the intake manifold according to signals from the ECM. The air induction system provides sufficient air for the engine operation. This system includes the throttle body, air intake device and idle control system components.

Relieving Fuel System Pressure

✽✽ CAUTION

Failure to relieve fuel pressure before repairs or disassembly can cause serious personal injury and/or property damage.

Fuel pressure is maintained within the fuel lines, even if the engine is **OFF** or has not been run in a period of time. This pressure must be safely relieved before any fuel-bearing line or component is loosened or removed.

1. Place a catch-pan under the joint to be disconnected. A large quantity of fuel will be released when the joint is opened.
2. Wear eye or full face protection.
3. Slowly release the joint using a wrench of the correct size. Counterhold the joint with a second wrench if possible.
4. Allow the pressurized fuel to bleed off slowly before disconnecting the joint.
5. Plug the opened lines immediately to prevent fuel spillage or the entry of dirt.
6. Dispose of the released fuel properly.

Fuel Pump

✽✽ CAUTION

Observe all applicable safety precautions when working around fuel. Whenever servicing the fuel system, always work in a well ventilated area. Do not allow fuel spray or vapors to come in contact with a spark or open flame. Keep a dry chemical fire extinguisher near the work area. Always keep fuel in a container specifically designed for fuel storage; also, always properly seal fuel containers to avoid the possibility of fire or explosion.

REMOVAL & INSTALLATION

▶ **See Figures 3, 4, 5, 6 and 7**

➡The fuel pump and sending unit are one unit.

❈❈ **CAUTION**

The fuel pump is located inside the fuel tank and is attached to the sending unit. Do not smoke or have any open flame in the work area when removing the fuel pump!

1983–91 Models

1. Disconnect the negative battery cable.
2. Position a suitable waste container under the fuel tank and drain the fuel from the tank.
3. Remove the fuel tank.
4. On non-All-Trac 4-Wheel Drive vehicles, remove the six screws from the fuel pump bracket. On All-Trac 4-Wheel Drive vehicles, there are seven screws to remove.
5. Withdraw the fuel pump bracket from the fuel tank. Remove the gasket from the fuel tank and discard it.
6. Remove the two nuts that hold the pump to the bracket and disconnect the wires from the fuel pump.
7. Pull the bracket from the bottom of the fuel pump.
8. Disconnect the fuel hose (discharge) from the fuel pump.
9. Remove the fuel filter rubber cushion and clip. Remove the filter from the pump.
10. Installation is the reverse of removal.
11. Install the bracket retaining screws and tighten to 35 inch lbs. (4 Nm). Fill the fuel tank and check for leaks.

1992–96 Models

▶ **See Figure 8**

➡Be sure this procedure is done in a well ventilated area.

1. Disconnect the negative battery cable.

2. Relieve the fuel pressure.
3. Remove the rear seat cushion.
4. Remove the floor service hole cover.
5. Disconnect the electrical fuel pump wiring at the fuel pump assembly. Check for any fuel leakage while in there.
6. Remove the gas cap, this will prevent any fuel gas spilling out of any high pressure lines.
7. Using SST 09631–22020 or an equivalent line (flare nut) wrench, disconnect the outlet pipe from the pump bracket.
8. Remove the pump bracket attaching screws.
9. Disconnect the return hoses from the pump bracket, then pull out the pump/bracket assembly.
10. Remove the nut and spring washer, then disconnect the wires from the pump bracket.
11. Remove the sending unit attaching screws, then remove the unit from the bracket.
12. Pull the lower side of the fuel pump from the bracket.
13. Unplug the connector to the fuel pump.
14. Disconnect the hose from the pump.
15. Separate the filter from the pump. Use a small screwdriver to remove the attaching clip.
16. Inspect all of the lines, hoses and fittings for any sign of corrosion, wear or damage to the surfaces. Check the pump outlet hose and the filter for restrictions.
17. When reassembling, ALWAYS replace the sealing gaskets with new ones. Also replace any rubber parts showing any sign of deterioration.
   To install:
18. Install the pump filter using a new clip. Install the rubber cushion under the filter.
19. Connect the outlet hose to the pump, then attach the pump to the bracket and tighten to 22–25 ft. lbs. (29–34 Nm).
20. Engage the connector to the fuel pump. Install the fuel sending unit to the pump bracket.
21. Install the fuel pump and bracket assembly onto the tank. Use new gaskets. Tighten the pump bracket retaining screws to 34 inch lbs. (4 Nm).
22. The remainder of installation is the reverse of removal. Tighten each component to specifications. Start the engine and check carefully for any sign of leakage around the tank and lines. Road test the vehicle for proper operation.

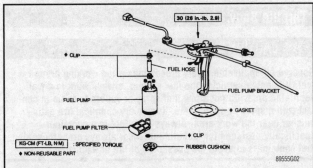

Fig. 3 The electric fuel pump has a filter; check it for clogging and tears

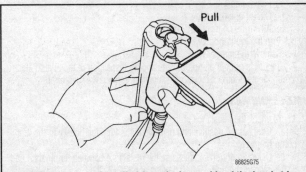

Fig. 4 The pump can be pulled from the lower side of the bracket in most cases

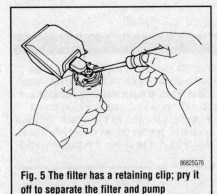

Fig. 5 The filter has a retaining clip; pry it off to separate the filter and pump

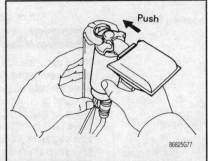

Fig. 6 Push the lower side of the pump into the bracket

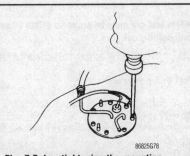

Fig. 7 Before tightening the mounting bolts, make sure the gasket is in place so there is no gaps

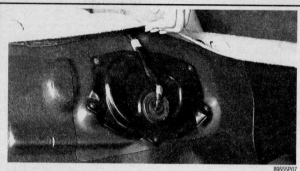

Fig. 8 Pull back the rug under the rear seat to access the fuel pump and sending unit cover

TESTING

Fuel Pump Operation

EXCEPT 1MZ-FE ENGINES

Since the fuel pump is concealed within the tank, it is difficult to test directly at the pump. It is possible to test the pump from under the hood, listening for pump function and feeling the fuel delivery lines for the build-up of pressure.

1. Turn the ignition switch **ON**, but do not start the engine.

2. Using a jumper wire, short both terminals of the fuel pump check connector. The check connector is located near the air cleaner. Connect the terminals labeled **FP** and **+B**. Special service connector 09843–18020 or equivalent can be used to perform this test.

3. Check that there is pressure in the hose running to the delivery pipe. You should hear fuel pressure noise and possibly hear the pump at the rear of the car.

4. If the fuel pump failed to function, it may indicate a faulty pump, but before removing the fuel pump, check the following items within the pump system:

   a. All fusible links

   b. All fuses (EFI—15A and IGN—7.5A)

   c. AM2—30A

   d. EFI main relay

   e. Fuel pump

   f. Circuit opening relay

   g. All wiring connections and grounds.

5. Turn the ignition to OFF.

6. Remove the jumper wire.

7. If there is no fuel pump pressure and an inspection of the related electrical components does not reveal a malfunction, replace the fuel pump.

1MZ-FE ENGINES

1. To check the resistance of the pump:

   a. Connect the positive and negative leads from the battery to the fuel pump harness.

   b. Using an ohmmeter, measure the resistance between terminals 4 and 5. Resistance should be 0.2–0.3 ohms at 68°F (20°C).

   c. If the resistance is not as specified, replace the fuel pump.

2. To check operation:

   a. Attach the positive lead from the battery to terminal 4 of the connector, and the negative lead to terminal 5. Check that the pump operates.

➡ **This test can must be proffered within 10 seconds to prevent the coil from burning out.**

3. If this test is not as specified, replace the fuel pump.

Fuel Pump Pressure

1. Before beginning the pressure test, make sure that the battery voltage is above 12 volts.

2. Turn the ignition key to the OFF position. Disconnect the negative battery cable.

3. Disengage the cold start injector connector or fuel filter inlet line.

4. Position a small plastic container or shop towel under the cold start injector pipe.

5. Remove the two union bolts, four gaskets and cold start injector pipe.

➡ **Loosen the union bolts slowly.**

6. Connect a suitable pressure gauge (SST No. 09628–45012 or equivalent) to the delivery pipe with two new gaskets and the union bolt. Tighten the union bolt to 13–22 ft. lbs. (17–29 Nm).

7. Thoroughly wipe up any fuel that may have spilled.

8. Reconnect the negative battery cable.

9. Remove the rubber cap from the fuel EFI check connector and short both the **+B** and **FP** terminals using a jumper wire.

10. Turn the ignition switch to the **ON** position.

11. Measure the fuel pressure on the gauge. On 1983–86 vehicles normal fuel pump pressure is 33–38 psi and on 1987–96 vehicles, 38–44 psi. If the fuel pressure exceeds the maximum limit, replace the fuel pressure regulator. If the pressure is below the minimum limit, check the following components:

   • Fuel hose and connections.

   • Fuel pump.

   • Fuel filter.

   • Fuel pressure regulator.

12. Remove the jumper wire.

13. Start the engine.

14. Disconnect the vacuum hose from the fuel pressure regulator and plug the end of the hose.

15. Measure the fuel pressure at idle. On 1983–86 vehicles normal fuel pump pressure is 33–38 psi and on 1987–96 vehicles, 38–44 psi. (265–304 kPa).

16. Unplug and reconnect the vacuum hose to the pressure regulator.

17. Measure the fuel pressure at idle again. On 1983–86 vehicles the pressure should be 27–31 psi and for 1987–96 vehicles, 31–37 psi. (206–255 kPa).

18. If the pressure is not as specified, check the vacuum hose and pressure regulator.

19. Stop the engine and check that the fuel pressure remains at 21 psi (147 kPa) or more for five minutes after the engine is turned off. If the fuel pressure is not as specified, check the fuel pump, pressure regulator and/or injectors.

20. Disconnect the negative battery cable and disconnect the test gauge carefully to prevent fuel spillage.

21. Install the cold start injector or filter pipe with new gaskets and the two new union bolts. Tighten the bolts to 13–22 ft. lbs. (17–29 Nm).

22. Attach the cold start injector connector.

23. Connect the negative battery cable.

24. Start the engine and check for leaks.

Throttle Body

✷✷ CAUTION

Observe all applicable safety precautions when working around fuel. Whenever servicing the fuel system, always work in a well ventilated area. Do not allow fuel spray or vapors to come in contact with a spark or open flame. Keep a dry chemical fire extinguisher near the work area. Always keep fuel in a container specifically designed for fuel storage; also, always properly seal fuel containers to avoid the possibility of fire or explosion.

REMOVAL & INSTALLATION

2S-ELC Engine

1. On 1986 vehicles, drain the cooling system.

✷✷ CAUTION

Never open, service or drain the radiator or cooling system when hot; serious burns can occur from the steam and hot coolant. Also, when draining engine coolant, keep in mind that cats and dogs are attracted to ethylene glycol antifreeze and could drink any that is left in an uncovered container or in puddles on the ground. This will prove fatal in sufficient quantities. Always drain coolant into a sealable container. Coolant should be reused unless it is contaminated or is several years old.

2. On vehicles equipped with automatic transaxle, disconnect the throttle cable from the throttle linkage.

3. Disconnect the accelerator cable from the throttle linkage and remove the accelerator cable return spring.

4. Remove the cable bracket from the throttle body.

5. Disconnect the air cleaner hose.

6. Disconnect and label the two water by-pass hoses, PCV throttle body hose, air inlet valve hose and all emission control vacuum hoses.

7. Disconnect the throttle position sensor wiring.

8. Remove the four bolts that secure the throttle body to the intake manifold.

9. Lift the throttle body and gasket from the intake manifold and remove from the vehicle.

10. Cover the intake manifold opening with masking tape to prevent the entry of foreign matter. Purchase a new gasket.

11. Using a soft bristle brush and carburetor cleaner, clean all the throttle body cast parts. Using low pressure compressed air, clean all the ports and passages.

12. Inspect and/or adjust the throttle valve and throttle position sensor as described in this Section. On 1987 vehicles, remove the Idle Speed Control (ISC) valve if required also detailed in this Section.

13. Installation is the reverse of removal. Install the ISC valve, if removed. Make sure that the gasket surface is clean and install the throttle body and gasket onto the intake manifold surface.

14. Install the four retaining bolts and tighten them to 9 ft. lbs. (12 Nm) in a criss-cross pattern.

15. Fill the cooling system to the proper level with a good brand of ethylene glycol coolant.

3S-FE Engine

▶ **See Figure 9**

1. Disconnect the negative battery cable.
2. Drain the cooling system.

✳✳ CAUTION

When draining the coolant, keep in mind that cats and dogs are attracted by the ethylene glycol antifreeze, and are quite likely to drink any that is left in an uncovered container or in puddles on the ground. This will prove fatal in sufficient quantity. Always drain the coolant into a sealable container. Coolant should be reused unless it is contaminated or several years old.

3. On vehicles equipped with automatic transaxle, disconnect the throttle cable from the throttle linkage.

4. Disconnect the accelerator cable from the throttle linkage.

5. Disconnect the air cleaner hose.

6. Detach the throttle position sensor wiring.

7. Disconnect the Idle Speed Control (ISC) control valve wiring.

8. Disconnect and label the two water by-pass hoses, PCV throttle body hose, air inlet valve hose and all emission control vacuum hoses.

9. Remove the four bolts that secure the throttle body to the intake manifold.

10. Lift the throttle body and throttle body gasket from the intake manifold and remove it from the vehicle.

11. Cover the intake manifold opening with masking tape to prevent the entry of foreign matter. Purchase a new gasket.

12. Using a soft bristle brush and carburetor cleaner, clean all the throttle body cast parts. Using low pressure compressed air, clean all the ports and passages.

13. Inspect and/or adjust the throttle valve and throttle position sensor as described in Section 4. Remove the ISC valve, if required.

14. Installation is the reverse of removal. Make sure that the gasket surface is clean and install the throttle body and gasket onto the intake manifold. Install the four retaining bolts and tighten them to 14 ft. lbs. (19 Nm).

15. Fill the cooling system to the proper level with a good brand of ethylene glycol coolant. Start the engine and check operation. Top off the coolant level if necessary.

5S-FE Engine

▶ **See Figure 10**

1. Turn the ignition key to the OFF position. Disconnect the negative battery cable.

2. Drain the engine coolant.

3. Disconnect the accelerator cable from the throttle linkage. If equipped with automatic transmission, disconnect the throttle cable from the linkage.

4. Remove the air cleaner cap, resonator and hose.

5. On 1995–96 models, remove the alternator and distributor. Then separate the front exhaust pipe from the catalytic converter and Remove the water outlet and bypass pipe.

6. On 1992–94 models, disconnect the Throttle Position Sensor and ISC valve wiring.

7. Label and disconnect the PCV and vacuum hoses from the throttle body.

8. Remove the retaining bolts holding the throttle body; remove the throttle body and its gasket.

9. Remove the coolant by-pass hoses and air hose after the throttle body is partially removed.

10. Clean the cast parts of the throttle body using a bristle brush and carburetor cleaner. Do not expose the throttle position sensor or other external components to the solvent. Use compressed air to clean and dry all passages in the throttle body.

11. If the throttle position sensor is to be replaced:
    a. Remove the mounting screws and extract the sensor.
    b. Make certain the throttle plate is fully closed. Place the sensor onto the throttle body so that the electrical connector is positioned properly.
    c. Temporarily install the retaining screws for the sensor.
    d. Adjust the throttle position sensor.

12. Installation is the reverse of removal. Place a new gasket on the intake manifold. The gasket is correctly installed in only one position: the protrusion or bulge in the gasket must face downward. Install the throttle body, tightening the retaining nuts and bolts to 14 ft. lbs. (19 Nm).

➡**The bolts must be installed correctly; the upper bolts are shorter than the lowers.**

13. Refill the cooling system. Start the engine, check for operation and top off the coolant level.

Fig. 9 The throttle body is retained by three bolts, remove them to extract the unit from the manifold

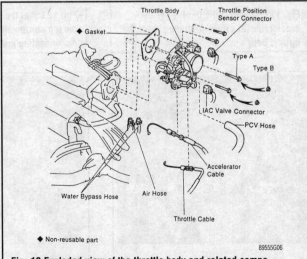

Fig. 10 Exploded view of the throttle body and related components—5S-FE engine

2VZ-FE Engine

1. Drain the coolant from the throttle body.
2. If equipped with automatic transmission, disconnect the throttle cable.
3. Disconnect the accelerator cable.
4. Remove the air flow meter, air cleaner cap and air intake hose as an assembly. Label and disconnect the air and vacuum hoses before removal.
5. Disconnect the TPS wiring.
6. Disconnect the PCV, coolant by-pass and emission hoses from the throttle body. If equipped with automatic transmission, remove the throttle cable bracket.
7. Remove the nuts and bolts holding the throttle body; remove the throttle body and the gasket.
8. Clean the cast parts of the throttle body using a bristle brush and carburetor cleaner. Do not expose the throttle position sensor to the solvent. Use compressed air to clean and dry all passages in the throttle body.
9. If the throttle position sensor is to be replaced:
    a. Remove the mounting screws and remove the sensor.
    b. Make certain the throttle plate is fully closed. Place the sensor onto the throttle body.
    c. Temporarily install the retaining screws for the sensor.
    d. Adjust the throttle position sensor.
10. Installation is the reverse of removal. Place a new gasket on the intake manifold. Install the throttle body, tightening the retaining nuts and bolts to 9 ft. lbs. (13 Nm).
11. Refill the engine coolant. Start the engine, check for operation and top off the coolant level.

3VZ-FE Engine

1. Drain the coolant from the engine.
2. Disconnect the accelerator cable and, if equipped with automatic transmission, the throttle cable.
3. Disconnect the air cleaner hose.
4. Detach the wiring from the throttle position sensor and the ISC valve.

5. Disconnect the PCV hose, the coolant by-pass hoses, the air tube hose and the emission system vacuum hoses.
6. Remove the retaining bolts; remove the throttle body and gasket.
7. Clean the cast parts of the throttle body using a bristle brush and carburetor cleaner. Do not expose the throttle position sensor or other external components to the solvent. Use compressed air to clean and dry all passages in the throttle body.
8. If the throttle position sensor is to be replaced:
    a. Remove the mounting screws and remove the sensor.
    b. Make certain the throttle plate is fully closed. With the throttle body held in its normal orientation, place the sensor onto the throttle body so that the electrical connector is in the correct position.
    c. Temporarily install the retaining screws for the sensor.
    d. Adjust the throttle position sensor.
9. Installation is the reverse of removal. Using a new gasket, install the throttle body and tighten the mounting bolts to 14 ft. lbs. (19 Nm).
10. Refill the coolant.

1MZ-FE Engine

♦ See Figures 11 thru 16

1. Disconnect the negative battery cable.
2. Drain the engine coolant.
3. Remove the air cleaner cap assembly.
4. Disconnect the accelerator cable. In automatic transaxles, disconnect the throttle body cable.
5. Disconnect the three upper throttle body vacuum hoses. There are markings on the top of the throttle body to identify each one of these.
6. Disconnect the TPS and IAC wiring.
7. Remove the linkage bracket attached to the side of the throttle body.
8. Loosen and remove the four throttle body retaining bolts and nuts. Pull the throttle body out slightly, then disconnect the hoses attached to the bottom of the IAC. Discard the throttle body gasket.
9. Installation is the reverse of removal. Using a new gasket, install the throttle body and tighten the mounting bolts to 14 ft. lbs. (19 Nm). Refill the coolant.

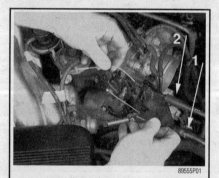

Fig. 11 Disconnect the throttle (1) and accelerator (2) cables from the side of the throttle body

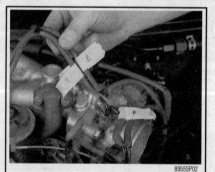

Fig. 12 Label the three hoses attached to the top portion of the throttle body before disconnecting them

Fig. 13 Remove these two bolts to detach the throttle bracket from the body

Fig. 14 The retaining nuts and bolts for throttle body removal

Fig. 15 With the throttle body pulled away slightly, disconnect the two back hoses

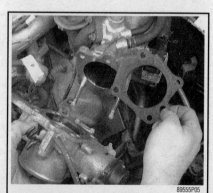

Fig. 16 Be sure to discard all of the old gasket material

Fuel Injectors

▶ See Figure 17

✳✳ CAUTION

Observe all applicable safety precautions when working around fuel. Whenever servicing the fuel system, always work in a well ventilated area. Do not allow fuel spray or vapors to come in contact with a spark or open flame. Keep a dry chemical fire extinguisher near the work area. Always keep fuel in a container specifically designed for fuel storage; also, always properly seal fuel containers to avoid the possibility of fire or explosion.

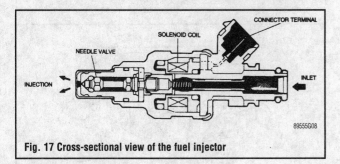

Fig. 17 Cross-sectional view of the fuel injector

REMOVAL & INSTALLATION

2S-ELC Engine

▶ See Figures 18 and 19

1. Disconnect the negative battery cable.
2. On 1985–86 vehicles, drain the cooling system.

✳✳ CAUTION

Never open, service or drain the radiator or cooling system when hot; serious burns can occur from the steam and hot coolant. Also, when draining engine coolant, keep in mind that cats and dogs are attracted to ethylene glycol antifreeze and could drink any that is left in an uncovered container or in puddles on the ground. This will prove fatal in sufficient quantities. Always drain coolant into a sealable container. Coolant should be reused unless it is contaminated or is several years old.

3. On 1983–84 vehicles, loosen the bolts and remove the throttle cable bracket from the throttle body. On 1985–86 vehicles, disconnect the throttle cable from the throttle linkage, if equipped with automatic transaxle and disconnect the accelerator cable from the throttle linkage.
4. Disconnect the air cleaner hose.
5. Disconnect the following hoses:
- Two water by-pass hoses from the throttle body.
- Two PCV valve hoses from the air intake chamber.
- Air valve hoses.
- Brake booster vacuum hose from the intake chamber.

- Fuel filter hose.
- Main and return fuel hoses.
- Label and disconnect the emission control hoses (1983–84)
- Vacuum sensing hose (1985–86)
- PS and A/C idle-up vacuum hoses (1985–86)
- Cruise control actuator vacuum hose (1985–86)

6. Disengage the cold start injector wire, throttle position sensor wire harness, four injector connectors and oxygen sensor connector (1985–86).
7. Place a towel or rag under the cold start injector pipe and remove the two union bolts and four gaskets. Remove the delivery pipe.

➡**Loosen the union pipe bolts slowly.**

8. Loosen the EGR valve pipe nut.
9. Remove the two nuts and four bolts and remove the air intake chamber and throttle body. Remove the gasket and purchase a new one.
10. Unbolt and remove the delivery pipe with the injectors attached.

➡**When removing the delivery pipe, take care not to drop it as damage to the injectors may result. Also, do not remove the injector cover.**

11. Remove the four insulators from the openings in the intake manifold.
12. Gently pull the injectors from the delivery pipe.
13. Remove the O-rings and grommets from the injectors and purchase new ones.

To install:

14. Install a new grommet and new O-ring onto each injector.

➡**Make sure that they are installed evenly to ensure a good seat and save yourself from having to take the injectors out and readjust or replace the O-rings.**

15. Lightly coat the O-rings with clean fuel and install the injectors into the delivery pipe.
16. Install the insulators into the intake manifold openings.
17. Install the injectors and delivery pipe into the intake manifold. Do not cock the injector, install it straight into the opening using a slight left to right twisting motion. Make sure that the injector connector is facing upward.
18. Go to each injector and rotate it by hand. The injector should rotate smoothly. Make sure that the injector connector is facing upward.

➡**If the injectors don't rotate smoothly, the O-rings are probably not installed correctly or the injectors are not installed evenly. If this is the case, you will have the pull the delivery pipe off the intake manifold and look at the O-rings to make sure that they are installed correctly. Adjust the O-rings and, if damaged, replace them.**

19. Install the four delivery pipe retaining bolts and tighten them to 8–11 ft. lbs. (10–15 Nm).
20. The remainder of installation is the reverse of removal. Tighten the air intake and throttle body with the four bolts, two nuts and new gasket to 15–18 ft. lbs. (20–24 Nm).
21. Check all fuel connections for leaks using the tip of your finger. Correct all fuel leaks immediately.
22. Remove the jumper wire.

3S-FE Engine

▶ See Figure 20

1. Disconnect the negative battery cable.
2. Disconnect the harness from the cold start injector.

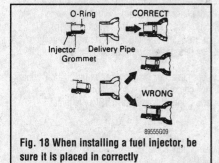

Fig. 18 When installing a fuel injector, be sure it is placed in correctly

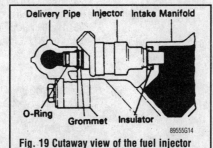

Fig. 19 Cutaway view of the fuel injector installed—1983–86 models

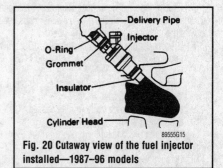

Fig. 20 Cutaway view of the fuel injector installed—1987–96 models

3. Place a towel or rag under the cold start injector pipe and remove the two union bolts, four gaskets and delivery pipe.

➡**Loosen the union pipe bolts slowly.**

4. Disconnect the vacuum sensing hose from the fuel pressure regulator.
5. Disconnect the fuel return pipe hose.
6. Remove the pulsation damper with the two gaskets. Discard the gaskets and purchase new ones.
7. Unbolt and remove the delivery pipe with the injectors attached.

➡**When removing the delivery pipe, take care not to drop it as damage to the injectors may result.**

8. Remove the four insulators and two spacers from the cylinder head.
9. Gently pull the injectors from the delivery pipe.
10. Remove the O-rings and grommets from the injectors and purchase new ones.

To install:

11. Install a new grommet and new O-ring onto each injector. Make sure that they are installed evenly, to ensure a good seat and save yourself from having to take the injectors out and readjust or replace the O-rings.
12. Lightly coat the O-rings with clean fuel.
13. Install the injectors into the delivery pipe. Do not cock the injector, install it straight into the opening using a light left to right twisting motion.
14. Place the four insulators and two spacers on the cylinder head.
15. Install the injectors together with the delivery pipe onto the cylinder head.
16. Go to each injector and rotate it by hand. The injector should rotate smoothly.

➡**If the injectors don't rotate smoothly, the O-rings are probably not installed correctly or the injectors are not installed evenly. If this is the case, you will have the pull the delivery pipe off the intake manifold and look at the O-rings to make sure that they are installed correctly. Adjust the O-rings and, if damaged, replace them.**

17. After the delivery pipe and injectors are properly in place, go to each injector and position the connector so that it is facing upward.
18. Install the two delivery pipe retaining bolts and tighten them to 9 ft. lbs. (12 Nm).
19. The remainder of installation is the reverse of removal. Tighten each component to specifications.
20. Short the **+B** and **Fp** terminals of the engine check connector with a jumper wire.
21. While the connector is shorted, pinch the fuel return hose. When the pinched, this causes the pressure in the high pressure fuel line to rise to 57 psi. (kPa) At this time any leaks in any part of the system should be apparent. Carefully look at each component for leakage and run the tip of your finger around each connection.

5S-FE Engine

▶ **See Figures 20, 21 and 22**

1. With the ignition in the **LOCK position**, disconnect the negative battery cable.
2. Drain the engine coolant. Disconnect the accelerator cable from the throttle body. If equipped with automatic transmission, disconnect the throttle cable.
3. Disengage the air intake temperature sensor connector.
4. Disconnect the cruise control actuator cable from the clamp on the resonator.
5. Loosen the air cleaner hose clamp bolt. Disconnect the air cleaner hose from the throttle body. Release the air cleaner clips and remove the air cleaner cap with the resonator and air cleaner hose.
6. Disconnect the wiring to the throttle position sensor and the ISC valve.
7. Label and disconnect the hoses for the PCV, EGR vacuum modulator and EVAP VSV.
8. Remove the 4 bolts holding the throttle body. Label and disconnect the hoses from the throttle body.
9. Remove the throttle body with its gasket.
10. Disconnect the PS vacuum hoses.
11. Label and disconnect the hoses from the EVAP Bi-metal Vacuum Switching Valve (BVSV).
12. Remove the EGR valve and the vacuum modulator.

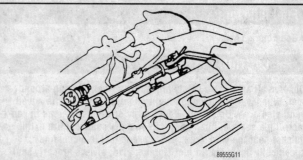

Fig. 21 Unbolt and remove the fuel delivery pipe and injectors as an assembly

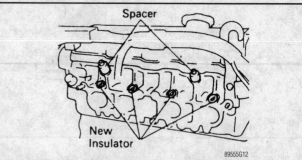

Fig. 22 Place new injector seals and spacers in position on the cylinder head—5S-FE engine shown

13. Disconnect the vacuum sensor hose at the air intake chamber, the brake booster vacuum hose and the vacuum sensing hose.
14. If equipped with air conditioning, disconnect the magnet switch VSV wiring.
15. Disconnect the ground straps from the intake manifold.
16. Disconnect the knock sensor and EGR Vacuum Switching Valve (VSV) wiring.
17. Free the engine wire harness by removing the bolt and wire clamp.
18. Remove the stays or supports holding the air intake chamber and the intake manifold.
19. Remove the intake manifold and remove the gasket.
20. Disconnect the wiring to each injector.
21. Loosen the pulsation damper and disconnect the fuel inlet pipe. Disconnect the fuel return hose.
22. Remove the retaining bolts; remove the delivery pipe or fuel rail along with the injectors. Do not drop any injectors during removal.
23. Remove the insulators and rail spacers from the head. Remove the injectors from the fuel rail.
24. Remove the O-ring and grommet from each injector.

To install:

25. Install a new grommet on each injector. Apply a light coat of gasoline to new O-rings and install them on each injector.
26. Install the injectors into the fuel rail while turning each left and right. After installation, check that the injectors turn freely in place; if not, remove the injector and inspect the O-ring for damage or deformation.
27. Place new insulators and spacers on the head.
28. Install the fuel rail and injectors; check that the injectors still turn freely in position. Position the injector connectors upward.
29. Install the retaining bolts, tightening them to 9 ft. lbs. (13 Nm).
30. Connect the fuel return hose. Install the fuel inlet pipe and pulsation damper to the delivery pipe. Use new gaskets; tighten the union bolt to 25 ft. lbs. (34 Nm).
31. Connect the wiring to each injector. The remained of installation is the reverse of removal. Tighten each component to specifications.
32. Refill the engine coolant. Connect the negative battery terminal.

2VZ-FE Engine

1. Disconnect the negative battery cable.
2. Drain the engine coolant.

3. If equipped with automatic transmission, disconnect the throttle control cable from the throttle body and bracket. On all vehicles, disconnect the accelerator cable and bracket from the throttle body and air plenum or intake chamber.

4. Disengage the air flow meter wiring and disconnect the air hoses. Loosen the clamp bolt and disconnect the cap clips; remove the air cleaner cover and the air flow meter with the air cleaner hose.

5. Label and disconnect the following hoses and electrical harnesses: PCV hoses, vacuum sensing (MAP) hose, fuel pressure vacuum solenoid valve hose, emission system vacuum hoses, ISC connector, throttle position sensor and EGR temperature sensor if so equipped.

6. Remove the right upper engine stay.

7. Disconnect the cold start injector harness and fuel hose.

8. Label and disconnect the brake booster vacuum hose, PS vacuum hose and air hose, cruise control vacuum hose, wire harness clamp and fuel pressure vacuum solenoid valve hose.

9. Remove the wire harness clamp and free the wire harness. Disconnect the EGR tube.

10. Remove the 2 bolts holding the engine hanger. Disconnect and remove the air plenum stay from the air plenum.

11. Remove the air plenum or intake chamber with its gasket.

12. Disconnect the cold start injector harness, the coolant temperature sensor harness and the six injector harnesses.

13. Disconnect the wire harness retaining clamps from the left side fuel rail.

14. Disconnect the fuel return hoses from the fuel pressure regulator and the No. 1 fuel rail. Disconnect the fuel inlet hose from the fuel filter.

15. Remove the No. 2 fuel line.

16. Remove the 2 bolts. Remove the left fuel rail together with the 3 injectors. Take great care not to drop an injector during removal.

17. Remove the 3 bolts, then remove the right fuel rail along with the injectors. Take great care not to drop an injector during removal.

18. Remove the injectors from the fuel rail. Remove the 6 insulators from the intake manifold and remove the spacers from the fuel rail mounting points.

To install:

19. Install a new grommet to each injector.

20. Lightly coat new O-rings with clean gasoline; install the O-rings on each injector.

21. Install the injectors into the fuel rails while turning the injector left and right. Once installed, the injector should turn freely. If any binding is felt, remove the injector and inspect the O-ring for crimping or damage.

22. Place the insulators and spacers in place on the manifold.

23. Install the right and left rail assemblies in position on the intake manifold. Again check that the injectors rotate freely. Turn the injector so the electrical connector faces upward.

24. Install the retaining bolts, tightening them to 9 ft. lbs. (13 Nm).

25. Install the No. 2 fuel pipe. The gaskets at the union bolts must be replaced. Tighten the fittings to 24 ft. lbs. (32 Nm).

26. Install the inlet hose to the fuel filter and connect the return hoses to the pressure regulator and No. 1 fuel line. The washers at the union bolts must be replaced with new ones.

27. Connect the wire harness clips to the left fuel rail.

28. Attach the wiring connectors to the injectors, the cold start injector and the coolant temperature sensor.

29. The remainder of installation is the reverse of removal. Tighten each component to specifications.

3VZ-FE Engine

▶ See Figure 23

1. With the ignition switch in the **LOCK** position, disconnect the negative battery terminal.

2. Drain the engine coolant.

3. Disconnect the accelerator cable from the throttle linkage.

4. If equipped with automatic transmission, disconnect the throttle cable from the linkage.

5. Remove the air cleaner cap, air flow meter and the air cleaner hose as a unit.

6. Remove the two 5mm bolts holding the V-cover; remove the cover.

7. Disconnect the EGR temperature wiring clamp from the set of emission control valves.

8. Label and remove the hoses from the fuel pressure control VSV. Disconnect the hoses, then separate the VSV wiring and remove the emission control valve set.

9. Label and disconnect the brake booster vacuum hose, PS air hose, PCV hose and IACV vacuum hose.

10. Disconnect the two ground straps.

11. Remove the wiring connector from the cold start injector. Disconnect the fuel line from the cold start injector.

12. Remove the No. 1 engine hanger and the air intake chamber support.

13. Remove the EGR pipe.

14. Remove the bolt and disconnect the hydraulic pressure pipe from the air intake chamber.

15. Disconnect the 3 hoses at the air intake plenum, disconnect the two coolant by-pass hoses and the EGR temperature sensor harness if so equipped.

16. Disconnect the throttle position sensor. Detach the connector for the Idle Speed Control (ISC) valve and remove the air hoses from the ISC valve. Remove the PS air hose.

17. Remove the bolts and nuts holding the air plenum, then lift off the unit and gasket.

18. Disconnect the fuel return hoses from the No. 1 fuel pipe; then separate the fuel inlet hose from the filter.

19. Disconnect the wiring from each injector.

20. Remove the No. 2 fuel pipe.

21. Remove the left delivery pipe or fuel rail; be careful not to drop the injectors during removal.

22. Remove the 3 injectors from the delivery pipe. Remove the rail spacers from the intake manifold.

23. Disconnect the two air hoses; remove the air pipe with the hoses attached.

24. Remove the right fuel rail and injectors. Take care not to drop an injector. Remove the injectors from the rail.

To install:

25. Install new grommets on each injector.

26. Apply a light coat of clean gasoline to new O-rings and install 2 on each injector.

27. Install each injector into the fuel rail while turning the injector left and right. Once installed, the injector should turn freely. If not, remove the injector and inspect the O-ring for damage or dislocation.

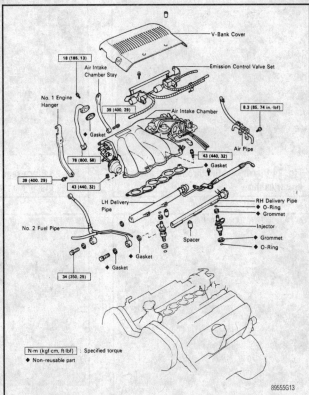

Fig. 23 Exploded view of the air intake chamber and fuel injectors— 3VZ-FE engine

28. Place the rail spacers on the manifold. Clean the injector ports and install the right rail and injector assembly. Again check that the injectors turn freely in place.

29. Position the injector wiring connector upward. Install the bolts holding the delivery pipe and tighten them to 9 ft. lbs. (13 Nm).

30. Install the air pipe and hoses; tighten the retaining bolts only to 74 inch lbs. (8.3 Nm).

31. Repeat Steps 28 and 29 to install the left side delivery pipe and injectors.

32. Install the No. 2 fuel pipe connecting the two fuel rails. Use new gaskets at each union bolt. Tighten the union bolts to 25 ft. lbs. (34 Nm).

33. Connect the IACV vacuum hose.

34. Attach the wiring connectors to their proper injectors.

35. Install the inlet hose to the fuel filter using new gaskets; tighten the bolt to 22 ft. lbs. (29 Nm). Connect the return hose to the No. 1 fuel pipe.

36. The remainder of installation is the reverse of removal. Tighten each component to specifications.

37. Refill the engine coolant.

1MZ-FE Engine

▶ See Figures 24 thru 33

1. Disconnect the negative battery cable.

❋❋ CAUTION

Work must be started approximately 90 seconds or longer after the negative battery cable has been disconnected, if equipped with an air bag.

2. Drain the engine coolant.

3. Disconnect the accelerator and throttle cables.

4. Remove the air cleaner and hose assembly.

5. Remove the V-bank cover.

6. Remove the emission valve control set, make sure to label all lines prior to removal.

7. Remove the No. 2 EGR pipe and discard the gaskets.

8. Remove the two bolts, and disconnect the hydraulic motor pressure pipe from the water inlet and air inlet chamber.

9. Remove the air intake chamber assembly. Disconnect the injector wiring.

10. Disconnect the air assist pipe from the bracket on the No. 1 fuel pipe. Remove the air assist hoses from the intake manifold.

11. Disconnect the fuel return hose from the No. 1 fuel pipe. Disconnect the fuel inlet hose for the fuel filter. Make sure you have a container handy to catch any split fuel.

12. Remove the delivery pipes and injectors by performing the following:

    a. Loosen the 2 union bolts holding the No. 2 fuel pipe to the delivery pipes.

    b. Disconnect the fuel return hose from the fuel pressure regulator.

    c. Remove the union bolt for the right hand delivery pipe, 2 gaskets, 2 bolts, left hand delivery pipe together with the 3 injectors and the No. 2 fuel pipe.

    d. Remove the union bolt for the delivery pipe and 2 gaskets from the No. 2 fuel pipe.

    e. Remove the 3 bolts, right hand delivery pipe together with the 3 injectors and the No. 1 fuel pipe.

    f. Remove the 4 spacers from the intake manifold.

    g. Pull out the 6 injectors from the delivery pipes. Remove the two O-rings and two grommets from each injector.

To install:

13. Install 2 new grommets to each injector. apply a light coat of fuel to the O-rings and install them to each injector.

    a. While turning the injector clockwise and counterclockwise, push it into the delivery pipes. Install the 6 injectors. Position the injector wiring outward.

    b. Place the 4 spacers into position on the intake manifold. Place the right hand delivery pipe and the No. 1 fuel pipe together with the 3 injectors in position on the intake manifold.

    c. Temporarily install the bolt holding the right side delivery pipe to the intake manifold.

    d. Place the left hand delivery pipe and the No. 2 fuel pipe together with the 3 injectors in position on the intake manifold.

Fig. 24 Disconnect the throttle and accelerator cables

Fig. 25 Place rags under any fuel hoses being disconnected

Fig. 26 Pull all of the hoses from the fuel rail

Fig. 27 Remove the end pipe attaching both of the injector rails

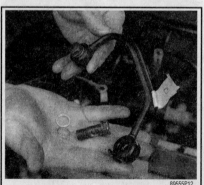

Fig. 28 The pipe contains a union bolt and two washers

Fig. 29 Lift the rail and remove the spacers

Fig. 30 Remove the injector with O-rings from the manifold

Fig. 31 Never reuse old O-rings when installing the old injector

Fig. 32 Remember to remove the grommets too

Fig. 33 The other side of the injector has two O-rings

e. Connect the fuel return hose to the fuel pressure regulator. Temporarily install the 2 bolts holding the left hand delivery pipe to the intake manifold.

f. Temporarily install the No. 2 fuel pipe to the left side delivery pipe with the union bolt and 2 new gaskets.

g. Check that the injectors rotate smoothly. If they do not, Replace the O-rings.

h. Position the injector connector outward. Tighten the 4 bolts holding the delivery pipes to the intake manifold and tighten to 7 ft. lbs. (10 Nm). Tighten the bolt holding the No. 1 fuel pipe to the intake manifold to 14 ft. lbs. (20 Nm). Tighten the 2 union bolts holding the no. 2 fuel pipe to the delivery pipes to 24 ft. lbs. (32 Nm).

14. Connect the fuel inlet and return hoses. make sure you use new gaskets and union bolt, tighten to 22 ft. lbs. (30 Nm). Connect the fuel return hose to the No. 1 fuel pipe. Pass the fuel return hose under the heater hoses.

15. Install the air assist hoses to the intake manifold and the and air assist pipe to the bracket on the No. 1 fuel pipe.

16. Engage the fuel injector wiring connectors.

17. The remainder of installation is the reverse of removal. Tighten each component to specifications.

18. Fill the engine with coolant, connect the negative battery cable.

19. Start the engine and top off the coolant level. Check vehicle operation.

TESTING

On-Vehicle Inspection

INJECTOR OPERATION

1. On V6 engines, remove the V-bank cover.
2. Start the engine.
3. Position the probe of the sound scope (or finger tip) under the base of the injector connector and have an assistant alternately increase the engine rpm and return it to idle.
4. Listen or feel for a change in the operating sound of the injector. The change should be proportional to the increase in engine rpm.
5. If no sound is heard or if the injector sound is unusual, check the connector and wiring, injector, resistor or the signal from the ECU.

INJECTOR RESISTANCE

Disconnect the wiring from the injector. With an ohmmeter, measure the resistance between the injector terminals. The resistance should be approximately 1.53.0 ohms for the 2S-ELC engine or 13.8 ohms for all other engines. If the resistance is not as specified, replace the injector. Reconnect the injector connector.

Off-Vehicle Inspection

INJECTOR VOLUME TEST

✴✴ CAUTION

To avoid personal injury, do not smoke or use any type of open flame when testing the injectors!

1. Remove the injector(s) from the vehicle and set aside.
2. Place a rag under the "banjo" fitting and, disconnect the fuel hose from the fuel filter outlet. Remove the gaskets and replace them with new ones.
3. Connect a hose and union (SST 09628–41045) to the fuel filter outlet connection with the new gaskets and tighten the union bolt.
4. Remove the fuel pressure regulator.
5. Connect the fuel return hose to the pressure regulator with the service union with a set of new gaskets and tighten the union bolt.
6. Install a new O-ring onto injector.
7. Connect the special tool to the injector with the service union and clamp the union and the tool to the injector with the service clamp.
8. Connect a length of rubber or vinyl hose to the injector tip to prevent fuel splashing and overspray.
9. Place the injector into a graduated cylinder with metric increments and connect the negative battery cable.
10. Turn the ignition switch **ON**, but DO NOT start the engine.
11. With a jumper wire, short the **+B** and **FP** terminals of the check connector on all engines except 1MZ-FE.
12. On the 1MZ-FE engine, connect the positive and negative leads from the battery to the fuel pump connector.
13. Connect wire (SST 09842-30070) to the injector and the battery for 15 seconds.
14. Measure the volume injected into the cylinder during the 15 second period. The volume should be 3.33.9 cu. inch (5464cc) for the 3.0L engine, 3.4–4.2 cu inch (56–69 cm) on 1MZ-FE engines or 2.73.4 cu. inch (4455cc) for all other engines. If all the injectors were tested, there should be no less than 0.3–0.4 cu. in. (5–6cc) difference between each injector.
15. If the actual volume does not agree with the specified volume, replace the injector.
16. Proceed to the "Check Leakage Rate" test.

LEAKAGE RATE

1. Leaving everything as it was from the injection test, disconnect the service tool test probes from the battery.
2. Check the injector tip for leakage for a period of one minute. An acceptable leakage rate is one drop.
3. If the leakage exceeds this amount, replace the injector.
4. Disconnect the negative battery cable and remove the all the test equipment.
5. Install the injector(s).

Fuel Pressure Regulator

REMOVAL & INSTALLATION

> ✳✳ **CAUTION**
>
> Observe all applicable safety precautions when working around fuel. Whenever servicing the fuel system, always work in a well ventilated area. Do not allow fuel spray or vapors to come in contact with a spark or open flame. Keep a dry chemical fire extinguisher near the work area. Always keep fuel in a container specifically designed for fuel storage; also, always properly seal fuel containers to avoid the possibility of fire or explosion.

2S-ELC and 3S-FE Engines

▶ **See Figures 34 and 35**

1. Disconnect the negative battery cable. Disconnect the vacuum sensing hose at the regulator.
2. Disconnect the fuel return hose.
3. Remove the retaining bolts and remove the regulator.
4. Reinstall in reverse order. Tighten the 2 retaining bolts to 48 inch lbs. (5.4 Nm).
5. Connect the negative battery cable.

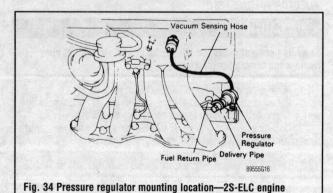

Fig. 34 Pressure regulator mounting location—2S-ELC engine

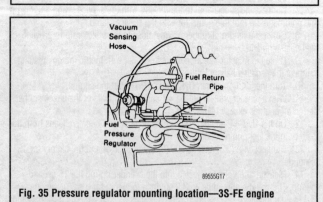

Fig. 35 Pressure regulator mounting location—3S-FE engine

5S-FE Engine

▶ **See Figure 36**

1. Turn the ignition key to the OFF position. Disconnect the negative battery cable.
2. Disconnect the vacuum hose at the fuel pressure regulator.
3. Disconnect the fuel return pipe from the fuel pressure regulator.
4. Remove the retaining bolts and remove the fuel pressure regulator.
5. Installation is the reverse of removal. Replace the O-ring, coating the new one with clean gasoline.
6. Install the pressure regulator. Tighten the retaining bolts to 48 inch lbs. (5 Nm).

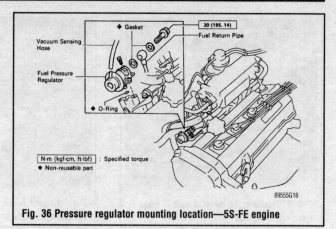

Fig. 36 Pressure regulator mounting location—5S-FE engine

7. Connect the fuel return line to the regulator. Replace the gaskets; tighten the union bolt to 14 ft. lbs. (19 Nm).

2VZ-FE Engines

1. Disconnect the negative battery cable. Disconnect the vacuum sensing hose at the regulator.
2. Disconnect the fuel return hose.
3. Loosen the locknut and remove the fuel pressure regulator.
4. Before installation, fully loosen the locknut. Lightly coat a new O-ring with gasoline and install it on the regulator.

To install:

5. Press the regulator into the fuel delivery pipe by hand. Turn the pressure regulator so that the vacuum pipe is vertical. Tighten the lock nut to 24 ft. lbs. (32 Nm).
6. Connect the fuel return hose and the vacuum hose. Connect the negative battery cable.

3VZ-FE Engine

1. Turn the ignition key to the OFF position. Disconnect the negative battery cable. Wait at least 90 seconds from the time the negative battery was disconnected to start work.
2. Remove the nuts holding the V-bank cover and remove the cover.
3. Disconnect the vacuum sensing hose and the fuel return hose from the pressure regulator.
4. Loosen the locknut and remove the pressure regulator.
5. Before installation, fully loosen the locknut. Lightly coat a new O-ring with gasoline and install it on the regulator.

To install:

6. Press the regulator into the fuel delivery pipe by hand. Turn the pressure regulator counterclockwise so that the fuel return pipe is pointing towards the air intake chamber and the vacuum port points straight up.
7. Tighten the locknut to 16 ft. lbs. (22 Nm).
8. Connect the fuel return hose. Install the vacuum hose.
9. Install the V-cover. Connect the negative battery cable.

1MZ-FE Engine

▶ **See Figures 37 and 38**

1. Turn the ignition key to the OFF position. Disconnect the negative battery cable.
2. Disconnect the air assist hose form the intake manifold.
3. Disconnect the vacuum sensing hose from the fuel pressure regulator.
4. Place a shop rag under the fuel return hose and disconnect the line from the pressure regulator.
5. Remove the 2 bolts and pull out the pressure regulator. Remove the O-ring and discard.

To install:

6. Apply a light coat of gasoline on the O-ring and place it on the pressure regulator.
7. Attach the pressure regulator to the delivery pipe.
8. Check the pressure regulator rotates smoothly.

Fig. 37 Unbolt and remove the fuel pressure regulator

Fig. 38 Remove and discard the old O-ring from the regulator

➡If the regulator does not rotate smoothly, the O-ring may be pinched, remove it, and repeat the installation steps.

9. Install the pressure regulator and tighten the 2 bolts to 69 inch lbs. (8 Nm).
10. Connect the fuel return line to the pressure regulator.

➡Be sure to insert the hose up to the stopper and clip it.

11. Connect the vacuum sensing hose. Connect the negative battery cable. Check for leaks.

Cold Start Injector

The cold start injector is mounted in the intake air stream. Controlled by the ECU, it provides additional fuel during cold engine start-up. Its function is controlled by both a timer circuit and as a function of coolant temperature. The 5S-FE and 1MZ-FE engines are not equipped with a cold start injector.

FUEL TANK

REMOVAL & INSTALLATION

▸ See Figures 40, 41 and 42

❋❋ CAUTION

To avoid personal injury, do not smoke or use any type of open flame when removing the fuel tank! Always use new gaskets on any fuel tank or fuel line component. During installation, make sure that the rubber protectors are installed with the fuel tank and make sure that all line or plug torque specification are observed. To reduce the amount of fuel that you will have to dispose of, use as much of the fuel as possible before draining the tank.

1. Raise and safely support the vehicle. Disconnect the negative battery cable and properly relieve the fuel system pressure.

REMOVAL & INSTALLATION

▸ See Figure 39

1. With the ignition **OFF**, disconnect the negative battery cable. For vehicles equipped with airbag systems, wait at least 90 seconds after disconnecting the battery before commencing any other work.
2. Disconnect the electrical harness from the cold start injector.
3. Place a container or towel under the cold start injector.
4. Slowly loosen the union bolt; contain fuel spillage. Remove the bolt and washers. Plug the fuel line immediately to prevent spillage and entry of dirt.
5. Remove the bolts holding the injector; remove the injector and gasket.
To install:
6. Using a new gasket, install the cold start injector. Tighten the bolts to 52–70 inch lbs. (6–8 Nm).
7. Install the fuel line with new gaskets. Tighten the union bolt to 11–15 ft. lbs. (15–20 Nm).

➡The gaskets at the fuel fitting must be replaced every time the joint is loosened or disassembled.

8. Connect the cold start injector harness. Reinstall the throttle body if it was removed.
9. Connect the negative battery cable.

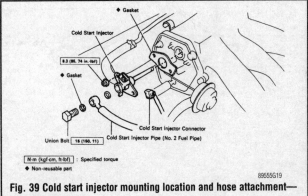

Fig. 39 Cold start injector mounting location and hose attachment— 3S-FE engine

TESTING

1. Switch the ignition **OFF**.
2. Disconnect the electrical wiring from the cold start injector
3. Use an ohmmeter to check the resistance of the injector. Correct resistance is 2-4 ohms 68°F (20°C). The resistance may vary slightly with the temperature of the injector. Use common sense and good judgment when testing.
4. If the resistance is not within specifications, it must be replaced.
5. Reconnect the wiring harness to the injector.

2. If equipped with a drain plug position a large capacity waste drain receptacle under the drain plug.
3. Remove the drain plug and gasket. Discard the gasket and purchase a new one.
4. If not equipped with a drain plug obtain an approved pumping device and drain a sufficient amount of fuel from the tank.
5. Remove the luggage compartment mat. Remove the cover over the tank sending unit and hose connections. Disconnect the gauge electrical harness and the vent, feed and fuel return hoses. Disconnect the fuel inlet filler neck.
6. With the aid of an assistant, support the tank and remove the tank strap bolts. Lower the tank and remove it from the vehicle.

➡To make the installation easier, label and tag all fuel lines and electrical connections.

7. Installation is the reverse of removal. Be careful not to twist or kink any of the hoses. Check for leaks.

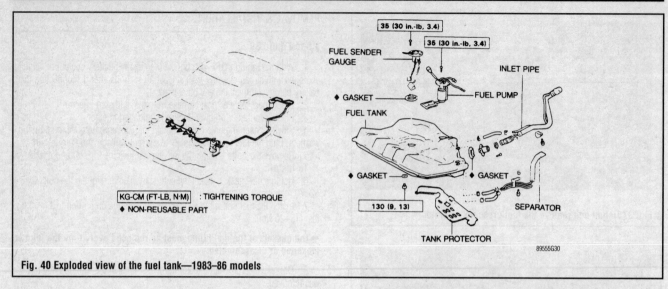

Fig. 40 Exploded view of the fuel tank—1983–86 models

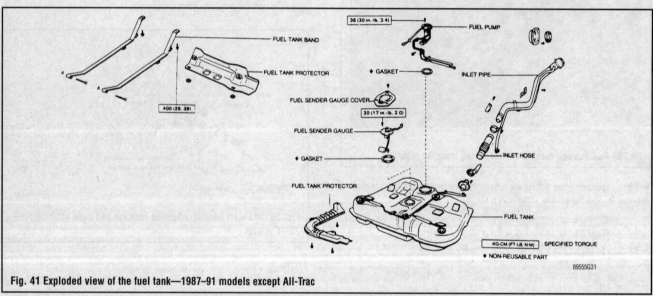

Fig. 41 Exploded view of the fuel tank—1987–91 models except All-Trac

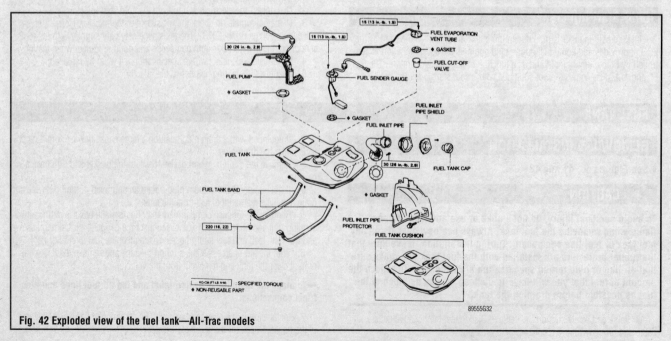

Fig. 42 Exploded view of the fuel tank—All-Trac models

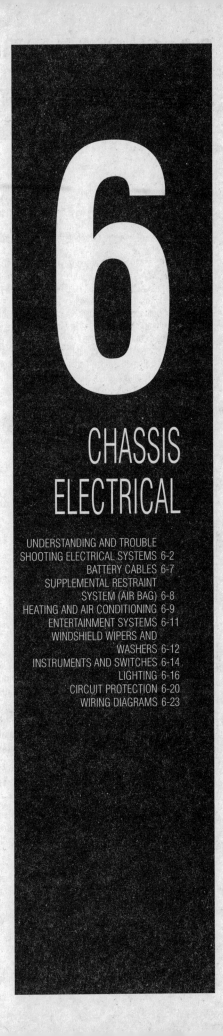

6

CHASSIS ELECTRICAL

UNDERSTANDING AND TROUBLESHOOTING ELECTRICAL SYSTEMS

Basic Electrical Theory

▶ See Figure 1

For any 12 volt, negative ground, electrical system to operate, the electricity must travel in a complete circuit. This simply means that current (power) from the positive (+) terminal of the battery must eventually return to the negative (-) terminal of the battery. Along the way, this current will travel through wires, fuses, switches and components. If, for any reason, the flow of current through the circuit is interrupted, the component fed by that circuit will cease to function properly.

Perhaps the easiest way to visualize a circuit is to think of connecting a light bulb (with two wires attached to it) to the battery—one wire attached to the negative (-) terminal of the battery and the other wire to the positive (+) terminal. With the two wires touching the battery terminals, the circuit would be complete and the light bulb would illuminate. Electricity would follow a path from the battery to the bulb and back to the battery. It's easy to see that with longer wires on our light bulb, it could be mounted anywhere. Further, one wire could be fitted with a switch so that the light could be turned on and off.

The normal automotive circuit differs from this simple example in two ways. First, instead of having a return wire from the bulb to the battery, the current travels through the frame of the vehicle. Since the negative (-) battery cable is attached to the frame (made of electrically conductive metal), the frame of the vehicle can serve as a ground wire to complete the circuit. Secondly, most automotive circuits contain multiple components which receive power from a single circuit. This lessens the amount of wire needed to power components on the vehicle.

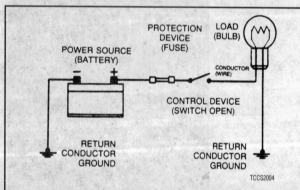

Fig. 1 This example illustrates a simple circuit. When the switch is closed, power from the positive (+) battery terminal flows through the fuse and the switch, and then to the light bulb. The light illuminates and the circuit is completed through the ground wire back to the negative (-) battery terminal. In reality, the two ground points shown in the illustration are attached to the metal frame of the vehicle, which completes the circuit back to the battery

HOW DOES ELECTRICITY WORK: THE WATER ANALOGY

Electricity is the flow of electrons—the subatomic particles that constitute the outer shell of an atom. Electrons spin in an orbit around the center core of an atom. The center core is comprised of protons (positive charge) and neutrons (neutral charge). Electrons have a negative charge and balance out the positive charge of the protons. When an outside force causes the number of electrons to unbalance the charge of the protons, the electrons will split off the atom and look for another atom to balance out. If this imbalance is kept up, electrons will continue to move and an electrical flow will exist.

Many people have been taught electrical theory using an analogy with water. In a comparison with water flowing through a pipe, the electrons would be the water and the wire is the pipe.

The flow of electricity can be measured much like the flow of water through a pipe. The unit of measurement used is amperes, frequently abbreviated as amps (a). You can compare amperage to the volume of water flowing through a pipe.

When connected to a circuit, an ammeter will measure the actual amount of current flowing through the circuit. When relatively few electrons flow through a circuit, the amperage is low. When many electrons flow, the amperage is high.

Water pressure is measured in units such as pounds per square inch (psi); The electrical pressure is measured in units called volts (v). When a voltmeter is connected to a circuit, it is measuring the electrical pressure.

The actual flow of electricity depends not only on voltage and amperage, but also on the resistance of the circuit. The higher the resistance, the higher the force necessary to push the current through the circuit. The standard unit for measuring resistance is an ohm. Resistance in a circuit varies depending on the amount and type of components used in the circuit. The main factors which determine resistance are:

• Material—some materials have more resistance than others. Those with high resistance are said to be insulators. Rubber materials (or rubber-like plastics) are some of the most common insulators used in vehicles as they have a very high resistance to electricity. Very low resistance materials are said to be conductors. Copper wire is among the best conductors. Silver is actually a superior conductor to copper and is used in some relay contacts, but its high cost prohibits its use as common wiring. Most automotive wiring is made of copper.

• Size—the larger the wire size being used, the less resistance the wire will have. This is why components which use large amounts of electricity usually have large wires supplying current to them.

• Length—for a given thickness of wire, the longer the wire, the greater the resistance. The shorter the wire, the less the resistance. When determining the proper wire for a circuit, both size and length must be considered to design a circuit that can handle the current needs of the component.

• Temperature—with many materials, the higher the temperature, the greater the resistance (positive temperature coefficient). Some materials exhibit the opposite trait of lower resistance with higher temperatures (negative temperature coefficient). These principles are used in many of the sensors on the engine.

OHM'S LAW

There is a direct relationship between current, voltage and resistance. The relationship between current, voltage and resistance can be summed up by a statement known as Ohm's law.

Voltage (E) is equal to amperage (I) times resistance (R): $E = I \times R$

Other forms of the formula are $R = E/I$ and $I = E/R$

In each of these formulas, E is the voltage in volts, I is the current in amps and R is the resistance in ohms. The basic point to remember is that as the resistance of a circuit goes up, the amount of current that flows in the circuit will go down, if voltage remains the same.

The amount of work that the electricity can perform is expressed as power. The unit of power is the watt (w). The relationship between power, voltage and current is expressed as:

Power (w) is equal to amperage (I) times voltage (E): $W = I \times E$

This is only true for direct current (DC) circuits; The alternating current formula is a tad different, but since the electrical circuits in most vehicles are DC type, we need not get into AC circuit theory.

Electrical Components

POWER SOURCE

Power is supplied to the vehicle by two devices: The battery and the alternator. The battery supplies electrical power during starting or during periods when the current demand of the vehicle's electrical system exceeds the output capacity of the alternator. The alternator supplies electrical current when the engine is running. Just not does the alternator supply the current needs of the vehicle, but it recharges the battery.

The Battery

In most modern vehicles, the battery is a lead/acid electrochemical device consisting of six 2 volt subsections (cells) connected in series, so that the unit is capable of producing approximately 12 volts of electrical pressure. Each sub-section consists of a series of positive and negative plates held a short distance apart in a solution of sulfuric acid and water.

The two types of plates are of dissimilar metals. This sets up a chemical reaction, and it is this reaction which produces current flow from the battery when its positive and negative terminals are connected to an electrical load . The power removed from the battery is replaced by the alternator, restoring the battery to its original chemical state.

The Alternator

On some vehicles there isn't an alternator, but a generator. The difference is that an alternator supplies alternating current which is then changed to direct current for use on the vehicle, while a generator produces direct current. Alternators tend to be more efficient and that is why they are used.

Alternators and generators are devices that consist of coils of wires wound together making big electromagnets. One group of coils spins within another set and the interaction of the magnetic fields causes a current to flow. This current is then drawn off the coils and fed into the vehicles electrical system.

GROUND

Two types of grounds are used in automotive electric circuits. Direct ground components are grounded to the frame through their mounting points. All other components use some sort of ground wire which is attached to the frame or chassis of the vehicle. The electrical current runs through the chassis of the vehicle and returns to the battery through the ground (-) cable; if you look, you'll see that the battery ground cable connects between the battery and the frame or chassis of the vehicle.

➡ **It should be noted that a good percentage of electrical problems can be traced to bad grounds.**

PROTECTIVE DEVICES

▶ **See Figure 2**

It is possible for large surges of current to pass through the electrical system of your vehicle. If this surge of current were to reach the load in the circuit, the surge could burn it out or severely damage it. It can also overload the wiring,

causing the harness to get hot and melt the insulation. To prevent this, fuses, circuit breakers and/or fusible links are connected into the supply wires of the electrical system. These items are nothing more than a built-in weak spot in the system. When an abnormal amount of current flows through the system, these protective devices work as follows to protect the circuit:

- Fuse—when an excessive electrical current passes through a fuse, the fuse "blows" (the conductor melts) and opens the circuit, preventing the passage of current.
- Circuit Breaker—a circuit breaker is basically a self-repairing fuse. It will open the circuit in the same fashion as a fuse, but when the surge subsides, the circuit breaker can be reset and does not need replacement.
- Fusible Link—a fusible link (fuse link or main link) is a short length of special, high temperature insulated wire that acts as a fuse. When an excessive electrical current passes through a fusible link, the thin gauge wire inside the link melts, creating an intentional open to protect the circuit. To repair the circuit, the link must be replaced. Some newer type fusible links are housed in plug-in modules, which are simply replaced like a fuse, while older type fusible links must be cut and spliced if they melt. Since this link is very early in the electrical path, it's the first place to look if nothing on the vehicle works, yet the battery seems to be charged and is properly connected.

✳ **CAUTION**

Always replace fuses, circuit breakers and fusible links with identically rated components. Under no circumstances should a component of higher or lower amperage rating be substituted.

SWITCHES & RELAYS

▶ **See Figures 3 and 4**

Switches are used in electrical circuits to control the passage of current. The most common use is to open and close circuits between the battery and the various electric devices in the system. Switches are rated according to the amount of amperage they can handle. If a sufficient amperage rated switch is not used in a circuit, the switch could overload and cause damage.

Some electrical components which require a large amount of current to operate use a special switch called a relay. Since these circuits carry a large amount of current, the thickness of the wire in the circuit is also greater. If this large wire were connected from the load to the control switch, the switch would have to carry the high amperage load and the fairing or dash would be twice as large to accommodate the increased size of the wiring harness. To prevent these problems, a relay is used.

Relays are composed of a coil and a set of contacts. When the coil has a current passed though it, a magnetic field is formed and this field causes the contacts to move together, completing the circuit. Most relays are normally open, preventing current from passing through the circuit, but they can take any elec-

Fig. 2 Most vehicles use one or more fuse panels. This one is located on the driver's side kick panel

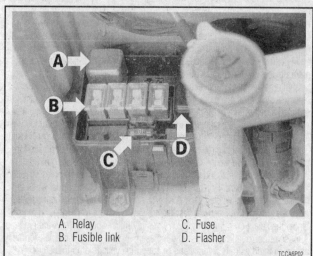

A. Relay
B. Fusible link
C. Fuse
D. Flasher

Fig. 3 The underhood fuse and relay panel usually contains fuses, relays, flashers and fusible links

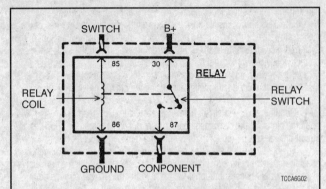

Fig. 4 Relays are composed of a coil and a switch. These two components are linked together so that when one operates, the other operates at the same time. The large wires in the circuit are connected from the battery to one side of the relay switch (B+) and from the opposite side of the relay switch to the load (component). Smaller wires are connected from the relay coil to the control switch for the circuit and from the opposite side of the relay coil to ground

trical form depending on the job they are intended to do. Relays can be considered "remote control switches." They allow a smaller current to operate devices that require higher amperages. When a small current operates the coil, a larger current is allowed to pass by the contacts. Some common circuits which may use relays are the horn, headlights, starter, electric fuel pump and other high draw circuits.

LOAD

Every electrical circuit must include a "load" (something to use the electricity coming from the source). Without this load, the battery would attempt to deliver its entire power supply from one pole to another. This is called a "short circuit." All this electricity would take a short cut to ground and cause a great amount of damage to other components in the circuit by developing a tremendous amount of heat. This condition could develop sufficient heat to melt the insulation on all the surrounding wires and reduce a multiple wire cable to a lump of plastic and copper.

WIRING & HARNESSES

The average vehicle contains meters and meters of wiring, with hundreds of individual connections. To protect the many wires from damage and to keep them from becoming a confusing tangle, they are organized into bundles, enclosed in plastic or taped together and called wiring harnesses. Different harnesses serve different parts of the vehicle. Individual wires are color coded to help trace them through a harness where sections are hidden from view.

Automotive wiring or circuit conductors can be either single strand wire, multi-strand wire or printed circuitry. Single strand wire has a solid metal core and is usually used inside such components as alternators, motors, relays and other devices. Multi-strand wire has a core made of many small strands of wire twisted together into a single conductor. Most of the wiring in an automotive electrical system is made up of multi-strand wire, either as a single conductor or grouped together in a harness. All wiring is color coded on the insulator, either as a solid color or as a colored wire with an identification stripe. A printed circuit is a thin film of copper or other conductor that is printed on an insulator backing. Occasionally, a printed circuit is sandwiched between two sheets of plastic for more protection and flexibility. A complete printed circuit, consisting of conductors, insulating material and connectors for lamps or other components is called a printed circuit board. Printed circuitry is used in place of individual wires or harnesses in places where space is limited, such as behind instrument panels.

Since automotive electrical systems are very sensitive to changes in resistance, the selection of properly sized wires is critical when systems are repaired. A loose or corroded connection or a replacement wire that is too small for the circuit will add extra resistance and an additional voltage drop to the circuit.

The wire gauge number is an expression of the cross-section area of the conductor. Vehicles from countries that use the metric system will typically describe the wire size as its cross-sectional area in square millimeters. In this

method, the larger the wire, the greater the number. Another common system for expressing wire size is the American Wire Gauge (AWG) system. As gauge number increases, area decreases and the wire becomes smaller. An 18 gauge wire is smaller than a 4 gauge wire. A wire with a higher gauge number will carry less current than a wire with a lower gauge number. Gauge wire size refers to the size of the strands of the conductor, not the size of the complete wire with insulator. It is possible, therefore, to have two wires of the same gauge with different diameters because one may have thicker insulation than the other.

It is essential to understand how a circuit works before trying to figure out why it doesn't. An electrical schematic shows the electrical current paths when a circuit is operating properly. Schematics break the entire electrical system down into individual circuits. In a schematic, usually no attempt is made to represent wiring and components as they physically appear on the vehicle; switches and other components are shown as simply as possible. Face views of harness connectors show the cavity or terminal locations in all multi-pin connectors to help locate test points.

CONNECTORS

▶ See Figures 5 and 6

Three types of connectors are commonly used in automotive applications—weatherproof, molded and hard shell.

• Weatherproof—these connectors are most commonly used where the connector is exposed to the elements. Terminals are protected against moisture and dirt by sealing rings which provide a weathertight seal. All repairs require the use of a special terminal and the tool required to service it. Unlike standard blade type terminals, these weatherproof terminals cannot be straightened once they are bent. Make certain that the connectors are properly seated and all of the sealing rings are in place when connecting leads.

Fig. 5 Hard shell (left) and weatherproof (right) connectors have replaceable terminals

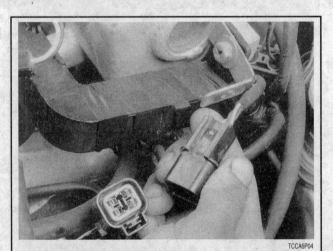

Fig. 6 Weatherproof connectors are most commonly used in the engine compartment or where the connector is exposed to the elements

• Molded—these connectors require complete replacement of the connector if found to be defective. This means splicing a new connector assembly into the harness. All splices should be soldered to insure proper contact. Use care when probing the connections or replacing terminals in them, as it is possible to create a short circuit between opposite terminals. If this happens to the wrong terminal pair, it is possible to damage certain components. Always use jumper wires between connectors for circuit checking and NEVER probe through weatherproof seals.

• Hard Shell—unlike molded connectors, the terminal contacts in hard-shell connectors can be replaced. Replacement usually involves the use of a special terminal removal tool that depresses the locking tangs (barbs) on the connector terminal and allows the connector to be removed from the rear of the shell. The connector shell should be replaced if it shows any evidence of burning, melting, cracks, or breaks. Replace individual terminals that are burnt, corroded, distorted or loose.

Test Equipment

Pinpointing the exact cause of trouble in an electrical circuit is most times accomplished by the use of special test equipment. The following describes different types of commonly used test equipment and briefly explains how to use them in diagnosis. In addition to the information covered below, the tool manufacturer's instructions booklet (provided with the tester) should be read and clearly understood before attempting any test procedures.

JUMPER WIRES

✳✳ CAUTION

Never use jumper wires made from a thinner gauge wire than the circuit being tested. If the jumper wire is of too small a gauge, it may overheat and possibly melt. Never use jumpers to bypass high resistance loads in a circuit. Bypassing resistances, in effect, creates a short circuit. This may, in turn, cause damage and fire. Jumper wires should only be used to bypass lengths of wire or to simulate switches.

Jumper wires are simple, yet extremely valuable, pieces of test equipment. They are basically test wires which are used to bypass sections of a circuit. Although jumper wires can be purchased, they are usually fabricated from lengths of standard automotive wire and whatever type of connector (alligator clip, spade connector or pin connector) that is required for the particular application being tested. In cramped, hard-to-reach areas, it is advisable to have insulated boots over the jumper wire terminals in order to prevent accidental grounding. It is also advisable to include a standard automotive fuse in any jumper wire. This is commonly referred to as a "fused jumper". By inserting an in-line fuse holder between a set of test leads, a fused jumper wire can be used for bypassing open circuits. Use a 5 amp fuse to provide protection against voltage spikes.

Jumper wires are used primarily to locate open electrical circuits, on either the ground (-) side of the circuit or on the power (+) side. If an electrical component fails to operate, connect the jumper wire between the component and a good ground. If the component operates only with the jumper installed, the ground circuit is open. If the ground circuit is good, but the component does not operate, the circuit between the power feed and component may be open. By moving the jumper wire successively back from the component toward the power source, you can isolate the area of the circuit where the open is located. When the component stops functioning, or the power is cut off, the open is in the segment of wire between the jumper and the point previously tested.

You can sometimes connect the jumper wire directly from the battery to the "hot" terminal of the component, but first make sure the component uses 12 volts in operation. Some electrical components, such as fuel injectors or sensors, are designed to operate on about 4 to 5 volts, and running 12 volts directly to these components will cause damage.

TEST LIGHTS

▶ See Figure 7

The test light is used to check circuits and components while electrical current is flowing through them. It is used for voltage and ground tests. To use a 12 volt test light, connect the ground clip to a good ground and probe wherever

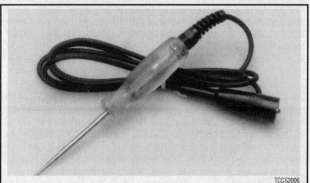

Fig. 7 A 12 volt test light is used to detect the presence of voltage in a circuit

necessary with the pick. The test light will illuminate when voltage is detected. This does not necessarily mean that 12 volts (or any particular amount of voltage) is present; it only means that some voltage is present. It is advisable before using the test light to touch its ground clip and probe across the battery posts or terminals to make sure the light is operating properly.

✳✳ WARNING

Do not use a test light to probe electronic ignition, spark plug or coil wires. Never use a pick-type test light to probe wiring on computer controlled systems unless specifically instructed to do so. Any wire insulation that is pierced by the test light probe should be taped and sealed with silicone after testing.

Like the jumper wire, the 12 volt test light is used to isolate opens in circuits. But, whereas the jumper wire is used to bypass the open to operate the load, the 12 volt test light is used to locate the presence of voltage in a circuit. If the test light illuminates, there is power up to that point in the circuit; if the test light does not illuminate, there is an open circuit (no power). Move the test light in successive steps back toward the power source until the light in the handle illuminates. The open is between the probe and a point which was previously probed.

The self-powered test light is similar in design to the 12 volt test light, but contains a 1.5 volt penlight battery in the handle. It is most often used in place of a multimeter to check for open or short circuits when power is isolated from the circuit (continuity test).

The battery in a self-powered test light does not provide much current. A weak battery may not provide enough power to illuminate the test light even when a complete circuit is made (especially if there is high resistance in the circuit). Always make sure that the test battery is strong. To check the battery, briefly touch the ground clip to the probe; if the light glows brightly, the battery is strong enough for testing.

➡A self-powered test light should not be used on any computer controlled system or component. The small amount of electricity transmitted by the test light is enough to damage many electronic automotive components.

MULTIMETERS

Multimeters are an extremely useful tool for troubleshooting electrical problems. They can be purchased in either analog or digital form and have a price range to suit any budget. A multimeter is a voltmeter, ammeter and ohmmeter (along with other features) combined into one instrument. It is often used when testing solid state circuits because of its high input impedance (usually 10 megaohms or more). A brief description of the multimeter main test functions follows:

• Voltmeter—the voltmeter is used to measure voltage at any point in a circuit, or to measure the voltage drop across any part of a circuit. Voltmeters usually have various scales and a selector switch to allow the reading of different voltage ranges. The voltmeter has a positive and a negative lead. To avoid damage to the meter, always connect the negative lead to the negative (-) side of the circuit (to ground or nearest the ground side of the circuit) and connect the positive lead to the positive (+) side of the circuit (to the power source or the nearest power source). Note that the negative voltmeter lead will always be black and that the positive voltmeter will always be some color other than black (usually red).

• Ohmmeter—the ohmmeter is designed to read resistance (measured in ohms) in a circuit or component. Most ohmmeters will have a selector switch which permits the measurement of different ranges of resistance (usually the selector switch allows the multiplication of the meter reading by 10, 100, 1,000 and 10,000). Some ohmmeters are "auto-ranging" which means the meter itself will determine which scale to use. Since the meters are powered by an internal battery, the ohmmeter can be used like a self-powered test light. When the ohmmeter is connected, current from the ohmmeter flows through the circuit or component being tested. Since the ohmmeter's internal resistance and voltage are known values, the amount of current flow through the meter depends on the resistance of the circuit or component being tested. The ohmmeter can also be used to perform a continuity test for suspected open circuits. In using the meter for making continuity checks, do not be concerned with the actual resistance readings. Zero resistance, or any ohm reading, indicates continuity in the circuit. Infinite resistance indicates an opening in the circuit. A high resistance reading where there should be none indicates a problem in the circuit. Checks for short circuits are made in the same manner as checks for open circuits, except that the circuit must be isolated from both power and normal ground. Infinite resistance indicates no continuity, while zero resistance indicates a dead short.

✳✳ WARNING

Never use an ohmmeter to check the resistance of a component or wire while there is voltage applied to the circuit.

• Ammeter—an ammeter measures the amount of current flowing through a circuit in units called amperes or amps. At normal operating voltage, most circuits have a characteristic amount of amperes, called "current draw" which can be measured using an ammeter. By referring to a specified current draw rating, then measuring the amperes and comparing the two values, one can determine what is happening within the circuit to aid in diagnosis. An open circuit, for example, will not allow any current to flow, so the ammeter reading will be zero. A damaged component or circuit will have an increased current draw, so the reading will be high. The ammeter is always connected in series with the circuit being tested. All of the current that normally flows through the circuit must also flow through the ammeter; if there is any other path for the current to follow, the ammeter reading will not be accurate. The ammeter itself has very little resistance to current flow and, therefore, will not affect the circuit, but it will measure current draw only when the circuit is closed and electricity is flowing. Excessive current draw can blow fuses and drain the battery, while a reduced current draw can cause motors to run slowly, lights to dim and other components to not operate properly.

Troubleshooting Electrical Systems

When diagnosing a specific problem, organized troubleshooting is a must. The complexity of a modern automotive vehicle demands that you approach any problem in a logical, organized manner. There are certain troubleshooting techniques, however, which are standard:

• Establish when the problem occurs. Does the problem appear only under certain conditions? Were there any noises, odors or other unusual symptoms? Isolate the problem area. To do this, make some simple tests and observations, then eliminate the systems that are working properly. Check for obvious problems, such as broken wires and loose or dirty connections. Always check the obvious before assuming something complicated is the cause.

• Test for problems systematically to determine the cause once the problem area is isolated. Are all the components functioning properly? Is there power going to electrical switches and motors. Performing careful, systematic checks will often turn up most causes on the first inspection, without wasting time checking components that have little or no relationship to the problem.

• Test all repairs after the work is done to make sure that the problem is fixed. Some causes can be traced to more than one component, so a careful verification of repair work is important in order to pick up additional malfunctions that may cause a problem to reappear or a different problem to arise. A blown fuse, for example, is a simple problem that may require more than

another fuse to repair. If you don't look for a problem that caused a fuse to blow, a shorted wire (for example) may go undetected.

Experience has shown that most problems tend to be the result of a fairly simple and obvious cause, such as loose or corroded connectors, bad grounds or damaged wire insulation which causes a short. This makes careful visual inspection of components during testing essential to quick and accurate troubleshooting.

Testing

OPEN CIRCUITS

▶ **See Figure 8**

This test already assumes the existence of an open in the circuit and it is used to help locate the open portion.

1. Isolate the circuit from power and ground.
2. Connect the self-powered test light or ohmmeter ground clip to the ground side of the circuit and probe sections of the circuit sequentially.
3. If the light is out or there is infinite resistance, the open is between the probe and the circuit ground.
4. If the light is on or the meter shows continuity, the open is between the probe and the end of the circuit toward the power source.

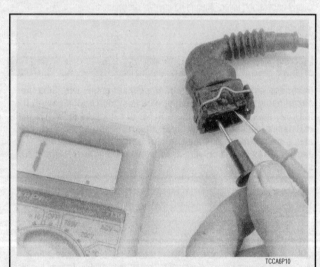

TCCA6P10

Fig. 8 The infinite reading on this multimeter indicates that the circuit is open

SHORT CIRCUITS

➡ **Never use a self-powered test light to perform checks for opens or shorts when power is applied to the circuit under test. The test light can be damaged by outside power.**

1. Isolate the circuit from power and ground.
2. Connect the self-powered test light or ohmmeter ground clip to a good ground and probe any easy-to-reach point in the circuit.
3. If the light comes on or there is continuity, there is a short somewhere in the circuit.
4. To isolate the short, probe a test point at either end of the isolated circuit (the light should be on or the meter should indicate continuity).
5. Leave the test light probe engaged and sequentially open connectors or switches, remove parts, etc. until the light goes out or continuity is broken.
6. When the light goes out, the short is between the last two circuit components which were opened.

VOLTAGE

This test determines voltage available from the battery and should be the first step in any electrical troubleshooting procedure after visual inspection. Many electrical problems, especially on computer controlled systems, can be caused by a low state of charge in the battery. Excessive corrosion at the battery cable terminals can cause poor contact that will prevent proper charging and full battery current flow.

1. Set the voltmeter selector switch to the 20V position.
2. Connect the multimeter negative lead to the battery's negative (-) post or terminal and the positive lead to the battery's positive (+) post or terminal.
3. Turn the ignition switch **ON** to provide a load.
4. A well charged battery should register over 12 volts. If the meter reads below 11.5 volts, the battery power may be insufficient to operate the electrical system properly.

VOLTAGE DROP

▶ **See Figure 9**

When current flows through a load, the voltage beyond the load drops. This voltage drop is due to the resistance created by the load and also by small resistances created by corrosion at the connectors and damaged insulation on the wires. The maximum allowable voltage drop under load is critical, especially if there is more than one load in the circuit, since all voltage drops are cumulative.

1. Set the voltmeter selector switch to the 20 volt position.
2. Connect the multimeter negative lead to a good ground.
3. Operate the circuit and check the voltage prior to the first component (load).
4. There should be little or no voltage drop in the circuit prior to the first component. If a voltage drop exists, the wire or connectors in the circuit are suspect.
5. While operating the first component in the circuit, probe the ground side of the component with the positive meter lead and observe the voltage readings. A small voltage drop should be noticed. This voltage drop is caused by the resistance of the component.
6. Repeat the test for each component (load) down the circuit.
7. If a large voltage drop is noticed, the preceding component, wire or connector is suspect.

RESISTANCE

▶ **See Figures 10 and 11**

✳✳ WARNING

Never use an ohmmeter with power applied to the circuit. The ohmmeter is designed to operate on its own power supply. The normal 12 volt electrical system voltage could damage the meter!

1. Isolate the circuit from the vehicle's power source.
2. Ensure that the ignition key is **OFF** when disconnecting any components or the battery.
3. Where necessary, also isolate at least one side of the circuit to be checked, in order to avoid reading parallel resistances. Parallel circuit resistances will always give a lower reading than the actual resistance of either of the branches.
4. Connect the meter leads to both sides of the circuit (wire or component) and read the actual measured ohms on the meter scale. Make sure the selector switch is set to the proper ohm scale for the circuit being tested, to avoid misreading the ohmmeter test value.

Wire and Connector Repair

Almost anyone can replace damaged wires, as long as the proper tools and parts are available. Wire and terminals are available to fit almost any need. Even the specialized weatherproof, molded and hard shell connectors are now available from aftermarket suppliers.

Be sure the ends of all the wires are fitted with the proper terminal hardware and connectors. Wrapping a wire around a stud is never a permanent solution and will only cause trouble later. Replace wires one at a time to avoid confusion. Always route wires exactly the same as the factory.

➡**If connector repair is necessary, only attempt it if you have the proper tools. Weatherproof and hard shell connectors require special tools to release the pins inside the connector. Attempting to repair these connectors with conventional hand tools will damage them.**

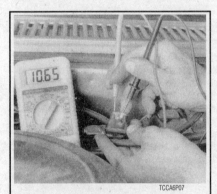

Fig. 9 This voltage drop test revealed high resistance (low voltage) in the circuit

Fig. 10 Checking the resistance of a coolant temperature sensor with an ohmmeter. Reading is 1.04 kilohms

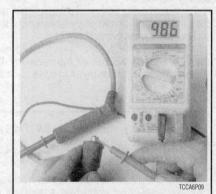

Fig. 11 Spark plug wires can be checked for excessive resistance using an ohmmeter

BATTERY CABLES

Disconnecting the Cables

When working on any electrical component on the vehicle, it is always a good idea to disconnect the negative (-) battery cable. This will prevent potential damage to many sensitive electrical components such as the Engine Control Module (ECM), radio, alternator, etc.

➡**Any time you disengage the battery cables, it is recommended that you disconnect the negative (-) battery cable first. This will prevent you from accidentally grounding the positive (+) terminal to the body of the vehicle when disconnecting it, thereby preventing damage to the previously mentioned components.**

Before you disconnect the cable(s), first turn the ignition to the **OFF** position. This will prevent a draw on the battery which could cause arcing (electricity trying to ground itself to the body of a vehicle, just like a spark jumping the plug gap) and, of course, damaging some components such as the alternator diodes and any electronic control units.

When the battery cable(s) are reconnected (negative cable last), be sure to check that your lights, windshield wipers and other electrically operated safety components are all working correctly. If your vehicle contains an Electronically Tuned Radio (ETR), don't forget to also reset your radio stations. Ditto for the clock.

SUPPLEMENTAL RESTRAINT SYSTEM (AIR BAG)

General Information

▶ **See Figure 12**

The air bag system used on Camrys is referred to as Supplemental Restraint System (SRS). The SRS provides additional protection for the driver, if a forward collision of sufficient force is encountered. The SRS assists the normal seatbelt restraining system by deploying an air bag, via the steering column.

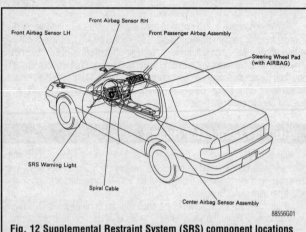

Fig. 12 Supplemental Restraint System (SRS) component locations

The center air bag sensor is the heart of the SRS. It consists of safing sensors, ignition control and drive circuit, diagnosis circuit, etc. The center air bag receives signals from the air bag sensors and determines whether the air bag must be activated or not. The center air bag sensor is also used to diagnose system malfunctions.

The air bag warning light circuit is equipped with an electrical connection check mechanism which detects when the connector to the center air bag sensor assembly is not properly connected.

All connectors in the air bag system are colored yellow. These connectors use gold-plated terminals with twin-lock mechanism. This design assures positive locking; there-by, preventing the terminals from coming apart.

SYSTEM OPERATION

When the ignition switch is turn to the **ON** or **ACC** position, the air bag warning lamp will turned ON for approximately 6 seconds. If no malfunctions are detected in the system, after the 6 second period have elapse, the warning light will go **OFF**.

The safing sensors are designed to go ON at a lower deceleration rate than the front or center air bag sensor. When the vehicle is involved in a frontal collision, the shock is great enough to overcome the predetermine level of the front or center air bag sensor. When a safing sensor and a front air bag sensor and/or the center air bag sensor go ON simultaneously, it causes the squib of the air bag to ignite and the air bag is deployed automatically. The inflated bag breaks open the steering wheel pad.

After air bag deployment have occurred, the gas is discharged through the discharge holes provided behind the bag. The bag become deflated as a result.

The connector of the air bag contains a short spring plate, which provides an activation prevention mechanism. When the connector is disconnected, the short spring plate automatically connects the power source and grounding terminals of the inflator module (squib).

SERVICE PRECAUTIONS

1. Work must be started after 90 seconds from the time the ignition switch is turned to the **LOCK** position and the negative battery cable has been disconnected. The SRS is equipped with a back-up power source so that if work is started within 90 seconds of disconnecting the negative battery cable, the SRS may deploy. When the negative terminal cable is disconnected from the battery, memory of the clock and radio will be canceled. Before you start working, make a note of the contents memorized by the audio memory system. When you have finished working, reset the audio systems and adjust the clock. Never use a back-up power supply from outside the vehicle.

2. In the event that of a minor frontal collision where the air bag does not deploy, the steering wheel pad, front air bag sensors and center air bag sensor assembly should be inspected.

3. Before repairs, remove the air bag sensors if shocks are likely to be applied to the sensors during repairs.

4. Never disassemble and repair the steering wheel pad, front air bag sensors or center air bag sensors.

5. Do not expose the steering wheel pad, front air bag sensors or center air bag sensor assembly directly to flames or hot air.

6. If the steering wheel pad, front air bag sensors or center air bag sensor assembly have been dropped, or there are cracks, dents or other defects in the case, bracket or connectors, have them replaced with new ones.

7. Information labels are attached to the periphery of the SRS components. Follow the instructions of the notices.

8. After arming the system, check for proper operation of the SRS warning light.

9. If the wiring harness in the SRS system is damaged, have the entire harness assembly replaced.

DISARMING THE SYSTEM

Work must be started only after 90 seconds from the time the ignition switch is turned to the **LOCK** position and the negative battery cable has been disconnected. The SRS is equipped with a back-up power source so that if work is started within 90 seconds of disconnecting the negative battery cable, the SRS may deploy. When the negative terminal cable is disconnected from the battery, memory of the clock and radio will be canceled. Before you start working, make a note of the contents memorized by the audio memory system. When you have finished work, reset the audio systems as before and adjust the clock. To avoid erasing the memory of each system, never use a back-up power supply from outside the vehicle.

ARMING THE SYSTEM

Reconnect the negative battery cable and perform the airbag warning light check by turning to the **ON** or **ACC** position, the air bag warning lamp will turned ON for approximately 6 seconds. If no malfunctions are detected in the system, after the 6 second period have elapse, the warning light will go **OFF**.

HEATING AND AIR CONDITIONING

➡️If your vehicle is equipped with air conditioning, refer to Section 1 for information regarding the implications of servicing your A/C system yourself. Only a MVAC-trained, EPA-certified, automotive technician should service the A/C system or its components.

Blower Motor

REMOVAL & INSTALLATION

1983–87 Models

▶ See Figure 13

1. Disconnect the negative battery cable.
2. Remove the parcel tray located under the dash.
3. Remove the two discharge duct bracket mounting screens, and then pull out the two brackets and the duct.
4. Remove the right side forward console cover.
5. Unscrew and remove the relay bracket located under the motor.
6. Disconnect the motor wiring. If equipped, unscrew and remove the A/C amplifier and route the wiring harness out of the way.
7. Remove the three mounting screws, and remove the motor, gasket, and blower assembly. If necessary, remove the blower mounting nut and washers and the separate the unit from the shaft.
8. Installation is the reverse of removal. Secure all components.
9. Cycle the blower through all the speeds to check for proper operation.

1988–91 Models

1. Disconnect the negative battery cable.
2. Remove the 3 screws attaching the retainer.
3. Remove the glove box. Pull out the duct between the blower motor assembly and the heater assembly.
4. Disconnect the blower motor wire in the case.
5. Disconnect the air source selector control cable at the blower motor assembly.
6. Loosen the nuts and bolts attaching the blower motor to the blower case, remove the blower motor from the vehicle.
7. Installation is the reverse of the removal procedure.
8. Check the blower for proper operation at all speeds.

1992–96 Models

▶ See Figures 14 and 15

1. Disconnect the negative battery cable. Wait at least 90 seconds to proceed work due to the SRS system.

✳✳ CAUTION

Some models covered by this manual may be equipped with a Supplemental Restraint System (SRS), which uses an air bag. When-

ever working near any of the SRS components, such as the impact sensors, the air bag module, steering column and instrument panel, disable the SRS, as described in Section 6.

2. Remove the lower instrument panel and the No. 2 panel under the passengers side of the vehicle.
3. Remove the wiring connector bracket.
4. Disconnect the harness attached to the motor, unscrew the motor and extract it from the vehicle.
5. Installation is the reverse of removal.

Heater Core

➡️If your vehicle is equipped with air conditioning, refer to Section 1 for information regarding the implications of servicing your A/C system yourself. Only a MVAC-trained, EPA-certified, automotive technician should service the A/C system or its components.

✳✳ CAUTION

Never open, service or drain the radiator or cooling system when hot; serious burns can occur from the steam and hot coolant. Also, when draining engine coolant, keep in mind that cats and dogs are attracted to ethylene glycol antifreeze and could drink any that is left in an uncovered container or in puddles on the ground. This will prove fatal in sufficient quantities. Always drain coolant into a sealable container. Coolant should be reused unless it is contaminated or is several years old.

REMOVAL & INSTALLATION

1983–91 Models

1. Disconnect the negative battery cable.
2. Position a suitable drain pan under the radiator, and partially drain the cooling system.
3. Remove the console, if so equipped, by removing the shift knob (manual transaxles), wiring connector, and console attaching screws.
4. Remove the carpeting from the tunnel.
5. If equipped, remove the cigarette lighter and ash tray.
6. Remove the package tray, if it makes access to the heater core easier.
7. On some models unscrew and remove the center air outlet.
8. Unscrew the bottom cover/intake assembly and withdraw.
9. Remove the cover from the heater control valve.
10. Unbolt and disconnect the heater control valve.
11. Loosen the hose clamps and disconnect the hoses from the core.
12. Remove the core from its housing.
13. Installation is the reverse of removal. Fill the radiator to the proper level with a good brand of ethylene glycol brand coolant.

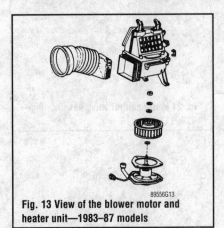

Fig. 13 View of the blower motor and heater unit—1983–87 models

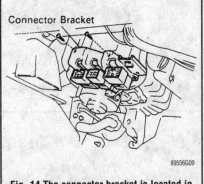

Fig. 14 The connector bracket is located in front of the motor

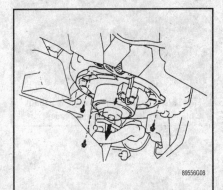

Fig. 15 The blower motor is attached with 3 retaining screws

14. Fill the cooling system to the proper level.
15. Reconnect the battery, then start and warm the engine, making sure that the cooling system stays full.
16. Stop the engine, pressurize the cooling system and check for leaks. Check the heater operation pressurized.

1992–96 Models

▶ See Figures 16, 17 and 18

1. Disconnect the negative battery cable.
2. From under the dash, remove the heater protector from the front of the A/C and heater unit. It is attached by two clips.
3. Unscrew and unclasp the heater core. Disconnect the heater pipes.
4. Pull the core out of the vehicle.
5. Installation is the reverse of removal.

Heater Water Control Valve

REMOVAL & INSTALLATION

▶ See Figures 19, 20 and 21

1. Partially drain the engine coolant from the radiator.
2. Mark and disconnect the cable from the heater control valve.
3. Disconnect the heater hoses from the heater control valve.

➡Be careful not to pull on the heater core tubes when removing the heater hoses, since the heater core can be easily damaged.

4. Remove the bolt and the heater control valve.
5. Installation is the reverse of removal. Fill the cooling system, then start and warm the engine, making sure it stays full.
6. Stop the engine, pressure test the cooling system and check for leaks. Check for proper heater operation.

Air Conditioning Components

REMOVAL & INSTALLATION

Repair or service of air conditioning components is not covered by this manual, because of the risk of personal injury or death, and because of the legal ramifications of servicing these components without the proper EPA certification and experience. Cost, personal injury or death, environmental damage, and legal considerations (such as the fact that it is a federal crime to vent refrigerant into the atmosphere), dictate that the A/C components on your vehicle should be serviced only by a Motor Vehicle Air Conditioning (MVAC) trained, and EPA certified automotive technician.

➡If your vehicle's A/C system uses R-12 refrigerant and is in need of recharging, the A/C system can be converted over to R-134a refrigerant (less environmentally harmful and expensive). Refer to Section 1 for additional information on R-12 to R-134a conversions, and for additional considerations dealing with your vehicle's A/C system.

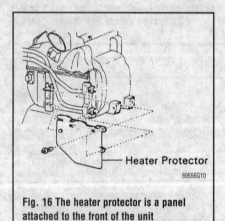

Fig. 16 The heater protector is a panel attached to the front of the unit

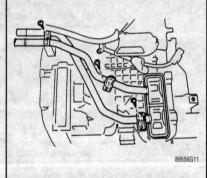

Fig. 17 There are three screws holding the pipe clamps

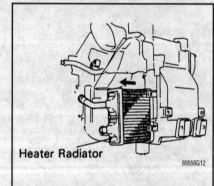

Heater Radiator

Fig. 18 Slide the core out in this direction from the unit

Fig. 19 The heater control valve is usually a plastic box located near the firewall

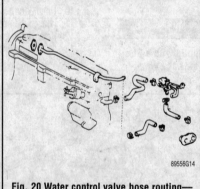

Fig. 20 Water control valve hose routing— 1983–87 models

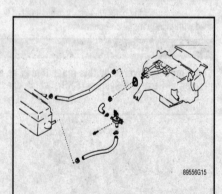

Fig. 21 Water control valve hose routing— 1988–91 models

ENTERTAINMENT SYSTEMS

Radio

REMOVAL & INSTALLATION

▶ See Figures 22, 23, 24 and 25

1. Disconnect the negative battery cable.

✳✳ CAUTION

On models with an airbag, wait at least 90 seconds from the time that the ignition switch is turned to the LOCK position and the battery is disconnected before performing any further work.

2. Remove the attaching screws from the trim panel.
3. Remove the trim panel, being careful of the concealed spring clips behind the panel.
4. Disconnect the wiring from the switches if so equipped mounted in the trim panel.
5. Remove the mounting screws from the radio.
6. Remove the radio from the dash until the wiring connectors are exposed.
7. Disconnect the electrical harness and the antenna cable from the body of the radio and remove the radio from the car.
8. Installation is the reverse of removal. Check radio system for proper operation.

Speakers

REMOVAL & INSTALLATION

Dash Mounted

▶ See Figure 26

1. Make sure that the radio is off.
2. Remove the speaker panel.
3. Remove the instrument panel box (some models).
4. Label and disconnect the speaker wires.
5. Remove the 2 screws and remove the speaker.
6. Installation is the reverse of removal be sure to secure all components.

Door Mounted

▶ See Figures 27, 28, 29 and 30

1. Make sure that the radio is off.
2. On some models the armrest must be removed.
3. If equipped. remove the clip and the screws securing the door pocket and remove the door pocket.
4. Remove the speaker cover usually attached by retaining screws or clips.
5. Remove the inner door panel.
6. Label and disconnect the speaker wires.
Remove the 4 screws and the speaker.
7. Installation is the reverse of removal, secure all components.

Fig. 22 Pry and remove the trim panel around the radio. Unplug the electrical connector

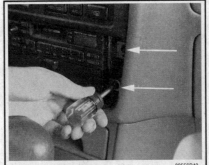

Fig. 23 Remove the upper and lower screws from both sides of the radio brackets

Fig. 24 Extract the radio with brackets and ashtray out of the dash

Fig. 25 Disconnect the wiring harness from the back of the radio, along with the antenna lead

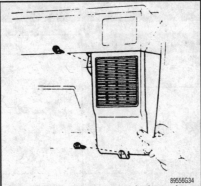

Fig. 26 View of the common dash speaker cover

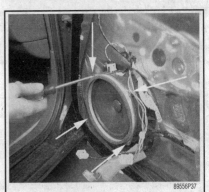

Fig. 27 Remove the four screws to extract the speaker from the door shell

Fig. 28 Extract the speaker and disconnect the wiring

Fig. 29 On some models, there is a tweeter in the door armrest that can be removed

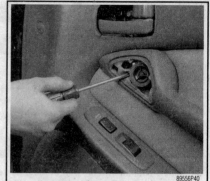

Fig. 30 Remove the screws retaining the speaker to remove it

Trunk Mounted

♦ See Figures 31, 32, 33 and 34

➡On some sedans and liftbacks the rear seat back and bottom must be removed to extract the package tray.

1. Remove the package tray trim (some models).
2. Label and disconnect the speaker wires in the trunk (some models).
3. Remove the screws and the speaker.
4. Installation is the reverse of removal, secure all the components.

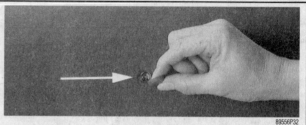

Fig. 31 Remove the caps and screws behind the seat for the rear package tray

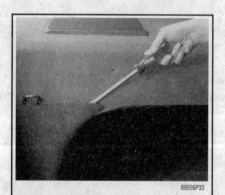

Fig. 32 Pry the side carpeted areas on either side of the package tray area

Fig. 33 Lift the package tray with speaker covers from the vehicle, be careful not to damage the third brake light

Fig. 34 Remove these three screws to extract the speaker from the rear dash

WINDSHIELD WIPERS AND WASHERS

Windshield Wiper Blade and Arm

REMOVAL & INSTALLATION

♦ See Figures 35, 36, 37 and 38

1. To remove the wiper blades, lift up on the spring release tab on the wiper blade-to-wiper arm connector.
2. Pull the blade assembly off the wiper arm.
3. Press the old wiper blade insert down, away from the blade assembly, to free it from the retaining clips on the blade ends. Slide the insert out of the blade. Slide the new insert into the blade assembly and bend the insert upward slightly to engage the retaining clips.

➡Prior to wiper arm removal, it is wise to mark the windshield-to-blade placement with crayon for installation. This will help with blade height.

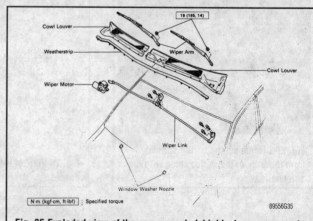

Fig. 35 Exploded view of the common windshield wiper components

Fig. 36 Remove the wiper arm nut

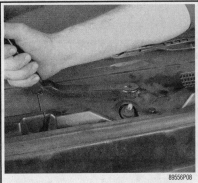

Fig. 37 Prior to arm removal, mark the location of the arm and shaft

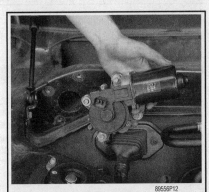

Fig. 38 Lift the arm up and off the linkage shaft

4. To replace a wiper arm, unscrew the acorn nut (a cap covers this retaining nut at the bottom of the wiper arm) which secures it to the pivot and carefully pull the arm upward and off the pivot. Install the arm by placing it on the pivot and tightening the nut to approximately 15 ft. lbs. (20 Nm). Remember that the arm MUST BE reinstalled in its EXACT previous position or it will not cover the correct area during use.

➡If one wiper arm does not move when turned on or only moves a little bit, check the retaining nut at the bottom of the arm. The extra effort of moving wet snow or leaves off the glass can cause the nut to come loose—will turn without moving the arm.

Windshield Wiper Motor

REMOVAL & INSTALLATION

Front

▶ See Figures 39, 40, 41 and 42

1. Disconnect the negative battery cable. Wait at least 90 seconds to work on vehicles equipped with air bags.

✳✳ CAUTION

Some models covered by this manual may be equipped with a Supplemental Restraint System (SRS), which uses an air bag. Whenever working near any of the SRS components, such as the impact sensors, the air bag module, steering column and instrument panel, disable the SRS, as described in Section 6.

2. Using a clip remover, remove the clips and the weatherstrip.
3. Disconnect the wiper motor harness.
4. Remove the cowl louver.
5. Disconnect the wiper link.

6. Remove the 4 bolts and remove the motor.
7. Installation is the reverse of removal. Attach all components and secure.

➡Return the motor to the PARK position before installing by cycling the motor on and off once. Do this before connecting the linkage.

Rear

1. Disconnect the negative battery terminal.
2. Remove the wiper arm and rear door trim cover. Disconnect the wiper motor wiring.
3. Remove the motor attaching bolts and withdraw the wiper motor along with the bracket.
4. Remove the mounting bracket from the old motor and transfer it to the new motor.

To install:

5. Install the wiper motor with bracket and secure.
6. Attach the wiring and install the rear door trim cover and wiper arm.

Fig. 39 Common view of the wiper motor mounted to the right side of the firewall

Fig. 40 Disconnect the wiring from the wiper motor

Fig. 41 Remove the cowl panel from the right side of the vehicle to access the motor linkage

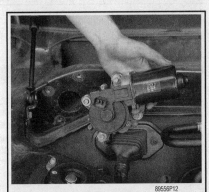

Fig. 42 After prying the motor from the linkage, pull the motor out

7. Connect the negative battery cable and check the motor for proper operation.

Windshield Washer Motor

REMOVAL & INSTALLATION

▶ **See Figures 43, 44, 45 and 46**

The windshield washer reservoir motor (pump) is located in the washer reservoir. The same pump is used for the front and rear washers.
1. Disconnect the negative battery cable.
2. Remove the washer reservoir/motor assembly from the vehicle.
3. Separate the washer fluid motor wiring from the harness.
4. Pull the motor from the rubber grommet retaining it to the washer reservoir.
5. Installation is the reverse of removal. Inspect the rubber grommet for deterioration and replace if necessary. Apply petroleum jelly to the motor before inserting it into the grommet.

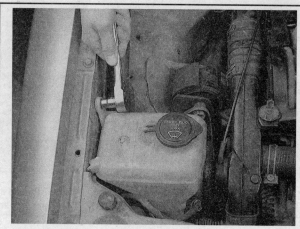
Fig. 43 Unbolt the washer reservoir . . .

Fig. 44 . . . then lift it out to access the wiring and hoses

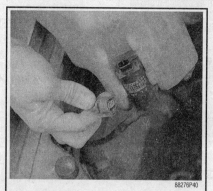
Fig. 45 Separate the wiring at the pump motor

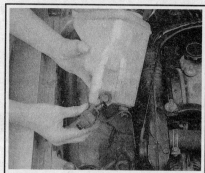
Fig. 46 Pull the motor from the grommet in the reservoir

INSTRUMENTS AND SWITCHES

Instrument Cluster

✴✴ WARNING

When working around a digital or electronic cluster, make sure that the circuitry is not damaged due to static electricity discharge. To lessen the probability of this happening, touch both hands to ground frequently to discharge any static.

REMOVAL & INSTALLATION

▶ **See Figures 47, 48, 49, 50 and 51**

1. Disconnect the negative battery cable. Wait at least 90 seconds for models equipped with an air bag.

✴✴ CAUTION

Some models covered by this manual may be equipped with a Supplemental Restraint System (SRS), which uses an air bag. Whenever working near any of the SRS components, such as the impact sensors, the air bag module, steering column and instrument panel, disable the SRS, as described in Section 6.

2. Remove the fuse box cover from under the left side of the instrument panel.
3. Remove the heater control knobs.
4. Using a screwdriver, carefully pry off the heater control panel.

5. Unscrew the cluster finish panel retaining screws and pull out the bottom of the panel.
6. Remove the combination meter.
7. Unplug all electrical harnesses and unhook the speedometer cable.
8. Installation is the reverse of removal. Secure all components.

Fig. 47 Pull the finish panel and disconnect the wiring harness from the back

Fig. 48 Unscrew the instrument cluster from the dash . . .

Fig. 49 . . . then extract the assembly

Fig. 50 Detach the cluster wiring, you may want to label them prior

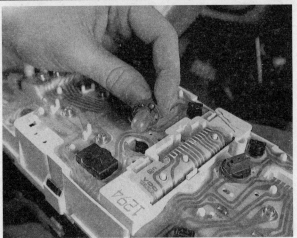

Fig. 51 Remove each bulb individually and inspect for replacement

Speedometer, Tachometer, and Gauges

REMOVAL & INSTALLATION

The gauges on all the models covered here can be replaced in the same basic manner. First, remove the instrument cluster and the front lens. Then, remove the gauge's attaching screws on either the front or the back of the cluster.

When replacing a speedometer or odometer assembly, the law requires the odometer reading of the replacement unit to be set to register the same mileage as the prior odometer. If the mileage cannot be set, the law requires that the replacement be set at zero and a proper label be installed on the drivers door frame to show the previous odometer reading and date of replacement.

Windshield Wiper/Washer Switch

REMOVAL & INSTALLATION

The windshield wiper/washer switch is part of the Combination Switch Assembly. Refer to Turn Signal/Combination Switch services procedures in Section 8 for additional information.

Rear Window Wiper/Washer Switch

REMOVAL & INSTALLATION

1. Disconnect the negative battery cable. Wait at least 90 seconds to perform work on models equipped with an air bag.

✳✳ CAUTION

Some models covered by this manual may be equipped with a Supplemental Restraint System (SRS), which uses an air bag. Whenever working near any of the SRS components, such as the impact sensors, the air bag module, steering column and instrument panel, disable the SRS, as described in Section 6.

2. From under the dash, disconnect wiring from the switch assembly.
3. Pull the switch from the panel.
4. Installation is the reverse of removal. Check system for proper operation.

Headlight Switch

REMOVAL & INSTALLATION

The headlight switch is part of the Combination Switch Assembly. Refer to Turn Signal/Combination Switch services procedures in Section 8 for additional information.

Dash-Mounted Switches

REMOVAL & INSTALLATION

✳✳ CAUTION

On models equipped with a Supplemental Restraint System (SRS) or "air bag," work must NOT be started until at least 90 seconds have passed from the time that both the ignition switch is turned to the LOCK position and the negative cable is disconnected from the battery.

Most dash-mounted switches can be removed using the same basic procedure. Remove the trim panel which the switch is secured to. Trim panels are usually secured by a series of screws and/or clips. Make sure you remove all attaching screws before attempting to pull on the panel. Do not use excessive force as trim panels are easily damaged. Once the trim panel has been removed, unplug the switch connector, then remove its retaining screws or pry it from the mounting clip. Always disconnect the negative battery cable first.

Horn

REMOVAL & INSTALLATION

♦ **See Figure 52**

The horn is located behind the grille. Remove the grille retaining bolts to access. Unbolt the one screw holding the horn assembly to the bracket.

Fig. 52 Remove the one bolt retaining the horn to the bracket

LIGHTING

Headlights

♦ **See Figure 53**

REMOVAL & INSTALLATION

Sealed Beam

♦ **See Figures 54 and 55**

➥**Before making a headlight replacement, make sure that the headlight switch is in the off position.**

1. Loosen the screws, release the clips and remove the headlight door. To release the clips, insert a flat blade screwdriver into the jaws of the clip and pry on the jaws.
2. Remove the beam unit retaining ring screws and remove the beam unit.
3. Compress the lock releases and disconnect the wire connector from the headlight. If the connector is tight, wiggle it while holding in the lock releases and pulling out.

➥**Never try to loosen the aim adjusting screws. If the screws are loosened, the headlights will have to be re-aimed by a qualified technician.**

4. When installing, use only a sealed beam unit with the same part number and wattage.

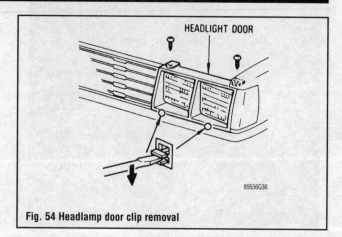

Fig. 54 Headlamp door clip removal

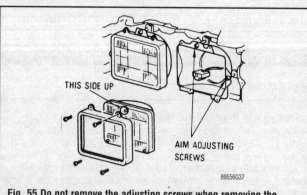

Fig. 55 Do not remove the adjusting screws when removing the head lamp sealed bulb

Composite

♦ **See Figures 56, 57 and 58**

➥**This procedure only applies to replaceable halogen headlight bulbs (such as Nos. 9004 and 9005); it does not pertain to sealed beam units.**

1. Open the vehicle's hood and secure it in an upright position.
2. Unfasten the locking ring which secures the bulb and socket assembly, then withdraw the assembly rearward.
3. If necessary, gently pry the socket's retaining clip over the projection on the bulb (use care not to break the clip.) Pull the bulb from the socket.

To install:

4. Before installing a light bulb into the socket, ensure that all electrical contact surfaces are free of corrosion or dirt.

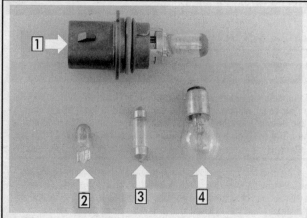

1. Halogen headlight bulb
2. Side marker light bulb
3. Dome light bulb
4. Turn signal/brake light bulb

Fig. 53 Examples of various types of automotive light bulbs

Fig. 56 Headlight bulbs are inside the sockets located in the engine compartment

Fig. 57 Detach the wiring from the back of the headlamp bulb

Fig. 58 Twist and pull the bulb out, but do not touch the bulb if it is still good

5. Line up the replacement headlight bulb with the socket. Firmly push the bulb onto the socket until the spring clip latches over the bulb's projection.

✳✳ WARNING

Do not touch the glass bulb with your fingers. Oil from your fingers can severely shorten the life of the bulb. If necessary, wipe off any dirt or oil from the bulb with rubbing alcohol before completing installation.

6. To ensure that the replacement bulb functions properly, activate the applicable switch to illuminate the bulb which was just replaced. (If this is a combination low and high beam bulb, be sure to check both intensities.) If the replacement light bulb does not illuminate, either it too is faulty or there is a problem in the bulb circuit or switch. Correct if necessary.

7. Position the headlight bulb and secure it with the locking ring.
8. Close the vehicle's hood.

Signal and Marker Lights

REMOVAL & INSTALLATION

Front Turn Signal and Parking Lights

◆ See Figures 59 thru 67

1. On some models you simply remove the lens screws or nuts and withdraw the assembly.
2. On others, remove the parking light cover clips to gain access to the parking light lens screws, if replacing that bulb.

Fig. 59 There is only one screw retaining the lamp into the bezel—1992–96 models

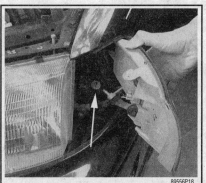

Fig. 60 Pull the parking lamp towards the front of the car to detach it from the socket

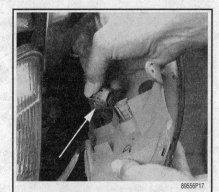

Fig. 61 Remove the wiring from the back of the parking lamp

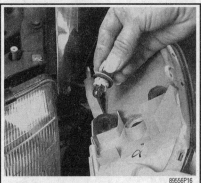

Fig. 62 Twist and remove the bulb from the parking lamp—1992–96 models

Fig. 63 On the front turnsignals, remove the one screw . . .

Fig. 64 . . then pull the lamp out and separate the harness from the bulb socket

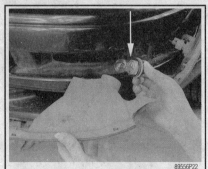

Fig. 65 All of the marker and signal lamps in the front have twist and remove bulb type sockets

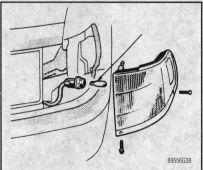

Fig. 66 Remove the retaining screws on the parking lamp and withdraw it—1983–91 models

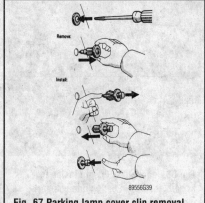

Fig. 67 Parking lamp cover clip removal

3. Remove the lens screws and the parking light lens or the turn signal lens.

4. Pull the bulb straight out of the socket for parking lights, and push in and turn to remove the turn signal bulb. Installation is the reverse of removal.

Rear Side Marker Lights

▶ See Figure 68

➡ On some models the side marker is part of the rear tail lamp assembly.

1. Unscrew the lamp from the outside of the car, then disconnect the wiring and withdraw the unit.

➡ On some models such as the 1986 sedan and all hatchbacks, you gain access to the bulb socket from the luggage compartment inside the vehicle.

2. Twist the socket and pull out from the inner lens housing.

3. Pull the bulb straight out of the socket. Installation is the reverse of removal.

Rear Turn Signal, Brake and Parking Lights

▶ See Figures 69, 70, 71 and 72

1. From the outside of the vehicle, remove the screws retaining the lamp housing to the body.

2. Remove the access cover in the luggage compartment.

3. Disconnect the wiring from the back of the lamp.

4. To replace the bulb, push in and rotate. Inspect the bulb and replace if necessary.

To install:

5. Position the lens to the body of the vehicle and secure with the screws.

6. Attach the wiring to the back of the lamp.

7. Install the access cover and secure.

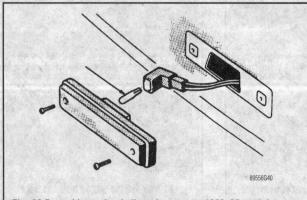

Fig. 68 Rear side marker bulb replacement—1983–85 models

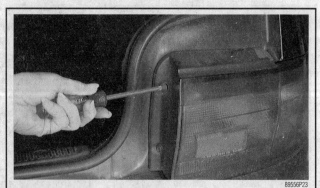

Fig. 69 To replace a bulb on the rear brake lamps, unscrew the housing from the outside—1994 sedan

Fig. 70 Pull the lamp assembly out . . .

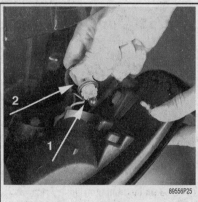

Fig. 71 View of the bulb (1) and socket (2)

Fig. 72 Slightly twist and pull the bulb out of the socket to replace

High-mount Brake Light

♦ See Figures 73 thru 79

1. Gently remove the lens with a suitable prying tool or remove the stop light cover screws and extract the cover.

➡Some models are equipped with clips to retain the cover. If this is the case, make sure new ones are obtained prior to removal, they often break during removal.

2. If equipped with a metal cover, remove to access the bulb.
3. Push in and rotate the bulb and remove on some models or just pull the bulb straight out. Installation is the reverse of removal.

Dome Light

♦ See Figures 80, 81 and 82

❊❊ CAUTION

Make sure that the dome light switch is off and that the doors are shut. Also, wear eye protection to avoid eye injury in case of broken glass.

Gently remove the lens with a suitable prying tool from the roof panel. Extract the bulb from the socket carefully. Insert a new bulb and snap the lens back into position.

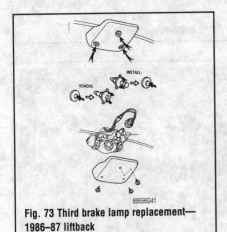

Fig. 73 Third brake lamp replacement— 1986–87 liftback

Fig. 74 On some third brake lights, carefully pry the lamp housing cover up

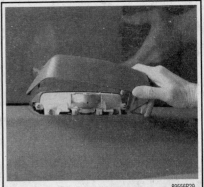

Fig. 75 Lift the cover off to access the lens and bulb

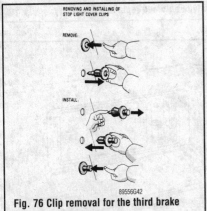

Fig. 76 Clip removal for the third brake lamp on most models

Fig. 77 Carefully remove the metal cover with a suitable pry tool

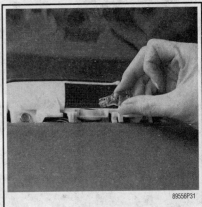

Fig. 78 Twist, remove and inspect the bulb

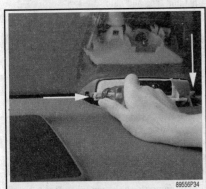

Fig. 79 Separate the housing from the body of the brake lamp

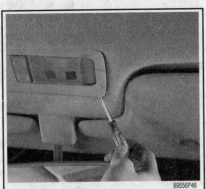

Fig. 80 Carefully pry the lens cover from the roof panel

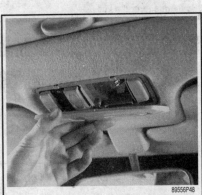

Fig. 81 Pull the lens and switch assembly off

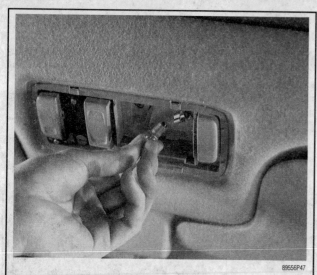

Fig. 82 Extract the bulb from the dome lamp housing

Cargo and Passenger Area Lamps

▶ See Figures 83, 84, 85 and 86

Twist, unscrew or gently remove the lens with a suitable prying tool. Extract the bulb from the socket. Reverse the removal procedure to install.

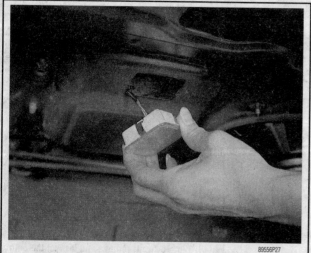

Fig. 83 Carefully pry out the lamp assembly from the cargo area to separate form the body

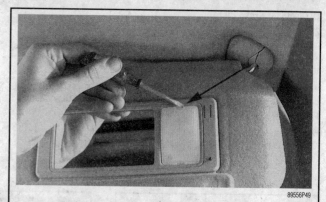

Fig. 84 Carefully pry at the notch in the lens to remove

Fig. 85 Extract the fuse type bulb and replace if necessary

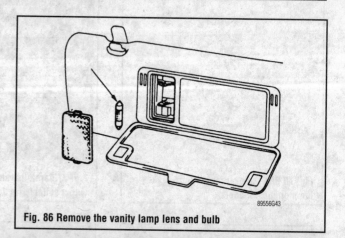

Fig. 86 Remove the vanity lamp lens and bulb

CIRCUIT PROTECTION

Fuses and Relays

There are several fuse blocks. They are located in the engine compartment, behind the right side kick panel, under the instrument panel or behind the left side kick panel.

REPLACEMENT

▶ See Figures 87 thru 93

If any light or electrical component in the vehicle does not work, its fuse may be blown. To determine the fuse that is the source of the problem, look on the lid of the fuse box as it will give the name and the circuit serviced by each fuse. To inspect a suspected blown fuse, pull the fuse straight out with the pull-out tool and look at the fuse carefully. If the thin wire that bridges the fuse terminals is broken, the fuse is bad and must be replaced. On a good fuse, the wire will be intact.

Sometimes it is difficult to make an accurate determination. If this is the case, try replacing the fuse with one that you know is good. If the fuse blows repeatedly, then this suggests that a short circuit lies somewhere in the electrical system and you should have the system checked.

✳✳ CAUTION

When making emergency replacements, only use fuses that have an equal or lower amperage rating than the one that is blown, to avoid damage and fire.

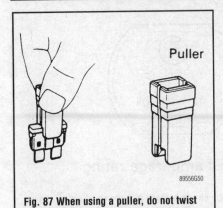

Fig. 87 When using a puller, do not twist or turn the fuse to remove

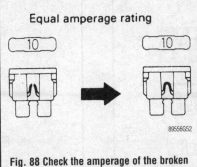

Fig. 88 Check the amperage of the broken fuse and only replace it with a new one of the same

Fig. 89 Once the cover is removed from the fuse box, you can identify each fuse and relay

Fig. 90 All circuit breakers and fuses pull out quick easily

Fig. 91 Another fuse block is located in the drivers side knee bolster behind a coin box—1994–96 models

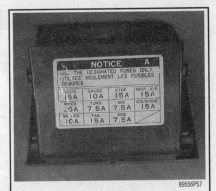

Fig. 92 On the back of the coin box on some models is a fuse listing

Fig. 93 Relays can be removed by pulling them from the block

When installing a new fuse, use one with the same amperage rating as the one being replaced. To install the a new fuse, first turn off all the electrical components and the ignition switch. Always use the fuse pull-out tool and install the fuse straight. Twisting of the fuse could cause the terminals to separate too much which may result in a bad connection. It may be a good idea to purchase some extra fuses and put them in the box in case of an emergency.

Fusible Links

In case of an overload in the circuits from the battery, the fusible links are designed to melt before damage to the engine wiring harness occurs. Headlight and other electrical component failure usually requires checking the fusible links for melting. Fusible links are located in the engine compartment next to the battery.

REPLACEMENT

▶ See Figures 94 and 95

The fusible link is replaced in a similar manner as the regular fuse, but a removal tool is not required.

✳✳ CAUTION

Never install a wire in place of a fusible link. Extensive damage and fire may occur.

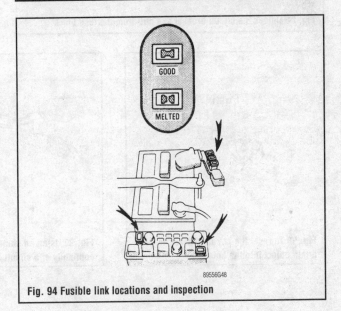

Fig. 94 Fusible link locations and inspection

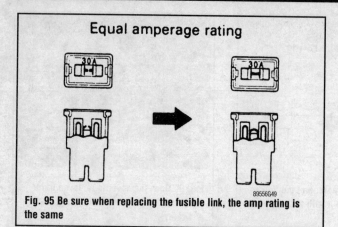

Equal amperage rating

Fig. 95 Be sure when replacing the fusible link, the amp rating is the same

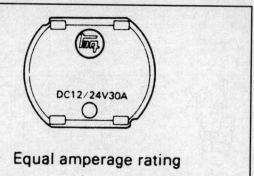

DC12/24V30A

Equal amperage rating

Fig. 97 Only replace the circuit breaker with the same amperage as the old

Circuit Breakers

In the event the rear window defogger, environmental control system, power windows, power door locks, power tail gate lock, sunroof or automatic shoulder belt does not work, check its circuit breaker. Circuit breakers are located in the passenger's or driver's side kick panel with the fuses.

REPLACEMENT

▶ **See Figures 96 and 97**

1. Turn the ignition switch to the **OFF** position.
2. Disconnect the negative battery cable. Wait at least 90 seconds before working on models with SRS system.

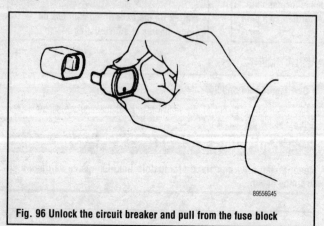

Fig. 96 Unlock the circuit breaker and pull from the fuse block

3. Remove the circuit breaker by unlocking its stopper and pulling it from its socket.

To install:

4. Carefully snap the breaker into place and be sure to secure.

➡**Always use a new circuit breaker with the same amperage as the old one. If the circuit breaker immediately trips or the component does not operate, the electrical system must be checked.**

5. Connect the negative battery cable.

RESETTING

▶ **See Figures 98 and 99**

1. Insert a thin object into the reset hole and push until a click is heard.
2. Using an ohmmeter, check that there is continuity between both terminals of the circuit breaker. If continuity is not as specified, replace the circuit breaker.

Flashers

REPLACEMENT

▶ **See Figure 100**

Locate the flasher and pull it from its socket. Most should pull directly out, if not check for clips on the side of the unit, release, then pull. Install a new one and check its operation. For example the location on 1992 models is position "C" in relay block 6.

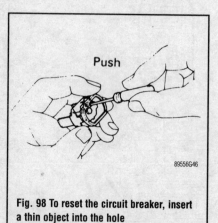

Push

Fig. 98 To reset the circuit breaker, insert a thin object into the hole

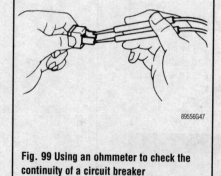

Fig. 99 Using an ohmmeter to check the continuity of a circuit breaker

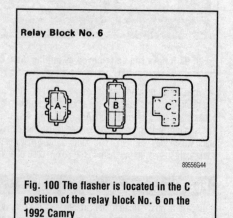

Relay Block No. 6

A B C

Fig. 100 The flasher is located in the C position of the relay block No. 6 on the 1992 Camry

WIRING DIAGRAMS

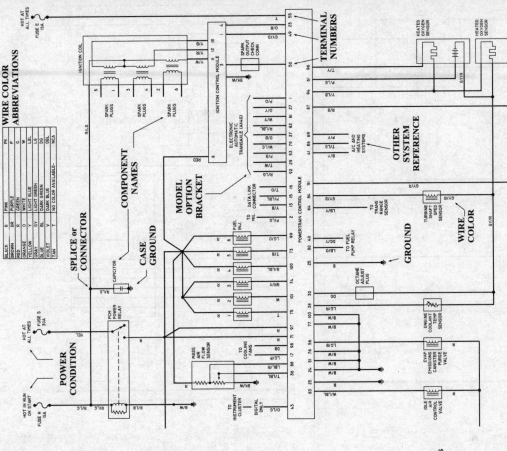

SAMPLE DIAGRAM: HOW TO READ & INTERPRET WIRING DIAGRAMS

DIAGRAM 1

INDEX OF WIRING DIAGRAMS

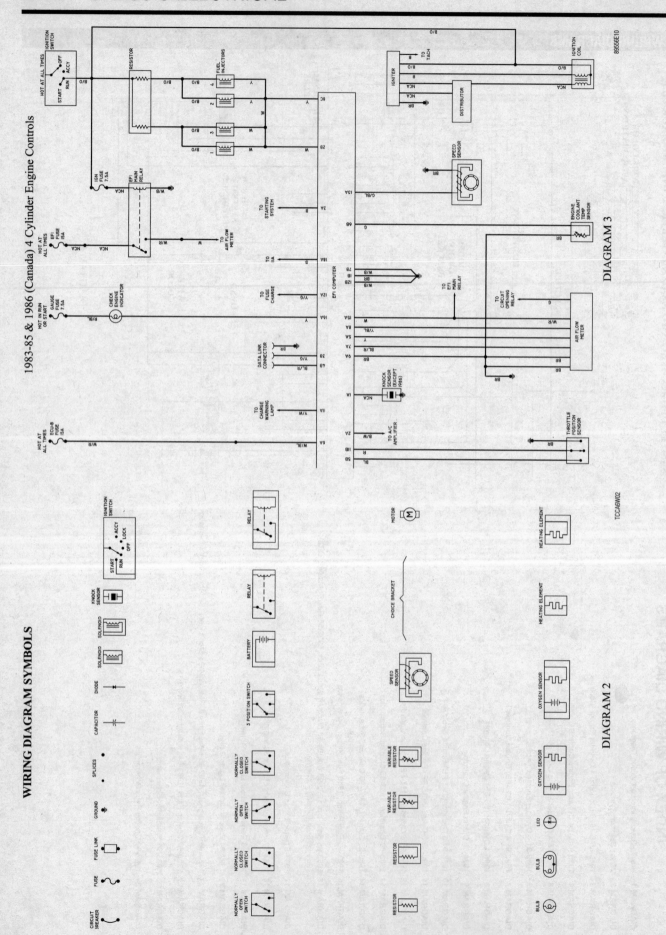

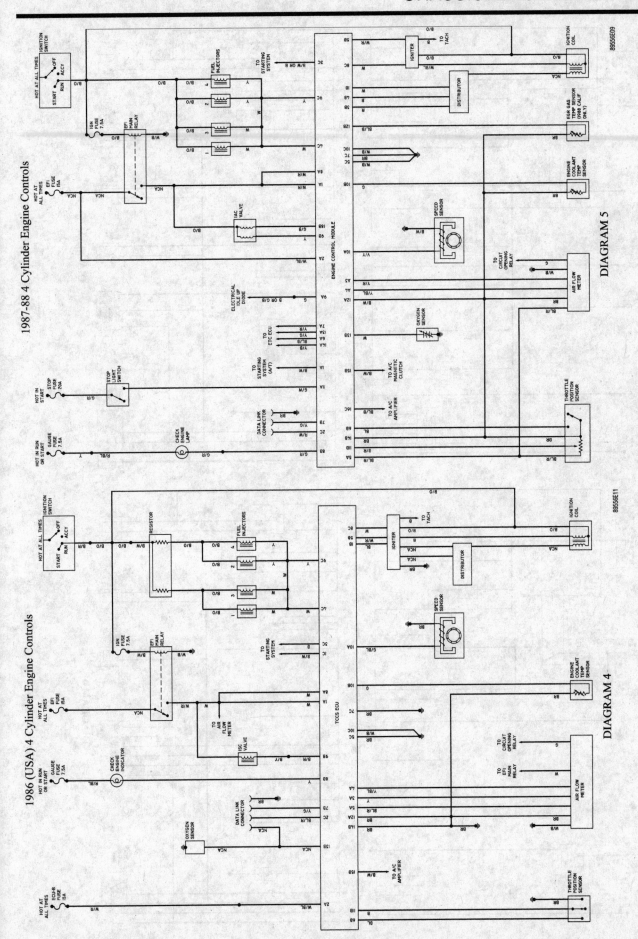

1987-88 4 Cylinder Engine Controls

DIAGRAM 5

1986 (USA) 4 Cylinder Engine Controls

DIAGRAM 4

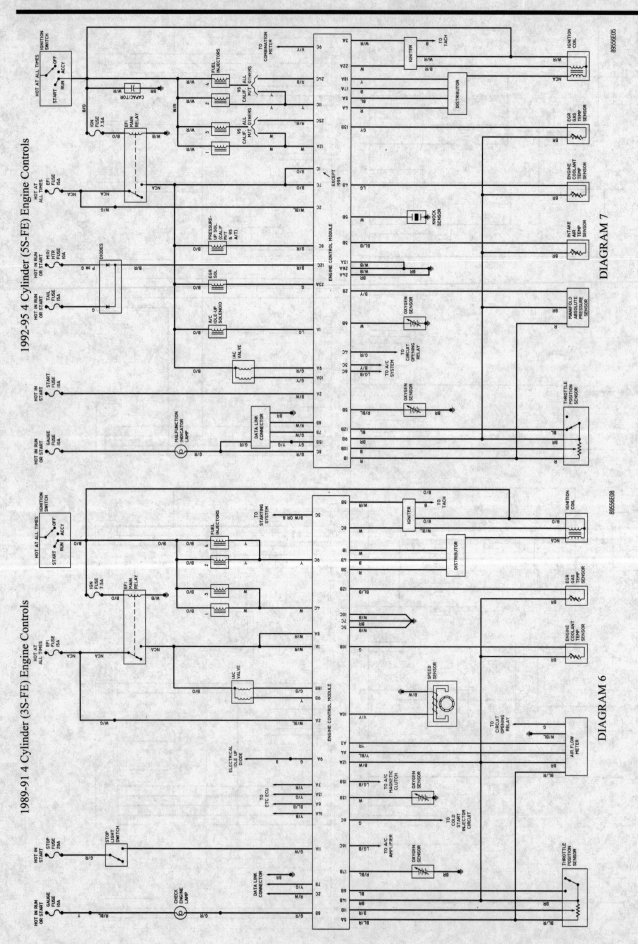

1992-95 4 Cylinder (5S-FE) Engine Controls

DIAGRAM 7

1989-91 4 Cylinder (3S-FE) Engine Controls

DIAGRAM 6

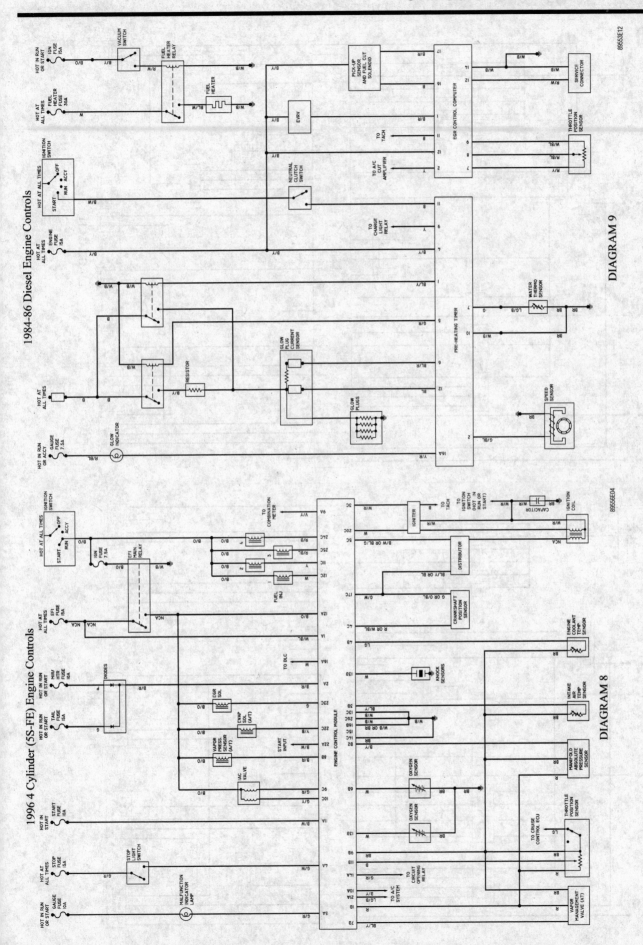

1984-86 Diesel Engine Controls

1996 4 Cylinder (5S-FE) Engine Controls

DIAGRAM 9

DIAGRAM 8

89553E12

89556E04

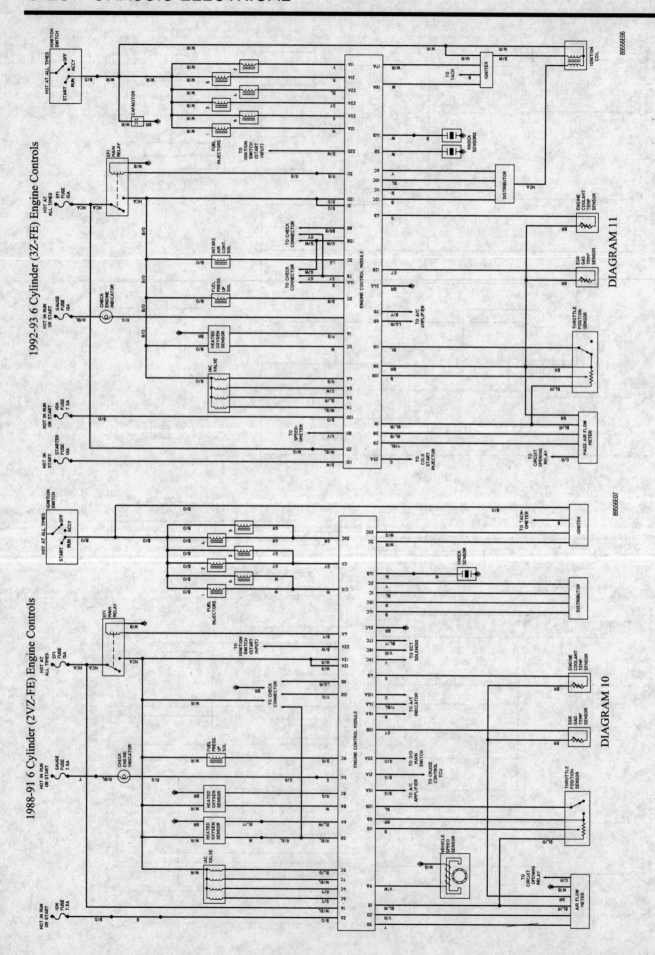

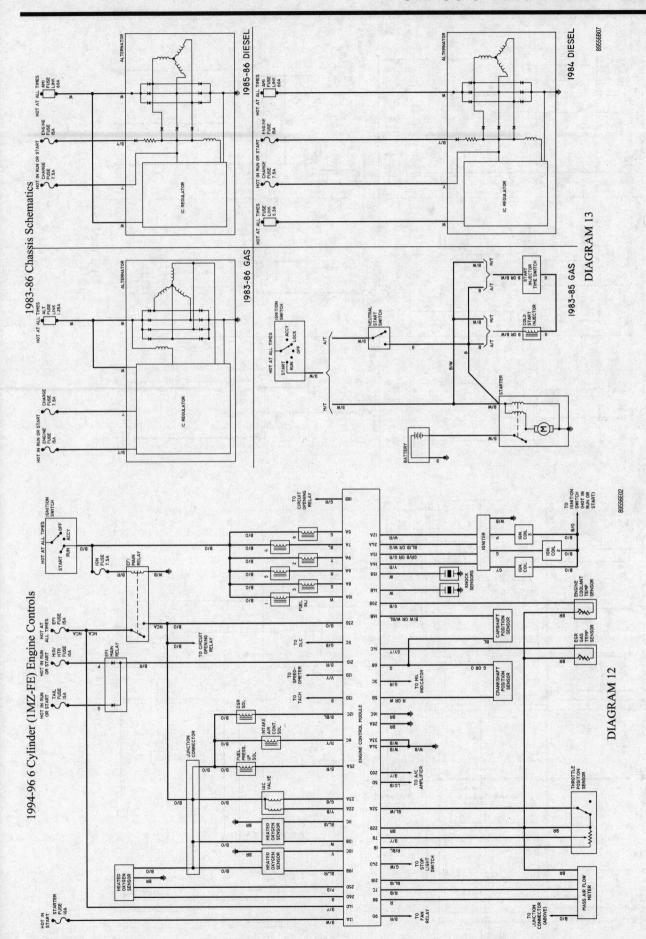

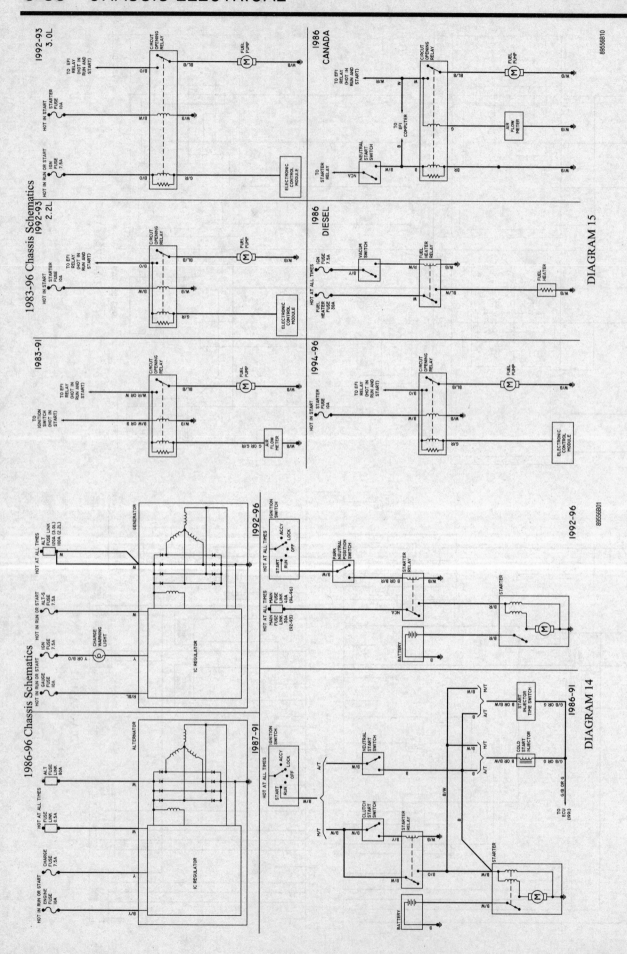

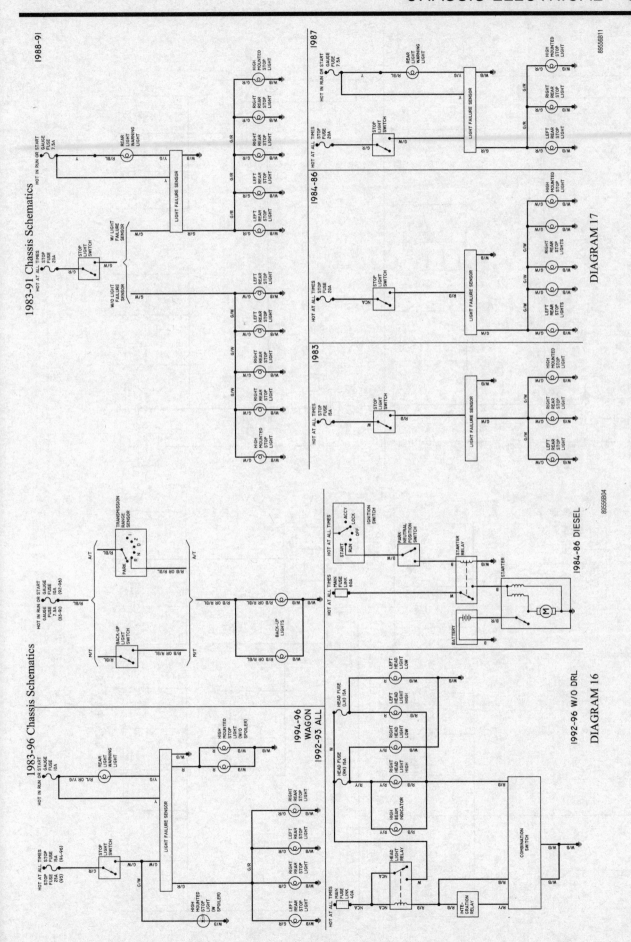

1988-91

1983-91 Chassis Schematics

1983-96 Chassis Schematics

1987

1984-86

1983

1984-86 DIESEL

1994-96 WAGON
1992-93 ALL

1992-96 W/O DRL

DIAGRAM 17

DIAGRAM 16

89556B11

89556B04

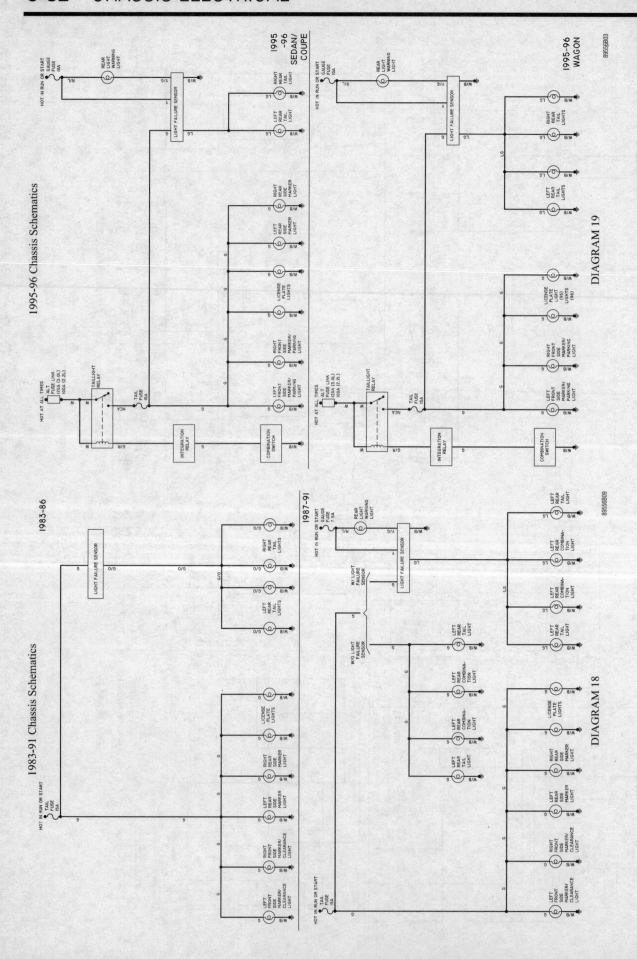

1995-96 Chassis Schematics

1983-91 Chassis Schematics

DIAGRAM 19

DIAGRAM 18

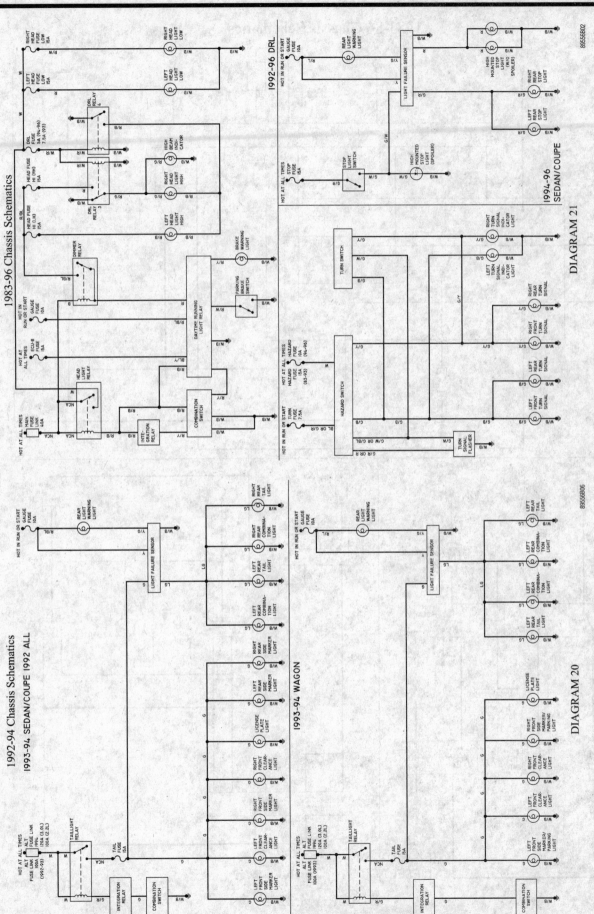

1983-96 Chassis Schematics

1992-94 Chassis Schematics
1993-94 SEDAN/COUPE 1992 ALL

1992-96 DRL

1994-96 SEDAN/COUPE

DIAGRAM 21

1993-94 WAGON

DIAGRAM 20

1983-86 Chassis Schematics

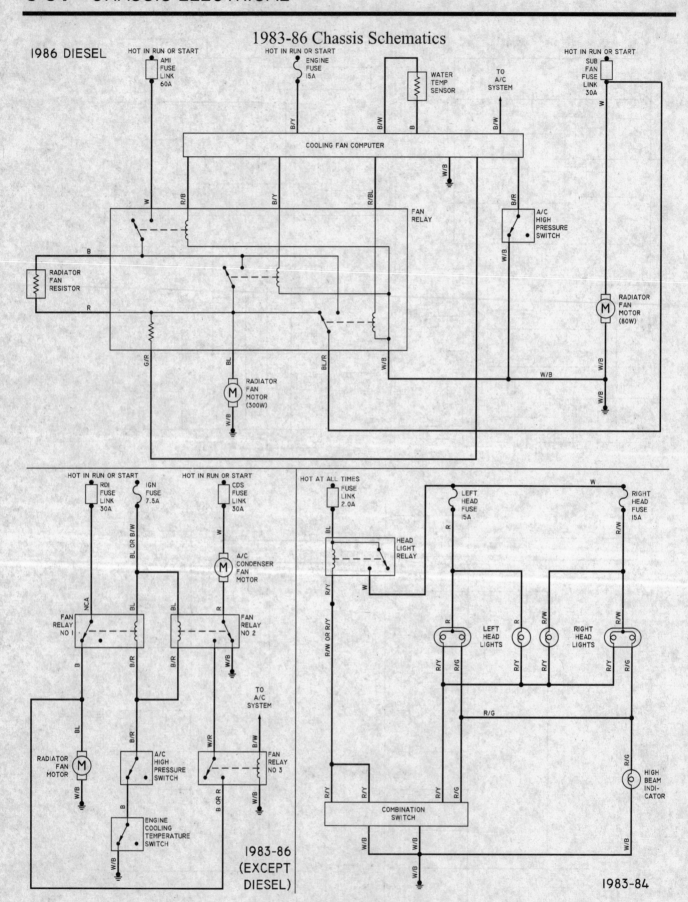

1983-86 (EXCEPT DIESEL)

1983-84

DIAGRAM 22

89556B12

1985-91 Chassis Schematics

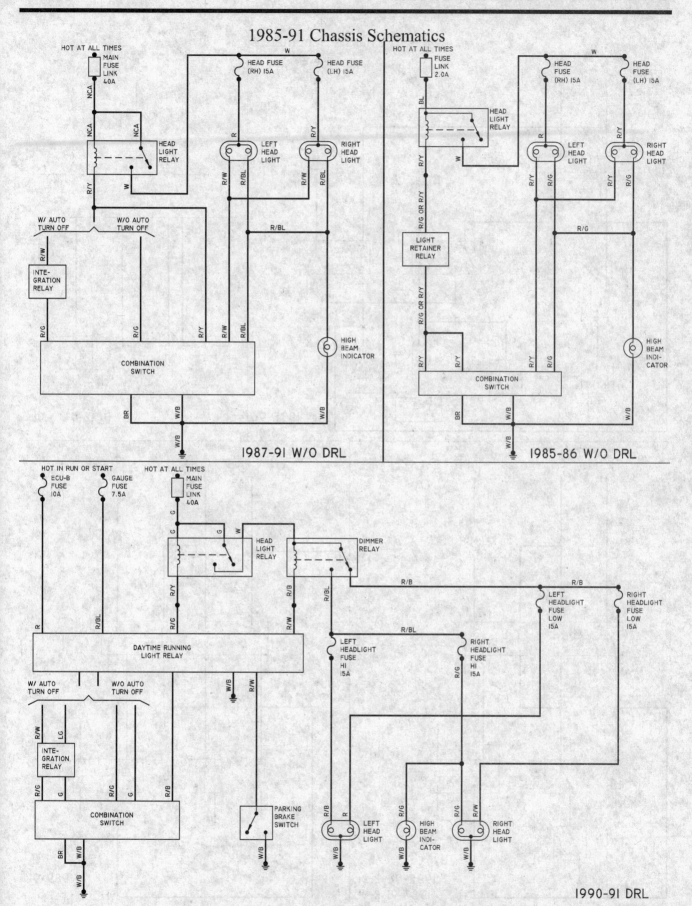

1987-91 W/O DRL

1985-86 W/O DRL

1990-91 DRL

DIAGRAM 23

89556B08

1987-96 Chassis Schematics

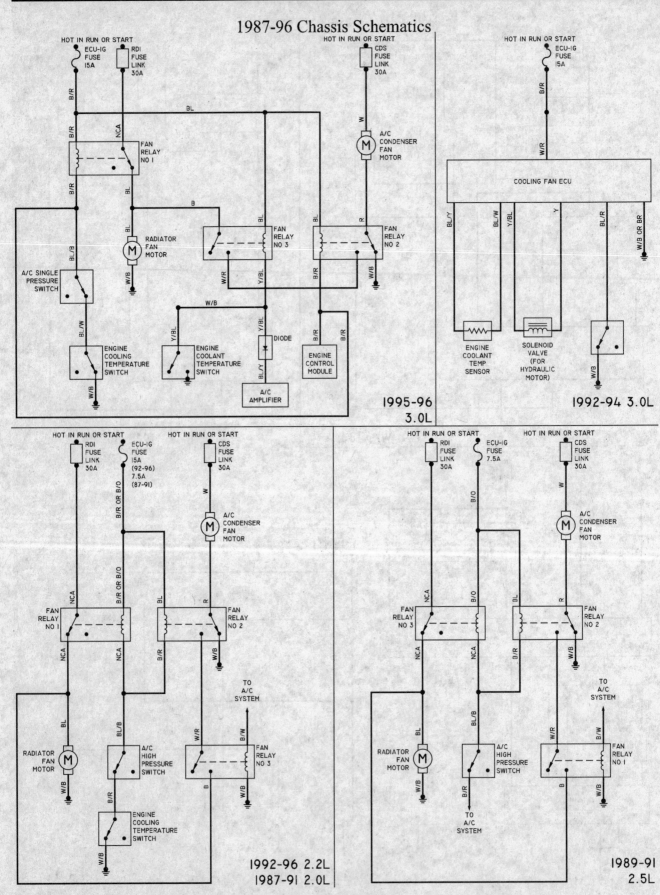

1995-96
3.0L

1992-94 3.0L

1992-96 2.2L
1987-91 2.0L

1989-91
2.5L

DIAGRAM 24

89556B05

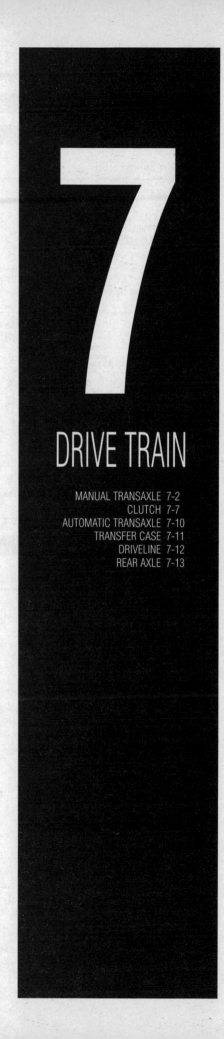

7

DRIVE TRAIN

MANUAL TRANSAXLE

Back-up Light Switch

REMOVAL & INSTALLATION

▶ **See Figure 1**

1. Disconnect the electrical harness from the back-up switch, which is mounted on the transaxle case.
2. Remove the ground strap.
3. Loosen and remove the back-up light switch from the transaxle case.
4. Remove the gasket. Discard the gasket and purchase a new one.
5. Installation is the reverse of removal. Secure the switch and gasket into the transaxle case and tighten to 30 ft. lbs. (40 Nm).

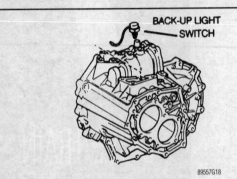

BACK-UP LIGHT SWITCH

89557G18

Fig. 1 The back-up light switch is located on the top of the manual transaxle

Manual Transaxle Assembly

REMOVAL & INSTALLATION

Except 4WD

1. Disconnect the negative battery cable.
2. Remove the air cleaner assembly for added working room.
3. On some models it may be necessary to remove the cruise control actuator.
4. Remove the clutch release cylinder and tube clamp and the cruise control actuator, if equipped.
5. Remove the retainer from the clutch tube bracket and unbolt and remove the bracket.
6. Remove the clips and washers that attach the transaxle control cables to the control levers. Remove the retaining clips and disconnect the transaxle control cables.
7. Remove the starter.
8. Disconnect the back-up light switch harness and ground strap.
9. Remove the upper transaxle mounting bolts.
10. Remove the front wheels.
11. Raise the vehicle and support it safely.
12. Remove the under covers.
13. Drain the fluid from the transaxle.
14. Disconnect the speedometer cable or sensor harness.
15. Remove the lower suspension crossmember.
16. Remove the front and rear engine mounting bolts and remove the engine mounting center member.
17. Have an assistant depress the brake pedal. Loosen the six mounting bolts and disconnect both driveshafts.
18. Remove the snapring from the center driveshaft bearing bracket. Remove the bearing bracket bolt and pull out the center driveshaft through the center bearing bracket. Discard the bolt and purchase a new one.
19. Disconnect the left steering knuckle from the lower arm. Pull the steering knuckle outward and remove the driveshaft.

20. On some models it may be necessary to remove the stabilizer bar.
21. On 1992–96 models, disconnect the steering gear housing from the front suspension member and disconnect the exhaust.
22. With a transaxle jack and block of wood, raise the transaxle and engine slightly and disconnect the left engine mounting.
23. Remove the transaxle mounting bolts from the engine.
24. Lower the left side of the engine and remove the transaxle. On 1992–96 models, remove the remaining components from the front suspension member and remove it. Then remove the transaxle as described.
Clean the mating surfaces of grease and dirt in preparation for reinstallation.
To install:
25. Move the transaxle into position so that the input shaft spline is aligned with the clutch disc.
26. Install the transaxle into the engine and secure with the lower mounting bolts. Install the remaining mounting bolts. On the 1983–86 models tighten the 10mm bolts to 29 ft. lbs. (39 Nm) and the 12mm bolts to 47 ft. lbs. (64 Nm). On 1987–92 models tighten the 10mm mounting bolts to 34 ft. lbs. (46 Nm) and 12mm bolts to 47 ft. lbs. (64 Nm). On the 1993–96 models, tighten bolt A to 47 ft. lbs. (64 Nm)., bolt B to 34 ft. lbs. (46 Nm) and bolt C to 18 ft. lbs. (25 Nm).
27. Connect the left engine mounting and tighten the mounting bolts to specifications. On 1992–96 models, install the front suspension member and other components related to it and tighten to specifications.
28. Install all the remaining components in the reverse order of removal. Tighten all components to specifications.
29. Fill the transaxle with the correct type and amount of fluid.
30. Connect the negative battery cable, the air cleaner and the cruise control actuator, if removed.
31. Check the front wheel alignment.
32. Perform a road test and check for any unusual noises or vibrations.

4WD Models

▶ **See Figures 2 and 3**

➡ **The transaxle on the All-Trac 4-Wheel Drive models is removed with the engine. For engine removal and installation procedures refer to Section 3.**

The cylinder block rib on these model engines contacts the transfer case. When disconnecting the transaxle from the engine the following points must be observed.

- After the engine has been secured to a suitable engine holding fixture, pull the transaxle straight out until there is approximately 50–75mm clearance between the engine and the transaxle case.
- Move the transmission case cover in the proper direction (follow directional arrow on the illustration).
- Support the transfer output shaft and pull out the entire transaxle assembly.
- Tighten the 12mm transaxle-to-engine mounting bolts to 47 ft. lbs. (64 Nm) and the 10mm bolts to 34 ft. lbs. (46 Nm).

Halfshafts

REMOVAL & INSTALLATION

▶ **See Figures 4 thru 13 (pg 3–5)**

1. Raise the front of the vehicle and support it safely.
2. Remove the front wheels.
3. Remove the cotter pin and locknut cap.
4. Have an assistant depress the brake pedal and loosen the bearing locknut.
5. Remove the engine under cover.
6. Remove the fender apron seal.
7. Disconnect the tie rod end from the steering knuckle.
8. On the slide out driveshafts proceed with the following:
   a. Disconnect the steering knuckle from the lower control arm.
   b. Use a plastic hammer and carefully tap the outer end of the halfshaft until it frees itself from the axle hub.

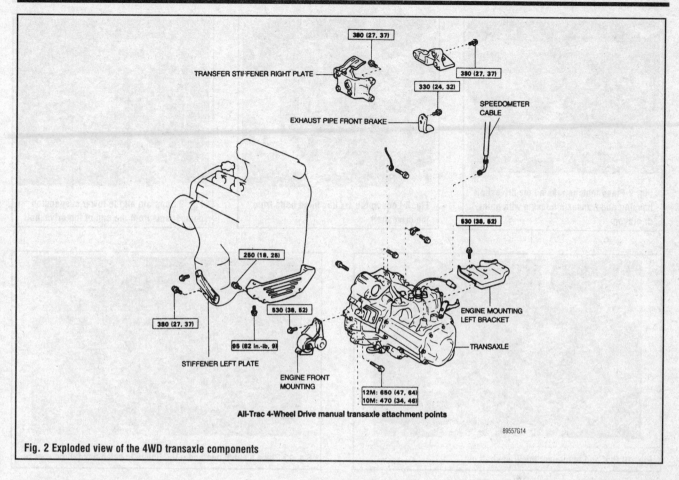

TRANSFER STIFFENER RIGHT PLATE

380 (27, 37)

380 (27, 37)

330 (24, 32)

EXHAUST PIPE FRONT BRAKE

SPEEDOMETER CABLE

530 (38, 52)

250 (18, 26)

530 (38, 52)

ENGINE MOUNTING LEFT BRACKET

380 (27, 37)

95 (82 in.-lb, 9)

TRANSAXLE

STIFFENER LEFT PLATE

ENGINE FRONT MOUNTING

12M: 650 (47, 64)
10M: 470 (34, 46)

All-Trac 4-Wheel Drive manual transaxle attachment points

89557G14

Fig. 2 Exploded view of the 4WD transaxle components

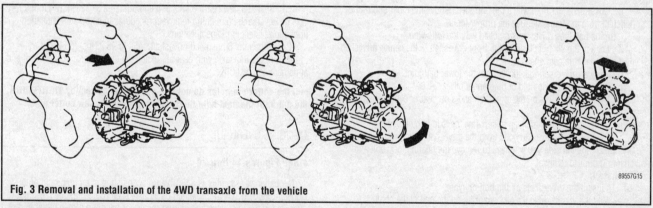

89557G15

Fig. 3 Removal and installation of the 4WD transaxle from the vehicle

89557P03

Fig. 4 Remove the locknut cap and cotter pin, make sure you discard the old cotter pin

89557P04

Fig. 5 Use a large breaker bar to loosen the axle hub nut

89557P05

Fig. 6 Inspect the threads of the nut and shaft

Fig. 7 Place matchmarks on the driveshaft housing and transaxle housing with paint or crayon

Fig. 8 Loosen the six hex head bolts from the driveshaft

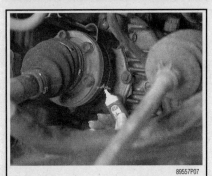

Fig. 9 Separate all the lower suspension components from the end of the driveshaft

Fig. 10 Pull and maneuver the driveshaft out

Fig. 11 Place a catch pan under the flange to catch any falling grease

c. Cover the outer boot with a rag and then remove the inner end of the halfshaft from the transaxle. Use the proper tools.

9. On the bolt type driveshafts proceed with the following:

a. Loosen the six nuts holding the front driveshaft to the center driveshaft or differential side gear shaft.

b. Separate the steering knuckle from the lower ball joint.

c. Drain the transaxle fluid or differential oil.

d. Place matchmarks on the driveshaft and side gear or center shaft using paint.

e. With a plastic hammer, tap to separate the axle hub and cover.

f. Remove the 6 hex head bolts from the driveshaft, then pry the assembly out. On the left side you will have to remove the bearing lock bolt and snapring prior to removal.

To install:

10. To install the driveshafts on the bolt on type:

a. On the left side, install a new snapring on the end of the shaft.

b. Coat gear oil to the side gear shaft and differential case sliding surface.

c. Using a brass bar and hammer, tap in the driveshaft until it makes contact with the pinion shaft.

➡Before installing the driveshaft, set the snapring opening side facing downward. Whether or not the side gear shaft is making contact with the pinion shaft can be known by the sound or feeling when driving it inward.

d. Check that there is 0.08–0.12 inch (2–3mm) of play in the axial direction and check that the driveshaft will not come out by trying to pull it completely out by hand.

e. Hand tighten the 6 hex driveshaft bolts.

f. On the right side, coat gear oil to the side gear shaft and differential case sliding surface.

g. Install the driveshaft to the transaxle through the bearing bracket, without damaging the oil seal lip.

h. Using a suitable tool, install a new snapring.

i. Install a new bearing lock bolt and tighten it to 32 Nm (24 ft. lbs.).

11. Reverse the remaining removal procedures to complete installation, tightening fasteners to specifications.

12. Tigthen the 6 hex head driveshaft bolts to 48 ft. lbs. (65 Nm).

13. Fill the transaxle with gear oil, install the fender apron, check front end alignment and test drive.

➡If the cotter pin holes do not line up, always correct by TIGHTENING the nut until the next hole lines up. Then install a new cotter pin

CV-JOINT OVERHAUL

▶ See Figures 14 thru 20

The halfshaft assembly is a flexible unit consisting of an inner and outer Constant Velocity (CV) joint joined by an axle shaft. Care must be taken not to over-extend the joint assembly during repairs or handling. When either end of the shaft is disconnected from the car, any over-extension could result in separation of the internal components and possible joint failure.

The CV joints are protected by rubber boots or seals, designed to keep the high-temperature grease in and the road grime and water out. The most common cause of joint failure is a ripped boot (tow hooks on halfshaft when car is being towed) which allows the lubricant to leave the joint, thus causing heavy wear. The boots are exposed to road hazards all the time and should be inspected frequently. Any time a boot is found to be damaged or slit, it should be replaced immediately.

➡Whenever the halfshaft is held in a vise, use pieces of wood in the jaws to protect the components from damage or deformation.

1. Mount the driveshaft in a vise and check that there is no play in the inboard and outboard joint.

2. Make sure that the inboard joint slides smoothly in the thrust direction.

3. Make sure that there is no excessive play in the radial direction of the inboard joint.

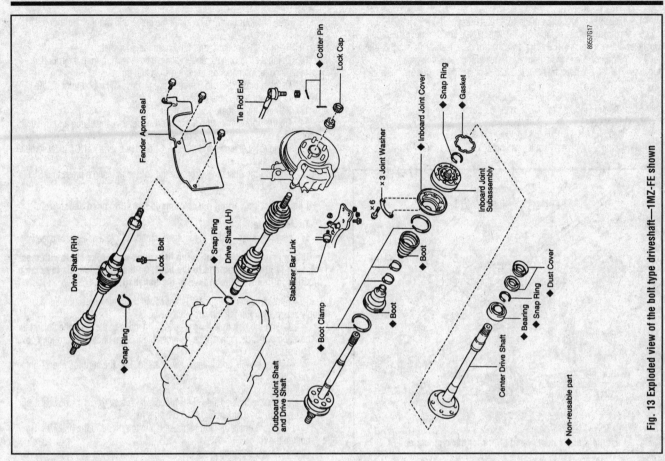

Fig. 13 Exploded view of the bolt type driveshaft—1MZ-FE shown

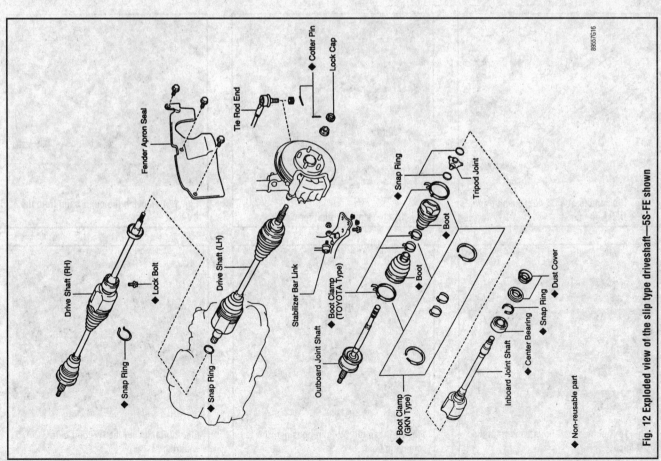

Fig. 12 Exploded view of the slip type driveshaft—5S-FE shown

4. Inspect the boots for damage (rips, punctures and cracks).

5. If your models is equipped with the bolt type shaft, remove the 6 bolts, 3 washers, and disconnect the center driveshaft or side gear shaft. Remove the joint gasket, discard and install nuts and washers to keep the inboard joint together. Tighten the bolts by hand to avoid scratching the surface.

6. On Toyota type:
   a. Remove the inboard joint boot clips.
   b. Slide the inboard joint toward the outboard joint.

7. On GNK type:
   a. Using pliers, remove the boot clamps.
   b. Using a side cutter, cut a small boot clamp and remove it.

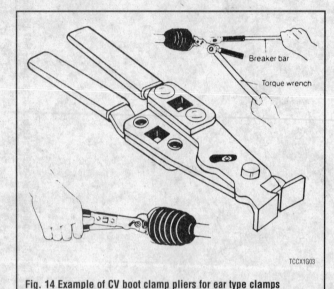

Fig. 14 Example of CV boot clamp pliers for ear type clamps

8. With chalk or paint, matchmark the inboard joint tulip and tripod. DO NOT use a punch.

9. Remove the inboard joint tulip from the driveshaft.

10. Using a snap ring expander, remove the snapring from the tripod.

11. Place matchmarks on the drive shaft and tripod.

12. Using a brass rod and hammer, evenly drive the tripod joint off the driveshaft without hitting the joint roller.

13. Remove the inboard joint boot.

14. On the right side, using a screw driver, remove the clamp and dynamic damper.

15. Remove the clamps and the outboard drive boot. DO NOT disassemble the outboard joint.

16. Remove the dust cover from the inboard joint using a press and SST 09950–00020 or equivalent.

➡**If equipped, be careful not to damage the ABS speed sensor rotor.**

To assemble:

17. Using a press, install the inboard joint tulip into a new dust cover.

➡**Before installing the boot, wrap the spline end of the shaft with masking tape to prevent damage to the boot. On the right side, fix the clamp position in line with the groove of the halfshaft.**

18. To assemble a new inboard joint cover, clean the contacting surface, apply seal packing to the inboard joint cover.
   a. Align the bolt holes of the cover with those of the joint, then insert the hexagon bolts. Using a plastic hammer, tap the rim of the inboard joint cover into place.
   b. Use the bolts and nuts and washers to keep the joint together. Tighten the bolts by hand.

19. Install the tripod, on Toyota types:
   a. Place the beveled side of the tripod axial spline toward the outboard joint.
   b. Align the matchmarks placed before removal.
   c. Using a brass bar and hammer, tap in the tripod to the halfshaft. Do not tap the roller.
   d. Using a snapring expander, install a new snapring.

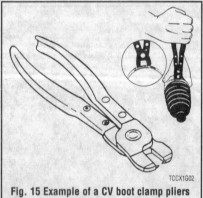

Fig. 15 Example of a CV boot clamp pliers for earless clamps

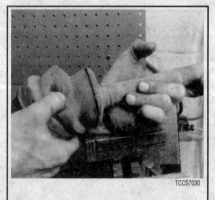

Fig. 16 Check the CV-boot for wear

Fig. 17 Removing the outer band from the CV-boot

Fig. 18 Removing the inner band from the CV-boot

Fig. 19 Clean the CV-joint housing prior to removing boot

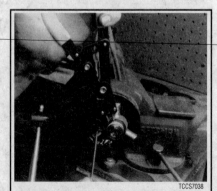

Fig. 20 Removing the CV-joint outer snapring

20. Pack the outboard tulip joint and the outboard boot with about 4.2–4.6 ounces of grease on Toyota types and 4.8–5.5 ounces on GNK types that was supplied with the boot kit.

21. Install the boot onto the outboard joint.

22. Pack the inboard tulip joint and boot with grease that was supplied with the boot kit.

23. Align the matchmarks on the tulip joint and tripod.

24. Install the inboard tulip joint onto the halfshaft.

25. Install the boot onto the halfshaft.

26. Make sure that the boot is properly installed on the halfshaft.

27. Before checking the standard length, bend the band and lock it.

28. Make sure that the boot is not stretched or squashed when the drive-shaft is at standard length.

Standard driveshaft length:
- 1983 vehicles—17.874 0.197 inch (454.0mm 5mm)
- 1984–86 vehicles—17.874 0.197 inch (454.0mm 5mm)
- Diesel engines LH—17.874 0.197 inch (454.0mm 5mm)
- Diesel engines RH—28.189 0.197 inch (716.0mm 5mm)
- 1987–88 vehicles (2WD)—17.744 0.197 inch (450.7mm 5mm)
- 1988 vehicles (4WD) with E56F2—15.98 inch (406mm)
- 1989 separated type axle, 4 cyl. (2WD)—17.744 0.197 inch (450.7mm 5mm)
- 1989 integrated type axle, 4 cyl. (2WD)—36.89 inch (937.0mm)

- 1989–90 With E56F5 Transaxle—20.178 0.197 inch (512.5 5mm)
- 1990–91 Toyota type, 4 cyl. LH—22.0 0.197 inch (558.7mm 5mm)
- 1990–91 Toyota type, 4 cyl. RH—33.27 0.197 inch (845.2mm 5mm)
- 1990–91 GKN type, 4 cyl. LH—25.67 0.236 inch (652.0mm 6mm)
- 1990–91 GKN type, 4 cyl. RH—36.89 0.236 inch (937.0 6mm)
- 1992–94 Toyota type 6 cyl. LH—17.953 inch (456.0mm)
- 1992–94 Toyota type 6 cyl. RH—17.953 inch (456.0mm)
- 1992–96 GKN type 6 cyl.—17.8090.079 inch (452.35 2.0mm)
- 1992–96 Toyota type 4 cyl. LH—23.940.197 inch (608.1 5.0mm)
- 1992–96 Toyota type 4 cyl. RH—34.10.197 inch (866.2 5.0mm)
- 1992–96 GKN type 4 cyl. LH—23.98 0.079 inch (609.2 2.0mm)
- 1992–94 GKN type 4 cyl. RH—34.67 0.079 inch (880.8 2.0mm)
- 1995–96 GKN type 4 cyl. RH—34.14 0.099 inch (867.3 2.5mm)

29. After making sure that the boots are in the shaft groove, bend the band and lock it on the Toyota type and pincer the band on the GKN type with the proper CV boot clamp tool. Tighten the small clamps the same way.

30. Pack in grease to the center driveshaft or side gear shaft. Use 42.554 g (1.51.9 oz.) for the Toyota type and 5160 g (1.82.1 oz.) for the GKN type.

31. Connect the driveshaft and the center driveshaft or the side gear shaft, placing a new gasket on the inboard joint without compressing the inboard boot.

32. Check to see that there is no play in the inboard and outboard joints and that the inboard joint slides smoothly in the thrust direction.

CLUTCH

Driven Disc and Pressure Plate

The clutch is a single dry disc type, with a diaphragm spring pressure plate. Clutch release bearings are sealed ball bearing units which need no lubrication and should never be washed in any kind of solvent.

REMOVAL & INSTALLATION

▶ **See Figures 21 thru 32**

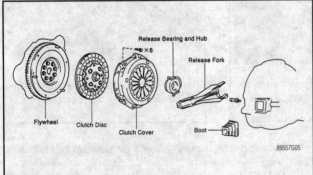

Fig. 21 Exploded view of the clutch components

✳✳ CAUTION

The clutch driven disc may contain asbestos, which has been determined to be a cancer causing agent. Never clean clutch surfaces with compressed air! Avoid inhaling any dust from any clutch surface! When cleaning clutch surfaces, use a commercially available brake cleaning fluid.

1. Remove the transaxle from the vehicle.
2. Matchmark the flywheel and the clutch cover with paint or chalk.
3. Loosen each set bolt one at a time until the spring tension is relieved.
4. Remove the set bolts completely and pull off the clutch cover with the clutch disc.

➡Do not drop the clutch disc. Do not allow grease or oil to get on any of the disc, pressure plate, or flywheel surfaces.

5. Unfasten the release bearing clips from the fork. Withdraw the release bearing assembly with the fork and then separate them.
6. Remove the fork boot.
7. Using calipers, measure the rivet head depth. Minimum depth is 0.30mm. If not within the limit, replace the clutch disc.
8. Using a dial indicator and V-blocks, measure the clutch disc runout. Maximum allowable runout is 0.78mm. If the runout is excessive, replace the clutch disc.
9. Using a dial indicator, measure the flywheel runout. Maximum runout is 0.10mm. If the runout is excessive, machine or replace the flywheel.

Fig. 22 Loosen and remove the clutch and pressure plate bolts evenly, a little at a time ....

Fig. 23 ... then carefully remove the clutch and pressure plate assembly from the flywheel

Fig. 24 Check across the flywheel surface, it should be flat

10. Using calipers, measure the diaphragm spring for depth and width and wear. Maximum depth is 0.60mm and maximum width is 5mm. Replace the clutch cover as necessary.

11. Grasp the release bearing and turn it while applying force in the axial direction. Replace the bearing and hub as required.

To install:

12. Insert proper alignment tool into the clutch disc and set them and the clutch cover in position.

13. Install the clutch disc bolts and tighten them evenly and gradually in a criss-cross pattern in several passes around the cover until they are snug.

14. Once the bolts are snug, tighten them in sequence to 14 ft. lbs. (19 Nm).

15. Using a dial indicator with a roller attachment, measure the diaphragm spring tip alignment. Maximum non-alignment is 0.05mm. Adjust the alignment as necessary using SST 09333–00013 or equivalent.

16. Apply molybdenum disulphide lithium base grease (NLGI No.2) to the following parts:
* Release fork and hub contact point.
* Release fork and push rod contact point.
* Release fork pivot point.
* Clutch disc spline.
* Inside groove of the release bearing hub.

Fig. 25 If necessary, lock the flywheel in place and remove the retaining bolts …

Fig. 26 … then remove the flywheel from the crankshaft in order replace it or have it machined

Fig. 27 Upon installation, it is usually a good idea to apply a thread-locking compound to the flywheel bolts

Fig. 28 Be sure that the flywheel surface is clean, before installing the clutch

Fig. 29 Install a clutch alignment arbor, to align the clutch assembly during installation

Fig. 30 You may want to use a thread locking compound on the clutch assembly bolts

17. Install the bearing assembly on the fork and then install them to the transaxle.

18. Install the boot.

19. Install the transaxle to the engine.

ADJUSTMENTS

Pedal Height

♦ See Figure 33

1. Check that the height of the clutch pedal is correct by measuring from the top of the pedal to the asphalt sheet on the kick panel. The pedal height should be within these specifications:
* 1983–85: 7.54–7.94 inch (191.5–201.5mm)
* 1986: 8.00–8.40 inch (203–213mm)
* 1987–89: 7.50–7.90 inch (191–201mm)
* 1990–91: 7.10–7.50 inch (181–191mm)
* 1992–96 except 3VZ-FE—6.33–6.72 inch (160.8–170.8mm)
* 1992–93 3VZ-FE—6.50–6.90 inch (164.7–174.7mm)

2. Remove the lower instrument panel and disconnect the air duct if necessary.

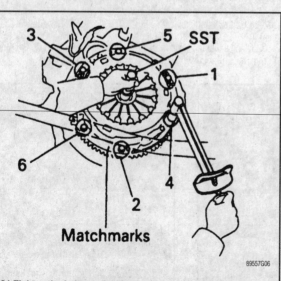

Fig. 31 Tighten the bolts on the clutch cover in this order

Fig. 32 Be sure to use a torque wrench to tighten all bolts

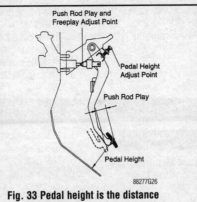

Fig. 33 Pedal height is the distance between the pedal and the floor board

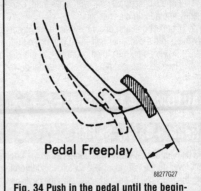

Fig. 34 Push in the pedal until the beginning of clutch resistance is felt

3. On vehicles except 1987–91 with cruise control, loosen the lock nut and turn the stopper bolt until the pedal height is correct and tighten the lock nut.

4. On the 1987–91 models with cruise control, loosen the lock nut on the clutch start switch, disconnect the wiring and adjust the switch to the correct position. Tighten the lock nut and reattach the wiring.

5. After the pedal height is adjusted, check the pedal free play and pushrod play.

Pedal Free-Play

▶ See Figure 34

Measure the clutch pedal free play and pushrod play by pressing on the clutch pedal with your finger and until resistance is felt. The clutch free play should be between 0.197–0.591 inch (5–15mm). Inadequate free play wears all parts of the clutch releasing mechanisms and may cause slippage. Excessive free play may cause inadequate release and hard shifting of gears.

If necessary, adjust the free play and pushrod play as follows:
1. Loosen the lock nut and turn the master cylinder push rod while depressing the clutch pedal lightly with your finger until the free play and pushrod play is correct.
2. Tighten the lock nut.
3. Check the pedal height.

Pushrod Play

Push in on the pedal with a finger softly until the resistance begins to increase somewhat. The push rod play at the pedal top should be: 0.039–0.197 inch (1.0–5.0mm).

Master Cylinder

REMOVAL & INSTALLATION

▶ See Figure 35

1. Wipe off and remove the reservoir tank cap.
2. Draw the fluid from the master cylinder with a syringe.

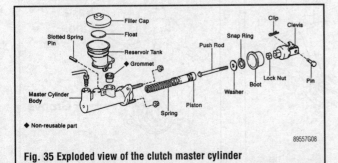

Fig. 35 Exploded view of the clutch master cylinder

3. Disconnect the clutch line tube fitting, using a line wrench.
4. On 1983–86 vehicles, remove the pedal return spring.
5. On 1886–91 vehicles, remove the lower instrument panel finish panel and disconnect the air duct from the panel.
6. Remove the clip and clevis pin with the spring washer. The spring washer is found on 1987–91 vehicles.
7. Remove the mounting nuts and remove the master cylinder.
8. Installation is the reverse of removal. Secure the master cylinder and tighten the mounting nuts to approximately 9 ft. lbs. (12 Nm).
9. Connect the clutch line tube and tighten the fitting to approximately 11 ft. lbs. (15 Nm).
10. Fill the reservoir with brake fluid and bleed the clutch system as described in this Section. Install the cap. Check for leaks.
11. Check and adjust the clutch pedal.

Slave Cylinder

REMOVAL & INSTALLATION

▶ See Figure 36

1. Place a small plastic container under the clutch line tube fitting and disconnect it, using a line wrench.
2. Remove the two retaining bolts.
3. Pull the release cylinder from its mounting.
4. Installation is the reverse of removal. Secure the cylinder bolts to approximately 9 ft. lbs. (12 Nm).
5. Connect and tighten the clutch line tube to 11 ft. lbs. (15 Nm). Fill the reservoir with brake fluid and bleed the clutch system as described in this Section. Check for leaks.

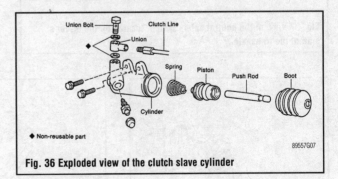

Fig. 36 Exploded view of the clutch slave cylinder

HYDRAULIC SYSTEM BLEEDING

➡ If any maintenance on the clutch system was performed or the system is suspected of containing air, bleed the system. Brake fluid will remove the paint from any surface. If the brake fluid spills onto any painted surface, wash it off immediately with soap and water.

1. Fill the clutch reservoir with brake fluid. Check the reservoir level frequently and add fluid as needed.
2. Connect one end of a vinyl tube to the bleeder plug and submerge the other end into a container half-filled with brake fluid.
3. Slowly pump the clutch pedal several times.
4. Have an assistant hold the clutch pedal down and loosen the bleeder plug until fluid starts to run out of the bleeder plug. You will notice air bubbles mixed in with the fluid.
5. Repeat Steps 2 and 3 until all the air bubbles are removed from the system.
6. Tighten the bleeder plug when all the air is gone.
7. Refill the master cylinder to the proper level as required.
8. Check the system for leaks.

AUTOMATIC TRANSAXLE

Neutral Safety Switch

The neutral safety switch is connected to the throttle cable and the manual shift lever on the transaxle. The switch, in addition to preventing vehicle start with the transaxle in gear, also actuates the back-up warning lights.

REMOVAL & INSTALLATION

▶ See Figures 37 and 38

1. Disconnect the neutral start switch harness.
2. With a pair of needle nose pliers, remove the clip that connects the manual control cable to the manual shift lever.
3. Unstake the lock nut and remove the manual shift lever.
4. Remove the neutral start switch with the seal gasket.
To install:
5. Install the neutral start switch making sure that the lip of the seal gasket is facing inward.
6. Install the manual shift lever.

7. Install the locknut and tighten to 61 inch lbs. (7 Nm). Stake the nut with the locking plate.
8. The remainder of installation is the reverse of removal. Check the operation of the switch and adjust as necessary.

ADJUSTMENT

▶ See Figures 39 and 40

If the engine starts with the shift selector in any position except Park or Neutral, adjust the switch as follows:
1. Loosen the two neutral start switch retaining bolts and move the shift selector to the Neutral range.
2. On 1983–85 vehicles, disconnect the neutral start switch harness and attach an ohmmeter across the terminals. Adjust the switch to the point at which there is continuity across the terminals.
3. On 1986–96 vehicles, align the groove and the neutral basic line. Maintain the alignment and tighten the bolts to 48 inch lbs. (5 Nm).

Automatic Transaxle

REMOVAL & INSTALLATION

The A540E and A540H transaxles should be removed along with the engine assembly. Refer to Section 3.
1. Disconnect the negative battery cable. Remove the air flow meter and the air cleaner assembly.
2. Disconnect the transaxle wire harness. Disconnect the neutral safety switch electrical harness and the cruise control actuator harness and cover, if equipped.
3. Disconnect the transaxle ground strap. Disconnect the throttle cable from the throttle linkage and disconnect the speed sensor harnesses, if equipped.
4. Remove the transaxle case protector. Disconnect the speedometer cable and control cable.
5. Disconnect the oil cooler hoses. Remove the upper starter retaining bolts, as required remove the starter assembly. Remove the upper transaxle housing bolts. Remove the engine rear mount insulator bracket set bolt.
6. Raise and support the vehicle safely. Drain the transaxle fluid.
7. Remove the left front fender apron seal. Disconnect both driveshafts and remove the exhaust pipe on 1992 vehicles.
8. Remove the suspension lower crossmember assembly. Remove the center driveshaft.

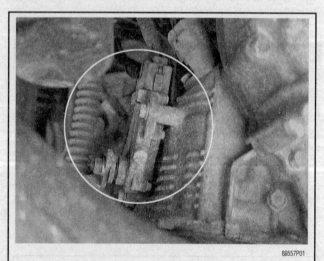

Fig. 37 View of the neutral safety switch, located on the driver's side of the transaxle

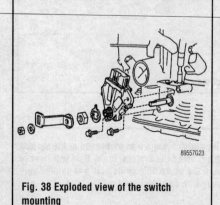

Fig. 38 Exploded view of the switch mounting

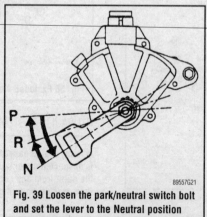

Fig. 39 Loosen the park/neutral switch bolt and set the lever to the Neutral position

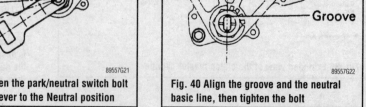

Fig. 40 Align the groove and the neutral basic line, then tighten the bolt

9. Remove the engine mounting center crossmember. Remove the stabilizer bar. Remove the left steering knuckle from the lower control arm.

10. Remove the torque converter cover. Remove the torque converter retaining bolts. On 1992 vehicles, remove the steering gear housing.

11. Properly support the engine and transaxle assembly. Remove the rear engine mounting bolts. Remove the remaining transaxle to engine retaining bolts.

12. Carefully remove the transaxle assembly from the vehicle.

To install:

13. Install the transaxle and tighten the 12mm transaxle housing bolts to 47 ft. lbs. (64 Nm); tighten the 10mm bolts to 34 ft. lbs. (46 Nm). Tighten the rear engine mount set bolts to 38 ft. lbs. (52 Nm). Tighten the torque converter mounting bolts to 20 ft. lbs. (27 Nm).

14. Reinstall the components in the reverse order of removal.

15. Install the transaxle cables, linkage and halfshafts.

16. Refill the transaxle with the approved fluid and check for leaks.

17. Lower the vehicle. Road test the vehicle and check operation.

Adjustments

Throttle Cable

▶ **See Figure 41**

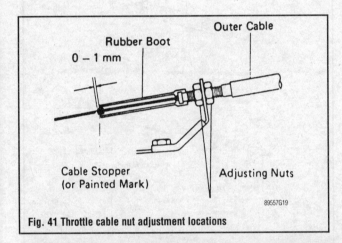

Fig. 41 Throttle cable nut adjustment locations

To inspect the throttle cable operation, remove the air cleaner and depress the accelerator cable all the way. Check that the throttle valve opens fully. If the throttle valve does not open fully, adjust the accelerator link as follows:

1. Remove the air cleaner.
2. Fully depress the accelerator cable.
3. Loosen the adjustment nuts.
4. Adjust the cable housing so that the distance between the end of boot and the stopper is 0.04 inch (01mm).
5. Tighten the adjusting nuts.
6. Recheck the adjustment.

Shift Cable

▶ **See Figure 42**

1. Loosen the swivel nut on the manual shaft lever.
2. Push the control lever to the right as far as it will go.
3. Bring the lever back two notches to the Neutral position.
4. Place the shifter in Neutral.
5. Hold the lever, lightly, toward the **R** range side and tighten the swivel nut.

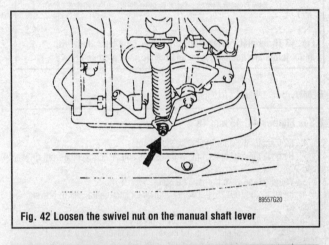

Fig. 42 Loosen the swivel nut on the manual shaft lever

Halfshafts

➡️ For illustrations and exploded views of the halfshafts and related components, refer to the Manual Transaxle section.

TRANSFER CASE

Extension Housing Seal

REMOVAL & INSTALLATION

The following procedure can be accomplished while the transfer case is in the vehicle.

1. Drain the transaxle oil.
2. Remove the propeller shaft.
3. Drive out the output shaft oil seal using a puller.

To install:

4. Place MP grease on the lip of the seal.
5. Drive in a new seal to a depth of 0.0430.075 inch (1.11.9mm).
6. Install the propeller shaft and fill the transaxle with the proper lubricant.

Side Gear Shaft Seal

REMOVAL & INSTALLATION

The following procedure can be accomplished while the transfer case is in the vehicle.

1. Remove both of the driveshafts.
2. Using a seal puller, remove the left side gear shaft seal.

3. On the A540H, remove the right side seal with a flatbladed tool.
4. Coat the seal lip with multi-purpose grease, then drive the new seal into the left side till the depth reaches about 0.02 inch (0.5mm).
5. On the A540H right side, perform the same procedure as on the left side.
6. Install both drive shafts.
7. Check the fluid levels, top off if necessary.

Transfer Case

REMOVAL & INSTALLATION

For ease of removal, the entire transaxle should be removed first.

1. Remove the bolts and the nuts retaining the unit to the transaxle.
2. Using a plastic hammer, remove the transfer assembly from the transaxle.

To install:

3. Make sure that the contact surfaces are clean and oil-free.
4. Apply seal packing (08826–00090) or equivalent to the transfer and install the transfer as soon as the packing is applied.

➡️ **Shift into 4th gear, and install the transfer assembly while turning the input shaft of the transaxle.**

5. Apply sealant to the bolt threads.
6. Tighten the 3 bolts and the 5 nuts to 51 ft. lbs. (69 Nm).

DRIVELINE

Driveshaft

♦ See Figure 43

The three piece driveshaft is a four joint type shaft. No. 1, 2 and 4 joints are hooked joints and the No.3 joint is a cross groove type constant velocity joint that ensures good flexibility and reduces vibration and noise. The driveshaft also uses two center support bearings to control vibration and suppress noise.

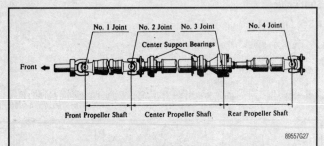

Fig. 43 Three piece driveshafts are a four joint type shaft—No. 1, 2 and 4 joints are hooked joints and the No. 3 is a cross groove

REMOVAL & INSTALLATION

♦ See Figures 44, 45 and 46

1. Matchmark the both front driveshaft flanges.
2. Remove the four bolts, nuts and washers and disconnect the front drive-shaft.
3. Withdraw the yoke from the transfer.
4. Insert a plug (09325–20010) or equivalent into the transfer to prevent oil leakage.
5. Have an assistant depress the brake pedal and hold it.
6. Place a piece of cloth into the inside of the universal joint cover.
7. Loosen the cross groove joint set bolts ½ turn.
8. Matchmark the intermediate and rear driveshafts.
9. Remove the four bolts, nuts and washers.
10. Remove the two bolts from the front center support bearing and remove the bearing and the washer.
11. Remove the rear front center support bearing and washers.

To install:

12. Install the center support bearing temporarily with the two bolts.
13. Align the matchmarks on the rear and intermediate flanges and connect the shafts with the four nuts, bolts and washers. Tighten the bolts to 54 ft. lbs. (73 Nm).
14. Remove the plug from the transfer and insert the yoke.
15. Align the matchmarks on both flanges. Install the bolts, nuts and washers and tighten to 54 ft. lbs. (73 Nm).
16. Have an assistant depress the brake pedal and hold it.
17. Using the removal tool, tighten the cross groove joint set bolts to 20 ft. lbs. (27 Nm).

18. Make sure that the vehicle is unloaded, and adjust the distance between the rear side of the boot cover and the shaft as shown in the accompanying figure.
19. Under the same unloaded conditions, adjust the distance between the rear side of the center bearing housing of the cushion to 0.393–0.472 inch (10–12mm) and tighten the bolts to 27 ft. lbs. (36 Nm).
20. Ensure that the center line of the bracket is at right angles at the shaft axial direction.

Center Bearing

♦ See Figure 47

Two center support bearings are used on All-Trac 4-Wheel Drive vehicles to control driveshaft noise and vibration and as a means of support for the intermediate driveshaft. The bearings use cushion rubber to bend the driveshaft to allow passage through the center of the bearing. To remove the bearing, refer to Driveshaft Removal and Installation.

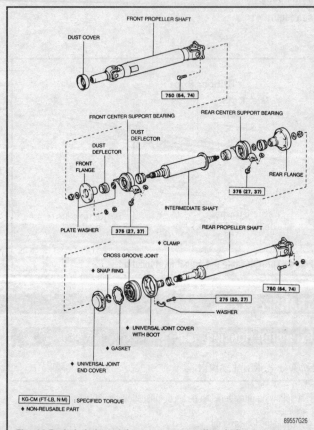

Fig. 44 Exploded view of the common propeller shaft components—All-Trac (4WD) models only

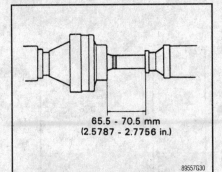

Fig. 45 Adjust the intervals between the rear side of the boot cover and shaft—All-Trac (4WD) models only

65.5 - 70.5 mm
(2.5787 - 2.7756 in.)

89557G30

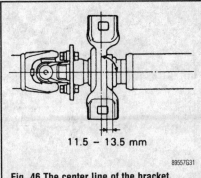

Fig. 46 The center line of the bracket should be at a right angle—All-Trac (4WD) models only

11.5 – 13.5 mm

89557G31

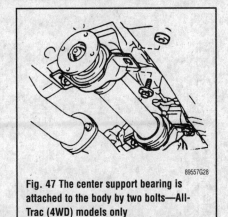

Fig. 47 The center support bearing is attached to the body by two bolts—All-Trac (4WD) models only

89557G28

REAR AXLE

Axle Shaft

REMOVAL & INSTALLATION

The following procedure applies to all 1988–91 4WD models only.
1. Raise and support the vehicle safely. Remove the rear wheels.
2. Remove the cotter pin, locknut cap and bearing nut.
3. Scribe matchmarks on the inner joint tulip and the side gear shaft flange. Loosen and remove the 4 nuts.
4. Disconnect the inner end of the shaft by punching it upward and then pull the outer end from the axle carrier. Remove the halfshaft.
5. Installation is the reverse of removal. Position the halfshaft into the axle carrier and pull the inner end down until the matchmarks are aligned.
6. Connect the halfshaft to the side gear shaft and tighten the nuts to 51 ft. lbs. (69 Nm). Install the bearing nut and tighten it to 137 ft. lbs. (186 Nm) with the brake pedal depressed. Install the cap and a new cotter pin.

Pinion Seal and Bearing

REMOVAL & INSTALLATION

♦ **See Figure 48**

The following procedure applies to all 1988–91 4WD models only.
1. Unbolt and remove the rear crossmember.
2. Matchmark the differential and driveshaft flanges.
3. Remove the four flange bolts, nuts and washers.
4. Disconnect the driveshaft from the differential.
5. With a hammer and a cold chisel, loosen the staked part of the locking nut.
6. Using SST No. 09330–00021 or equivalent to hold the flange, remove the locking nut.
7. Remove the plate washer.
8. Remove the companion flange.
9. Using a seal puller (SST 09308–10010) or equivalent, remove the front oil seal and then remove the oils slinger.
10. Using a bearing puller (SST 09556–22010) or equivalent, remove the front bearing.
11. Remove the front bearing spacer. Purchase a new spacer, bearing and oil seal as required.
To install the front seal and bearing
12. Install a new bearing spacer and bearing onto the shaft.
13. Install the oils slinger onto the shaft.
14. Using a seal driver, install the new oil seal to a depth of 0.078 inch (2mm).
15. Coat the lip of the new oil seal with multi-purpose grease.
16. Using the removal tool, install the companion flange.
17. Install the plate washer.

18. Coat the threads of the new nut with gear oil.
19. Using the removal tool to hold the flange, tighten the companion flange to 80 ft. lbs. (108 Nm).
20. Check and adjust the drive pinion preload as follows:
    a. Using a inch lb. torque wrench, measure the preload of the backlash between the drive pinion and the ring gear. Preload for a new bearing is 9–14 inch lbs. (1–1.5mm) and 4–7 inch lbs. (0.4–0.7mm) for a used bearing.
    b. If the preload is greater that the specified limit, replace the bearing spacer.
    c. If the preload is less than specification, re-tighten the nut in 9 ft. lbs. (12 Nm) increments until the specified preload is reached. Do not exceed a maximum torque of 174 ft. lbs. (235 Nm).
    d. If the maximum torque is exceeded, replace the bearing spacer and repeat the bearing preload procedure. Preload CANNOT be reduced by simply backing off on the pinion nut.
21. Stake the drive pinion nut.
22. Align the driveshaft and differential flange matchmarks.
23. Install the flange bolts and tighten to 54 ft. lbs. (73 Nm).
24. Install the rear crossmember and tighten the retaining bolts to 53 ft. lbs. (71 Nm).
25. Remove the differential FILL plug (the uppermost plug) and check the oil level. Fill the differential to the proper level with new API GL-5 hypoid gear oil.
26. Install and tighten the fill plug with a new gasket. Tighten the plug to 29 ft. lbs. (39 Nm).
27. Take the vehicle for a road test and inspect for leaks.

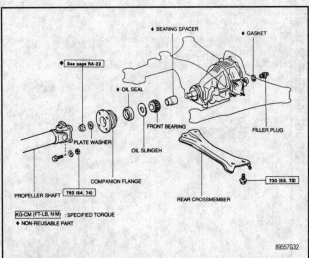

89557G32

Fig. 48 The differential oil seal is in between the companion flange and oil slinger—All-Trac (4WD) models only

TORQUE SPECIFICATIONS

E53 Manual Transaxle:

	US	METRIC
Back-up light switch	33 ft. lbs.	45 Nm
Differential case-to-differential case	46 ft. lbs.	63 Nm
Engine-to-stiffener plate	13 ft. lbs.	18 Nm
Oil pump-to-cover	8 ft. lbs.	10 Nm
Transaxle case-to-transaxle case	46 ft. lbs.	63 Nm
Transaxle case-to-oil pump	13 ft. lbs.	17 Nm
Transaxle case-to-rear bearing retainer	31 ft. lbs.	42 Nm
Transaxle case-to-case cover	22 ft. lbs.	29 Nm
Transaxle-to-stiffener plate	27 ft. lbs.	37 Nm
Transaxle-to-starter	29 ft. lbs.	39 Nm

Automatic Transaxle:

		US	METRIC
Drain plug	1983-85	22 ft. lbs.	30 Nm
	1986-96	36 ft. lbs.	49 Nm
Neutral safety switch-to-case bolt		48 inch lbs.	5 Nm
Neutral safety switch nut		61 inch lbs.	7 Nm
Oil pan		43 inch lbs.	5 Nm
Oil strainer		8 ft. lbs.	11 Nm
Transaxle-to-engine	10mm	32 ft. lbs.	43 Nm
	12mm	47 ft. lbs.	64 Nm
Torque converter-to-driveplate		20 ft. lbs.	27 Nm

Driveshaft:

		US	METRIC
Center support bearing-to-body		27 ft. lbs.	37 Nm
Cross groove joint set bolt		20 ft. lbs.	27 Nm
Intermediate shaft-to-center support			
bearing-to-flange	1st	134 ft. lbs.	181 Nm
	3rd	51 ft. lbs.	69 Nm
Propeller shaft-to-differential		54 ft. lbs.	74 Nm
Propeller shaft-to-intermediate shaft		54 ft. lbs.	74 Nm

Rear Axle:

	US	METRIC
Axle shaft bearing lock nut	137 ft. lbs.	186 Nm
Axle shaft-to-side gear shaft	51 ft. lbs.	69 Nm
Carrier-to-carrier cover	34 ft. lbs.	47 Nm
Companion flange-to-propeller shaft	54 ft. lbs.	74 Nm
Fill plug	29 ft. lbs.	39 Nm
Differential-to-support member under side	70 ft. lbs.	95 Nm
Differential-to-support member rear side	108 ft. lbs.	147 Nm

89557C02

TORQUE SPECIFICATIONS

Clutch		US	METRIC
Bleeder plug	1986-87	8 ft. lbs.	11 Nm
	1992-96	6 ft. lbs.	8 Nm
Clutch cover-to-flywheel		14 ft. lbs.	19 Nm
Clutch line union		11 ft. lbs.	15 Nm
Master cylinder set bolt		9 ft. lbs.	12 Nm
Release (slave) cylinder		9 ft. lbs.	12 Nm
Reservoir tank-to-cylinder	1986-87	18 ft. lbs.	24 Nm
Release fork support	1989-91	35 ft. lbs.	47 Nm
	1992-96	29 ft. lbs.	39 Nm

89557C03

TORQUE SPECIFICATIONS

S51 Manual Transaxle:

		US	METRIC
Back-up light switch		33 ft. lbs.	45 Nm
Transaxle case-to-transaxle case		22 ft. lbs.	30 Nm
Transaxle case-transaxle case co	1983-84	13 ft. lbs.	18 Nm
	1985-96	22 ft. lbs.	30 Nm
Drain plug	1983-88	29 ft. lbs.	39 Nm
	1988-96	36 ft. lbs.	49 Nm
Fill plug	1983-88	29 ft. lbs.	39 Nm
	1989-96	36 ft. lbs.	49 Nm
Transaxle-to-engine	1983-86 10mm	29 ft. lbs.	39 Nm
	12mm	47 ft. lbs.	64 Nm
	1987-92 10mm	34 ft. lbs.	46 Nm
	12mm	47 ft. lbs.	64 Nm
	1993-96 A	34 ft. lbs.	46 Nm
	B	18 ft. lbs.	25 Nm
	C		

E56F and E56F5 Manual Transaxle:

	US	METRIC
Back-up light switch	33 ft. lbs.	45 Nm
Shift and selector lever-to-transaxle	14 ft. lbs.	20 Nm
Transaxle-to-transfer	51 ft. lbs.	69 Nm
Transaxle case-to-transaxle case	22 ft. lbs.	29 Nm
Transaxle case-to-transaxle case cover	22 ft. lbs.	29 Nm
Transfer case-to-transaxle right case	33 ft. lbs.	44 Nm
Transfer case-to-inspection hole cover	12 ft. lbs.	16 Nm
Transfer right case-to-transfer case cover	13 ft. lbs.	17 Nm

E52 Manual Transaxle:

	US	METRIC
Back-up light switch	33 ft. lbs.	45 Nm
Center driveshaft bearing locknut	24 ft. lbs.	32 Nm
Differential case-to-differential case	46 ft. lbs.	63 Nm
Drain plug	29 ft. lbs.	39 Nm
Driveshaft-to-center driveshaft	48 ft. lbs.	65 Nm
Elbow-to-transaxle	20 ft. lbs.	27 Nm
Filler plug	29 ft. lbs.	39 Nm
Front wheel bearing locknut	137 ft. lbs.	186 Nm
Oil pump-to-cover	8 ft. lbs.	10 Nm
Selecting bell crank set bolt	14 ft. lbs.	20 Nm
Transaxle case-to-transaxle case	22 ft. lbs.	30 Nm
Transaxle case-to-case cover	22 ft. lbs.	30 Nm
Transaxle case-to-oil pump	13 ft. lbs.	17 Nm
Transaxle-to-front engine mounting	38 ft. lbs.	52 Nm
Transaxle-to-stiffener plate	27 ft. lbs.	37 Nm
Transaxle-to-engine mounting left stay	38 ft. lbs.	52 Nm
Transaxle-to-rear end plate	18 ft. lbs.	25 Nm
Transaxle-to-case protector	18 ft. lbs.	25 Nm

89557C01

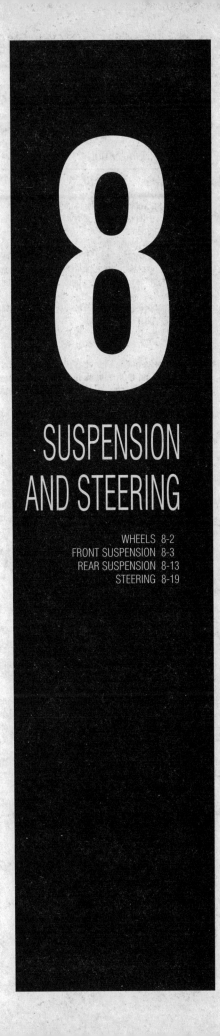

8

SUSPENSION AND STEERING

WHEELS

Wheel Assembly

REMOVAL & INSTALLATION

▶ See Figure 1

1. Park the vehicle on a level surface.
2. Remove the jack, tire iron and, if necessary, the spare tire from their storage compartments.
3. Check the owner's manual or refer to Section 1 of this manual for the jacking points on your vehicle. Then, place the jack in the proper position.
4. If equipped with lug nut trim caps, remove them by either unscrewing or pulling them off the lug nuts, as appropriate. Consult the owner's manual, if necessary.
5. If equipped with a wheel cover or hub cap, insert the tapered end of the tire iron in the groove and pry off the cover.
6. Apply the parking brake and block the diagonally opposite wheel with a wheel chock or two.

➡ Wheel chocks may be purchased at your local auto parts store, or a block of wood cut into wedges may be used. If possible, keep one or two of the chocks in your tire storage compartment, in case any of the tires has to be removed on the side of the road.

7. If equipped with an automatic transmission/transaxle, place the selector lever in **P** or Park; with a manual transmission/transaxle, place the shifter in Reverse.
8. With the tires still on the ground, use the tire iron/wrench to break the lug nuts loose.

➡ If a nut is stuck, never use heat to loosen it or damage to the wheel and bearings may occur. If the nuts are seized, one or two heavy hammer blows directly on the end of the bolt usually loosens the rust. Be careful, as continued pounding will likely damage the brake drum or rotor.

9. Using the jack, raise the vehicle until the tire is clear of the ground. Support the vehicle safely using jackstands.
10. Remove the lug nuts, then remove the tire and wheel assembly.
    To install:
11. Make sure the wheel and hub mating surfaces, as well as the wheel lug studs, are clean and free of all foreign material. Always remove rust from the wheel mounting surface and the brake rotor or drum. Failure to do so may cause the lug nuts to loosen in service.
12. Install the tire and wheel assembly and hand-tighten the lug nuts.
13. Using the tire wrench, tighten all the lug nuts, in a crisscross pattern, until they are snug.
14. Raise the vehicle and withdraw the jackstand, then lower the vehicle.
15. Using a torque wrench, tighten the lug nuts in a crisscross pattern to 137 ft. lbs. (186 Nm). Check your owner's manual or refer to Section 1 of this manual for the proper tightening sequence.

✳✳ WARNING

Do not overtighten the lug nuts, as this may cause the wheel studs to stretch or the brake disc (rotor) to warp.

16. If so equipped, install the wheel cover or hub cap. Make sure the valve stem protrudes through the proper opening before tapping the wheel cover into position.
17. If equipped, install the lug nut trim caps by pushing them or screwing them on, as applicable.
18. Remove the jack from under the vehicle, and place the jack and tire iron/wrench in their storage compartments. Remove the wheel chock(s).
19. If you have removed a flat or damaged tire, place it in the storage compartment of the vehicle and take it to your local repair station to have it fixed or replaced as soon as possible.

INSPECTION

Inspect the tires for lacerations, puncture marks, nails and other sharp objects. Repair or replace as necessary. Also check the tires for treadwear and air pressure as outlined in Section 1 of this manual. Check the wheel assemblies for dents, cracks, rust and metal fatigue. Repair or replace as necessary.

Wheel Lug Studs

REMOVAL & INSTALLATION

Disc Brakes

▶ See Figure 2

1. Raise and support the appropriate end of the vehicle safely using jackstands, then remove the wheel.
2. Remove the brake pads and caliper. Support the caliper aside using wire or a coat hanger. For details, please refer to Section 9 of this manual.
3. Remove the outer wheel bearing and lift off the rotor. For details on wheel bearing removal, installation and adjustment, please refer to Section 1 of this manual.
4. Properly support the rotor using press bars, then drive the stud out using an arbor press.

➡ If a press is not available, CAREFULLY drive the old stud out using a blunt drift. MAKE SURE the rotor is properly and evenly supported or it may be damaged.

To install:
5. Clean the stud hole with a wire brush and start the new stud with a hammer and drift pin. Do not use any lubricant or thread sealer.
6. Finish installing the stud with the press.

➡ If a press is not available, start the lug stud through the bore in the hub, then position about 4 flat washers over the stud and thread the lug

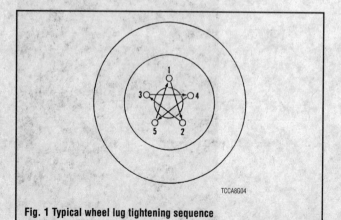

Fig. 1 Typical wheel lug tightening sequence

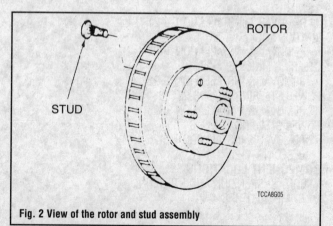

Fig. 2 View of the rotor and stud assembly

nut. Hold the hub/rotor while tightening the lug nut, and the stud should be drawn into position. **MAKE SURE THE STUD IS FULLY SEATED,** then remove the lug nut and washers.

7. The remainder of installation is the reverse of removal. Tighten the lug nuts to 137 ft. lbs. (186 Nm).

Drum Brakes

▶ **See Figures 3, 4 and 5**

1. Raise the vehicle and safely support it with jackstands, then remove the wheel.
2. Remove the brake drum.
3. If necessary to provide clearance, remove the brake shoes, as outlined in Section 9 of this manual.

4. Using a large C-clamp and socket, press the stud from the axle flange.
5. Coat the serrated part of the stud with liquid soap and place it into the hole.

To install:

6. Position about 4 flat washers over the stud and thread the lug nut. Hold the flange while tightening the lug nut, and the stud should be drawn into position. **MAKE SURE THE STUD IS FULLY SEATED,** then remove the lug nut and washers.

7. If applicable, install the brake shoes.
8. Install the brake drum.
9. Install the wheel, then remove the jackstands and carefully lower the vehicle.
10. Tighten the lug nuts to 137 ft. lbs. (186 Nm).

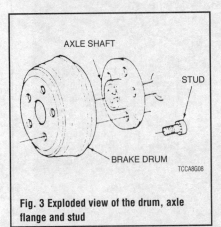

Fig. 3 Exploded view of the drum, axle flange and stud

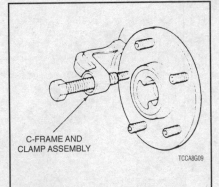

Fig. 4 Use a C-clamp and socket to press out the stud

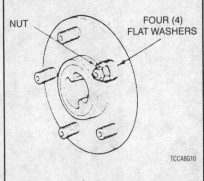

Fig. 5 Force the stud onto the axle flange using washers and a lug nut

FRONT SUSPENSION

Coil Springs

REMOVAL & INSTALLATION

▶ **See Figures 6 and 7**

1. Remove the shock absorber assembly with coil spring out from under the vehicle.
2. To disassemble the shock absorber from the coil spring, install 2 nuts and a bolt to the bracket at the lower part of the shock absorber and secure it in a vice.
3. Using a special coil spring compressor, such as 09727–30020 or equivalent, compress the coil spring. Do not use an impact wrench, it will damage the compression tool.
4. Renmove the cap from the suspension support. Using a retaining tool to hold the seat, such as 09729–22031 or equivalent remove the nut.
5. Remove the following components:
- Suspension support

- Dust seal
- Spring seat
- Upper insulator and coil spring
- Spring bumper and lower insulator

To install:

6. Install the lower insulator. Attach the spring bumper to the piston rod.
7. Using the compressor tool, such as 09727–30020 or equivalent, compress the coil spring. Install the coil spring to the shock absorber.

➡**Fit the lower end of the coil spring into the gap of the spring seat of the shock absorber.**

8. Install the upper insulator. Place the spring seat to the shock with the OUT mark facing the outside of the vehicle. Install the dust seal and suspension support.
9. Install the retaining tool, such as 09729–22031 or equivalent to hold the spring seat, install a new nut. Tighten the nut to 34–36 ft. lbs. (47–49 Nm). Install the cap and remove the compression tool.
10. Pack the upper suspension support with MP grease.
11. Install the coil and shock absorber assembly into the vehicle.

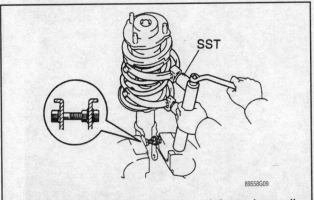

Fig. 6 View of the common spring compressor being used on a coil

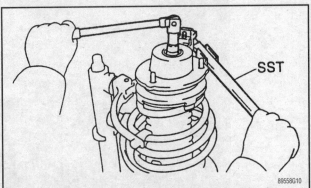

Fig. 7 Hold the suspension support using a retaining tool and remove the nut

FRONT SUSPENSION AND STEERING COMPONENTS

1. Tie rod end
2. Lower control arm
3. Steering knuckle
4. Ball joint (attached to arm)
5. Halfshaft

MacPherson Struts

REMOVAL & INSTALLATION

1983–86 Models

▶ **See Figure 8**

1. Raise and support the front end on jackstands placed under the frame pads.
2. Remove the front wheels.
3. Using a line nut wrench, disconnect the brake tube and flexible hose from the clamp. Drain the brake fluid into a plastic container.
4. Using needle nose pliers, remove the two clips and E-rings from the brake tube support bracket.
5. Remove the two retaining bolts and separate the brake pad from the brake caliper.

➡ **Do not disconnect the brake hose from the caliper.**

6. Matchmark the shock absorber lower mounting bracket with the camber adjusting cam.
7. Remove the nuts and bolts and disconnect the steering knuckle and the shock absorber.
8. Remove the three bolts from the top of the suspension support.
9. Remove the shock absorber from the body.

➡ **Cover the driveshaft boot with a cloth to prevent damage.**

To install:

10. Position the shock absorber onto the body and install the three nuts. Tighten the nuts to 27 ft. lbs. (36 Nm).
11. Coat the threads of the steering knuckle retaining nuts with clean engine oil.
12. Connect the steering knuckle to the shock absorber lower bracket. Insert the mounting bolts from the rear side and align the matchmarks made on the camber adjusting cam. Tighten the nuts to 157 ft. lbs. (213 Nm).
13. There is a bearing located under the suspension support dust cover. Remove the dust cover and pack the bearing with multi-purpose grease. Once packed, reinstall the dust cover.
14. Install the brake caliper and tighten the retaining bolts to 65 ft. lbs. (88 Nm).
15. Install the two clips and E-rings. Connect the brake tube to the flexible hose.
16. Bleed the brake lines as described in Section 9. Have the front wheel alignment checked.

1987–88 Models

1. Raise and support the front end on jackstands placed under the frame pads.
2. Remove the front wheels.
3. Disconnect the brake from the caliper by removing the union bolt from the banjo fitting. Drain the brake fluid into a plastic container.

➡ **The union bolt uses gaskets to seal the bolt to the caliper. Discard the bolt gaskets and purchase new ones.**

4. Using needle nose pliers, remove the clip from the brake tube support bracket.
5. Pull the brake hose from the support bracket.
6. Matchmark the shock absorber lower mounting bracket with the camber adjusting cam.
7. Remove the nuts and bolts and disconnect the steering knuckle and the shock absorber.
8. Remove the three bolts from the top of the suspension support.
9. Remove the shock absorber from the body.

➡ **Cover the driveshaft boot with a cloth to prevent damage.**

10. Installation is the reverse of removal. Position the shock absorber onto the body and install the three nuts. Tighten the nuts to 47 ft. lbs. (64 Nm).
11. Attach the steering knuckle to the shock absorber lower bracket. Insert the mounting bolts from the rear side and align the matchmarks made on the camber adjusting cam. Tighten the nuts to 166 ft. lbs. (224 Nm).
12. There is a bearing located under the suspension support dust cover. Remove the dust cover and pack the bearing with multi-purpose grease. Once packed, reinstall the dust cover.
13. Bleed the brake lines as described in Section 9. Align the front suspension.

1989–96 Models

▶ **See Figures 9 thru 16**

1. Remove the hubcap and loosen the lug nuts.
2. Raise and support the vehicle safely.

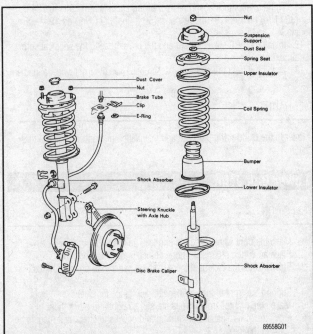

Fig. 8 View of the front shock absorber assembly and related components—1983 models

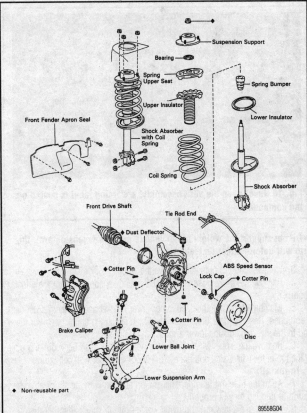

Fig. 9 View of the front shock absorber assembly and related components—1995–96 models

Fig. 10 View of the front shock absorber assembly lower mounting bolt locations

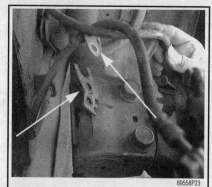

Fig. 11 Unbolt and set aside the brake hose attached to the strut

Fig. 12 Remove the two strut mounting bolts

Fig. 13 A long bolt and nut retain the lower portion of the strut assembly

Fig. 14 Lower the vehicle and remove the three upper bearing support nuts on the strut tower

Fig. 15 With the aide of a helper, remove the strut from the under side of the vehicle

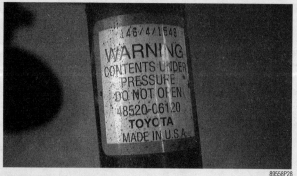

Fig. 16 Never open the strut assembly, a warning label is posted on the component

→Do not support the weight of the vehicle on the suspension arm; the arm will deform under its weight.

3. Unfasten the lug nuts and remove the wheel.

4. Remove the brake hose and the ABS speed sensor wire from the shock absorber.

5. Matchmark on the shock absorber lower bracket and camber adjust cam, if equipped. Remove the 2 bolts and nuts which attach the shock absorber lower end to the steering knuckle lower arm.

6. Remove the 3 nuts which secure the upper shock absorber mounting plate to the top of the wheel arch and remove the shock absorber with coil spring.

To install:

7. Align the hole in the upper suspension support with the shock absorber piston or end, so they fit properly.

8. Always use a new nut and nylon washer on the shock absorber piston rod end when securing it to the upper suspension support. Tighten the nut to 29–40 ft. lbs. (39–54 Nm).

→Do not use an impact wrench to tighten the nut.

9. Coat the suspension support bearing with multipurpose grease prior to installation. Pack the space in the upper support with multipurpose grease, also, after installation.

10. Tighten the 3 suspension support-to-wheel arch nuts to 47 ft. lbs. (64 Nm). On 1992–96 models tighten to 59 ft. lbs. (80 Nm).

11. Tighten the shock absorber-to-steering knuckle arm bolts to 224 ft. lbs. (304 Nm) on 1989–91 models and 156 ft. lbs. (211 Nm) on 1992–96 models.

12. Install the ABS speed sensor and the brake hose to the shock absorber, if equipped.

13. Install the front tire and wheel assembly. Have the front wheel alignment checked.

OVERHAUL

Refer to the Coil Spring Removal and Installation procedure earlier in this section.

Lower Ball Joint

INSPECTION

1. Make the front wheels straight and jack up the front of the vehicle.

2. Place an 8 inch (203mm) wooden block under one front tire.

3. Slowly lower the jack until there is about half a load on the front coil spring.

4. Support the front of the vehicle with jackstands for safety.

5. Make sure that the front wheels are still straight and block them.

6. Move the lower suspension arm up and down and check that there is no vertical play in the joint.

7. If there is play in the joint, replace it.

8. Repeat the procedure for the other side.

REMOVAL & INSTALLATION

▶ **See Figure 17**

1983–87 Models

1. Remove the lower suspension arm as described in this Section.
2. Clamp the lower arm in a vise.
3. Remove the cotter pin and the nut.
4. On 1983–86 vehicles, temporarily install the nut to prevent the ball joint from falling out.
5. Using a ball joint puller such as SST 09628–62011 or equivalent, remove the ball joint from the lower arm.
6. Installation is the reverse of removal. Secure the castellated nut and tighten to 67 ft. lbs. (91 Nm).
7. Install a new cotter pin.
8. Install the lower arm and tighten to specifications.

09628–62011
Ball Joint Puller

89558G07

Fig. 17 View of a common ball joint puller. This one is available from Toyota, part #09628-62011

1988–91 Models

▶ **See Figure 18**

1. Raise and support the vehicle safely. Remove the wheels.
2. Remove the bolts attaching the ball joint to the steering knuckle.
3. Remove the stabilizer bar nut, retainer and cushion.
4. Remove the nut attaching the lower arm shaft to the lower arm.
5. Remove the lower suspension crossmember (2 bolts and 4 nuts).
6. Remove the lower control arm and lower arm shaft as an assembly.
7. Grip the lower arm assembly in a vise and remove the ball joint cotter pin and retaining nut. With a ball joint removal tool, pull the ball joint out of the control arm.

To install:

8. Position the ball joint in the lower arm and tighten the nut to 67 ft. lbs. (91 Nm) for 1988 or 90 ft. lbs. (123 Nm) for 1989–91. Install a new cotter pin.
9. Install the lower arm to the stabilizer bar and then install the lower arm shaft to the body. Install the lower arm nut and retainer. Screw on a new stabilizer bar end nut and retainer.

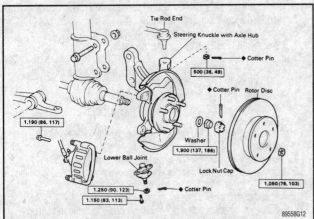

Fig. 18 View of the ball joint and related components—1988–91 models

89558G12

10. Connect the ball joint to the steering knuckle and tighten the bolts to 94 ft. lbs. (127 Nm) for 1988 or 83 ft. lbs. (113 Nm) for 1989–91. Align the holes for the ABS speed sensor in the dust deflector and steering knuckle.
11. Install the suspension lower crossmember. Tighten the inner bolts to 32 ft. lbs. (43 Nm) and the outer ones to 153 ft. lbs. (207 Nm).
12. Install the wheels and lower the vehicle. Bounce it several times to set the suspension.
13. Tighten the stabilizer bar end nut and the lower arm shaft-to-lower arm bolt to 156 ft. lbs. (212 Nm).
14. Check the ABS speed sensor signal and front wheel alignment.

1992–96 Models

▶ **See Figure 19**

1. Raise the front of the vehicle and support it safely. Remove the front wheels.
2. Remove side fender apron seal.
3. Remove the steering knuckle with the axle hub, from the vehicle. See appropriate procedure of this Section for aid in removing the knuckle.
4. Pry the dust deflector from the knuckle.
5. Remove the cotter pin and the nut from the ball joint stud. Discard the old cotter pin.
6. Using two armed puller tool, remove the lower ball joint from the steering knuckle.
7. Installation is the reverse of removal. Install the lower ball joint onto the steering knuckle and tighten nut to 94 ft. lbs. (127 Nm). Install new cotter pin.
8. Using the appropriate driver, install new dust deflector. Align the holes for the ABS speed sensor in the dust deflector and steering knuckle.

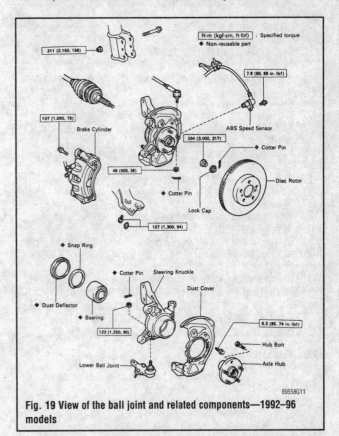

89558G11

Fig. 19 View of the ball joint and related components—1992–96 models

Stabilizer Bar

REMOVAL & INSTALLATION

1983–86 Models

1. Remove the engine under covers.
2. On 1985–86 vehicles, remove the center support member as follows:

a. Remove the two access hole covers from the center engine mounting member.

b. Remove the bolts from the front and rear mountings.

c. Unbolt the center mounting member.

3. Remove both stabilizer bar brackets from the body.

4. On one side, disconnect the lower stabilizer end from the lower control arm.

5. Unbolt and remove the lower control arm on the other side.

6. Remove the stabilizer bar, retainer and spacer.

To install:

7. Install the spacer first and then the retainer.

8. Make the nut finger tight.

9. Pry the bar forward and install the brackets. Tighten the bracket retaining bolts to 83 ft. lbs. (112 Nm).

10. Install the lower arm on one side and tighten the stabilizer bar nut to 86 ft. lbs. (116 Nm).

11. On 1985–86 vehicles, install the center support member as follows:

a. Position the members and install the mounting bolts. Tighten the mounting bolts to 29 ft. lbs. (39 Nm).

b. Install the front and rear mountings and tighten the bolts to 29 ft. lbs. (39 Nm).

c. Install the access covers.

12. Install the engine under covers.

13. Have the front wheel alignment checked.

1987–91 Models

1. Raise the front of the vehicle and support it safely. Remove the front wheels.

2. Unbolt and remove the suspension lower crossmember from the bottom of the vehicle.

3. Remove the nuts attaching the stabilizer bar to the lower arm.

4. Remove the stabilizer bar bracket.

5. Remove the control cable clamp from the engine center mounting member.

6. Unbolt and remove the center mounting member.

7. Withdraw the stabilizer bar from the lower suspension arms.

8. Note their position and remove the spacers and retainers from the bar.

To install:

9. Install the spacers and retainers onto the stabilizer bar in their original order.

10. Connect the stabilizer bar to the lower arms.

11. Install the retainers and temporarily install two new nuts onto the stabilizer bar. They will be tightened later.

12. Install the stabilizer bar brackets with cushions. Tighten the retaining bolts to 94 ft. lbs. (127 Nm)S

13. The remained of installation is the reverse of removal. Install the engine center mounting member and tighten the outside bolts to 153 ft. lbs. (206 Nm) and the inside bolts to 32 ft. lbs. (43 Nm).

14. Install the suspension lower crossmember. Tighten the outside bolts to 153 ft. lbs. (207 Nm) and the inside bolts to 32 ft. lbs. (43 Nm).

15. Bounce the vehicle up and down a few times to stabilize the suspension.

16. Tighten the stabilizer bar nuts to 156 ft. lbs. (212 Nm).

17. Have the front wheel alignment checked.

1992–96 Models

1. Raise the front of the vehicle and support it safely. Remove the front wheels.

2. Remove both right and left side fender apron seals.

3. Remove the cotter pin and the nut from both side tie rod end studs. Using puller, disconnect right and left tie rod ends from the steering knuckle

4. Remove stabilizer bar links (bolts) from each control arm.

5. Remove the right and left bushing retainers and the bar bushings.

6. Remove the front exhaust pipe.

7. Remove the steering gear box mounting bolts and nuts.

8. Lift the steering gear box and remove the stabilizer bar from the vehicle.

To install:

9. Lift the steering gear box and install bar into position.

10. Install the steering gear box mounting bolts and nuts and tighten to 134 ft. lbs. (181 Nm).

11. Install the front exhaust pipe.

12. Install the left and the right stabilizer bar bushings, bushing retainers, and secure with the retaining bolts. Tighten the retainer bolts to 14 ft. lbs. (19 Nm).

13. Install both side stabilizer bar links and tighten to 47 ft. lbs. (64 Nm) on 1992–94 models and 29 ft. lbs. (39 Nm) on 1995–96 models.

14. Connect both side tie rod ends to the steering knuckles and tighten the nut to 36 ft. lbs. (49 Nm).

15. Install the left and the right fender apron seals and the front wheels.

Lower Control Arm

REMOVAL & INSTALLATION

1983–86 Models

1. Raise the front of the vehicle and support it with jackstands. Remove the front wheels.

2. Loosen and remove the two bolts attaching the ball joint to the steering knuckle.

3. Remove the nut that holds the stabilizer bar to the lower control arm.

4. Loosen the lower control arm bolt.

5. Wiggle the stabilizer bar back and forth and pull out the bolt.

6. Remove the lower control arm.

✳✳ CAUTION

Do not pull on the driveshaft!

7. Remove the retainer and the spacer from the stabilizer bar.

8. Remove and install the ball joint, if necessary.

To install:

9. Install the spacer first and then the retainer. Pass the lower arm through the stabilizer.

10. While pushing on the bar and having an assistant pry on the arm with a crescent wrench, temporarily install the bolt.

11. Install the retainer and finger tighten the stabilizer bar nut.

12. Connect the lower arm to the steering knuckle and tighten the bolts to 83 ft. lbs. (112 Nm).

13. Install the front wheels and lower the vehicle.

14. Bounce the vehicle up and down several times to settle the suspension.

15. Tighten the stabilizer bar nut to 86 ft. lbs. (116 Nm).

16. Tighten the lower control arm bolt to 83 ft. lbs. (112 Nm).

17. Have the front wheel alignment checked.

1987 Models

1. Raise the front of the vehicle and support it safely.

2. Remove the front wheels.

3. Separate the lower ball joint from the steering knuckle.

4. Remove the nut holding the stabilizer bar to the lower arm.

5. Remove the nut holding the lower arm shaft to the lower arm.

6. Unbolt and remove the lower suspension crossmember.

7. Remove the lower arm shaft mounting nut and bolt.

8. Remove the lower arm with the lower arm shaft.

9. Remove and install the ball joint as necessary.

To install:

10. First insert the lower arm into the stabilizer bar, and then install the lower arm shaft into the body.

11. Temporarily install the lower arm nut and retainer.

12. Temporarily install the new stabilizer nut with the retainer to hold the stabilizer bar to the lower arm.

13. Connect the steering knuckle to the lower ball joint and tighten the two bolts to 94 ft. lbs. (127 Nm).

14. Temporarily install the lower arm shaft to the body.

15. Install the suspension lower cross member. Tighten the outside bolts to 153 ft. lbs. (207 Nm) and the inside bolts to 32 ft. lbs. (43 Nm).

16. Install the front wheels and lower the vehicle.

17. Bounce the vehicle up and down several times to settle the suspension.

18. Tighten the lower suspension arm nuts to 156 ft. lbs. (212 Nm).

19. Have the front wheel alignment checked.

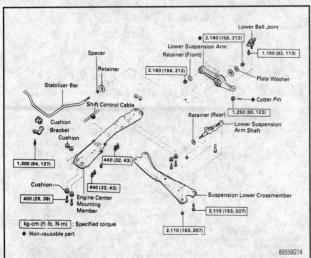

Fig. 20 View of the lower control arm and front suspension components—1990 shown

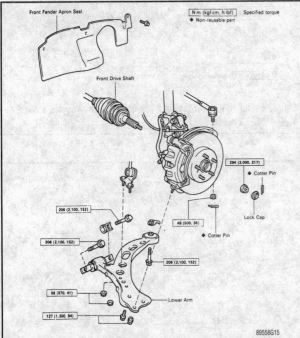

Fig. 21 Exploded view of the lower control arm mounting bolt locations

1988–91 Models

▶ **See Figure 20**

1. Raise the vehicle and support safely. Remove the front wheels and the fender apron seal.
2. Disconnect the lower arm from the steering knuckle, at the ball joint.
3. Disconnect the stabilizer bar from the lower arm.
4. Remove the crossmember and lower arm as an assembly. Remove the lower suspension with the lower suspension arm shaft.

To install:

5. Install the crossmember and lower arm assemblies. Loosely install the lower arm bushing bolts. Tighten the crossmember bolts to 112 ft. lbs. (152 Nm).
6. Install the ball joint bolts and tighten to 90 ft. lbs. (123 Nm).
7. Install the stabilizer nut loosely.
8. Install the front wheels and lower the vehicle. Bounce up and down to stabilize the suspension. With the vehicle weight on the suspension, tighten the lower control arm bushing and stabilizer nuts to 156 ft. lbs. (212 Nm).
9. Align the front end.

1992–96 Models

▶ **See Figures 21 thru 26**

1. Raise the vehicle and support safely. Remove the front wheels and the fender apron seal.
2. While applying the front brakes, remove the drive shaft lock nut.
3. Disconnect and separate the tie rod end from the steering knuckle.
4. Remove the left and right stabilizer end brackets from the lower arms.
5. Remove the 2 nuts and one bolt to disconnect the lower arm from the ball joint.
6. Remove the bolt and nut (with arm attached) from the rear of the arm.

➡ **There is a nut with an arm attached to it to prevent nut rotation.**

7. Remove the pivot bolts from where it attaches to the subframe. Remove the spacer from the one pivot bolt. Maneuver the arm from its mounting area.

To install:

8. Slide the control arm into the rear biscuit then place the rest of the arm into position.
9. Install the lower arm bushing stopper to the lower arm shaft. Install the pivot bolt where they attach to the subframe and tighten to 152 ft. lbs. (206 Nm).
10. Tighten the bolts on the rear biscuit of the control arm to 152 ft. lbs. (206 Nm).
11. Connect the lower arm to the lower ball joint and tighten the fasteners to 94 ft. lbs. (127 Nm).
12. Install both side stabilizer end brackets to the lower arm and tighten to 41 ft. lbs. (56 Nm).
13. Connect the tie rod end to the steering knuckle and tighten nut to 36 ft. lbs. (49 Nm). Install new cotter pin.
14. Install the drive shaft lock nut and tighten to 217 ft. lbs. (294 Nm). Install new cotter pin.
15. Install front fender apron seal and the front wheel. Tighten the lugnuts to 76 ft. lbs. (103 Nm).

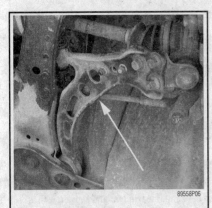

Fig. 22 View of the lower control arm

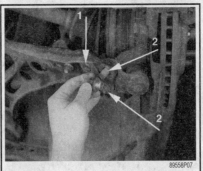

Fig. 23 Remove the bolt (1) and two nuts (2) to separate the lower control arm from the ball joint

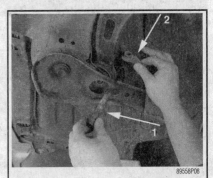

Fig. 24 Remove the long bolt and nut with attaching arm from the lower control arm towards the rear of the vehicle

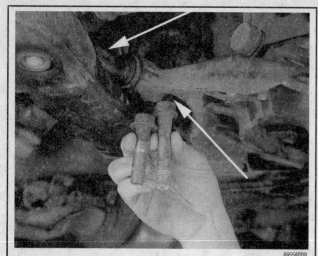

Fig. 25 Remove the two pivot bolts connecting the control arm to the subframe

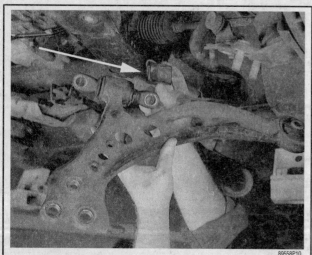

Fig. 26 Maneuver the control arm out from under the vehicle, make sure not to loose the spacer during separation

Steering Knuckle

On all models, the steering knuckle is attached to the axle hub. Both components are removed as an assembly.

Front Hub and Bearing

REMOVAL & INSTALLATION

1983–91 Models

▶ See Figures 27 and 28

1. Raise the front of the vehicle and support it safely.
2. Remove the front wheels.
3. Remove the cotter pin and the bearing lock nut cap. Discard the cotter pin.
4. Have an assistant depress the brake pedal and loosen the bearing lock nut.
5. Disconnect the brake caliper from the steering knuckle and support it with a piece of wire.
6. Remove the disc rotor and disconnect the ABS wheel speed sensor.

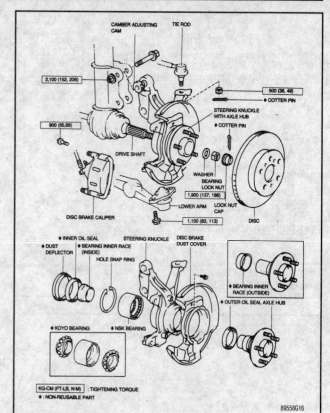

Fig. 27 Exploded view of the axle hub and steering knuckle assembly—1986–89 models

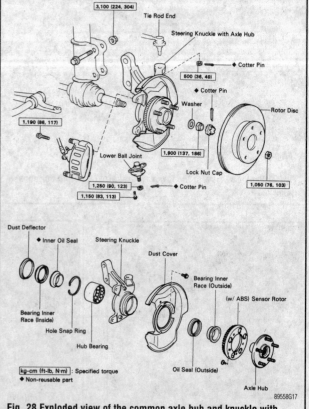

Fig. 28 Exploded view of the common axle hub and knuckle with ABS—1990–91 models

7. Remove the castellated nut from the tie rod end.

8. Using SST No. 09628–62011 or equivalent two-armed puller, disconnect the tie rod from the steering knuckle.

9. Place alignment marks on the steering knuckle and camber adjust cam.

10. Unbolt and separate the steering knuckle from the shock absorber.

11. Remove the cotter pin, nut and disconnect the steering knuckle from the lower suspension arm using a suitable two-armed puller.

12. With a rubber mallet, tap the driveshaft and pull the axle hub and steering knuckle from the driveshaft. Cover the drive boot with a rag.

13. Proceed to "Bearing Replacement" in this Section to remove and install the wheel bearing and oil seals.

To install:

14. Attach the steering knuckle to the lower suspension arm and temporarily install the nut.

15. Attach the steering knuckle to the shock absorber lower bracket temporarily. Insert the bolts from the rear side and align the matchmarks made on the adjusting cam. Tighten the bolts as follows:

- 1983–86 models—152 ft. lbs. (206 Nm)
- 1987–88 models—166 ft. lbs. (226 Nm)
- 1989–91 models—224 ft. lbs. (304 Nm)

16. Connect the tie rod to the steering knuckle. Tighten the castellated nut to 36 ft. lbs. (49 Nm). Secure the nut with a new cotter pin.

17. On 1983–96 models, tighten the steering knuckle-to-lower arm retaining bolts to 83 ft. lbs. (112 Nm).

18. Connect the ball joint to the lower suspension arm with the castellated nut and a new cotter pin. On 1987–88 models, tighten the nut to 67 ft. lbs. (91 Nm). On 1989–91 vehicles, tighten the nut to 90 ft. lbs. (123 Nm).

19. Connect the ABS wheel speed sensor and position the rotor disc onto the axle hub.

20. Connect the brake caliper to the steering knuckle.

21. Have an assistant depress the brake pedal and tighten the bearing lock nut to 137 ft. lbs. (186 Nm).

22. Install the adjusting nut cap with a new cotter pin. Using pliers, separate the cotter pin prongs and wrap them around the flats of the nut.

23. Install the front wheels and lower the vehicle.

24. Have the front wheel alignment checked.

1992—96 Models

▶ **See Figure 29**

1. Raise the vehicle and support safely. Remove the front wheels and the fender apron seal.

2. Check the bearing backlash and axle hub deviation.

   a. Remove the two brake caliper set bolts.

   b. Hang the caliper using stiff wire on the shock absorber assembly.

   c. Remove the rotor.

   d. Place a dial indicator near the center of the axle hub and check the backlash in the bearing shaft direction.

   e. Backlash maximum should read 0.0020 inch (0.05mm). If the specification is greater than this, replace the bearing.

   f. Using the dial indicator, check the deviation at the surface of the axle hub outside and hub bolt. Maximum is 0.0020 inch (0.05mm). If greater than specified, replace the axle hub.

3. Install the rotor and caliper assembly. Remove the cotter pin and lock cap off the center hub nut. Discard the cotter pin.

4. While applying the front brakes, remove the drive shaft lock nut.

5. Disconnect and separate the tie rod end from the steering knuckle.

6. Remove the left and right stabilizer end brackets from the lower arms.

7. Remove the 2 nuts and disconnect the lower arm from the ball joint.

8. Remove the drive shaft from the axle hub. Secure the shaft out of the way using wire. Be careful not to damage the shaft boot or ABS sensor rotor.

9. Remove the 2 brake caliper mounting bolts and remove the caliper. Support caliper from the vehicle using wire. Remove the brake rotor.

10. If equipped with ABS, remove the sensor from the steering knuckle.

11. Remove the 2 nuts on the lower end of the shock and remove the steering knuckle and hub assembly.

To install:

12. Install the steering knuckle and hub assembly onto the vehicle and temporarily install the lower shock bolts.

13. Connect the lower ball joint to the lower arm and tighten the bolt and nuts to 94 ft. lbs. (127 Nm).

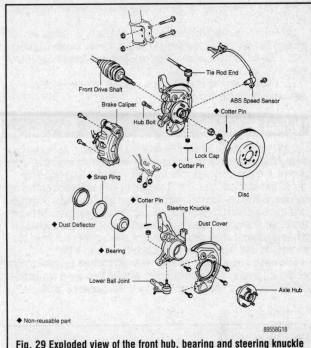

◆ Non-reusable part

89558G18

Fig. 29 Exploded view of the front hub, bearing and steering knuckle assembly—1992–96 models

14. Connect the tie rod to the knuckle and tighten the nut to 36 ft. lbs. (49 Nm). Install new cotter pin.

15. Tighten the nuts on the lower end of the shock to 156 ft. lbs. (211 Nm).

16. Install both side stabilizer end brackets to the lower arm and tighten to 43 ft. lbs. (58 Nm).

17. Install the front ABS sensor and tighten to 69 inch lbs. (8 Nm).

18. Install the front brake rotor and caliper. Tighten the caliper mounting bolts to 79 ft. lbs. (107 Nm).

19. Install the drive shaft locknut, and while applying the brakes, tighten to 217 ft. lbs. (294 Nm). Install lock cap and new cotter pin.

20. Install front fender apron seal and the front wheel. Tighten the front wheel to 76 ft. lbs. (103 Nm).

BEARING REPLACEMENT

1. Clamp the steering knuckle in a vise with soft jaws to protect the knuckle.

2. Using screw driver, carefully pry the dust deflector from the hub.

3. Drive out the bearing inner oil seal from the knuckle. On 1983–86 vehicles the seal is extracted with a puller. On 1987–96 vehicles, the seal is pried from the knuckle bore.

4. After the seal is removed, use snapring pliers to remove the hole snapring from the knuckle bore.

5. Unbolt and separate the dust deflector from the steering knuckle.

6. Using a two-armed mechanical puller, pull the axle hub from the dust deflector.

7. Using the puller, remove the inner (inside) bearing race from the bearing.

8. Using Torx® wrench, remove the sensor control rotor from the axle hub.

9. Using the puller, remove the outer bearing race. Set the outer race aside.

10. Remove the outer bearing seal in the same manner as the inner seal.

11. Take the inner (outside) race and install it inside the bearing.

12. With a piece of brass stock, tap the bearing from the steering knuckle.

To install bearing:

13. Clean all the oil seal and bearing seating surfaces with a clean, dry rag.

14. Install SST No. 09608–32010 into the bore of the steering knuckle and press the bearing into the bore. Leave the tool in place.

15. Turn and insert the side lip of the new outer oil seal into the factory tool and drive the seal into the steering knuckle.

16. Attach the brake disc cover to the steering knuckle with the bolts.

17. Apply multi-purpose grease between the oil seal lip, oil seal and bearing and press the hub into the knuckle.

18. Install a new snapring in the knuckle.

19. Press a new oil seal into the knuckle and coat the seal with multi-purpose grease.

20. Press the dust deflector into the knuckle. Make sure on vehicles with ABS, you align the holes for the speed sensor in the dust deflector and steering knuckle.

21. Connect the ball joint to the steering knuckle and tighten the bolts to 94 ft. lbs. (127 Nm).

22. Install the steering knuckle and hub assembly onto the vehicle as described earlier in this Section.

Wheel Alignment

If the tires are worn unevenly, if the vehicle is not stable on the highway or if the handling seems uneven in spirited driving, the wheel alignment should be checked. If an alignment problem is suspected, first check for improper tire inflation and other possible causes. These can be worn suspension or steering components, accident damage or even unmatched tires. If any worn or damaged components are found, they must be replaced before the wheels can be properly aligned. Wheel alignment requires very expensive equipment and involves minute adjustments which must be accurate; it should only be performed by a trained technician. Take your vehicle to a properly equipped shop.

Following is a description of the alignment angles which are adjustable on most vehicles and how they affect vehicle handling. Although these angles can apply to both the front and rear wheels, usually only the front suspension is adjustable.

CASTER

▶ **See Figure 30**

Looking at a vehicle from the side, caster angle describes the steering axis rather than a wheel angle. The steering knuckle is attached to a control arm or shock absorber at the top and a control arm at the bottom. The wheel pivots around the line between these points to steer the vehicle. When the upper point is tilted back, this is described as positive caster. Having a positive caster tends to make the wheels self-centering, increasing directional stability. Excessive positive caster makes the wheels hard to steer, while an uneven caster will cause a pull to one side. Overloading the vehicle or sagging rear springs will affect caster, as will raising the rear of the vehicle. If the rear of the vehicle is lower than normal, the caster becomes more positive.

CAMBER

▶ **See Figure 31**

Looking from the front of the vehicle, camber is the inward or outward tilt of the top of wheels. When the tops of the wheels are tilted in, this is negative camber; if they are tilted out, it is positive. In a turn, a slight amount of negative camber helps maximize contact of the tire with the road. However, too much negative camber compromises straight-line stability, increases bump steer and torque steer.

TOE

▶ **See Figure 32**

Looking down at the wheels from above the vehicle, toe angle is the distance between the front of the wheels, relative to the distance between the back of the wheels. If the wheels are closer at the front, they are said to be toed-in or to have negative toe. A small amount of negative toe enhances directional stability and provides a smoother ride on the highway.

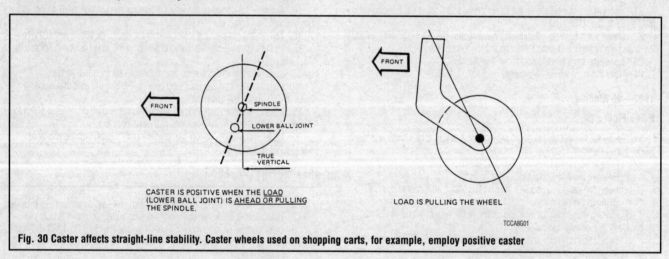

CASTER IS POSITIVE WHEN THE <u>LOAD</u> (LOWER BALL JOINT) IS <u>AHEAD OR PULLING</u> THE SPINDLE.

LOAD IS PULLING THE WHEEL

TCCA8G01

Fig. 30 Caster affects straight-line stability. Caster wheels used on shopping carts, for example, employ positive caster

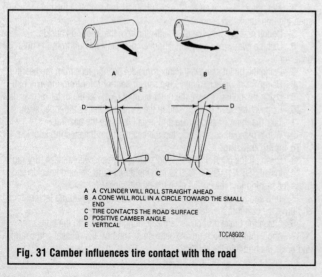

A A CYLINDER WILL ROLL STRAIGHT AHEAD
B A CONE WILL ROLL IN A CIRCLE TOWARD THE SMALL END
C TIRE CONTACTS THE ROAD SURFACE
D POSITIVE CAMBER ANGLE
E VERTICAL

TCCA8G02

Fig. 31 Camber influences tire contact with the road

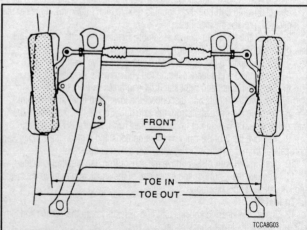

FRONT

TOE IN
TOE OUT

TCCA8G03

Fig. 32 With toe-in, the distance between the wheels is closer at the front than at the rear

REAR SUSPENSION

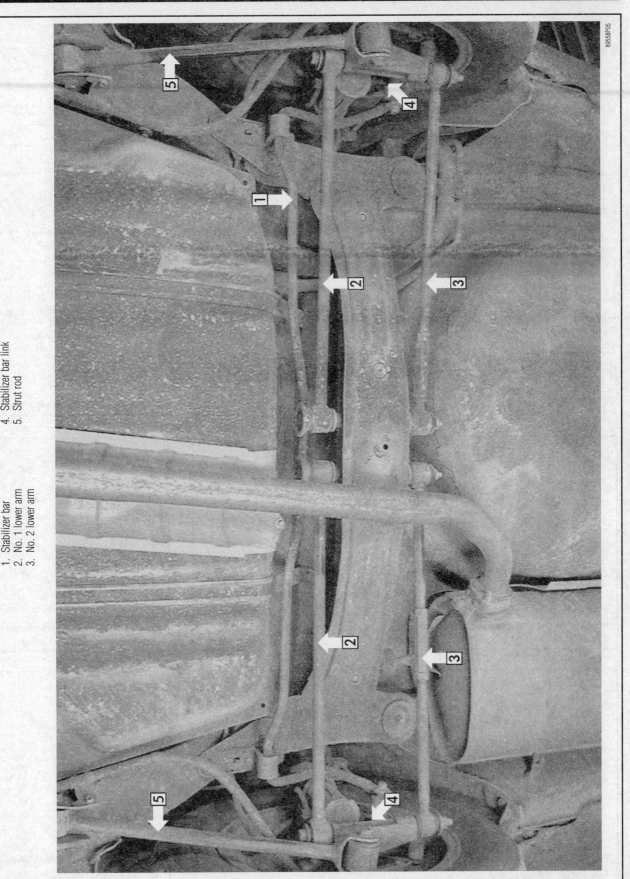

REAR SUSPENSION COMPONENTS

1. Stabilizer bar
2. No. 1 lower arm
3. No. 2 lower arm
4. Stabilizer bar link
5. Strut rod

Coil Springs

REMOVAL & INSTALLATION

▶ **See Figures 33 thru 40**

1. Remove the shock absorber assembly with coil spring out from under the vehicle.

2. To disassemble the shock from the coil spring, install 2 nuts and a bolt to the bracket at the lower part of the shock absorber and secure it in a vice.

3. Using a special coil spring compressor, such as 09727–30020 or equivalent, compress the coil spring. Do not use an impact wrench, it will damage the compression tool.

4. Remove the cap from the suspension support. Using a retaining tool to hold the seat, such as 09729–22031 or equivalent remove the nut.

5. Remove the following components:
- Suspension support
- Dust seal
- Spring seat
- Upper insulator and coil spring
- Spring bumper and lower insulator

To install:

6. Install the lower insulator. Attach the spring bumper to the piston rod.

7. Using the compressor tool, such as 09727–30020 or equivalent, compress the coil spring. Install the coil spring to the shock absorber.

➡**Fit the lower end of the coil spring into the gap of the spring seat of the shock absorber.**

8. Install the upper insulator to the upper support. Match the bolt of the upper support with the cut-off part of the insulator. Install the upper support and piston rod.

9. Install the retaining tool, such as 09729–22031 or equivalent to hold the spring seat, install a new nut. Tighten the nut to 34–36 ft. lbs. (47–49 Nm).

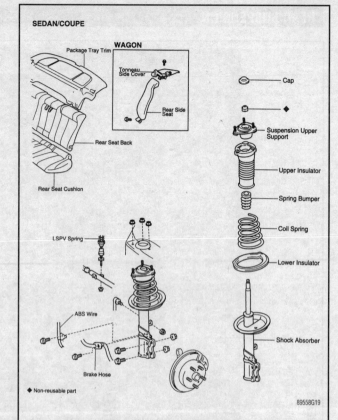

Fig. 33 Exploded view of the rear coil and shock assembly

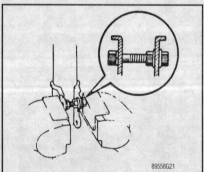

Fig. 34 Install a bolt and two nuts as shown to the end of the shock and place the assembly in a vise

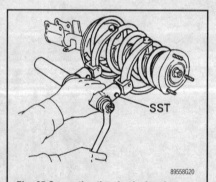

Fig. 35 Separating the shock absorber from the coil spring with a compressor tool

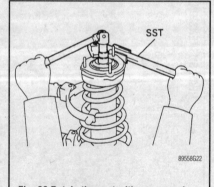

Fig. 36 Retain the seat with one wrench and remove the nut with another

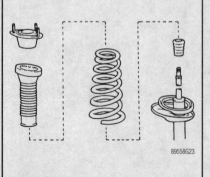

Fig. 37 Placement order of the coil and strut components

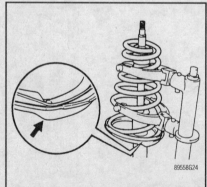

Fig. 38 Fit the lower end of the coil into the gap of the seat

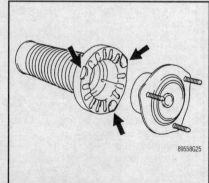

Fig. 39 Match the bolt of the upper support with the cut-off of insulator

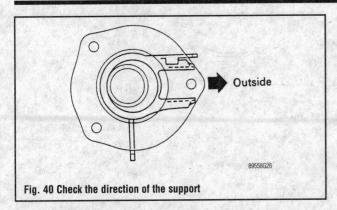

Fig. 40 Check the direction of the support

10. Rotate the upper support and set it in the direction shown in the illustration. Remove the SST, then check the direction of the upper support.
11. Install the cap.
12. Pack the upper suspension support with MP grease.
13. Install the coil and shock absorber assembly into the vehicle.

MacPherson Struts

REMOVAL & INSTALLATION

1983–86 Models

1. On 4-door sedan, remove the package tray and vent duct.
2. On hatchback, remove the speaker grilles.
3. Disconnect the brake line from the wheel cylinder.

✳✳ CAUTION

Brake fluid contains polyglycol ethers and polyglycols. Avoid contact with the eyes and wash your hands thoroughly after handling brake fluid. If you do get brake fluid in your eyes, flush your eyes with clean, running water for 15 minutes. If eye irritation persists, or if you have taken brake fluid internally, IMMEDIATELY seek medical assistance.

4. Remove the brake line from the brake hose.
5. Disconnect the brake hose from its bracket on the shock absorber.
6. Loosen, but do not remove, the nut holding the suspension support to the shock absorber.
7. Unbolt the shock absorber from the rear arm.
8. Unbolt and extract the shock absorber from the body.
To install:
9. Attach the shock absorber to the body and tighten the 3 nuts to 17 ft. lbs. (25 Nm).
10. Engage the shock absorber bracket with the carrier and install the hardware. Tighten the nuts to 119 ft. lbs. (162 Nm).
11. Tighten the center suspension support nut to 36 ft. lbs. (49 Nm). There is a bearing located under the suspension support dust cover. Remove the dust cover and pack the bearing with multi-purpose grease. Once packed, reinstall the dust cover.
12. The remainder of installation is the reverse of removal. Tighten each component to specifications.
13. Have the rear wheel alignment checked.

1987–88 Models

1. On wagon models, remove the toneau cover holder.
2. Loosen the rear wheel lug nuts, raise the rear of the vehicle and support it safely. Block the front wheels.
3. Remove the rear wheels.
4. Using the proper size flare nut wrench, disconnect the backing plate hardware.
5. With a flare nut and a back-up wrench, disconnect the brake tube from the brake hose and use a small plastic container to collect the brake fluid.
6. Undo the clip and disconnect the brake hose from the shock absorber.

➡Before the axle bolts are removed, the axle carrier must be supported with a jack.

7. Support the axle carrier with a floor jack and remove the mounting bolts and nut. Disconnect the axle carrier from the shock absorber.
8. Support the shock absorber firmly by hand and remove the three mounting nuts. Remove the shock absorber from the body.
To install:
9. Position the shock absorber onto the body and support it firmly by hand. Install the three nuts and tighten them to 23 ft. lbs. (31 Nm).
10. Attach the axle carrier to the shock absorber with the nuts and bolts. Tighten the nuts to 166 ft. lbs. (226 Nm).
11. The remainder of installation is the reverse of removal. Tighten each component to specifications.
12. Bleed the brake lines as described in Section 9.
13. Have the rear wheel alignment checked.

1989–96 Models

▸ See Figures 41 and 42

1. On the 4-door sedan, remove the package tray and vent duct. On 1992–96 models, it will be necessary to remove the rear seat back.
2. On the hatchback, remove the speaker grilles.
3. On the wagon models remove the tonnue cover and rear seat back.
4. Loosen the rear wheel lug nuts, raise the rear of the vehicle and support it safely. Block the front wheels.
5. Remove the rear wheels.
6. Disconnect the brake hose and the ABS speed sensor from the shock absorber.
7. If equipped with ABS, disconnect the Load Sensing Proportioning Valve (LSPV) spring from the lower arm.
8. Disconnect the stabilizer bar link from the shock absorber.
9. Support the rear axle and loosen the 2 bolts from the lower end of the shock absorber.
10. From inside the vehicle, unbolt the upper support.
11. Lower the rear axle carrier and remove the two bolts.
12. Remove the shock absorber from the vehicle.

Fig. 41 A rubber cap covers the rear shock absorber tower nut

Fig. 42 The upper shock absorber tower is retained by the center nut (circled) and three surrounding nuts

To install:

13. Install the shock absorber assembly onto the vehicle.
14. Connect the brake hose and the ABS speed sensor to the shock absorber.
15. Connect the stabilizer bar link to the shock absorber.
16. Install the wheel and tire assembly.
17. During installation, please observe the following tighten specifications:
    a. Tighten the shock absorber-to-body bolts to 29 ft. lbs. (39 Nm).
    b. Tighten the shock absorber-to-axle carrier nuts to 166 ft. lbs. (226 Nm) on 1988–91 vehicles and 188 ft. lbs. (255 Nm) on 1992–96 vehicles.
    c. Tighten the suspension support-to-shock absorber nut to 36 ft. lbs. (49 Nm) on 1988–91 vehicles. On 1992–96 models, tighten the stabilizer bar link to shock absorber retainers to 47 ft. lbs. (64 Nm).
18. Install the rear seat back, vent duct and the package tray as required.

OVERHAUL

Refer to the Coil Spring removal and installation procedure earlier in this section.

Suspension Arms

REMOVAL & INSTALLATION

▶ **See Figures 43, 44 and 45**

1983–86 Models

1. Loosen the rear wheel lug nuts. Raise the rear of the vehicle with a floor jack and support the body with safety stands. Remove the rear wheels.
2. Remove the nut and bolt that connects the No. 2 suspension arm to the axle carrier.
3. Note and record the position of the cam plate mark, then remove the nut and bolt that connects the No. 2 suspension arm to the body. Remove the No. 2 suspension arm.

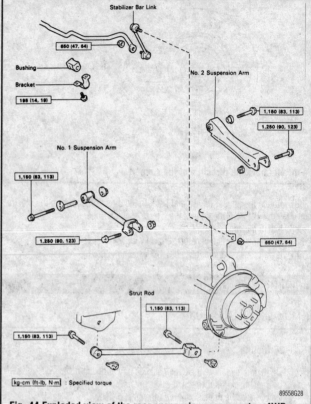

kg-cm (ft-lb, N·m) : Specified torque

89558G28

Fig. 44 Exploded view of the rear suspension components—4WD models

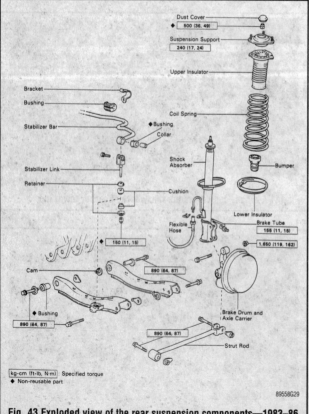

kg-cm (ft-lb, N·m): Specified torque
◆ Non-reusable part

89558G29

Fig. 43 Exploded view of the rear suspension components—1983–86 models

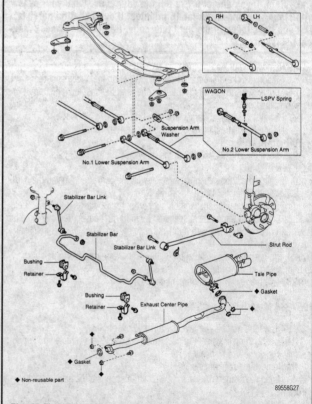

◆ Non-reusable part

89558G27

Fig. 45 Exploded view of the rear suspension arms and strut rod— 1992–96 models

4. On 1984–86 vehicles, remove the nut, retainer and cushion that connects the No. 1 suspension arm to the stabilizer bar link. Discard the nut and purchase a new one.

5. Disconnect the No. 1 suspension arm from the axle carrier by removing the nut and bolt. Remove the nut and bolt that connects the No. 2 suspension arm to the body.

6. Press the old side body bushing from the No. 1 suspension arm and press in a new bushing. The new bushing need not be lubricated to install it.

7. To install, engage the No. 1 suspension arm with the body and install the nut and bolt so that it is finger tight. The lip of the nut should be resting on the flange of the bracket and not over it.

8. On 1984–86 vehicles, connect the stabilizer link to the No. 1 suspension arm with the cushions, retainers and the new nut. Tighten the nut to 11 ft. lbs. (16 Nm).

9. Engage the No. 1 suspension arm with the axle carrier and install the nut and bolt so that they are finger tight. When doing this, insert the lip of the nut into the hole in the arm.

10. Position the No. 2 suspension arm onto the body and temporarily install the cam and bolt.

11. Align the cam plate mark with its original position. Temporarily install the nut and bolt that connects the suspension arm to the body.

12. Install the rear wheels and remove the safety stands.

13. Lower the vehicle and bounce the rear end a few to times to allow the rear suspension to stabilize.

14. Now that the vehicle weight is on the suspension, tighten all the previously finger tightened bolts to 64 ft. lbs. (87 Nm).

15. Have the rear alignment checked.

1987–91 Models

▶ See Figure 46

1. Raise the vehicle and support safely. Remove the rear wheels.

2. Remove the nut from the axle carrier. Remove the mounting bolts from the strut rod and disconnect from the carrier.

3. Disconnect the Load Sensing Proportioning Valve (LSPV) spring from the lower arm if equipped.

4. Disconnect No. 1 and No. 2 suspension arms from the axle carrier.

5. Remove the fasteners and pull the fuel tank protector down from the vehicle.

6. Place matchmarks on the toe adjust cam and suspension member.

7. Remove the service hole cover(s). Loosen the bolt and remove the toe adjust plate No. 2.

8. Remove the bolt with toe adjust cam, disconnect the No. 2 suspension arm and remove from the vehicle.

9. Remove the nut retainer from the body and remove the No. 1 suspension arm.

To install:

10. Install the stamped suspension arm No. 1 with the identification mark **L** for left and **R** for right on the proper side. Temporarily install the suspension arms with the bolt, washer and nut. Do not tighten at this time. Install with the bushing slit side towards the rear.

11. Face the paint mark on the No. 2 suspension arms toward the rear of the vehicle. Install the bushing with the slit side towards the rear of the vehicle.

12. Loosely install the bolt into the axle carrier. Connect the Load Sensing Proportioning Valve (LSPV) spring to the lower arm and tighten to 9 ft. lbs. (13 Nm).

13. Connect the strut bar to the axle carrier and temporarily install the bolt and nut.

14. Install the fuel tank protector, rear wheels and lower the vehicle. Bounce the suspension up and down a few times.

15. Tighten the strut rod bolts to 83 ft. lbs. (113 Nm) and the suspension arm nuts (inside and outside) to 134 ft. lbs. (181 Nm).

16. Have the rear wheel alignment checked.

1992–96 Models

▶ See Figures 47 thru 53

1. Raise the vehicle and support safely. Remove the rear wheel.

2. Remove the nut from the axle carrier. Remove the mounting bolts from the strut rod and disconnect from the carrier.

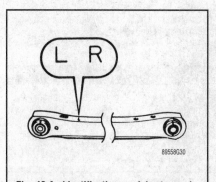

Fig. 46 An identification mark is stamped into the rear suspension arm on some models

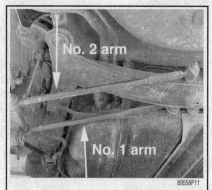

Fig. 47 View of the No. 1 and No. 2 rear lower arms

Fig. 48 A large bolt running through the knuckle secures the No.1 and No. 2 arms

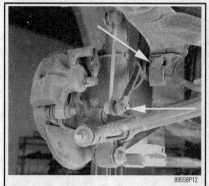

Fig. 49 The rear stabilizer bar is attaches on both sides at these two locations

Fig. 50 The strut rod runs from the knuckle to the body

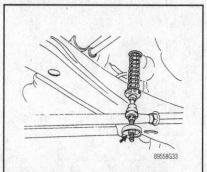

Fig. 51 Disconnect the Load Sensing Proportioning Valve (LSPV) spring from the lower arm

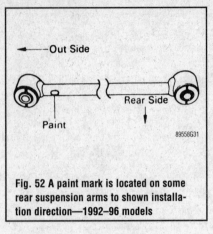

Fig. 52 A paint mark is located on some rear suspension arms to shown installation direction—1992–96 models

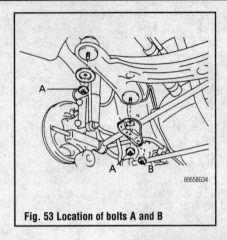

Fig. 53 Location of bolts A and B

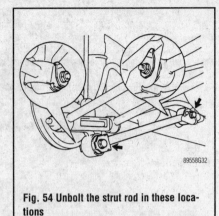

Fig. 54 Unbolt the strut rod in these locations

3. Disconnect the Load Sensing Proportioning Valve (LSPV) spring from the lower arm if equipped.

4. Remove the No. 2 arm by removing the 3 nuts and washers.

5. Remove the right and left stabilizer bar bushing retainers.

6. Remove the exhaust center and tail pipes.

7. Support the suspension member with a jack. Remove the 6 nuts a and the left and right suspension member lower stopper. Lower the suspension member.

8. Remove the No. 1 arm with the 2 bolts and washer.

To install:

9. Install the No. 1 arm with the washer and two bolts. Face the paint mark towards the rear. Do not tighten at this time.

10. Jack up the suspension member. Install the member lower supports and the six nuts. Tighten nut A to 83 ft. lbs. and B to 28 ft. lbs. (38 Nm).

11. Install the exhaust system and the left and right stabilizer bar retainers. Tighten the retainer bolts to 14 ft. lbs. (19 Nm).

12. Face the paint mark on the No. 2 suspension arm toward the rear of the vehicle. Temporarily install the two lock nuts..

13. Connect the Load Sensing Proportioning Valve (LSPV) spring to the lower arm and tighten to 9 ft. lbs. (13 Nm).

14. Connect the strut bar to the axle carrier and temporarily install the bolt and nut.

15. Tighten the nut on the outside of the lower arms to 134 ft. lbs. (181 Nm).

16. Install the rear wheels and lower the vehicle. Bounce the suspension up and down a few times.

17. Jack up the vehicle and support the body with stands.

18. Remove the rear wheel. Support the rear axle carrier with a jack. Tighten the nut on the outside of the lower arm to 134 ft. lbs. (181 Nm). Tighten the strut rod set bolts to 83 ft. lbs. (113 Nm).

19. Install the rear wheel and lower the vehicle. Tighten the lug nuts.

20. Inspect and adjust the rear wheel alignment.

21. Tighten the No. 2 lower arm and locknuts to 41 ft. lbs. (56 Nm) if necessary.

Strut Rod

REMOVAL & INSTALLATION

♦ **See Figures 50 and 54**

1. Loosen the rear wheel lug nuts. Raise the rear of the vehicle with a floor jack and support the body with safety stands. Remove the rear wheels.

2. Disconnect the strut rod from the axle carrier and the body by removing the two nuts and bolts.

3. Remove the strut rod.

To install:

4. Position the strut rod onto the body and axle carrier and install the nuts and bolts finger tight. Make sure that the lip of the nut is resting on the flange of the bracket.

5. Install the rear wheels and remove the safety stands.

6. Lower the vehicle and bounce the rear end a few to times to allow the rear suspension to stabilize.

7. Tighten the mounting bolts to 83 ft. lbs. (113 Nm).

8. Have the rear wheel alignment checked.

Stabilizer Bar

REMOVAL & INSTALLATION

1. Loosen the rear wheel lug nuts. Raise the rear of the vehicle with a floor jack and support the body with safety stands. Remove the rear wheels.

2. Remove the nut, retainer and cushion that connects the No. 1 suspension arm to the stabilizer bar.

3. On some vehicles, it may be necessary to support the fuel tank and remove the tank band from the body.

4. Disconnect the stabilizer bar from the body by removing the bolts. Remove the stabilizer bar from the vehicle with bushings and brackets. If the bushings appear to be worn or cracked, replace them.

5. Installation is the reverse of removal. Temporarily connect the stabilizer bar to the body with the bushings, brackets and bolts.

6. Connect the stabilizer bar links to the No. 1 suspension arm with the retainers, cushions and nuts. Tighten the center bracket bolts to 14 ft. lbs. (19 Nm). Tighten the stabilizer-to-body bolts to 14 ft. lbs. (19 Nm) and the stabilizer link to stabilizer bar bolts to 47 ft. lbs. (64 Nm).

7. Have the rear wheel alignment checked.

Rear Wheel Bearings

On models with ABS the rear wheel bearing can not be separated from the rear hub. On some models without rear ABS the rear bearing can be removed from the hub. On these models it is required to obtain a bearing puller such as 09950–20017 to separate the bearing from the hub.

REMOVAL & INSTALLATION

♦ **See Figures 55 and 56**

1. Raise and support the vehicle safely.

2. Remove the rear wheel and tire assembly.

3. Remove the brake drum or if equipped with disc brakes, remove the caliper and the rotor from the axle carrier. Suspend the caliper with a wire.

➡ **If the rear brake drum is difficult to remove, insert a suitable prying tool (a bent wire or coat hanger will do the job nicely) through the hole in the backing plate and hold the automatic adjusting lever away from the adjusting bolt. With a brake tool, reduce the brake shoe adjustment tension by turning the adjusting bolt. The same can be done through the front of the disc on rear disc brakes, to reduce the tension applied by the parking brake shoes.**

4. Disconnect and plug the brake line at the backing plate.

5. Remove the 4 axle hub-to-carrier bolts and slide off the hub and brake assembly. Remove the O-ring from the backing plate.

6. Remove the bolt and nut attaching the carrier to the strut rod.

7. Remove the bolt and nut attaching the carrier to the No. 1 suspension arm.

8. Remove the bolt and nut attaching the carrier to the No. 2 suspension arm.

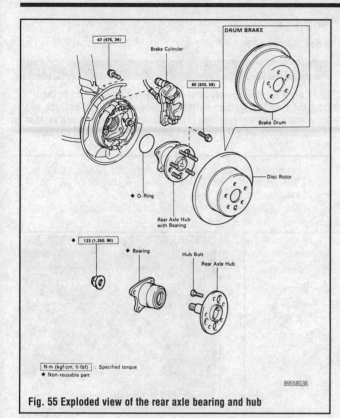

Fig. 55 Exploded view of the rear axle bearing and hub

Fig. 56 Remove the four bolts retaining the axle hub, use this large hole in the hub to access them

9. Unbolt the carrier from the rear strut tube and remove the carrier.

10. Using a hammer and cold chisel, loosen the staked part of the hub nut and remove the nut.

11. Using a 2-armed puller or 09950–20017, press the axle shaft from the hub.

12. Remove the bearing inner race (inside).

13. Using a 2-armed puller again, pull off the bearing inner race (outside) over the bearing and then press it out of the hub.

To install:

14. Position a new bearing inner race (outside) on the bearing and then press a new oil seal into the hub. Coat the lip of the seal with grease.

15. Position a new bearing inner race (inside) on the bearing and then press the inner race with the hub onto the axle shaft.

16. Install the nut and tighten it to 90 ft. lbs. (123 Nm). Stake the nut with a brass drift.

17. Position the axle carrier on the strut tube and tighten the nuts to 119 ft. lbs. (162 Nm) on 1983–86 vehicles, 166 ft. lbs. (226 Nm) on 1987–91 models and 188 ft. lbs. (255 Nm) on 1992–96 models.

18. Install the bolt and nut attaching the carrier to the No. 2 suspension arm; finger tighten it only.

➡**Make sure that the lip of the nut is in the hole on the arm.**

19. Install the bolt and nut attaching the carrier to the No. 1 suspension arm; finger tighten it only.

➡**Make sure that the lip of the nut is in the hole on the arm.**

20. Install the strut rod-to-carrier bolt so that the lip of the nut is in the groove on the bracket.

21. Install a new O-ring onto the axle carrier. Install the axle hub and brake backing plate. Tighten the four bolts to 59 ft. lbs. (80 Nm).

22. Reconnect and tighten the brake line to the wheel cylinder. Install the brake drum and wheel and tire assemblies. Tighten the lug nuts to 76 ft. lbs. (103 Nm).

23. Bleed the brakes. The brake bleeding procedure is detailed in Section 9.

24. Lower the vehicle and bounce the rear end a few times to stabilize the rear suspension.

25. Tighten the suspension arm bolts and the strut rod bolt to 64 ft. lbs. (87 Nm) on 1983–86 vehicles. On 1987–96 vehicles, tighten the strut rod-to-axle carrier bolts to 83 ft. lbs. (112 Nm) and the No.1 and No. 2 suspension arm-to-carrier bolts to 134 ft. lbs. (181 Nm).

STEERING

Steering Wheel

✳✳ CAUTION

On vehicles equipped with an air bag, the negative battery cable must be disconnected for a minimum of 90 seconds before working on the system. Failure to do so may result in deployment of the air bag and possible personal injury.

REMOVAL & INSTALLATION

1983–88 Models

✳✳ WARNING

Do not attempt to remove or install the steering wheel by hammering on it. Damage to the energy absorbing steering column could result.

1. Park the vehicle so that the front wheels are straight and make sure the steering wheel in the neutral position.

2. On 1983–86 US vehicles and 1987–88 vehicles equipped with tilt steering, remove the screw at the lower portion of the steering wheel pad and **gently** pull the pad upward and outward to remove it. On Canadian and 1987–88 vehicles without tilt steering, just pull the steering wheel pad upward and outward (gently). On Canadian models, the horn plate will be removed with the pad.

3. Loosen and remove the steering wheel nut.

4. Using a suitable metric threaded puller, remove the steering wheel.

To install:

5. Position the steering wheel onto the shaft and "walk" the steering wheel down the main shaft and install the nut.

6. Make sure that the steering wheel is at the center point and hold it there. Tighten the nut to 26 ft. lbs. (35 Nm) and check the center point again. Install the steering wheel pad in the reverse of the removal procedure.

1989–96 Models

WITHOUT AIR BAG

✳✳ WARNING

Do not attempt to remove or install the steering wheel by hammering on it. Damage to the energy-absorbing steering column could result.

1. Disconnect the negative battery cable. Position the front wheels straight ahead.

2. Unfasten the horn and turn signal multi-connector(s) at the base of the steering column shroud.

3. If equipped with a 3 spoked wheel, loosen the trim pad retaining screws from the back side of the steering wheel. The 2 spoke steering wheel is removed in the same manner as the three spoke, except that the trim pad should be pried off with a small prybar. Remove the pad by lifting it toward the top of the wheel.

4. Lift the trim pad and horn button assembly from the wheel.

5. Remove the steering wheel hub retaining nut.

6. Scribe matchmarks on the hub and shaft to aid in correct installation.

7. Use a suitable puller to remove the steering wheel.

8. Installation is the reverse of removal. Tighten the wheel retaining nut to 26 ft. lbs. (35 Nm).

WITH AIR BAG

▶ See Figures 57 thru 69

✳✳ CAUTION

Work must be started only after 90 seconds or longer has passed from the time the ignition switch is turned to the LOCK position and the negative battery terminal is disconnected. If the air bag system is disconnected with the ignition switch at the ON or ACC, deployment could occur.

1. Disconnect the negative battery cable. Remember, have the ignition key in the **LOCK** position and wait 90 seconds prior to working on the SRS system.

2. Place the front wheels facing straight ahead.

3. Remove the steering wheel lower No. 2 and No. 3 covers.

Fig. 57 Remove the two side trim covering the Torx® screws

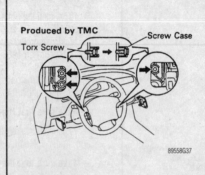

Fig. 58 Torx® screw locations on the TMC steering wheel pad

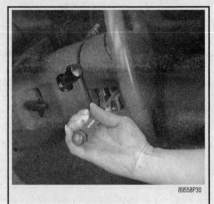

Fig. 59 Remove the screws . . . .

Fig. 60 . . . then pull the pad off the steering wheel slightly

Fig. 61 Disconnect the SRS wiring from the back side of the pad

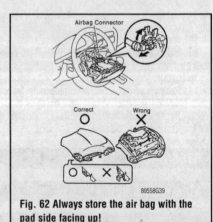

Fig. 62 Always store the air bag with the pad side facing up!

Fig. 63 Remove the steering wheel nut from the shaft . . .

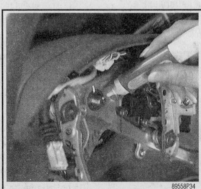

Fig. 64 . . . then matchmark the shaft and wheel with paint

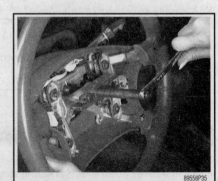

Fig. 65 Place a steering wheel puller on the end of the shaft and tighten to extract the wheel

Fig. 66 Disconnect any wiring from the combination switch etc . . .

Fig. 67 . . . then pull the steering wheel off

Fig. 68 Read the spiral cable warning and directions prior to installation

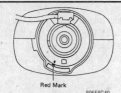

Red Mark

Fig. 69 Make sure the mark on the cable is aligned correctly

4. Using a Torx® wrench T30, loosen the screws until the groove trailing the screw circumference catches on the screw case. Models produced by TMC have 3 screws and models produced by TMM have 3 screws.

➡**Loosen the screws until the groove along the screw circumference catches on the screw case.**

5. Pull the wheel pad out from the steering wheel and disconnect the air bag wiring.

6. Walk over to a table and place the air bag down with the pad facing upwards only.

7. Remove the steering wheel nut. Place matchmarks on the wheel and steering shaft.

8. Using a steering wheel puller SST 09950–50010 or equivalent, remove the steering wheel.

To install:

9. Turn the spiral cable on the combination switch counterclockwise by hand until it becomes harder to turn. Then rotate the cable clockwise about 3 turns to align the alignment mark (usually red).

10. Install the steering wheel, align the matchmarks and tighten the nut to 26 ft. lbs. (35 Nm).

11. Connect the air bag wiring and install the steering pad. Confirm that the groove of the Torx® screws is caught on the screw case. Tighten the Torx® screws to 78 inch lbs. (9 Nm).

✳✳ CAUTION

If the wheel pad/air bag has been dropped by accident, replace it with a new one. If not, the air bag may go off without warning during normal operation of the vehicle.

12. Install the screw covers.

13. Connect the battery cable, check operation and the steering wheel center point.

14. Reset the radio and clock.

Turn Signal (Combination Switch)

REMOVAL & INSTALLATION

◆ **See Figures 70 and 71**

1. Disconnect the negative battery cable. On vehicles equipped with an air bag, wait at least 90 seconds before working on the vehicle.

✳✳ CAUTION

Some models covered by this manual may be equipped with a Supplemental Restraint System (SRS), which uses an air bag. Whenever working near any of the SRS components, such as the impact sensors, the air bag module, steering column and instrument panel, disable the SRS, as described in Section 6.

2. Remove the steering wheel, as outlined in this section.

3. Remove the instrument lower finish panel (as required), air duct and upper and lower column covers.

4. Disconnect the combination switch wiring.

5. On air bag equipped vehicles, disconnect the cable wiring, remove the spiral cable housing attaching screws and slide the cable assembly from the front of the combination switch.

6. Remove the screws that attach the combination switch to its mounting brackets and extract the assembly from the vehicle.

To install:

7. Position the combination switch onto the mounting bracket and install the retaining screws.

8. Connect the electrical wiring.

9. Install the upper/lower column covers, air duct and instrument lower finish panel.

10. Turn the spiral cable on the combination switch counterclockwise by hand until it becomes harder to turn. Then rotate the cable clockwise about 3 turns to align the alignment mark.

11. Install the steering wheel onto the shaft and tighten nut to 26 ft. lbs. (35 Nm).

12. Connect the air bag wiring and install the steering pad.

13. Connect the battery cable, check operation and the steering wheel center point.

14. Connect the negative battery cable. Check all combination switch functions for proper operation. Check the steering wheel center point.

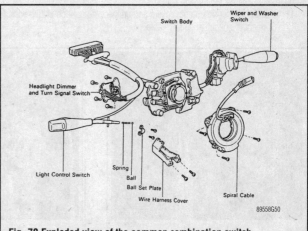

Fig. 70 Exploded view of the common combination switch

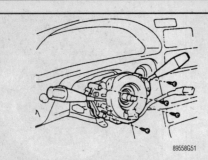

Fig. 71 Most combination switches are attached with several screws

Ignition Lock/Switch

REMOVAL & INSTALLATION

1. Disconnect the negative battery cable. If equipped with an air bag, wait at least 90 seconds before working on the vehicle.

✳✳ CAUTION

Some models covered by this manual may be equipped with a Supplemental Restraint System (SRS), which uses an air bag. Whenever working near any of the SRS components, such as the impact sensors, the air bag module, steering column and instrument panel, disable the SRS, as described in Section 6.

2. Remove the lower steering column cover. Unfasten the ignition switch connector under the instrument panel.
3. Remove the screws which secure the upper and lower halves of the steering column cover.
4. Turn the lock cylinder to the **ACC** position with the ignition key.
5. Push the lock cylinder stop in with a small, round object (cotter pin, punch, etc.).

➡**On some vehicles, it may be necessary to remove the steering wheel and combination switch first.**

6. Withdraw the lock cylinder from the lock housing while depressing the stop tab.
7. To remove the ignition switch, unfasten its securing screws and withdraw the switch from the lock housing.
To install:
8. Align the locking cam with the hole in the ignition switch and insert the switch into the lock housing.
9. Secure the switch with its screw(s).
10. Make sure both the lock cylinder and column lock are in the **ACC** position. Slide the cylinder into the lock housing until the stop tab engages the hole in the lock.
11. Install the steering column covers and connect the ignition switch wiring.
12. Connect the negative battery cable.

Steering Linkage

REMOVAL & INSTALLATION

Tie Rod Ends

▶ **See Figures 72 thru 78**

1. Loosen the front wheel lug nuts.
2. Raise the front of the vehicle and support the body with safety stands.
3. Remove the front wheels.
4. With a wire brush remove all the dirt and grease from the tie rod end, clamp bolt or lock nut and threads.
5. Remove the cotter pin.
6. Loosen the locknut from the tie rod by retaining the rod with a second wrench. There is a cut-out on the end of the tie rod near the steering knuckle.
7. Use white crayon or similar marker to place alignment marks on the tie rods and rack ends.
8. Place a tie rod puller on the end and separate the end from the knuckle.
9. Remove the castellated nut, then unscrew the tie rod end from the steering rack. Counting the number of turns it takes to completely free the tie rod end from the steering rack is also a good reference for installation of the tie rod to its original position.
To install:
10. Install the lock nut or clamp bolt. Screw the tie rod end onto the rack until the marks on the tie rod are aligned with the marks on the rack. The tie rod ends must be screwed equally on both sides of the rack.
11. Adjust the toe-in.
12. On tie rod ends with clamps, tighten the clamp nut to 14 ft. lbs. (19 Nm). On tie rod ends with lock nuts, tighten the nut to 41 ft. lbs. (55 Nm).
13. Connect the tie rod ends to the steering knuckle arm and tighten the nuts to 36 ft. lbs. (49 Nm). Install a new cotter pin and wrap the prongs firmly around the flats of the nuts.
14. Install the front wheels and lower the vehicle.

Fig. 72 The tie rod end is attached to the steering knuckle with a cotter pin (2) and castellated nut (1)

Fig. 73 Remove the tie rod end cotter pin and discard it

Fig. 74 Use two wrenches to loosen the lock nut on the inner end of the tie rod

Fig. 75 Place matchmarks on the tie rod end and rack end threads

Fig. 76 Using a tie rod puller to separate the end form the knuckle

Fig. 77 Remove the nut and pull the end from the knuckle

Fig. 78 Inspect the end and threads if reusing

Power Steering Gear

REMOVAL & INSTALLATION

Except 4WD

1983–93 MODELS

▶ See Figure 79

1. Raise and support the vehicle safely. Remove the front wheels.
2. Remove the cotter pin and nut holding the knuckle arm to the tie rod end. Using a tie rod puller, disconnect the tie rod end from the knuckle arm.
3. On some engines it is necessary to remove the lower crossmember, remove the engine under cover, center engine mount member and the rear engine mount.
4. On 1983–86 vehicles equipped with manual transaxle, remove the four retaining clips and disconnect the two control cables from the transaxle.
5. Using SST No. 09631–22020 or equivalent, disconnect the return line and the pressure line from the control valve housing. Use a small plastic container to catch the fluid.
6. Remove the rear engine mounting and bracket as required.
7. Remove the steering gear housing brackets. Slide the gear housing to the right side and then to the left side to remove the housing.

To install:

8. Install the grommets to the gear housing.
9. Install the steering gear onto the body and support by hand.
10. On 1983–86 vehicles, install the left mounting bracket so that the flat surface is facing upward (paint mark on left side of the bracket down). On 1987–93 vehicles, install the brackets in the same way they were removed. Install the nuts and bolts and tighten them to 43 ft. lbs. (58 Nm)..
11. Install the rear engine mounting bracket and tighten the retaining bolts to 38 ft. lbs. (52 Nm).
12. On 1983–86 vehicles, connect the mounting to the bracket and tighten the bolts to 58 ft. lbs. (78 Nm).
13. Install the center member with the mounting bolts. Tighten the body mount bolts to 29 ft. lbs. (39 Nm) and the engine mount bolts to 32 ft. lbs. (43 Nm).
14. On 1987–88 vehicles, install the lower crossmember and tighten the outer bolts to 129 ft. lbs. (174 Nm), inner bolts to 29 ft. lbs. (39 Nm) and install

the engine under covers. On 1992–93 vehicles, install the lower cross member and tighten the outer bolts to 153 ft. lbs. (207 Nm).
15. Connect the pressure and return lines and tighten the connector nuts to 33 ft. lbs. (44 Nm).
16. Install the universal joint and tighten the retaining bolts to 26–33 ft. lbs. (35–44 Nm).
17. Connect the tie rods to the steering knuckle with the castellated nut. Tighten the nut to 36 ft. lbs. (49 Nm) and install a new cotter pin. The prongs of the cotter pin should be firmly wrapped around the flats of the nut.
18. On 1983–86 vehicles, connect the transaxle control cables.
19. Install the front wheels and lower the vehicle.
20. Fill the power steering reservoir tank to the proper level with Dexron®II or III ATF.
21. Bleed the system as described in this Section.
22. Check for leaks, adjust the toe-in and check the steering wheel center point.

1994–96 MODELS

▶ See Figures 80 and 81

1. Disconnect the negative battery cable. Wait at least 90 seconds before working on the vehicle to allow the SRS system to disarm.

❈❈ CAUTION

Some models covered by this manual may be equipped with a Supplemental Restraint System (SRS), which uses an air bag. Whenever working near any of the SRS components, such as the impact sensors, the air bag module, steering column and instrument panel, disable the SRS, as described in Section 6.

2. Remove the right and left side fender apron seals.
3. Disconnect the right and left tie rod ends.
4. Place matrchmarks on the intermediate shaft and control valve set. Loosen the two bolts A and B. Remove bolt A and side the shaft out from under the vehicle.
5. Disconnect the power steering line clamp.
6. Disconnect the pressure and feed lines.
7. Unbolt the stabilizer bar, but do not remove it.
8. On the 1MZ-FE engine, remove the heated oxygen sensor.
9. Lift up the stabilizer bar and remove the 2 gear assembly set bolts and nuts. Remove the gear assembly from the left side of the vehicle.

To install:

10. Install the gear assembly from the left side of the vehicle. Be careful not to damage the power steering lines. Lift the stabilizer bar and install the set bolts. Tighten the 2 set bolts and nuts to 134 ft. lbs. (181 Nm).
11. On the 1MZ-FE engine, install the heated oxygen sensor.
12. Position the stabilizer bar and tighten the bolt to 14 ft. lbs. (19 Nm) and the nut to 29 ft. lbs. (39 Nm).
13. Attach the pressure and feed return lines. Tighten them to 15 ft. lbs. (20 Nm).

➡ **Use a torque wrench with a fulcrum length of 11.81 inch (300mm).**

14. Connect the clamp to the lines and tighten the nut to 7 ft. lbs. 910 Nm).
15. Connect the intermediate shaft. Make sure to align the matchmarks on the joint and main shaft. Tighten to 26 ft. lbs. (35 Nm).

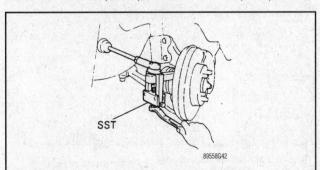

Fig. 79 Remove the nut and pull the end from the knuckle

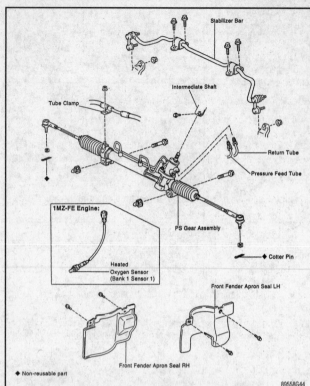

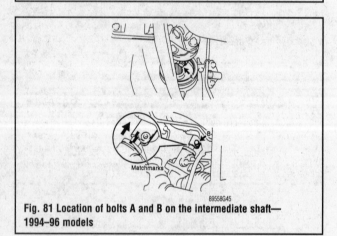

Fig. 80 Exploded view of the power steering gear and related components—1994–96 models

Fig. 81 Location of bolts A and B on the intermediate shaft—1994–96 models

16. Connect the tie rod ends.

17. Install the fender apron seals and securely tighten the bolts.

18. Remove the steering wheel pad. Be cautious of the SRS system, refer to Section 6.

19. Remove the steering wheel. Refer to Steering Wheel Removal and Installation procedure.

➡️**When removing the steering wheel for this procedure, there is no reason to apply matchmarks.**

20. Positon the front wheels facing straight ahead. Do this with the front of the vehicle on jackstands.

21. Center the spiral cable.

22. Install the steering wheel at the straight ahead position. Temporarily tighten the wheel set nut. Attach the wiring.

23. Bleed the power steering system.

24. Check the steering wheel center point. Tighten the steering nut to 26 ft. lbs. (35 Nm).

25. Check the front wheel alignment.

4WD

▶ **See Figure 82**

1. Loosen the front wheel lug nuts. Raise the front of the vehicle and support the body with safety stands. Remove the front wheels.

2. Matchmark the universal joint with the control valve shaft. Loosen the upper U-joint set bolt and remove the lower bolt. Pull the U-joint upward from the control valve shaft.

3. Remove the cotter pin and nut holding the knuckle arm to the tie rod end. Using a tie rod puller, disconnect the tie rod end from the knuckle arm.

4. Disconnect the speedometer cable. Removal of the front exhaust pipe is required on some models.

5. Using SST No. 09631–22020 or equivalent flare nut wrench, disconnect the return line and the pressure line from the control valve housing. Use a small plastic container to catch the fluid.

6. Matchmark the driveshaft to the intermediate shaft flange. Remove the flange bolts, separate the flanges and pull the prop shaft out. Install SST No. 09325–20010 into the intermediate shaft.

7. If more clearance is required to remove the gear, jack up the front of the engine carefully. DO NOT over-tilt the engine.

8. Disconnect the steering gear support brackets. Slide the gear housing to the right to position the left tie rod end in the body panel. Then, pull the steering gear assembly through the opening in the left lower side of the vehicle body.

✳✳ CAUTION

Be careful not to damage the pressure tubes and transaxle control cables.

9. Remove the gear housing grommets.

To install:

10. Install the grommets to the gear housing.

11. Install the steering gear onto the body and tighten the mounting bracket bolts and nuts to 43 ft. lbs. (59 Nm).

12. Install the drive shaft making sure to align the matchmarks. Tighten the bolts to 54 ft. lbs. (74 Nm).

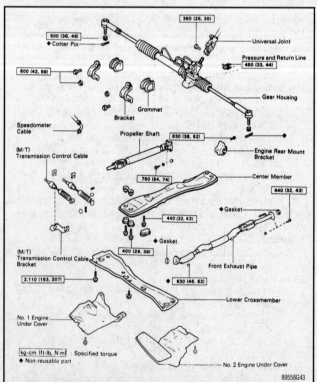

Fig. 82 Exploded view of the common 4WD power steering gear assembly and related components

13. Connect the return line and the pressure line to the control valve housing and tighten the line union nuts to 33 ft. lbs. (45 Nm).

14. Connect the tie rod end to the knuckle arm and tighten to 36 ft. lbs. (49 Nm) Install new cotter pin.

Align the matchmark on the universal joint and the control valve shaft. Push the U-joint downward onto the control valve shaft. Tighten the bolt to 26 ft. lbs. (35 Nm).

15. Install the front wheels onto the vehicle.

Power Steering Pump

REMOVAL & INSTALLATION

1983–86 Models

1. Remove the cap from the power steering reservoir tank and remove as much fluid as possible using a syringe such as a turkey baster. Have a coffee can or small plastic container ready to collect the fluid.

2. On the 1983 and on all gasoline models, disconnect the pressure line hose from the pipe extension. Remove the union seat from the pressure hose. Drain the hose into a container.

3. Loosen the hose clamp and pull the return line hose from its connection. Drain the hose.

➡ **Tie the hose ends up high, so that the fluid cannot flow out of them. Drain or plug the pump to prevent fluid leakage.**

4. Remove the power steering pump drive belt.

5. Remove the bolt from the rear mounting brace. Remove the front bracket bolts and withdraw the pump.

6. Disconnect the pressure line hose from the pump.

To install:

7. If any gasket or seals were removed, discard them and purchase new ones.

8. On gasoline models, install the pressure line hose with new gaskets by aligning the tip of the plate with the pump housing. Tighten the union bolt to 34 ft. lbs. (46 Nm).

9. Position the pump onto the mounting bracket and temporarily install mounting bolt(s).

10. Adjust the drive belt tension.

11. Push the return hose onto it's fitting and secure it with the clamp. Fill the reservoir tank to the proper level with Dexron®III ATF.

12. Bleed the system as described in this Section.

13. Check for all connections and hoses for leaks.

1987–88 Models

1. Loosen the right wheel lug nuts, raise the vehicle and support it safely.

2. Remove the right front wheel.

3. Unbolt and remove the lower crossmember.

4. Disconnect the vacuum hose from the air control valve.

5. Loosen the clamp on the return hose and pull the hose from it's connection.

6. Remove the union bolt with the two gaskets and disconnect the return hose from the pump.

7. Loosen the two mounting bolts and push the pump downward until you can remove the drive belt from the pulley. Remove the bolts completely and remove the pump.

To install:

8. Connect the pump to the mounting bracket temporarily with the two bolts and slip the drive belt over the pulley. Adjust the drive belt tension and tighten the bolts to 29 ft. lbs. (39 Nm).

9. Connect the pressure tube to the pump with two new gaskets. Tighten the union bolt to 38 ft. lbs. (52 Nm).

10. Connect the return hose to the pump and tighten the clamp.

11. Connect the vacuum hose to the air control valve.

12. Install the cross member. Tighten the center bolts to 29 ft. lbs. (39 Nm) and the outer bolts to 153 ft. lbs. (207 Nm).

13. Install the right front wheel and lower the vehicle.

14. Fill the reservoir tank to the proper level with Dexron®II ATF.

15. Bleed the system as described in this Section.

16. Check for all connections and hoses for leaks.

1989–92 Models

1. Raise and support the vehicle safely. Remove the fan shroud.

2. Remove the right front wheel and the engine under cover. Remove the lower suspension crossmember.

3. Unfasten the nut from the center of the pump pulley. Disconnect the vacuum hose from the air control valve, if equipped.

➡ **Use the drive belt as a brake to keep the pulley from rotating.**

4. Withdraw the drive belt.

5. If equipped with an idler pulley, push on the drive belt to hold the pulley in place and remove the pulley set nut. Loosen the idler pulley set nut and adjusting bolt. Remove the drive belt and loosen the drive pulley to remove the Woodruff key.

6. Remove the pulley and the Woodruff key from the pump shaft.

7. Detach and plug the intake and outlet hoses from the pump reservoir.

➡ **Tie the hose ends up high so the fluid cannot flow out of them. Drain or plug the pump to prevent fluid leakage.**

8. Remove the bolt from the rear mounting brace.

9. Remove the front bracket bolts and withdraw the pump from the lower side of the vehicle.

To install:

10. Tighten the pump pulley mounting bolt to 25–39 ft. lbs. (34–53 Nm).

11. Tighten the 5 outer mounting bolts on the lower crossmember to 154 ft. lbs. (209 Nm).

12. Adjust the pump drive belt tension. The belt should deflect 0.130.93 inch (3.323.6mm) under thumb pressure applied midway between the air pump and the power steering pump.

13. Fill the reservoir with Dexron®II automatic transmission fluid. Bleed the air from the system.

1993–96 Models

1. Remove the left and right front apron seals.

2. Dsiconnect the return line. Be careful not to spill fluid on the belt.

3. Disocnnect the pressure feed line. Remove the union bolt and gasket.

4. On the 5S-FE engines, label and disconnect the vacuum hoses from the pump.

5. Loosen the adjustment bolts and remove the belt.

6. Loosen the upper bolt enough so that the lower bolt can be removed. The upper bolt can not be removed.

7. Installation is the reverse of removal. Install the pump and temporarily tighten the 2 bolts.

8. Install the drive belt and adjust the tension. Tighten the bolts to 32 ft. lbs. (43 Nm).

9. Attach the pressure feed line. Make sure a new gasket is used. The stopper of the line must be touching the front bracket, then tighten the bolt to 38 ft. lbs. (51 Nm).

10. Bleed the power steering system.

BLEEDING

1. Raise and support the vehicle safely.

2. Fill the pump reservoir with the proper fluid.

3. Rotate the steering wheel from lock-to-lock several times. Add fluid if necessary.

4. With the steering wheel turned fully to one lock, crank the starter while watching the fluid level in the reservoir.

➡ **Do not start the engine. Operate the starter with a remote starter switch or have an assistant do it from inside the vehicle. Do not run the starter for prolonged periods.**

5. Repeat Step 4 with the steering wheel turned to the opposite lock.

6. Start the engine. With the engine idling, turn the steering wheel from lock-to-lock several times.

7. Lower the front of the vehicle and repeat the previous step.

8. Center the wheel at the midpoint of its travel. Stop the engine.

9. The fluid level should not have risen more than 0.2 inch (5mm). If it does, repeat Step 7.

10. Check for fluid leakage.

TORQUE SPECIFICATIONS

Front:			US	METRIC
Wheel lug nuts			137 ft. lbs.	186 Nm
Coil spring seat nut			34-36 ft. lbs.	47-49 Nm
Upper strut mount nuts	1983-86		27 ft. lbs.	36 Nm
	1987-91		47 ft. lbs.	64 Nm
	1992-96		59 ft. lbs.	80 Nm
Tie rod end locknut	1983-91		41 ft. lbs.	56 Nm
	1992-96		54 ft. lbs.	74 Nm
Tie rod clamp nut			14 ft. lbs.	19 Nm
Steering knuckle-to-strut	1983-86		157 ft. lbs.	213 Nm
	1987-88		166 ft. lbs.	224 Nm
	1989-91		224 ft. lbs.	304 Nm
	1992-96		156 ft. lbs.	211 Nm
Steering knuckle-to-caliper	1983-91		86 ft lbs.	117 Nm
	1992-96		79 ft. lbs.	107 Nm
Steering knuckle-to-tie rod end			36 ft. lbs.	49 Nm
Axle hub nut	1983-91		137 ft. lbs.	186 Nm
	1992-96		217 ft. lbs.	294 Nm
Ball joint-to-lower control arm	1983-88		67 ft. lbs.	91 Nm
	1989-91		90 ft. lbs.	123 Nm
Ball joint-to-steering knuckle	1992-96		94 ft. lbs.	127 Nm
	1983-91		83 ft. lbs.	113 Nm
	1992-96		90 ft. lbs.	123 Nm
Center driveshaft bearing bracket bolt		V6	47 ft. lbs.	64 Nm
Driveshaft-to-center driveshaft		V6	48 ft. lbs.	65 Nm
Driveshaft-to-side gear shaft			48 ft. lbs.	65 Nm
Driveshaft bearing bracket/lock bolt		GNK	24 ft. lbs.	32 Nm
		TOYOT.	47 ft. lbs.	64 Nm
Driveshaft bearing bracket-to-stay			47 ft. lbs.	64 Nm
Suspension upper support-to-body	1983-91		47 ft. lbs.	64 Nm
	1992-96		59 ft. lbs.	80 Nm
Suspension upper support-to-piston rod	1983-91		34 ft. lbs.	47 Nm
	1992-96		36 ft. lbs.	49 Nm
Stabilizer bar-to-lower suspension arm	1990-91		156 ft. lbs.	212 Nm
Stabilizer bar bracket-to-body	1983-86		83 ft. lbs.	112 Nm
	1987-91		94 ft. lbs.	127 Nm
Stabilizer bar bushing retainer	1992-96		14 ft. lbs.	19 Nm
Stabilizer bar link set nut	1992-93		47 ft. lbs.	64 Nm
	1994-96		29 ft. lbs.	39 Nm
Steering gear box set nut	1992-96		134 ft. lbs.	181 Nm
Steering wheel nut			25 ft. lbs.	36 Nm
Torx head nuts			78 inch lbs.	9 Nm
Rear:				
Axle bearing set bolt	1992-96		59 ft. lbs.	80 Nm
Bearing locknut without ABS			90 ft lbs.	123 Nm
Axle carrier-to-strut	1983-86		119 ft. lbs.	162 Nm
	1987-91		166 ft. lbs.	226 Nm

89558C01

TORQUE SPECIFICATIONS

Rear:			US	METRIC
Axle carrier-to-strut continued	1992-96		188 ft. lbs.	255 Nm
Axle hub-to-carrier	1983-91		59 ft. lbs.	80 Nm
No. 1 and No. 2 suspension	1983-86		65 ft. lbs.	87 Nm
arm-to-carrier	1987-91	2WD	134 ft. lbs.	181 Nm
	1983-91	4WD	90 f. lbs.	123 Nm
Driveshaft-to-side gear shaft	1983-91	4WD	51 ft. lbs.	69 Nm
Piston rod-to-suspension support	1983-91		36 ft. lbs.	49 Nm
Upper shock nuts	1983-86		17 ft. lbs.	25 Nm
	1987-88		23 ft. lbs.	31 Nm
	1989-96		29 ft. lbs.	39 Nm
Suspension support-to-body	1983-91		29 ft. lbs.	39 Nm
No. 1 arm-to-body	1983-91		83 ft. lbs.	113 Nm
No. 2 arm-to-body	1983-91		83 ft. lbs.	113 Nm
Strut rod-to-body	1983-91		83 ft. lbs.	113 Nm
Stabilizer bar-0to-bar link	1983-91		47 ft. lbs.	64 Nm
Shock absorber-to-bar link	1983-91		47 ft. lbs.	64 Nm
Stabilizer bar bracket-to-body	1983-91		14 ft. lbs.	19 Nm
Hub nut	1983-91		76 ft. lbs.	103 Nm

89558C02

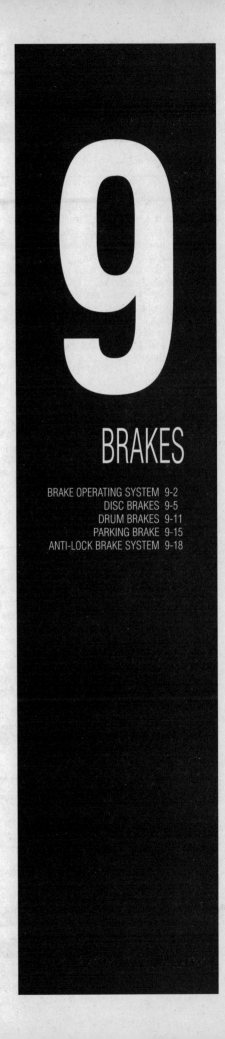

9
BRAKES

BRAKE OPERATING SYSTEM

Basic Operating Principles

DISC BRAKES

Instead of the traditional expanding brakes that press outward against a circular drum, disc brake systems utilize a disc (rotor) with brake pads positioned on either side of it. An easily-seen analogy is the hand brake arrangement on a bicycle. The pads squeeze onto the rim of the bike wheel, slowing its motion. Automobile disc brakes use the identical principle but apply the braking effort to a separate disc instead of the wheel.

The disc (rotor) is a casting, usually equipped with cooling fins between the two braking surfaces. This enables air to circulate between the braking surfaces making them less sensitive to heat buildup and more resistant to fade. Dirt and water do not drastically affect braking action since contaminants are thrown off by the centrifugal action of the rotor or scraped off the by the pads. Also, the equal clamping action of the two brake pads tends to ensure uniform, straight line stops. Disc brakes are inherently self-adjusting. There are three general types of disc brake:

1. A fixed caliper.
2. A floating caliper.
3. A sliding caliper.

The fixed caliper design uses two pistons mounted on either side of the rotor (in each side of the caliper). The caliper is mounted rigidly and does not move.

The sliding and floating designs are quite similar. In fact, these two types are often lumped together. In both designs, the pad on the inside of the rotor is moved into contact with the rotor by hydraulic force. The caliper, which is not held in a fixed position, moves slightly, bringing the outside pad into contact with the rotor. There are various methods of attaching floating calipers. Some pivot at the bottom or top, and some slide on mounting bolts. In any event, the end result is the same.

DRUM BRAKES

Drum brakes employ two brake shoes mounted on a stationary backing plate. These shoes are positioned inside a circular drum which rotates with the wheel assembly. The shoes are held in place by springs. This allows them to slide toward the drums (when they are applied) while keeping the linings and drums in alignment. The shoes are actuated by a wheel cylinder which is mounted at the top of the backing plate. When the brakes are applied, hydraulic pressure forces the wheel cylinder's actuating links outward. Since these links bear directly against the top of the brake shoes, the tops of the shoes are then forced against the inner side of the drum. This action forces the bottoms of the two shoes to contact the brake drum by rotating the entire assembly slightly (known as servo action). When pressure within the wheel cylinder is relaxed, return springs pull the shoes back away from the drum.

Brake Light Switch

REMOVAL & INSTALLATION

1. Turn the ignition key to the OFF position. Disconnect the negative battery cable.
2. Remove the instrument lower finish panel and the air duct if required to gain access to the stoplight switch. Disconnect the stoplight switch wiring.
3. Remove the switch mounting nut, then slide the switch from the mounting bracket on the pedal.
4. Installation is the reverse of removal. Depress the brake pedal and verify that the brake lights illuminate.

Master Cylinder

✳✳ WARNING

Clean, high quality brake fluid is essential to the safe and proper operation of the brake system. You should always buy the highest quality brake fluid that is available. If the brake fluid becomes contaminated, drain and flush the system, then refill the master cylinder with new fluid. Never reuse any brake fluid. Any brake fluid that is removed from the system should be discarded.

REMOVAL & INSTALLATION

▶ **See Figures 1, 2, 3, 4 and 5**

➡**Before the master cylinder is reinstalled, the brake booster pushrod must be adjusted. This adjustment requires the use of a measuring tool No. 09397–00010 or its equivalent.**

1. Open the hood and disconnect the level warning switch harness. Disconnect the negative battery cable. Wait at least 90 seconds prior to working on the vehicle if equipped with SRS.

✳✳ CAUTION

Some models covered by this manual may be equipped with a Supplemental Restraint System (SRS), which uses an air bag. Whenever working near any of the SRS components, such as the impact sensors, the air bag module, steering column and instrument panel, disable the SRS, as described in Section 6.

2. Remove the cap from the master cylinder and drain the fluid out with the use a turkey baster or similar syringe. Deposit the fluid into a container.
3. Disconnect the brake tubes from the master cylinder. Drain the fluid from the lines into the container. Plug the lines to prevent fluid from leaking onto and damaging painted surfaces or the entry of moisture into the brake system.

Fig. 1 Remove the brake fluid in the reservoir

Fig. 2 Using a line wrench, disconnect the brake line from the master cylinder, then plug to prevent leakage

Fig. 3 Unplug the connector from the reservoir

Fig. 4 Unbolt and pull the master cylinder from the brake booster

Fig. 5 Remove and discard the old gasket

4. Remove the three nuts that attach the master cylinder and 3-way union to the brake booster.

5. Remove the master cylinder from the booster studs. Remove and discard the old gasket.

To install:

6. Clean the brake booster gasket and the master cylinder flange surfaces. Install a new gasket onto the brake booster.

7. Adjust the length of the brake booster push rod as follows:

a. Set the measuring tool (09737–00010 or equivalent) on the master cylinder with the gasket and lower the pin of the tool until it lightly contacts the position.

b. Turn the measuring tool upside-down and position it onto the booster.

c. Measure the clearance between the booster push rod and the pin head of the tool. There must be zero clearance. To obtain zero clearance, adjust the push rod length until the push rod light contacts the head of the pin.

8. Before installing the master cylinder, make sure that the **UP** mark is in the correct position. Install the master cylinder over the mounting studs and tighten the three nuts to 9 ft. lbs. (13 Nm).

9. Connect the tubes to the master cylinder outlet plugs and tighten the union nuts to 11 ft. lbs. (15 Nm).

10. Connect the level warning switch wiring.

11. Fill the brake fluid reservoir to the proper level with clean brake fluid and bleed the brake system as described in this section.

12. Check for leaks. Check and/or adjust the brake pedal.

Power Brake Booster

REMOVAL & INSTALLATION

▶ **See Figure 6**

➡ **Before the brake booster is reinstalled, the brake booster pushrod must be adjusted so that there is zero clearance between it and the master cylinder. This adjustment requires the use of a brake booster pushrod gauge such as SST No. 09737–00010 or its equivalent.**

1. If necessary, remove the instrument lower finish panel, air duct and floor mats to gain access to the brake booster linkage.

2. Remove the master cylinder from the vehicle.

3. On some models, loosen the clamp screw and push down on the charcoal canister slightly to access the booster lower bolts.

4. Loosen the hose clamp and disconnect the vacuum hose from the booster.

5. On 1983–86 vehicles, disconnect the wiring from the brake light switch.

6. From inside the vehicle, remove the pedal return spring, clip and the clevis pin with the locknut. Remove the four mounting nuts and the clevis.

7. Pull the booster and gasket from the fire wall.

To install:

8. Adjust the length of the brake booster push rod as follows:

a. Set the measuring tool (09737–00010 or equivalent) on the master cylinder with the gasket and lower the pin of the tool until it lightly contacts the position.

b. Turn the measuring tool upside-down and position it onto the booster.

c. Measure the clearance between the booster push rod and the pin head of the tool. There must be zero clearance. To obtain zero clearance, adjust the push rod length until the push rod light contacts the head of the pin.

9. Connect the clevis pin with locknut to the booster and install the brake booster with a new gasket.

10. Install the mounting nuts and tighten them to 9 ft. lbs. (13 Nm).

11. Insert the clevis pin through the clevis and the brake pedal. Secure the pin with the retaining clip.

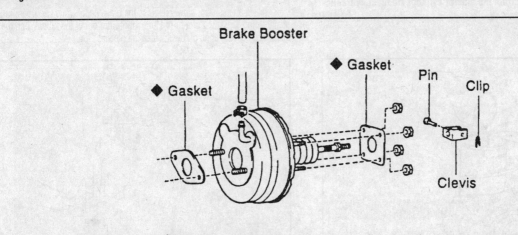

Fig. 6 Exploded view of the brake booster with attaching master cylinder

12. Install the pedal return spring. On 1983–86 vehicles, connect the brake light switch wiring.

13. The remainder of installation is the reverse of removal. Tighten each component to specifications.

14. Fill the brake fluid reservoir to the proper level with clean brake fluid and bleed the master cylinder as described in this Section.

15. Check for leaks. Check and/or adjust the brake pedal.

16. Perform a brake booster operational check and air tightness check as detailed below.

Proportioning Valve

A proportioning valve is used to reduce the hydraulic pressure to the rear brakes because of weight transfer during high speed stops. This helps to keep the rear brakes from locking up by improving front to rear brake balance.

REMOVAL & INSTALLATION

1. Disconnect the brake lines from the valve unions.
2. Remove the valve mounting bolt, if used, and remove the valve.

➡ If the proportioning valve is defective, it must be replaced as an assembly; it cannot be rebuilt.

To install:

3. Place the valve in line and attach with the mounting bolts.
4. Attach all brake lines to the valve.
5. Bleed the brake system. Test drive the vehicle for proper operation.

Bleeding the Brake System

❋❋ CAUTION

Brake fluid contains polyglycol ethers and polyglycols. Avoid contact with the eyes and wash your hands thoroughly after handling brake fluid. If you do get brake fluid in your eyes, flush your eyes with clean, running water for 15 minutes. If eye irritation persists, or if you have taken brake fluid internally, IMMEDIATELY seek medical assistance.

On vehicles equipped with anti-lock brakes (ABS), please refer to the appropriate procedure later in this section.

➡ If any maintenance or repairs were performed on the brake system, or if air is suspected in the system, the system must be bled. If the master cylinder has been overhauled or if the fluid reservoir was run dry, start the bleeding procedure with the master cylinder. Otherwise (and after bleeding the master cylinder), start with the wheel cylinder which is farthest from the master cylinder (longest hydraulic line).

❋❋ WARNING

Clean, high quality brake fluid is essential to the safe and proper operation of the brake system. You should always buy the highest quality brake fluid that is available. If the brake fluid becomes contaminated, drain and flush the system, then refill the master cylinder with new fluid. Never reuse any brake fluid. Any brake fluid that is removed from the system should be discarded. Also, do not allow any brake fluid to come in contact with a painted surface; it will damage the paint.

MASTER CYLINDER

◗ See Figures 7, 8 and 9

❋❋ CAUTION

Brake fluid contains polyglycol ethers and polyglycols. Avoid contact with the eyes and wash your hands thoroughly after handling brake fluid. If you do get brake fluid in your eyes, flush your eyes with clean, running water for 15 minutes. If eye irritation persists, or if you have taken brake fluid internally, IMMEDIATELY seek medical assistance.

1. Check the fluid level in the master cylinder reservoir and add fluid as required to bring to the proper level.
2. Disconnect the brake lines from the master cylinder. Place a few shop rags around the master cylinder port holes.
3. Have an assistant depress the brake pedal and hold it in the down position, fluid will spew from the cylinder.
4. While the pedal is depressed, block the port holes of the master cylinder with your finger.
5. Repeat the procedure three or four times.
6. Bleed the brake system, if needed.

BRAKE SYSTEM

◗ See Figure 10

➡ Start the brake system bleeding procedure on the wheel cylinder that is the furthest away from the master cylinder. To bleed the brakes you will need a supply of brake fluid, a long piece of clear vinyl tubing and a small container that is half full of brake fluid.

1. Clean all the dirt and grease from the caliper or wheel cylinder bleeder plug and remove the protective cap. Connect one end of a clear vinyl tube to the fitting.
2. Insert the other end of the tube into a jar which is half filled with brake fluid.
3. Have an assistant slowly depress the brake pedal while you open the bleeder plug $FR1/3½ of a turn. Fluid should run out of the tube. When the pedal is at its full range of travel, close the bleeder plug.

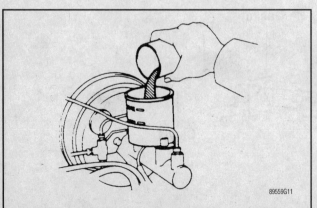

89559G11

Fig. 7 Add brake fluid to the master cylinder to the full position

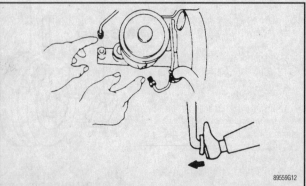

89559G12

Fig. 8 Once the brake lines are disconnected, have an assistant depress and hold the pedal down

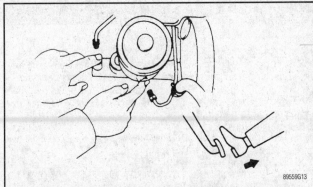

Fig. 9 Place your fingers on the cylinder port holes to keep fluid from spewing out while the pedal is depressed

4. Have your assistant slowly pump the brake pedal. Repeat Step 3 until there are no more air bubbles in the fluid.

5. Repeat the procedure for each wheel cylinder. Add brake fluid to the master cylinder reservoir every few pumps, so that it does not completely drain during bleeding.

Fig. 10 Place a tube on the bleeder plug with an attached jar to catch the fluid from the system when bleeding the brakes

DISC BRAKES

※※ CAUTION

Brake fluid contains polyglycol ethers and polyglycols. Avoid contact with the eyes and wash your hands thoroughly after handling brake fluid. If you do get brake fluid in your eyes, flush your eyes with clean, running water for 15 minutes. If eye irritation persists, or if you have taken brake fluid internally, IMMEDIATELY seek medical assistance.

Brake Pads

REMOVAL & INSTALLATION

▸ See Figures 11, 12 and 13

※※ CAUTION

Brake pads contain asbestos, which has been determined to be a cancer causing agent. Never clean the brake surfaces with compressed air! Avoid inhaling any dust from any brake surfaces. When cleaning brake surfaces, use a commercially available brake cleaning fluid.

1983–88 Models

1. Loosen the wheel lugs slightly, then raise and safely support the front of the car. Remove the wheel(s) and temporarily attach the rotor disc with two of the wheel nuts.

2. Remove the two bolts from the torque plate.

3. Remove the brake cylinder and suspend it with a piece of wire from the strut spring so that the brake hose in not under stress. DO NOT disconnect the brake hose.

4. Remove the two anti-squeal springs, two brake pads, two anti-squeal shims, two wear indicator plates and four pad support plates. Note the various positions of the parts removed to make installation easier.

5. Check the rotor thickness and disc runout as described in this Section.

To install:

6. Install the four pad support plates and a new pad wear indicator plate on the inside brake pad.

➡Make sure that the arrow on the pad wear indicator is pointing in the rotating direction of the disc.

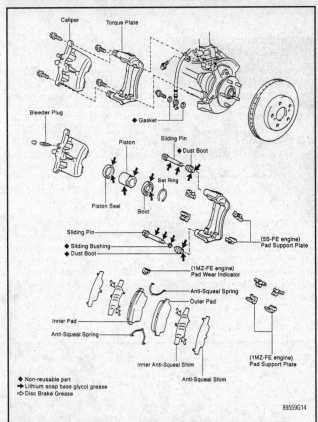

Fig. 11 Exploded view of the front single piston disc brake components

7. Install the new brake pads onto the support plates, then install the two anti-squeal springs. Do not allow oil and grease to come in contact with the surface of the pads.

8. Remove the master cylinder cap and take a small amount of brake fluid from the reservoir. Force the piston back into the caliper bore using a large C-type clamp to accommodate the greater thickness of the new brake pads. Always do one wheel at a time, because at this point there is the possibility of the oppo-

site piston extending out of the caliper bore. If the piston is difficult to push into the caliper, loosen the bleeder plug and allow fluid to exit the caliper while depressing the piston into the caliper bore.

9. Remove the supporting wire and position the brake cylinder carefully to avoid wedging the dust boot. Install the cylinder installation bolts. On 1983–86

vehicles, tighten the bolts to 18 ft. lbs. (24 Nm) and 29 ft. lbs. (39 Nm) on 1987–88 vehicles.

10. Install the wheels and lower the vehicle.

11. Check the master cylinder level to ensure that it is on the **MAX** line. Before moving the vehicle, make sure to pump the brake pedal to seat the pads against the rotors.

1989–96 Models

♦ **See Figures 14 thru 30**

1. Loosen the lug nuts slightly for the wheels.
2. Raise and support the vehicle safely.
3. Remove the wheels.
4. On rear brake pads, remove the brake hose mounting bracket attached to the strut.
5. Siphon a sufficient quantity of brake fluid from the master cylinder reservoir to prevent any brake fluid from overflowing the master cylinder when removing or installing new pads. This is necessary as the piston must be forced into the caliper bore to provide sufficient clearance when installing the pads.
6. Grasp the caliper from behind and carefully pull it to seat the piston in its bore.
7. On some models it will be necessary to remove the 2 caliper mounting pins (bolts), then remove the caliper assembly. Suspend the caliper with a wire. On other calipers, remove just the lower bolt and lift the caliper up and suspend it from a wire. Do not disconnect the brake line.
8. Slide out the old brake pads along with any anti-squeal shims, springs, pad wear indicators and pad support plates. Make sure to note the position of all assorted pad hardware.

To install:

9. Check the brake disc (rotor) for thickness and run-out. Inspect the caliper and piston assembly for breaks, cracks, fluid seepage or other damage. Overhaul or replace as necessary.

10. Install the pad support plates into the torque plate.

11. Install the pad wear indicators onto the pads. Be sure the arrow on the indicator plate is pointing in the direction of rotation.

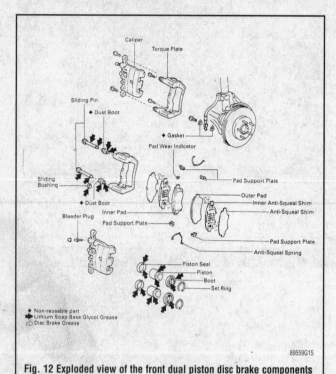

Fig. 12 Exploded view of the front dual piston disc brake components

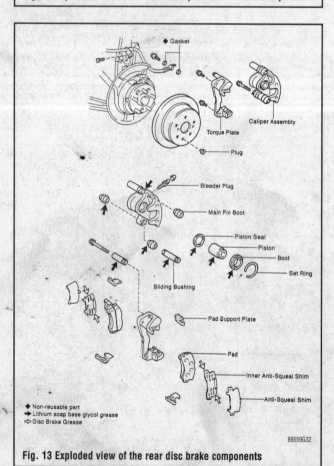

Fig. 13 Exploded view of the rear disc brake components

Fig. 14 Remove the lower caliper bolt using two wrenches, one to retain and one to loosen—front shown

Fig. 15 The lower bolt is a small one as seen here

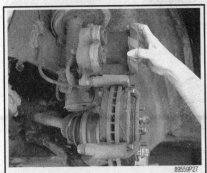

Fig. 16 Lift up the outer portion of the caliper and suspend with wire if necessary—front shown

Fig. 17 Remove the upper and lower anti squeal springs attached to the edges of the pads—front

Fig. 18 Pull the outer pad towards you to remove—front shown

Fig. 19 Pull the shim from the pad and save if not supplied in the new set of pads—front shown

Fig. 20 Remove the four pad support plates which look like clips on either side of the pads—front shown

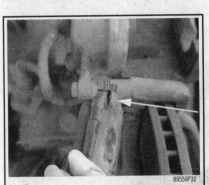

Fig. 21 The pad wear indicators are located on the top of the pads—front shown

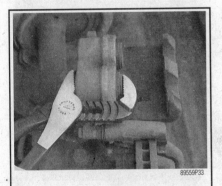

Fig. 22 Compress the caliper piston before placing over the pads when assembling

Fig. 23 On rear disc pads, disconnect the brake hose mounting from the strut

Fig. 24 Remove the lower bolt of the caliper ...

Fig. 25 ... then lift the caliper outer portion up and secure with wire—rear disc pads shown

Fig. 26 Slide the front pad out towards you to remove it from the caliper—rear disc pads shown

Fig. 27 Disc pads are usually equipped with two anti squeal shims, make sure you remove both of them

Fig. 28 Be careful not to loose or bend the clips

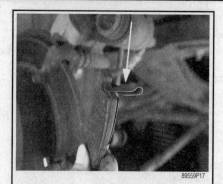

Fig. 29 Be sure to install the support plates in the correct direction

Fig. 30 Compress the piston enough to place the caliper back into position—rear pads shown

12. Install the anti-squeal shims on the outside of each pad and then install the pad assemblies into the torque plate.

13. Position the caliper back down over the pads. If it won't fit, use a C-clamp or hammer handle and carefully force the piston into its bore.

14. On front pads, install and tighten the caliper mounting bolts to 29 ft. lbs. (39 Nm) on 1989–91 vehicles, and 25 ft. lbs. (34 Nm) on 1992–96 models.

15. On rear brake pads, install and tighten the caliper mounting bolt to 14 ft. lbs. (20 Nm).

16. Attach the rear brake hose bracket and tighten the bolt to 21 ft. lbs. (29 Nm).

17. Install the wheels and lower the vehicle. Check the brake fluid level. Before moving the vehicle, make sure to pump the brake pedal to seat the pads against the rotors.

INSPECTION

If you hear a squealing noise coming from the brakes while driving, check the brake lining thickness and pad wear indicator by looking into the inspection hole on the brake cylinder with the wheels removed and the vehicle properly supported. The wear indicator is designed to emit the squealing noise when the brake pad wears down to 2.5mm at which time the pad wear plate and the rotor disc rub against each other. If there are traces of the pad wear indicator contacting the rotor disc, the brake pads should be replaced.

To inspect the brake lining thickness, look through the inspection hole and measure the lining thickness using a machinists rule. Also looks for signs of uneven wear. Standard thickness is 10mm. The **minimum** allowable thickness is 0.039 inch. (1mm) at which time the brake pads must be replaced.

➡Always replace the pads on both wheels. When inspecting or replacing the brake pads, check the surface of the disc rotors for scoring, wear and runout. The rotors should be resurfaced if badly scored or replaced if badly worn.

Brake Caliper

REMOVAL & INSTALLATION

▸ **See Figures 31 thru 40**

1. Loosen the wheel lug nuts slightly.
2. Raise and support the vehicle safely.
3. Remove the wheels.
4. Disconnect the brake hose from the caliper. Plug the end of the hose to prevent loss of fluid. Some brake lines have a union bolt and gasket type line attached to the caliper. Do not loose the washers.

➡**Have a container handy to catch brake fluid from the disconnected lines.**

5. Hold the sliding pin and remove the bolts that attach the caliper to the torque plate.
6. With two hands, lift up and remove the caliper assembly.
7. Installation is the reverse of the removal procedure. Grease the caliper pins and bolts with Lithium grease or equivalent. Tighten the caliper bolt(s) for the front wheels to 20–27 ft. lbs. (27–41 Nm). On the rear wheels tighten the main pin to 20 ft. lbs. (26 Nm) and the bolt to 14 ft. lbs. (20 Nm). Fill and bleed the system. Before moving the vehicle, make sure to pump the brake pedal to seat the pads against the rotors.

OVERHAUL

▸ **See Figures 41 thru 48**

➡Some vehicles may be equipped dual piston calipers. The procedure to overhaul the caliper is essentially the same with the exception of multiple pistons, O-rings and dust boots.

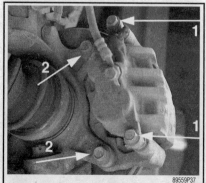

Fig. 31 Caliper sliding pins (1) and mounting bolts (2)

Fig. 32 The brake caliper is attached by these two bolts—rear brakes shown

Fig. 33 Unbolt the brake hose form the strut assembly

Fig. 34 Pull the hose and place away from the caliper assembly

Fig. 35 Disconnect the hose from the back of the caliper, do not loose the washers

Fig. 36 Remove the sliding pin from the caliper

Fig. 37 Removing the caliper assembly from the rotor—front shown

Fig. 38 Remove the caliper assembly from the rotor—rear shown

Fig. 39 Always apply caliper grease to the sliding pin before installing—front shown

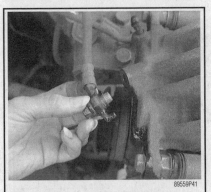

Fig. 40 Make sure the bolt and washers are placed in order on the banjo fitting

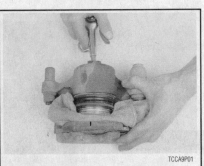

Fig. 41 For some types of calipers, use compressed air to drive the piston out of the caliper, but make sure to keep your fingers clear

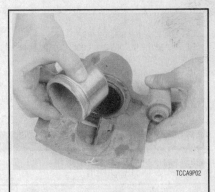

Fig. 42 Withdraw the piston from the caliper bore

1. Remove the caliper from the vehicle and place on a clean workbench.

✳✳ CAUTION

NEVER place your fingers in front of the pistons in an attempt to catch or protect the pistons when applying compressed air. This could result in personal injury!

➡Depending upon the vehicle, there are two different ways to remove the piston from the caliper. Refer to the brake pad replacement procedure to make sure you have the correct procedure for your vehicle.

2. The first method is as follows:
   a. Stuff a shop towel or a block of wood into the caliper to catch the piston.
   b. Remove the caliper piston using compressed air applied into the caliper inlet hole. Inspect the piston for scoring, nicks, corrosion and/or worn or damaged chrome plating. The piston must be replaced if any of these conditions are found.

3. For the second method, you must rotate the piston to retract it from the caliper.

4. If equipped, remove the anti-rattle clip.

5. Use a prytool to remove the caliper boot, being careful not to scratch the housing bore.

6. Remove the piston seals from the groove in the caliper bore.

7. Carefully loosen the brake bleeder valve cap and valve from the caliper housing.

8. Inspect the caliper bores, pistons and mounting threads for scoring or excessive wear.

9. Use crocus cloth to polish out light corrosion from the piston and bore.

10. Clean all parts with denatured alcohol and dry with compressed air.

To assemble:

11. Lubricate and install the bleeder valve and cap.

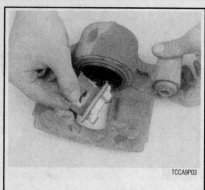

Fig. 43 On some vehicles, you must remove the anti-rattle clip

Fig. 44 Use a prytool to carefully pry around the edge of the boot . . .

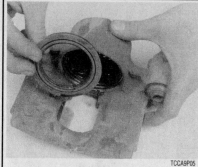

Fig. 45 . . . then remove the boot from the caliper housing, taking care not to score or damage the bore

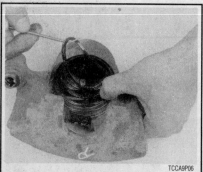

Fig. 46 Use extreme caution when removing the piston seal; DO NOT scratch the caliper bore

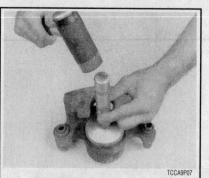

Fig. 47 Use the proper size driving tool and a mallet to properly seal the boots in the caliper housing

Fig. 48 There are tools, such as this Mighty-Vac, available to assist in proper brake system bleeding

12. Install the new seals into the caliper bore grooves, making sure they are not twisted.

13. Lubricate the piston bore.

14. Install the pistons and boots into the bores of the calipers and push to the bottom of the bores.

15. Use a suitable driving tool to seat the boots in the housing.

16. Install the caliper in the vehicle.

17. Install the wheel and tire assembly, then carefully lower the vehicle.

18. Properly bleed the brake system.

Brake Disc (Rotor)

REMOVAL & INSTALLATION

▶ See Figures 49 and 50

1. Loosen the wheel lugs slightly, then raise and safely support the of the car. Remove the front wheel(s) and temporarily attach the rotor disc with two of the wheel nuts.

2. Unbolt and remove the torque plate from the steering knuckle.

3. Remove the two wheel nuts and pull the disc from the axle hub.

4. Installation is the reverse of removal. For the front rotor, install the torque plate onto the steering knuckle. On 1983–84 vehicles, tighten the plate bolts to 70 ft. lbs. (95 Nm); 1985–86, 65 ft. lbs. (88 Nm); 1987–91, 79 ft. lbs. (107 Nm); 1992–96, 73 ft. lbs. (103 Nm).

5. On rear brake rotors install the torque plate onto the steering knuckle, and tighten the plate bolts to 34 ft. lbs. (47 Nm).

6. Remove the wheel nuts and install the wheels. Secure the wheel lugs. Before moving the vehicle, make sure to pump the brake pedal to seat the brake pads against the rotors.

Fig. 49 Removing the front rotor from the axle hub—front shown

INSPECTION

Front

Examine the disc. If it is worn, warped or scored, it must be replaced. Check the thickness of the disc against the specifications given in the Disc and Pad

Fig. 50 Using two hands, pull the rotor off the hub—rear shown

Specifications chart. If it is below specifications, replace it. Use a micrometer to measure the thickness.

The disc run-out should be measured before the disc is removed and again, after the disc is installed. Use a dial indicator mounted on a magnet type stand (attached to the shock absorber shaft) to determine runout. Position the dial so the stylus is 0.394 inch (10mm) from the outer edge of the rotor disc. The maximum allowable runout on 1983–86 and 1989 vehicles is 0.0059 inch (0.15mm). The maximum allowable runout for 1987–88 vehicles is 0.0031 inch (0.08mm). The maximum allowable runout on 1990–91 vehicles is 0.0027 inch (0.07mm). The maximum allowable runout on 1992–96 vehicles is 0.0020 inch (0.05mm). If runout exceeds the specification, replace the disc.

➡Be sure that the wheel bearing nut is properly tightened. If it is not, an inaccurate run-out reading may be obtained. If different run-out readings are obtained with the same disc, between removal and installation, this is probably the cause.

Rear

Examine the disc. If it is worn, warped or scored, it must be replaced. Check the thickness of the disc against the specifications given in the Disc and Pad Specifications chart. If it is below specifications, replace it. Use a micrometer to measure the thickness.

The disc run-out should be measured before the disc is removed and again, after the disc is installed. Use a dial indicator mounted on a magnet type stand (attached to the shock absorber shaft) to determine runout. Position the dial so the stylus is 0.394 inch (10mm) from the outer edge of the rotor disc. The maximum allowable runout 0.0059 inch (0.15mm). If the runout exceeds the specification, replace the disc.

DRUM BRAKES

❖❖ CAUTION

Brake shoes may contain asbestos, which has been determined to be a cancer causing agent. Never clean the brake surfaces with compressed air! Avoid inhaling any dust from any brake surface. When cleaning brake surfaces, use a commercially available brake cleaning fluid.

Brake Drums

REMOVAL & INSTALLATION

◗ See Figures 51 and 52

1. Loosen the rear wheel lug nuts slightly. Release the parking brake.
2. Block the front wheels, raise the rear of the car, and safely support it with jackstands.
3. Remove the lug nuts and the wheel.
4. Tap the drum lightly with a mallet to free the drum if resistance is felt. Sometimes brake drums are stubborn. If the drum is difficult to remove, perform the following:

    a. Insert the end of a bent wire (a coat hanger will do nicely) through the hole in the brake drum and hold the automatic adjusting lever away from the adjuster.

    b. Reduce the brake shoe adjustment by turning the adjuster bolt with a brake adjuster tool. The drum should now be loose enough to remove without much effort.

5. Installation is the reverse of removal.
6. If the adjuster was loosened to remove the drum, turn the adjuster bolt to adjust the length to the shortest possible amount.

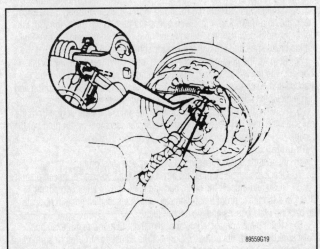

Fig. 51 Insert a bent wire or brake tool through the hole in the drum and hold the adjuster lever away from the lever

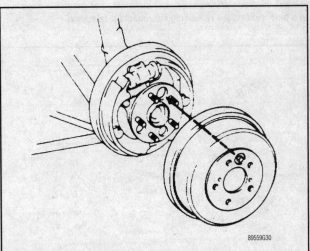

Fig. 52 Align the adjusting hole on the drum with the largest hole in the axle carrier when installing

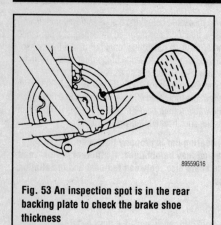

Fig. 53 An inspection spot is in the rear backing plate to check the brake shoe thickness

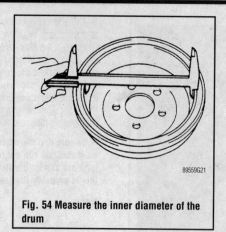

Fig. 54 Measure the inner diameter of the drum

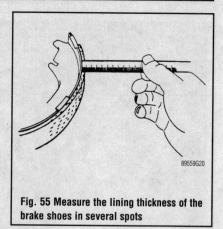

Fig. 55 Measure the lining thickness of the brake shoes in several spots

7. Retighten the lug nuts and pump the brake pedal before moving the vehicle.

INSPECTION

▶ See Figures 53 and 54

1. Remove the inspection hole plug from the backing plate, and with the aide of a flashlight, check the lining thickness. The minimum lining thickness is 0.039 inch (1.0mm). If the lining does not meet the minimum specification, replace the shoes.
2. Remove the brake drum and clean it thoroughly.
3. Inspect the drum for scoring, cracks, grooves and out-of-roundness. Replace or turn the drum, as required. Light scoring may be removed by dressing the drum with fine grit emery cloth. Heavy scoring will require the use of a brake drum lathe to turn the drum.
4. Using inside calipers, measure the inside diameter of the drum. The maximum allowable diameter for 1983–86 vehicles is 7.913 inch (201mm). The maximum allowable diameter for 1987–96 vehicles is 9.079 inch (230.6mm). If the drum exceeds the maximum diameter, replace it.

Brake Shoes

INSPECTION

▶ See Figure 55

➡When servicing drum brakes, only dissemble and assemble one side at a time, leaving the remaining side intact for reference.

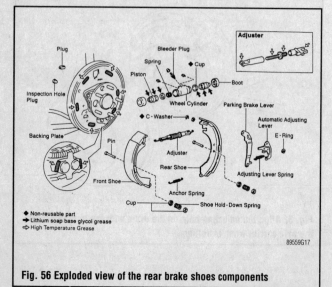

Fig. 56 Exploded view of the rear brake shoes components

1. Inspect all parts for rust and damage.
2. Measure the lining thickness. The minimum allowable thickness is 0.039 inch (1.0mm). If the lining does not meet the minimum specification, replace it.

➡If one of the brake shoes needs to be replaced, replace all the rear shoes in order to maintain even braking.

3. Measure inside diameter of the drum as detailed in this Section.
4. Place the shoe into the drum and check that the lining is in proper contact with the drum's surface. If the contact is improper, repair the lining with a brake shoe grinder or replace the shoe.
5. To measure the clearance between brake shoe and parking brake lever, temporarily install the parking brake and automatic adjusting levers onto the rear shoe, using a new C-washer. With a feeler gauge, measure the clearance between the shoe and the lever. The clearance should be within 0–0.013 inch (0–0.35mm). If the clearance is not as specified, use a shim to adjust it. When the clearance is correct, stake the C-washer with pliers.

REMOVAL AND INSTALLATION

▶ See Figures 56 thru 63

1. Raise and support the vehicle safely. Remove the wheels.
2. Perform the brake drum removal procedure as previously detailed. Do one set of shoes at a time. Note the position and direction of each component part so that they may be reinstalled in the correct order.

➡Do not depress the brake pedal once the brake drum has been removed.

3. Carefully unhook the return spring from the leading (front) brake shoe. Grasp the hold-down spring pin with pliers and turn it until its in line with the slot in the hold-down spring. Remove the hold-down spring and the pin. Pull out the brake shoe and unhook the anchor spring from the lower edge.
4. Remove the hold-down spring from the trailing (rear) shoe. Pull the shoe out with the adjuster strut, automatic adjuster assembly and springs attached and disconnect the parking brake cable. Unhook the return spring and then remove the adjusting strut. Remove the anchor spring.
5. Remove the adjusting strut. Unhook the adjusting lever spring from the rear shoe and then remove the automatic adjuster assembly by popping out the C-clip.

To install:

6. Inspect the shoes for signs of unusual wear or scoring.
7. Check the wheel cylinder for any sign of fluid seepage or frozen pistons.
8. Clean and inspect the brake backing plate and all other components. Check that the brake drum inner diameter is within specified limits. Lubricate the backing plate bosses and the anchor plate.
9. Mount the automatic adjuster assembly onto a new rear brake shoe. Make sure the C-clip fits properly. Connect the adjusting strut/return spring and then install the adjusting spring.
10. Connect the parking brake cable to the rear shoe and then position the shoe so the lower end rides in the anchor plate and the upper end is against the boot in the wheel cylinder. Install the pin and the hold-down spring. Rotate the pin so the crimped edge is held by the retainer.
11. Install the anchor spring between the front and rear shoes and then

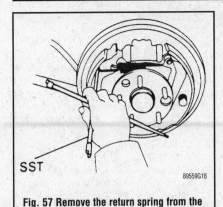

Fig. 57 Remove the return spring from the front brake shoe

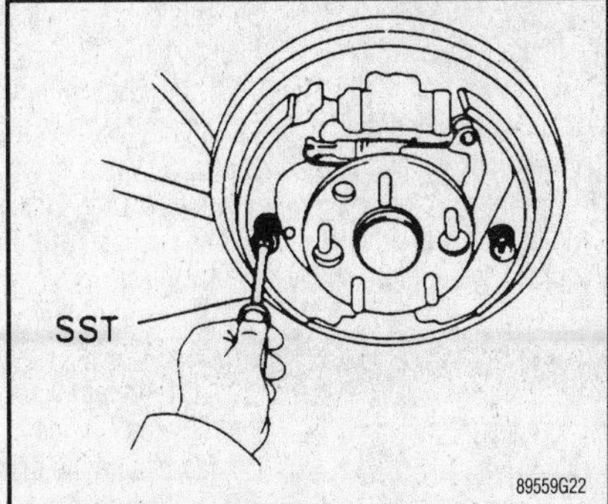

Fig. 58 Using a hold-down spring brake tool, remove the spring, cup and pin from the front shoe

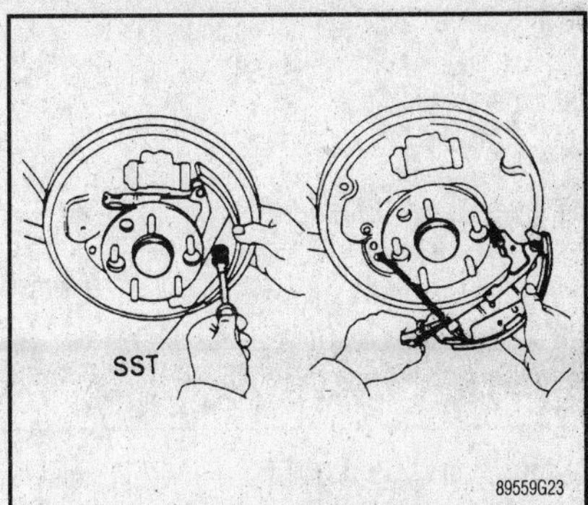

Fig. 59 Remove the hold-down spring from the rear brake shoe, then disconnect the cable

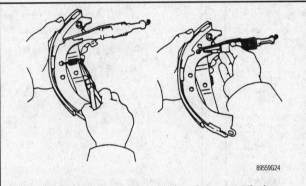

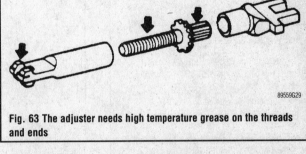

Fig. 60 Remove the adjusting lever spring, then extract the lever with the return spring

Fig. 63 The adjuster needs high temperature grease on the threads and ends

stretch the spring enough so the front shoe will fit as the rear did in Step 10. Install the hold-down spring and pin. Connect the return spring/adjusting strut between the 2 shoes and connect it so it rides freely.

12. Check that the automatic adjuster is operating properly; the adjusting bolt should turn when the parking brake lever (in the brake assembly, not in the vehicle!) is moved. Adjust the strut as short as possible and then install the brake drum. Set and release the parking brake several times.

13. Install the wheel and lower the vehicle. Check the level of brake fluid in the master cylinder.

ADJUSTMENTS

All models are equipped with self-adjusting rear drum brakes. Under normal conditions, adjustment of the rear brake shoes should not be necessary. However, if an initial adjustment is required insert the blade of a brake adjuster tool or a screw driver into the hole in the brake drum and turn the adjuster slowly. The tension is set correctly if the tire and wheel assembly will rotate approximately 3 times when spun with moderate force. Do not over adjust the brake shoes. Before adjusting the rear drum brake shoes, make sure emergency brake is in the OFF position, and all cables are free.

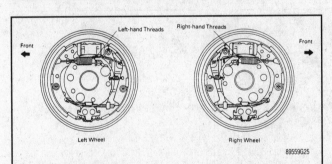

Fig. 61 Assemble the brake shoe components in the correct direction as shown

Wheel Cylinder

REMOVAL & INSTALLATION

♦ See Figures 64 and 65

1. Plug the master cylinder inlet to prevent hydraulic fluid from leaking. Raise and safely support the vehicle.

✳✳ CAUTION

Brake fluid contains polyglycol ethers and polyglycols. Avoid contact with the eyes and wash your hands thoroughly after handling brake fluid. If you do get brake fluid in your eyes, flush your eyes with clean, running water for 15 minutes. If eye irritation persists, or if you have taken brake fluid internally, IMMEDIATELY seek medical assistance.

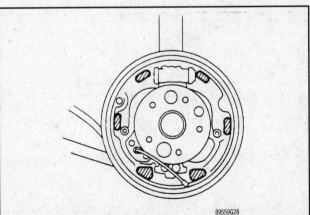

Fig. 62 Apply high temperature grease to the backing plate in these locations

2. Remove the brake drums and shoes.

3. Working from behind the backing plate, disconnect the hydraulic line from the wheel cylinder.

4. Unfasten the screws retaining the wheel cylinder and withdraw the cylinder.

5. Installation is the reverse of removal. Secure the wheel cylinder retaining bolts to 7 ft. lbs. (10 Nm).

6. Make all the necessary adjustments. Fill the master cylinder to the proper level with clean brake fluid bleed the brake system. Check the brake system for leaks.

OVERHAUL

♦ **See Figures 66 thru 75**

Wheel cylinder overhaul kits may be available, but often at little or no savings over a reconditioned wheel cylinder. It often makes sense with these components to substitute a new or reconditioned part instead of attempting an overhaul.

If no replacement is available, or you would prefer to overhaul your wheel cylinders, the following procedure may be used. When rebuilding and installing wheel cylinders, avoid getting any contaminants into the system. Always use clean, new, high quality brake fluid. If dirty or improper fluid has been used, it will be necessary to drain the entire system, flush the system with proper brake fluid, replace all rubber components, then refill and bleed the system.

1. Remove the wheel cylinder from the vehicle and place on a clean workbench.

2. First remove and discard the old rubber boots, then withdraw the pistons. Piston cylinders are equipped with seals and a spring assembly, all located behind the pistons in the cylinder bore.

3. Remove the remaining inner components, seals and spring assembly. Compressed air may be useful in removing these components. If no compressed air is available, be VERY careful not to score the wheel cylinder bore

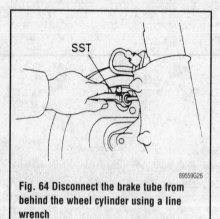

Fig. 64 Disconnect the brake tube from behind the wheel cylinder using a line wrench

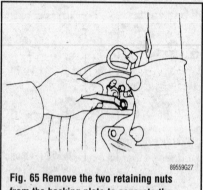

Fig. 65 Remove the two retaining nuts from the backing plate to separate the wheel cylinder from the backing plate

Fig. 66 Remove the outer boots from the wheel cylinder

Fig. 67 Compressed air can be used to remove the pistons and seals

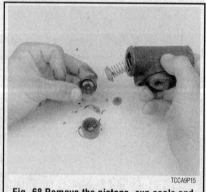

Fig. 68 Remove the pistons, cup seals and spring from the cylinder

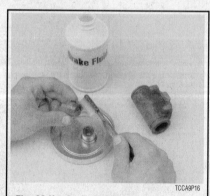

Fig. 69 Use brake fluid and a soft brush to clean the pistons ...

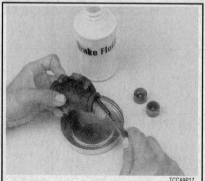

Fig. 70 ... and the bore of the wheel cylinder

Fig. 71 Once cleaned and inspected, the wheel cylinder is ready for assembly

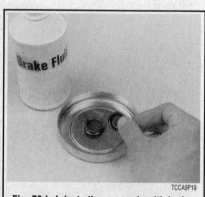

Fig. 72 Lubricate the cup seals with brake fluid

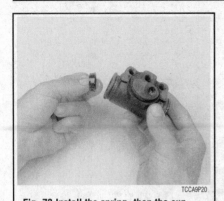

Fig. 73 Install the spring, then the cup seals in the bore

Fig. 74 Lightly lubricate the pistons, then install them

Fig. 75 The boots can now be installed over the wheel cylinder ends

when removing parts from it. Discard all components for which replacements were supplied in the rebuild kit.

4. Wash the cylinder and metal parts in denatured alcohol or clean brake fluid.

✳✳ WARNING

Never use a mineral-based solvent such as gasoline, kerosene or paint thinner for cleaning purposes. These solvents will swell rubber components and quickly deteriorate them.

5. Allow the parts to air dry or use compressed air. Do not use rags for cleaning, since lint will remain in the cylinder bore.

6. Inspect the piston and replace it if it shows scratches.

7. Lubricate the cylinder bore and seals using clean brake fluid.

8. Position the spring assembly.

9. Install the inner seals, then the pistons.

10. Insert the new boots into the counterbores by hand. Do not lubricate the boots.

11. Install the wheel cylinder.

PARKING BRAKE

PARKING BRAKE SHOE COMPONENTS

1.	Adjuster	5.	Hold-down spring and cup
2.	Front shoe	6.	Return spring
3.	Rear shoe	7.	Shoe strut
4.	Brake cable	8.	Strut spring

89559P24

Cables

REMOVAL & INSTALLATION

Pedal Operated Front Cable

1. Remove the left inner kick panel to access the parking brake pedal assembly.
2. Remove the retainer clip from the pin on the pedal assembly. Withdraw the pin from the bracket and the eye of the cable.
3. Remove the spring clip holding the cable to the brake pedal assembly, then extract the cable.
4. Disconnect the rear portion of the front parking brake wire and remove from the vehicle.
5. Installation is the reverse of the removal procedure.

Lever Operated Intermediate Wire

1. Raise and safely support the vehicle.
2. Remove the parking brake lever console box.
3. Remove the retainer nut located on the top of the lever shaft.
4. From under the vehicle disconnect the cable from the equalizer and extract the intermediate cable from the lever assembly. Remove the cable from the vehicle.
5. Installation is the reverse the removal procedure. Tighten the cable retainer nut to 9 ft. lbs. (13 Nm).

Rear Cable

1. Raise and safely support the vehicle.
2. Remove the tire and wheel assembly from the vehicle.
3. Working from underneath of the car, loosen the locknut on the parking brake cable equalizer.
4. Remove the brake drum or rotor from the vehicle.
5. Remove the rear brake shoe and disconnect the parking cable from the shoe.
6. Remove the rear cable from the equalizer assembly and remove the cable from the vehicle.
7. Installation is the reverse of the removal procedure.

ADJUSTMENT

Lever Type

▶ **See Figure 76**

➡**Before any adjustment is attempted, make sure that the rear brake shoe clearance is correct and that the automatic self adjuster is properly adjusted.**

1. Pull the parking brake lever all the way up and count the number of clicks. The travel number should be between 5 to 8 clicks, if not perform the following steps.

2. If the brake system requires adjustment, loosen the cable lock nut which is located at the rear of the parking brake lever. On some models remove the rear console box. On some vehicles, the adjustment and lock nuts are located under the vehicle, beneath the lever assembly. Raise and safely support the vehicle as required.
3. Take up the slack in the parking brake cable by rotating the adjusting nut with another open end wrench.
   a. To loosen the brake cable, turn the adjustment nut counterclockwise.
   b. To increase the tension on the brake cable, turn the adjustment nut clockwise.
4. Tighten the lock nut to 48 inch lbs. (5 Nm), using care not to disturb the setting of the adjusting nut.
5. If removed, install the rear console box.
6. Check the rotation of the rear wheels to be sure the brakes are not dragging.

Pedal Type

▶ **See Figures 77 and 78**

1. Slowly press the parking brake pedal and count the number of clicks. The travel number should be between 3 to 6 clicks. If it is not, perform the following procedure:
   a. Remove the hole cover. in the center console.
   b. Loosen the lock nut and turn the adjusting nut until the lever travel is correct.
   c. Tighten the locknut to 9 ft. lbs. (13 Nm).
   d. Install the hole cover.

Brake Shoes

REMOVAL & INSTALLATION

▶ **See Figures 79, 80, and 81**

➡**Some of the parking brake assembly springs are color coded green, blue, white. The remainder of the springs have no color. Make sure that all springs are installed in their proper locations.**

1. Loosen the rear wheel lugs slightly and raise the rear of the vehicle and support it safely. Remove the rear wheels.
2. Remove the two mounting bolts and disconnect the rear disc brake assembly. Suspend the disc with wire from the strut spring or a convenient location on the body.
3. Pull the rotor disc from the axle hub. If the rotor disc is stubborn, return the shoe adjuster until the wheel spins freely, and remove the disc.
4. Using a suitable spring removal tool, remove the return springs.
5. Remove the shoe strut with the adjuster spring.
6. Slide the front shoe out and remove the adjuster. Unhook the tension spring and remove the front shoe.
7. Slide the rear shoe out and remove the tension spring. Disconnect the parking brake cable from the lever. Remove the shoe hold down spring cups, springs and pins.
   To install:

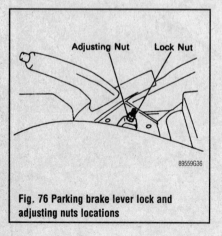

Fig. 76 Parking brake lever lock and adjusting nuts locations

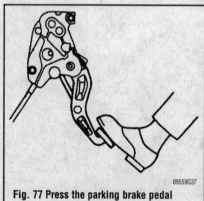

Fig. 77 Press the parking brake pedal down and count the number of clicks

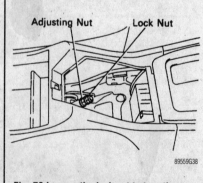

Fig. 78 Loosen the lock nut to turn the adjusting nut for adjustments

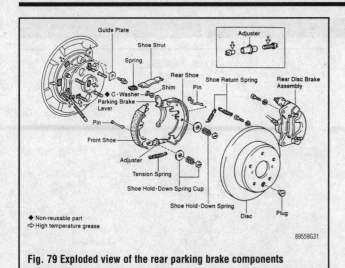

Fig. 79 Exploded view of the rear parking brake components

Fig. 80 Rear disc parking brake adjustment plug

8. Lubricate all shoe sliding surfaces of the backing plate and the threads and head of the adjuster with a high temperature Lithium grease or equivalent.

9. Connect the parking brake cable to the to the rear shoe lever. Install the shoe hold down springs, cups and pins.

10. Slide the rear shoe in between the hold down spring cup and the backing plate.

✷✷ CAUTION

Do not allow the brake shoe rubbing surface to come in contact with the grease on the backing plate.

11. Hook the one end of the tension spring to the rear shoe and connect the front shoe to the other end of the spring. Install the adjuster between the front and rear shoes. Slide the front shoe in between the hold down spring cup and the backing plate.

12. Install the strut so that the spring end is forward.

13. Install the front and then the rear return springs using the removal tool.

14. Before installing the disc, lightly polish the disc and shoe surfaces with a fine grit emery cloth. Position the rotor disc onto the axle hub so that the hole on the rear axle shaft is aligned with the service hole on the disc.

15. Adjust the parking brake shoe clearance, then settle the parking brake shoes and disc.

16. Attach the disc brake assembly to the backing plate and tighten the bolt to 34 ft. lbs. (47 Nm).

17. Install the rear wheels and lower the vehicle.

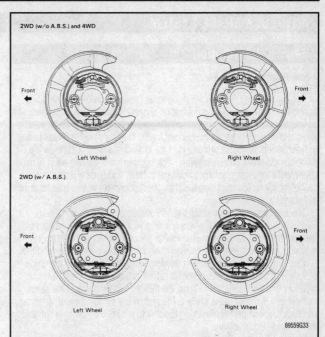

Fig. 81 Assemble the parking brake components in the correct direction

ADJUSTMENTS

◆ See Figure 82

1. Temporarily install the hub nuts on the outside of the disc.

2. Remove the hole plug.

3. Turn the adjuster with an adjuster brake tool and expand the shoes until the disc locks.

4. Return the adjuster 8 notches.

5. Install the hole plug.

6. Settle the shoes and disc on lever type:

   a. With the parking brake release button pushed in, pull the lever with 22 lbs. of force.

7. Settle the shoes and disc on pedal type:

   a. Depress the parking brake pedal with 33 lbs. of force.

   b. Drive the vehicle at about 31 mph (50 km) on a safe, level and dry road for about a quarter of a mile.

   c. Repeat this procedure 2 or 3 times.

8. Recehck and adjust the parking brake or lever travel.

Fig. 82 Once put back together, adjust the shoe clearance with a brake tool through the adjuster hole

ANTI-LOCK BRAKE SYSTEM

General Information

◆ **See Figures 83 and 84**

Anti-lock braking systems are designed to prevent locked-wheel skidding during hard braking or during braking on slippery surfaces. The front wheels of a vehicle cannot apply steering force if they are locked and sliding; the vehicle will continue in its previous direction of travel. The four wheel anti-lock brake systems found on Toyota vehicles hold the individual wheels just below the point of locking. By preventing wheel lock-up, maximum braking effort is maintained while preventing loss of directional control. Additionally, some steering capability is maintained during the stop. The ABS system will operate regardless of road surface conditions.

There are conditions for which the ABS system provides no benefit. Hydroplaning occurs when the tires ride on a film of water, losing contact with the paved surface. This renders the vehicle uncontrollable until road contact is regained. Extreme steering maneuvers at high speed or cornering beyond the limits of tire adhesion can result in skidding which is independent of vehicle braking. For this reason, the system is named antilock rather than antiskid.

Under normal braking conditions, the ABS system functions in the same manner as a standard brake system. The system is a combination of electrical and hydraulic components, working together to control the flow of brake fluid to the wheels when necessary.

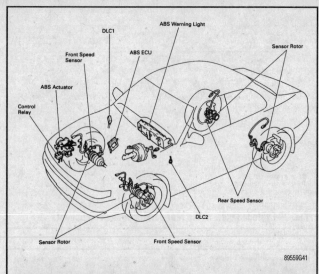

Fig. 84 Exploded view of the Nippondenso ABS system components

notice some pulsation in the body of the vehicle during a hard stop; this is generally due to suspension shudder as the brake pressures are altered rapidly and the forces transfer to the vehicle.

Although the ABS system prevents wheel lockup under hard braking, as brake pressure increases, wheel slip is allowed to increase as well. This slip will result in some tire chirp during ABS operation. The sound should not be interpreted as lockup but rather than as indication of the system holding the wheel(s) just outside the point of lockup. Additionally, the final few feet of an ABS engaged stop may be completed with the wheels locked; the electronic controls do not operate below 4 mph (6.4 kph).

The speed of each wheel (or the front wheels and driveshaft in 3 sensor systems) is monitored by the speed sensor. A toothed wheel rotates in front of the sensor, generating a small AC voltage which is transmitted to the ABS controller. The ABS computer compares the signals and reacts to rapid loss of wheel speed at a particular wheel by engaging the ABS system. Each speed sensor is individually removable. In most cases, the toothed wheels may be replaced if damaged, but disassembly of other components such as hub and knuckle, constant velocity joints or axles may be required.

A computer interprets inputs from the speed sensors, the brake lights, the brake warning lamp circuit, and, on some vehicles, the fuel injection system and/or a deceleration sensor. After processing the inputs, the computer controls output electrical signals to the hydraulic control solenoids, causing them to increase, decrease or hold brake line pressures. Additionally, the computer oversees operation of the pump motor and the ABS warning lamp.

Additionally, the computer constantly monitors system signals, performs a system actuation test immediately after engine start-up and can assign and store diagnostic fault codes if any errors are noted.

The ABS actuator, also called the hydraulic unit, contains the control solenoids for each brake circuit. The pump which maintains the system pressure during ABS braking is also within this unit. The solenoid relay and pump motor relays are mounted externally on the actuator. The ABS actuator can only be changed as a unit; with the exception of the relays, individual components cannot be replaced.

The deceleration sensor, used only on 4WD vehicles, advises the computer of vehicle deceleration. The computer uses this information in addition to the wheel speed sensor signals to decide if ABS control is necessary.

The ABS or ANTILOCK dashboard warning lamp is controlled by the ABS controller. The lamp will illuminate briefly when the ignition switch is turned **ON** as a bulb check. The lamp should then extinguish and remain out during vehicle operation. If only the ABS warning lamp illuminates while driving, the controller has noted a fault within the ABS system. ABS function is halted, but normal braking is maintained.

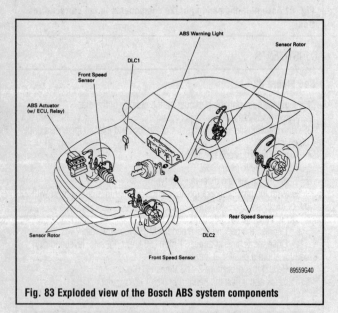

Fig. 83 Exploded view of the Bosch ABS system components

The Anti-lock Brake System Computer (ABS ECU) is the electronic brain of the system, receiving and interpreting speed signals from the speed sensors. The ABS ECU will enter anti-lock mode when it senses impending wheel lock at any wheel and immediately controls the brake line pressure(s) to the affected wheel(s). The actuator assembly is separate from the master cylinder and booster. It contains the wheel circuit valves used to control the brake fluid pressure to each wheel circuit.

During anti-lock braking, line pressures are controlled or modulated by the rapid cycling of electronic valves within the actuator. These valves can allow pressures within the system to increase, remain constant or decrease depending on the needs of the moment as registered by the ABS ECU. The front wheels are controlled individually. Depending on the model, the rear wheel circuits may receive the same electrical signal or be under individual control.

The operator may hear a popping or clicking sound as the pump and/or control valves cycle on and off during normal operation. The sounds are due to normal operation and are not indicative of a system problem. Under most conditions, the sounds are only faintly audible. If ABS is engaged, the operator may

SYSTEM COMPONENTS

Speed Sensors

The speed of each wheel is monitored by a sensor. A toothed wheel (sensor rotor) rotates in front of the sensor, generating a small AC voltage which is transmitted to the ABS controller. The ABS computer compares the signals and reacts to rapid loss of wheel speed at a particular wheel by engaging the ABS system. Each speed sensor is individually removable. In most cases, the toothed wheels may be replaced if damaged, but disassembly of other components such as hub and knuckle, constant velocity joints or axles may be required.

ABS Controller

This computer-based unit interprets inputs from the speed sensors, the brake lights and the brake warning lamp circuit. After processing the inputs, the unit controls output electrical signals to the hydraulic control solenoids, causing them to increase, decrease or hold brake line pressures. Additionally, the controller oversees operation of the pump motor and the ABS warning lamp.

Additionally, the controller constantly monitors system signals, performs a system actuation test immediately after engine start-up and can assign and store diagnostic fault codes if any errors are noted.

ABS Actuator

Also called the hydraulic unit, the actuator contains the control solenoids for each brake circuit. The pump which maintains the system pressure during ABS braking is also within this unit. The control relay is mounted externally near the actuator. The ABS actuator can only be replaced as a unit; with the exception of the relay, individual components cannot be replaced.

ABS Warning Lamp

▶ See Figures 85 and 86

The ABS dashboard warning lamp is controlled by the ABS controller. The lamp will illuminate briefly when the ignition switch is turned **ON** as a bulb

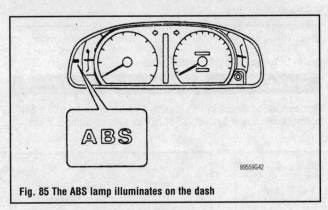

89559G42

Fig. 85 The ABS lamp illuminates on the dash

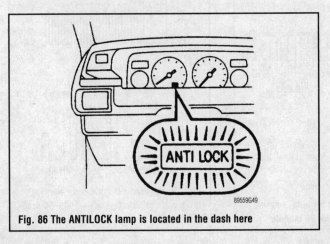

89559G49

Fig. 86 The ANTILOCK lamp is located in the dash here

check. The lamp should then extinguish and remain out during vehicle operation. If only the ABS warning lamp illuminates while driving, the controller has noted a fault within the ABS system. ABS function is halted, but normal braking is maintained.

Diagnosis and Testing

SYSTEM PRECAUTIONS

- Certain components within the ABS system are not intended to be serviced or repaired individually. Only those components with removal and installation procedures should be serviced.
- Do not use rubber hoses or other parts not specifically specified for the ABS system. When using repair kits, replace all parts included in the kit. Partial or incorrect repair may lead to functional problems and require the replacement of components.
- Lubricate rubber parts with clean, fresh brake fluid to ease assembly. Do not use lubricated shop air to clean parts; damage to rubber components may result.
- Use only DOT 3 brake fluid from an unopened container.
- If any hydraulic component or line is removed or replaced, it may be necessary to bleed the entire system.
- A clean repair area is essential. Always clean the reservoir and cap thoroughly before removing the cap. The slightest amount of dirt in the fluid may plug an orifice and impair the system function. Perform repairs after components have been thoroughly cleaned; use only denatured alcohol to clean components. Do not allow ABS components to come into contact with any substance containing mineral oil; this includes used shop rags.
- The anti-lock brake controller is a microprocessor similar to other computer units in the vehicle. Insure that the ignition switch is **OFF** before removing or installing controller harnesses. Avoid static electricity discharge at or near the controller.
- If any arc welding is to be done on the vehicle, the ABS controller should be disconnected before welding operations begin.
- If the vehicle is to be baked after paint repairs, disconnect and remove the ABSC from the vehicle.

DEPRESSURIZING THE SYSTEM

The system operates on low hydraulic pressure and requires no special system depressurization prior to the opening of hydraulic lines or other system repairs. Simply verify the ignition switch is **OFF** and pump/motor is not running.

DIAGNOSTIC CODES

If a malfunction occurs, the system will identify the problem and the computer will assign and store a fault code for the fault(s). The dashboard warning lamp will be illuminated to inform the driver that a fault has been found.

During diagnostics, the system will transmit the stored code(s) by flashing the dashboard warning lamp. If two or more codes are stored, they will be displayed from lowest number to highest, regardless of the order of occurrence. The system does not display the diagnostic codes while the vehicle is running.

INITIAL CHECKS

Visual Inspection

Before diagnosing an apparent ABS problem, make absolutely certain that the normal braking system is in correct working order. Many common brake problems (dragging parking brake, fluid seepage, etc.) will affect the ABS system. A visual check of specific system components may reveal problems creating an apparent ABS malfunction. Performing this inspection may reveal a simple failure, thus eliminating extended diagnostic time.

1. Inspect the tire pressures; they must be approximately equal for the system to operate correctly.
2. Inspect the brake fluid level in the reservoir.
3. Inspect brake lines, hoses, master cylinder assembly, brake calipers and cylinders for leakage.

4. Visually check brake lines and hoses for excessive wear, heat damage, punctures, contact with other parts, missing clips or holders, blockage or crimping.

5. Check the calipers or wheel cylinders for rust or corrosion. Check for proper sliding action if applicable.

6. Check the caliper and wheel cylinder pistons for freedom of motion during application and release.

7. Inspect the wheel speed sensors for proper mounting and connections.

8. Inspect the sensor wheels for broken teeth or poor mounting.

9. Inspect the wheels and tires on the vehicle. They must be of the same size and type to generate accurate speed signals.

10. Confirm the fault occurrence with the operator. Certain driver induced faults, such as not releasing the parking brake fully, will set a fault code and trigger the dash warning light(s). Excessive wheel spin on low-traction surfaces, high speed acceleration or riding the brake pedal may also set fault codes and trigger a warning lamp. These induced faults are not system failures but examples of vehicle performance outside the parameters of the control unit

11. Many system shutdowns are due to loss of sensor signals to or from the controller. The most common cause is not a failed sensor but a loose, corroded or dirty connector. Incorrect adjustment of the wheel speed sensor will cause a loss of wheel speed signal. Check harness and component connectors carefully.

READING CODES

▶ **See Figures 87 thru 92**

1. Start the engine and drive at a speed over 4 mph (6.4 kph). Listen carefully for actuator operation as the vehicle passes 4 mph (6.4 kph). If the brake is not applied, the controller cycles each solenoid and operates the pump motor briefly as an initial system check.

2. Return the vehicle to the workplace and turn the ignition switch **OFF**. Check battery condition; approximately 12 volts is required to operate the system.

3. Turn the ignition switch **ON** and check that the dashboard warning lamp (ABS or ANTILOCK) comes on for 3 seconds. If the lamp does not come on, repair the fuse, bulb or wiring.

4. On 1989–91 vehicles, read the stored diagnostic code(s), if any, as follows:

  a. With the ignition **ON**, disconnect the service wiring at the actuator.

  b. If a fault code has been set, the dashboard warning lamp will begin to blink 4 seconds later. The number of flashes corresponds to the first digit of a 2digit code; after a 1.5 second pause, the second digit is transmitted. If a second code is stored, it will be displayed after a 2.5 second pause. Once all codes have been displayed, the entire series will repeat after a 4 second pause.

  c. If no codes have been stored, the warning lamp will flash continuously every ½ second with no variation.

5. On 1992–94 vehicles, read the stored diagnostic code(s), if any as follows:

  a. With the ignition **ON**, disconnect the service wiring at the actuator.

  b. Using a jumper wire (SST 09843–18020) or equivalent, connect terminals **Tc** and **E1** of the check connector. Remove the short pin from terminals Wa and Wb of the check connector.

  c. If a fault code has been set, the dashboard warning lamp will begin to blink 4 seconds later. The number of flashes corresponds to the first digit of a 2-digit code; after a 1.5 second pause, the second digit is transmitted. If a second code is stored, it will be displayed after a 2.5 second pause. Once all codes have been displayed, the entire series will repeat after a 4 second pause.

  d. If no codes have been stored, the warning lamp will flash continuously every ½ second with no variation.

6. On 1995–96 vehicles, read the stored diagnostic code(s), if any as follows:

  a. Disconnect the short pin from the DLC1.

  b. Using a jumper wire, connect terminals Tc and E1 of the DLC2 or DLC1.

  c. Turn the ignition switch to the **ON** position.

  d. Read the diagnostic code from the ABS warning lamp. If not code appears, inspect the diagnostic circuit or the ABS circuit.

  e. After completing the check, disconnect the terminals Tc and E1 and turn off the display. If two or more malfunctions are displayed at the same time, the lowest numbered trouble code will be displayed first.

7. Clear the trouble codes.

CLEARING DIAGNOSTIC CODES

With the system set to read codes (short pin disconnected and jumper wire in place), turn the ignition switch **ON**. Apply the brake pedal 8 or more times within 3 seconds.

After the rapid pedal application, the dash warning lamp should display constant flashing, indicating a normal system. If codes are still displayed, make certain the repairs made to the system are correct. Also inspect the brake light switch at the brake pedal for any binding or sticking.

Once the codes are cleared, disconnect the jumper wire. Reinstall the short pin. The dash warning lamp should go out.

ABS Actuator

REMOVAL & INSTALLATION

▶ **See Figure 93**

1. Disconnect the negative battery cable.

✳✳ CAUTION

Some models covered by this manual may be equipped with a Supplemental Restraint System (SRS), which uses an air bag. When-

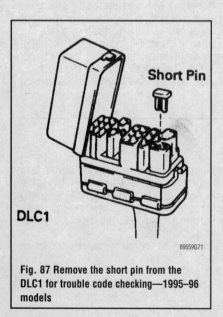

Fig. 87 Remove the short pin from the DLC1 for trouble code checking—1995–96 models

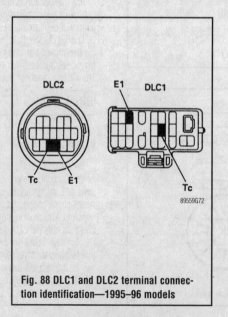

Fig. 88 DLC1 and DLC2 terminal connection identification—1995–96 models

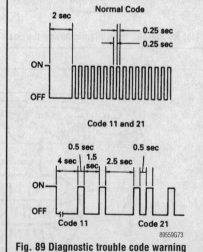

Fig. 89 Diagnostic trouble code warning lamp code blink reference—1995–96 models

Code	ABS Warning Light Blinking Pattern	Diagnosis	
11	ON / OFF	Open circuit in ABS control (solenoid) relay circuit	BE3931
12	ON / OFF	Short circuit in ABS control (solenoid) relay circuit	BE3931
13	ON / OFF	Open circuit in ABS control (motor) relay circuit	BE3931
14	ON / OFF	Short circuit in ABS control (motor) relay circuit	BE3931
21	ON / OFF	Open or short circuit in 3-position solenoid circuit for right front wheel	BE3932
22	ON / OFF	Open or short circuit in 3-position solenoid circuit for left front wheel	BE3932
23	ON / OFF	Open or short circuit in 3-position solenoid circuit for right rear wheel	BE3932
24	ON / OFF	Open or short circuit in 3-position solenoid circuit for left rear wheel	BE3932
31	ON / OFF	Right front wheel speed sensor signal malfunction	BE3933
32	ON / OFF	Left front wheel speed sensor signal malfunction	BE3933
33	ON / OFF	Right rear wheel speed sensor signal malfunction	BE3933
34	ON / OFF	Left rear wheel speed sensor signal malfunction	BE3933
35	ON / OFF	Open circuit in left front or right rear speed sensor circuit	BE3933
36	ON / OFF	Open circuit in right front or left rear speed sensor circuit	BE3933
37	ON / OFF	Faulty rear speed sensor rotor	BE3933
41	ON / OFF	Low battery positive voltage or abnormally high battery positive voltage	BE3934
51	ON / OFF	Pump motor is locked / Open in pump motor ground	BE3935
Always ON	ON	Malfunction in ECU	

Fig. 90 Diagnostic trouble codes—1995–96 models

89559G86

Code	ABS Warning Light Blinking Pattern	Diagnosis	
11	ON / OFF	Open or short circuit in ABS solenoid relay circuit	BE3931
13	ON / OFF	Open or short circuit in ABS motor relay circuit	BE3931
21	ON / OFF	Open or short circuit in 3-position solenoid circuit for right front wheel	BE3932
22	ON / OFF	Open or short circuit in 3-position solenoid circuit for left front wheel	BE3932
23	ON / OFF	Open or short circuit in 3-position solenoid circuit for rear wheels	BE3932
31	ON / OFF	Right front wheel speed sensor signal malfunction	BE3933
32	ON / OFF	Left front wheel speed sensor signal malfunction	BE3933
33	ON / OFF	Right rear wheel speed sensor signal malfunction	BE3933
34	ON / OFF	Left rear wheel speed sensor signal malfunction	BE3933
35	ON / OFF	Open circuit in right front speed sensor circuit	BE3933
36	ON / OFF	Open circuit in left front speed sensor circuit	BE3933
37	ON / OFF	Faulty rear speed sensor rotor	BE3933
38	ON / OFF	Open circuit in right rear speed sensor circuit	BE3933
39	ON / OFF	Open circuit in left rear speed sensor circuit	BE3933
41	ON / OFF	Low battery positive voltage	BE3934
51	ON / OFF	Pump motor is locked / Open in pump motor circuit in actuator	BE3935
62	ON / OFF	Malfunction in ECU	BE3936

Fig. 91 Diagnostic trouble codes—1989–94 models

89559G87

DIAGNOSTIC CODE

Code No.	Light Pattern	Diagnosis	Malfunctioning Part
	ON ⎍⎍⎍⎍⎍⎍⎍⎍⎍ OFF	All speed sensors and sensor rotors are normal	
71	⎍⎍⎍⎍⎍⎍⎍‿⎍‿	Low voltage of front right speed sensor signal	• Front right speed sensor • Sensor installation
72	⎍⎍⎍⎍⎍⎍‿⎍⎍‿	Low voltage of front left speed sensor signal	• Front left speed sensor • Sensor installation
73	⎍⎍⎍⎍⎍‿⎍⎍‿	Low voltage of rear right speed sensor signal	• Rear right speed sensor • Sensor installation
74	⎍⎍⎍⎍‿⎍⎍⎍‿	Low voltage of rear left speed sensor signal	• Rear left speed sensor • Sensor installation
75	⎍⎍⎍⎍⎍⎍⎍⎍⎍‿	Abnormal change of front right speed sensor signal	• Front right sensor rotor
76	⎍⎍⎍⎍⎍⎍‿⎍⎍⎍⎍‿	Abnormal change of front left speed sensor signal	• Front left sensor rotor
77	⎍⎍⎍⎍‿⎍⎍⎍⎍‿	Abnormal change of rear right speed sensor signal	• Rear right sensor rotor
78	⎍⎍⎍⎍⎍⎍‿⎍⎍⎍⎍⎍‿	Abnormal change of rear left speed sensor signal	• Rear left sensor rotor

89559G88

Fig. 92 Diagnostic trouble codes for speed sensors

89559P08

Fig. 93 The ABS actuator is located on the right side of the vehicle against the fender well

ever working near any of the SRS components, such as the impact sensors, the air bag module, steering column and instrument panel, **disable the SRS, as described in Section 6.**

2. Label and disconnect the electrical connectors.
3. Remove the fluid in the brake actuator with a suitable syringe.
4. Remove the engine coolant reserve tank and the windshield washer tank as required.
5. If necessary, remove the A/C joint tube mounting bolt and the two power steering hose clamp bolts.
6. Disconnect the hydraulic lines from the brake actuator. Plug the ends of the lines to prevent loss of fluid.
7. Detach the hydraulic fluid pressure differential switch wiring connectors.
8. Loosen the brake actuator reservoir mounting nuts.
9. Unfasten the nuts and remove the ABS actuator assembly.

10. Installation is the reverse of removal. Before tightening the mounting nuts or bolts, screw the hydraulic line into the cylinder body a few turns.
11. Install the actuator and tighten the ABS assembly bolts to 14 ft. lbs. (19 Nm).
12. Attach and tighten the hydraulic lines to 11 ft. lbs. (15 Nm).
13. After installation is completed, fill the reservoir and bleed the brake system. Drive the vehicle for at least 20 seconds at 19 mph 930 km) to make sure the ABS lamp does not illuminate. If it does, read the DTC codes.

Front Speed Sensor

TESTING

▶ **See Figures 94 and 95**

1. Remove the bolt from the pipe clamp of the wire harness for the sensor.
2. Disconnect the speed sensor wiring.
3. Mesarure the resistance between terminals 1 and 2 of the speed sensor body and ground. Resistance should be:
   • 1989–91 models—0.85–1.30 kilohms.
   • 1992–94 models—0.92–1.22 kilohms
   • 1995–96 models—0.6–1.8 kilohms
4. If the resistance is not within specifications, replace the sensor.
5. Check that there is no continuity between each terminal and the sensor body on 1989–94 models. there should be 1 milohm on models 1995–96.

REMOVAL & INSTALLATION

1989–91 Models

1. Raise and safely support the front of the vehicle.
2. Remove the tire and wheel. Remove the fender shield as required, to access the wire connector.
3. Disconnect the wheel speed sensor lead from the ABS harness. Remove any retaining bolts or clips holding the harness in place.

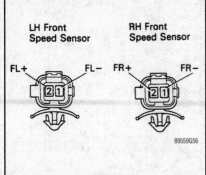

Fig. 94 Front speed sensor terminal identification—1989–91 models

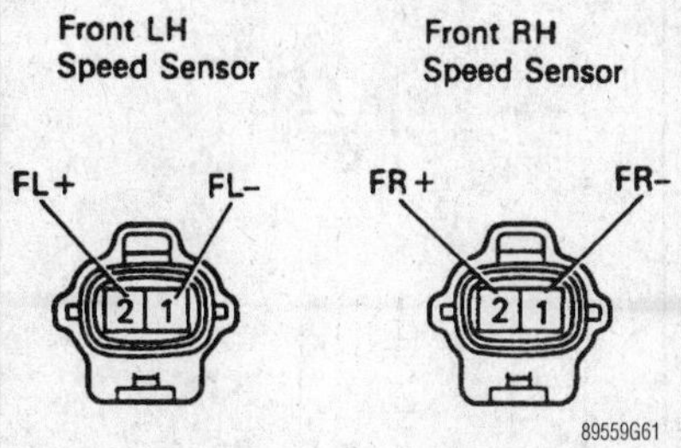

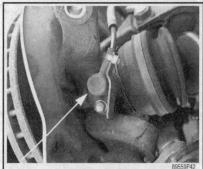

Fig. 95 Front speed sensor terminal identification—1992–96 models

Fig. 96 The front speed sensor is attached to the back of the knuckle with one bolt—1992–96 models

➡Clips and retainers must be reinstalled in their exact original location. Take careful note of the position of each retainer and of the correct harness routing during removal.

4. Remove the single bolt holding the speed sensor.

5. Carefully remove the sensor straight out of its mount. Do not subject the sensor to shock or vibration; protect the tip of the sensor at all times.

6. Installation is the reverse of removal. Secure the sensor retaining bolt to 69 inch lbs. (8 Nm).

1992–96 Models

▶ See Figure 96

1. Remove the inner fender shield.

2. Disconnect the speed sensor harness.

3. Remove the harness and the sensor retainers and remove the sensor from the vehicle.

4. Installation is the reverse of removal. Secure the sensor, tighten the retainers to 69 inch lbs. (8 Nm).

Rear Speed Sensor

TESTING

▶ See Figures 97, 98 and 99

1. Remove the rear seat cushion and side seat back.

2. Disconnect the speed sensor wiring harness from the switch.

3. Mesaure the resistance between terminals 1 and 2 of the speed sensor body and ground. Resistance should be:
- 1989–91 models—0.85–1.50 kilohms.
- 1992–94 models—1.05–1.45 kilohms
- 1995–96 models—0.9–1.3 kilohms

4. If the resistance is not within specifications, replace the sensor.

5. Check that there is no continuity between each terminal and the sensor body on 1989–94 models. there should be 1 milohm on models 1995–96.

REMOVAL & INSTALLATION

2WD Vehicle

1989–91 MODELS

1. Remove the rear seat cushion. Disconnect the sensor cable connector; feed the sensor cable through the grommet.

2. Raise and safely support the rear of the vehicle.

3. Remove the wheel and tire.

4. Remove the clips and retainers holding the sensor cable to the body and suspension arm.

5. Remove the upper axle carrier mounting bolt and nut.

6. Remove the brake caliper and brake disc. Suspend the caliper from stiff wire; do not let it hang by the hose.

7. Remove the 4 bolts holding the hub and remove the hub.

8. Remove the backing plate with the parking brake assembly and O-ring.

9. Remove the speed sensor retaining bolt and remove the sensor from the backing plate.

To install:

10. Position the sensor on the backing plate and install the retaining bolt. Tighten the bolt to 69 inch lbs. (8 Nm).

11. Install the backing plate with the parking brake assembly in place.

12. Install a new O-ring on the axle carrier. Install the hub and tighten the 4 mounting bolts to 59 ft. lbs. (80 Nm).

13. Align the hole on the axle hub and the service hole on the brake disc. Install the disc.

14. The remainder of installation is the reverse of removal. Tighten each component to specifications.

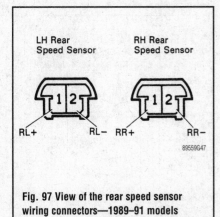

Fig. 97 View of the rear speed sensor wiring connectors—1989–91 models

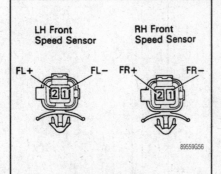

Fig. 98 Rear speed sensor terminal identification—1992–96 models

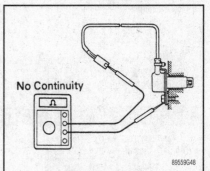

Fig. 99 Testing the continuity of the rear speed sensor terminal and body with an ohmmeter

Fig. 100 The rear speed sensor is attached to the back of the rear hub

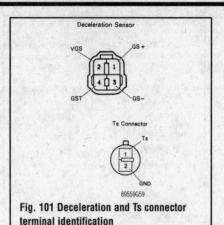

Fig. 101 Deceleration and Ts connector terminal identification

Fig. 102 Check the warning light blinks about 1 time every second

1992–96 MODELS

▶ See Figure 100

1. Remove the rear seat cushion. Disconnect the sensor cable wiring; feed the sensor cable through the grommet.
2. Raise and safely support the rear of the vehicle.
3. Remove the wheel and tire.
4. Remove the clips and retainers holding the sensor cable to the body and suspension arm. Remove the sensor from the vehicle.

To install:

5. Place the speed sensor into position on the axle carrier. Tighten the mounting bolt to 69 inch lbs. (8 Nm).
6. Feed the harness connector through to the interior and connect the harnesses together.
7. Install the grommet securely. Install the sensor harness with clamps and bolts and tighten to 48 inch lbs. (5 Nm).

4WD Vehicle

1. Raise and safely support the rear of the vehicle.
2. Remove the tire and wheel.
3. Disconnect the wheel speed sensor lead from the ABS harness. Remove any retaining bolts or clips holding the harness in place.

➡Clips and retainers must be reinstalled in their exact original location. Take careful note of the position of each retainer and of the correct harness routing during removal.

4. Remove the single bolt holding the speed sensor.
5. Carefully remove the sensor straight out of its mount. Do not subject the sensor to shock or vibration; protect the tip of the sensor at all times.

To install:

6. Before installation, make certain all traces of paint are removed from the hub carrier surface. A clean metal-to-metal contact is required. Fit the sensor into position. Make certain the sensor sits flush against the mounting surface; it must not be crooked.
7. Install the retaining bolt. Tighten the bolt to 69 inch lbs. (8 Nm).
8. Route the sensor cable correctly and install the harness clips and retainers. The cable must be in its original position and completely clear of moving components.
9. Connect the sensor cable to the ABS harness.
10. Install the wheel and tire.
11. Lower the vehicle to the ground.

Deceleration Sensor and ABS ECU

This procedure is for the 4WD models only. The ABS ECU can be located in the engine compartment and trunk area on 2WD models.

TESTING

▶ See Figures 101 and 102

➡The following procedures require driving the vehicle while it is in the diagnostic mode. The anti-lock system will be disabled; only normal braking function will be available.

1. Check the battery voltage with the engine off; voltage should be approximately 12 volts.
2. With the ignition switch **ON**, make certain the ABS warning lamp comes on for about 3 seconds and then goes out. Turn the ignition switch **OFF**.
3. Remove the rubber cap from the Ts connector located in front of the actuator. Use a jumper wire to connect the 2 terminals.
4. Apply the parking brake fully, depress the brake pedal and start the engine.
5. After a short delay, the ABS dashboard warning lamp should flash about once every second. This is slower than the usual system flashing when transmitting a code.
6. Release the parking brake and drive the vehicle straight ahead at 12.4 mph (20 kph) or greater speed. Lightly depress the brake pedal; there should be no change in the flashing dashboard lamp.
7. Continue to drive at the same speed and apply the brakes moderately. The warning lamp should stop flashing and remain on during braking only. Once the brake is released, flashing continues at the previous rate.
8. Continue driving at the same speed; apply the brakes strongly. The dash warning lamp should remain on during the braking period and change to a rapid flash when the brakes are released.
9. If the warning lamp display does not meet specifications, check the installation of the deceleration sensor. It must be correctly and securely installed. If installation is proper, replace the sensor and retest the system.
10. Stop the vehicle and turn the ignition switch **OFF**. Remove the jumper wire from the check connector.

REMOVAL & INSTALLATION

▶ See Figure 103

1. Remove the ABS ECU cover and the ECU from the mounting bracket.
2. Disconnect the wiring from the ECU and remove the computer from the vehicle.
3. Remove the 2 mounting screws from the deceleration sensor and remove the sensor from the vehicle.
4. Installation is the reverse of removal. Secure the sensor to the bracket and tighten to 28 inch lbs. (3 Nm).
5. Position the computer and install it with the 5 screws, tighten them to 28 inch lbs. (3 Nm).

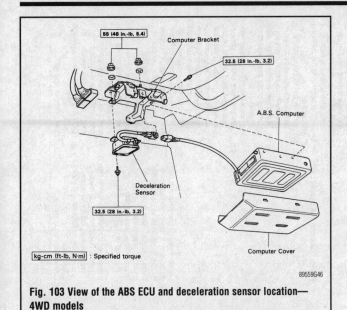

Fig. 103 View of the ABS ECU and deceleration sensor location— 4WD models

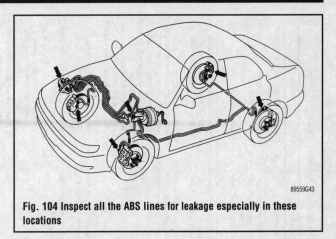

Fig. 104 Inspect all the ABS lines for leakage especially in these locations

Sensor Ring (Rotor)

The wheel mounted sensor rings are integral parts of either the wheel hub or the axle shaft; if the ring is damaged, the hub or shaft must be replaced. For axle shaft and wheel hub removal and installation procedures, please refer to the appropriate section of this repair manual.

Bleeding The ABS System

▶ See Figure 104

The brake fluid reservoir is located on top of the master cylinder. While no special procedures are needed to fill the fluid, the reservoir cap and surrounding area must be wiped clean of all dirt and debris before removing the cap. The slightest dirt in the fluid can cause a system malfunction. Use only DOT 3 fluid from an unopened container. Use of old, polluted or non-approved fluid can seriously impair the function of the system.

Bleeding is performed in the usual manner, using either a pressure bleeder or the 2-person manual method. If a pressure bleeder is used, it must be of the diaphragm type with an internal diaphragm separating the air chamber from the fluid. Tighten each bleeder plug to 74 inch lbs. (8 Nm).

Always begin the bleeding with the longest brake line, then the next longest, and so on. If the master cylinder has been repaired or if the reservoir has been emptied, the master cylinder will need to be bled before the individual lines and calipers. During any bleeding procedure, make certain to maintain the fluid level above the MIN line on the reservoir. When the bleeding procedure is complete, fill the reservoir to the MAX line before reinstalling the cap.

BRAKE SPECIFICATIONS
All measurements in inches unless noted

Year	Model	Master Cylinder Bore	Brake Disc Original Thickness	Brake Disc Minimum Thickness	Brake Disc Maximum Runout	Brake Drum Diameter Original Inside Diameter	Brake Drum Diameter Max. Wear Limit	Brake Drum Diameter Maximum Machine Diameter	Minimum Lining Thickness Front	Minimum Lining Thickness Rear
1983	Camry	—	0.866	0.827	0.0059	7.874	7.913	—	0.039	0.039
1984	Camry	—	0.866	0.827	0.0059	7.874	7.913	—	0.039	0.039
1985	Camry	—	0.866	0.827	0.0059	7.874	7.913	—	0.039	0.039
1986	Camry	—	0.866	0.827	0.0059	7.874	7.913	—	0.039	0.039
1987	Camry	—	0.866	0.827	0.0051	9.000	9.079	—	0.039	0.039
1988	Camry	—	0.984	0.945	0.0031	9.000	9.079	—	0.039	0.039
1989	Camry	—	0.984 ①	0.945 ②	0.0028 ③	9.000	9.079	—	0.039	0.039
1991	Camry	—	0.984 ①	0.945 ②	0.0028 ③	9.000	9.079	—	0.039	0.039
1992	Camry	—	1.102 ①	1.024 ②	0.0020 ③	9.000	9.079	—	0.039	0.039
1993	Camry	—	1.102 ①	1.024 ②	0.0020 ③	9.000	9.079	—	0.039	0.039
1994	Camry	—	1.102 ①	1.024 ②	0.0020 ③	9.000	9.079	—	0.039	0.039
1995	Camry	—	1.102 ①	1.024 ②	0.0020 ③	9.000	9.079	—	0.039	0.039
1996	Camry	—	1.102 ①	1.024 ②	0.0020 ③	9.000	9.079	—	0.039	0.039
1997	Camry	—	1.102 ①	1.024 ②	0.0020 ③	9.000	7.913	—	0.039	0.039

① Rear disc STD: 0.394 inch
② Rear disc Limit: 0.354 inch
③ Rear disc runout: 0.0059 inch

89559C01

Troubleshooting the Brake System

Problem	Cause	Solution
Low brake pedal (excessive pedal travel required for braking action.)	Excessive clearance between rear linings and drums caused by inoperative automatic adjusters	Make 10 to 15 alternate forward and reverse brake stops to adjust brakes. If brake pedal does not come up, repair or replace adjuster parts as necessary.
	Worn rear brakelining	Inspect and replace lining if worn beyond minimum thickness specification.
	Bent, distorted brakeshoes, front or rear	Replace brakeshoes in axle sets
	Air in hydraulic system	Remove air from system. Refer to Brake Bleeding.
Low brake pedal (pedal may go to floor with steady pressure applied.)	Fluid leak in hydraulic system	Fill master cylinder to fill line; have helper apply brakes and check calipers, wheel cylinders, differential valve tubes, hoses and fittings for leaks. Repair or replace as necessary.
	Air in hydraulic system	Remove air from system. Refer to Brake Bleeding.
	Incorrect or non-recommended brake fluid (fluid evaporates at below normal temp).	Flush hydraulic system with clean brake fluid. Refill with correct-type fluid.
	Master cylinder piston seals worn, or master cylinder bore is scored, worn or corroded	Repair or replace master cylinder
Low brake pedal (pedal goes to floor on first application—o.k. on subsequent applications.)	Disc brake pads sticking on abutment surfaces of anchor plate. Caused by a build-up of dirt, rust, or corrosion on abutment surfaces	Clean abutment surfaces
Fading brake pedal (pedal height decreases with steady pressure applied.)	Fluid leak in hydraulic system	Fill master cylinder reservoirs to fill mark, have helper apply brakes, check calipers, wheel cylinders, differential valve, tubes, hoses, and fittings for fluid leaks. Repair or replace parts as necessary.
	Master cylinder piston seals worn, or master cylinder bore is scored, worn or corroded	Repair or replace master cylinder
Decreasing brake pedal travel (pedal travel required for braking action decreases and may be accompanied by a hard pedal.)	Caliper or wheel cylinder pistons sticking or seized	Repair or replace the calipers, or wheel cylinders
	Master cylinder compensator ports blocked (preventing fluid return to reservoirs) or pistons sticking or seized in master cylinder bore	Repair or replace the master cylinder
	Power brake unit binding internally	Test unit according to the following procedure: (a) Shift transmission into neutral and start engine (b) Increase engine speed to 1500 rpm, close throttle and fully depress brake pedal (c) Slow release brake pedal and stop engine (d) Have helper remove vacuum check valve and hose from power unit. Observe for backward movement of brake pedal. (e) If the pedal moves backward, the power unit has an internal bind—replace power unit

TCCA9C001

Troubleshooting the Brake System (cont.)

Problem	Cause	Solution
Spongy brake pedal (pedal has abnormally soft, springy, spongy feel when depressed.)	Air in hydraulic system	Remove air from system. Refer to Brake Bleeding.
	Brakeshoes bent or distorted	Replace brakeshoes
	Brakelining not yet seated with drums and rotors	Burnish brakes
	Rear drum brakes not properly adjusted	Adjust brakes
Hard brake pedal (excessive pedal pressure required to stop vehicle. May be accompanied by brake fade.)	Loose or leaking power brake unit vacuum hose	Tighten connections or replace leaking hose
	Incorrect or poor quality brakelining	Replace with lining in axle sets
	Bent, broken, distorted brakeshoes	Replace brakeshoes
	Calipers binding or dragging on mounting pins. Rear brakeshoes dragging on support plate.	Replace mounting pins and bushings. Clean rust or burrs from rear brake support plate ledges and lubricate ledges with molydisulfide grease. NOTE: If ledges are deeply grooved or scored, do not attempt to sand or grind them smooth—replace support plate.
		Repair or replace parts as necessary.
	Caliper, wheel cylinder, or master cylinder pistons sticking or seized	
	Power brake unit vacuum check valve malfunction	Test valve according to the following procedure: (a) Start engine, increase engine speed to 1500 rpm, close throttle and immediately stop engine (b) Wait at least 90 seconds then depress brake pedal (c) If brakes are not vacuum assisted for 2 or more applications, check valve is faulty
	Power brake unit has internal bind	Test unit according to the following procedure. (a) With engine stopped, apply brakes several times to exhaust all vacuum in system (b) Shift transmission into neutral, depress brake pedal and start engine (c) If pedal height decreases with foot pressure and less pressure is required to hold pedal in applied position, power unit vacuum system is operating normally. Test power unit. If power unit exhibits a bind condition, replace the power unit.
	Master cylinder compensator ports (at bottom of reservoirs) blocked by dirt, scale, rust, or have small burrs (blocked ports prevent fluid return to reservoirs).	Repair or replace master cylinder CAUTION: Do not attempt to clean blocked ports with wire, pencils, or similar implements. Use compressed air only.
	Brake hoses, tubes, fittings clogged or restricted	Use compressed air to check or unclog parts. Replace any damaged parts.
	Brake fluid contaminated with improper fluids (motor oil, transmission fluid, causing rubber components to swell and stick in bores	Replace all rubber components, combination valve and hoses. Flush entire brake system with DOT 3 brake fluid or equivalent.
	Low engine vacuum	Adjust or repair engine

TCCA9C002

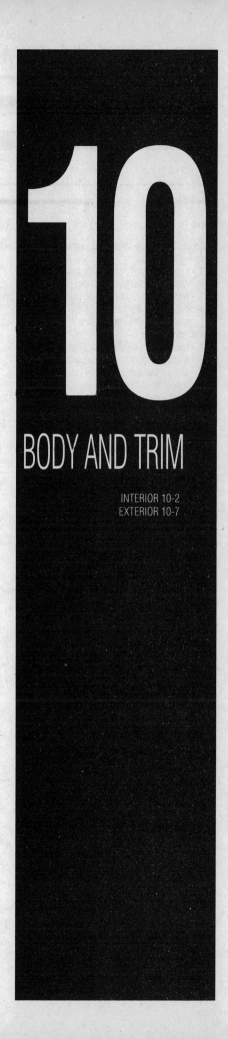

10

BODY AND TRIM

EXTERIOR

Doors

ADJUSTMENT

▶ See Figure 1

Front

To adjust the door in forward, rearward and vertical directions, perform the following adjustment:
1. Loosen the body side hinge bolts or nuts.
2. Adjust the door to the desired position.
3. Secure the body side hinge bolts or nuts and check the door for proper alignment. Tighten the bolts to 21 ft. lbs. (28 Nm).

To adjust the door in left, right and vertical directions, perform the following adjustments:
4. Loosen the door side hinge bolts slightly.
5. Adjust the door to the desired position.
6. Secure the door side hinge bolts and check the door for proper alignment. Tighten the bolts to 21 ft. lbs. (28 Nm).

To adjust the door lock striker, perform the following procedure:
7. Check that the door fit and the door lock linkages are adjusted properly.
8. Slightly loosen the striker mounting screws and tap striker with a hammer until the desired position is obtained.
9. Tighten the striker mounting screws.

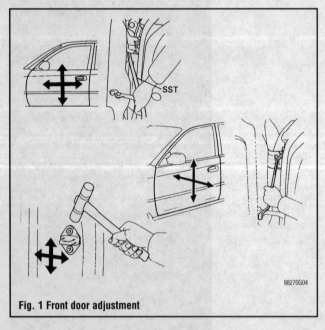

Fig. 1 Front door adjustment

Rear

▶ See Figure 2

To adjust the door in the forward/rearward and vertical directions perform the following:
1. Remove the rear seat cushion and rear seat back.
2. Remove the roof side inner garnish.
3. Remove the rear seat side garnish.
4. Unscrew and remove the front door scuff plate.
5. Remove the center pillar lower garnish.
6. Loosen the body side hinge nuts to adjust. Tighten them to 21 ft. lbs. 928 Nm).
7. Install the center pillar lower garnish.
8. Secure the front door scuff plate.
9. Install the rear seat side garnish.

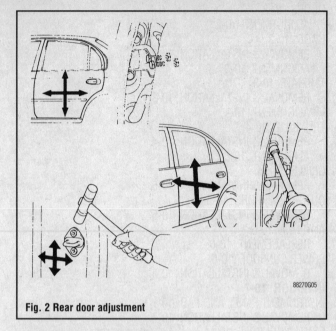

Fig. 2 Rear door adjustment

10. Attach the roof side inner garnish.
11. Install the rear seatback and rear seat cushion. Tighten the bolts to 14 ft. lbs. (19 Nm).
To adjust the door in the left/right and vertical positions perform the following:
12. Loosen the door side hinge bolts to adjust.
13. Substitue the standard bolt for the centering the bolt. Tighten to 21 ft. lbs. (28 Nm).
To adjust the door lock striker, perform the following procedure:
14. Check that the door fit and the door lock linkages are adjusted properly.
15. Slightly loosen the striker mounting screws and tap striker with a hammer until the desired position is obtained.
16. Tighten the striker mounting screws.

Hood

REMOVAL & INSTALLATION

▶ See Figures 3, 4, 5, 6 and 7

1. Open the hood completely.
2. Protect the cowl panel and hood from scratches during this operation. Apply protection tape or cover body surfaces before starting work.

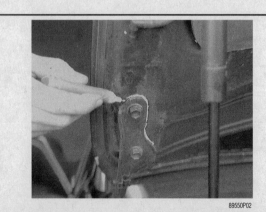

Fig. 3 Scribe marks on the hood where the hinge mates the area

Fig. 4 Disconnect the windshield washer hose

Fig. 5 Remove the clip retaining the upper portion of the hood struts

Fig. 6 With an assistant holding the hood in place, slide the strut off the hood

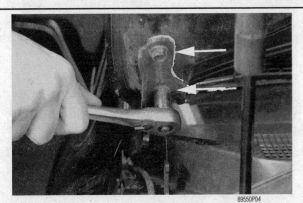

Fig. 7 Have a helper secure the hood, then remove the attaching bolts

3. Scribe a mark showing the location of each hinge on the hood to aid in alignment during installation.

4. Disconnect any windshield washer hoses.

5. Prop the hood in the upright position. Disconnect the hood prop cylinder(s) from the hood (if equipped).

6. Have an assistant help hold the hood while you remove the hood-to-hinge bolts. Use care not to damage hood or vehicle during hood removal.

7. Lift the hood off of the vehicle.

8. Installation is the reverse of removal. Open the hood and adjust so that all clearances are the same and the hood panel is flush with the body.

9. After all adjustments are complete, tighten hinge mounting bolts to 10 ft. lbs. (14 Nm).

ALIGNMENT

▶ See Figures 8, 9 and 10

Since the centering bolt, which has a chamfered shoulder, is used as the hood hinge and the lock set bolt, the hood and lock can't be adjusted with it on. To adjust properly, remove the hinge centering bolt and substitute a bolt with a washer for the centering bolt.

To adjust the hood forward or rearward and left or right directions, adjust the hood by loosening the side hinge bolts and moving the hood to the desired position. Secure the hinge bolts to 10 ft. lbs. (14 Nm).

To adjust the front edge of the hood in a vertical direction, turn the cushions as required.

To adjust the hood lock, remove the clips holding the radiator upper seal to the upper radiator support. Remove the upper seal from the vehicle and adjust the lock by loosening the lock retainer bolts. Tighten the hood lock mounting bolts to 69 inch lbs. (8 Nm) and reinstall the radiator upper seal when adjustment is complete.

Tailgate

REMOVAL & INSTALLATION

▶ See Figure 11

1. Open the tailgate completely.

2. Remove the inner trim panel.

3. Disengage the electrical connector from the combination light and the electric solenoid as required. Remove the harness and position out of the way.

4. Scribe the hinge location on the tailgate to aid in installation.

5. Disconnect the damper stay from the tailgate and position out of the way. Disconnect the rear defroster wiring, if equipped.

6. Remove the tailgate-to-hinge bolts and remove the tailgate from the vehicle.

7. Installation is the reverse of removal. Secure all components.

8. Close the tailgate slowly to check for proper alignment, and adjust as required.

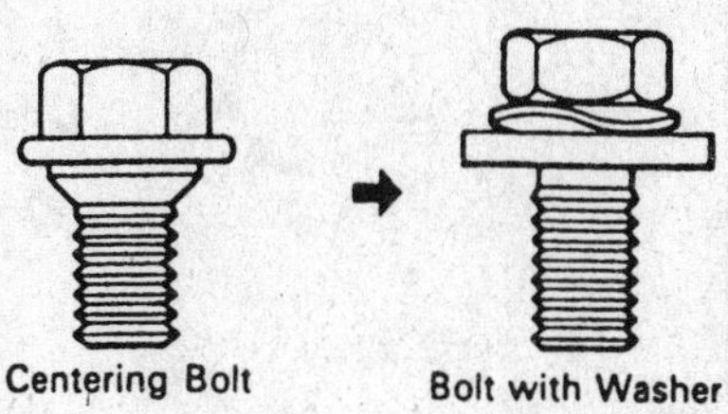

Fig. 8 Shouldered centering bolt which is to be removed during hood adjustment

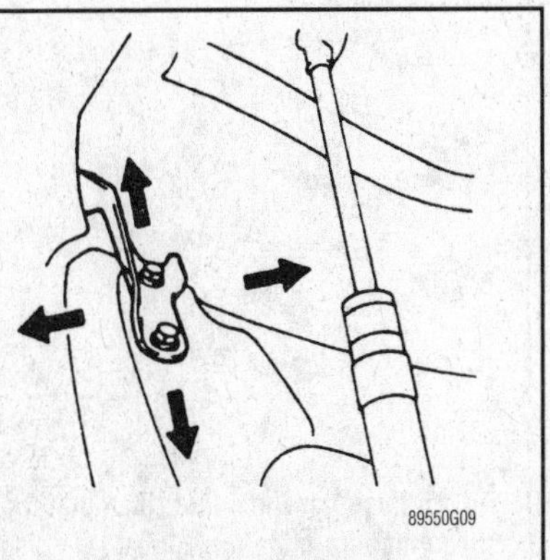

Fig. 9 Hood adjustment directions

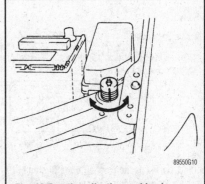

Fig. 10 Turn the adjusting cushion in either direction

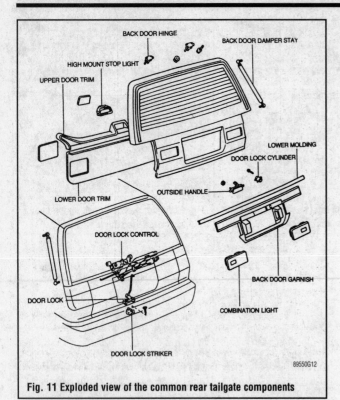

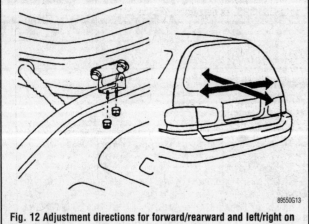

Fig. 11 Exploded view of the common rear tailgate components

ALIGNMENT

▶ See Figures 12 and 13

To adjust the door in forward/rearward and left/right directions, loosen the hinge bolts and position the tailgate as required. Tighten to 9 ft. lbs. (13 Nm).

To adjust the tailgate lock striker, loosen the mounting bolts and using a plastic hammer, tap the striker to the desired position. Removing of the lower trim panel is normally required to access the striker.

Vertical adjustment of the door edge is made by removing or adding shims under the hinges.

Trunk Lid

REMOVAL & INSTALLATION

▶ See Figures 14, 15 and 16

1. Remove the luggage compartment trim to access the hinge bolts.
2. Using a pry tool or SST 09804–24010, push down on the torsion bar at one end and pull the luggage compartment lid hinge from the torsion bar.
3. Slowly lift the tool and remove the torsion bar from the bracket.
4. Repeat the last 2 steps for the other side of the trunk lid to remove that torsion bar.
5. Prop the hood in the upright position and scribe the hinge locations in the trunk lid.
6. Remove the hinge-to-trunk lid mounting bolts and remove the trunk lid from the vehicle.

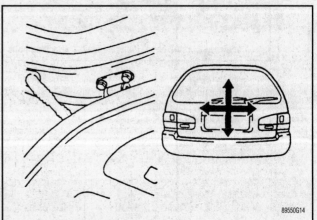

Fig. 12 Adjustment directions for forward/rearward and left/right on the tailgate

Fig. 13 Adjustment directions for left/right and vertical on the tailgate

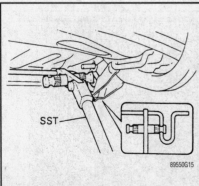

Fig. 14 Insert the prytool to the torsion bar on the hinge side

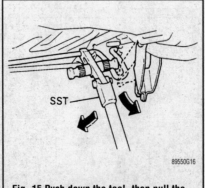

Fig. 15 Push down the tool, then pull the trunk hinge from the torsion bar

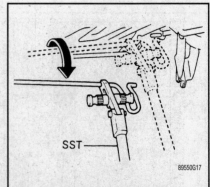

Fig. 16 Slowly lift the tool and separate the torsion bar from the bracket

7. Installation is the reverse of removal. Install the torsion bar to the side and center brackets, and the pry tool or SST 09804-24010, install the torsion bar to the hinges.

ALIGNMENT

To adjust the door in forward/rearward and left/right directions, loosen the hinge bolts and position the tailgate as required. Tighten the hinge bolts to 69 inch lbs. (8 Nm).

To adjust the tailgate lock striker, loosen the mounting bolts and using a plastic hammer and a brass bar, tap the striker to the desired position.

Vertical adjustment of the door edge is made by removing or adding washes to shim the hinge bolts.

Grille

REMOVAL & INSTALLATION

♦ See Figures 17 and 18

The grille can be removed without removing any other parts. The grille is held on by a number of fasteners. Raise the hood and look for screws placed vertically in front of the metalwork. Remove the retainer screws and lift the grille from the vehicle. During installation, make sure that all the retainers are installed in their original locations.

Outside Mirrors

REMOVAL & INSTALLATION

The mirrors on these models can be removed from the door without disassembling the door liner or other components. Both left and right outside mirrors may be either manual, manual remote (small lever on the inside to adjust the mirror) or electric remote. If the mirror glass is damaged, replacements may be available through your dealer or a reputable glass shop in your area. If the plastic housing is damaged or cracked, the entire unit will need to be replaced.

Manual

♦ See Figure 19

1. Remove the set screw and the adjustment knob, if equipped.
2. Remove the delta cover; that's the triangular black inner cover. It can be removed with a blunt plastic or wooden tool. Don't use a metal prytool; the plastic will be marred.
3. Depending on the style of mirror, there may be concealment plugs or other minor parts under the delta cover—remove them.
4. Support the mirror housing from the outside and remove the three bolts or nuts holding the mirror to the door.
5. Remove the mirror assembly.
6. Installation is the reverse of removal.

Power

♦ See Figures 20 and 21

1. Turn the ignition key to the OFF position. Disconnect the negative battery cable. Wait at least 90 seconds from the time the negative battery was disconnected to start work.

✳✳ CAUTION

Some models covered by this manual may be equipped with a Supplemental Restraint System (SRS), which uses an air bag. Whenever working near any of the SRS components, such as the impact sensors, the air bag module, steering column and instrument panel, disable the SRS, as described in Section 6.

Fig. 17 Only two bolts retain the grille on late model Camrys

Fig. 18 Once the retainers are detached, pull the grille out from the front of the vehicle

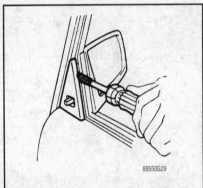

Fig. 19 Use a tapped ended tool to pry the trim from the mirror

Fig. 20 Remove the delta cover from the inside of the door

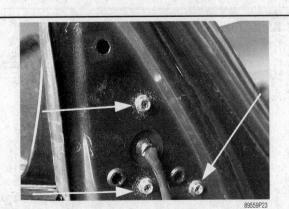

Fig. 21 Location of the three retaining screws

2. Remove the delta cover; that's the triangular black inner cover. It can be removed with a blunt plastic or wooden tool. Don't use a metal prytool; the plastic will be marred.

3. Depending on the style of mirror, there may be concealment plugs or other minor parts under the delta cover—remove them.

4. Depending on the type of door trim, you may need to remove the door inner panel to access the electrical wiring harness for the mirror.

5. Support the mirror housing from the outside and remove the three bolts or nuts holding the mirror to the door.

6. If the wiring to the electric mirror was not disconnected previously, detach it now. Some connectors can only be reached after the mirror is free of the door. Remove the mirror assembly.

7. Installation is the reverse of removal. Cycle the mirror several times to make sure that it works properly.

Antenna

REPLACEMENT

Manual

If your antenna mast is the type where you can unscrew the mast from the fender, simply do so with a pair of pliers. Most damaged antennas are simply the result of a car wash or similar mishap, in which the mast is bent.

Some antenna masts are attached to the side of the windshield pillar on the drivers side. Simply unscrew the two plastic holders and proceed with cable removal.

Disconnect the antenna cable at the radio by pulling it straight out of the set. Depending on access, this may require loosening the radio and pulling it out of the dash. Working under the instrument panel, disengage the cable from its retainers.

➡ **On some models, it may be necessary to remove the instrument panel pad to get at the cable.**

Outside, unsnap the cap from the antenna base. Remove the screw(s) and lift off the antenna base, pulling the cable with it, carefully. When reinstalling, make certain the antenna mount area is clean and free of rust and dirt. The antenna must make a proper ground contact through its base to work properly. Install the screws and route the cable into the interior. Make certain the cable is retained in the clips, etc. Attach the cable to the radio; reinstall the radio if it was removed.

Power

Some models are equipped with a power antenna located in the trunk. Turn the ignition key to the **OFF** position. Disconnect the negative battery cable. To access the antenna, simply remove the trim panel from the interior of the vehicle. Detach the electrical wiring harness from the component. Unbolt the unit. The antenna may have a mounting nut retaining it to the outside of the quarter panel. Remove this nut and retainer to slip the unit out from inside the car. Pull the unit out from the vehicle.

Installation is the reverse to install. Connect the negative battery cable and check component operation.

Power Sunroof

REMOVAL & INSTALLATION

▸ **See Figures 22 and 23**

1. Disconnect the negative battery cable.
2. Using a taped flat-bladed tool, remove the cover and the power roof switch.
3. Remove the inner rear view mirror, sun visors, and the front assist grip, if equipped.
4. Remove the front pillar garnishes and remove the front side of the headliner. On some models, it may be necessary to remove the upper and the lower side garnishes to allow enough clearance for the headliner.

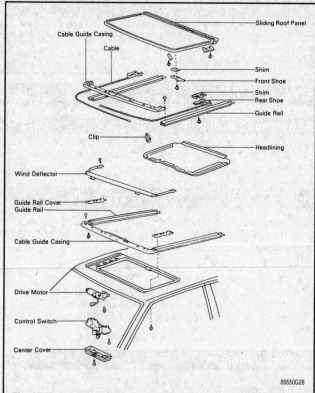

Fig. 22 Exploded view of the common sliding roof—1983–91 models

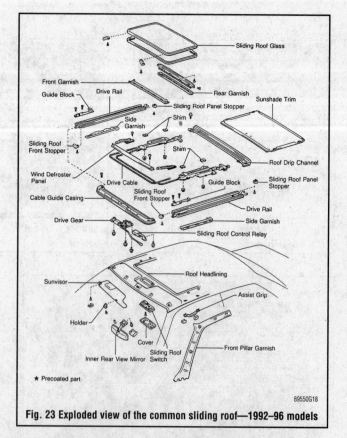

Fig. 23 Exploded view of the common sliding roof—1992–96 models

5. On some models, remove the four screws from the wind deflector and extract it from the vehicle.

6. On 1992–96 models, disconnect and remove the sliding roof control relay.

7. Disconnect the electrical wiring, remove the fasteners and remove the drive motor.

8. Remove the side guide rail trim covers.

9. Apply tape to the vehicle to protect the finish and remove the screws holding the glass into the roof.

10. Remove the roof from the vehicle lifting outward and slightly forward. Take notice of shim positioning and install in original location on installation.

11. Installation is the reverse of removal.

INTERIOR

Instrument Panel and Pad

▶ See Figures 24, 25 and 26

Always apply protection tape to the body adjacent to the component when removing or installing. When prying off the body components with a screwdriver or scraper, etc. be sure to apply protection tape to the tip of the blade to prevent damage to the component or paint. This will not be a sure way to keep the component from being damaged. Careful use of a tool in this matter is necessary. There are tools specifically made to remove trim pieces of a vehicle that can be purchased at your local parts store.

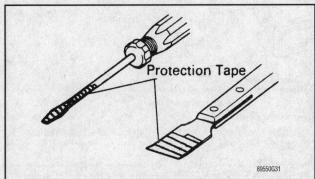

Fig. 24 If a special trim removal tool is not accessible, tape the end of the prytool and use with care

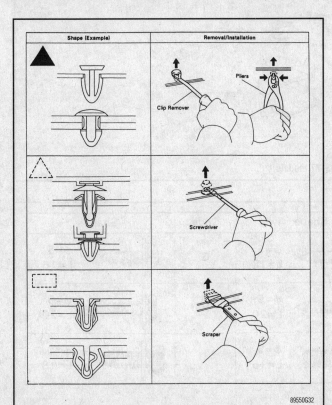

Fig. 25 Clip types and removal suggestions

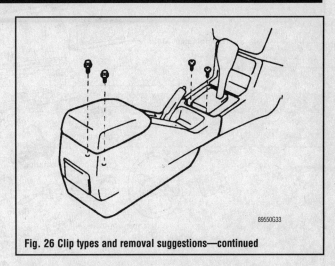

Fig. 26 Clip types and removal suggestions—continued

REMOVAL & INSTALLATION

1983–92 Models

▶ See Figures 27, 28, 29, 30 and 31

1. Turn the ignition key to the OFF position. Disconnect the negative battery cable. Wait at least 90 seconds from the time the negative battery was disconnected to start work.

✳✳ CAUTION

Some models covered by this manual may be equipped with a Supplemental Restraint System (SRS), which uses an air bag. Whenever working near any of the SRS components, such as the impact sensors, the air bag module, steering column and instrument panel, disable the SRS, as described in Section 6.

2. Remove the retainer clips from the front pillar garnish and remove the trim by pulling gently.

3. Remove the right and left speaker covers and the speakers.

4. Remove the hood release lever.

5. Remove right and left side kick panel trim covers.

6. Remove the steering wheel.

7. Remove the upper and the lower steering column covers.

8. Remove the retainer screws in the lower dash trim panel and remove the panel. Label and disconnect the electrical wiring as required.

9. On 1992 models, remove the floor console upper trim panel to gain access to the mounting screws. Remove the mounting screws in the front floor console and the rear console box. Remove the floor console from the vehicle.

10. Remove the glove compartment and glove compartment door.

11. Remove the center cluster finish panel.

12. Remove the stereo and the junction block mounted to the lower portion of the instrument panel.

13. Remove the combination switch on the steering column and the combination meter assembly from the front of the instrument panel. Disconnect all connectors.

14. Pull off the heater control knobs, remove the retaining screws and remove the heater control assembly from the vehicle.

15. Remove the side defroster ducts, lower ducts, and the discharge registers.

16. Remove the mounting bolts from the instrument panel and remove instrument panel from the vehicle.

17. Installation is the reverse of removal.

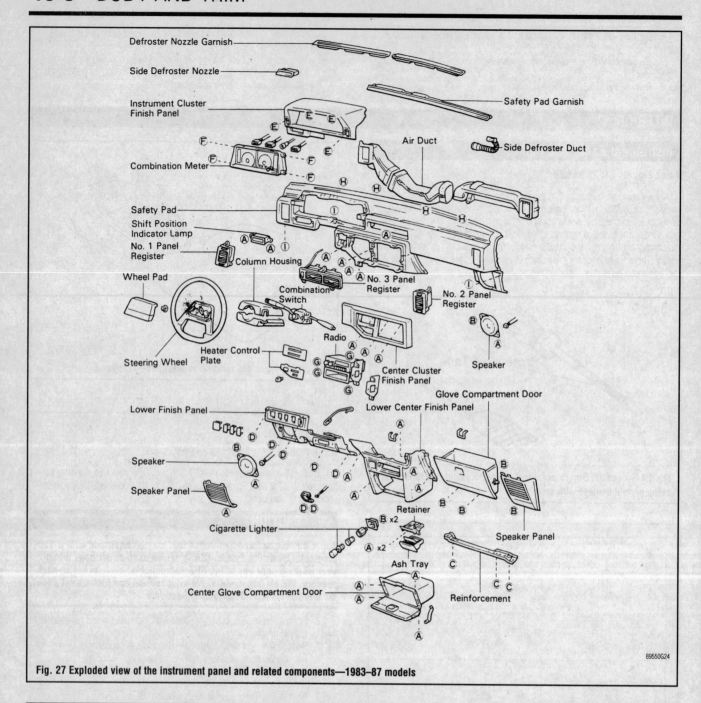

Fig. 27 Exploded view of the instrument panel and related components—1983–87 models

89550G24

Code	Shape		Code	Shape		Code	Shape	
A		$\phi=5$ L=16	D		$\phi=5$ L=18	G		$\phi=5$ L=16
B		$\phi=5$ L=14	E		$\phi=5$ L=20	H		$\phi=5$ L=20
C		$\phi=5$ L=16	F		$\phi=5$ L=16	I		$\phi=6$ L=18

Fig. 28 Various types of instrument panel bolts—1983—87 models

89550G23

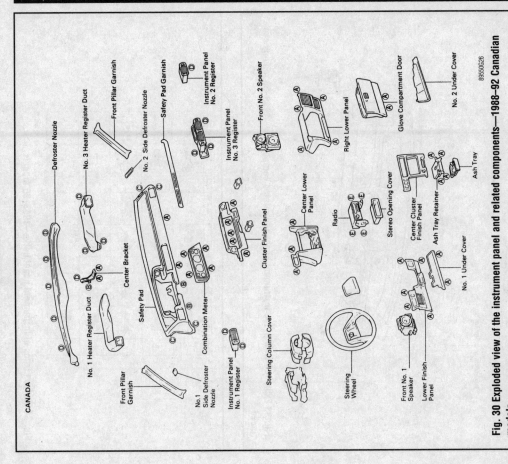

Fig. 30 Exploded view of the instrument panel and related components—1988–92 Canadian models

88550G26

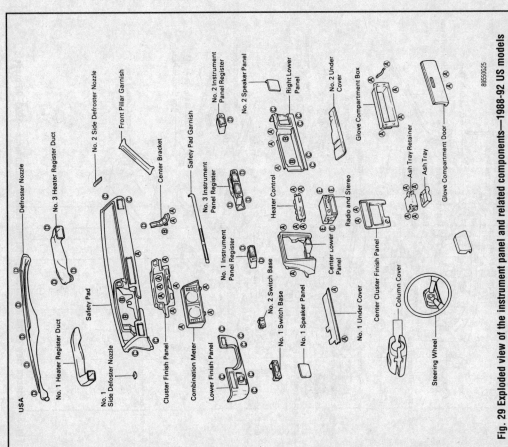

Fig. 29 Exploded view of the instrument panel and related components—1988–92 US models

88550G25

Code	Shape	Size	Code	Shape	Size	Code	Shape	Size
A		$\phi = 5.2\ (0.21)$ $L = 16\ (0.63)$	B		$\phi = 6\ (0.24)$	C		$\phi = 6\ (0.24)$ $L = 20\ (0.79)$

Code	Shape	Size	Code	Shape	Size
D		$\phi = 5\ (0.20)$ $L = 14\ (0.55)$	E		$\phi = 5\ (0.20)$ $L = 18\ (0.71)$

mm (in.)

Fig. 31 Various types of instrument panel bolts—1988–92 models

88550G27

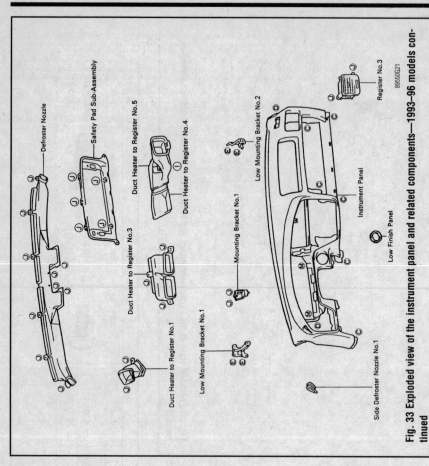

Fig. 33 Exploded view of the instrument panel and related components—1993–96 models continued

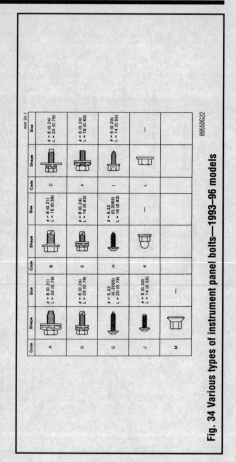

Fig. 34 Various types of instrument panel bolts—1993–96 models

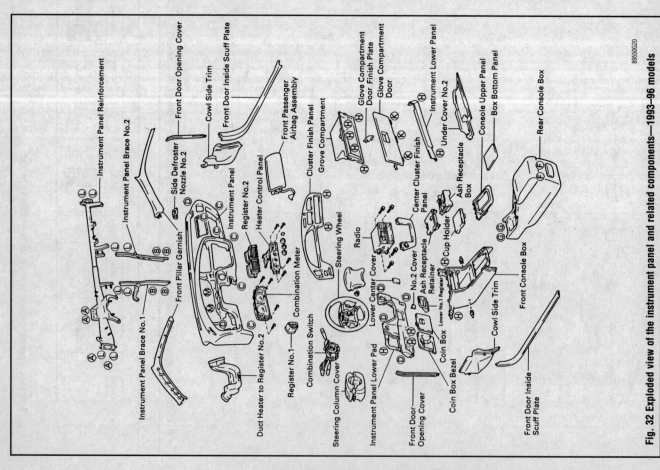

Fig. 32 Exploded view of the instrument panel and related components—1993–96 models

1993–96 Models

▶ **See Figures 32, 33, 34, 35 and 36**

1. Turn the ignition key to the OFF position. Disconnect the negative battery cable. Wait at least 90 seconds from the time the negative battery was disconnected to start work.

✳✳ **CAUTION**

Some models covered by this manual may be equipped with a Supplemental Restraint System (SRS), which uses an air bag. Whenever working near any of the SRS components, such as the impact sensors, the air bag module, steering column and instrument panel, disable the SRS, as described in Section 6.

2. Remove the front pillar garnish. on sedans, remove the clips by hand. On Wagons, pull the garnish rearwards to remove it. And on the coupe models, the rear garnish must be removed before the front pillar garnish.

3. Unscrew and remove the scuff plates from the inner door wells.

4. Remove the front door opening cover by pulling on it.

5. Slide the hood lock lever forwards and remove it.

6. Remove the clip and the cowl side trim by pulling on it.

7. Remove the steering wheel.

8. Unsecure the upper console panel, make sure to take the end of the tool prior to removal.

9. Remove the 2 bolts and 2 screws to extract the rear console box.

10. Press on the sides of the coin box while pulling it outwards to remove.

11. Remove the 2 screws and the coin bezel, then remove the 4 bolts, the screw and lower instrument panel pad.

12. Remove the combination switch.

13. Pull out the under cover No. 2.

14. Remove the instrument lower panel.

15. Remove the front lower console box.

16. Remove the glove box door. Remove the door box compartment finish plate inside the instrument panel box. Pull up on the airbag connector and disconnect it.

➡ **When handling the airbag connector, take care not to damage the wiring harness.**

17. Remove the compartment assembly screws and extract the unit from the dash.

18. Remove the center cluster finish panel, when extracting the panel remember there is wiring behind needed to be disconnected.

19. Unscrew and extract the No. 1 and No. 2 registers.

20. Remove the radio form the dash.

21. Remove the combination meter.

22. Pull out the heater control knobs. Remove the 5 screws and hang the heater control out of the way. Disconnect the air mix damper control cable. Remove the heater control.

23. Remove the clip and the No. 1 register No. 2.

24. On the passengers side airbag, remove the left side installation bolt. Remove the 5 bolts and 2 clips.

✳✳ **CAUTION**

Do not store the air bag assembly with the airbag door facing down. Never disassemble the airbag assembly.

25. Remove the No. 2 side defroster nozzle.

26. When removing the instrument panel, disconnect the wiring, then remove the connector holder. Detach any other wiring in the area, then remove the mounting bolts and nuts. Extract the panel from the dash. Remove the heater duct and register for the No. 4 and 5.

To install:

27. Attach the instrument panel wiring to the appropriate harnesses. Place the panel into position and tighten the bolts and nuts to 69 inch lbs. (8 Nm).

28. Attach the No. 2 side defroster nozzle.

29. Attach the passengers side airbag. Refer to the airbag precautions in Section 5. Tighten the bolts to the following:

- 8mm bolts—15 ft. lbs. (20 Nm)
- 6mm bolts—69 inch lbs. (8 Nm)
- Left side installation bolt—69 inch lbs. (8 Nm)

30. The remainder of installation is the reverse of removal. Tighten each component to specifications.

31. Reset all of the electrical components such as radio and clock.

Center Console

REMOVAL & INSTALLATION

▶ **See Figures 37 and 38**

1. Disconnect the negative battery cable. Wait at least 90 seconds from the time the negative battery was disconnected to start work.

✳✳ **CAUTION**

Some models covered by this manual may be equipped with a Supplemental Restraint System (SRS), which uses an air bag. Whenever working near any of the SRS components, such as the impact sensors, the air bag module, steering column and instrument panel, disable the SRS, as described in Section 6.

2. Remove the floor console upper trim panel to gain access to the mounting screws.

3. Remove the mounting screws in the front floor console and in the rear console box.

4. Remove the floor console from the vehicle.

5. Reverse the removal procedure to install.

Fig. 35 Unscrew the center cluster finish panel from around the instrument panel

Fig. 36 Pull the finish panel away from the dash

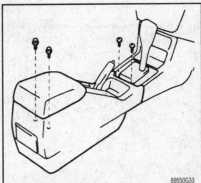

Fig. 37 Remove the rear center console retaining bolts

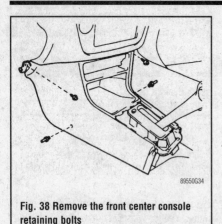

Fig. 38 Remove the front center console
retaining bolts

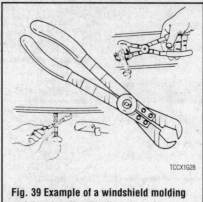

Fig. 39 Example of a windshield molding
and door handle clip pliers

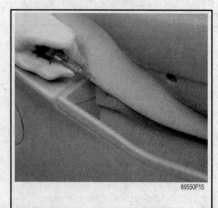

Fig. 40 Slide a piece of cloth under the
door window handle and push up to
release the snapring

Door Panels

REMOVAL & INSTALLATION

▶ See Figure 39

Front Door

1983–86 MODELS

▶ See Figure 40

1. Remove the inside door handle bezel and the armrest.
2. On vehicles not equipped with power windows, place a soft cloth under the window and pull upwards on the cloth to release the snapring. Remove the regulator handle.
3. On manual mirrors, remove the setting screw and knob. Tape the end of a thin screwdriver or a trim removal tool and pry the retainer loose to remove the cover.
4. Push on the center of the clip with a thin object to remove it.
5. Tape the end of a thin bladed tool use a trim removal tool, then insert it between the door panel and door. Slide the tool until you hit a retaining pin, then, carefully, pry the pin out of the door. Do this with each pin until the panel is free. On vehicles equipped with power windows, disconnect the electrical wiring after the panel is free.
6. Installation is the reverse of removal. Secure all components.

1987–88 MODELS

1. On vehicles without power windows, place a soft cloth under the window and pull upwards on the cloth to release the snapring. Remove the regulator handle and plate.
2. Remove the screw from the inside handle and slide the handle forward. Disconnect and remove the handle from the control link.
3. On manual mirrors, remove the setting screw and knob. Tape the end of a thin bladed tool or use a trim removal tool and pry the retainer loose to remove the cover.
4. Remove the two screws from the armrest.
5. Remove the two caps and two screws from the trim panel.
6. Tape the end of a thin bladed tool or use a trim removal tool, then insert the tool between the door panel and door and pry the panel loose. On vehicles equipped with power windows, door lock and mirror, disconnect the electrical wiring after the panel is free.
7. Installation is the reverse of removal.

1989–96 MODELS

▶ See Figures 41 thru 46

1. On vehicles without power windows, place a soft cloth under the window regulator handle and pull upwards on the cloth to release the snapring. Remove the regulator handle and plate.
2. Remove the screw from the inside handle and slide the handle forward. Disconnect and remove the handle from the control link.
3. On manual mirrors, remove the setting screw and knob. Tape the end of a thin flat-bladed tool and pry the retainer loose to remove the cover.
4. If equipped with power windows, remove the power window switch from the and armrest.
5. Remove the mounting screws and remove the armrest from the door panel. Remove the inside door handle bezel by pushing rearward.
6. Remove the door courtesy light by pulling outward. Disconnect the electrical wiring.
7. Remove the two screw caps and speaker cover(s). Remove six screws from the trim panel.
8. Remove the door pocket from the panel.
9. Tape the end of a thin bladed tool, then insert the tool between the door panel and door and pry the panel outward. Disconnect the electrical wiring after the panel is free and remove the panel from the vehicle.
10. Installation is the reverse of removal.

Fig. 41 Using a taped prytool, carefully
remove the bezel portion of the handle

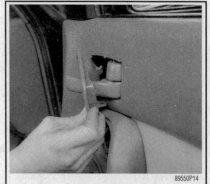

Fig. 42 Remove the bezel by pulling
towards the tip of the handle

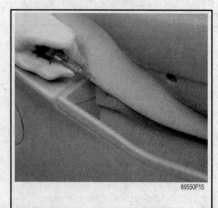

Fig. 43 Remove any screw covers ...

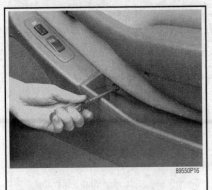

Fig. 44 . . . and extract any retaining screws from the door panel

Fig. 45 Carefully pry the edge of the door panel around the outer edges, then remove the door panel

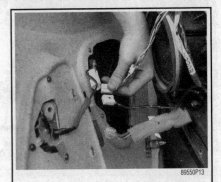

Fig. 46 Once the door panel is removed, make sure to disconnect all wiring

Rear Door

1983–86 MODELS

1. Remove the inside door handle bezel.
2. Remove the armrest and ashtray.
3. On vehicles without power windows, place a soft cloth under the window and pull upwards on the cloth to release the snapring. Remove the regulator handle.
4. Tape the end of a thin bladed tool, then insert the tool between the door panel and door. Slide the tool until you hit a retaining pin, then, carefully, pry the pin out of the door. Do this with each pin until the panel is free.
5. On vehicles equipped with power windows, door lock and mirror, disconnect the electrical connector after the panel is free.
6. On 1983–84 vehicles, remove the three upper mounting screws and remove the upper trim panel.
7. On 1983–84 vehicles, install the upper trim panel with the attaching screws.
8. Engage the electrical connector, if equipped, and install the trim panel onto the door.
9. With the door window fully closed, install the window regulator and handle.

1987–88 MODELS

1. On vehicles without power windows, place a soft cloth under the window and pull upwards on the cloth to release the snapring. Remove the regulator handle and plate.
2. Remove the screw from the inside handle and slide the handle forward. Disconnect and remove the handle from the control link.
3. Remove the two screws from the armrest.
4. Tape the end of a screwdriver and insert it between the trim retainers and the door panel to pry it loose.
5. Once released, remove the door trim with the inner weatherstrip.
6. Installation is the reverse of removal. Secure all components accordingly.
7. With the door window fully closed, install the window regulator and handle as shown in the illustration.

1989–96 MODELS

1. On vehicles without power windows, place a soft cloth under the window regulator handle and pull upwards on the cloth to release the snapring. Remove the regulator handle and plate.
2. If equipped with power windows, tape the end of a thin bladed tool and insert it between the window switch and the armrest. Pry the switch from the armrest and disconnect the wiring.
3. Tape the end of a bladed tool, pry the inside door handle bezel rearward, and remove.
4. Remove the screw caps and remove the retaining screws.
5. Use the bladed tool, and insert it between the trim retainers and the door panel to pry it loose.
6. Pull the trim panel upwards and remove from the door.

To install:

7. Install the door trim panel onto the door from above. Tap the top of the door panel to insure it is fully seated on door panel.
8. Install all trim retainers and secure.
9. Install the power window switch onto the armrest and secure.
10. With the door window fully closed, install the window regulator and handle.

Door Locks

REMOVAL & INSTALLATION

▶ **See Figures 47, 48 and 49**

1. Turn the ignition key to the **OFF** position. Disconnect the negative battery cable.
2. Remove the door panel and watershield. Remove the service hole cover.
3. Disconnect the door outside opening linkage. Remove the two mounting bolts and remove the door handle if in need of replacement.
4. Disconnect the lock cylinder control linkage.
5. Remove the lock knob and the child protector lock lever knob.

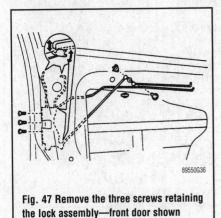

Fig. 47 Remove the three screws retaining the lock assembly—front door shown

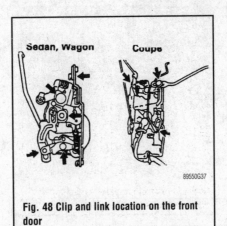

Fig. 48 Clip and link location on the front door

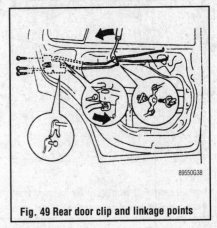

Fig. 49 Rear door clip and linkage points

6. Remove the three lock assembly retaining screws and the door lock. If equipped with power locks, disconnect the electrical wiring.

7. To remove the lock cylinder, remove the lock cylinder retaining clip and pull the cylinder from the door.

8. Install and secure all components in the reverse order of removal.

Tailgate Lock

REMOVAL & INSTALLATION

1. Turn the ignition key to the **OFF** position. Disconnect the negative battery cable.

2. Remove the back door inside garnish.

3. Remove the link protector.

4. Disconnect the links from the door control and door lock cylinder.

5. Remove the bolts and the door lock control with the solenoid.

6. To remove the door lock cylinder, remove the retaining screws and then remove the cylinder.

7. Install and secure all components in the reverse order of removal.

Sedan Trunk Lock

REMOVAL & INSTALLATION

Remove the inside trunk garnish. Remove the bolts and the door lock control with the solenoid, if equipped. The installation is the reverse of the removal procedure.

Door Glass and Regulator

REMOVAL & INSTALLATION

Front Door

♦ See Figures 50, 51 and 52

1. Disconnect the negative battery cable.

2. Remove the front door panel to gain access to the regulator assembly.

3. Remove the service hole cover.

4. Lower the regulator until the door glass is in the fully open position.

5. Remove the two glass channel mount bolts.

6. Pull the glass up and out of the door.

7. If equipped, unbolt and remove the inside door panel frame.

8. If equipped with power windows, disconnect the electrical wiring.

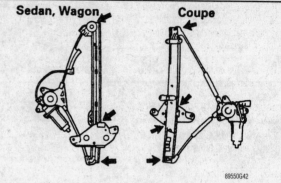

Fig. 51 View of the front window regulator in models with power windows

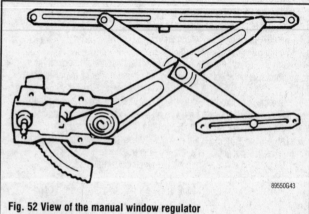

Fig. 52 View of the manual window regulator

9. Remove the equalizer arm bracket mounting bolts.

10. Remove the window regulator mounting bolts and remove the regulator (with the power window motor attached) through the service hole.

To install:

11. Coat all the window regulator sliding surfaces with multi-purpose grease.

12. Place the regulator (with the power window motor) through the service hole and install the mounting bolts. Connect the power window connector if equipped.

13. Place the door glass into the door cavity.

14. Install and secure all remaining components in the reverse order of removal.

15. With the equalizer arm, raise the glass to the almost closed position and make sure that the leading and trailing edges of the glass are equidistant from the top of the glass channel. If not, adjust the equalizer arm to achieve an even fit.

Rear Door

1. Disconnect the negative battery cable.

2. Remove the front door panel to gain access to the regulator assembly.

3. Remove the service hole cover.

4. Remove the clips from the outer edge of the belt molding and remove the rear door belt molding from the vehicle.

5. Remove the door glass run.

6. Remove the division bar by removing the two screws under the weatherstripping, the screw from the panel and pulling the glass run from the division bar. Pull the bar from the door.

7. Remove the glass mounting screws and remove the door glass.

8. To remove the quarter window, remove the glass along with the weatherstrip by pulling assembly forward.

9. To remove the regulator, unbolt from door panel and remove from vehicle. If equipped with power windows, disconnect the electrical connector and remove the regulator with the power window motor attached.

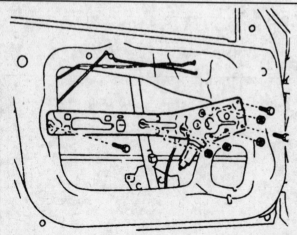

Fig. 50 Removing front door inside panel frame by removing these bolts and nuts

10. Install and secure all components in the reverse order of removal.

11. With the equalizer arm, raise the glass to the almost closed position and make sure that the leading and trailing edges of the glass are equidistant from the top of the glass channel. If not, adjust the equalizer arm to achieve an even fit.

12. With the door glass fully closed, adjust the door glass stopper so it lightly makes contact with the glass plate.

Electric Window Motor

The power window motor, if equipped, is attached to the window regulator. If service is required, remove the window regulator from the inside of the door panel and detach the motor from the regulator. Removal and installation of the regulator is described in this section.

Inside Rear View Mirror

REPLACEMENT

The inside mirror is held to its bracket by screws. Usually these are covered by a colored plastic housing which must be removed for access. These covers can be stubborn; take care not to gouge the plastic during removal.

Once exposed, the screws are easily removed. The mirror mounts are designed to break away under impact, thus protecting your head and face from serious injury in an accident.

Reassembly requires only common sense (which means you can do it wrong—pay attention); make sure everything fits without being forced and don't overtighten any screws or bolts.

Seats

REMOVAL & INSTALLATION

Front seats are held to the floor with four bolts each.

The sedan rear seat is retained by two clips at the front and two bolts at the rear. The side seat cushion is held in by one bolt located on the bottom. To remove, lift up and out.

The hatchback rear seat cushion is retained by four bolts, while the seat back is bolted to its hinges.

When installing the seats, tighten the front seat bolts to 27 ft. lbs. (37 Nm); the sedan rear seat bolts to 9 ft. lbs. (12 Nm); the hatchback seat cushion front bolts to 27 ft. lbs. (37 Nm); the hatchback seat cushion rear bolts to 14 ft. lbs. (19 Nm); the seat back-to-center hinge bolts to 69 inch lbs.; the seat back-to-side hinge bolts to 13 ft. lbs. (17 Nm).

TORQUE SPECIFICATIONS

	US	METRIC
Front bumper		
arm-to-body	78 inch lbs.	9 Nm
reinforcement-to-bumper arm	78 inch lbs.	9 Nm
reinforcement extension-to-body	15 ft. lbs.	21 Nm
Rear bumper		
arm-to-body	59 ft. lbs.	79 Nm
reinforcement-to-arm	32 ft. lbs.	43 Nm
cover-to-body	52 inch lbs.	6 Nm
Hood		
hinge-to-hood	10 ft. lbs.	14 Nm
lock-to-body	69 inch lbs.	8 Nm
Front and rear doors		
lock-to-panel	48 inch lbs.	5 Nm
regulator-to-frame	48 inch lbs.	5 Nm
regulator-to-panel	48 inch lbs.	5 Nm
Back door		
door hinge-to-body	9 ft. lbs.	13 Nm
door hinge-to-door	9 ft. lbs.	13 Nm
door lock-to-door	7 ft. lbs.	10 Nm
damper stay-to-body	78 inch lbs.	9 Nm
damper stay-to-door	78 inch lbs.	9 Nm
Trunk		
door hinge-to-compartment door	69 inch lbs.	8 Nm
Sliding roof		
drive gear-to-body	48 inch lbs.	5 Nm
Seats		
front track-to-body	27 ft. lbs.	37 Nm
rear seatback-to-body	13 ft. lbs.	18 Nm
rear seatback-to-hinge	13 ft. lbs.	18 Nm
rear seatback-to-hinge (fold down)	13 ft. lbs.	18 Nm
second rear side back-to-body	11-13 ft. lbs.	15-18 Nm
second seatback-to-hinge	13 ft. lbs.	18 Nm
second seatback hinge-to-body	13 ft. lbs.	18 Nm
second cushion hinge-to-body	13 ft. lbs.	18 Nm
third seatback link-to-bracket	13 ft. lbs.	18 Nm
third bracket-to-body	13 ft. lbs.	18 Nm
Adjusters		
power front adjuster-to-cushion frame	13 ft. lbs.	18 Nm
power front adjuster-to-seatback frame	13 ft. lbs.	18 Nm
manual front adjuster-to-cushion frame	13 ft. lbs.	18 Nm
manual front adjuster-to-seatback board	13 ft. lbs.	18 Nm
Fold-down seat		
seat lock control-to-seatback frame	13 ft. lbs.	18 Nm
front seat adjuster-to-seatback board	13 ft. lbs.	18 Nm

89550C01

GLOSSARY

AIR/FUEL RATIO: The ratio of air-to-gasoline by weight in the fuel mixture drawn into the engine.

AIR INJECTION: One method of reducing harmful exhaust emissions by injecting air into each of the exhaust ports of an engine. The fresh air entering the hot exhaust manifold causes any remaining fuel to be burned before it can exit the tailpipe.

ALTERNATOR: A device used for converting mechanical energy into electrical energy.

AMMETER: An instrument, calibrated in amperes, used to measure the flow of an electrical current in a circuit. Ammeters are always connected in series with the circuit being tested.

AMPERE: The rate of flow of electrical current present when one volt of electrical pressure is applied against one ohm of electrical resistance.

ANALOG COMPUTER: Any microprocessor that uses similar (analogous) electrical signals to make its calculations.

ARMATURE: A laminated, soft iron core wrapped by a wire that converts electrical energy to mechanical energy as in a motor or relay. When rotated in a magnetic field, it changes mechanical energy into electrical energy as in a generator.

ATMOSPHERIC PRESSURE: The pressure on the Earth's surface caused by the weight of the air in the atmosphere. At sea level, this pressure is 14.7 psi at 32°F (101 kPa at 0°C).

ATOMIZATION: The breaking down of a liquid into a fine mist that can be suspended in air.

AXIAL PLAY: Movement parallel to a shaft or bearing bore.

BACKFIRE: The sudden combustion of gases in the intake or exhaust system that results in a loud explosion.

BACKLASH: The clearance or play between two parts, such as meshed gears.

BACKPRESSURE: Restrictions in the exhaust system that slow the exit of exhaust gases from the combustion chamber.

BAKELITE: A heat resistant, plastic insulator material commonly used in printed circuit boards and transistorized components.

BALL BEARING: A bearing made up of hardened inner and outer races between which hardened steel balls roll.

BALLAST RESISTOR: A resistor in the primary ignition circuit that lowers voltage after the engine is started to reduce wear on ignition components.

BEARING: A friction reducing, supportive device usually located between a stationary part and a moving part.

BIMETAL TEMPERATURE SENSOR: Any sensor or switch made of two dissimilar types of metal that bend when heated or cooled due to the different expansion rates of the alloys. These types of sensors usually function as an on/off switch.

BLOWBY: Combustion gases, composed of water vapor and unburned fuel, that leak past the piston rings into the crankcase during normal engine operation. These gases are removed by the PCV system to prevent the buildup of harmful acids in the crankcase.

BRAKE PAD: A brake shoe and lining assembly used with disc brakes.

BRAKE SHOE: The backing for the brake lining. The term is, however, usually applied to the assembly of the brake backing and lining.

BUSHING: A liner, usually removable, for a bearing; an anti-friction liner used in place of a bearing.

CALIPER: A hydraulically activated device in a disc brake system, which is mounted straddling the brake rotor (disc). The caliper contains at least one piston and two brake pads. Hydraulic pressure on the piston(s) forces the pads against the rotor.

CAMSHAFT: A shaft in the engine on which are the lobes (cams) which operate the valves. The camshaft is driven by the crankshaft, via a belt, chain or gears, at one half the crankshaft speed.

CAPACITOR: A device which stores an electrical charge.

CARBON MONOXIDE (CO): A colorless, odorless gas given off as a normal byproduct of combustion. It is poisonous and extremely dangerous in confined areas, building up slowly to toxic levels without warning if adequate ventilation is not available.

CARBURETOR: A device, usually mounted on the intake manifold of an engine, which mixes the air and fuel in the proper proportion to allow even combustion.

CATALYTIC CONVERTER: A device installed in the exhaust system, like a muffler, that converts harmful byproducts of combustion into carbon dioxide and water vapor by means of a heat-producing chemical reaction.

CENTRIFUGAL ADVANCE: A mechanical method of advancing the spark timing by using flyweights in the distributor that react to centrifugal force generated by the distributor shaft rotation.

CHECK VALVE: Any one-way valve installed to permit the flow of air, fuel or vacuum in one direction only.

CHOKE: A device, usually a moveable valve, placed in the intake path of a carburetor to restrict the flow of air.

CIRCUIT: Any unbroken path through which an electrical current can flow. Also used to describe fuel flow in some instances.

CIRCUIT BREAKER: A switch which protects an electrical circuit from overload by opening the circuit when the current flow exceeds a predetermined level. Some circuit breakers must be reset manually, while most reset automatically.

COIL (IGNITION): A transformer in the ignition circuit which steps up the voltage provided to the spark plugs.

COMBINATION MANIFOLD: An assembly which includes both the intake and exhaust manifolds in one casting.

COMBINATION VALVE: A device used in some fuel systems that routes fuel vapors to a charcoal storage canister instead of venting them into the atmosphere. The valve relieves fuel tank pressure and allows fresh air into the tank as the fuel level drops to prevent a vapor lock situation.

COMPRESSION RATIO: The comparison of the total volume of the cylinder and combustion chamber with the piston at BDC and the piston at TDC.

CONDENSER: 1. An electrical device which acts to store an electrical charge, preventing voltage surges. 2. A radiator-like device in the air conditioning system in which refrigerant gas condenses into a liquid, giving off heat.

CONDUCTOR: Any material through which an electrical current can be transmitted easily.

CONTINUITY: Continuous or complete circuit. Can be checked with an ohmmeter.

COUNTERSHAFT: An intermediate shaft which is rotated by a mainshaft and transmits, in turn, that rotation to a working part.

CRANKCASE: The lower part of an engine in which the crankshaft and related parts operate.

CRANKSHAFT: The main driving shaft of an engine which receives reciprocating motion from the pistons and converts it to rotary motion.

CYLINDER: In an engine, the round hole in the engine block in which the piston(s) ride.

CYLINDER BLOCK: The main structural member of an engine in which is found the cylinders, crankshaft and other principal parts.

CYLINDER HEAD: The detachable portion of the engine, usually fastened to the top of the cylinder block and containing all or most of the combustion chambers. On overhead valve engines, it contains the valves and their operating parts. On overhead cam engines, it contains the camshaft as well.

DEAD CENTER: The extreme top or bottom of the piston stroke.

DETONATION: An unwanted explosion of the air/fuel mixture in the combustion chamber caused by excess heat and compression, advanced timing, or an overly lean mixture. Also referred to as "ping".

DIAPHRAGM: A thin, flexible wall separating two cavities, such as in a vacuum advance unit.

DIESELING: A condition in which hot spots in the combustion chamber cause the engine to run on after the key is turned off.

DIFFERENTIAL: A geared assembly which allows the transmission of motion between drive axles, giving one axle the ability to turn faster than the other.

DIODE: An electrical device that will allow current to flow in one direction only.

DISC BRAKE: A hydraulic braking assembly consisting of a brake disc, or rotor, mounted on an axle, and a caliper assembly containing, usually two brake pads which are activated by hydraulic pressure. The pads are forced against the sides of the disc, creating friction which slows the vehicle.

DISTRIBUTOR: A mechanically driven device on an engine which is responsible for electrically firing the spark plug at a predetermined point of the piston stroke.

DOWEL PIN: A pin, inserted in mating holes in two different parts allowing those parts to maintain a fixed relationship.

DRUM BRAKE: A braking system which consists of two brake shoes and one or two wheel cylinders, mounted on a fixed backing plate, and a brake drum, mounted on an axle, which revolves around the assembly.

DWELL: The rate, measured in degrees of shaft rotation, at which an electrical circuit cycles on and off.

ELECTRONIC CONTROL UNIT (ECU): Ignition module, module, amplifier or igniter. See Module for definition.

ELECTRONIC IGNITION: A system in which the timing and firing of the spark plugs is controlled by an electronic control unit, usually called a module. These systems have no points or condenser.

END-PLAY: The measured amount of axial movement in a shaft.

ENGINE: A device that converts heat into mechanical energy.

EXHAUST MANIFOLD: A set of cast passages or pipes which conduct exhaust gases from the engine.

FEELER GAUGE: A blade, usually metal, or precisely predetermined thickness, used to measure the clearance between two parts.

FIRING ORDER: The order in which combustion occurs in the cylinders of an engine. Also the order in which spark is distributed to the plugs by the distributor.

FLOODING: The presence of too much fuel in the intake manifold and combustion chamber which prevents the air/fuel mixture from firing, thereby causing a no-start situation.

FLYWHEEL: A disc shaped part bolted to the rear end of the crankshaft. Around the outer perimeter is affixed the ring gear. The starter drive engages the ring gear, turning the flywheel, which rotates the crankshaft, imparting the initial starting motion to the engine.

FOOT POUND (ft. lbs. or sometimes, ft.lb.): The amount of energy or work needed to raise an item weighing one pound, a distance of one foot.

FUSE: A protective device in a circuit which prevents circuit overload by breaking the circuit when a specific amperage is present. The device is constructed around a strip or wire of a lower amperage rating than the circuit it is designed to protect. When an amperage higher than that stamped on the fuse is present in the circuit, the strip or wire melts, opening the circuit.

GEAR RATIO: The ratio between the number of teeth on meshing gears.

GENERATOR: A device which converts mechanical energy into electrical energy.

HEAT RANGE: The measure of a spark plug's ability to dissipate heat from its firing end. The higher the heat range, the hotter the plug fires.

HUB: The center part of a wheel or gear.

HYDROCARBON (HC): Any chemical compound made up of hydrogen and carbon. A major pollutant formed by the engine as a byproduct of combustion.

HYDROMETER: An instrument used to measure the specific gravity of a solution.

INCH POUND (inch lbs.; sometimes in.lb. or in. lbs.): One twelfth of a foot pound.

INDUCTION: A means of transferring electrical energy in the form of a magnetic field. Principle used in the ignition coil to increase voltage.

INJECTOR: A device which receives metered fuel under relatively low pressure and is activated to inject the fuel into the engine under relatively high pressure at a predetermined time.

INPUT SHAFT: The shaft to which torque is applied, usually carrying the driving gear or gears.

INTAKE MANIFOLD: A casting of passages or pipes used to conduct air or a fuel/air mixture to the cylinders.

JOURNAL: The bearing surface within which a shaft operates.

KEY: A small block usually fitted in a notch between a shaft and a hub to prevent slippage of the two parts.

MANIFOLD: A casting of passages or set of pipes which connect the cylinders to an inlet or outlet source.

MANIFOLD VACUUM: Low pressure in an engine intake manifold formed just below the throttle plates. Manifold vacuum is highest at idle and drops under acceleration.

MASTER CYLINDER: The primary fluid pressurizing device in a hydraulic system. In automotive use, it is found in brake and hydraulic clutch systems and is pedal activated, either directly or, in a power brake system, through the power booster.

MODULE: Electronic control unit, amplifier or igniter of solid state or integrated design which controls the current flow in the ignition primary circuit based on input from the pick-up coil. When the module opens the primary circuit, high secondary voltage is induced in the coil.

NEEDLE BEARING: A bearing which consists of a number (usually a large number) of long, thin rollers.

OHM: (Ω) The unit used to measure the resistance of conductor-to-electrical flow. One ohm is the amount of resistance that limits current flow to one ampere in a circuit with one volt of pressure.

OHMMETER: An instrument used for measuring the resistance, in ohms, in an electrical circuit.

OUTPUT SHAFT: The shaft which transmits torque from a device, such as a transmission.

OVERDRIVE: A gear assembly which produces more shaft revolutions than that transmitted to it.

OVERHEAD CAMSHAFT (OHC): An engine configuration in which the camshaft is mounted on top of the cylinder head and operates the valve either directly or by means of rocker arms.

OVERHEAD VALVE (OHV): An engine configuration in which all of the valves are located in the cylinder head and the camshaft is located in the cylinder block. The camshaft operates the valves via lifters and pushrods.

OXIDES OF NITROGEN (NOx): Chemical compounds of nitrogen produced as a byproduct of combustion. They combine with hydrocarbons to produce smog.

OXYGEN SENSOR: Use with the feedback system to sense the presence of oxygen in the exhaust gas and signal the computer which can reference the voltage signal to an air/fuel ratio.

PINION: The smaller of two meshing gears.

PISTON RING: An open-ended ring with fits into a groove on the outer diameter of the piston. Its chief function is to form a seal between the piston and cylinder wall. Most automotive pistons have three rings: two for compression sealing; one for oil sealing.

PRELOAD: A predetermined load placed on a bearing during assembly or by adjustment.

PRIMARY CIRCUIT: the low voltage side of the ignition system which consists of the ignition switch, ballast resistor or resistance wire, bypass, coil, electronic control unit and pick-up coil as well as the connecting wires and harnesses.

PRESS FIT: The mating of two parts under pressure, due to the inner diameter of one being smaller than the outer diameter of the other, or vice versa; an interference fit.

RACE: The surface on the inner or outer ring of a bearing on which the balls, needles or rollers move.

REGULATOR: A device which maintains the amperage and/or voltage levels of a circuit at predetermined values.

RELAY: A switch which automatically opens and/or closes a circuit.

RESISTANCE: The opposition to the flow of current through a circuit or electrical device, and is measured in ohms. Resistance is equal to the voltage divided by the amperage.

RESISTOR: A device, usually made of wire, which offers a preset amount of resistance in an electrical circuit.

RING GEAR: The name given to a ring-shaped gear attached to a differential case, or affixed to a flywheel or as part of a planetary gear set.

ROLLER BEARING: A bearing made up of hardened inner and outer races between which hardened steel rollers move.

ROTOR: 1. The disc-shaped part of a disc brake assembly, upon which the brake pads bear; also called, brake disc. 2. The device mounted atop the distributor shaft, which passes current to the distributor cap tower contacts.

SECONDARY CIRCUIT: The high voltage side of the ignition system, usually above 20,000 volts. The secondary includes the ignition coil, coil wire, distributor cap and rotor, spark plug wires and spark plugs.

SENDING UNIT: A mechanical, electrical, hydraulic or electro-magnetic device which transmits information to a gauge.

SENSOR: Any device designed to measure engine operating conditions or ambient pressures and temperatures. Usually electronic in nature and designed to send a voltage signal to an on-board computer, some sensors may operate as a simple on/off switch or they may provide a variable voltage signal (like a potentiometer) as conditions or measured parameters change.

SHIM: Spacers of precise, predetermined thickness used between parts to establish a proper working relationship.

SLAVE CYLINDER: In automotive use, a device in the hydraulic clutch system which is activated by hydraulic force, disengaging the clutch.

SOLENOID: A coil used to produce a magnetic field, the effect of which is to produce work.

SPARK PLUG: A device screwed into the combustion chamber of a spark ignition engine. The basic construction is a conductive core inside of a ceramic insulator, mounted in an outer conductive base. An electrical charge from the spark plug wire travels along the conductive core and jumps a preset air gap to a grounding point or points at the end of the conductive base. The resultant spark ignites the fuel/air mixture in the combustion chamber.

SPLINES: Ridges machined or cast onto the outer diameter of a shaft or inner diameter of a bore to enable parts to mate without rotation.

TACHOMETER: A device used to measure the rotary speed of an engine, shaft, gear, etc., usually in rotations per minute.

THERMOSTAT: A valve, located in the cooling system of an engine, which is closed when cold and opens gradually in response to engine heating, controlling the temperature of the coolant and rate of coolant flow.

TOP DEAD CENTER (TDC): The point at which the piston reaches the top of its travel on the compression stroke.

TORQUE: The twisting force applied to an object.

TORQUE CONVERTER: A turbine used to transmit power from a driving member to a driven member via hydraulic action, providing changes in drive ratio and torque. In automotive use, it links the driveplate at the rear of the engine to the automatic transmission.

TRANSDUCER: A device used to change a force into an electrical signal.

TRANSISTOR: A semi-conductor component which can be actuated by a small voltage to perform an electrical switching function.

TUNE-UP: A regular maintenance function, usually associated with the replacement and adjustment of parts and components in the electrical and fuel systems of a vehicle for the purpose of attaining optimum performance.

TURBOCHARGER: An exhaust driven pump which compresses intake air and forces it into the combustion chambers at higher than atmospheric pressures. The increased air pressure allows more fuel to be burned and results in increased horsepower being produced.

VACUUM ADVANCE: A device which advances the ignition timing in response to increased engine vacuum.

VACUUM GAUGE: An instrument used to measure the presence of vacuum in a chamber.

VALVE: A device which control the pressure, direction of flow or rate of flow of a liquid or gas.

VALVE CLEARANCE: The measured gap between the end of the valve stem and the rocker arm, cam lobe or follower that activates the valve.

VISCOSITY: The rating of a liquid's internal resistance to flow.

VOLTMETER: An instrument used for measuring electrical force in units called volts. Voltmeters are always connected parallel with the circuit being tested.

WHEEL CYLINDER: Found in the automotive drum brake assembly, it is a device, actuated by hydraulic pressure, which, through internal pistons, pushes the brake shoes outward against the drums.

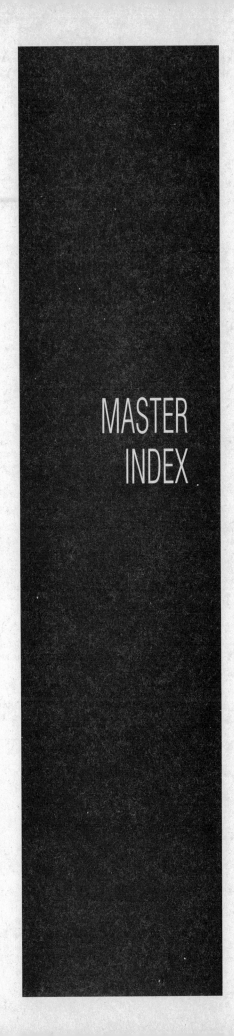

MASTER
INDEX